DIPLOMA IN CORPORAT

PAPER 2 – CORPORATE FIN

STRATEGY AND ADVICE

STUDY TEXT

CW01604714

APPROVED WORKBOOK

ICAEW

PARTNER IN LEARNING

BPP LEARNING MEDIA

Published August 2019

ISBN 9781 5097 1608 1

British Library Cataloguing-in-Publication Data
A catalogue record for this book
is available from the British Library

Published by

BPP Learning Media Ltd
BPP House, Aldine Place
London W12 8AA

www.bpp.com/learningmedia

Printed in United Kingdom by RICOH UK Limited

Unit 2
Wells Place
Merstham
RH1 3LG
United Kingdom

Your learning materials, published by BPP Learning Media Ltd, are printed on paper obtained from traceable sustainable sources.

All rights reserved. No part of this publication may be reproduced, stored in a retrieval system or transmitted in any form or by any means, electronic, mechanical, photocopying, recording or otherwise, without the prior written permission of BPP Learning Media.

The contents of this book are intended as a guide and not professional advice. Although every effort has been made to ensure that the contents of this book are correct at the time of going to press, BPP Learning Media makes no warranty that the information in this book is accurate or complete and accept no liability for any loss or damage suffered by any person acting or refraining from acting as a result of the material in this book.

Every effort has been made to contact the copyright holders of any material reproduced within this publication. If any have been inadvertently overlooked, BPP Learning Media will be pleased to make the appropriate credits in any subsequent reprints or editions.

© BPP Learning Media Ltd 2019

BPP LEARNING MEDIA

A note about copyright

Dear Customer

What does the little © mean and why does it matter?

Your market-leading BPP books, course materials and e-learning materials do not write and update themselves. People write them: on their own behalf or as employees of an organisation that invests in this activity. Copyright law protects their livelihoods. It does so by creating rights over the use of the content.

Breach of copyright is a form of theft – as well being a criminal offence in some jurisdictions, it is potentially a serious breach of professional ethics.

With current technology, things might seem a bit hazy but, basically, without the express permission of BPP Learning Media:

- Photocopying our materials is a breach of copyright
- Scanning, ripcasting or conversion of our digital materials into different file formats, uploading them to facebook or emailing them to your friends is a breach of copyright

You can, of course, sell your books, in the form in which you have brought them – once you have finished with them. (Is this fair to your fellow students? We update for a reason.) But the e-products are sold on a single user license basis: we do not supply 'unlock' codes to people who have bought them second-hand.

And what about outside the UK? BPP Learning Media strives to make our materials available at prices students can afford by local printing arrangements, pricing policies and partnerships which are clearly listed on our website. A tiny minority ignore this and indulge in criminal activity by illegally photocopying out material or supporting organisations that do. If they act illegally and unethically in one area, can you really trust them?

CONTENTS

Updates

From time to time we may need to publish updates to one of our titles. This can be for a variety of reasons, from a small change in regulation to the identification of errata.

You should check our updates/errata page regularly for anything that may affect your learning materials. All updates are available free of charge on our updates page on our website at:

http://www.bpp.com/about-bpp/aboutBPP/StudentInfo#q4

PART A

Corporate finance strategy and advice

Introduction

Welcome to the Study Text for Paper 2 of the Corporate Finance Qualification, Corporate Finance Strategy and Advice. This chapter details the syllabus for Paper 2 and cross-references the requirements to the material contained in this Study Text.

SYLLABUS

Aim

The aim of the syllabus is to provide students with a detailed understanding of issues, disciplines, regulations and strategies involved in advising on and implementing companies' corporate finance objectives. This covers the following areas: changes in control and restructuring; mergers and acquisitions; debt and equity issues; and strategic financial management.

New content to support the four areas above is introduced in this paper, covering, for domestic and international businesses: business strategy; mergers and acquisitions; and corporate performance and reconstructions. This module will also ensure that candidates can analyse and evaluate complex business issues and provide advice upon them.

Students will also find significant areas of overlap in the syllabus with Paper 1, Corporate Finance Techniques and Theory. Much of the material for Paper 1 is also potentially examinable in Paper 2, Corporate Finance Strategy and Advice. The examiners will be ascertaining whether students can apply this knowledge in more complex business scenarios.

Entry to Corporate Finance Strategy and Advice

Candidates embarking on this module of the Diploma in Corporate Finance will have passed CISI Certificate in Corporate Finance or the ACA.

It is strongly recommended that candidates have passed the Corporate Finance Techniques and Theory module before embarking on this module of the Diploma in Corporate Finance.

Assessment

The module will draw from across the syllabus and be assessed through a four-hour open-book case study. Candidates will be expected to demonstrate that they can apply their understanding to a case study based upon a real corporate finance scenario. Scenarios will encompass the four major areas of: changes in control and restructuring; mergers and acquisitions; debt and equity issues; and strategic financial management. Scenarios may contain elements of all these areas.

Questions will be phrased to allow candidates to demonstrate the depth of their ability in their area of professional expertise. Examiners and markers will ensure that there is a consistent approach and depth and relevance in answers is appropriate.

Candidates will be required to use professional judgement to identify and evaluate alternatives and determine the appropriate solution or solutions to compliance and other issues, giving due consideration to the commercial impact of their recommendations.

Safeguards will be put in place to ensure consistency of perspective in answers.

The application of the knowledge gained through the Techniques and Theory syllabus will be enhanced by study of the content areas listed below. This includes deeper study of some of the areas already touched upon in the Techniques and Theory syllabus.

Knowledge Levels

The level of knowledge required in this module is that required for the solution of complex problems except where indicated with a **(G)**, where knowledge is required only at a level for the solution of straightforward problems.

Syllabus and BPP Study Text Coverage

1. Corporate Strategy

Candidates will be able to analyse and evaluate information relating to the strategy of domestic and international businesses and give relevant advice. Corporate strategy questions will make up approximately 15–35% of the total marks in the examination.

In the assessment, candidates may be required to:

SYLLABUS		BPP STUDY TEXT
a.	Analyse information about business entities of any form in complex scenarios and evaluate strategy using appropriate tools, including:	Chapters 1, 2
	• SWOT analysis	
	• PEST analysis	
	• Porter's 5 Forces analysis	
b.	Give relevant and appropriate advice on	Chapters 1, 2, 10, 19
	• Business strategy	
	• Growth by acquisition versus organic growth	
	• Disposals and the disposal process	

2. Mergers and Acquisitions

Candidates will be able to analyse and evaluate information relating to mergers and acquisitions of domestic and international businesses and give relevant advice. Mergers and Acquisitions questions will make up approximately 35–50% of the total marks in the examination.

In the assessment, candidates may be required to:

SYLLABUS		BPP STUDY TEXT
a.	Analyse and evaluate information about business entities of any form in complex scenarios and give relevant and appropriate advice on:	
	• Financing acquisitions	Chapters 5, 6, 7, 11
	• The financial effect of an acquisition on the enlarged group	Chapters 3,4, 11
	• Advanced valuation (modelling free cash flows, multiples and comparable company analysis)	Chapters 4, 10
	• Creating shareholder value from acquisitions, including post acquisition integration and synergy analysis	Chapter 10
	• Restructuring, including schemes of arrangement	Chapters 12, 19
	• Due diligence (both buy and sell side)	Paper 1 material

3. Corporate Performance and Reconstructions

Candidates will be able to analyse and evaluate information relating to corporate performance and reconstructions of domestic and international businesses and give relevant advice. Corporate Performance and Reconstructions questions will make up approximately 35–50% of the total marks in the examination.

In the assessment, candidates may be required to:

SYLLABUS		BPP STUDY TEXT
a.	Analyse and evaluate information about business entities of any form in complex scenarios and give relevant and appropriate advice on:	
	• Advanced corporate performance, including economic value added (EVA)	Chapter 18
	• Reconstructions and business recovery	Chapter 19
	• Schemes of arrangement	Chapters 12, 19
	• The role of private equity	Chapter 6

Supporting material for sections 2 and 3 above

In the assessment of section 2 Mergers and Acquisitions and section 3 Corporate Performance and Reconstructions, candidates may be required to:

SYLLABUS		BPP STUDY TEXT
a.	Distinguish between the activities of the advisory team, including:	Chapter 9
	• Sponsors	
	• Nominated advisors (NOMAD)	
	• Financial advisers	
	• Stockbrokers	
	• Lawyers	
	• Reporting accountants	
	• PR / marketing	
	• Valuers / competent persons	
b.	Illustrate the role of the advisory team in respect of:	Chapters 7, 9
	• Pricing and timing	
	• Underwriting	
	• Market dynamics	
	• Global markets/issues	
	• Limitations of strategic reviews	
	• Long-term goals	
	• American and global depositary receipts (ADR/GDR)	
	• Dual listings	
c.	Distinguish between the various sources and methods of raising capital and the most appropriate method for a given circumstance	Chapters 3,4, 5, 6, 7
d.	Explain the principal factors involved in the Main market, AIM market and ISDX market flotations **(G)**	Chapter 8
e.	Analyse the preparations for a flotation:	Chapter 8
	• Suitability	
	• Responsibilities of a sponsor / nomad / ISDX adviser	
	• Pre-flotation considerations	
	• Taxation implications	

SYLLABUS		BPP STUDY TEXT
f.	Explain the principal factors involved in private equity investment, including:	Chapter 6
	• Houses and fund structure	
	• Key characteristics of private equity backed businesses	
	• Typical process	
	• Debt packages	
	• Mezzanine	
	• Management team	
	• Due diligence – scope and nature	
	• Legal documents	
g.	Interpret the regulatory requirements for a quoted transaction, including:	Chapters 8, 14
	• Listing Rules	
	• Prospectus Rules	
	• The Takeover Code	
	• Disclosure and Transparency Rules	
	• Financial Services and Markets Act 2000 ss.21, 72-103, 397 and related orders	
	• FCA Conduct of Business sourcebook	
	• Market abuse regime	
	• AIM Rules	
	• ISDX Rules	
	• Companies Act	
h.	Critically evaluate the main methods of conducting a quoted flotation:	Chapter 7
	• Offer for sale	
	• Placing	
	• Introduction	
	• Reverse takeover	
i.	Discuss the pricing mechanisms available when raising capital via an IPO or flotation	Chapter 7
j.	Critically evaluate methods of raising capital available to quoted companies and the issues surrounding these, including:	Chapter 7
	• Vendor placings	
	• Rights issues	
	• Placing and open offer (and claw-backs)	
	• Public to private	
	• Regulatory considerations	
	• Pre-emption rights	
	• Schemes of arrangement	

SYLLABUS		BPP STUDY TEXT
	• Pre-Emption Group, The Investment Association and other relevant guidelines	
	• Demerger	
	• Private investment in public equity	
k.	Explain the nature and purpose of secondary and dual listings	Chapter 7
l.	Interpret and apply the continuing obligations requirements of quoted companies	Chapters 8, 13
m.	Discuss the requirements and purpose of regulations relating to the disclosure of price sensitive information	Chapter 12
n.	Evaluate the regulatory requirements in respect of shareholder notifications and their intended purpose	Chapters 12, 14
o.	Evaluate the regulatory requirements surrounding acquisitions and disposals:	Chapters 12, 14
	• AIM and ISDX Rules **(G)**	
	• Listing Rules	
	• Companies Act	
	• Takeover Code	
	• Criminal Justice Act	
	• Insider dealing	
	• Financial Services and Markets Act 2000 s.397	
	• Disclosure and transparency disclosures	
p.	Critically appraise the techniques and concepts of employee share participation and pensions arrangements, examining the following concepts and techniques used in share participation arrangements:	Chapter 16
	• Approved share option scheme	
	• Non approved share option scheme	
	• Long term incentive plans (LTIPs)	
	• Investment Performance Council (IPC) guidelines	
	• Other options and warrants	
	• SAYE plans	
q.	Critically evaluate the various stakeholder relationships, stakeholders' expectations and management of them:	Chapter 17
	• Categories of institutional and other investors	
	• Management of investor expectations	
	• Analysts' and shareholders' meetings	
r.	Evaluate the appropriateness, advantages and limitations of the following methods of disseminating information:	Chapters 12, 17
	• Public announcements	
	• Investment advertising rules	
	• Press conferences and PR	
	• Private meetings	
	• Selective disclosure notifications of inside information	

SYLLABUS			BPP STUDY TEXT
s.	Examine the role of directors and discuss their duties and obligations in relation to:		Chapter 8, 13, 17
	•	Related party transactions	
	•	Board committees	
	•	Directors' dealings	
	•	Conflicts of interest	
	•	Non-executive directors	
	•	Corporate governance	
	•	Responsibilities to stakeholders	
t.	Discuss the requirements for continuing advice arising from:		Chapters 14, 15
	•	Dividend policy	
	•	Regulatory bodies	
		– Bank of England	
		– London Stock Exchange	
		– Financial Conduct Authority	
u.	Discuss the requirements for the management of inside and confidential information:		Chapters 12, 14
	•	Current best practice for the management of confidential and price sensitive information	
	•	Familiarity with current events including market conduct, regulatory breaches and industry developments	

The Strategic Environment

chapter 1

Contents

1 Introduction

An analysis of strategy is concerned with the direction and scope of an organisation over the long term. Organisations make decisions on strategy with the aim of achieving advantage in a changing environment, through the configuration of resources and competences. Strategic decisions are made under conditions of complexity and uncertainty; they have wide impact on the organisation and often lead to major change. Corporate financiers need to be able to evaluate company strategy to assess achievability of forecasts and appropriateness of capital structure. Strategic analysis is also a key part of the M&A process. This chapter, and the following chapter, will give you an insight into some important tools which can be deployed to assess the strategic direction of an entity.

We begin by looking at the conclusions of academics Johnson, Scholes and Whittington on the scope and nature of strategic decisions that an organisation will confront.

2 Strategic Decisions

Johnson, Scholes and Whittington (2008) explored the significance of strategy by considering the subject matter of strategic decisions. They discern six general areas for decision-making that will normally be regarded as strategic.

(a) The organisation's **long-term direction**: no specific timescale is envisaged, but you should think in terms in excess of one year and more probably of about five years or more.

(b) The **scope of an organisation's activities**: this will include both the overall roles and purposes the organisation accepts for itself and the activities it undertakes in pursuit of them. Strategic planning considers the whole organisation.

(c) For commercial organisations and for many not-for-profit organisations too, strategy will be about gaining some kind of **advantage in competition.**

(d) Strategic management in some organisations will take the form of **adapting their activities to fit the business environment.** In its simplest form, this will involve adapting products and services to gradually changing **customer requirements.**

(e) A contrasting approach will be to **exploit unique resources** and the organisation's **special competences** in particular. This approach sees the business environment as **something that can be changed** by the organisations' own actions.

(f) Strategic decisions are affected by the **values and expectations** of all of the organisation's **stakeholders.** Stakeholders are people who have a legitimate interest in what the organisation does.

Having defined the matters that require decisions of a strategic nature, Johnson, Scholes and Whittington go on to describe some important characteristics of the strategic decisions. Decisions about strategy are likely to be **complex** since there are likely to be a number of significant factors to take into consideration and a variety of possible outcomes to balance against one another. There is likely to be a high degree of **uncertainty** surrounding a strategic decision, both about the precise nature of current circumstances and about the likely consequences of any course of action. Strategic decisions have extensive impact on **operational decision-making**; that is, decisions at lower levels in the organisation. Strategic decisions thus affect the organisation as a whole and require processes that cross operational and functional boundaries within it. An **integrated approach** is therefore required. Strategic decisions are likely to lead to **change** within the organisation as resource capacity is adjusted to permit new courses of action. Changes with implications for **organisational culture** are particularly complex and difficult to manage.

3 Analysing the Environment

The starting point to appraise the validity of an organisation's strategic decisions is an evaluation of the strategic environment. All organisations are open systems: they exist within a complex environment and have a variety of interchanges with that environment, both receiving inputs from it and providing outputs to it. Organisations try to control the nature of their outputs, but very few of them can control more than a few of the inputs they receive. Understanding the nature of the business environment and the changes taking place within it is therefore an essential part of strategic business analysis.

The environment may be divided for convenience into three concentric layers: the macro-environment; the industry or sector; and competitors and markets within the sector. The layers and the elements interact with one another.

Various tools can be used to analysis these three different layers, summarised as follows:

Environmental element	Basis of analysis
Macro-environment	PESTEL Yip's Key Drivers of Change Porter's Diamond
Industry or sector	Porter's Five Forces Industry Life Cycle
Competitors and markets	Strategic groups Market segments Critical success factors

4 The Macro-environment

The macro-environment may be analysed using the PESTEL framework. PESTEL is a mnemonic which summarises the key environmental pressures that an entity faces, as follows:

- **P**olitical environment
- **E**conomic environment
- **S**ociocultural environment
- **T**echnological environment
- **E**nvironmental protection
- **L**egal issues

Macro-environmental influences

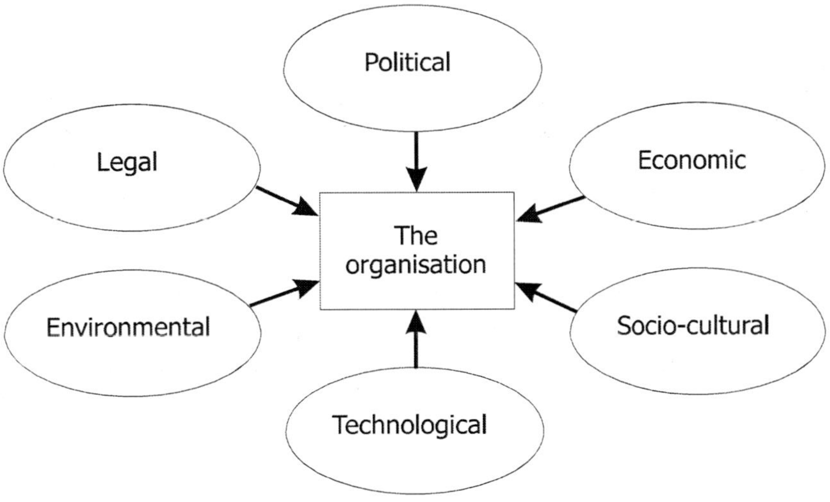

PESTEL is a useful checklist for general environmental factors, but in the real world these factors are often interlinked. Any single environmental development can have implications for all six PESTEL aspects. In particular, political, social and economic affairs tend to be closely related. What sort of factors should you consider when using PESTEL? The following factors raises some issues that are worthy of consideration. The list is not exhaustive and it is essential for you to consider the specifics of any company provided in an exam scenario.

The political environment

Government is responsible for providing a stable framework for economic activity and, in particular, for maintaining and improving the physical, social and market infrastructure. Public policy on competition and consumer protection is particularly relevant to business strategy.

Government policy

Government policy affects the whole economy, and governments are responsible for enforcing and creating a stable framework in which business can be done. A report by the World Bank indicated that the quality of government policy is important in providing three things.

- Physical infrastructure (eg transport)
- Social infrastructure (education, a welfare safety net, law enforcement, equal opportunities)
- Market infrastructure (enforceable contracts, policing corruption)

Political risk

The political risk in a decision is the risk that political factors will invalidate the strategy and perhaps severely damage the firm. Examples are wars, political chaos, corruption and nationalisation.

A political risk checklist was outlined by Jeannet and Hennessey. Companies should ask the following six questions:

1 How stable is the host country's political system?

2 How strong is the host government's commitment to specific rules of the game, such as ownership or contractual rights, given its ideology and power position?

3 How long is the government likely to remain in power?

4 If the present government is succeeded, how would the specific rules of the game change?

5 What would be the effects of any expected changes in the specific rules of the game?

6 In light of those effects, what decisions and actions should be taken now?

The economic environment

The economic environment affects firms at national and international level, both in the general level of economic activity and in particular variables, such as exchange rates, interest rates and inflation.

The economic environment is an important influence at local and national level.

Factor	Impact
Overall growth or fall in gross domestic product	Increased/decreased demand
Local economic trends	Type of industry in the area. Level of rents. Labour rates. House prices.
Inflation	Low in most countries; distorts business decisions; wage inflation compensates for price inflation
Interest rates	Impacts cost of debt
Tax levels	Affects customer demand and company profitability and reinvestment levels
Government spending	Impacts government suppliers (eg construction firms)
The business cycle	Economic activity is always punctuated by periods of growth followed by decline, simply because of the nature of trade. Government policy can cause, exacerbate or mitigate such trends, but cannot abolish the business cycle.

The forecast state of the economy will influence the planning process for organisations which operate within it. In times of boom and increased demand and consumption, the overall planning problem will be to identify the demand. Conversely, in times of recession, the emphasis will be on cost-effectiveness, continuing profitability, survival and competition.

Impact of international factors on the economic environment

Factor	Impact
Exchange rates	Cost of imports, selling prices and value of exports; cost of hedging against fluctuations
Characteristics of overseas markets	Desirable overseas markets (demand) or sources of supply (cheap imports?)
International capital markets	Generally, advanced economies accept that supply and demand set the value of their currencies, using interest rates only to control inflation.
Large multinational companies (MNCs)	MNCs have huge turnovers and significant political influence because of governments' desire to attract capital investment.
Government policy on trade/protection	Cost of barriers to trade, effect on supplier interests of free trade, erection of reciprocal barriers, possibility of dumping

The sociocultural environment

The social and cultural environment features long-term social trends and people's beliefs and attitudes. Factors that influence strategy include population growth; population age; population geography; ethnicity; household and family structure; social structure; employment patterns; population wealth.

Implications of demographic change

(a) Changes in patterns of demand: an ageing population suggests increased demand for health care services: a young growing population has a growing demand for schools, housing and work.

(b) Location of demand: population shift eg rural depopulation

(c) Recruitment policies: need to take account of rising retirement ages

(d) Wealth and tax. Patterns of poverty and hence need for welfare provisions may change. The tax base may alter.

Culture

Through contact with a particular culture, individuals learn a language, acquire values and learn habits of behaviour and thought.

(a) Beliefs and values. Beliefs are what we feel to be the case on the basis of objective and subjective information. Values are beliefs which are relatively enduring, relatively general and fairly widely accepted as a guide to culturally appropriate behaviour.

(b) Customs: modes of behaviour which represent culturally accepted ways of behaving in response to given situations

(c) Artefacts: all the physical tools designed by human beings for their physical and psychological well-being: works of art, technology, products

(d) Rituals. A ritual is a type of activity which takes on symbolic meaning, consisting of a fixed sequence of behaviour repeated over time.

The learning and sharing of culture is made possible by language (both written and spoken, verbal and non-verbal).

Knowledge of the culture of a society is clearly of value to businesses in a number of ways. Culture influences tastes and lifestyles and therefore influences the sorts of products and services a business should offer. Marketers can adapt their products accordingly, and be fairly sure of a sizeable market. This is particularly important in export markets. Human resource managers may need to tackle cultural differences in recruitment. For example, some ethnic minorities have different body language which may be hard for some interviewers to interpret.

Cultural change might have to be planned for.

The technological environment

Technological developments can affect all aspects of business, not just product and services.

Technology contributes to overall economic growth via gains in productivity (more output per units of input); reduced costs (eg transportation technology) and new types of product.

Effects of technological change on organisations

(a) The type of products or services that are made and sold.

(b) The way in which products are made (eg process automation, new raw materials).

(c) The way in which goods and services are sold. The growth of direct selling via the internet has had a significant impact on the implementation of business strategy

(d) The way in which markets are identified. Database systems make it much easier to analyse the market place.

(e) The way in which firms are managed. IT encourages delayering of organisational hierarchies, homeworking, and better communication. Technology has also enabled greater integration between buyers and suppliers.

(f) The means and extent of communications with external clients.

The impact of recent technological change also has potentially important social consequences, which in turn have an impact on business.

(a) Homeworking. Whereas people were once collected together to work in factories, home working will become more important.

(b) Knowledge work. Certain sorts of skill, related to interpretation of data and information processes, are likely to become more valued than manual or physical skills.

(c) Services. Technology increases manufacturing productivity, releasing human resources for service jobs. These jobs require greater interpersonal skills (eg in dealing with customers).

Environmental protection

The physical environment is important for logistical reasons, as a source of resources, and because of increasing regulation.

The importance of physical environmental conditions

(a) Resource inputs. Managing physical resources successfully (eg oil companies, mining companies) is a good source of profits.

(b) Logistics. The physical environment presents logistical problems or opportunities to organisations.

(c) Government. The physical environment is under government influence.

    (i) Local authority town planning departments can influence where a building and necessary infrastructure can be sited.

    (ii) Governments can set regulations about some of the organisation's environmental interactions.

(d) Disasters. In some countries, the physical environment can pose a major threat to organisations.

The impact of business activity on the physical environment is now a major concern. Companies are under pressure to incorporate measures to protect the environment into their plans. This presents both challenges and opportunities, since some measures will impose costs, but others will allow significant savings. There is also a new range of markets for goods and services designed to protect or have minimum impact on the environment.

Martin Bennett and Peter James looked at the ways in which a company's concern for the environment can impact on its performance:

(a) Short-term savings through waste minimisation and energy efficiency schemes can be substantial.

(b) Pressures on businesses for environmental action are increasing.

(c) Companies with poor environmental performance may face increased cost of capital because investors and lenders demand a higher risk premium.

(d) There are a growing number of energy and environmental taxes, such as landfill tax.

(e) Accidents and long-term environmental effects can result in large financial liabilities.

(f) Pressure group campaigns can cause damage to reputation and/or additional costs.

(g) Environmental legislation may cause some products to be phased out, but in doing so can provide opportunities for new products to replace them.

(h) The cost of processing input which becomes waste is equivalent to 5–10% of some organisation's revenue.

They go on to suggest six main ways in which business and environmental benefits can be achieved:

(a) Integrating the environment into capital expenditure decisions (by considering environmental opposition to projects which could affect cash flows, for example).

(b) Understanding and managing environmental costs. Environmental costs are often 'hidden' in overheads and environmental and energy costs are often not allocated to the relevant budgets.

(c) Introducing waste minimisation schemes.

(d) Understanding and managing life cycle costs. For many products, the greatest environmental impact occurs upstream (such as mining raw materials) or downstream from production (such as energy to operate equipment). This has led to producers being made responsible for dealing with the disposal of products such as cars, and government and third party measures to influence raw material choices. Organisations therefore need to identify, control and make provision for environmental life cycle costs and work with suppliers and customers to identify environmental cost reduction opportunities.

(e) Measuring environmental performance. Business is under increasing pressure to measure all aspects of environmental performance, both for statutory disclosure reasons and due to demands for more environmental data from customers.

(f) Involving management accountants in a strategic approach to environment-related management accounting and performance evaluation.

Such analysis and action should help organisations to better understand present and future environmental costs and benefits.

John Elkington, chairman of the think-tank SustainAbility Ltd, has said that sustainability now embraces not only environmental and economic questions, but also social and ethical dimensions. He writes about the **triple bottom line**, which means that businesses must increasingly recognise that the challenge now is to help deliver simultaneously:

- Economic prosperity
- Environmental quality
- Social equity

Elkington quotes the example of Kvaerner, the Norwegian construction company, to show how important it is to control material and energy usage. An environmental report compiled by the company listed the following:

- A 20% cut in insurance premiums would be worth $15 million
- A 1% reduction in absence due to sick leave is worth $30 million
- A 1% reduction in material and energy consumption is worth $60 million

The legal environment

Various legal factors affect all companies:

Factor	Example
General legal framework: contract, tort, agency	Basic ways of doing business; negligence proceedings; ownership; rights and responsibilities, property
Criminal law	Theft; insider dealing; bribery; deception; industrial espionage
Company law	Directors and their duties; reporting requirements; takeover proceedings; shareholders' rights; insolvency
Employment law	Trade Union recognition; minimum wage; unfair dismissal; redundancy; maternity; Equal Opportunities
Health and safety	Fire precautions; safety procedures
Data protection	Use of information about employees and customers
Marketing and sales	Laws to protect consumers (eg refunds and replacement, 'cooling off' period after credit agreements); what is or isn't allowed in advertising
Environment	Pollution control; waste disposal
Tax law	Corporation tax payment; Collection of income tax (PAYE) and National Insurance contributions; sales tax (VAT)
Competition law	General illegality of cartels

5 Macro-economic Change

Yip identifies four aspects of globalisation as key drivers of change in the macro-environment:

- Market globalisation
- Cost globalisation
- Government activity and policy
- Global competition

Market globalisation

Gradual globalisation of markets is taking place because of the interplay of a number of forces. It is impossible to isolate a simple chain of causation here. Consumer tastes are becoming more homogeneous eg in entertainment. As markets globalise, firms supplying them become global customers for their own inputs and seek global suppliers. Improvements in global communications and logistics reduce costs, make globalisation easier and allow the creation of global brands. The latter feeds back to the homogenisation of taste.

Cost globalisation

Economies of scale are a major source of cost advantage: companies in some industries, such as some electronics manufacture, can continue to gain such economies even as they (the companies) expand up to global size. Experience effects can continue to drive down costs in the same way. An organisation undertaking any activity learns to do it more efficiently over time, as it gains more experience of carrying out that activity. This increased efficiency reduces unit costs. Sourcing efficiencies may be achieved by central procurement from global lowest-cost suppliers. Country-specific cost advantages, such as low labour costs or a favourable exchange rate, encourage purchasers to search globally for suppliers. High costs of product development can be spread over longer production runs if products are standardised and sold globally.

Government policy

The climate of government opinion has been increasingly sympathetic to free trade, though producer special interests and popular discontent continue to hamper it. Technical standardisation in both manufacturing and services has also encouraged increased trade, while some governments have been active in seeking foreign direct investment.

Global competition

Competitive forces seem to have had global effects. Existing high levels of international trade encourage further interaction between competitors as a matter of routine. The existence of global competitors and global customers in an industry prompts purely national firms to start trading globally so as to be able to compete on an even footing.

6 Porter's Diamond

Michael Porter identifies four principal determinants of national competitive advantage:

- Factor conditions
- Firm strategy structure and rivalry
- Demand conditions
- Related and supporting industries

Porter's The Competitive Advantage of Nations, suggests that some nations' industries are more internationally competitive than others. Porter does not believe that countries or nations as such are competitive, but rather that the conditions within a country may help firms to compete.

The original explanation for national success was the theory of comparative advantage. This held that relative opportunity costs determined the appropriateness of particular economic activities in relation to other countries. (Opportunity cost is defined as the value of that which must be given up in order to acquire or achieve something.)

Porter argues that comparative advantage is too general a concept to explain the success of individual companies and industries. He suggests that industries that require high technology and highly skilled employees are less affected than low technology industries by the relative costs of their inputs of raw materials and basic labour as determined by the national endowment of factors of production.

We must therefore look elsewhere for the determinants of national competitive advantage.

Porter identifies four principal factors, which are outlined in the diagram below. Porter refers to this as the diamond.

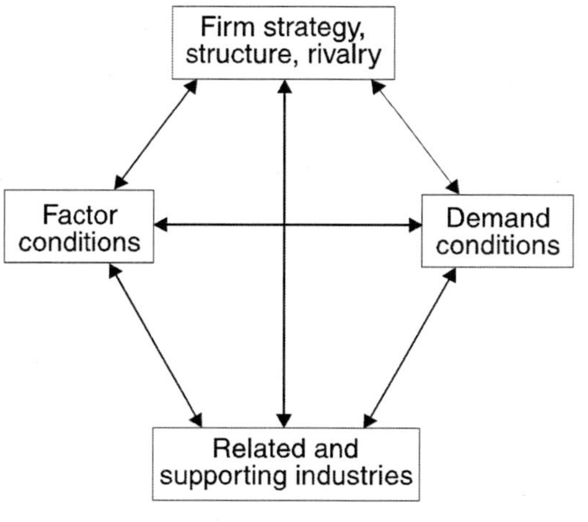

Analysing the diamond

Factor conditions

Factor conditions are a country's endowment of inputs to production.

- Human resources (skills, price, motivation, industrial relations)
- Physical resources (land, minerals, climate, location relative to other nations)
- Knowledge (scientific and technical know-how, educational institutions)
- Capital (amounts available for investment, how it is deployed)
- Infrastructure (transport, communications, housing)

Porter distinguishes between **basic** and **advanced** factors.

(a) **Basic** factors are natural resources, climate, semiskilled and unskilled labour. They are inherent, or at best their creation involves little investment. They are unsustainable as a source of national competitive advantage, since they are widely available.

(b) **Advanced** factors are associated with a well-developed scientific and technological infrastructure and include modern digital communications infrastructure, highly educated people, research laboratories and so on. They are necessary to achieve high order competitive advantages such as differentiated products and proprietary production technology.

An abundance of factors is not enough. It is the efficiency with which they are deployed that matters. Porter also notes that generalised factors, such as transport infrastructure do not provide as decisive and sustainable bases for competitive advantage as do specialised factors. These are factors that are relevant to a limited range of industries, such as knowledge bases in particular fields and logistic systems developed for particular goods or raw materials. Such factors are integral to innovation and very difficult to move to other countries.

Demand conditions: the home market

The home market determines how firms perceive, interpret and respond to buyer needs. This information puts pressure on firms to innovate and provides a launch pad for global ambitions.

(a) There are no cultural impediments to communication.

(b) The segmentation of the home market shapes a firm's priorities: companies will be successful globally in segments which are similar to the home market.

(c) Sophisticated and demanding buyers set standards. If the home market sets high standards, achieving these high standards will put a firm in a strong position to be competitive on the international market.

(d) Anticipation of buyer needs: if consumer needs are expressed in the home market earlier than in the world market, the firm benefits from experience.

(e) The rate of growth. Slow growing home markets do not encourage the adoption of state of the art technology.

(f) Early saturation of the home market will encourage a firm to export.

Related and supporting industries

Competitive success in one industry is linked to success in related industries. Domestic suppliers are preferable to foreign suppliers, as they offer continuing close co-operation and co-ordination. The process of innovation is also enhanced when suppliers are of high quality, since information is transmitted rapidly and problems are solved by joint effort.

Firm strategy, structure and rivalry

Management style and industrial structure. Nations are likely to display competitive advantage in industries that are culturally suited to their normal management practices and industrial structures.

Influencing the diamond

A nation's competitive industries tend to be clustered. Porter believes clustering to be a key to national competitive advantage. A cluster is a linking of industries through relationships that are either vertical (buyer-supplier) or horizontal (common customers, technology, skills).

How does a country create a diamond of competitive advantage? Governments cannot compete: only firms can do that. Governments can influence the context in which an industry operates and can create opportunities and pressures for innovation.

(a) Factors of production provide the seed corn.

(b) Related and supporting industries can also be a foundation, if the competences within them can be configured in a new way.

(c) Government policy should support cluster development and promote high standards of education, research and commercially relevant technologies. Although, government is not one of the four primary factors on the diamond, governments can play a crucial role in developing national competitive advantage. For example, governments can help shape levels of infrastructure and education in a country, and can directly affect a country's attractiveness as an investment location through their tax policies.

(d) Extraordinary demand in the home market based on national peculiarities and conditions can set the demand conditions determinant in the diamond.

However, while Porter's theory suggests that clustering will help international competitiveness, the cluster approach is not guaranteed to be successful.

If a firm wishes to compete in an industry in which there is no national competitive advantage, it can take a number of steps to succeed:

(a) Compete in the most challenging market, to emulate domestic rivalry and to obtain information. If a firm can compete successfully in such a market, even if this only means carving out a small niche, it should do well elsewhere.

(b) Spread research and development activities to countries where there is an established research base or industry cluster already.

(c) Be prepared to invest heavily in innovation.

(d) Invest in human resources, both in the firm and the industry as a whole. This might mean investing in training programmes.

(e) Look out for new technologies which will change the rules of the industry. The UK with its large efficient research base should have some creative ideas.

(f) Collaborate with foreign companies. American motor companies, successfully learned Japanese production techniques.

(g) Supply overseas companies. Japanese car plants in the UK have encouraged greater quality in UK components suppliers. Inward investment provides important learning opportunities for domestic companies.

(h) Source components from overseas.

(i) Exert pressure on politicians and opinion formers to create better conditions for the diamond to develop (eg in education).

7 INDUSTRY AND SECTOR

Industries tend not to be stable: such features as location, products, customers and rate of growth all tend to be more or less variable. One important feature of this instability is the way in which the boundaries of an industry can change. Previously distinct industries can converge: their technologies, activities and products start to mingle or become complementary and their member firms start to compete or collaborate. This process can be supply-led or demand-led.

Supply-led convergence occurs where suppliers discover links with suppliers in other industries and move together to cooperate in building new markets. Such convergence is common in the public sector, where government departments are regularly merged and reorganised. Government can also promote supply-led convergence in the private sector, especially by deregulation, as has happened in the UK financial services industry. Demand-led convergence occurs when customers treat the products of different industries as substitutable, as in the case of mobile and fixed line telephones, or complementary, as in the case of air travel and car hire.

8 Porter's Five Forces

The competitive environment is structured by five forces: threat of new entrants; substitute products; the bargaining power of customers; the bargaining power of suppliers; competitive rivalry. In discussing competition, Porter (Competitive Strategy) distinguishes between factors that characterise the nature of competition. In one industry compared with another, some factors make one industry as a whole potentially more profitable than another (ie yielding a bigger return on investment). Factors within a particular industry lead to the competitive strategies that individual firms might select.

Five competitive forces influence the state of competition in an industry, and collectively determine the profit potential of the industry as a whole:

- The threat of new entrants to the industry
- The threat of substitute products or services
- The bargaining power of customers
- The bargaining power of suppliers
- The rivalry amongst current competitors in the industry

Each of these factors is considered further below.

The threat of new entrants (and barriers to entry to keep them out)

A new entrant into an industry will bring extra capacity and more competition (and so could, in turn, drive down profits). The strength of this threat is likely to vary from industry to industry and depends on two things: firstly, the strength of the barriers to entry. Barriers to entry discourage new entrants. Secondly, the strengthening of the threat depends upon the likely response of existing competitors to the new entrant.

Barriers to entry can arise from:

(a) **Scale economies**. High fixed costs often imply a high breakeven point, and a high breakeven point depends on a large volume of sales. If the market as a whole is not growing, the new entrant has to capture a large slice of the market from existing competitors.

(b) **Product differentiation**. Existing firms in an industry may have built up a good brand image and strong customer loyalty over a long period of time. A few firms may promote a large number of brands to crowd out the competition.

(c) **Capital requirements.** When capital investment requirements are high, the barrier against new entrants will be strong, particularly when the investment would possibly be high-risk.

(d) **Knowledge requirements**. As well as high capital requirements, knowledge and know-how are also a barrier to entry. It is much more difficult to enter an industry which requires significant specialist knowledge, and skills, than an industry where no specialist skills are required.

(e) **Switching costs**. Switching costs refer to the costs (time, money, convenience) that a customer would have to incur by switching from one supplier's products to another's.

(f) **Access to distribution channels.** Distribution channels carry a manufacturer's products to the end-buyer. New distribution channels are difficult to establish, and existing distribution channels hard to gain access to.

(g) **Cost advantages** of existing producers, independent of economies of scale include:

(i) Patent rights
(ii) Experience and know-how
(iii) Government subsidies and regulations
(iv) Favoured access to raw materials

Entry barriers might be lowered by the impact of change for example, changes in the environment, technological changes or new distribution channels for products or services (eg the internet).

The threat from substitute products

A substitute product is a good or service produced by another industry which satisfies the same customer needs. Substitutes are always present, but they can be easy to overlook because they may be very different from the industry's product. It is very easy to misunderstand the nature of substitute products in Porter's model: while they provide competition, they are not goods or services produced by competitors in the same industry.

When the threat of substitutes is high, industry profitability suffers. Substitute products or services limit an industry's profit potential by placing a ceiling on prices (because buyers will switch to the substitute if it offers a better value alternative).

The threat of a substitute is high if it offers an attractive alternative to the industry's product in terms of price and performance, or if the buyer's cost of switching to the substitute is low.

The bargaining power of customers

Customers want better quality products and services at a lower price. Satisfying this might force down the profitability of suppliers in the industry. Just how strong the position of customers will be depends on a number of factors:

- How much the customer buys
- How many buyers there are: if there are relatively few buyers but each is large relative to the supplier, then the buyers will be powerful
- How critical the product is to the customer's own business (if the customer is completely reliant on a product this will reduce the customer's bargaining power)
- Switching costs (ie the cost of switching supplier)
- Whether the products are standard items (hence easily copied) or specialised
- The customer's own profitability: a customer who makes low profits will be forced to insist on low prices from suppliers
- Customer's ability to bypass the supplier (or take over the supplier)
- The skills of the customer purchasing staff, or the price-awareness of consumers
- When product quality is important to the customer, the customer is less likely to be price-sensitive, and so the industry might be more profitable as a consequence

The bargaining power of suppliers

Suppliers can exert pressure for higher prices. The ability of suppliers to get higher prices depends on several factors:

- Whether there are just one or two dominant suppliers to the industry, able to charge monopoly or oligopoly prices

- The threat of new entrants or substitute products to the supplier's industry
- Whether the suppliers have other customers outside the industry, and do not rely on the industry for the majority of their sales
- The importance of the supplier's product to the customer's business
- Whether the supplier has a differentiated product which buyers need to obtain
- Whether switching costs for customers would be high

The rivalry amongst current competitors in the industry

The intensity of competitive rivalry within an industry will affect the profitability of the industry as a whole. Competitive actions might take the form of price competition, advertising battles, sales promotion campaigns, introducing new products for the market, improving after sales service or providing guarantees or warranties. Competition can stimulate demand, expanding the market, or it can leave demand unchanged, in which case individual competitors will make less money, unless they are able to cut costs.

Factors determining the intensity of competition

(a) **Market growth**. Rivalry is intensified when firms are competing for a greater market share in a total market where growth is slow or stagnant. For example, supermarkets Tesco, Sainsbury's and Asda are becoming increasingly competitive in their attempt to maintain their market share, in the context of the rise of discount retailers Aldi and Lidl.

(b) **Cost structure**. High fixed costs are a temptation to compete on price, as in the short run any contribution from sales is better than none at all. A perishable product produces the same effect.

(c) **Switching**. Suppliers will compete if buyers can, and do, switch easily.

(d) **Capacity**. A supplier might need to achieve a substantial increase in output capacity, in order to obtain reductions in unit costs.

(e) **Uncertainty**. When one firm is not sure what another is up to, there is a tendency to respond to the uncertainty by formulating a more competitive strategy.

(f) **Strategic importance**. If success is a prime strategic objective, firms will be likely to act very competitively to meet their targets.

(g) **Exit barriers** make it difficult for an existing supplier to leave the industry. These can take many forms.

   (i) **Non-current assets with a low break-up value** (eg there may be no other use for them, or they may be old)

   (ii) The **cost of redundancy payments** to employees

   (iii) If the firm is a division or subsidiary of a larger enterprise, the **effect of withdrawal on the other operations within the group**

   (iv) The **reluctance of managers to admit defeat**, their loyalty to employees and their fear for their own jobs

   (v) **Government pressures** on major employers not to shut down operations, especially when competition comes from foreign producers rather than other domestic producers

9 The Industry Life Cycle

It may be possible to discern an industry life cycle, which will have wider implications for the nature of competition and competitive advantage. This cycle reflects changes in demand and the spread of technical knowledge among producers. Innovation creates the new industry, and this is normally product innovation. Later, innovation shifts to processes in order to maintain margins. The overall progress of the industry lifecycle is illustrated below.

	Inception	Growth	Maturity/ shakeout	Decline
Product characteristics	Basic, no standards established	Improved design and quality, differentiated	Standardised product with little differentiation	Varied quality but fairly undifferentiated
Competitors	None to few	Many entrants	Competition increases, weaker players leave	Few remain. Competition may be on price
Buyers	Early adopters, prosperous, curious must be induced	More customers attracted and aware	Mass market, brand switching common	Enthusiasts, traditionalists, sophisticates
Profits	Negative – high first mover advantage	Good, possibly starting to decline	Eroding under pressure of competition	Variable
Technology	No standards established	Technologies become more standardised	Technology is understood across the industry	Technology is understood across the industry
Production processes	Small scale batch production. Specialised distributors	Mass production. Distribution networks expanded	Long production runs. Cost efficiency critical	Overcapacity. Production is reduced

Each phase has different implications for competitive behaviour and corporate strategy for example if an industry is growing, the organisations in that industry can grow as the market develops. In a mature industry, growth can only be achieved by stealing market share from other competitors and typically the market becomes more fragmented.

Costs faced by organisations will also vary at different stages in the industry lifecycle. For example, research and development costs will be very high in the inception phase. Production costs may be low during the maturity stage as processes have been refined and contracts negotiated, but marketing expenditure may be high in order to protect market share.

Financial returns to an industry also vary according to the lifecycle stage.

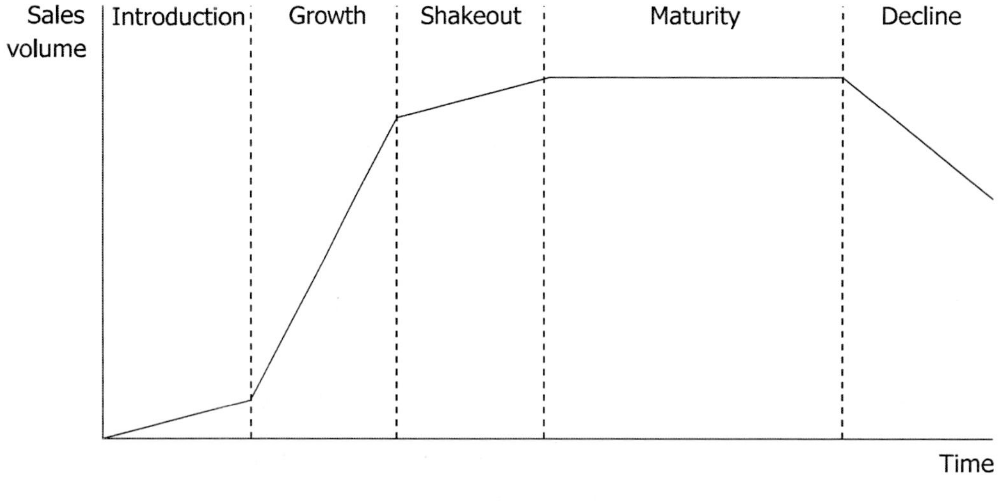

The characteristics of the industry at the different phases of the lifecycle are shown in the table below.

	Inception	Growth	Shakeout	Maturity	Decline
Customers	Experimenters, innovators	Early adopters	Growing selectivity of purchase	Mass market, Products well known	Price competition Commodity product
R&D	High	Extend product before competition	Seek lower cost methods of supply to access new markets	Low	
Company	Early mover Production focused	React to more competitors with increased marketing mass production	Potential consolidation through taking-over rivals. Long production runs	Battles over market share. Seek cost reduction. Long production runs	Cost control or exit
Competitors	A few No major barriers to entry	More entrants to the market	Many competitors, price cutting but weeding out of weaker players	Depending on industry, a few large competitors Difficult for newcomers to dislodge entrenched companies	Price-based competition, fewer competitors
Profitability	Low or negative, as an investment	Growing	Levelling off	Stable, high or under pressure	Falling, unless cost control

The industry life cycle has strategic implications for organisations operating in that industry. Management must pursue different strategies at each stage.

Inception stage

- Attract trend-setting buyer groups by promotion of technical novelty or fashion
- Price high (skim) to cash in on novelty, or price low (penetration) to gain adoption and high initial share
- Support product despite poor current financial results
- Review investment program periodically in light of success of launch (eg delay or bring forward capacity increases)
- Build channels of distribution
- Monitor success of rival technologies and competitor products

Growth stage

- Ensure capacity expands sufficiently to meet firm's target market share objectives
- Penetrate market, possibly by reducing price
- Maintain barriers to entry (eg fight patent infringements, keep price competitive)
- High promotion of benefits to attract early majority of potential buyers
- Build brand awareness to resist impact from new entrants

- Ensure investors are aware of potential of new products to ensure support for financial strategy
- Search for additional markets and product refinements (ie market penetration)
- Consider methods of expanding and reducing costs of production (eg contract manufacturing overseas, building own factory in a low cost location)
- Product development

Shakeout phase

- Monitor industry for potential mergers and rationalisation behaviour
- Periodic review of production and financial forecasts in light of sales growth rates
- Shift business model from customer acquisition to extracting revenue from existing customers
- Seek to extend growth by finding new markets or technologies

Maturity phase

- Maximise current financial returns from product
- Defend market position by matching pricing and promotion of rivals
- Modify markets by positioning product to gain acceptance from non-buyers (eg new outlets or suggested new uses)
- Modify the product to make it cheaper or of greater benefit
- Intensify distribution
- Leverage the existing customer database to gain additional incomes
- Engage in integration activities with rivals (eg mergers, mutual agreements on competition)
- Ensure successor industries are ready for launch to pick up market

Decline phase

- Harvest cash flows by minimising spending on promotion or product refinement
- Simplify range by weeding out variations
- Narrow distribution to target loyal customers and reduce stocking costs
- Evaluate exit barriers and identify the optimum time to leave the industry (eg leases ending, need for renewal investment)
- Seek potential exit strategy (eg buyer for business, firms willing to buy licences etc)
- The response of competitors is particularly important – there may be threats as they attempt to defend their position, or opportunities, eg when a competitor leaves the market

	Inception	Growth	Maturity	Decline
Product	• Correct any problems in product design • Improve features to develop competitive advantage	• Ensure product quality is maintained despite volume growth • Look at ways to improve quality and design to sustain competitive advantage	• Product efficiency • Cost control • Quality control (minimise defective products) • Only the most productive/ efficient firms will survive	• Assess if it is possible to modify product so that life cycle is started again
Marketing	• Establish product position and target markets • Develop product awareness (advertising; promotion)	• Market penetration • Establish market niche for product • Establish brand loyalty: heavy media use, product samples and other promotions • Establish distribution capabilities to support increased production	• Marketing aimed at maintaining customer loyalty	• Advertising and promotion is minimised
HR	• Establish staff requirements • Recruiting staff	• Training and development of staff to deal with competitive pressures as competition gets tougher	• Personnel incentives to improve productivity and efficiency	• Staff transferred to products in earlier stages of life cycle
Finance	• Arrange funding for product development and marketing • Assess capital requirements for production facilities which may be needed for increased capacity in growth phase			• Liquidation (worst case scenario)

The industry life cycle model is an important concept that may illuminate some aspects of strategic thought. Like other models, it has some value for analysis, for forecasting trends and for suggesting possible courses of action, but it would be a mistake to attempt to apply it to all industries at all times. Proper attention must always be paid to current circumstances and options.

10 Implications of Strategic Theories on Company Action

How do we fit all this together to enable us to produce insightful and meaning analysis of an entity's strategic position and its development? It is important to remember the purpose of all environmental analysis ideas is to provide input into the process of designing a **practical business strategy**. One very useful way of thinking about the implications of environmental information is to consider it in terms of summarised **opportunities and threats.**

Threats

For a commercial organisation, the most urgent threats are likely to emerge from within the immediate industry arena. The **five forces** model provides a good summary of the threats inherent here, supplemented by strategic group analysis. Recognising threats in the wider PESTEL environment is, perhaps, more difficult, since it covers such an enormous range of factors.

Opportunities

Opportunities may take the form of **strategic gaps**: these are potentially profitable aspects of the competitive environment that are not being exploited by rivals. Johnson, Scholes and Whittington give several examples of how these might arise:

(a) Potential **substitutes** for existing products might be created. This is largely a technology-based opportunity, but an important route to the development of substitutes is the imaginative development of new uses for existing products and methods.

(b) Other **strategic groups** may present opportunities, especially if there are changes in the macro-environment, such as deregulation or opening of new markets in developing countries.

(c) It may be possible to target **different strategic customers.** In the case of consumer goods, the development of internet selling means that the ultimate user is displacing the distributor as the strategic customer.

(d) There may be potential to market **complementary products.** For example, capital goods manufacturers routinely offer credit services to assist the customer to buy.

(e) New **market segments** may have potential, though there may be a need to adapt the product.

All of the environmental factors affecting an organisation can be summarised as either opportunities or threats. The diagram below illustrates this.

External forces

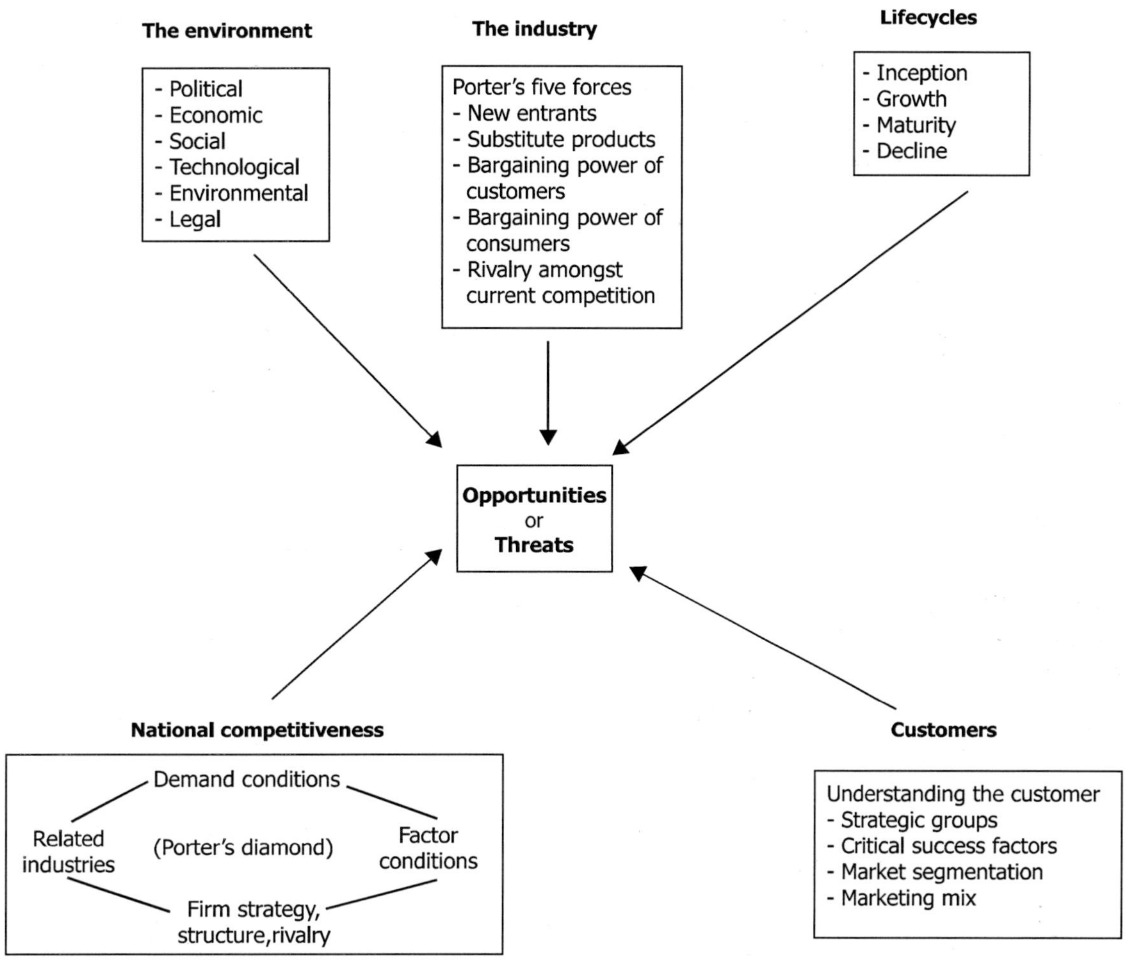

11 SWOT ANALYSIS

The **SWOT analysis** combines the results of the environmental analysis above, with a consideration of the organisation's internal operations. It uses a single framework for assessing the firm's current and future strategic fit, or lack of it, with the environment. It is an analysis of the organisation's strengths and weaknesses, and the opportunities and threats offered by the environment.

A complete awareness of the organisation's environment and its internal capacities is **necessary** for a rational consideration of future strategy. The threads must be drawn together so that potential strategies may be developed and assessed. This is done by combining the internal and external analyses into a SWOT analysis or corporate appraisal.

Effective SWOT analysis does not simply require a categorisation of information, it also requires some **evaluation of the relative importance** of the various factors under consideration.

(a) These features are only of relevance if they are **perceived to exist by the consumers.** Listing corporate features that internal personnel regard as strengths/weaknesses is of little relevance if they are not perceived as such by the organisation's consumers.

(b) In the same vein, threats and opportunities are conditions presented by the external environment and they should be independent of the firm.

The SWOT can now be used guiding strategy formulation.

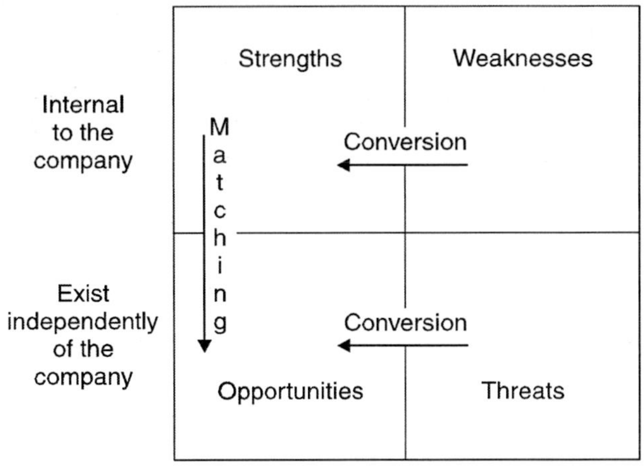

(a) **Match strengths with market opportunities**

Strengths that do not match any available opportunity are of limited use while opportunities which do not have any matching strengths are of little immediate value.

(b) **Conversion**

This requires the development of strategies that will convert weaknesses into strengths in order to take advantage of some particular opportunity, or converting threats into opportunities which can then be matched by existing strengths.

12 Levels of Strategy in an Organisation

There are three main levels of strategy in an organisation:

- Corporate: the general direction of the whole organisation
- Business: how the organisation or its SBUs tackle particular markets
- Operational/functional: specific strategies for different departments of the business

The distinction between corporate and business strategy arises because of the development of the divisionalised business organisation, which typically has a corporate centre and a number of strategic business units (SBUs) dealing with particular markets. Chandler described how four large US corporations found that the best way to divide strategic responsibility was to have the corporate HQ allocate resources and exercise overall financial control while the SBUs were each responsible for their own product-market strategies. Operational strategies are then developed for component parts of SBUs.

Defining aspects of corporate strategy

Characteristic	Comment
Scope of activities	Strategy and strategic management impact upon the whole organisation: all parts of the business operation should support and further the strategic plan.
Expectations of stakeholders	There may be a mission statement, but in any case, stakeholder expectations must be prioritised and managed.
Resources	Strategy involves choices about allocating or obtaining corporate resources now and in future.

Business-level strategy

Business-level strategy is about the particular and distinct combination of products and markets dealt with by one business unit. A business unit might be a small, independent organisation or part of a larger one. In the first case, business and corporate strategy merge with one another; in the second, SBU level strategies must be co-ordinated with corporate strategy and with each other.

Operational strategies

Operational strategies are concerned with how the component parts of an organisation deliver effectively the corporate- and business-level strategies in terms of resources, processes and people.

Much operational strategy is created by individual business functions and delivered by them.

Characteristic	Comment
Marketing	Devising products and services, pricing, promoting and distributing them, in order to satisfy customer needs at a profit. Marketing and corporate strategies are interrelated.
Production	Factory location, manufacturing techniques, outsourcing and so on.
Finance	Ensuring that the firm has enough financial resources to fund its other strategies by identifying sources of finance and using them effectively.
Human resources management	Secure personnel of the right skills in the right quantity at the right time, and to ensure that they have the right skills and values to promote the firm's overall goals.
Information systems	A firm's information systems are becoming increasingly important, as an item of expenditure, as administrative support and as a tool for competitive strength. Not all information technology applications are strategic, and the strategic value of IT will vary from case to case.
R&D	New products and techniques.

13 Elements of Strategic Management

Johnson, Scholes and Whittington analyse strategic management into three main elements.

- **Strategic position**
- **Strategic choices**
- **Strategy into action** (implementation)

Strategic position

The strategic managers must attempt to understand the organisation's strategic position. There are three main groups of influences to consider: the environment; strategic capability and the expectations of stakeholders.

The environment

The environment of business includes wider political, economic, social, technological, environmentally conscious and legal forces as well as the more immediate pressures of business competition. It is both complex and subject to constant change, to an extent that probably precludes complete understanding. However, if the more salient aspects of the environment can be identified and described, they may be diagnosed into opportunities and threats.

Strategic capability

The organisation's resources and competences make up its strategic capability. This may be analysed into strengths and weaknesses; these influence, enable or constrain possible future strategic choices.

Stakeholders' expectations

Strategy is made in order to achieve the organisation's purpose. This may have a formal, even legal, definition and corporate governance may be a relevant issue. Consideration must also be given to the expectations of stakeholder groups that have a less formal relationship with the organisation. Stakeholder power and interest influence the direction in which strategy evolves, as do ethical issues.

Strategic choices

Strategic choices are made at both the corporate and business unit level. At the level of the business unit, these choices are about how to achieve competitive advantage and are based on an understanding of customers and markets. At the corporate level, strategy is primarily about scope: this is concerned with the overall product/business portfolio, the spread of markets and the relationship between business units and the corporate centre.

Strategic choices must also be made about the direction and method of development.

Strategy into action (implementation)

Strategies must be made to work in practice. Major issues here include structuring, enabling and change:

(a) Structuring includes processes, relationships, organisation structure and how these elements work together.

(b) Enabling is the complex two-way process by which the organisation's resources are managed to both support and to create strategies.

(c) Change is a very common feature of strategic development and the management of change is an important feature of strategic implementation.

Johnson, Scholes and Whittington represent these three elements as a Venn diagram as illustrated below:

Strategic Choices

chapter 2

Contents

1 Introduction

Strategic choice often relates to business expansion, which thus impacts directly on the corporate finance arena. This chapter considers the strategic choices that an organisation is faced with in terms of securing growth in line with strategic objectives. We look at the strategic arguments that exist for different methods of expansion and what are the relevant factors for consideration.

2 Diversity of Products and Markets

Expansion can be achieved via diversification – either related or unrelated. Johnson, Scholes and Whittington suggest three reasons why all types of diversification may be advantageous.

(a) Economies of scope (as opposed to economies of scale) may result from the greater use of under-utilised resources. These benefits are often referred to in terms of "synergy" and can take several forms:

   (i) **Marketing synergy** is achieved by extending the use of marketing facilities such as distribution channels; sales staff and administration; and warehousing.

   (ii) **Operating synergy** arises from the better use of operational facilities and personnel, bulk purchasing, and a greater spread of fixed costs whereby the firm's competence can be transferred to making new products.

   (iii) **Investment synergy** comes from the wider use of a common investment in non-current assets, working capital or research, such as the joint use of plant, common raw material inventory and transfer of research and development from one product to another.

   (iv) **Management synergy** is the advantage to be gained where management skills concerning current operations are easily transferred to new operations because of the similarity of problems in the two industries.

(b) Corporate management skills may be extendible across a range of unrelated businesses. In a way this is also a kind of synergy, in which the corporate parent represents the resource that can be more intensively utilised. This kind of approach is commonly seen in consumer goods groups that deploy brand management skills across a diverse range of products and markets.

(c) Diversification can increase market power via cross-subsidisation. A high margin business can subsidise a low margin one, enabling it to create a price advantage over its rivals and building market share. Eventually, it may achieve a dominant position that enables it to increase its prices and recoup earlier group losses.

Johnson, Scholes and Whittington also discuss **three questionable reasons** that may be advanced to justify a policy of diversification:

(a) **Response to environmental change** can be justified as a reason to diversify if it is undertaken in order to protect existing shareholder value by, for example, responding to the emergence of new and threatening technology developments. However, the environmental change reasoning is sometimes used as a cover for what is actually a move to protect the interests of top management; typically, this will lead to ill-considered acquisitions that destroy value.

(b) **Risk spreading** can be a valid reason for an owner-managed business to diversify, but financial theory suggests that shareholders in large corporations can manage their risk exposure better by diversifying their own portfolios.

(c) The **expectations of powerful stakeholders** can lead to inappropriate strategies generally.

3 Related Diversification

Related diversification is development beyond current products and markets but within the capabilities or value network of the organisation.

The argument of synergy is often used to justify related diversification. However, achieving synergy can be difficult and requires considerable strategic skill, both to recognise synergistic potential and to achieve it in practice. Simply undertaking more and more value activities is not necessarily a route to improved performance: each activity undertaken must be managed in a skilful and appropriate manner. A number of very large corporations have de-merged with success. Also, the management of external relationships with suppliers, customers and collaborators is emerging as an effective alternative to expansion.

Horizontal integration makes use of current capabilities by development into activities that are competitive with or directly complementary to a company's present activities. An example would be a TV company that moved into film production.

Vertical integration occurs when a company expands backwards or forwards within its existing value network and thus becomes its own supplier or distributor. For example, backward integration would occur if a milk processing business acquired its own dairy farms rather than buying raw milk from independent farmers. If a cloth manufacturer began to produce shirts instead of selling all of its cloth to other shirt manufacturers, this would be **forward integration**.

Vertical integration has its greatest potential for success when the final customer's needs are not being properly satisfied. If there is potential for improving the satisfaction of the end user by improving the links in the value network, then an integration strategy may succeed. Examples would be where there is a premium on speed, as in the marketing of fresh foodstuffs, or when complex technical features require great attention to quality procedures.

Advantages of vertical integration

- A secure supply of components or materials, hence lower supplier bargaining power
- Stronger relationships with the final consumer of the product
- A share of the profits at all stages of the value network
- More effective pursuit of a differentiation strategy
- Creation of barriers to entry

Disadvantages of vertical integration

(a) Overconcentration. A company places 'more eggs in the same end-market basket' (Ansoff, I). Such a policy is fairly inflexible, more sensitive to instabilities and increases the firm's dependence on a particular aspect of economic demand.

(b) The firm fails to benefit from any economies of scale or technical advances in the industry into which it has diversified. This is why, in the publishing industry, most printing is subcontracted to specialist printing firms, who can work machinery to capacity by doing work for many firms.

4 Unrelated Diversification

Unrelated diversification is the development of products or services beyond the current capabilities or value network. Unrelated diversification produces a conglomerate. Conglomerate diversification can succeed when managed by particularly talented strategic leaders who deploy an effective dominant logic; dominant logic is the term used by *Prahalad and Bettis* to signify a cognitive orientation or world-view based on sound judgement and experience.

Potential advantages of conglomerate diversification

Bear in mind our discussion of questionable reasons for diversification when considering these points:

(a) **Risk-spreading.** Entering new products into new markets can compensate for the failure of current products and markets.

(b) **Improved profit opportunities.** An improvement of the **overall profitability and flexibility** of the firm may arise through acquisition in industries with better prospects than those of the acquiring firms.

(c) **Escape** from a declining market

(d) **Use a company's image and reputation** in one market to develop into another where corporate image and reputation could be vital ingredients for success

Potential disadvantages of conglomerate diversification

(a) **Shareholders would rather diversify their own portfolios.** Having companies in a group, with little synergy with one another, or even worse, negative synergy, actually destroys shareholder value.

(b) The **dilution of shareholders' earnings** if diversification is into growth industries with high P/E ratios.

(c) **Lack of a common identity and purpose** in a conglomerate organisation. A conglomerate will only be successful if it has a high quality of management and financial ability at central headquarters, where the diverse operations are brought together.

(d) **Failure in one of the businesses will drag down the rest**, as it will eat up resources.

(e) **Lack of management experience.**

5 International Diversification

Globalisation

There have been several factors at work which have resulted in the increase in world trade since the middle of last century:

(a) **Import substitution.** A country aims to produce manufactured goods which it previously imported, by protecting local producers. This has had limited success.

(b) **Export-led growth.** The success of this particular strategy has depended on the existence of open markets elsewhere. Japan, South Korea, Taiwan have chosen this route.

(c) **Market convergence**. Transnational market segments have developed whose characteristics are more homogeneous than the different segments within a given geographic market. Youth culture is an important influence here.

This has meant a proliferation of suppliers exporting to, or trading in, a wider variety of places. In many domestic markets it is now likely that the same international companies will be competing with one another. However, the existence of global markets should not be taken for granted in terms of all products and services, or indeed in all territories.

(a) Some **services** are still subject to managed trade (for example, some countries prohibit firms from other countries from selling insurance). Trade in services has been liberalised under the auspices of the World Trade Organisation.

(b) **Immigration.** There is unlikely ever to be a global market for labour, given the disparity in skills between different countries and restrictions on immigration.

(c) The market for some goods is much more globalised than for others.

(i) Upmarket luxury goods may not be required or afforded by people in developing nations.

(ii) Some goods can be sold almost anywhere, but to limited degrees. Television sets are consumer durables in some countries, but still luxury or relatively expensive items in other ones.

(iii) Other goods are needed almost everywhere. In oil a truly global industry exists in both production (eg North Sea, Venezuela, Russia, Azerbaijan, Gulf states) and consumption (any country using cars and buses, not to mention those with chemical industries based on oil).

Developing the global business

Ohmae describes five stages in the evolution of a global business:

(a) **Exporting**. The product is saleable in overseas markets and they are exploited by means of foreign intermediaries such as agents and distributors. Foreign sales are a profitable extension of domestic operations. Little or no adjustment is made to the product in order to reap economies of scale. This is a low risk strategy, since there is little financial commitment, but the company is very much dependent on the effort and motivation of its foreign intermediaries.

(b) **Overseas branches**. Existing and potential export sales are high enough to justify largely replacing the foreign intermediaries with the company's own foreign sales and service branches. Financial commitment increases with increasing business, as does exchange rate and political risk. If the company is aiming to achieve globalisation, it is at this stage that it begins to acquire the local knowledge and experience that it will need.

(c) **Overseas production**. Export sales are now so high that shipping and other exporting-related costs represent an opportunity for savings by establishing overseas production. At the same time, overseas production can exploit cheap labour and other resources. Some functions, such as R&D and marketing are centralised and there is centralised control of manufacturing operations with regular reports to headquarters. World-wide synergies and economies of scale are sought and decisions on adapting to local conditions are made at headquarters. Products are still largely standardised.

(d) **Insiderisation**. The company clones itself in its overseas markets, completing the corporate functionality in each location rather than restricting itself to marketing. The aim is to develop a full marketing capability and offer products suited to local requirements. This approach reduces exchange rate and political risk but requires financial commitment. Economies of scale will be lost and there may be inefficiencies of co-ordination.

(e) **The global company**. The global company differs from the multinational in that it has a **geocentric** management orientation. It takes a world view while recognising local differences and similarities. It minimises its local adaptation of products and the rest of the marketing mix to those things that actually add customer value and it makes use of the best of its global facilities and people to promote overall excellence. It is likely to centralise functions such as R&D, finance and HR, though not necessarily all in the same place. At the same time its operations will be controlled locally. The primary skill of the global company is to integrate learning, skills, competences and technologies in order to achieve global efficiencies combined with local responsiveness. It manages the value chain so that each part is centred in an optimal location. It is subject to a number of problems:

- Differing cultural values may undermine the global corporate identity.
- Senior executives with the right mix of attitudes and skills are likely to be scarce.
- It is subject to a wide range of environmental risks, particularly political ones.

Ohmae suggests there are five reasons why companies are moving towards the global stage. He calls these the **five Cs**:

(a) **Customer**. Market convergence is driven by widespread customer demand for products with similar characteristics.

(b) **Company**. The search for economies of scale drives expansion towards the global scale.

(c) **Competition.** The very existence of global competitors motivates companies to expand for reasons of prestige and competitiveness. They may also be amenable to cost-reducing strategic alliances.

(d) **Currency**. Exchange rate risk can be managed most easily when a company has major cash flows in the countries in which it operates.

(e) **Country**. Multiple locations enable a company to exploit both absolute and comparative advantage. They also enable it to promote itself as locally oriented in each country, thus enhancing its image with the local government and markets.

There are other factors encouraging the globalisation of world trade:

(a) **Financial factors** such as Third World debt; often lenders require the initiation of economic reforms as a condition of the loan. This can lead to a reduction in local protectionism and a consequent increase in trade.

(b) **Country/continent** connections, such as that between the UK and the Commonwealth which foster trade and tourism.

(c) **Legal and regulatory factors** such as industrial standards and protection of intellectual property, which encourage the development and spread of standardised technology and design.

(d) **Markets** trading in international commodities; commodities are not physically exchanged, only the rights to ownership. A buyer can, thanks to efficient systems of trading and modern communications, buy a commodity in its country of origin for delivery to a specific destination at some future time.

(e) **The internet**; major companies are developing on-line systems of internal co-ordination and procurement.

(f) **Government policy** in many countries seeks to control the balance of payments by discouraging imports. Government policy towards importers will also reflect their quite proper desire to expand their economies and hence employment and improve the local standard of living. Local manufacture may thus be the only way to access some markets.

Designs for global businesses

Bartlett and Ghoshal find that the pressures driving globalisation exist independently of the need for local responsiveness; and that both vary from industry to industry. The relationship between these pressures influences both the management orientation and the structure of the company that operates internationally.

(a) The **global company**, if active in more than one industry, is likely to be organised in product divisions with global scope. Efficiency is likely to be a key strategic competency.

(b) Companies operating in industries that require **little local differentiation** and at the same time are not subject to pressure for globalisation will tend to be structured with an international or export division.

(c) The **multinational environment** drives a polycentric orientation, with largely autonomous local operating companies. Responsiveness to local demand is likely to be a key strategic competency.

(d) The **transnational environment** is particularly difficult to respond to. Global scale is desirable but local conditions require differentiated approaches. The structural response may be the global heterarchy. Each regional or national unit achieves global scale and influence within the overall organisation by exploiting its specialised competences on behalf of the whole company. Some headquarters functions, such as R&D may be diffused across the organisation. The role of the global strategic apex is to promote a corporate culture and shared values that will promote co-operation and co-ordination.

Market selection

In making a decision as to which market(s) to enter the firm must start by establishing its objectives. Here are some examples.

(a) What proportion of total sales will be overseas?

(b) What are the longer term objectives?

(c) Will it enter one, a few, or many markets? In most cases it is better to start by selling in countries with which there is some familiarity and then expand into other countries gradually as experience is gained. Reasons to enter fewer countries at first include the following.

- (i) Market entry and market control costs are high
- (ii) Product and market communications modification costs are high
- (iii) There is a large market and potential growth in the initial countries chosen
- (iv) Dominant competitors can establish high barriers to entry

(d) What types of country should it enter (in terms of environmental factors, economic development, language used, cultural similarities and so on)? Three major criteria should be as follows.

- (i) Market attractiveness
- (ii) Competitive advantage
- (iii) Risk

The matrix below can be used to bring together these three major criteria and assist managers in their decisions.

Evaluating which markets to enter

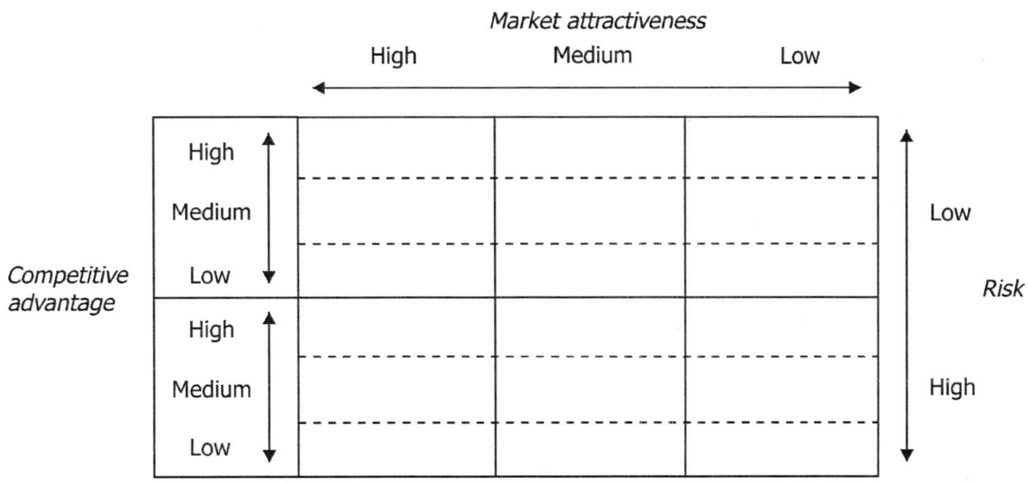

Source: Kotler

(a) **Market attractiveness**. This concerns such indicators as GNP/head and forecast demand, and market accessibility.

(b) **Competitive advantage**. This is principally dependent on prior experience in similar markets, language and cultural understanding.

(c) **Risk**. This involves an analysis of political stability, the possibility of government intervention and similar external influences.

The best markets to enter are those located at the top left of the diagram. The worst are those in the bottom right corner. Obtaining the information needed to reach this decision requires detailed and often costly international marketing research and analysis. Making these decisions is not easy, and a fairly elaborate screening process will be instituted.

In international business there are several categories of risk:

(a) **Political risk** relates to factors as diverse as wars, nationalisation, arguments between governments etc.

(b) **Business risk.** This arises from the possibility that the business idea itself might be flawed. As with political risk, it is not unique to international marketing, but firms might be exposed to more sources of risk arising from failures to understand the market.

(c) **Currency risk.** This arises out of the volatility of foreign exchange rates. Given that there is a possibility for speculation and that capital flows are free, such risks are increasing.

(d) **Profit repatriation risk.** Government actions may make it hard to repatriate profits.

Modes of entry to foreign markets

If an organisation has decided to enter an overseas market, the way it does so is of crucial strategic importance. Broadly, three ways of entering foreign markets can be identified: **indirect exports**, **direct exports** and **overseas manufacture**.

Choice of mode

The most suitable mode of entry varies:

(a) **Among firms in the same industry** (eg a new exporter as opposed to a long-established exporter)

(b) **According to the market** (eg some countries limit imports to protect domestic manufacturers whereas others promote free trade)

(c) **Over time** (eg as some countries become more, or less, hostile to direct inward investment by foreign companies)

A large number of considerations apply:

Consideration	Comment
The firm's marketing objectives	These relate to volume, time scale and coverage of market segments. Thus setting up an overseas production facility would be inappropriate if sales are expected to be low in volume.
The firm's size	A small firm is less likely than a large one to possess sufficient resources to set up and run a production facility overseas.
Mode availability	Some countries only allow a restricted level of imports, but will welcome a firm if it builds manufacturing facilities which provide jobs and limit the outflow of foreign exchange.
Mode quality	All modes may be possible in theory, but some are of questionable quality or practicality. The lack of suitably qualified distributors or agents would preclude the export, direct or indirect, of high technology goods needing installation, maintenance and servicing by personnel with specialist technical skills.
Human resources requirements	When a firm is unable to recruit suitable staff either at home or overseas, indirect exporting or the use of agents based overseas may be the only realistic option.

Consideration	Comment
Market feedback information	In some cases a firm can receive feedback information about the market and its marketing effort from its sales staff or distribution channels. In these circumstances direct export or joint ventures may be preferred to indirect export.
Learning curve requirements	Firms which intend a heavy future involvement in an overseas market might need to gain the experience that close involvement in an overseas market can bring. This argues against the use of indirect exporting as the mode of entry.
Risks	Firms might prefer the indirect export mode as assets are safer from expropriation.
Control needs	Production overseas by a wholly owned subsidiary gives a firm absolute control while indirect exporting offers only limited control over the marketing mix to the exporter.

Exporting

Goods are made at home but sold abroad. It is the easiest, cheapest and most commonly used route into a new foreign market.

Advantages of exporting

(a) Exporters can **concentrate production** in a single location, giving **economies of scale** and **consistency of product quality**.

(b) Firms lacking experience can try international marketing on a **small scale**.

(c) Firms can **test** their international marketing plans and strategies before risking investment in overseas operations.

(d) Exporting **minimises operating costs**, administrative overheads and personnel requirements.

Indirect exports

Indirect exporting is where a firm's goods are sold abroad by other organisations who can offer greater market knowledge.

(a) **Export houses** are firms which facilitate exporting on behalf of the producer. Usually the producer has little control over the market and the marketing effort.

(b) **Specialist export management firms** perform the same functions as an in-house export department but are normally remunerated by way of commission.

(c) **UK buying offices of foreign stores and governments**

(d) **Complementary exporting** ('piggy back exporting') occurs when one producing organisation (the carrier) uses its own established international marketing channels to market (either as distributor, or agent or merchant) the products of another producer (the rider) as well as its own.

Direct exports

Direct exporting occurs where the producing organisation itself performs the export tasks rather than using an intermediary. Sales are made directly to customers overseas who may be the wholesalers, retailers or final users.

(a) **Sales to final user.** Typical customers include industrial users, governments or mail order customers.

(b) Strictly speaking an **overseas export agent** or distributor is an overseas firm hired to effect a sales contract between the principal (ie the exporter) and a customer. Agents do not take title to goods; they earn a commission (or profit).

(c) **Company branch offices abroad.** A firm can establish its own office in a foreign market for the purpose of marketing and distribution as this gives greater control.

A firm can manufacture its products overseas, either by itself or by using an overseas manufacturer.

Overseas production

Benefits of overseas manufacture

- A better understanding of customers in the overseas market
- Economies of scale in large markets
- Production costs are lower in some countries than at home
- Lower storage and transportation costs
- Overcomes the effects of tariff and non-tariff barriers
- Manufacture in the overseas market may help win orders from the public sector

Contract manufacture

Licensing is a quite common arrangement as it avoids the cost and problems of setting up overseas.

In the case of contract manufacture a firm (the contractor) makes a contract with another firm (the contractee) abroad whereby the contractee manufactures or assembles a product on behalf of the contractor. Contract manufacture is suited to countries where the small size of the market discourages investment in plant and to firms whose main strengths are in marketing rather than production.

Advantages of contract manufacture

- No need to invest in plant overseas
- Lower risks associated with currency fluctuations
- Risk of asset expropriation is minimised.
- Control of marketing is retained by the contractor.
- Lower transport costs and, sometimes, lower production costs

Disadvantages of contract manufacture

- Suitable overseas producers cannot always be easily identified.
- The need to train the contractee producer's personnel
- The contractee producer may eventually become a competitor.
- Quality control problems in manufacturing may arise

Joint ventures

Some governments discourage or even prohibit foreign firms setting up independent operations, so joint ventures are the only option. That said, a joint venture with an indigenous firm provides local knowledge, quickly.

Wholly owned overseas production

Production capacity can be built from scratch, or, alternatively, an existing firm can be acquired.

(a) **Acquisition** has all the benefits and drawbacks of acquiring a domestic company.

(b) **Creating new capacity** can be beneficial if there are no likely candidates for takeover, or if acquisition is prohibited by the government.

Advantages

(a) The firm does not have to share its profits with partners of any kind.
(b) The firm does not have to share or delegate decision-making.
(c) There are none of the communication problems that arise in joint ventures.
(d) The firm is able to operate completely integrated international systems.
(e) The firm gains a more varied experience from overseas production.

Disadvantages

(a) The investment needed prevents some firms from setting up operations overseas.

(b) Suitable managers may be difficult to recruit at home or abroad.

(c) Some overseas governments discourage, and sometimes prohibit, 100% ownership of an enterprise by a foreign company.

(d) This mode of entry forgoes the benefits of an overseas partner's market knowledge, distribution system and other local expertise.

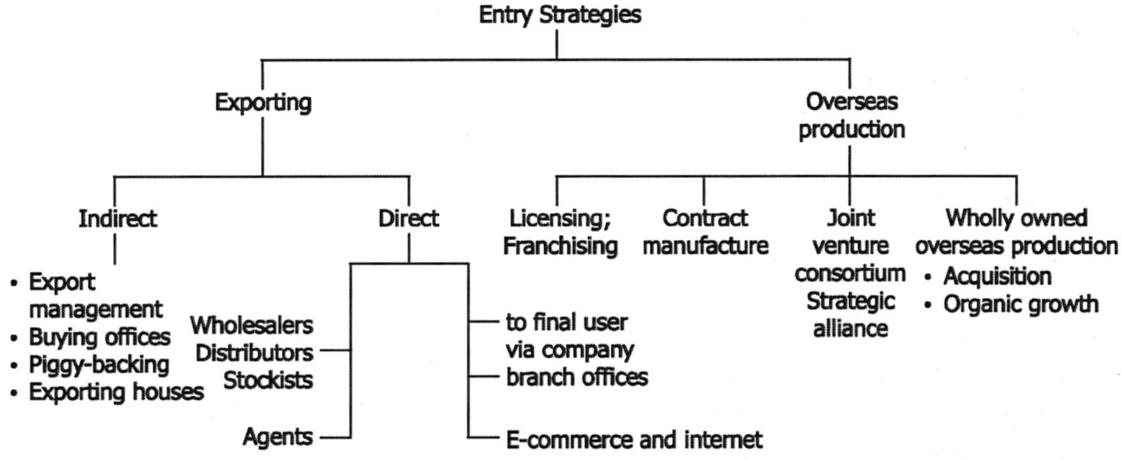

	Exporting	Overseas production
Advantages	Concentrates production; small start possible; minimises overheads	Lower distribution costs; overcomes trade barriers; possibly lower production costs
Key issues	Exchange rates, protectionism	Political risk; partnership; managing overseas facilities; more risky
Involvement	Usually less involved, but an exporter might depend on the **overseas** market	Usually more involved, but overseas subsidiaries might act independently: varying levels of control and risk

6 THE CORPORATE PARENT AND VALUE CREATION

Johnson, Scholes and Whittington propose three main value-creating roles for the corporate parent:

(a) **Envisioning** is the process of creating a clear vision of **corporate intent.** This is important for three reasons:

  (i) The **corporate parent** itself needs a clear view of its own role if it is to avoid wasteful activity.

  (ii) **External stakeholders** in general and existing and potential **investors** in particular need a clear understanding of corporate intent if they are to understand what the organisation does and to make appropriate decisions about their relationships with it.

  (iii) The **managers** responsible for the performance of individual business divisions need to know how their work fits in to the corporate scheme so that they know what is expected of them. Their motivation also depends to some extent on having a reasonable belief that the corporate parent knows what it is doing.

(b) **Intervention** to improve performance or develop business strategy takes a number of forms:

  (i) **Monitoring and control** of performance against plans, targets and intentions
  (ii) Action to develop SBU (Strategic Business Unit) **strategic capability**
  (iii) **Coaching** and **training**
  (iv) Promoting **collaboration** between SBUs and the creation of **synergies**

(c) The corporate parent may provide **services**, **resources** and **expertise** to its SBUs.

  (i) Financial assistance
  (ii) Resource sharing
  (iii) Managerial assistance
  (iv) Central services, such as HRM, purchasing and treasury
  (v) Knowledge creation and management
  (vi) Access to external networks

It might be argued that external market forces and mechanisms such as takeover-enforced management change are capable of dealing with these issues without incurring the overhead cost associated with the existence of a corporate parent. Johnson, Scholes and Whittington suggest that the corporate parent is likely to produce better results since it has both access to inside information and the co-operation of the SBU managers.

Value destruction

The existence of the corporate parent imposes **costs** related to its size, therefore **it must create value at least equal to these costs** if it is to be worth having. This may be challenging. In addition, the activities of the corporate parent may be economically disadvantageous.

(a) The corporate hierarchy provides an arena for **managers' political ambition**. There is power to be achieved, but at a distance from the commercial realities of life in the SBUs. This is attractive to many.

(b) The **size and complexity** of a very large corporation can hinder or obscure the development of a clear and useful **corporate vision**.

(c) Corporate processes and hierarchy can **slow decision-making**, **stunt enterprise** and **absorb the energies** of SBU managers. This has the effect of blunting market responsiveness and harming overall efficiency.

Strategic rationale

Johnson, Scholes and Whittington identify three approaches to value creation that the corporate parent might adopt. They call these approaches **strategic rationales.**

Portfolio managers

The **portfolio manager** provides a service to investors by applying financial disciplines. It seeks out **undervalued companies** as purchase targets, acquires them, and improves their value and performance. Improvement may be achieved by asset stripping (the sale of attractive but inessential non-current assets), by disposing of under-performing elements or by installing new management. Portfolio managers **keep their own costs low** and provide **few central services.** Their SBUs are largely autonomous and their managers are judged by financial results. Typically, this type of corporate parent presides over a **widely diversified conglomerate**; our earlier remarks about diversification and strategic success apply here.

Synergy managers

The **synergy manager**, reasonably enough, pursues economies of scope; that is, the benefits of synergy. We have already discussed potential sources of synergy: here we may simply remark that the synergy manager aims to achieve high efficiency in the **shared use of resources and competences.** To do this, it must overcome some difficulties:

(a) The **costs** involved in sharing
(b) The impact of **self-interest** among SBU managers
(c) **Incompatibility of systems and culture** among SBUs
(d) Variation in **local conditions**

Synergy managers must be **determined** if they are to achieve their goals. The central staff must integrate and control the efforts of the SBUs, which means they must be familiar with all of their operations and may reduce managerial motivation within the SBUs. The corporate parent must also be realistic about its ability to leverage the resources and competences it believes to offer synergistic benefits: it is easy to become subject to the **illusion of synergy.**

Parental developers

The **parental developer** adds value to its SBUs by deploying its own specific competences to aid them in their operations and development. To do this requires certain qualities in the corporate parent:

(a) It must have **actual, demonstrable competences** to deploy, otherwise its efforts will be mere interference and a distraction to the SBUs.

(b) Since it is unlikely that it can be equally good at everything, it must be prepared to divest itself of capabilities that can be **provided externally at lower cost.**

(c) It must have sufficient understanding of its SBUs to discern genuine **opportunities for intervention.**

The parental developer may encounter a problem in the form of a high-performing SBU that offers no opportunities for the deployment of its competences. Logically, it would dispose of this business, since its relationship with it can only be one of adding cost, but the likelihood of any corporate parent actually doing this seems low. Alternatively, it could attempt to change its role in respect of such a SBU and become a portfolio manager or synergy manager. The danger of doing this is the potential for loss of focus and confusion as to just what it should be doing.

7 The Corporate Portfolio

A corporate parent of any type will have to make decisions about acquiring, nurturing and disposing of subsidiaries.

Four **major strategies** can be pursued with respect to products, market segments and, indeed, SBUs:

(a) **Build.** A build strategy forgoes short term earnings and profits in order to increase market share.

(b) **Hold.** A hold strategy seeks to maintain the current position.

(c) **Harvest.** A harvesting strategy seeks short-term earning and profits at the expense of long-term development.

(d) **Divest.** Divestment reduces negative cash flow and releases resources for use elsewhere.

A number of strategic tools have been developed to assist the decision process. These tools help the corporate parent to manage its portfolio of SBUs against three criteria:

(a) **Balance**, in relation to markets and corporate needs
(b) **Attractiveness**, in terms of profitability and growth
(c) **Strategic fit**, in terms of potential synergy and parenting capability

The balance and attractiveness criteria are addressed by a range of matrix-based tools; strategic fit is the subject of a single model, the Ashridge portfolio display.

The Boston classification

The **Boston Consulting Group** (BCG) developed a matrix based on empirical research that assesses businesses in terms of potential cash generation and cash expenditure requirements. SBUs are categorised in terms of **market growth rate** and **relative market share**:

(a) Assessing rate of **market growth** as high or low depends on the conditions in the market. No single percentage rate can be set, since new markets may grow explosively while mature ones grow hardly at all. High market growth rate can indicate good opportunities for profitable operations. However, intense competition in a high growth market can erode profit, while a slowly growing market with high barriers to entry can be very profitable.

(b) **Relative market share** is assessed as a ratio: it is market share compared with the market share of the **largest competitor**. Thus a relative market share greater than unity indicates that the SBU is the market leader. BGG settled on market share as a way of **estimating costs** and thus **profit potential**, because both costs and market share are connected with **production experience**: as experience in satisfying a particular market demand for value increases, market share can be expected to increase also, and costs to fall.

		Relative market share	
		High	*Low*
Market growth	*High*	Stars	Question marks
	Low	Cash cows	Dogs

The portfolio should be balanced, with cash cows providing finance for stars and question marks; and a minimum of dogs.

(a) In the short term, **stars** require capital expenditure in excess of the cash they generate, in order to maintain their position in their competitive growth market, but promise high returns in the future. Strategy: **build.**

(b) In due course, stars will become **cash cows.** Cash cows need very little capital expenditure, since mature markets are likely to be quite stable, and they generate high levels of cash income. Cash cows can be used to finance the stars. Strategy: **hold** or **harvest** if weak.

(c) **Question marks** must be assessed as to whether they justify considerable capital expenditure in the hope of increasing their market share, or should they be allowed to die quietly as they are squeezed out of the expanding market by rival products? Strategy: **build** or **harvest.**

(d) **Dogs** may be ex-cash cows that have now fallen on hard times. Although they will show only a modest net cash outflow, or even a modest net cash inflow, they are cash traps which tie up funds and provide a poor return on investment. However, they may have a useful role, either to complete a product range or to keep competitors out. There are also many smaller niche businesses in markets that are difficult to consolidate that would count as dogs but which are quite successful. Strategy: **divest** or **hold.**

The BCG matrix must be used with care:

(a) It may be difficult to define 'high' and 'low' on both axes of the matrix.

(b) The matrix has been used to assess **products** rather than **SBUs,** but Johnson, Scholes and Whittington say this should not be done; nor should it be applied to broad markets that include many market segments. They do, however, recommend it for assessing a **portfolio of international operations**, though with three caveats:

  (i) The permitted forms of activity and ownership vary from country to country.
  (ii) Political risk is not considered.
  (iii) Shared resources are not considered.

(c) The matrix is built around cash flows but **innovative capacity** may be the critical resource.

The public sector portfolio matrix

Montanari and Bracker proposed a matrix for the analysis of services provided by public sector bodies. This might be applied at the level of local or national government, or an executive agency with a portfolio of services. The axes are an assessment of service efficiency and public attractiveness: naturally, political support for a service or organisation depends to a great extent on the extent to which the public need and appreciate it.

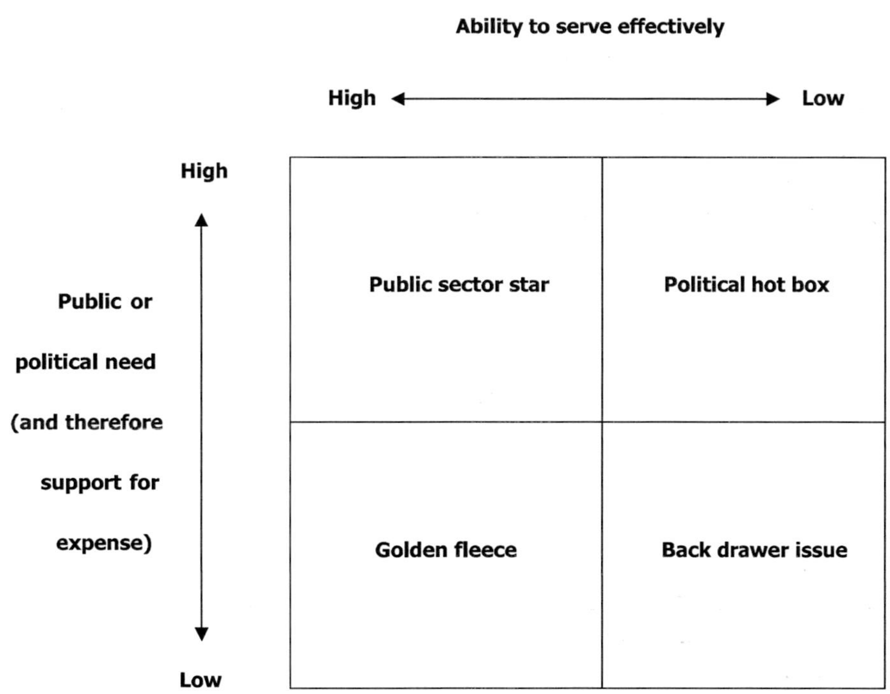

(a) A **public sector star** is something that the system is doing well and should not change. They are essential to the viability of the system.

(b) **Political hot boxes** are services that the public want, or which are mandated, but for which there are not adequate resources or competences.

(c) **Golden fleeces** are services that are done well but for which there is low demand. They may therefore be perceived to be undesirable uses for limited resources. They are potential targets for cost cutting.

(d) **Back drawer issues** are unappreciated and have low priority for funding. They are obvious candidates for cuts, but if managers perceive them as essential, they should attempt to increase support for them and move them into the **political hot box** category.

The Ashridge portfolio display

The Ashridge portfolio display is concerned with **strategic fit**, that is, the role of the corporate parent and the suitability of the range of SBUs it manages. The principles embodied in the model can be approached from two directions:

(a) Corporate parents should build portfolios of businesses that they can develop effectively.
(b) Corporate parents should seek to build parenting skills that are relevant to their portfolios.

The coherence of the corporation overall may be assessed by reference to two variables:

(a) **'Feel'**: the degree of fit between the parent's skills, resources and other characteristics and the SBUs' core strategic functions (CSF)

(b) **'Benefit'**: the degree of fit between the opportunities the SBUs present for parenting and the parent's skills resources and other characteristics

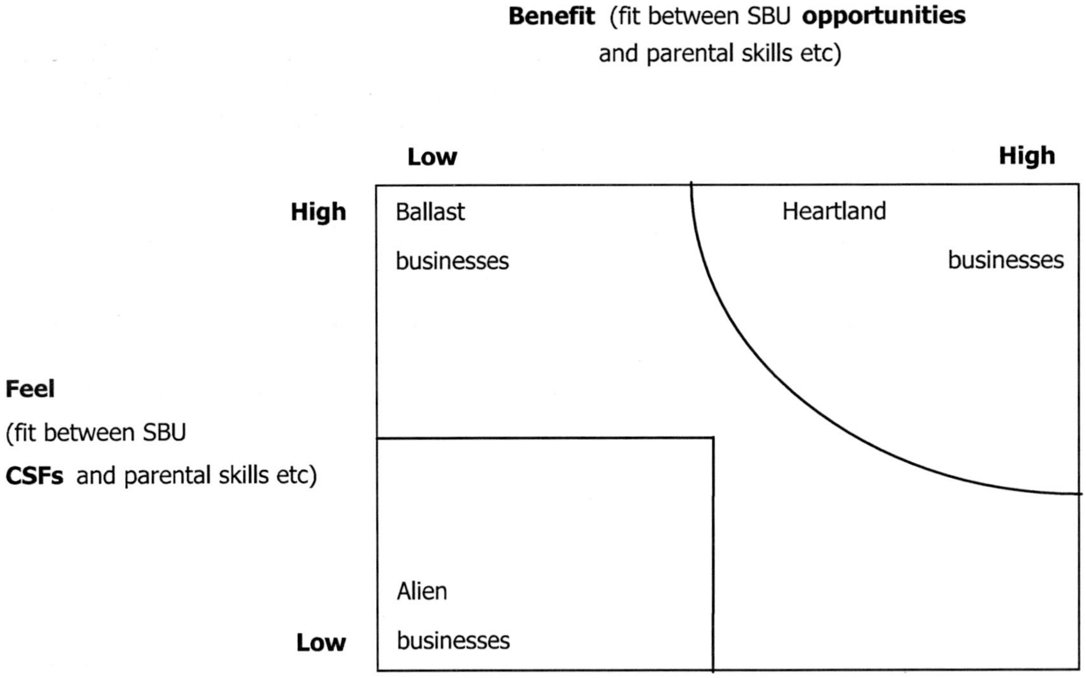

(a) **Heartland businesses** can benefit from the attention of the parent without risk of harm from unsuitable developments.

(b) **Ballast businesses** are well-understood by the parent, but need little assistance. They would do just as well if they were independent businesses. They should bear as little central cost as possible.

(c) **Value trap businesses** provide good opportunities for parenting, but these opportunities do not relate to the SBU's CSFs. They should only be retained if they can be moved into the heartland; this will require the parent to acquire new skills and resources.

(d) **Alien businesses** have no place in the portfolio. They need the attention of a skilled parent, but the actual parent does not have the skills and resources required to help them.

This analysis reverses the usual approach to portfolio management: it does not ask what the value of the SBUs is to the centre, but what value the centre can add to the SBUs. This raises two questions:

(a) Is the **cost burden** of the parent **commensurate with the value it adds**? For example, if the corporate parent's role is limited to, say, relations with the financial markets, it should be small and economically run.

(b) If a corporate parent has a justifiably interventionist role, **how many SBUs can it parent effectively**?

The trend in business recent years has been decentralisation of decision-making and a move towards **facilitiation** by the parent rather than active intervention. A similar trend towards privatisation and deregulation has been apparent in the public sector.

Better off tests

Michael Porter suggests that one of the key issues behind acquisitions should be in realising synergies between the existing company and the new acquisition.

To this end, he suggests that potential acquisitions should be assessed against three tests:

- **Better off test** – Will the company being acquired be better off after the acquisition? Will it gain competitive advantage from being in the group? Will the group be better off as a result of acquiring the company?
- **Attractiveness test** – Is the target industry structurally attractive? (Porter originally developed his tests in relation to diversification, and so was looking at companies making acquisitions in unrelated industries. However, the point about 'attractiveness' could be applied more generally to look at target companies, or countries.)
- **Cost of entry** – The cost of the acquisition (or the cost of entering a new market) must not capitalise all future profits from that acquisition (or market). In other words, will the future cash flows from the acquisition be greater than the amounts paid to acquire it?

Porter also identified another key point in relation to successful acquisitions, which could be called the **parenting test**. Has the company making the acquisition got the necessary skills as a corporate parent to get the best value out of the company being acquired? For example, have they got any experience of previous acquisitions?

8 Business Unit Strategy: Generic Strategies

Competitive advantage is anything which gives one organisation an edge over its rivals. *Porter* argues that a firm should adopt a competitive strategy intended to achieve competitive advantage for the firm.

Competitive strategy means 'taking offensive or defensive actions to create a dependable position in an industry, to cope successfully with ... competitive forces and thereby yield a superior return on investment for the firm. Firms have discovered many different approaches to this end, and the best strategy for a given firm is ultimately a unique construction reflecting its particular circumstances'. (Porter)

The choice of competitive strategy

Porter believes there are three **generic strategies** for competitive advantage.

Cost leadership and differentiation are industry-wide strategies. Focus involves segmentation but also the pursuit, **within the chosen segment only**, of a strategy of cost leadership or differentiation.

Cost leadership

A cost leadership strategy seeks to achieve the position of lowest-cost producer in the **industry as a whole**. By producing at the lowest cost, the manufacturer can compete on price with every other producer in the industry, and earn the higher unit profits, if the manufacturer so chooses.

How to achieve overall cost leadership

(a) Set up production facilities to obtain **economies of scale**

(b) Use the **latest technology** to reduce costs and/or enhance productivity (or use cheap labour if available)

(c) In high technology industries, and in industries depending on labour skills for product design and production methods, exploit the **learning curve effect**. By producing more items than any other competitor, a firm can benefit more from the learning curve, and achieve lower average costs.

(d) Concentrate on improving productivity

(e) **Minimise overhead costs**

(f) **Get favourable access to sources of supply**

Differentiation

A differentiation strategy assumes that competitive advantage can be gained through **particular characteristics** of a firm's products. Products may be divided into three categories:

(a) **Breakthrough products** offer a radical performance advantage over competition, perhaps at a drastically lower price.

(b) **Improved products** are not radically different from their competition but are obviously superior in terms of better performance at a competitive price.

(c) **Competitive products** derive their appeal from a particular compromise of cost and performance. For example, cars are not all sold at rock-bottom prices, nor do they all provide immaculate comfort and performance. They compete with each other by trying to offer a more attractive compromise than rival models.

How to differentiate

(a) **Build up a brand image**

(b) **Give the product special features** to make it stand out

(c) **Exploit other activities of the value chain** (for example, quality of after-sales service or speed of delivery).

Generic strategies and the five forces

Competitive force	Advantages		Disadvantages	
	Cost leadership	Differentiation	Cost leadership	Differentiation
New entrants	Economies of scale raise entry barriers	Brand loyalty and perceived uniqueness are entry barriers.		
Substitutes	Firm is not so vulnerable as its less cost-effective competitors to the threat of substitutes.	Customer loyalty is a weapon against substitutes.		
Customers	Customers cannot drive down prices further than the next most efficient competitor.	Customers have no comparable alternative. Brand loyalty should lower price sensitivity.		Customers may no longer need the differentiating factor. Sooner or later customers become price sensitive.
Suppliers	Flexibility to deal with cost increases	Higher margins can offset vulnerability to supplier price rises.	Increase in input costs can reduce price advantages.	
Industry rivalry	Firm remains profitable when rivals go under through excessive price competition.	Unique features reduce direct competition.	Technological change will require capital investment, or make production cheaper for competitors. Competitors learn via imitation. Cost concerns ignore product design or marketing issues.	Imitation narrows differentiation.

Focus (or niche) strategy

In a focus strategy, a firm concentrates its attention on one or more particular segments or niches of the market, and does not try to serve the entire market with a single product.

(a) A **cost focus strategy:** aim to be a cost leader for a particular segment. This type of strategy is often found in the printing, clothes manufacture and car repair industries.

(b) A **differentiation focus strategy:** pursue differentiation for a chosen segment. Luxury goods suppliers are the prime exponents of such a strategy.

Porter suggests that a focus strategy can achieve competitive advantage when '**broad-scope**' businesses fall into one of two errors:

(a) **Underperformance** occurs when a product does not fully meet the needs of a segment and offers the opportunity for a **differentiation focus** player.

(b) **Overperformance** gives a segment more than it really wants and provides an opportunity for a **cost focus** player.

Advantages

(a) A niche is more secure and a firm can insulate itself from competition.

(b) The firm does not spread itself too thinly.

(c) Both cost leadership and differentiation require **superior performance** – life is easier in a niche, where there may be little or no competition.

Drawbacks of a focus strategy

(a) The firm sacrifices economies of scale which would be gained by serving a wider market.
(b) Competitors can move into the segment, with increased resources.
(c) The segment's needs may eventually become less distinct from the main market.

Which strategy?

Although there is a risk with any of the generic strategies, Porter argues that a firm *must* pursue one of them. A **stuck-in-the-middle** strategy is almost certain to make only low profits. 'This firm lacks the market share, capital investment and resolve to play the low-cost game, the industry-wide differentiation necessary to obviate the need for a low-cost position, or the focus to create differentiation or a low-cost position in a more limited sphere.'

It is also important that both cost leadership and differentiation require superior performance. Therefore, most businesses should pursue some form of focus strategy as it is easier to dominate a niche than a complete market.

Conceptual difficulties with generic strategy

In practice, it is rarely simple to draw hard and fast distinctions between the generic strategies as there are conceptual problems underlying them.

(a) **Cost leadership**

(i) **Internal focus.** Cost refers to internal measures, rather than the market demand. It can be used to gain market share: but it is the **market share which is important,** not cost leadership as such.

(ii) **Only one firm.** If cost leadership applies cross the whole industry, only one firm will pursue this strategy successfully. However, the position is not clear-cut:

- More than one firm might **aspire** to cost leadership, especially in dynamic markets where new technologies are frequently introduced.
- The boundary between cost leadership and cost focus might be blurred.
- Firms competing market-wide might have different competences or advantages that confer cost leadership in different segments.

(iii) **Higher margins can be used for differentiation.** Having low costs does *not* mean you have to charge lower prices or compete on price. A cost leader can choose to 'invest higher margins in R&D or marketing'. Being a cost leader arguably gives producers more freedom to choose *other* competitive strategies.

(b) **Differentiation**. Porter assumes that a differentiated product will always be sold at a **higher price**.

(i) However, a **differentiated product** may be sold at the same price as competing products in order to **increase market share**.

(ii) **Choice of competitor.** Differentiation from whom? Who are the competitors? Do they serve other market segments? Do they compete on the same basis?

(iii) **Source of differentiation**. This can include **all** aspects of the firm's offer, not only the product. Restaurants aim to create an atmosphere or 'ambience', as well as serving food of good quality.

Focus probably has fewer conceptual difficulties, as it ties in very neatly with ideas of market segmentation. In practice most companies pursue this strategy to some extent, by designing products/services to meet the needs of particular target markets.

'Stuck-in-the-middle' is therefore what many companies actually pursue quite successfully. Any number of strategies can be pursued, with different approaches to **price** and the **perceived added value** (ie the differentiation factor) in the eyes of the customer.

The strategy clock

Porter's basic concept of generic strategies has been the subject of further discussion. Johnson, Scholes and Whittington, quoting *Bowman,* describe the strategic options using the **strategy clock.**

The eight strategies shown on the clock represent different approaches to creating value for the customer and each customer will buy from the provider whose offering most closely matches their own view of the proper relationship between price and perceived benefits.

Each position on the clock has its own **critical success factor**, since each strategy is defined in market terms. Positions 1 and 2 will attract customers who are price conscious above all, with position 2 giving a little more emphasis to serviceability. These are typical approaches in commodity markets. By contrast, strategies 4 and 5 are relevant to consumers who require a customised product.

The Strategy Clock

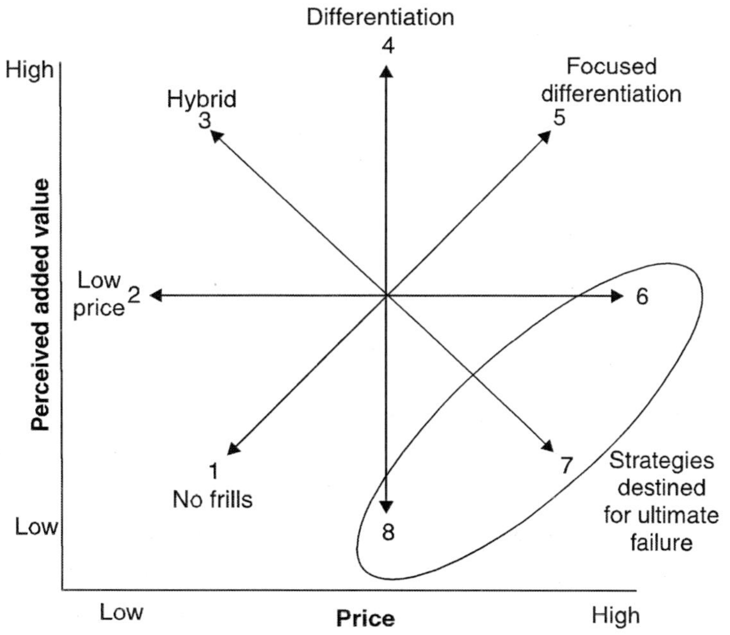

Price-based strategies

Strategies 1 and 2 are price-based strategies.

(a) A **no frills** strategy is appropriate under several conditions. It can be used for commodity-like products and the most price-conscious customers. It is also suitable where customers' switching costs are low and where there is little opportunity for competition on product features. This strategy may be used for market entry, to gain experience and build volume.

(b) A **low price** strategy offers better value than competitors. This can lead to price war and thence to reduced margins and lack of reinvestment for all players and Porter's generic strategy of **cost leadership** is appropriate to a firm adopting this strategy.

Differentiation strategies

Strategies 3, 4 and 5 are all differentiation strategies. Each one represents a different trade-off between market share (with its cost advantages) and margin (with its direct impact on profit). Differentiation can be created in three ways:

- Product features
- Marketing, including powerful brand promotion
- Core competences

The **hybrid** strategy seeks both differentiation and a lower price than competitors. The cost base must be low enough to permit reduced prices and reinvestment to maintain differentiation. This strategy may be more advantageous than differentiation alone under certain circumstances:

- If it leads to growth in market share
- If differentiation rests on core competences and costs can be reduced elsewhere
- If a low price approach is suited to a particular market segment
- Where it is used as a market entry strategy

The basic **differentiation** strategy comes in two variants, depending on whether a price premium is charged or a competitive price is accepted in order to build market share. The pursuit of a differentiation strategy requires detailed and accurate **market intelligence**. The **strategic customers** and their preferences must be clearly identified, as must the competitors and their likely responses. The chosen basis for differentiation should be inherently difficult to imitate, and will probably need to be developed over time.

A strategy of **focussed differentiation** seeks a high price premium in return for a high degree of differentiation. This implies concentration on a well-defined and probably quite restricted market segment. **Centres of excellence** in the public sector pursue a similar strategy.

(a) Focus is a common start-up strategy: expansion may prompt or require a gradual move to a less focussed differentiation.

(b) It is difficult to pursue focus with only part of an organisation: the less focussed part, even if it is to some extent differentiated, can damage the brand values of the focussed part.

(c) In the public sector, stakeholders expecting universal provision will object to focus on particular segments.

(d) Focus is aimed at a specific segment: if the non-focussed product is improved enough to become acceptable to this segment, the advantage of focus will be eroded. Alternatively, competitors may make even more focussed offerings to sub-segments, again eroding the focuser's original advantage.

Failure strategies

Combinations 6, 7 and 8 are likely to result in failure.

The SWOT matrix

We have already introduced SWOT Analysis; however, it will be useful to review it here, because each of the general classes of strategy it suggests could be useful to consider alongside the strategy clock, particularly when considering cash flows and the availability of resources. The SWOT matrix is also a relevant tool when developing product-market strategies, which we look at later in this chapter.

	External factors (opportunities: threats)	
Internal factors (strengths: weaknesses)	**SO** Use strengths to maximise opportunities (maxi-maxi strategy)	**ST** Use strengths to minimise threats (maxi-mini strategy)
	WO Minimise weaknesses by taking advantage of opportunities (mini-maxi strategy)	**WT** Minimise weaknesses and avoid threats (mini-mini strategy)

SO This is a strong position. A company might look to use this strength to expand globally or develop new products, building on its existing reputation.

ST This is a less strong position than 'SO' but an 'ST' company still has strengths it can draw on. Consider this example: A clothing manufacturing company with an established reputation for good quality products is now facing competition from cheap overseas competitors. The clothing company should adopt a differentiation strategy to use its reputation and brand to try to reduce the competitive threat. However, this strategy may not be successful if the cheap, imported clothes are also good quality, in which case the established company will need to consider moving its manufacturing plant abroad to a low cost location, and compete using a low price strategy.

WO A company has identified opportunities in the external environment, but internal organisational weaknesses (for example, inadequate manufacturing capacity, or poor distribution or marketing networks) prevent it taking advantage of them. In this case, the company either needs to re-engineer its processes, or collaborate with a company which has the resources it needs. If the 'WO' company has sufficient funds, it may consider acquiring a company with the resources it needs (although it is unlikely that a 'WO' company will have sufficient funds to be able to do this).

WT A company faced with internal weaknesses and external threats may be in a precarious position and be forced into defensive strategies, for example, restructuring, or downsizing. Alternatively it may look for a merger with another company, or, in the worst case scenario, it will have to go into liquidation.

An organisation in such a defensive position can only ever use strategy to protect itself. It cannot create success because it has neither the internal strengths nor the external opportunities needed to do so.

Successful companies, even if they temporarily use SO, WO and WT strategies, will attempt to get into a situation where they can work from strengths to take advantage of opportunities (SO strategy). They will strive to overcome weakness and make them strengths; and if they face threats, they will cope with them so that they can focus on opportunities.

9 SUSTAINING COMPETITIVE ADVANTAGE

Sustaining price-based strategies

(a) **Low margins** can be sustained either by increased volumes or by cross-subsidisation from another business unit.

(b) A **cost leader** can operate at a price advantage, but to be sustainable, cost leaders must constantly and aggressively drive down all of their costs.

(c) A cost leader or a company with extensive financial resources can win a **price war**.

(d) A **no-frills strategy** can succeed in the long term if it is aimed at a segment that particularly appreciates low price.

Sustaining differentiation

Sustaining differentiation is difficult. To begin with, it is more than just being *different*: the difference must be **valued by customers**. Secondly, a difference that a competitor can easily imitate gives no sustainable advantage.

(a) **Attempts at imitation can be obstructed** by, for example, securing preferred access to customers or suppliers through bidding or licensing procedures.

(b) Some resources are **inherently immobile**. This can be the result of **intangibility**, as in the case of brands; high customer switching costs, as with proprietary technology; or **co-specialisation**, which occurs when organisations' value chains are intimately linked.

(c) **Cost advantage** can be used to sustain differentiation rather than price advantage by investing in innovation, brand management or quality improvement.

Lock-in

Lock-in is achieved in a market when a company's product becomes the **industry standard**. Direct competitors are reduced to minor niches and **compatibility** with the industry standard becomes a prerequisite for complementary products.

Factors affecting lock-in

(a) **Perception of dominance**: potential competitors and suppliers of complementary products will only conform to an attempt to set standards if they perceive the standard-setter as dominant in the market, usually in terms of market share.

(b) **First mover advantage**: a standard is more likely to be set early in the lifecycle of a new product than when it is mature.

(c) **Self-reinforcement**: once dominance is achieved, conforming with the standard becomes necessary for survival.

(d) **Fierce defence**: a firm that achieves lock-in will defend its position vigorously.

Lock-in is also known as the **delta model**, which is the term used by *Hax and Wilde*, who described it in their book of the same name.

Strategy and hypercompetition

Repositioning on the strategy clock

Repositioning may be possible. For example, a firm using a no frills strategy may move towards higher quality combined with a low price; that is from position 1 on the clock to position 2. Similarly, a differentiator may attempt to create a new market segment or niche and move towards a more focussed kind of differentiation

Counterattacking against market-based moves

Market-based strategies that work under less competitive conditions are often successfully counterattacked.

(a) **First mover advantage can be undermined** by leapfrogging into the lead with an improved product or making a flank attack on a new segment.

(b) **Product/market moves can be imitated**, thus preventing the competitor from achieving advantage.

Attacking barriers to entry

(a) **Rapid technological advance** shortens lifecycles and can allow competitors to outflank an initially **robust** strategic capability.

(b) Attempts to dominate particular market segments or geographic markets may be overcome in several ways.

- (i) **Economies of scale** in a market can be countered by utilising the effects of similar economies achieved from a dominant position in another one. An example would be entering a foreign market with an undifferentiated product already established in the home market. **Cross subsidy** can also be used, perhaps to enable initial price competition.

- (ii) Dominance of the market's current pattern of **distribution** can be overcome by developing a different approach, such as selling by mail order rather than through retail outlets.

(c) Small competitors can **avoid direct confrontation** with resource-heavy dominant players by concentrating on niches, building trading alliances and by merging with other small companies.

Principles of hypercompetitive strategy

(a) **Pre-empt imitation and remain unpredictable** by competing in new ways. This may involve destroying current advantages in order to develop new ones.

(b) To attack **competitors' weaknesses** is to provoke them to overcome them.

(c) A **series of small moves** disguises the strategy and provides a succession of temporary advantages.

(d) **Misleading signals** of strategic intent can be used to confuse.

Collaboration as a strategy

Organisations do not only compete. **Collaboration** between buyers and sellers and between potential competitors can reduce costs below those of operating independently.

(a) Buyers and sellers may collaborate to ensure high quality, share the cost of research or reduce inventory levels, for example. Where high quality is of great important, becoming an **accredited supplier** can be difficult, but will **enhance selling power.**

(b) Collaboration between members of a fragmented market **increases buying power**, as when small retailers co-operate to buy in large quantities.

(c) Collaboration between suppliers in an industry over such matters as marketing and research and development can help to **build barriers** to entry and against substitutes.

(d) On the other hand, collaboration may be the best way to obtain entry to some foreign markets; **aspiring entrants** can obtain local knowledge and access to the local infrastructure. Indeed, some governments require entrants to take a local partner.

(e) Suppliers may collaborate with consumers for a variety of reasons: examples include self-assembly of furniture and self-assessment of tax liability. Such **co-production** can help to hold down **costs** and increase a sense of **ownership.**

(f) **Knowledge sharing** may be required in the public sector, as a form of best practice. Also, collaboration may be required to improve standards, secure best value from spending or solve problems that cut across agency boundaries.

10 Using the Value Chain in Competitive Strategy

The value chain model can be used to analyse a business's operations in order to establish where it achieves **competitive advantage through the creation of value.** It can also show where there is potential for **improved value addition** (especially in relationship to competitors) and where activities are being performed that do not add value; the aim here should be to eliminate such activities, or at least to reconfigure them so that they do contribute some value. However, using the value chain in this way, as with using any strategic management tool, requires careful thought and sound judgement. This may well involve the use of other strategic concepts, such as differentiation, competences and critical success factors, focussing the strategist's attention on areas where they might be applied.

Other uses of the value chain

As well as using the value chain to establish where it creates value for the customer, an organisation can also use the model in other strategically valuable ways:

- Identification of critical success factors
- Identification of activities suitable for out sourcing
- Identification of areas where value activities are not mutually supporting
- Identification of opportunities to use information strategically

11 Product-market Strategy: Direction of Growth

Product-market strategies involve determining which products should be sold in which markets, by market penetration, market development, product development and diversification. Diversification is assumed to be risky, especially diversification that is entirely unrelated to current products and markets. Alliances of various kinds are a possible approach to diversification. Withdrawal may be a valid option.

Product-market mix is a short hand term for the **products and services** a firm sells (or a service which a public sector organisation provides) and the **markets** it sells them to.

The importance of market share

Like some of the portfolio matrix tools we looked at, the PIMS (Profit Impact of Market Strategy) framework regards competitive strength and market attractiveness as important determinants of profitability. However, perhaps the single most significant factor to emerge from the PIMS data is the link between profitability and relative market share. You will recall that relative market share was one of the axes of the BCG matrix.

There is a definite, observable correlation between market share and return on investment. This is probably the result of lower costs resulting from economies of scale. Economies of scale due to increasing market share are particularly evident in purchasing and the utilisation of non-current assets.

Product-market mix

Ansoff drew up a **growth vector matrix**, describing how a combination of a firm's activities in current and new markets, with existing and new products can lead to **growth**. Ansoff's original model was a 4 cell matrix based on product and market, shown as the heart of the diagram below. *Lynch* has produced an enhanced model that he calls the **market options matrix.** This adds the external options shown in the diagram. Withdrawal, demerger and privatisation are discussed at the end of this section.

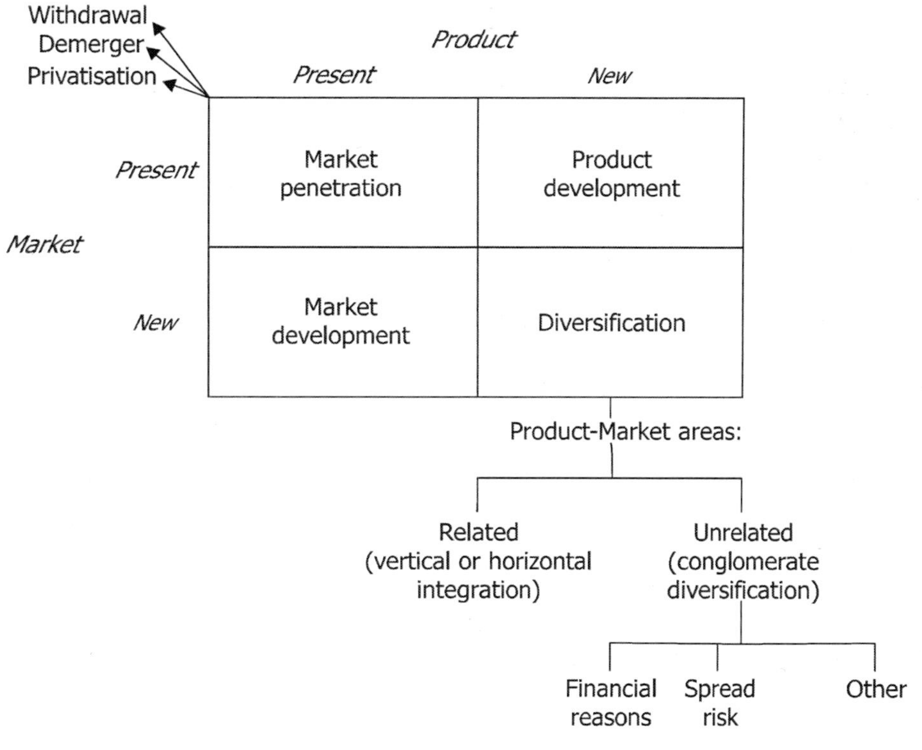

Current products and current markets: market penetration

Market penetration. The firm seeks to do four things:

(a) **Maintain or to increase its share** of current markets with current products, eg through competitive pricing, advertising, sales promotion

(b) Secure dominance of growth markets

(c) Restructure a mature market by driving out competitors

(d) Increase usage by existing customers (eg airmiles, loyalty cards)

This is a relatively **low risk** strategy since it requires no capital investment. As such it is attractive to the unadventurous type of company.

Consolidation

To consolidate is to seek to maintain current market share. This may be an appropriate strategy when the firm is already the market leader; if availability of funds is limited; or when an owner-manager is approaching retirement or wishes to avoid the loss of personal control that is a likely consequence of growth. Also, if it seems that profitability does **not** correlate with market share, consolidation may be a sensible option.

(a) Consolidation does not mean neglect. It is unlikely that competitors will halt their efforts, so the firm must continue to enhance its market offer in order to maintain its relative position.

(b) PIMS data indicates that **high product quality** is important if a consolidation strategy is to succeed. It can compensate to some extent for both a low market share and a low level of marketing expenditure.

Present products and new markets: market development

Market development is the process by which the firm seeks new markets for its current products. There are many possible approaches. Here are some examples:

(a) **New geographical areas** and export markets (eg a radio station building a new transmitter to reach a new audience)

(b) **Different package sizes** for food and other domestic items so that both those who buy in bulk and those who buy in small quantities are catered for

(c) **New distribution channels** to attract new customers (eg organic food sold in supermarkets not just specialist shops)

(d) **Differential pricing policies** to attract different types of customer and create **new market segments.** For example, travel companies have developed a market for cheap long-stay winter breaks in warmer countries for retired couples.

This approach to strategy is also low in risk since it also requires little capital investment.

New products and present markets: product development

Product development is the launch of new products to existing markets. This has several advantages:

(a) The company can exploit its existing marketing arrangements such as promotional methods and distribution channels at low cost.

(b) The company should already have good knowledge of its customers and their wants and habits.

(c) Competitors will be forced to respond.

(d) The cost of entry to the market will go up.

This strategy is **riskier** than both market penetration and market development since it is likely to require **major investment** in the new product development process and, for physical products, in suitable production facilities.

New products: new markets (diversification)

Diversification occurs when a company decides to make **new products for new markets**. It should have a clear idea about what it expects to gain from diversification.

(a) **Growth.** New products and new markets should be selected which offer prospects for growth which the existing product-market mix does not.

(b) **Investing surplus** funds not required for other expansion needs, bearing in mind that the funds could be returned to shareholders. Diversification is a high risk strategy, having many of the characteristics of a new business start-up. It is likely to require the deployment of **new competences.**

Diversification and synergy

Synergy combined results produce a better rate of return than would be achieved by the same resources used independently. Synergy is used to justify diversification.

Obtaining synergy

Synergy is probably difficult to achieve in practice when one company takes over another. All too often, the expectations of synergy that help to justify a business combination fail to materialise. Synergy is probably more discussed in takeover bids than actually implemented.

Other strategies

Withdrawal may be an appropriate strategy under certain circumstances.

(a) Products may simply disappear when they reach the end of their life cycles.

(b) Underperforming products may be weeded out.

(c) Sale of subsidiary businesses for reasons of corporate strategy, such as finance, change of objectives, lack of strategic fit

(d) Sale of assets to raise funds and release other resources

Exit barriers make this difficult.

(a) Cost barriers include redundancy costs and the difficulty of selling assets.

(b) Managers might fail to grasp the idea of decision-relevant costs ('we've spent all this money, so we must go on').

(c) Political barriers include government attitudes. Defence is an example.

(d) Marketing considerations may delay withdrawal. A product might be a loss-leader for others, or might contribute to the company's reputation for its breadth of coverage.

(e) Psychology. Managers hate to admit failure, and there might be a desire to avoid embarrassment.

(f) People might wrongly assume that carrying on is a low risk strategy.

Divestment and **demerger** have become more common as companies seek to reverse the diversification strategies they once pursued. There are several reasons for this:

(a) To **rationalise** a business as a result of a strategic appraisal, perhaps as a result of portfolio analysis. Another reason might be to concentrate on core competences and synergies.

(b) To sell off **subsidiary companies** at a profit, perhaps as an exit route after managing a turn-round.

(c) To allow market valuation to reflect growth and income prospects. Where a low growth, steady income operation exists alongside a potentially high growth new venture, the joint P/E is likely to be too high for the cash cow and too low for the star. The danger is that a predator will take over the whole operation and split the business in two, allowing each part to settle at its own level.

(d) Satisfy investors: diversified conglomerates are unfashionable. Modern investment thinking is that investors prefer to provide their own portfolio diversification.

(e) To **raise funds** to invest elsewhere or to reduce debt.

Demerger can realise underlying asset values in terms of share valuation. ICI's demerger of its attractive pharmaceuticals business led to the shares in the two demerged companies trading at a higher combined valuation than those of the original single form.

Privatisation has been pursued by governments all over the world to raise funds and transform culture and performance.

12 Method of Growth

The **method of growth** can vary.

- Companies can grow organically, building up their own products and developing their own market.
- They may choose to acquire these ready-made by buying other companies. Acquisitions are risky because of the incompatibility of different companies.
- Many firms grown by other means, such as joint ventures, franchising and alliances.

Organic growth

Organic growth (sometimes referred to as **internal development**) is the primary method of growth for many organisations, for a number of reasons. Organic growth is achieved through the development of internal resources.

Reasons for pursuing organic growth

(a) **Learning.** The process of developing a new product gives the firm the best understanding of the market and the product.

(b) **Innovation.** It might be the only sensible way to pursue genuine technological innovations, and exploit them.

(c) There is **no suitable target for acquisition.**

(d) Organic growth can be **planned more meticulously** and offers little disruption.

(e) It is often **more convenient** for managers, as organic growth can be financed easily from the company's current cash flows, without having to raise extra money.

(f) The **same style of management and corporate culture** can be maintained.

(g) **Hidden or unforeseen losses are less likely** with organic growth than with acquisitions.

(h) **Economies of scale** can be achieved from more **efficient use of central head office** functions such as finance, purchasing, personnel and management services.

Problems with organic growth

(a) **Time –** sometimes it takes a long time to descend a **learning curve**.

(b) **Barriers to entry** (eg distribution networks) are harder to overcome: for example a brand image may be built up from scratch.

(c) The firm will have to **acquire the resources independently.**

(d) Organic growth may be **too slow for the dynamics of the market.**

Organic growth is probably ideal for market penetration, and suitable for product or market development, but it might be a problem with extensive diversification projects.

Acquisitions and mergers

The purpose of acquisitions

(a) **Marketing advantages**

(i) Buy in a new product range
(ii) Buy a market presence (especially true if acquiring a company overseas)
(iii) Unify sales departments or to rationalise distribution and advertising
(iv) Eliminate competition or to protect an existing market

(b) **Production advantages**

(i) Gain a higher utilisation of production facilities
(ii) Buy in technology and skills
(iii) Obtain greater production capacity
(iv) Safeguard future supplies of raw materials
(v) Improve purchasing by buying in bulk

(c) **Finance and management**

(i) Buy a high quality management team, which exists in the acquired company
(ii) Obtain cash resources where the acquired company is very liquid
(iii) Gain undervalued assets or surplus assets that can be sold off
(iv) Obtain tax advantages (eg purchase of a tax loss company)

(d) **Risk-spreading**

(e) **Independence**. A company threatened by a take-over might take over another company, just to make itself bigger and so a more expensive target for the predator company.

(f) **Overcome barriers to entry**

Many acquisitions **do** have a logic, and the **acquired company can be improved** with the extra resources and better management. Furthermore, much of the criticisms of **takeovers** has been directed more against the notion of **conglomerate diversification** as a strategy rather than takeover as a **method of growth**.

Problems with acquisitions and mergers

(a) **Cost**. They might be too expensive, especially if resisted by the directors of the target company. Proposed acquisitions might be referred to the government under the terms of anti-monopoly legislation.

(b) **Customers** of the target company might resent a sudden takeover and consider going to other suppliers for their goods.

(c) **Incompatibility.** In general, the problems of assimilating new products, customers, suppliers, markets, employees and different systems of operating might create 'indigestion' and management overload in the acquiring company. A proposed merger between two UK financial institutions was called off because of incompatible information systems.

(d) **Asymmetric information.** *John Kay* suggests that the acquisitions market for companies is rarely efficient.

(i) The existing management 'always knows more about what is for sale than the potential purchaser. ... Successful bidders are often only the people who were willing to pay too much – that is the reason why their bid succeeds'.

(ii) 'At the same time, good buys may be ignored, because there is no potential purchaser confident that he really is making a good buy.'

(e) **Driven by the personal goals** of the acquiring company's managers, as a form of sport, perhaps.

(f) **Corporate financiers and banks** have a stake in the acquisitions process as they can charge fees for advice.

(g) **Poor success record of acquisitions.** Takeovers benefit the shareholders of the acquired company often more than the acquirer. According to the Economist Intelligence Unit, there is a consensus that fewer than half all acquisitions are successful.

(h) **Firms rarely take into account non-financial factors.** A survey by London Business School examining 40 acquisitions (in the UK and USA) revealed some major flaws.

(i) All acquirers conducted financial audits, but only 37% conducted anything approaching a management audit: despite detailed audits of equipment, property, finances etc, few bothered with people.

(ii) Some major problems of implementation relate to **human resources and personnel issues** such as morale, performance assessment and culture. Especially in service industries and 'knowledge-based' or creative businesses, many of the firm's assets are effectively the staff. If key managers or personnel leave, the business will suffer.

Joint ventures

Short of mergers and takeovers, there are other ways by which companies can co-operate.

(a) **Consortia:** organisations co-operate on specific business areas such as purchasing or research.

(b) **Joint ventures:** two firms (or more) join forces for manufacturing, financial and marketing purposes and each has a share in both the equity and the management of the business.

(i) **Share costs.** As the capital outlay is shared, joint ventures are especially attractive to smaller or risk-averse firms, or where very expensive new technologies are being researched and developed (such as in the civil aerospace or petrochemical industries).

(ii) **Cut risk.** A joint venture can reduce the risk of government intervention if a local firm is involved (eg *Club Mediterranée* pays much attention to this factor).

(iii) Participating enterprises **benefit from all sources of profit.**

(iv) **Close control** over marketing and other operations

(v) Overseas joint ventures provide **local knowledge, quickly.**

(vi) **Synergies.** One firm's production expertise can be supplemented by the other's marketing and distribution facility.

(c) A **licensing agreement** is a commercial contract whereby the licenser gives something of value to the licensee in exchange for certain performances and payments.

  (i) The licenser may provide rights to produce a patented product or to use a patented process or trademark as well as advice and assistance on marketing and technical issues.

  (ii) The licenser receives a **royalty.**

(d) **Subcontracting** is also a type of alliance. Co-operative arrangements also feature in supply chain management, JIT and quality programmes.

Disadvantages of joint ventures

(a) **Conflicts of interest** between the different parties

(b) **Disagreements** may arise over profit shares, amounts invested, the management of the joint venture, and the marketing strategy.

(c) One partner may wish to **withdraw** from the arrangement.

(d) There may be a temptation to neglect **core competences.** Acquisition of competences from partners may be possible, but alliances are unlikely to create new ones.

EXAMPLE

In May 2010, the US glass packaging manufacturer Owens-Illinois Inc. announced that it is teaming up with a Thai company to buy four plants in China and Southeast Asia that make beverage and food containers.

The joint venture of Owens-Illinois and Thailand's Berli Jucker Public Co. signed a deal to buy Faser & Neave Holdings' Malaya Glass plants in Sichuan Province, China; Saraburi Province, Thailand; Johor Bahru, Malaysia and Ho Chi Minh City, Vietnam.

The plants make containers for the beer, non-alcoholic beverage and food markets, and employ about 1,900 people.

The joint venture is buying the plants for $221.7 million, according to a news release. Owens-Illinois will pay $132.4 million of the total.

The plants in Malaysia and Vietnam will be operated by a joint venture owned 50% by Owens-Illinois and 50% by Berli Jucker. The acquired interest in the Chinese plant will be managed as part of Owens-Illinois' existing China operations. Berli Jucker will assume majority ownership of the Thai operation.

Owens-Illinois Chairman and CEO Al Strucken said the deal fits his company's objective of seeking 'a leadership position in China and Southeast Asia.'

He said the plant in Schuan expands its presence in China, while the joint venture gives it a competitive position in the growing markets in Vietnam and Malaysia.

Franchising

Franchising is a method of expanding the business on less capital than would otherwise be possible, because **franchisees** not only pay a capital lump sum to the franchiser to enter the franchise but they also bear some of the running costs of the new outlets. For suitable businesses, it is an **alternative business strategy to raising extra capital** for growth. Probably the most well-known franchisers are *McDonalds,* but other franchisers include *Budget Rent-a-car, Dyno-rod, Express Dairy, Holiday Inn, Kall-Kwik Printing, Kentucky Fried Chicken, Sketchley Cleaners* and *Body Shop.*

The franchiser and franchisee each provide different inputs to the business.

(a) The **franchiser**

(i) Name, and any goodwill associated with it

(ii) Systems and business methods, business strategy and managerial know-how

(iii) Support services, such as advertising, training, research and development, and help with site decoration

(b) The **franchisee**

(i) Capital, personal involvement and local market knowledge
(ii) Payment to the franchiser for rights and for support services
(iii) Responsibility for the day-to-day running, and the ultimate profitability of the franchise

Advantages of franchising

(a) **Reduces capital requirements.** Firms often franchise because they cannot readily raise the capital required to set up company-owned stores. John Y. Brown, the former president of Kentucky Fried Chicken, maintained that it would have cost KFC $450 million to establish its first 2,700 stores if it had run them as company-owned stores, and this was a sum that was not available to the corporation in the early stages of its life.

(b) **Reduces managerial resources required.** A firm may be able to raise the capital required for growth, but it may lack the managerial resources required to set up a network of company-owned stores. Recruiting and training managers and staff accounts for a significant percentage of the cost of growth of a firm.

Under a franchise agreement, the franchisees supply the staff required for the day-to-day running of the operation.

(c) **Improves return on promotional expenditure through speed of growth.** A retail firm's brand and brand image are crucial to the success of its stores. Companies often develop their brand through extensive advertising and promotion, but this only translates into sales if they have a number of stores that customers can visit after seeing their advertisements.

To reap the benefits of its national or regional advertising efforts, the company needs to attain the minimum efficient scale, in terms of number of stores, as quickly as possible.

Because franchising provides quicker access to capital and managerial resources, a firm can expand more quickly through franchising than through opening new company-owned stores. Faster expansion through franchising, in turn, should allow companies to achieve a favourable return on their promotional campaigns.

(d) **Benefits of specialisation.** Because the franchisee and the franchiser both contribute different resources to the franchise, franchising provides an effective way of reducing costs: each party concentrates on their core areas, and increases their efficiency in those areas.

In general, franchisers are more cost-efficient than franchisees in performing functions that decrease in cost with a substantial level of output. By contrast, franchisees are more efficient in performing functions which are more efficient at a smaller scale. For example, in the fast-food business, product development and national promotion are more efficiently handled on a large scale (by the franchiser), whereas the production of food itself is handled better on a relatively smaller scale (by the franchisee).

(e) **Low head office costs.** The franchiser only needs a small number of head office staff because there is a considerable delegation of operational responsibility to the franchisees. For example, in the fast-food business, the franchisees provide the staff who work in the restaurants, and so the franchisees incur the HR and payroll costs associated with that.

(f) **Reduced supervision costs.** Company-owned retail stores are run by employee managers who may often perform poorly if they are not supervised. A company, therefore, has to supervise its store managers, and this will result in central overhead costs. However, under a franchise arrangement, because franchisees have invested capital in their own stores, and because their earnings come from the profits of those stores, they are motivated to work hard to maximise the success of the stores. Consequently the franchiser will have much lower supervision costs.

(g) **Risk Management.** When opening new stores, a corporation does not know with certainty the business potential and the chances of success of different locations. Under a franchising arrangement, the franchiser can judge the profitability potential of different sites without incurring a significant business risk. If a particular store fails, the franchisee bears the brunt of the failure.

However, franchising also helps franchisees reduce their risks. Franchised stores typically open more quickly, and become profitable more quickly, than independent company-owned stores. The franchisee benefits from the franchiser's managerial experience and from the established brand name. In effect, when a franchisee enters a lease agreement with the franchiser, it is leasing managerial know-how and brand recognition, as well as the physical store it is operating.

Disadvantages of franchising

(a) **Profits are shared.** The franchisee receives the revenue from the customer at the point of sale and then pays the franchiser a share of the profits.

(b) The **search for competent candidates** is both costly and time consuming where the franchiser requires many outlets (eg McDonald's in the UK).

(c) **Control** over franchisees

(d) **Risk to reputation.** A franchisee can damage the public perception of a brand by providing inferior goods or services.

(e) **Potential for conflict.** There may be disagreement over the respective rights and obligations of the franchiser and franchisee, for example over the level of support to be provided or the fees payable. These terms need to be clearly set out in a contact when the franchise is granted to reduce the chances of conflict arising. Conflict may also occur if either side is acting in bad faith, for example if the franchisee is providing inferior goods or services which risk damaging the franchiser's brand.

Alliances

Some firms enter long-term **strategic alliances** with others for a variety of reasons:

(a) They share development costs of a particular technology.

(b) The regulatory environment prohibits takeovers (eg most major airlines are in strategic alliances because in most countries – including the US – there are limits to the level of control an 'outsider' can have over an airline).

(c) Complementary markets or technology

(d) **Learning.** Alliances can also be a 'learning' exercise in which each partner tries to learn as much as possible from the other.

(e) **Technology.** New technology offers many uncertainties and many opportunities. Such alliances provide funds for expensive research projects, spreading risk.

(f) **The alliance itself can generate innovations.**

(g) The alliance can involve **'testing' the firm's core competence** in different conditions, which can suggest ways to improve it.

(h) Regulation may prevent take over.

Strategic alliances only go so far, as there may be disputes over control of strategic assets.

Choosing alliance partners

Hooley et al suggest the following factors should be considered in choosing alliance partners.

Drivers	What benefits are offered by collaboration?
Partners	Which partners should be chosen?
Facilitators	Does the external environment favour a partnership?
Components	Activities and processes in the network
Effectiveness	Does the previous history of alliances generate good results? Is the alliance just a temporary blip? For example, in the airline industry, there are many strategic alliances, but these arise in part because there are legal barriers to cross-border ownership.
Market-orientation	Alliance partners are harder to control and may not have the same commitment to the end-user.

Alliances have some limitations

(a) **Core competence**. Each organisation should be able to focus on its core competence. Alliances do not enable it to create new competences.

(b) **Strategic priorities.** If a key aspect of strategic delivery is handed over to a partner, the firm loses flexibility. A core competence may not be enough to provide a comprehensive customer benefit.

13 Strategy and Market Position

So far in this chapter we have considered the broader aspects of strategy as they affect the overall stance of the organisation. In this section we will examine some of the options that apply most appropriately to the strategic management of individual products or brands. An appreciation of scale is important when considering strategy. The strategies we discuss below may be regarded as detailed strategy for a major global organisation. On the other hand, they may constitute the essence of corporate strategy for a smaller company.

Most of the material in this section is based on Strategic Marketing Management by Wilson, Gilligan and Pearson.

Strategies for market leaders

PIMS research has revealed the advantages of being the market leader. A company in this position may try to do three things:

(a) **Expand the total market** by seeking increased usage levels; and new uses and users. These aims correspond to market penetration and market development.

(b) **Protect the current market share**. The most common way of doing this is by means of continuous product innovation.

(c) **Expand market share**. This may be pursued by enhancing the attractiveness of the product offering in almost any way, including increased promotion, aggressive pricing and improved distribution.

Military analogies have been used to describe defensive strategies for market leaders.

Strategies for market challengers

The market challenger seeks to **build market share** in the hope of eventually overtaking the existing leader. However, this does not necessarily mean attacking the market leader head-on. This is a risky strategy in any case, because of the leader's resources in cash, promotion and innovation. Instead, the challenger may attack smaller regional firms or companies of similar size to itself that are vulnerable through lack of resources or poor management.

Military analogies have also been used to describe the challenger's attacking options.

Strategies for market followers

The market follower accepts the status quo and thus avoids the cost and risk associated with innovation in product, price or distribution strategy. Such a **me-too** strategy is based on the leader's approach. This can be both profitable and stable. However, to be consistently successful, such a strategy must not simply imitate. The follower should compete in the most appropriate segments, maintain its customer base and ensure that its turnover grows in line with the general expansion of the market. It should be aware that it may constitute an attractive target for market challengers. The follower must therefore control its costs and exploit appropriate opportunities.

Strategies for market nichers

Avoiding competition by **niching** is a profitable strategy for small firms generally and for larger organisations where competition is intense. The key to niching is **specialisation**, but there are other considerations:

(a) The chosen market must have some growth potential while being uninteresting to major competitors.

(b) The firm must be able to serve its customers sufficiently well to build up sufficient goodwill to fend off any attacks.

(c) It must be possible to build up sufficient size to be profitable and purchase efficiently.

Serving a single niche can be risky: a sudden change in the market can lead to rapid decline. **Multiple niching** can overcome this problem.

14 Success Criteria

Organisations must select strategies to pursue in a rational way. JS&W suggest three **success criteria** to guide strategy choice:

- **Suitability**
- **Feasibility**
- **Acceptability**

Suitability

Suitability relates to the **strategic logic** of the strategy. The strategy should fit the organisation's current strategic position and should satisfy a range of requirements:

- **Exploit** strengths: that is, **unique** resources and **core competences**
- **Rectify** an organisation's **weaknesses**, or deal with problems identified in it
- **Neutralise** or deflect environmental **threats**

- Help the firm to **seize opportunities**
- **Satisfy the goals** of organisation
- **Fill the gap** identified by gap analysis
- Generate/maintain **competitive advantage**
- Involve an acceptable level of **risk**
- Suit the **politics** and corporate **culture**

A number of techniques can be used to assess suitability. These are discussed below.

Life cycle analysis

The **product life cycle** concept may be used to assess potential strategies.

The **industry life cycle** may be combined with an appraisal of the company's strength in its markets using a **life cycle/portfolio matrix**. This was originally designed by consultants **Arthur D Little.**

STAGES OF INDUSTRY MATURITY

COMPETITIVE POSITION	Embryonic	Growth	Mature	Ageing
Dominant	Fast grow Start up	Fast grow Attain cost leadership Renew Defend position	Defend position Attain cost leadership Renew Fast grow	Defend position Focus Renew Grow with industry
Strong	Start up Differentiate Fast grow	Fast grow Catch up Attain cost leadership Differentiate	Attain cost leadership Renew, focus Differentiate Grow with industry	Find niche Hold niche Hang in Grow with industry Harvest
Favourable	Start up Differentiate Focus Fast grow	Differentiate, focus Catch up Grow with industry	Harvest, hang in Find niche, hold niche Renew, turnaround Differentiate, focus Grow with industry	Retrench Turnaround
Tenable	Start up Grow with industry Focus	Harvest, catch up Hold niche, hang in Find niche Turnaround Focus Grow with industry	Harvest Turnaround Find niche Retrench	Divest Retrench
Weak	Find niche Catch up Grow with industry	Turnaround Retrench	Withdraw Divest	Withdraw

The position of the company on the **industry maturity** axis of this matrix depends on the assessment of eight factors including market growth rate, growth potential and number of competitors. Each stage has its own strategic implications. For instance, an ageing market will be subject to falling demand, so heavy marketing expenditure is unlikely to be justified.

Competitive position

(a) A **dominant** position allows the company to exert influence over the behaviour of competitors. It is rare in the private sector.

(b) A **strong** position gives considerable freedom of choice over strategy.

(c) A **favourable** position arises in a fragmented market, often when the company has strengths to exploit.

(d) A **tenable** position is vulnerable to competition and profitability may depend on specialisation.

(e) A **weak** position arises from inability to compete effectively. Firms of any size can find themselves in this condition.

Business profile analysis

In **business profile analysis** the expected effects of a strategy on the corporation are forecast. A business profile is then created by scoring the forecast state against the favourable parameters established by the empirical findings of PIMS research. There are eleven of these parameters; they relate to market position, financial strength, quality and operational efficiency. The forecast profile may be compared with the current profile in order to assess the proposed strategy for suitability.

Strategy screening

It is not enough merely to assess strategies for suitability. Eventually choices must be made. Such choices may be assisted by **strategy screening** methods, which include **ranking, decision trees** and **scenario planning**. Scenarios have already been described. Potential strategies may be screened by assessing their suitability against each potential scenario. This leads not so much to a choice as to the establishment of a series of **contingency plans**.

Consistency

Strategies must be internally consistent: generic strategy, market options choice and method of development must all work together satisfactorily. For example a strategy of cost leadership would not be supported by a decision to acquire a chain of luxury distributors.

Feasibility

Feasibility asks whether the strategy can be implemented and, in particular, if the organisation has adequate **strategic capability**. The Ms model can provide a framework to use here.

Machinery	Has the organisation got the machinery required to deliver this strategy? Can any new machinery be obtained?
Make-up	Is the organisational structure appropriate to the strategy?
Management	Does the management team have the skills required to deliver the strategy?
Markets	Does the organisation have strong enough products or a strong enough brand for the strategy to work?
Materials	Does the organisation have access to the materials required to deliver the strategy?
Men and women	Will the strategy require extra staff? Will the strategy require staff to acquire new skills? If so, how long will this take?
Methods	Can the strategy be implemented, given the organisation's current production methods (either in-house or outsourced)?
Money	Can the organisation raise any finances that may be required? Will it be able to keep up with repayments if loan funding is required?

In addition, the organisation also needs to assess whether it has the ability to deal with the likely **responses that competitors** will make, and enough **time** to implement the strategy.

Strategies which do not make use of the existing competences and which therefore call for new competences to be acquired, might not be feasible, since gaining competences takes time and can be costly.

Two important financial approaches to assessing the feasibility of particular strategies are **funds flow** analysis and **breakeven** analysis. The principles of both should be familiar to you from your earlier studies in financial and management accounting.

Resource deployment analysis makes a wider assessment of feasibility in terms of **resources** and **competences.** The resources and competences required for each potential strategy are assessed and compared with those of the firm. A two stage approach may be followed.

(a) Does the firm have the necessary resources and competences to achieve the **threshold** requirements for each strategy?

(b) Does the firm have the core competences and **unique resources** to maintain **competitive advantage**?

When assessing feasibility in this way, it is important to remember that it may be possible to acquire new competences and resources or to stretch existing ones. Such innovation is likely to be difficult to imitate.

Acceptability

The acceptability of a strategy depends on expected performance outcomes and the extent to which these are acceptable to stakeholders.

(a) **Financial considerations.** Strategies will be evaluated by considering how far they contribute to meeting the dominant objective of increasing shareholder wealth.

There are a number of the financial indicators which should be considered to assess the acceptability of a strategy:

(i) Return on investment

(ii) Profits

(iii) Growth

(iv) EPS

(v) Cash flow

(vi) Price/Earnings

(vii) Market capitalisation

(viii) Cost-benefit analysis

Profitability analysis techniques include **forecast ROCE, payback period** and **NPV**, all of which you should be familiar with. These methods should not be overemphasised.

(i) They are developed for assessing **projects** where cash flows are predictable. This is unlikely to be easy with wider **strategies.**

(ii) There may be **intangible** costs and benefits associated with a strategy, such as an enhanced product range or image or a loss of market share. **Cost-benefit analysis** is probably more appropriate for dealing with such development. See below.

Shareholder value analysis has the potential to provide a more realistic assessment of overall strategy than traditional financial measures such as NPV and forecast ROCE. This is because its emphasis on value management and understanding the organisation's system of value drivers requires managers to take an integrated view of current and potential future strategies and their overall effects.

(b) **Customers** may object to a strategy if it means reducing service, but on the other hand they may have no choice.

(c) **Banks** are interested in the implications for cash resources, debt levels and so on.

(d) **Government.** A strategy involving a takeover may be prohibited under competition legislation.

(e) **The public.** The environmental impact may cause key stakeholders to protest. For example, out of town superstores are now frowned upon by national and local government in the UK.

(f) **Risk.** Different shareholders have different attitudes to risk. A strategy which changed the risk/return profile, for whatever reason, may not be acceptable. Financial ratio projections and sensitivity analysis may be useful in the assessment of risk.

Cost-benefit analysis may be an appropriate approach to acceptability where intangible effects are important, which is particularly the case in the public sector. This type of analysis attempts to put a monetary value on intangibles such as safety and amenity so that the impact of a strategy on all parties may be assessed.

Strategy selection

Planning and enforced choice

The techniques dealt with in this chapter are appropriate to the use of the rational model and may be useful when less formal approaches are taken. They also have a role when strategic developments are **imposed from outside** the organisation. This may come about, for instance, as a result of a major change in the environment, as when the oil shocks of the 1970s stimulated off-shore production, or because of the influence of a dominant stakeholder.

Formal evaluation of imposed strategy

(a) The first role of formal evaluation is to assess the degree of **risk** inherent in the imposed strategy. This may indicate that a medium-term programme to reduce risk is required; this could be incorporated into the overall plan.

(b) Secondly, techniques such as **scenario planning** can be used to establish contingency plans in case the imposed strategy leads to unacceptably low performance.

Real options

The selection of a particular course of strategic action may offer **options for future strategy**. The availability of such an option should be considered when evaluating strategies.

A possible course of action may open up further possibilities: one important case is the possibility of making further, follow-on investments. This is equivalent to a call option in financial strategy. For example, if a manufacturing business decides to open a retail outlet, it acquires the option to stock complementary products from other manufacturers. If the NPV of the basic outlet strategy is assessed as negative, this negative sum represents the price of the option to expand the range at a future date.

Using this type of conceptual approach allows more subtle evaluation of possible strategies to be undertaken and permits more sophisticated choices to be made between alternatives. In particular, the option to abandon a chosen strategy at low cost will make that strategy more attractive than one with a high cost of abandonment. This choice might rise where there are two possible approaches to manufacturing a new product.

(a) Purchase of high efficiency, highly specialised machinery
(b) Purchase of lower efficiency, general purpose machinery

Option (a) may offer lower costs if the venture succeeds, but the ability to use option (b)'s machinery for another purpose reduces its cost of abandonment should the venture fail.

COST OF CAPITAL

chapter 3

Contents

1 Introduction

This chapter examines some important considerations related to the calculation of cost of capital. A cost of capital or required return of finance providers is an essential element of cash based valuation. The Dividend Valuation Model states that the value of any asset can be determined as the present value of future cash returns discounted at the investors' required return. To value a company or its equity we must therefore ascertain the required return of the investors.

There are various possible components to a company's financing:

- Equity shares
- Minority interest
- Preference/non-equity shares
- Debt (both on and off balance sheet)

In order to generate a weighted average cost of capital the required return and approximate weightings by market value of each component must be calculated.

2 Cost of Equity

Introduction

Various methodologies for deriving the cost of equity financing exist. Each of the approaches is considered in detail below along with the ability of each of these methods to be applied in a practical and workable manner with regard to companies.

3 Dividend Valuation Model (DVM)

Whilst the DVM can be applied to generate valuations, it can also be applied in reverse to derive the required return of investors. If we have a known value of equity and a known set of future cash returns from that equity then the required return of investors can be derived as the internal rate of return of the cash flows.

For equity there are two shortcut methods that we can derive, which are when we have:

- A constant dividend as in the case of preference shares
- A constant growth rate for the dividend (or constant after a certain time) which may be suitable for ordinary shares

We can only utilise these formulae for non-redeemable shares. If we are ever dealing with redeemable securities we are likely to need to resort to first principles.

Relevant Cash Flows

The financing cash flows involved are

Time	Inflow/(Outflow)
0	Market value ex-div
$1 - \infty$	(Dividends paid)

Notes:

1 The inflow at t_0 is the ex-div market value. We assume that a company will only issue shares ex-div, which, in practice, is what happens.

2 If the shares currently in issue are presently cum-div then we must calculate the ex-div value using the equation

$$E_{ex\ div} = E_{cum\ div} - d_0$$

Where

- $E_{ex\ div}$ is the ex-div market value of the shares
- $E_{cum\ div}$ is the cum-div market value of the shares
- d_0 is the dividend about to be paid now

Constant Dividend

Investor Viewpoint

The investor will be looking to satisfy his required return. If his required rate of return on equity is r_e and the annual perpetuity return is d then he will be willing to pay, and hence the ex-div market value (assuming that the first dividend will be paid in one year's time and hence we can correctly apply the perpetuity discount factor) will be

$$E_{ex\ div} = \frac{d}{r_e}$$

ie the market value is determined by the investor based on his expectations of future returns and his own required rate of return.

EXAMPLE

If shareholders require the return on their investment in a certain share to be 10%, and they expect the share to yield a dividend of 10p pa in perpetuity, what will be the market value of the shares?

SOLUTION

The ex-div market value of the share will be determined by shareholders to be

$$E_{ex\text{-}div} = \frac{d}{r_e}$$

$$E_{ex\text{-}div} = \frac{10p}{0.1}$$

£1.00

This may appear to be over-simplistic, and you may feel that in practice there are many other factors that influence share price. We will discuss these other factors shortly. However, the above is an illustration of the dividend valuation model which provides a good starting point for any analysis.

Company Viewpoint

So the investor determines the market price of the shares, and if the company wants to price them higher it will simply not sell any. We now need to establish the cost to the company of raising and servicing this finance, which, as we noted above, is the IRR of the financing flows. The IRR is the discount rate at which the NPV is zero. If the cost to the company, the cost of equity, is k_e then discounting the relevant flows at this rate will yield this zero NPV. Considering all of the financing flows we get

Time	Cash Flow £	Discount Factor	Present Value £
0	$E_{ex\ div}$	1	$E_{ex\ div}$
1 — ∞	(d)	$\frac{1}{k_e}$	$\frac{(d)}{k_e}$
	IRR ⇒	NPV =	0

Hence for a constant dividend

$$E_{ex\ div} = \frac{d}{k_e}$$

Rearranging this to solve for k_e we get

$$k_e = \frac{d}{E_{ex\ div}}$$

EXAMPLE

Based on the above scenario, calculate the cost of equity for the company.

SOLUTION

$$k_e = \frac{d}{E_{ex\ div}}$$

$$k_e = \frac{10p}{£1.00}$$

$$k_e = 10\%$$

Conclusion

The effective rate of return that a company will have to pay to shareholders by way of dividend will be whatever rate of return the shareholders demand, eg if shareholders demand 20% then the company will effectively be having to pay 20%.

The formulae that are relevant for establishing either the market value of the shares or the cost of capital to the company are

$$E_{ex\ div} = \frac{d}{k_e}$$

$$k_e\ (= r_e) = \frac{d}{E_{ex\ div}}$$

Where

- $E_{ex\ div}$ is the ex-div market value of the shares which can be calculated as
  - $E_{ex\ div} = E_{cum\ div} - d$
  - $E_{cum\ div}$ is the cum-div market value of the shares
  - d is the dividend about to be paid now
- k_e is the cost of equity finance to the company
- r_e is the investors' required rate of return

The constant dividend model is unlikely to be a good approximation for equity shares. It is, however, very useful in deriving the cost of preference share capital and the value of untraded preference shares (derived by discounting the constant dividend at the dividend yield of a comparable company's traded preference shares).

Practical Points

Although the above should cause no problem arithmetically, it does pose many problems from a practical point of view. The assumptions inherent in this analysis are as follows.

Investors

No one investor will have the power to affect the market value of a quoted share, and therefore in the dividend valuation model we are considering the expectations and required returns of all investors as if they act as a rational and homogeneous mass.

Expected Receipts

The model is based on expectations and not on actual receipts. As a result there are many extraneous events which may change expectations and hence the market values of the share (eg press comments). In particular, profit announcements will affect expectations of dividends and hence the market value as is indeed the case in practice.

Required Returns

The model is based on the shareholders' required return (r_e) which will be determined by two factors:

- The rates of return that may be earned elsewhere
- The risk perceived in the investment

Both of these factors are relevant in practice in the way predicted by the model, in that if interest rates rise, share prices fall, and more risky shares have higher required rates of return.

Capital Gains

The model would appear to ignore capital gains and therefore be applicable only to those investors who require income. This is not the case however. Capital gains in share prices arise from either:

- Speculative demand; or
- Long-term growth.

Speculative gains result from higher expectations of receipts, whether justified or not. For example, if a rumour gets round that a company is going to announce higher dividends, then the share price will increase.

Long-term growth in share prices will only occur if the company is steadily expanding and steadily increasing its dividends. It is this continual increase in the expected dividend stream that will result (per the model) in increases in the share price.

4 CONSTANT GROWTH IN DIVIDENDS

Introduction

For ordinary share capital, it is unrealistic to expect a dividend to remain constant. It is more likely that dividends would grow in the future. If, for the moment, we were to assume a constant rate of growth at the rate of g per annum, then our future dividend stream would be:

Time	Based on the previous year	Based on the time = 0 dividend
0	d_0	d_0
1	$d_1 = d_0 \times (1 + g) =$	$d_0 \times (1 + g)$
2	$d_2 = d_1 \times (1 + g) =$	$d_0 \times (1 + g)^2$
3	$d_3 = d_2 \times (1 + g) =$	$d_0 \times (1 + g)^3$
n		$d_0 \times (1 + g)^n$

Investor Viewpoint

If the shareholders' required rate of return is r_e per annum, then the market value will be the present value of this dividend stream discounted at the rate r_e, ie:

$$E_{ex\ div} = \frac{d_1}{1 + r_e} + \frac{d_2}{(1 + r_e)^2} + \frac{d_3}{(1 + r_e)^3} + ... + \frac{d_n}{(1 + r_e)^n} + ...$$

and substituting for the dividends we get

$$E_{ex\ div} = \frac{d_0 \times (1 + g)}{1 + r_e} + \frac{d_0 \times (1 + g)^2}{(1 + r_e)^2} + \frac{d_0 \times (1 + g)^3}{(1 + r_e)^3} + ... + \frac{d_0 \times (1 + g)^n}{(1 + r_e)^n} + ...$$

As we can see here, growth is acting like inflation in that it is increasing the actual cash flow each year. Since this is a perpetuity stream, we could calculate the effective discount rate and apply it in the perpetuity discount factor formula ($\frac{1}{r}$) as follows.

If r = effective discount factor, then

$$\frac{1}{1+r} = \frac{(1+g)}{1+r_e}$$

Hence

$$1 + r = \frac{1+r_e}{(1+g)}$$

$$r = \frac{1+r_e}{(1+g)} - 1$$

$$r = \frac{1+r_e-(1+g)}{(1+g)}$$

$$r = \frac{r_e-g}{(1+g)}$$

Therefore

$$\frac{1}{r} = \frac{(1+g)}{r_e-g}$$

Hence we have

$$E_{ex\ div} = \frac{d_0}{r} = \frac{d_0 \times (1+g)}{r_e-g}$$

Giving

$$\mathbf{E_{ex\ div} = \frac{d_1}{r_e-g}}$$

Where

- $E_{ex\ div}$ is the ex-div market value of the shares which may need to be calculated using:
  - $E_{ex\ div} = E_{cum\ div} - d_0$
  - $E_{cum\ div}$ is the cum-div market value of the shares
  - d_0 is the dividend about to be paid now if we are cum-div
- d_1 is the expected dividend in one years time which may need to be calculated as $d_1 = d_0 \times (1 + g)$
- r_e is the investors' required rate of return
- g is the expected annual growth rate of the dividends

Company Viewpoint

Again, from the company's viewpoint it must satisfy the shareholders' requirements otherwise the share price will fall. As we noted above, the cost of capital to the company in this situation is equal to the investors' required rate of return. That is

$$k_e = r_e$$

and hence from the company's viewpoint

$$E_{ex\ div} = \frac{d_1}{k_e - g}$$

Which can be rearranged as follows

$$k_e - g = \frac{d_1}{E_{ex\ div}}$$

$$\mathbf{k_e = \frac{d_1}{E_{ex\ div}} + g}$$

Where

- d_1 is the expected dividend in one year's time
- $E_{ex\ div}$ is the market value determined by the investor
- g is the expected annual growth rate of the dividends

EXAMPLE

A company is about to pay a dividend of 10p on its £1 ordinary shares. The shares are currently quoted at £2.30. The dividend is expected to grow at the rate of 10% pa Calculate the cost of equity for the company.

SOLUTION

Since we are about to pay the dividend we will assume that the share is currently cum-div. Hence, since we need the ex-div value we must use the expression

$$E_{ex\ div} = E_{cum\ div} - d_0$$

to calculate the ex-div price as

$$E_{ex\ div} = £2.30 - 10p = £2.20$$

Then, using the above formula for the cost of equity, we get

$$k_e = \frac{d_1}{E_{ex\ div}} + g$$

$$k_e = \frac{10p \times 1.1}{£2.20} + 10\%$$

$$k_e = \frac{11p}{£2.20} + 10\%$$

$$k_e = 5\% + 10\% = 15\%\ pa$$

Conclusion

Formulae

The formulae that are relevant for establishing either the market value of the shares or the cost of capital to the company are

$$E_{ex\ div} = \frac{d_1}{k_e - g}$$

$$k_e\ (= r_e) = \frac{d_1}{E_{ex\ div}} + g$$

Where

- $E_{ex\ div}$ is the ex-div market value of the shares determined by the investor
  - $E_{ex\ div} = E_{cum\ div} - d_0$, where:
    - $E_{cum\ div}$ is the cum-div market value of the shares
    - d_0 is the dividend about to be paid now if we are cum-div
- d_1 is the expected dividend in one year's time which could be calculated as $d_1 = d_0 \times (1 + g)$
- k_e is the cost of equity finance to the company
- r_e is the investors' required rate of return
- g is the expected annual growth rate of the dividends

Note: this is the general term for equity which covers both the constant growth and constant dividend situations. If we have a constant dividend then we have no growth, ie $g = 0$. If we substitute this in the above equations we obtain the constant dividend ones.

Market Value, not Nominal Value used in Calculations

We are not interested in how much the shares were originally issued for since this money has already been invested. The original cost of capital is irrelevant, we need to satisfy our shareholder's *current* requirements and maintain their current wealth which may be considerably different from that at the original issue date.

What we are concerned with here is the likely future cost of equity finance. The best indicator of this is the return currently being demanded by people buying our existing shares on the Stock Exchange, ie if shareholders can purchase our existing shares and get a return of 10% on their investment, then presumably we would have to offer 10% on any new shares issued to make them attractive.

Limitations of Cost of Equity Calculations

In establishing these formulae we have:

- Assumed that the dividend valuation model is valid, that is that investors do know their required rates of return and use them to evaluate their investment opportunities.

  This may, in practice, be fairly reasonable in that in assessing an investment opportunity, an investor will look to the returns available elsewhere and probably will, possibly unconsciously, establish a required return. However, in practice there will certainly be other factors influencing market values.

- Assumed that, as the company issuing the shares, we have accurate knowledge of these shareholder expectations. Since shareholders are basing the market value on their expectations of dividends, it is these expectations that we should be using in our calculations of the cost of equity.
- Alternatively assumed that the current market price of any shares is stable and at equilibrium, thus providing a reasonable basis for the calculations.
- Assumed that dividends are constant or experience constant growth. In practice these assumptions are not unreasonable. Companies do tend to try to achieve a standard dividend policy such as this.
- Assumed up to now that dividends are payable at annual intervals. This is unlikely to be the case in practice, however we can modify the formulae to deal with non-annual flows, hence this should not be regarded as something that refutes the ideas.
- So far ignored both corporate and personal taxation, these are considered later in our analysis of the cost of debt.

Finally

We obviously have no problem establishing the current dividend and therefore the main difficulty is establishing the expected rate of growth of dividends.

Growth Rates

One problem that we have currently left unanswered is how do we establish the investors' expectations regarding the dividend growth rate. There are two possible ways in which we could tackle this, which are:

- Look at the past dividend growth rates
- Consider what causes growth

Past Dividends

Shareholders' expectations of future dividend growth will be based on many factors, but perhaps the most obvious indicator is the rate of past dividend growth.

If dividends have been growing at the rate of 5% pa for a number of years, it will be reasonable (in the absence of any further information) to assume that this rate of growth will continue in the future. Since past dividend information will be available we will be able to ascertain this compound growth rate by using the formula

$$\text{Dividend this year} = \text{Dividend n years ago} \times (1 + g)^n$$

OR

$$(1 + g) = \sqrt[n]{\frac{\text{Dividend this year}}{\text{Dividend n years ago}}}$$

EXAMPLE

The dividend paid by a company in 2011 was £12,634. In 2016 they are proposing to pay a dividend of £22,265. Estimate the growth rate for the dividends.

SOLUTION

Each year the dividend grow by a factor of (1 + g), hence over the five years from 2011 to 2016 the dividends will have grown by $(1 + g)^5$. Thus

$£22,265 = £12,634 \times (1 + g)^5$

or

$$(1 + g) = \sqrt[5]{\frac{£22,265}{£12,634}}$$

$$(1 + g) = \sqrt[5]{1.7623}$$

$$(1 + g) = 1.12$$

$$g = 0.12 \text{ or } 12\% \text{ pa}$$

5 Causes of Growth

Introduction

Our alternative method is to consider what causes growth in dividends, or may cause growth in the future since it is investors' expectations of the future that we are concerned with. In the short term dividends will fluctuate for many reasons, but in the context of cost of capital we are only concerned with the shareholders' expectations of long-term growth.

If a company fully distributes all of its profits in any year, then at the end of the year (start of next year) it will be in exactly the same position as it was at the start of the year. It will not have grown.

Long-term growth results from retaining a portion of earnings and reinvesting them to generate higher earnings and higher dividends in the future.

EXAMPLE

A company can generate a profit after tax of 10% in a year based on its opening capital employed. Its policy is to distribute 80% of all profits and retain 20%. What will be the dividend growth rate?

SOLUTION

Based on this information we could calculate the profits and net assets for the next two years as follows.

	Year 1	Year 2
Opening capital employed	£100,000	£102,000
Rate of return	10%	10%
	£	£
Profit after tax	10,000	10,200
Dividend (80% of net income)	(8,000)	(8,160)
Retained profit	2,000	2,040

In Year 1 we generate a profit of £10,000 (£100,000 × 10%), of which 80% is distributed and £2,000 (20%) retained.

Thus at the start of Year 2 our net assets will have increased by this £2,000 retained profit to a figure of £102,000. Hence in this year we will generate a profit after tax of £10,200 (£102,000 × 10%) and distribute £8,160 (£10,200 × 80%).

Looking at the dividends, we can see that they have grown by 2%, ie the retention of profit has resulted in 2% dividend growth. But this is not all, as all of the value figures (capital employed, profit after tax, retained profits) have increased by 2%. We do not just have growth in income, we also have capital growth.

This 2% growth (dividend growth and capital growth) stems from the fact that in year 2 we are getting a 10% return on the opening net assets in year 1 plus a 10% return on the retained profits from year 1. These retained profits represent 20% of the total profits, hence we are getting an additional 10% return on 20% of the profits - 2% overall (10% × 20%).

Summary

This leads to the expression that we could have used to calculate the growth rate directly using the rb model or Gordon's Growth model, specifically

$$\mathbf{g = r \times b}$$

Where

- r = rate of return on reinvested capital
- b = proportion of profits retained and reinvested

Applying this gives

$$g = 10\% \times 20\% = 2\%$$

as we established above.

Do not regard consideration of past dividends as being conceptually different to the rb model. It is the retention and reinvestment that caused the growth to occur in the past, and provided that the company does not intend to change its policy, the two approaches should lead to the same result.

The Effect of Inflation on Dividend Growth

In practice dividends do not grow at a constant rate and, although this will result from changes in a company's retention policy, the main reason will be due to the effects of inflation.

Inflation will cause the value of all transactions to increase and hence profits and dividends to rise without any corresponding increase in the activity levels of the business. We therefore need to build this factor in to our analysis which we can do as follows.

$$\mathbf{(1 + g) = (1 + rb) \times (1 + i)}$$

Where

- r = real rate of return on investment before the effects of inflation
- b = proportion of profits retained and reinvested
- i = annual rate of inflation

EXAMPLE

If our above company generated a return of 10% pa excluding the effects of inflation, and inflation was running at 5% pa what will be the growth rate of the dividends?

SOLUTION

Looking at this situation and adding the effects of the inflation, we get

	Year 1	Year 2	
Existing earnings	10,000	10,500	(£10,000 × 1.05)
Additional earnings from reinvestment		210	(£2,000 × 10% × 1.05)
Profit after tax	10,000	10,710	
Dividend (80%)	(8,000)	(8,568)	
	2,000	2,142	

As we can see from this, the growth rate for all factors has now been 7.1% pa which is exactly what we would get by applying the above formula, as follows.

$$(1 + g) = (1 + rb) \times (1 + i)$$

$$(1 + g) = 1.02 \times 1.05 = 1.071$$

$$g = 0.071 \text{ or } 7.1\% \text{ pa}$$

Before continuing, note that the return from reinvestment of 10% is the real return, ie the return that we would expect in the absence of inflation. The actual return based on actual cash receipts, would be higher. In this example, with inflation at 5%, the actual return would be 15.5% ((1.10 × 1.05) – 1).

In practice, we would not expect a constant rate of inflation and hence the actual return on reinvestment will vary. However, it is certainly more likely that the real return on reinvestment will be reasonably constant, on the assumption that the company will continue to invest in the same type of project.

6 Non-Constant Growth

Introduction

There may be circumstances when we can foresee one growth rate for a given period, followed by another thereafter. How can we evaluate the share in this circumstance?

The solution is to split the problem into two.

Future Market Value

The first step is to calculate the market value from the point from which a constant future growth rate can be seen using the normal constant growth formula.

In applying this formula remember that we are calculating the market value today based on the dividend in one year's time. Similarly we can use this formula to calculate the market value in, say, four years based on the dividend in five year's time. More generally, the market value at any point in time (n) can be calculated based on the dividend one year later (n + 1), ie the present value of the future cash flows from that date, as

$$E_n = \frac{d_{n+1}}{r_e - g}$$

Where E_n is the ex-div market value at time n. This time will be the relevant time to use when discounting back to current market values.

Current Market Value

Calculate the current market value by discounting the earlier dividends (those prior to d_{n+1}) plus this future value back to present values.

The points to take care about are that all dividends should be considered once and once only, and, as ever, be careful with the timing of the flows when calculating the current value. This is best illustrated with an example.

EXAMPLE

A share has just paid a dividend of 10p per share. It is expected that the dividends will grow at the rate of 10% pa for the next five years, then 5% pa thereafter. The investors require a rate of return of 15% on these shares and this is not expected to alter in the future. What is the current market value of the shares?

SOLUTION

Future Market Value

There is a constant growth rate of 5% pa following time five, hence we can evaluate the market value at time five based on this as

$$E_5 = \frac{d_6}{r_e - g}$$

$$E_5 = \frac{10p \times 1.10^5 \times 1.05}{0.15 - 0.05}$$

$$E_5 = \frac{16.910}{0.10} = 169.104p$$

Current Market Value

The future value considers all dividends from time five. We now need to build in all the rest as follows.

Time	Cash Flow £	Discount Factor	Present Value £
1	$d_1 = 10p \times 1.10 = 11p$	$\frac{1}{1.15}$	9.565
2	$d_2 = 10p \times 1.10_2 = 12.1p$	$\frac{1}{1.15^2}$	9.149
3	$d_3 = 10p \times 1.10_3 = 13.31p$	$\frac{1}{1.15^3}$	8.752
4	$d_4 = 10p \times 1.10_4 = 14.641p$	$\frac{1}{1.15^4}$	8.371
5	$d_5 = 10p \times 1.10_5 = 16.105p$	$\frac{1}{1.15^5}$	8.007
5	$E_5 = 169.104p$	$\frac{1}{1.15^5}$	84.074
			127.918

Problems in Applying the DVM

Attempting to apply the dividend valuation model to generate a cost of equity is problematic for any company. Below we consider some of the main practical problems.

Known Share Price

For listed companies a share price will be available. However, where a corporate financier is seeking to generate a valuation to support a company's entry onto an exchange, or where a venture capitalist wishes to evaluate an unlisted company, no quoted share price will be available. In such circumstances the dividend valuation model can only be utilised to derive the required return of equity for a company of similar risk characteristics to the company under consideration. In many cases there will not even be a comparable quoted company of similar size, activities or characteristics to use as a guide.

Known Future Cash Returns

Equity shares provide unknown future cash returns. The only solution is therefore to estimate what the market believes the future cash returns may be. It should be noted that what is required here is not an estimate of what the actual cash returns will be (as would be used in the forecast from which the valuation is derived) but rather what the general market expectation is. It is the market as a whole which determines the price and therefore it is only from an estimate of what returns the market expects that the required return of investors can be derived.

Attempting to ascertain what future cash returns the marketplace expects from an equity is self-evidently problematic. The only practical solution to the problem is to rely upon analyst consensus views which are likely to influence the market view. Any new company in a new sector is unlikely to have positive earnings in its first few years of operation, and is almost certainly not going to be paying out dividends to its shareholders. Hence, even where a stock is already listed, has been operating for several years and is covered by several securities analysts, it remains probable that almost all of the future cash returns must be estimated without any objective guidance.

Conclusions

Given the absence of any objective guidance with regard to the market consensus view as to the future cash returns available for some stocks, the dividend valuation model does not provide a useful mechanism for the generation of a cost of equity in such cases. The methodology will be excessively subjective if the user is required to use their own estimate of the general market view. Indeed, there is a risk of producing entirely circular valuations if the user were to input their own estimates of future cash returns into the dividend valuation model to derive a cost of equity, and this cost of equity were then used to discount those same projected cash returns.

7 Capital Asset Pricing Model (CAPM)

The ubiquitous CAPM is the leading methodology for deriving the cost of equity capital within International financial markets. Whilst many have questioned its ability to explain stock returns it has proved remarkably resilient to criticism over the last decades and very few market participants have used any alternative methodology for any sustained period of time.

The theoretical basis of the CAPM is examined first along with some general criticisms. The particular problems of applying CAPM are considered in detail later.

General

Modern portfolio theory shows how one can appraise investments from the point of view of companies and individuals by evaluating the impact of the investment on the risk-return profile of the current portfolio of investments.

The primary weakness of this method is that it remains dependent on individuals' risk-return preferences which, for corporate investment appraisal in particular, is inconvenient as a result of:

- The difficulties involved in ascertaining such risk-return preferences
- The problem caused to a company by an investment which is acceptable to only a section of its shareholders

The introduction of the market portfolio, representing a fully diversified portfolio any investor would choose to invest in, raises the possibility of avoiding these difficulties.

For investors who are well-diversified, all investments could be appraised in relation to the Capital Market Line, which represents all possible combinations of the market portfolio and a risk free asset. Investors with differing risk-return preferences will now choose to hold some combination of the market portfolio and the risk-free investment.

If a diversified investor invests a proportion of his funds (b) in the market portfolio and the remainder (1 – b) in the risk free investment then his expected return and risk can be calculated using portfolio theory equations as

Return

$$r = r_f + b(r_m - r_f)$$

Risk

$$\sigma = \sqrt{b^2\sigma_m^2} = b\sigma_m$$

What we can see is that to benefit from a proportion of the *risk premium* $(r_m - r_f)$ we must face the same proportion of the market portfolio risk σ_m.

Alternatively, if we know what proportion of the market portfolio risk we are willing to face, we can establish the likely return that can be achieved, ie if

σ_s = risk we are willing to face

σ_m = market portfolio risk

then the proportion of funds that we would invest in the market portfolio would be

$$b = \frac{\sigma_s}{\sigma_m}$$

and the return that we could then expect as a diversified investor for this level of risk would be

$$r = r_f + b(r_m - r_f)$$

Clearly therefore, any alternative investment opportunity with this level of risk must offer a higher return if it is to be attractive to the investor.

Thus this equation gives the minimum acceptable return for a given level of risk for the diversified investor, ie the required rate of return with which to appraise the investment opportunity.

This, in essence, is the Capital Asset Pricing Model, though clearly, there is much more to it.

8 Systematic and Unsystematic Risk

Introduction

We have seen that an investment's total risk (the variability of its returns about its expected return) can be measured by its standard deviation. This total risk can be split into two components.

Systematic (or Market) Risk

This measures the variability in the investment's returns which are caused by general market fluctuations. It cannot be diversified away because it is a 'fact of the market'. Even if an investor held all quoted UK shares they would still be subject to some risk as history has shown. This risk will be caused by such general economic factors as:

- Inflation rates
- Interest rates
- Tax rates

Unsystematic (or Specific) Risk

This is the remainder which reflects factors specific to the investment or the industry in which the company operates. It is this element of an investment's risk that can be diversified away. Since the unsystematic risk is not common to all companies/segments of the market, it can be eliminated within a well-diversified portfolio.

Relevance

The importance of the above to a well-diversified investor is as follows.

Unsystematic Risk is Irrelevant

If an investor is well diversified, unsystematic risk should be of no concern as it will be diversified away within his overall portfolio. In this situation the only risk the investor is left facing is the systematic risk.

Required Return Depends on Systematic Risk

Investors demand a return commensurate with the risk they face. Since our investor faces only the systematic risk of his investment, the returns he demands will be based on this, ie the premium for risk will be a function of systematic risk only, not the total risk of the investment.

We must measure the level of systematic risk present in any particular investment and use this measure to set a target return which would be sufficient to compensate for that risk. The investment's expected return may be then compared against this required rate to determine whether it should be accepted or rejected.

Betas and Required Returns

Portfolio theory introduced the Capital Market Line (CML). It shows the best combinations of risk and return which can currently be obtained on the market by diversified investors, through combinations of the market portfolio (m) and risk-free securities. No investor should be content with a portfolio falling beneath the CML.

If an investment carries a risk of 50% of the standard deviation of m ($0.5\sigma_m$) then the return must be equal to r_f plus a risk premium equal to 50% ($r_m - r_f$) in order to place it on the CML representing an acceptable level of return. **Note.** The risk referred to here is only systematic risk as we noted above since we are assuming unsystematic risk to have been diversified away by the diversified investor.

Now changing the risk axis from an absolute measure (the standard deviation as a percentage) to a relative one where σ_m is 1, our investment which has a risk of 50% of σ_m will appear with a relative measure of risk of 0.5.

In other words our horizontal axis is now showing risk represented by a sort of index number which we call a beta factor (β) such that for our investment above

$$\beta = \frac{50\% \times \sigma_m}{\sigma_m} = 0.5$$

This change of axis creates the Security Market Line (SML).

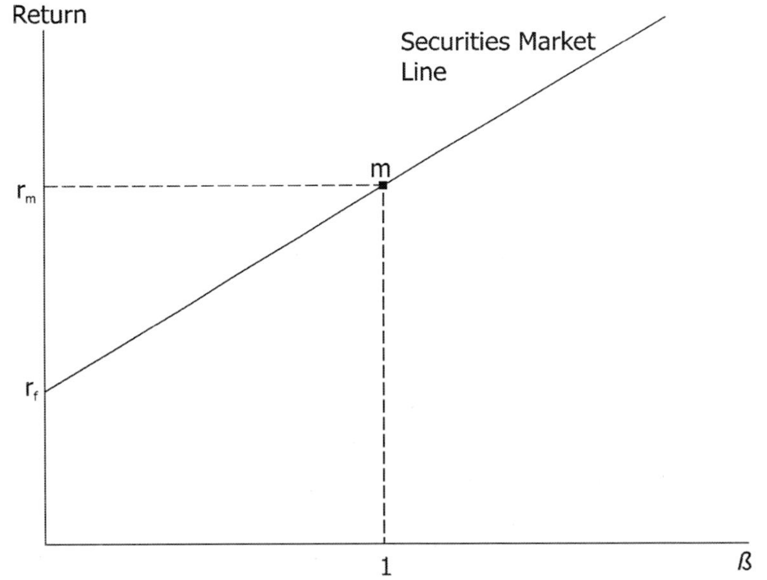

Hence, for an investment whose relative risk is given by β, the required return is given by the Capital Asset Pricing Model (CAPM) formula.

$$r = r_f + \beta(r_m - r_f)$$

Where

- r_m= the return expected from the market portfolio
- r_f = the return offered by a risk-free security
- β = the risk of the investment opportunity relative to that of the market portfolio (systematic risk only)

EXAMPLE

For example, suppose that the risk-free rate of return is 6%, and the market is expected to return 14%, what return would a diversified investor expect from an investment with a * of

- 0
- 0.5
- 1
- 1.5

SOLUTION

Using

$$r = r_f + \beta(r_m - r_f)$$

Gives

β = 0

$$r = 6\% + 0 \times (14\% - 6\%) = 6\%$$

β = 0.5

$$r = 6\% + 0.5 \times (14\% - 6\%) = 10\%$$

β = 1

$$r = 6\% + 1 \times (14\% - 6\%) = 14\%$$

β = 1.5

$$r = 6\% + 1.5 \times (14\% - 6\%) = 18\%$$

The Security Market Line

Investment appraisal under CAPM amounts to plotting investments' expected returns and betas on the SML graph. An investment lying above the SML would be accepted by any investor (or any company) as it is offering a return higher than could normally be expected for that given level of risk, ie it is undervalued. An investment lying beneath the SML would be rejected as its current return is too low, ie it is overvalued. An investment lying on the SML is currently correctly priced in the market. An investor or company should be indifferent to the choice between buying it or not.

Note. When utilising CAPM it is important to bear in mind that you must appraise the investment in isolation (effectively as a separate company), without reference to the investing group or company. The CAPM formula gives the impact of the investment on a well diversified investor's portfolio.

9 BETAS

Introduction

What it Means

The beta of an investment is a relative measure of the *systematic risk* of an investment.

In general terms:

- The sign of the beta (+/–) indicates whether, on average, the investments returns move with (+) the market, rising and falling when it does, or in the opposite direction (–) to the market.
- The scale or value of the beta indicates the relative volatility.

A beta of 0.5 (or –0.5) for instance, would indicate that on average the investment's returns move one half as much as the market's do in the same (opposite) direction. If the market fell by 6% we would expect the investment to fall (rise) by 3%; if the market rose by 6% we would expect the investment's returns to rise (fall) by 3% etc.

Summary

$\beta > 1$

On average, the investment's returns will move in the same direction as the market's returns, but to a greater extent.

$\beta = 1$

On average, the investment's returns will move in the same direction as the market's returns, and to the same extent.

$0 < \beta < 1$

On average, the investment's returns will move in the same direction as the market's returns, but to a lesser extent.

$\beta = 0$

The investment's returns are uncorrelated with those of the market. This would be the case if the investment were risk-free, but more generally this situation will arise when all of the investment's risk is unsystematic.

$\beta < 0$

On average, the investment's returns will move in the opposite direction to the market, to a lesser extent if $\beta > -1$, to the same extent if $\beta = -1$, and to a greater extent if $\beta < -1$.

Use of Betas

We can use the β for an investment to establish from the CAPM formula what the appropriate risk adjusted required rate of return is in order to appraise the investment.

EXAMPLE

A new one-year investment opportunity requires an initial investment of £1m and is expected to give a return of £1.2m at the end of the year.

Assume the market return is 14%, and risk-free return is 6%.

The investment's beta has been estimated at 1.5.

Assuming investors are well-diversified, should the investment be accepted and what value would we place on the investment?

SOLUTION

Required Rate of Return

The required return given by the CAPM would be

$$r = r_f + \beta(r_m - r_f)$$

$$r = 6\% + 1.5(14\% - 6\%)$$

$$r = 6\% + 12\% = 18\%$$

Investments Return and Appraisal

The return on the investment will be 20% (£1.2m return from a £1.0m investment), hence it should be accepted. It is offering a better level of return for its level of (systematic) risk than can currently be obtained elsewhere on the market.

Value of Investment

To value the investment, the investors will use the required rate given by the CAPM as a risk adjusted discount rate to find the present value of its future returns (the usual market value approach) giving

Time	Cash Flow £'000	Discount Factor	Present Value £'000
0	(1,000)	1	(1,000)
1	1,200	$\frac{1}{1.18}$	1,017
Net present value			17

The £1.017m is the value of the investment's returns to well-diversified investors (hence the market value of the investment). It is the maximum price that they should be prepared to pay for such returns.

The investment is accepted because it is worth £17,000 more than it costs.

Although the impact of the investment may differ from quoted company to quoted company (it might correlate positively with some companies' returns, negatively with others') the impact on any company's well-diversified investors is found by looking at the impact on the market portfolio.

If capital markets are efficient, then all quoted shares should be correctly valued (any share which was undervalued would be the subject of buying pressure, which would force its price up to the fair value). CAPM shows that a share's market value should be that which equates the expected return from the share with the required return for the share's beta.

Calculation of Betas

Systematic Risk

To get a beta we need to know the systematic risk element of the investment we are considering (σ_s). We have said that systematic risk is that part of the total risk that is related to the market portfolio. The correlation coefficient between two investment opportunities is a measure of this relationship, hence

$$\sigma_s = \sigma_i \, cor_{im}$$

Where

- σ_s = the investments systematic risk
- σ_i = the investments total risk (systematic and unsystematic)
- cor_{im} = correlation coefficient between the returns of the investment and those of the market portfolios

For instance, if an investment were perfectly correlated with the market so that all its fluctuations could be fully explained by fluctuations in the market, then all of its risk would be systematic $\sigma_s = \sigma_i$ If an investment were uncorrelated to the market, then its systematic risk would be zero, and all its risk would be unsystematic. Between those extremes come varying proportions of systematic and unsystematic risk.

Note that the relationship between these risks (total, systematic and unsystematic) is

$$\sigma_i^2 = \sigma_s^2 + \sigma_u^2$$

Where

- σ_i = the investment's total risk (standard deviation)
- σ_s = the investment's systematic risk
- σ_u = the investment's unsystematic risk

ie the investment's total variance is the sum of its systematic and unsystematic variances.

The Beta Coefficient

Remember that beta is an index number showing the systematic risk of an investment relative to the market portfolio, ie

$$\beta = \frac{\sigma_s}{\sigma_m}$$

and from $\sigma_s = cor_{im}\sigma_i$ above we can establish

$$\beta = \frac{\sigma_s}{\sigma_m} = \frac{cor_{im}\sigma_i}{\sigma_m} = \frac{cor_{im}\sigma_i\sigma_m}{\sigma_m^2} = \frac{\text{Covariance}_{(i,m)}}{\text{Variance of the Market}}$$

If the covariance or correlation coefficient between the investment and the market can be established, the beta can be calculated. Alternatively, if we establish the systematic risk we can establish the beta.

Calculation of Beta Coefficients in Practice

Beta factors are calculated in practice for shares quoted on the Stock Exchange and are available from a large number of data providers.

The method of calculation is very much based on the above ideas regarding the average variability of the returns from investments relative to those of the market, involving the use of linear regression analysis. If the historical return on the FTSE index (representing the market) over and above the risk-free return is plotted on a scatter diagram against the corresponding returns of a security i also over and above r_f, then following might be observed.

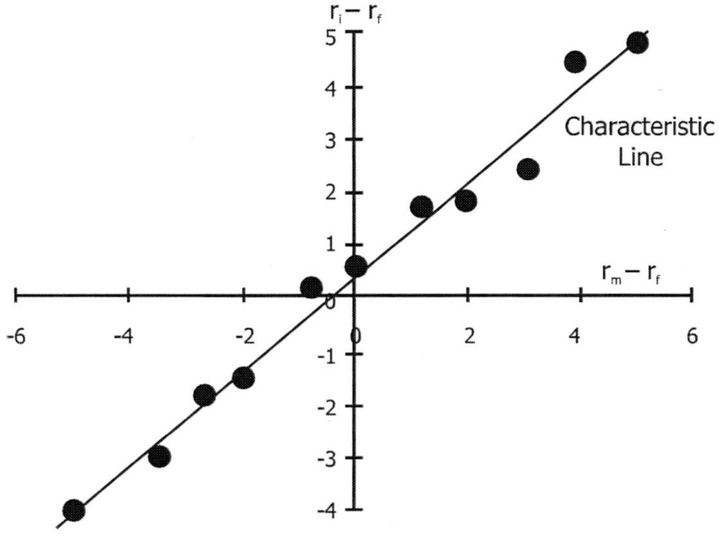

If the linear regression line of best fit is found it will show the average relationship between the two sets of returns. This line is known as the security's characteristic line.

The results of a regression analysis give the terms for the linear regression equation

$$y = a + bx$$

Where

$y = r_i - r_f$

$x = r_m - r_f$

b indicates the volatility of i's return relative to the market returns. If the slope is greater than 45% (ie greater than 1) then i's returns tend to be more volatile than those of the market. This is exactly how we have earlier defined an investment's beta factor. Hence, beta is estimated by the slope of the regression line which can be calculated as

$$\beta = \frac{n\Sigma xy - \Sigma x \Sigma y}{n\Sigma x^2 - (\Sigma x)^2};$$

a is the intercept on the vertical axis and is known as the alpha factor (α_i). It indicates that i has a premium larger than that predicted by the CAPM. If the expected return from the CAPM equals the actual return then $\alpha_i = 0$, thus α_i represents an **abnormal return.**

Note. Using $y = r_i$ and $x = r_m$ gives the correct calculation of beta but mis-states the alpha value. If we simply want to establish the beta, however, this may simplify things.

EXAMPLE

Observations over a period of time over which the risk-free rate was constant at 6% pa showed the following returns from the market and an investment.

Period	Market r_m %	Investment r_i %
1	12	9
2	13	9
3	14	10
4	15	10
5	16	12
Mean	14	10

Calculate

- The beta for the investment.
- The total risk of the investment which should be split into systematic and unsystematic components.

The abnormal return from the investment.

SOLUTION

Period	r_m %	r_i %	r_m^2 %	r_i^2 %	X r_{m-f} %	Y r_{i-f} %	x^2 %	xy %
1	12	9	144	81	6	3	36	18
2	13	9	169	81	7	3	49	21
3	14	10	196	100	8	4	64	32
4	15	10	225	100	9	4	81	36
5	16	12	256	144	10	6	100	60
			990	506	40	20	330	167

Beta Coefficient

Inserting these results in the regression equation gives

$$\beta = \frac{n\Sigma xy - \Sigma x\Sigma y}{n\Sigma x^2 - (\Sigma x)^2} = \frac{5 \times 167 - 40 \times 20}{5 \times 330 - 40^2}$$

$$\beta = \frac{35}{50} = 0.7$$

Risk

Total Risk

The total risk of the investment (its standard deviation) can be calculated as

$$\sigma_i = \sqrt{\frac{\sum fr^2 - n\bar{r}^2}{n-1}}$$

$$\sigma_i = \sqrt{\frac{506 - 5 \times 10^2}{4}} = \sqrt{\frac{6}{4}} = 1.2247\%$$

Systematic Risk

The systematic element of that risk can be established from

$$\beta = \frac{\sigma_s}{\sigma_m}$$

or

$$\sigma_s = \beta\sigma_m$$

Now

$$\sigma_m = \sqrt{\frac{\sum fr^2 - n\bar{r}^2}{n-1}}$$

$$\sigma_m = \sqrt{\frac{990 - 5 \times 14^2}{4}} = \sqrt{\frac{10}{4}} = 1.5811\%$$

Therefore

$$\sigma_s = \beta\sigma_m = 0.7 \times 1.5811\% = 1.1068\%$$

Unsystematic Risk

This can be established using

$$\sigma_i^2 = \sigma_s^2 + \sigma_u^2$$

giving

$$1.2247^2 = 1.1068^2 + \sigma_u^2$$

$$1.5 = 1.225 + \sigma_u^2$$

$$\sigma_u^2 = 0.275$$

$$\sigma_u = 0.5244\%$$

Abnormal Return

Using the CAPM formula the expected return is

$$r = r_f + \beta(r_m - r_f)$$

$$r = 6 + 0.7(14 - 6) = 11.6\%$$

The observed average return has been 10%, hence there is an abnormal return of −1.6%.

10 Assumptions and Limitations of CAPM

The Assumptions

CAPM is based on a number of assumptions:

- Investors are rational and risk averse, they seek to maximise the expected utility of their wealth.
- Investors are only concerned with a security's expected return and its systematic risk.
- The capital market is perfect and in equilibrium, which means in particular:
  - It is not dominated by any individual investors
  - There are no transaction costs, for instance commissions or taxes, or other imperfections
  - All securities are fairly valued, hence r_m is a realistic return
- All investors have the same expectations regarding the probability distributions of returns from each security, thus they have the same opportunity set and efficient frontier.
- There exists a risk-free rate at which all investors may borrow or lend without limit.

The realism and relevance of many of these assumptions may be questioned. The first two are probably not too far fetched, but the others are clearly invalid. The question is, are the effects of these invalid assumptions significant enough to invalidate the whole theory, or do they just produce minor distortions which can be separately dealt with?

It is worth noting that extensions made to CAPM which seek to relax these basic assumptions give results which are still broadly in line with the basic theory.

Much research has been carried out over the years to try to establish to what extent CAPM is valid. The model has proved surprisingly resilient to such testing, and it seems that β is a valid and fairly complete measure of risk. It is, however, worth noting that academic research (notably the work of Fama and French) indicates the explanatory power of CAPM is limited and appears to be worsening through time.

The Limitations

Aside from the limitations stemming from the CAPM's assumptions, the following limitations are worth considering.

Single-Period (One Year) Model

The required rate of return derived from the model is only valid as long as the inputs (r_m, r_f, β) are valid. As a result of annual budgets which tend to effect tax rates and interest rates we can expect that one or more of these factors will change over a year. As such, the returns that we consider when using CAPM is the holding period return over that time.

Few investment opportunities last for one year only; however, we can extend the model to more than one time period if we assume that all relevant factors (such as risk-free rate and market rate) remain constant over the period covered.

Only Applicable to Diversified Portfolios

The model assumes that the overall portfolio held is diversified and equates to the market as a whole. If we were dealing with a small undiversified portfolio, then a portfolio theory approach would be more applicable.

Single Economy Model

The CAPM was established as a single economy model. At the time of its development as a model it was broadly reasonable to assume that countries operated as single economies. With the relaxation of exchange controls and the increase in the globalisation of the international capital markets and growth of cross-border investment, it is becoming less and less reasonable to assume countries represent single, independent economies. Data providers will calculate betas for European stocks by regressing that stock against that country's equity market regardless of whether that stock's operations are restricted to that country and without regard to the fact that many European countries are now within unitary economic governance. Applying the CAPM on a country by country basis leads to the rather strange conclusion that if a company is listed in France the required return of shareholders may well be different to if the company sought a listing in Germany.

Problems in Estimating the Beta

One significant problem in applying the CAPM to early stage stocks relates to the availability of reliable beta measures. To generate a beta across short periods requires measurement of the stock against an index on a very regular basis if the beta is to have any statistical validity. This in turn can introduce a non-trading bias whereby stocks that are not actively traded will appear to have static prices even when the index is changing. This is not, of course, indicative of low sensitivity to systematic risk but rather a function of the stock's lack of liquidity.

Measurement of beta over relatively short reference periods may also distort the beta since it may not provide sufficient breadth of market behaviour. For example, if the market were consistently rising over the beta measurement period, this would tend to exaggerate the beta of market leaders (which appear to behave in the same manner as the market, but to a greater extent) and understate the beta of laggards (where the stock would not appear to rise in response to systematic risk factors).

For some stocks, with a relatively long market history, the CAPM may provide a reasonable methodology to estimate the cost of equity. For those with a short history of trading, it will be possible to generate betas of probably limited reliability by using short measurement periods. Bloomberg, for example, will measure returns weekly over just two years to generate a beta.

For those stocks which are newly listed or not even listed at present, the CAPM will be extremely difficult to apply. A couple of possible solutions are:

- To utilise a beta which does not rely on measurement of stock returns against an index, or
- To utilise the beta of a company of similar risk characteristics as the company under consideration if a reliable beta for a comparable company is available.

The first solution obviously requires a rigorous methodology for beta calculation from alternative data. To attempt to generate a methodology from first principles in this context is bound to be extremely difficult. It is something of a leap of faith to assume that the beta provided represents a reasonable assessment of a stock's systematic sensitivity.

The second solution is obviously also problematic in that finding a company of comparable risk characteristics is very subjective and may be difficult to find any materially similar companies.

11 The Effects of Gearing on Investment Appraisal

Introduction

If a company is geared then we could draw up a simple balance sheet with assets on the left and financing on the right as

Asset value	Equity value	E
	Debt value	D
Asset value	Total value	V

The basic business risk of the operations will cause the asset values and the earnings they generate to vary. Very little, if any, of this variation will be borne by the debt holders, it will be borne by the shareholders.

With the variation in asset values being spread over much smaller equity values, the percentage variability in this figure will be much larger. As a result, the risk to shareholders is much higher in a geared company than it would be were the company ungeared, when the risk to shareholders would simply be this business risk. This additional risk is the effect of financial gearing.

12 Geared Betas

Definition

Asset/Earnings/Ungeared Beta

The asset/earnings/ungeared beta is a measure of the basic business risk to the asset values/earnings. It therefore represents the risk shareholders would face were the company ungeared.

Equity/Dividend/Geared Beta

The equity, dividend or geared beta is a measure of the risk to shareholders in the geared company. The difference between the equity and asset betas will reflect the financial risk.

Relating Asset and Equity Betas

Ignoring Corporation Tax

Suppose we buy all of the firm's debt **and** equity, then we would own 100% of the assets and their returns. In the absence of corporation tax there is no difference in value between geared and ungeared companies as the investor is receiving the same total return (the full operating profit which will be distributed to the one investor either as interest or dividends) at the same total risk (the risk in the operating profits).

As a result any variability in asset values and earnings in the ungeared company will exactly match the variability of assets and earnings in the geared company, both in absolute and relative terms.

It follows that the asset beta or beta of the ungeared company will equal the beta of the portfolio of debt and equity in the geared company, ie the overall risk of this investment portfolio would be the asset or ungeared beta (β_u).

We have seen above how betas can be combined. Since we hold all the equity and all the debt, the beta of this combination must be the weighted average of the equity or geared beta (β_g) and the debt beta (β_d).

$$\beta_u = \beta_g \times \frac{E_g}{V_g} + \beta_d \times \frac{D}{V_g}$$

Where

- β_u = the asset/earnings/ungeared beta
- β_g = the equity/dividend/geared beta
- β_d = debt beta
- E_g = market value of the firms equity
- D = market value of the firms debt
- V_g = the total market value of the firm ($V_g = E_g + D$)

Rearranging this to solve for β_g we get

$$\beta_u \times V_g = \beta_g \times E_g + \beta_d \times D$$

$$\beta_g \times E_g = \beta_u \times V_g - \beta_d \times D$$

$$\beta_g = \beta_u \times \frac{V_g}{E_g} - \beta_d \times \frac{D}{E_g}$$

Now $V_g = E_g + D$ hence

$$\beta_g = \beta_u \times \frac{E_g + D}{E_g} - \beta_d \times \frac{D}{E_g}$$

$$\beta_g = \beta_u \times \frac{E_g}{E_g} + \beta_u \times \frac{D}{E_g} - \beta_d \times \frac{D}{E_g}$$

$$\beta_g = \beta_u + (\beta_u - \beta_d) \times \frac{D}{E_g}$$

and if we assume that $\beta_d = 0$ (ie debt is risk free), then this reduces to

$$\beta_g = \beta_u\left(1 + \frac{D}{E_g}\right) \text{ or } \beta_g = \beta_u \times \frac{V_g}{E_g}$$

Including Corporation Tax

When we include the effects of corporation tax we must remember that interest payments on debt attract tax relief, whereas dividend payments on equity do not. The tax charge in a geared company will, therefore, be lower as a result of this tax relief, hence the total available to pay out as either interest or dividends will be higher.

EXAMPLE

Total pay-out by the company	**Ungeared £**	**Geared £**
Earnings	1,000	1,000
Interest	–	(400)
Profit before tax	1,000	600
Corporation tax at 20%	(200)	(120)
Profit after tax = Dividends	800	480
Total received by the investors		
Interest	–	400
Dividends	800	480
	800	880

In this example, the geared company can afford to pay out more in total to its investor than the ungeared company. The difference of £80 (£880 – £800) is due to the tax relief on the interest of £400 × 20%.

Our investor who has financed all the company will receive a greater total return in absolute terms, though the variability (risk) in absolute terms is the same. He is therefore facing a lower risk in relative terms as a result of receiving this tax relief on interest. To incorporate this effect the equation needs to be amended as follows:

$$\beta_g = \beta_u + (\beta_u - \beta_d) \times \frac{D(1 - T_c)}{E_g}$$

and if we assume that $\beta_d = 0$ (ie debt is risk free), then this reduces to

$$\beta_g = \beta_u\left(1 + \frac{D(1 - T_c)}{E_g}\right)$$

13 ARBITRAGE PRICING THEORY

Introduction

Arbitrage pricing theory (APT), like the CAPM, is an equilibrium model of asset pricing. Although the CAPM made certain strong assumptions about investor preferences (for example, investors were assumed to be risk-averse), APT makes no such strong assumptions. That is, APT is not based on the idea that investors look at portfolios in terms of expected returns and standard deviations, rather APT requires only that investors prefer higher levels of wealth to lower levels of wealth.

APT therefore provides:

- An alternative pricing model to CAPM
- A basis for portfolio strategies where a portfolio is sensitive to various factors
- A basis for performance measurement

Basic Model

APT gives the expected return from a security based on:

- The value taken by various factors to which the security is sensitive
- The sensitivity of the security to those factors

as

$$r_i = a_i + b_{i1}F_1 + b_{i2}F_2 + \cdots + b_{in}F_n$$

Where

- r_i = return from the investment i
- F_1, F_2 ... F_n = are the factors that influence the returns of security i
- b_{i1}, b_{i2} ... b_{i2} = the sensitivity of the security to these factors
- a_i = expected return from the security if each factor has a value of zero

Note: $F_1 \cdots F_n$ are factors common to all securities and may be factors such as

Equities	Bonds
Interest rates	Coupon
Inflation rates	Duration
GDP growth rates	Interest rates
Tax rates	Default risk
FTSE index growth rate	Conversion options

For the purposes of the theory it is necessary to assume that there are many securities and that the sensitivities to the factors differ substantially among securities.

Pure Factor Portfolios

Construction

In such a world, a number of investment strategies exist. Particularly interesting is the strategy involving portfolios that represent *pure factor portfolios*. Given enough securities with different characteristics, it should be possible to construct a portfolio that has unit sensitivity (ie a sensitivity of 1) to one particular factor and no sensitivity to any other factors, and zero non-factor risk.

The approach is to combine positions in the securities to hedge out the sensitivity of the portfolio to all but one factor.

EXAMPLE

Three securities have the following sensitivities.

Security	b_{i1}	b_{i2}
a	(0.40)	1.75
b	1.60	(0.75)
c	0.67	(0.25)

An investor has £1,000 to invest and puts £300 in security a and £700 in security b, with nothing in c. If we use X_i to denote the proportion of his funds invested in each security then $X_a = 0.3$, $X_b = 0.7$, $X_c = 0$. What will be the sensitivity of this portfolio to the two factors.

SOLUTION

Pure Factor 1 Portfolio

Factor 1

$b_{p1} = b_{a1} \times X_a + b_{b1} \times X_b + b_{c1} \times X_c$

$b_{p1} = (-0.40) \times 0.3 + 1.60 \times 0.7 + 0.67 \times 0 = 1.0$

Factor 2

$b_{p2} = b_{a2} \times X_a + b_{b2} \times X_b + b_{c2} \times X_c$

$b_{p2} = 1.75 \times 0.3 + (-0.75) \times 0.7 + (-0.25) \times 0 = 0.0$

Thus, by choosing the proportions appropriately, the investor could create a portfolio (call it p1) that is sensitive only to factor 1, hence

$$r_{p1} = a_{p1} + F_1$$

Since $b_{p1} = 1$, $b_{p2} = 0$ for this portfolio, this would be a pure factor 1 portfolio.

By design, its return moves with the first factor on a one-for-one basis.

Pure Factor 2 Portfolio

An alternative strategy could create a **pure factor** 2 portfolio. If the investor with £1,000 decided to invest £625 in securities like a and £375 in securities like c, the sensitivities of the resulting portfolio would be

Factor 1

$b_{p1} = b_{a1} \times X_a + b_{b1} \times X_b + b_{c1} \times X_c$

$b_{p1} = (-0.40) \times 0.625 + 1.60 \times 0.0 + 0.67 \times 0.375 = 0.0$

Factor 2

$b_{p2} = b_{a2} \times X_a + b_{b2} \times X_b + b_{c2} \times X_c$

$b_{p2} = 1.75 \times 0.625 + (-0.75) \times 0.0 + (-0.25) \times 0.375 = 1.0$

The result would be a portfolio (call it p2) sensitive only to factor 2

$r_{p2} = a_{p2} + F_2$

Practice

In a market with many securities of diverse characteristics, it would be theoretically possible to create **pure factor** portfolios that are sensitive to only one factor. In practice, the required conditions are not met completely, meaning it is only possible to create **impure factor** portfolios that are sensitive primarily (but not exclusively) to one factor.

Although APT assumes that pure factor portfolios can be created, it should be kept in mind that the reasonableness of the assumption is not of concern. Instead, it is the accuracy of the predictions of APT that are of importance.

Expected Returns on Factor Portfolios

Portfolio Returns

The expected return from a pure factor portfolio will depend on the expected value of the relevant factor. It is convenient to break this expected return into two parts

- The risk-free rate.
- The rest, which is typically indicated by the Greek letter *lambda,* λ and may be regarded as the **expected return premium per unit of sensitivity to the factor.**

Thus, the expected return on a pure factor 1 portfolio is

$$r_{p1} = a_{p1} + F_1 = r_f + \lambda_1$$

similarly the expected return on a pure factor 2 portfolio is

$$r_{p2} = a_{p2} + F_2 = r_f + \lambda_2$$

EXAMPLE

If r_f = 7% and r_{p1} = 16.6% then

$$r_{p1} = r_f + \lambda_1$$

gives

$$16.6 = 7.0 + \lambda_1$$

$$\lambda_1 = 9.6\%$$

If r_{p2} = 13.4% then

$$r_{p2} = r_f + \lambda_2$$

gives

$$13.4 = 7.0 + \lambda_2$$

$$\lambda_2 = 6.4\%$$

This means that the expected return premiums per unit of sensitivity to factors 1 and 2 are 9.6% and 6.4% respectively.

It is possible that many alternative combinations of securities could be used to construct a pure factor 1 portfolio. Will each such combination have the same expected return? Under the theory, the answer is yes, otherwise some **arbitrage profit opportunity** would exist. Whereas pure factor portfolios may not be unique in their composition, their expected returns should be, as a result of the operations of arbitrageurs.

Risk Free Returns

The presence of a risk-free rate is a natural part of APT. With a great many diverse securities, it will be possible to construct a portfolio that has zero sensitivity to every factor and is sufficiently diversified to have insignificant non-factor risk. Its expected return, which will be virtually risk-free, can be used as a base from which other expected returns are measured.

Derivation of the Theory

Expected Returns on Securities

By splitting funds among a risk-free portfolio and pure factor portfolio, it is possible for the investor to form a portfolio with almost any sensitivity to each factor.

For example, assume that the return on security i is related to factors 1 and 2 as follows.

$$r_i = a_i + 0.8F_1 + 1.5F_2$$

Thus, if an investor had £1,000 to invest, he could put it all in security k and have an expected return of

$$\overline{r}_i = a_i + 0.8\overline{F}_1 + 1.5\overline{F}_2$$

Where

- $\bar{r}_i$ = the expected return
- $\bar{F}_1$ = the expected value of F_1
- $\bar{F}_2$ = the expected value of F_2

Now, consider an alternative strategy in which £1,300 is borrowed at the risk-free rate to supplement the investor's £1,000. This means that the proportion invested in the risk-free asset is (–£1,300/£1,000) = –1.3 = X_f . Of the resulting £2,300 available for investment, £800 is invested in a pure factor 1 portfolio and the remaining £1,500 is invested in a pure factor 2 portfolio. This means that the proportions invested in these two portfolios are (£800/£1,000) = 0.8 =X_1 and (£1,500/£1,000) = 1.5 = X_2 respectively. The expected return on the resulting portfolio p, can be calculated as a weighted average of its three components.

$$\bar{r}_p = (X_f \times r_f) + (X_1 \times \bar{r}_{p1}) + (X_2 \times \bar{r}_{p2})$$

$$\bar{r}_p = (-1.3 \times r_f) + (0.8 \times \bar{r}_{p1}) + (1.5 \times \bar{r}_{p2})$$

$$\bar{r}_p = (-1.3 \times r_f) + (0.8 \times (r_f + \lambda_1)) + (1.5 \times (r_f + \lambda_2))$$

$$\bar{r}_p = -1.3r_f + 0.8r_f + 0.8\lambda_1 + 1.5r_f + 1.5\lambda_2$$

$$\bar{r}_p = r_f + 0.8\lambda_1 + 1.5\lambda_2$$

Now, compare portfolio p with security i. Each has a sensitivity of 0.8 to factor 1 and a sensitivity of 1.5 to factor 2.

Conclusion

The conclusion is that the expected return of security i would be equal to the expected return of portfolio p in equilibrium. That is, arbitrage would ensure that the expected return of security i would be

$$\bar{r}_i = r_f + 0.8\lambda_1 + 1.5\lambda_2$$

More generally, for any security i

$$\bar{r}_i = r_f + b_{i1}\lambda_1 + b_{i2}\lambda_2$$

This equation is the asset pricing equation of APT. In words, it states that

The expected return of security will be related to its sensitivity to each factor. Moreover, the relationship will be linear, with a common intercept term that is equal to the risk-free rate.

Comparison to CAPM

Like the equation obtained from CAPM, the APT equation asserts that there is a linear relationship between expected returns and the various relevant attributes of securities. CAPM can be viewed simply as a single factor model in which the factor is the market risk premium ($r_m - r_f$) and the sensitivity is the beta (β).

Practical Use

APT is silent about how many factors exist and what they represent. In turn, this means that APT is silent about the lambda values such as λ_1 and λ_2 in the equations, they can be positive, negative, or zero. Identification of factors and the associated lambda values involves both empirical work and judgement.

The APT equation refers to equilibrium expected returns for a security. However, disequilibrium can be represented with this equation in a manner similar to the CAPM. In particular, an alpha term can be added to the right-hand side of the equation to indicate the amount of mispricing.

An overpriced security would have negative alpha. This would mean that its expected return would be less than its equilibrium expected return of $\overline{r}_i = r_f + b_{i1}\lambda_1 + b_{i2}\lambda_2$. In turn, this suggests that the security is not an attractive one to purchase (or to hold onto if it is already owned). Similarly, an under priced security would have a positive alpha, meaning its expected return would be greater than its equilibrium return, and that it is an attractive security to purchase.

Problems in Applying APT in the Real World

There are effectively two insurmountable problems in attempting to apply APT in practice. The first is that there are limited providers of APT inputs.

The second problem is that, like the CAPM, generation of sensitivities to the relevant risk factors (whatever they may be determined to be) progresses along the same lines as calculation of betas. Hence where a stock is seeking a listing or is relatively newly listed, reliable sensitivities can not be readily ascertained even if data were provided for markets outside of the US.

14 Cost of Debt

Introduction

General

Again, to raise finance we must interest the potential investor, ie satisfy his required rate of return. As for shares, the market value will be determined by the investor based on his:

- Expectations of receipts
- Required rate of return

Once again we will apply the dividend valuation model ideas, that the market value of an investment will equal the present value of the investors' future expected receipts discounted at the investors' required rate of return. Hence our aim is similar in that we wish to calculate the IRR of the financing flows and establish any short cut methods available.

There are, however, some differences between equity and debt that we need to consider, specifically:

- Debt is most commonly redeemable, whereas equity tends to be irredeemable
- The return paid by companies to debt investors (interest) is allowable for corporation tax relief, dividends are not

Possible Ability to Redeem

We were able to establish short cut IRR's for equity since we assumed that it is irredeemable and that we could, therefore, apply the perpetuity discount factor ($\frac{1}{r}$).

If finance is redeemable, however, this formula will not be appropriate. Our evaluation for debt must, therefore, be split between:

- Irredeemable debt
- Redeemable debt

15 Effects of Taxation

Introduction

The rate of return demanded by investors determines the market value of the investment and hence the rate that the company has to pay on its borrowings. One relevant cash flow effect that we have not considered so far is tax. We will consider separately the effect of corporation tax on equity and on debt and then personal tax.

Corporation Tax

UK companies pay corporation tax on their taxable profits. at the UK main rate of corporation tax is 20% on taxable profits, which include capital gains. Tax due on each year's profits is generally paid by quarterly instalments (two within and two after the year end) or nine months after the company's year end for smaller companies.

A number of adjustments are made to reported profits to find taxable profits. Looking specifically at financing flows, dividend payments are **not** an allowable deduction for corporation tax purposes, although interest payments are. That is, any interest payments go to reduce a company's corporation tax charge but dividends do not.

Equity

A company deducts the net dividend paid to the investor from its **after-tax** profits, as we have already stated it does not impact on taxable profits.

Ignoring the effects of personal tax, the amount received by the investor is equal to the impact on the net assets of the company. As a result the ultimate cost to the company, the cost of equity, is equal to the investors' required rate of return before the effects of personal taxes.

Normally in cost of capital calculations, however, we assume that dividends and corporation tax are payable together on the last day of the accounting period. We ignore the time delay between the two events.

Debt

Irredeemables

For debt, the amount received by the investor before the effects of personal taxes is the **gross** interest which is the amount paid by the company from its profits **before** tax.

This expense attracts corporation tax relief, hence the impact on the net assets of the company is less than the amount received in the hands of the investor. It follows from this that the cost to the company, the cost of debt, is less than the required rate of return of the investor before personal taxes.

For example, if a company paid £10 interest to an investor, he would receive £10 gross income before personal tax but the company would only suffer a £8 reduction in net assets (£10 × 80%) with corporation tax at 20%.

As we noted above, the market value will be determined by the investor based on his receipts (the gross interest) and his required rate of return. The company will have to accept this value in order to raise debt finance, and the cost of debt finance to the company will again be the IRR of the financing flows. Now, however, one of the relevant financing flows we will have to consider will be the corporation tax relief on the interest paid.

Redeemable Debt

Although interest is tax allowable, the redemption proceeds are not. Thus, for redeemable debt, not all of the payments by the company attract corporation tax relief, although the interest payments still do.

Income Tax

The effect of income tax is slightly less obvious, since the only direct effect is on the investor, whereas it is only the cost to the company that is of concern to us here.

It would be reasonable to assume that when investors consider returns from investments, it is the amount net of income tax that they are most concerned with. However, all rational investors will be aware that this return is very much dependant on their own rate of personal tax, and hence their required after personal tax return will reflect this.

For example, if irredeemable gilts are yielding 10%, a 40% taxpayer knows that he will only receive a 6% return (10% × 60%) whereas a tax exempt individual will receive the full 10%.

Thus it is perhaps correct to consider investors' pre-personal tax required rates of return as this is the only point where such requirements will be consistent regardless of the personal tax situation of the investor.

Conclusion

Equity

Tax has no impact on our cost of equity calculations.

Debt

Interest payments attract tax relief, reducing the net cost to the company. As a result our calculations may have two elements:

- Calculation of the market value based on the gross receipts and the investors' required rate of return (sometimes referred to as the **pre-tax cost of debt**)
- Calculation of the cost to the company based on the net (of corporation tax) interest and the market value set by the investor (referred to as the **post-tax cost of debt**)

Dealing with Taxation

It is conventional to use a post-tax cost of debt for valuations. However, the assumption of instant tax relief becomes highly inappropriate for companies at even relatively early stages of their life cycle if the company is not going to be generating earnings subject to tax for some time, and therefore not receiving any cash flow benefit from tax relief.

There is no satisfactory way to deal with the often substantial delay that may be experienced by stocks in receiving tax relief on any interest payments that can be made within the conventional framework. Some analysts have ignored tax relief on debt until such time as the company is expected to become profitable. This, however, ignores the fact that the interest payments made whilst the company is loss-making does eventually yield tax benefits, since it increased the losses made by the company in the early years which are then used to offset profits in the later years.

Perhaps the easiest solution to the problem lies in discarding the conventional approach. If the tax benefits generated from interest payments are dealt with in the cash flow forecast then the timing of tax relief can be properly reflected in the forecast tax charges. This would require calculations of forecast taxes to proceed on a realistic rather than a notional basis as is required under the conventional methodology (where taxes are calculated on earnings before interest rather than after interest so as not to double-count the tax relief on interest payments already dealt with in the cost of capital). This alternative approach would then only require the required return of debtholders to be calculated rather than the cost of debt to the company.

This alternative approach does, however, have a significant drawback. Using the conventional approach would allow for a valuation to be undertaken without explicit forecasting of interest payable under the free cash flow to the enterprise approach. The alternative methodology, whilst it allows for proper expression of the timing of tax relief on interest payments, does require a forecast of interest payable in each year in order to generate a tax charge net of tax relief on interest payments within the cash flow forecast. In turn this requires forecasting of debt issued and debt repaid throughout the forecast period, and many of the benefits of avoiding financial flow forecasting within the free cash flow to the enterprise valuation framework disappear.

Irredeemable Debt

Investors' Viewpoint

Irredeemable debt is analogous to shares with a constant dividend in that investors expect a constant interest stream in perpetuity.

By following the same logic as for equity we can say that market value of debt (D) will be determined by

$$D_{ex\ int} = \frac{i_{gross}}{r_d}$$

Where

- $D_{ex\ int}$ is the ex-interest market value of the bond determined by the investor.
  - $D_{ex\ int} = D_{cum\ int} - i_{gross}$, where
    - $D_{cum\ int}$ is the cum-interest market value of the bond.
    - i_{gross} is the *gross* interest about to be paid now if we are cum-int.
- r_d is the investors' required rate of return for debt.

Company Viewpoint

From the company's viewpoint, it must pay this interest in perpetuity. However, this attracts tax relief, hence the net cost to the company is the interest net of corporation tax relief (i_{net}), and thus the cost of debt (k_d) to the company is given by

$$k_d = \frac{i_{net}}{D_{ex\ int}}$$

EXAMPLE

A company has in issue some 8% irredeemable debentures. The investors' required rate of return on debt is 10%, and the rate of corporation tax is 30%. Calculate the company's cost of debt.

SOLUTION

Market Value

We must firstly establish the market value for, say, a £100 nominal value of the debenture as determined by the investor based on the pre-tax cost of debt as follows.

$$D_{ex\ int} = \frac{i_{gross}}{r_d}$$

$$D_{ex\ int} = \frac{£8}{10\%}$$

$$D_{ex\ int} = £80$$

Cost of Debt

We can now use this value to establish the cost to the company (the post-tax cost of debt) as follows.

$$k_d = \frac{i_{net}}{D_{ex\ int}}$$

$$k_d = \frac{£8 \text{x} 0.7}{£80}$$

$$k_d = 7.0\% \text{ pa}$$

Conclusion

What we have found is that the cost of debt to the company is 30% lower than the investors' required rate of return (7% = 10% × 70%) as all the interest payments attract 30% corporation tax relief.

We have, however, made a few assumptions here, specifically:

- We have ignored personal tax.
- We have assumed interest to be payable at annual intervals.

Half-Yearly Interest

In practice, interest would almost certainly be payable half-yearly and our assumption above would clearly limit the accuracy of our cost of capital calculations. We do not need, however, to make this assumption, as we can utilise the equivalent period interest rate formula to calculate the appropriate rate for the shorter period and continue with the calculations in the same way.

EXAMPLE

Assume the 8% debentures are quoted at £80 with interest payable half-yearly and corporation tax at 30%. The next interest payment will be in six months. Calculate the cost of debt.

SOLUTION

The debenture will pay £4 gross interest every six months in perpetuity, which, after corporation tax relief, will cost the company £2.80 (£4 × 70%). The cost of debt is, therefore

$$k_d = \frac{i_{net}}{D_{ex\ int}}$$

$$k_d = \frac{£2.80}{£80}$$

$$k_d = 3.50\% \text{ per six months}$$

We have used the six monthly payment, hence we have the six monthly rate. What we need is the annual rate which we get as follows

$$1 + k_d = 1.035^2 = 1.071225$$

$$k_d = 0.071225 \text{ or } 7.12\% \text{ pa}$$

16 REDEEMABLE DEBT

Introduction

The types of finance that we are considering here are:

- Redeemable debt
- Convertible debt
- Bank loans and short term variable rate debt

Most debt instruments issued by companies repay the capital sum entirely at the redemption date. Certain bank loans along with leases and hire purchase (HP) redeem the capital on an ongoing basis. We will need to consider each alternative where appropriate. Let us look at each in turn, starting with plain redeemable debt.

Investors' Viewpoint

Applying our basic dividend valuation model idea, the market value of the debt will be the present value of the future expected receipts discounted at the investors' required rate of return.

EXAMPLE

A company intends to issue 8% bonds with a nominal value of £100 which will be redeemed at £110 in five years' time. The investors' required rate of return is 10% pa Establish the price at which the bonds will be issued, ie the market value of the bonds.

SOLUTION

Since the market value is the present value of the future expected receipts, we need to do a present value calculation.

Time	Cash Flow £	Discount Factor	Present Value £
1–5	8.00	$\frac{1}{0.1}\left(1-\frac{1}{(1.1)_5}\right) = 3.791$	30.33
5	110.00	$\frac{1}{1.1_5}$	68.30
Net present value			98.63

Company Viewpoint

The company will receive tax relief on any interest it charges against the profit and loss account. Since the effective interest charges to the profit and loss account will equate to the required return of the debtholders, the tax relief can be accounted for by reducing the required return of debtholders down by the relevant rate of tax relief.

As we noted above, we make a simplification in that we assume no time delay in receiving the tax benefit, which is not quite true.

EXAMPLE

Based on the above, if the tax rate is 20% calculate the cost of debt to the company.

SOLUTION

We can deduce the cost of debt to the company using

kd = rd (1-tax)

= 10% (1-0.2)

= 8% p.a.

Convertible Debt

Convertible debt carries a fixed rate of interest and gives the holder the option to convert it into equity at a certain future date, under terms specified by the company. The impact of this is that the ultimate redemption proceeds may be either:

- A cash alternative; or
- Shares.

What we must do for this situation is to establish which will be preferable at the conversion date and include that as the redemption proceeds in the above calculations.

We can get the market value of the shares at the redemption date by establishing the current market value and growth rate (perhaps by using cost of equity calculations described above) and extrapolating forward.

EXAMPLE

We will use the above example but now assume that the debt is convertible in five years at the investors option on the basis of 40 shares for every £100 nominal value of stock held. We are also given or have calculated that the current share price is £2.30 and its growth rate is 4% pa. Establish the value and cost of debt.

SOLUTION

Conversion Option

We need to firstly establish the relevant cash flows, hence need to determine whether we will be converting or not.

We could calculate the share price in five years as

$$E_5 = E_0\,(1 + g)^5$$

Where E_n is the market value of equity at time n, giving

$$E_5 = £2.30 \times 1.04^5$$
$$E_5 = £2.80$$

Hence in five years the value of 40 shares will be £112 (£2.80 × 40). Our investor is therefore faced with the option of accepting either:

- £110 cash; or
- Shares with a value of £112.

On the assumption that he is rational, he will prefer the shares. We can now follow through the rest of the calculations using £112 as the redemption proceeds as follows.

Market Value

Time	Cash Flow £	Discount Factor	Present Value £
1–5	8.00	$\frac{1}{0.1}\left(1-\frac{1}{(1.1)^5}\right) = 3.791$	30.33
5	112.00	$\frac{1}{1.1^5}$	69.54
Market Value			99.87

Cost of Debt

kd = rd (1-tax)

= 10% (1-0.3)

= 7% p.a.

Variable Rate Debt

Where we have variable rate debt, the interest rate that we will be paying will exactly equal the investors' required rate of return. The lender varies the rate to ensure that it does.

In this situation if the market value of the debt is equal to the redemption proceeds (eg for a bank loan), the formulae that we established for irredeemables **will be applicable.**

EXAMPLE

A company has £100 nominal value variable rate bonds in issue redeemable at par in five years. The bonds are currently paying interest at 10% (the investors' required rate of return or pre-tax cost of capital). Tax is at 20%. Calculate the cost of debt to the company, ie the post-tax cost of debt.

SOLUTION

Following the approach that we have been applying in all of the above examples

Market Value

Time	Cash Flow £	Discount Factor	Present Value £
1–5	10.00	$\frac{1}{0.1}\left(1-\frac{1}{(1.1)^5}\right) = 3.791$	37.91
5	100.00	$\frac{1}{1.1^5}$	62.09
Market Value			100.00

In fact we did not need to do this calculation. If the investment is paying exactly the return that is being demanded, then it will be valued at par.

Cost of Debt

The company will suffer the interest net of corporation tax, ie interest of £8 (£10 × 80%) an effective rate of 8% pa. Our assertion is that this will be the cost to them, ie the post tax cost of capital. We can prove this by discounting all the financing flows at this rate which, if we are correct, will give an NPV of zero (since an IRR is the discount rate at which the cost of capital is zero).

Ongoing Capital Repayments

Where we have ongoing capital repayments, ie we pay regular instalments which are part interest and part capital, then to establish the cost of debt we are trying to calculate the IRR of an annuity.

This can be done by the above first principles method, however there is a short cut if we have discount factor tables.

EXAMPLE

We have borrowed £8,200 which is being repaid in 6 annual instalments of £1,800 (after tax relief on the interest element). Calculate the post-tax cost of debt.

SOLUTION

Setting up the cash flows involved where AF6 is the six year annuity discount factor at the IRR (discount rate at which the NPV is zero), we get

Time	Cash Flow £	Discount Factor	Present Value £
0	8,200	1	8,200
1–5	(1,800)	AF6	(8,200)
Net present value			–

Since AF6 is the annuity factor at the IRR, the present value of the related flow must be £8,200 to make the NPV zero.

Thus

$$AF6 = \frac{£8,200}{£1,800} = 4.556$$

the related rate of 8.5%, ie k_d = 8.5% pa

17 COST OF DEBT SUMMARY

Introduction

The market value is determined by the investor based on his required rate of return (the **pre-tax cost of debt**).

The cost to the company (the **post-tax cost of debt)** the required return of the debtholders reduced down for the corporation tax savings yielded from interest charged to the profit and loss account.

Irredeemables

The relevant formulae are

$$D_{ex\ int} = \frac{i_{gross}}{r_d}$$

$$k_d = \frac{i_{net}}{D_{ex\ int}}$$

Where

- $D_{ex\ int}$ is the ex-interest market value of the bond determined by the investor
  - $D_{ex\ int} = D_{cum\ int} - i_{gross}$, where:
    - $D_{cum\ int}$ is the cum-div market value of the shares
- i is the interest about to be paid now if we are cum-int, either gross or net as noted
- r_d is the investors' required rate of return for debt (the pre-tax cost of debt)
- k_d is the cost to the company (the post-tax cost of debt)

Redeemables

Reduce the debtholders required return for corporation tax savings unless

- There are ongoing repayments of capital and annuity discount factor tables are available.

18 The Weighted Average Cost of Capital

Introduction

So far we have considered the cost to capital with respect to each source separately In practice, a company is likely to be financed by both debt and equity together. If we wish to calculate an overall weighted average cost of capital for the enterprise then we must include all elements of financing in our calculation.

The weighted average cost of capital (WACC) is an overall combined cost of capital for the company reflecting all sources of finance which can be calculated using the formula

$$WACC = k_e \times \frac{E}{V} + k_d \times \frac{D}{V}$$

Where

- k_e is the cost of equity
- k_d is the post-tax cost of debt
- E is the market value of the firm's equity
- D is the market value of the firm's debt
- V is the total market value of the firm (V = E + D)

EXAMPLE

A company is financed from three sources, ordinary shares, preference shares and irredeemable debt. By using the basic cost of capital calculations above we have established the following.

Category	K_e / K_d %	E / D £'000
Ordinary shares	18	12,000
Preference shares	12	2,000
Irredeemable debt	8	6,000

Calculate the WACC.

SOLUTION

Formula

Applying the above formula we get

$$\text{WACC} = \text{ke} \times \frac{E}{V} + \text{kd} \times \frac{D}{V}$$

$$\text{WACC} = 18\% \times \frac{12{,}000}{20{,}000} + 12\% \times \frac{2{,}000}{20{,}000} + 8\% \times \frac{6{,}000}{20{,}000}$$

$$\text{WACC} = 10.8\% + 1.2\% + 2.4\% = 14.4\% \text{ pa}$$

Conclusion

A company must generate this level of return from its existing projects overall if it to be able to service all of its providers of finance and, hence, maintain the market value of the company. The WACC is therefore the appropriate benchmark required return for analysis (such as comparison of ROCE – WACC) and for discounting the free cash flow to the enterprise to derive an enterprise value.

The relevant formulae are

$$\textbf{WACC} = k_e \times \frac{E}{V} + k_d \times \frac{D}{V}$$

Where

- k_e is the cost of equity
- k_d is the post-tax cost of debt
- E is the market value of the firm's equity
- D is the market value of the firm's debt
- V is the total market value of the firm (V = E + D)

CAPITAL STRUCTURE

chapter 4

Contents

1 INTRODUCTION

Provision of advice on the suitability of capital structure is at the heart of the work of the corporate financier and will have a similar prominence in the material that the examiner will be looking to assess for Paper 2. This chapter examines the impact on capital structure on cost of capital and critically assesses theories on capital structure, concluding as to their usefulness and practical relevance for corporate finance advice.

2 HOW CAPITAL STRUCTURE AFFECTS WACC

The Calculation of WACC

Let us remind ourselves as to how the WACC of a company is calculated.

$$\text{WACC} = k_e \times \frac{E}{V} + k_d \times \frac{D}{V}$$

Where

k_e is the cost of equity.

k_d is the post-tax cost of debt.

E is the market value of the firms equity.

D is the market value of the firms debt.

V is the total market value of the firm (V = E + D).

What will be the effect on the overall value of WACC as the market value of debt increases relative to the market value of equity in this equation?

Debt is Cheaper than Equity

Debt is less risky than equity for investors and therefore requires a lower rate of return. In addition, interest payments attract corporation tax relief, hence the cost of debt will be lower than the cost of equity. The effect of this is that as a company gears up, its WACC will be reduced due the higher proportion of the cheaper debt financing in the company's overall financial structure.

Increased Gearing Increases the Risk to Equity

Higher debt levels increase the variability of returns to equity. This can be seen from comparing the returns of two companies with different levels of gearing in two different economic scenarios.

	Ungeared		**Geared**	
	Year 1	**Year 2**	**Year 1**	**Year 2**
	£'000	**£'000**	**£'000**	**£'000**
Profits before interest	1,000	500	1,000	500
Interest	–	–	(400)	(400)
Profits after interest	1,000	500	600	100

It can be seen that, whereas returns to equity fall by 50% (from 1,000 to 500) for the ungeared company, they fall by over 83% (from 600 to 100) for the geared company.

As a result of this increased risk, equity investors in the geared company will require a higher rate of return, ie the cost of equity will tend to rise. This increase in required returns for equity (k_e) will tend to increase a company's WACC as it gears up.

Two Conflicting Forces

It can be seen that increased gearing affects the WACC in two conflicting ways.

- It tends to be reduced due to the greater proportion of lower cost debt finance.
- It tends to be pulled up by the increasing cost of equity.

These two factors are accepted facts, however how they combine is the subject of various theories.

The net impact of gearing on a company's WACC has been considered by two main theories, the traditional theory and the theory of Modigliani and Miller (M & M).

3 The Traditional Theory of Gearing

The Theory

An Ungeared Company

Clearly in an ungeared company the WACC will be one and the same as its cost of equity, since it only has the one source of finance. This situation will, however, change as we increase gearing and these two influences will conflict.

Effect of Gearing on the Cost of Equity

The traditionalists believed that at low levels of gearing the company's cost of equity remains fairly constant. Equity investors are not concerned with low levels of gearing and believe that it does not significantly affect the risk of their investment. As such, they do not require any significant extra return to compensate them for the additional gearing risk.

As debt levels increase, however, shareholders will become more concerned about the increased gearing risk attached to their investment. At some stage, this concern will translate into higher required rates of return to compensate equity investors for the additional risk.

The traditionalists believed that when a particular threshold of gearing is exceeded, shareholders are suddenly galvanised into action and start demanding significantly higher rates of return. This means that, while at low levels of gearing the cost of equity is relatively constant, at higher levels it increases sharply.

The traditionalists did not however identify what specifically a high level of gearing was.

Effect of Gearing on the Cost of Debt

The cost of debt remains constant at low to medium levels of gearing. However, at higher levels it increases to compensate debt investors for increased default risk.

Overall Impact of Gearing on WACC

At lower levels of gearing, equity finance is being replaced by cheaper debt finance. However, the cost of the remaining equity does not increase significantly for reasons noted above. This means that the WACC of the company will initially fall.

At higher levels of gearing, the introduction of cheap debt still has a downward pull on the company's WACC. However there is now also a significant upward pull, due to increases in the cost of equity. The net effect of these two conflicting forces is that the WACC starts to rise.

At very high levels of gearing, increases in the cost of debt means that the WACC increases even more dramatically.

Graphically

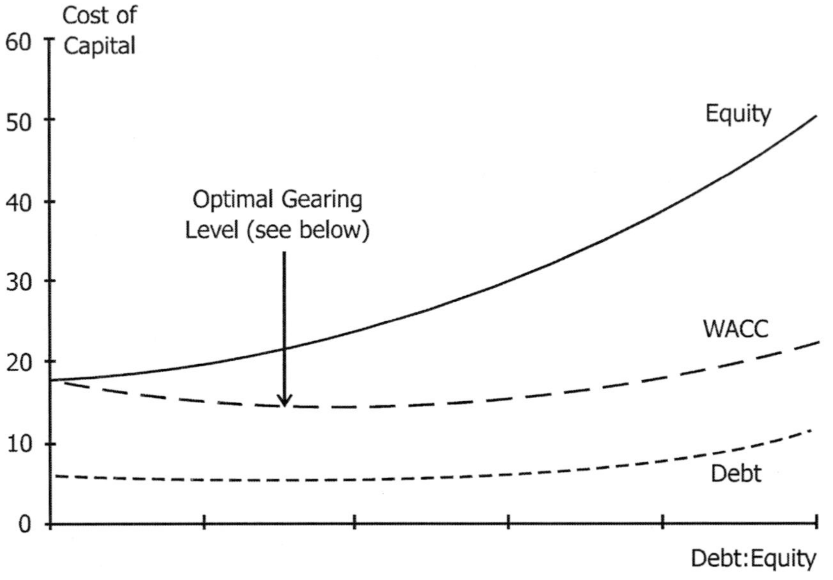

Implications for Capital Structure

The implication of the above for a company is that it will have an optimal level of gearing which will minimise its WACC. A low WACC will be beneficial since it will enable the company to accept more projects with positive net present values, hence, all other things being equal, it will maximise the market value of the company given its current projects.

Companies should, therefore, always raise finance so as to move towards their optimal gearing level and their minimum WACC. A company on the far left of the graph should raise debt finance for new projects, a company which has gone too far to the right should raise equity finance to reduce gearing levels.

Once the company has hit its optimal capital structure, it should aim to stay there and always raise finance in such a way as to achieve this. Since it would be impracticable to constantly raise a mixture of debt and equity for each new project, the company should first issue debt and then issue equity, meaning that it oscillates around its optimal point rather than remaining precisely on it.

Implications for Investment Appraisal

When a company is appraising a project, it needs to consider two factors:

- Whether the project itself is worthwhile
- Whether it should be financed by debt or equity

A worthwhile project is one that has a positive net present value. Worthwhile finance is finance which reduces or does not increase the company's WACC, which can be established by considering the marginal cost of capital.

Marginal Cost of Capital

The marginal cost of capital is the total cost to the company of any additional source of finance.

If the cost of the new finance is lower than the existing cost of funds, it is a good method of finance and will result in a lowering of the company's overall WACC. If it is higher than the existing WACC, it will have an adverse effect, causing the WACC to increase.

The marginal cost of capital can be calculated as

$$\textbf{Marginal Cost of Capital} = \frac{\text{Total additional finance costs}}{\text{Total new finance raised}}$$

Where the total additional finance costs will be made up of two components:

- Direct cost of any extra interest paid
- Indirect cost of any additional dividend demanded by the shareholders to maintain the market value of their shares (their wealth), in order to compensate them for the additional risk that they are facing

EXAMPLE

A company is at present all equity financed with a market value of £10m. It is paying a constant total dividend of £2.5m and has a cost of equity (and hence a WACC) of 25%.

It is considering a new project in the same business area as its existing investments which will require investment of £1m and will give annual income of £0.19m in perpetuity.

The company is considering financing the investment by raising irredeemable debt which will cost 5%. If it does this, then the existing shareholders will perceive additional gearing risk to their investment. As a result, they will require an increased return on their equity of 26%.

Is the project worthwhile and is the financing method appropriate (ignoring the effects of tax)?

SOLUTION

The Financing Method

Considering the finance first of all, it is likely that the company is correct in wanting to issue debt, since it is at present ungeared. The traditional theory indicates that low levels of gearing cause no problems for the company.

In order to make a more exact evaluation of the financing method, we need to calculate its cost and compare it to the existing cost of capital for the company.

The Marginal Cost of Raising the Finance

The cost of the new source of finance comes from two sources. The obvious source is the requirement to pay 5% interest on the borrowings made. If this was the end of the story then the new finance would clearly be much cheaper than the existing 25% cost of equity.

However, an additional cost is the increase in the required return of the equity shareholders which will occur as a result of the increase in borrowings. In order to keep shareholders happy, a higher dividend will need to be paid to compensate them for their additional risk. If the dividend is not increased then the market value of the shares will fall to £9.6 million, being the present value of the existing dividend of £2.5 million discounted at a discount rate of 26% $\left(\frac{£2.5m}{0.26}\right)$.

The new total dividend can be calculated as the dividend that would maintain the value of the equity at £10m when discounted at the new required return of 26%. The new dividend will therefore need to be £2.6m (£10m × 26%). The increase in the total finance cost is thus:

Increase in Total Cost	**£'000**
Interest payments (5% × £1m)	50
Increase in dividends required (£2.6m - £2.5m)	100
Total additional finance costs	150

Since the company has raised £1m at an annual cost of £150,000, the cost of this finance in percentage terms is 15%.

Since the marginal cost of finance is less than the current WACC of 25%, the method of finance is good and the WACC of the company will fall after the finance is raised.

Is the Project Worthwhile?

The project itself is generating annual returns of £190,000 and therefore gives a return of 19% on the investment required of £1m.

If it was being funded by equity, it would clearly not be worthwhile, since equity investors are demanding a return of 25% from an ungeared company in this business area. However, the method of finance being used only needs a return in excess of 15% for the project to have a positive net present value and therefore it can be accepted.

If the project had been giving returns of say £0.3m a year, then it would have been acceptable even with equity finance. However, the company should always aim to maximise its opportunities and, rather than simply remain ungeared, it should investigate different sources of finance to ensure it raises funds in the most cost effective way possible.

The New WACC of the Company

The new WACC of the company can be calculated by using the normal formula. The new market value of the company's equity will first need to be calculated by discounting the new total dividend at 26%.

The new total dividend is:

Increase in Total Cost	**£'000**
Old dividend	2,500
Dividend from new project (£190,000 – £50,000)	140
	2,640

The market value of the equity is therefore £10,153,846 $\left(\frac{£2,640,000}{0.26}\right)$ and the new WACC of the company can be calculated as

$$\text{WACC} = k_e \times \frac{E}{V} + k_d \times \frac{D}{V}$$

$$\text{WACC} = 26\% \times \frac{10,154}{10,154 + 1,000} + 5\% \times \frac{1,000}{10,154 + 1,000}$$

$$\text{WACC} = 24\%$$

It can be seen that the WACC has fallen as we anticipated since the marginal cost of capital is lower than the WACC.

The Limitations of the Traditional Theory

The chief weaknesses of the theory are:

- It is vague and imprecise
- It does not advance possible reasons why the changes in cost of equity occur and only suggests that people 'become concerned' at some stage
- It does not identify at what specific level of gearing a company's cost of equity will suddenly start to increase, merely asserting that this is the case
- A company will have to research itself through trial and error to establish the impact of gearing on its WACC
- The theory assumes that a low WACC is desirable. While this is probably the case, a more encompassing objective for management would be to increase the market value of the company through effective trading. Shareholders would rather see share price increases through sustainable operational factors than have a company with a reduced WACC, though as we noted earlier, the two (share prices and WACC) are inter-related

4 Modigliani and Miller (M & M)

M & M's Basic Assumptions

Introduction

M & M adopted a very different approach from that of the traditionalists. The advantage of M & M's approach is that it highlights specific reasons for the effect of gearing on a company's market value and WACC.

The disadvantage of the approach is that it has many limiting assumptions which make it difficult to apply in the real world.

M & M's Assumptions - A Perfect Capital Market

Investors Make Rational Decisions

M & M assume that investors are rational and hence their actions are logical and can be predicted.

There are no Dealing Costs when Buying and Selling Securities

This enables investors to buy and sell securities on the basis of their value rather than being deterred by transaction costs. It enables arbitrage to take place so that all companies should be fairly valued since if they are not they will be sold.

All Investors have Costless Access to all Relevant Information

This again enables companies to be fairly valued by the market place.

Companies and Individuals can all Borrow and Lend at One Rate of Interest

This means that there is no advantage to corporate gearing as opposed to personal gearing so that there is no incentive for an investor to want to buy shares in a geared company on the basis of interest rates alone.

The lack of a borrowing and depositing spread means that the actions of individuals are not constrained by the transaction cost this implies. Arbitrage can therefore take place to ensure all companies are fairly valued.

Debt is Risk Free

This is a simplification which can be relaxed. Its advantage is that it means that a company can never become insolvent which simplifies the analysis

There is no Taxation

This simplification will be relaxed but it is convenient to initially consider the situation where no tax exists before adding in tax refinements.

M & M's Basic Theory

M & M considered two equivalent companies, ie companies that are precisely the same in all respects except for the fact that one is ungeared and one is geared. The financial results for these two companies are as follows.

	Ungeared £	Geared £
Earnings	1,000	1,000
Interest	–	(400)
Dividends	1,000	600

Both companies pay out all their earnings each year, either as interest to debt investors or dividends to equity investors, or a combination of both.

M & M pointed out that the total pay-outs of both companies are the same at £1,000. Whether these pay-outs are called dividends or interest is irrelevant. Since both companies generate the same cash flows in the hands of their investors they must have the same total market value.

The combined value of Company G's equity and its debt must be equal to the value of Company U's equity, ie

$$E_u = V_g = (E_g + D)$$

Where

- E_u = market value of the equity of the ungeared company
- E_g = market value of the equity of the geared company
- D = market value of the debt of the geared company
- V_g = total market value of the geared company

Any single investor would be indifferent between owning all of Company U's equity and receiving £1,000, all of which is called a dividend, and owning all of Company G's debt plus equity and receiving £1,000, part of which is called interest and part of which is called dividends.

Splitting the ownership between a number of people should still not affect the total market value - the total cake remains the same however it is shared out among different investors.

Since the total market values (debt plus equity) of both companies are the same and the total pay-outs (dividends plus interest) are the same, the WACC for both companies must be the same.

These ideas can be expressed on a graph as with the traditional theory. However, since M & M's theory is constructed in an academically rigorous fashion, the axes of the graph need to be defined more carefully.

Graphically

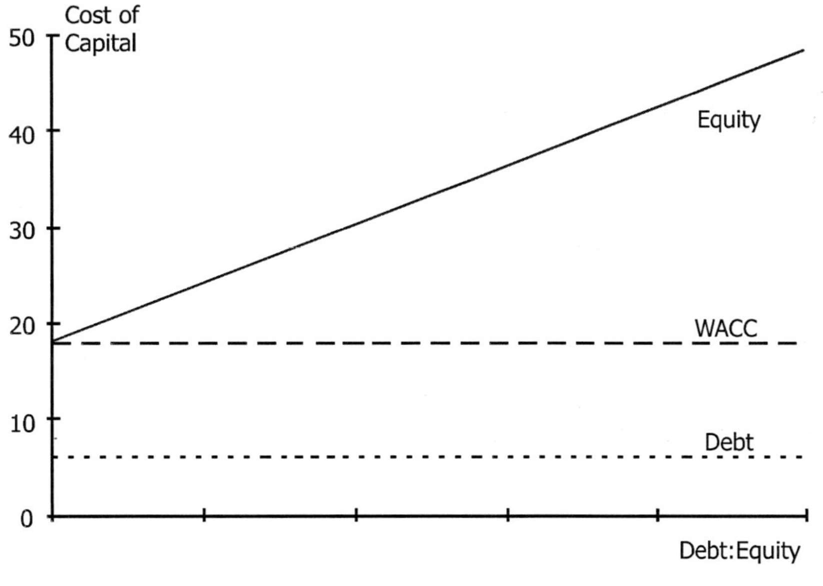

Since debt is risk free, it has the same cost regardless of the level of gearing. The WACC likewise remains constant whatever the level of gearing, as we have seen above.

Given these two lines and the way in which gearing has been defined as Debt:Equity $\frac{D}{E}$, it can be shown that the cost of equity must rise in a straight line as indicated, as we will see later.

Implications for Capital Structure and Investment Appraisal

The conclusion that can be drawn is that in the absence of tax the benefits of cheap debt finance are exactly counterbalanced by the increased returns required by equity investors, meaning that the company's WACC remains constant.

Since a company's market value and its WACC remain constant regardless of how it has financed itself, the financing decision is irrelevant. All that matters is that any project has a positive net present value when discounted at the company's existing WACC (assuming the project is in the same business risk class as the remainder of the company's investments).

Formulae

Thanks to M & M's rigorous academic approach, it is possible to develop formula which will exactly predict the change in the cost of a company's equity and the market value of its equity at different gearing levels. These formulae are as follows:

Market Values

$$V_g = (E_g + D) = V_u \; (= E_u)$$

Where

- E_g = market value of the equity of the geared company
- E_u = market value of the equity of the ungeared company
- D = market value of the debt of the geared company
- V_g = total market value of the geared company
- V_u = total market value of the ungeared company

WACC

$$WACC_g = WACC_u$$

Where

- $WACC_g$ = WACC of the geared company
- $WACC_u$ = WACC of the ungeared company (which will also be its cost of equity)

Cost of Equity

$$k_g = k_u + (k_u - r_f) \times \frac{D}{E_g}$$

Where

- k_g = cost of equity of the geared company
- k_u = cost of equity of the ungeared company (which will also be its WACC)
- r_f = the cost of debt for the geared company, which is the risk free rate of interest

EXAMPLE

An ungeared company with a market value of £10m pays all of its earnings out as a constant annual dividend of £2m and thus has a cost of equity of 20% $\left(\frac{£2m}{£10m}\right)$.

It decides to reorganise its capital structure and raises £1m of irredeemable debt at a cost of 5%. It uses the £1m to redeem part of its equity.

What is the new

- Total market value Vg?
- Market value of equity Eg?
- Cost of equity kg?
- WACC?

SOLUTION

New Total Market Value

Assuming that M & M's theory applies, the market value of the company must remain the same as before, ie £10m.

New Market Value of Equity

Since the debt has a market value of £1m, we can calculate the market value of the equity as

$$E_u = V_g = (E_g + D)$$
$$£10m = (E_g + £1m)$$
$$E_g = £9m$$

the equity in the geared company must have a market value of £9m.

New Cost of Equity

Basic Principles

The new cost of equity can be calculated using our basic cost of capital equations as the new dividend divided by the new market value of the equity.

The new constant dividend will be the total earnings of the company of £2m less the interest payment of £50,000 (£1m × 5%), ie £1.95m.

The cost of equity in this geared company is therefore

$$k_g = \frac{d_1}{E_{ex\ div}} + g$$

$$k_g = \frac{1.95}{9.00} + 0$$

$$k_g = 21.67\%$$

M & M Formula

Alternatively we could have used M&M's formula

$$k_g = k_u + (k_u - r_f) \times \frac{D}{E}$$

We know that

- k_u = 20%
- r_f = 5%
- D = £1m
- E = £9m

Giving

$$k_g = 20 + (20 - 5) \times \frac{£1m}{£9m}$$

$$k_g = 21.67\%$$

What is the New WACC?

First Principles

The new WACC will be given by the calculation

$$WACC = k_g \times \frac{E}{V} + k_d \times \frac{D}{V}$$

Giving

$$WACC = 21.67\% \times \frac{£9m}{£9m + £1m} + 5\% \times \frac{£1m}{£9m + £1m}$$

$$WACC = 20\%$$

M & M Formula

It can be seen that the WACC has remained unchanged at 20% as was predicted by the M&M equation

$$WACC_g = WACC_u$$

Conclusion

The above illustration does not prove that M & M's theories are correct, it merely shows that, given M & M's assumptions and accepting that the total market value of the company cannot change, the equations produced by M & M will hold good.

Corporation Tax

Having established that, in the limited circumstances above, a company's capital structure is irrelevant, M & M then considered one of the major limitations in their analysis, ie ignoring the existence of corporation tax. They continued to assume, however, that there was no personal tax.

Generally, when a company pays interest to debt investors, it is eligible for tax relief, whereas payments to equity investors do not qualify as an allowable expense for the company. The implication of this different tax treatment for the two equivalent companies above can be seen by comparing their earnings streams.

Assuming corporation tax at 20%,

Total pay-out by the company	Ungeared £	Geared £
Earnings	1,000	1,000
Interest	–	(400)
Profit before tax	1,000	600
Corporation tax at 20%	(200)	(120)
Profit after tax = Dividends	800	480
Total received by the investors		
Interest	–	400
Dividends	800	480
	800	880

In this case, the geared company can afford to pay out more in total to its investors than the ungeared company. The difference of £80 (£880 – £800) is due to the tax relief on the interest of £400 × 20%.

The fact that pay-outs in total from the geared company exceed pay-outs in total from the ungeared company means that a rational investor would pay more to acquire the debt and equity together of the geared company than the equity of the ungeared one.

The total market value of the geared company (debt plus equity) will, therefore, exceed the market value of the ungeared company's equity.

The effect of this on a company's WACC as it increases its level of gearing can be seen from the following graph.

Graphically

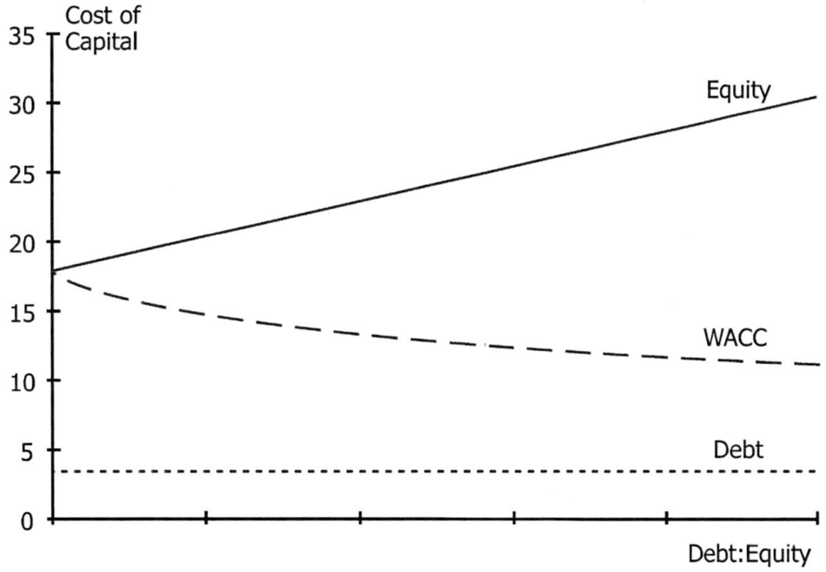

As the company borrows more money and substitutes debt for equity funding, the cost of equity rises to reflect the increased gearing risk. However, due to the tax relief on interest payments, the cost of debt to the company is now cheaper than before.

This means that the benefit of cheap debt more than compensates for the increase in the cost of equity. The net effect is that the WACC falls in a curved line, constantly decreasing as the level of debt increases but never quite falling to the level of the cost of debt.

Adapting the Formulae for Corporation Tax

The formulae introduced above can be adapted slightly to take account of corporation tax. All the symbols used are as above, with the additional symbol T_c being used for the rate of corporation tax.

Market Values

$$V_g = V_u + D \times T_c$$

Where

- V_g = total market value of the geared company
- V_u = total market value of the ungeared company
- D = market value of the debt of the geared company
- T_c = rate of corporation tax

This formula confirms what we stated earlier, that the total market value of the geared company exceeds that of the ungeared company. The exact amount by which its market value is higher will be the present value of the extra payments.

The extra payment amounts to the tax relief on the irredeemable risk free interest payments, ie the interest payments times the tax rate. The present value of these flows will therefore be the present value of the interest payments (the market value of the debt) times the tax rate. Hence the extra value is given by $D \times T_c$, sometimes referred to as the present value of the tax shield. We expand on this a little more later.

WACC

$$WACC_g = WACC_u \times \left(1 - T_c \frac{D}{V_g}\right)$$

Where

- $WACC_g$ = WACC of the geared company
- $WACC_u$ = WACC of the ungeared company (which will also be its cost of equity)

This formula confirms that the WACC of the geared company is lower than that of the ungeared company. The higher the level of corporation tax or the higher the level of gearing, the lower the WACC becomes.

Cost of Equity

$$k_g = k_u + (k_u - r_f) \times \frac{D}{E_g} \times (1 - T_c)$$

Where

- k_g = cost of equity of the geared company.
- k_u = cost of equity of the ungeared company (which will also be its WACC).
- r_f = the required return to debt investors, which is assumed to be risk free.

This confirms that the cost of equity in the geared company is higher than that in the ungeared company, due to gearing risk.

Note. In all three equations, if corporation tax is nil, then they become the same as the equations introduced earlier in the absence of corporation tax.

EXAMPLE

An ungeared company with a market value of £10m has constant profits before tax of £4m and suffers corporation tax at a rate of 40%. All post tax profits are paid out as a dividend. Its dividend is therefore £2.4m and it has a cost of equity of 24% $\left(\frac{£2.4m}{£10.0m}\right)$

The company decides to issue £2m of irredeemable debt at the risk free rate of interest of 5%. It uses the proceeds to repay equity finance.

What is the new

- Total market value V_g?
- Market value of equity E_g?
- Cost of equity k_g?
- WACC?

SOLUTION

Total Market Value

Assuming that M & M applies, the total value of the company's equity plus debt will be given by

$$V_g = V_u + D \times T_c$$

Giving

$$V_g = £10m + £2m \times 40\%$$
$$V_g = £10.8m$$

Market Value of Equity

We can then calculate the market value of the equity in the geared company using

$$V_g = E_g + D$$

Giving

$$£10.8m = E_g + £2m$$
$$E_g = £8.8m$$

Cost of Equity

First Principles

The new cost of equity will be given by the new dividend divided by the new market value of the equity. The new dividend is the revised profit after tax:

	£'000
Earnings	4,000
Interest (£2 million × 5%)	(100)
Profit before tax	3,900
Corporation tax at 40%	(1,560)
Profit after tax = Dividends	2,340

The cost of equity can be calculated using

$$k_g = \frac{d_1}{E_{ex\,div}} + g$$

Giving

$$k_g = \frac{£2.34m}{£8.8m} + 0$$

$$k_g = 26.59\%$$

M & M Formula

Undertaking this same calculation but applying M&M's formula

$$k_g = k_u + (k_u - r_f) \times \frac{D}{E} \times (1 - T_c)$$

Giving

$$k_g = 24\% + (24\% - 5\%) \times \frac{£2m}{£8.8m} \times (1 - 0.4)$$

$$k_g = 26.59\%$$

New WACC

First Principles

The new WACC is the weighted average of the new cost of equity and the **post tax** cost of debt of 3% (5% × 0.6) which can be found by using the equation

$$WACC = k_g \times \frac{E_g}{V_g} + k_d \times \frac{D}{V_g}$$

Giving

$$WACC = 26.59\% \times \frac{£8.8m}{£10.8m} + 3\% \times \frac{£2m}{£10.8m}$$

$$WACC = 22.22\%$$

M & M Formula

We can obtain the same solution by using the M&M formula.

$$WACC_g = WACC_u \times \left(1 - T_C \frac{D}{V_g}\right)$$

Giving

$$WACC_g = 24\% \times \left(1 - 0.4 \frac{£2m}{£10.8m}\right)$$

$$WACC_g = 22.22\%$$

As before, we have not proved the validity of M & M's equations, rather we have shown that they are mutually consistent.

Quantifying the Extra Value of the Geared Company

We have stated that the total market value of the geared company exceeds that of the ungeared company by $D \times T_c$. We can now show why this is the case.

The Benefit of the Tax Shield

The higher pay-outs are caused by the tax relief on the irredeemable debt interest, typically referred as the tax shield. In the above illustration this was £40,000 (40% × £100,000).

Note. Whatever the level of earnings in the two equivalent companies, the difference in total pay-outs will always be £40,000. For example, if earnings were £5m, the ungeared company would pay out £3m of dividends (£5m × 60%) and the geared company would pay out £100,000 of interest and £2.94m of dividends (£4.9m × 60%) – a total of £3.04m, £40,000 higher than in the ungeared company.

The Market Value of the Tax Shield

The difference in value between the two companies will be given by the present value of this extra cash flow of £40,000 a year in perpetuity, discounted at an appropriate required rate of return.

Since the tax relief relates to interest, which is a risk free flow in M & M's model, the appropriate rate of return to use to evaluate this flow would be this risk free rate of 5%. The present value of the tax relief is therefore £800,000 $\left(\frac{£40,000}{5\%}\right)$

A more general expression would be that the present value of the tax relief is

$$\text{PV tax relief} = \left(\frac{i_{gross} \times T_c}{r_f}\right)$$

Where

- i_{gross} = annual interest payment on the irredeemable debt
- r_f = risk free rate of return

Now we know that $\frac{i_{gross}}{r_f}$ is the expression which gives the market value of debt (D). Here, $\frac{£100,000}{5\%}$ = £2 million. Therefore, we can say that

$$\text{PV tax relief} = D \times T_c$$

In this case, 40% x £2m = £800,000.

This proves the formula

$$\mathbf{V_g = V_u + D \times T_c}$$

Where

- V_g = total market value of the geared company
- V_u = total market value of the ungeared company
- D = market value of the debt of the geared company
- T_c = rate of corporation tax

Implications for Capital Structure and Investment Appraisal

Companies Should Finance all Projects Solely by Debt

M&M's theory of capital structure with corporation tax indicates that companies should gear up indefinitely. Any new project should always be funded by debt.

The relevant rate for project appraisal will then be the marginal cost of raising the funds as under the traditional theory. This will be calculated using the same principles as with the traditional theory but with the added sophistication of working out the new required return for equity (k_g) using M & M's formula.

After a while the marginal cost of raising the new debt would almost be equivalent to the company's cost of debt. This will be when the WACC of the company has fallen so that it is almost the same as the cost of debt.

Financial Distress

It is obvious, however, that this is a ridiculous conclusion to make in the real world. A more reasonable proposition would be that a company should initially borrow money due to the tax benefits of paying interest rather than dividends.

When gearing reaches a particular level, however, all investors will perceive significant risks of insolvency and as a result both the cost of equity (k_g) and the cost of debt (k_d) will rise. That is, debt will no longer be risk free and M & M's equations will no longer apply.

As a result the company will be prevented from raising any more debt without incurring a financing cost penalty. Once it has reached this stage, a company should raise finance to maintain its gearing at this level.

There are a number of different techniques a company can use to establish its maximum gearing level (its **debt capacity**), which are dealt with below.

The Costs of Financial Distress

Introduction

In M & M's original propositions, debt was considered to be risk free and the company was considered not to have any risk of failing. However, corporate failure is an unfortunate and expensive reality.

If a company actually becomes insolvent and has to be liquidated, there are many administrative and other costs to be borne (such as liquidators' fees) which would not otherwise have been suffered.

Even if a company does not become insolvent but merely has a rough ride for several years, there will be additional costs. These will arise because, among other factors, the management will need to spend extra time speaking to debt and equity investors and will be restricted in their actions due to loan covenants which proscribe various courses of action.

Corporate Value is Reduced by the Cost of Financial Distress

These additional costs of financial distress will reduce pay-outs to investors. As a company borrows more money, the probability that these cash outflows will occur increases, reducing the value of the company. This fall in value needs to be incorporated into M & M's equation linking the value of the geared and ungeared company.

$$V_g = V_u + D \times T_c - PV_{fd}$$

Where PV_{fd} is the expected present value of the cash outflows due to financial distress.

M & M concluded that a company should gear up to take advantage of any tax benefits available, but only to the extent that the marginal benefits exceed the marginal costs of financial distress.

5 The Pecking Order Theory of Gearing

The Theory

Directors Follow the Line of Least Resistance

The pecking order theory of gearing takes a much more human viewpoint as to how gearing levels are established in practice. It states that when directors raise funds, they do it in the way which will cause least aggravation. As such, the theory (as explained by Myers) largely ignores the 'static payoff' theory proposed by Modigliani and Miller.

Retained Profits or 'Internal Equity'

As a result of the above, the first method of raising funds is to retain profits in the company rather than paying them out as a dividend. This is easy to do and is also very cheap. The problem is that retained profits (often referred to as 'internal equity') may be insufficient to fund new projects. Furthermore, investors may not wish to see their dividends cut. This is referred to as dividends being 'sticky'.

Debt Finance

If retained profits are insufficient, then the directors will turn to debt finance. This can be raised in larger sums than may be the case with retained profits and is still fairly cheap and easy to raise. As with internal equity, however, there is a limitation due to the debt capacity of the business.

External Equity

When the debt capacity of the business has been reached, the directors will turn to shareholders and ask for additional investment. This 'external equity' is the last port of call because it is expensive (involving underwriting fees, prospectus etc) and time consuming.

Implications of the Theory

Profitable Companies Have Less Need to Borrow

This theory would suggest that highly profitable companies should have very low levels of gearing, since much of their capital requirements can be funded from retained profits. Companies which are less profitable will have to borrow money to fund new investment and will therefore be more highly geared.

This is the opposite conclusion to M & M's theory, which would suggest that profitable companies have less risk of financial distress and should therefore be more highly geared. Nevertheless, it does seem to be borne out to some extent in practice.

Asymmetry of Information

The theory highlights the problems of asymmetry of information between directors and shareholders as a reason for the unwillingness to issue new equity. The argument is that investors will not wish to buy new equity, believing that the directors are only issuing the equity because they believe that the company's equity is overvalued. If the company were undervalued, then the directors would not wish to issue equity as it would involve a transfer of value from existing shareholders to new shareholders. As a result, investors assume that equity issues imply bad news about the company and will not subscribe except at a low price.

To avoid this problem, directors will prefer to use internal equity or debt.

Practical Factors Affecting Gearing Levels

Cash Flows

Cash flow analysis focuses on the ability of the company to pay interest on its borrowings and repay the capital at the required date. A prudent approach to establishing an appropriate level of gearing from a cash flow viewpoint would be to assume that the company is in a recession and to forecast the level of cash it will be able to generate from its operations. The maximum level of borrowings that could be serviced by this cash flow would be a prudent debt capacity level.

Asset Backing

Asset backing looks at the value of the assets in the company and determines whether they would be sufficient to redeem the loans if sold. As such it could be seen as a banker's method of establishing debt capacity. Shareholders will be interested in the company as a going concern and will not want to see all the assets sold off to repay loans.

Nevertheless it provides a useful indicator of a safe level of borrowings for an asset based company. It would of course be less relevant for a service based company with very few tangible assets but large cash flows.

Business Risk

Generally, companies which have a high level of business risk should borrow less than companies with a low level of business risk. For example, a company involved in the manufacture and distribution of computers and related software is in a highly volatile sector.

Operating profits and cash flows in such companies can be very good in times of prosperity but disastrous in a recession. Such a company should not borrow too much money since there is a high risk that in any one year it will default on its loans. By contrast, a utility, such as a company operating in the water sector, is likely to have fairly stable earnings and as such can be more highly geared.

Ratios

Ratios such as interest cover and debt to equity can be calculated for a company and compared to sector average. This does not take into account the specific factors affecting a company and as such is of limited use. However, it does give an indication of what investors perceive to be acceptable levels of gearing for a particular sector.

Maturity Structure

The repayment timetable for loans should link in with the expected operating cash flows of the company. It is no use to a property developer to have to repay its loans before it has finished building and sold a development. In such a case, a deep discount bond, where minimal interest is paid over the life of the loan and one large **balloon** repayment is made at the end of the loan may be appropriate.

Generally companies should aim to have a wide range of maturity dates to ensure that there are not excessive demands on the company's cash flow at any one date. In particular, a company should ensure that it does not have too much short term debt which it is unable to refinance.

Debt and the Money Market

chapter 5

Contents

1 Introduction

You are expected to be very familiar with different sources of capital and the practical implications of different alternatives. This chapter focusses on debt finance, both listed and unlisted. Corporate finance advice also entails understanding the liquidity position of a company in the short term and thus the consideration of money market instruments is included. Paper 2 examination requirements are likely to focus on your ability to suggest funding alternatives, as opposed to a rote listing of capital instrument characteristics.

2 Bank Finance

We consider below the main forms of bank funding, looking at the main characteristics and uses of each type of finance.

Term Loans

Term loan facilities are suitable for cash flow lending situations in which the loan proceeds are used for long-term needs, such as to finance equipment acquisitions, permanent working investment, stock repurchases, and the refunding of existing maturities of short-term debt as they become due. Some features of term loans are as follows:

- The loan may be **amortised** (ie repaid in instalments over the term of the loan) or **bullet** repayment (ie repaid in one single instalment at the end of the term).
- The interest rate may be **fixed or floating**. The floating rate is expressed as a fixed spread over a variable interest rate such as the London Interbank Offered Rate (LIBOR).
- It may be a **senior** loan or **subordinated**. Senior debt is debt provided by a bank which is designated the senior lender, and which therefore has priority in receiving interest and capital repayments and ranks ahead of other lenders on a winding-up. It is generally secured (see below). Subordinated debt is debt where the rights and returns are subordinated to those of the senior lender. It is therefore typically more expensive for the company than senior debt.

Commercial mortgage

A commercial mortgage is a flexible method of purchasing or improving a freehold or leasehold property. It may be owner occupied or for investment, commercial or industrial purposes. In essence, it is a long-term loan from the bank, secured on the property concerned. The main features are that it is provided over a long term, the interest base can be either floating or fixed, and the amount granted is based on the open market valuation of the property.

Syndicated loans

A syndicated loan is a loan provided by two or more banks to one or more borrowers. The loan is syndicated – spread among the banking community – usually because it is for a larger amount that one bank is prepared to lend on its own. The terms and conditions on which the loan is to be made by the banks to the borrower are set out in a loan agreement, to which all lenders and the borrower are a party. Consequently, all lenders are bound by the same terms, which are enforced on their behalf by the lead arranger.

Overdraft

Some borrowers will borrow on a **demand basis**. This means that the bank itself can demand immediate repayment at any time. The usual mechanism for this is the overdraft – where a company's account is allowed to go into debit up to a certain limit. This is highly flexible for the borrower since it can alter the balance of its borrowings at will. However, it imposes a high degree of risk on the borrower, since the bank can demand repayment immediately (although banks will often quote a non-binding 'review date'), and the borrower would have to seek emergency refinancing from another source. The interest rate for UK overdrafts is normally variable, calculated by reference to a margin above the base rate. Given the flexibility of this source of finance for the borrowing, overdrafts are a relatively more expensive form of funding for a business.

Revolving credits

A revolving credit is a formal legal agreement in which the bank agrees to lend up to a certain amount for a specific purpose over a specified period of time, usually two to five years. The borrower has complete flexibility in borrowing all or a portion of the total amount as necessary and repaying any amount at any time during the life of the commitment. In other words, revolving credit arrangements do not have set repayment schedules. The interest basis is normally variable, calculated by reference to a margin above LIBOR, payable on the amounts drawn down. Additionally, the borrower must pay a commitment fee on amounts not drawn down.

Factoring

Factoring means selling trade debts for immediate cash to a 'factor' who charges commission. Most factors offer three basic services, although clients are under no obligation to take them all.

The services provided by a factor are as follows:

- An accounting, credit checking and debt collection service
- Credit insurance against bad debts, for 'approved' debts
- The provision of immediate cash against invoices, up to 75-85% of the face value of the invoices and, because of the credit insurance, a guarantee of payment of the remainder within an agreed period of time

Invoice discounting is similar to factoring, except that only the financing service is used; copies of invoices sent to customers are discounted with a financial institution. The trading company still collects the debts as agents for the financial institution and remits the cash on receipt.

In summary, factoring generally refers to purchasing a client's entire turnover (excluding cash sales), whereas invoice discounting refers to purchasing individual debts on a 'one-off' basis.

3 Leasing

Leasing is a tax-effective source of finance for the acquisition of a non-current asset. A lease is an agreement in which the owner of an item (eg a business asset) or a piece of real estate allows someone else to use it for a specified time, in return for a rental. The owner of the leased asset is the lessor and the user of the asset is the lessee.

In certain circumstances, it can be seen that leasing is equivalent to raising finance from a bank to purchase an asset. Consider two alternative situations.

Borrowing Money to Buy an Asset

A plc borrows £100,000 from a bank at a rate of 15%, repayable over three years, with three annual repayments of £44,000. It uses the cash to purchase an asset with a useful life of three years.

Leasing an Asset

B plc takes out a three-year lease on the same asset. The lease payments are £44,000 a year, payable annually in arrears. The lease is not cancellable.

A plc and B plc have the same effective commercial situation. The cash flows for both companies are precisely the same, being three annual outflows of £44,000. The benefits received from the asset are exactly the same for both companies.

Legally, however, the two situations are different. A plc has two separate transactions, borrowing money and buying an asset. B plc has only one transaction, renting an asset.

Finance Leases

The term 'finance lease' has been coined to describe a lease that is virtually equivalent to borrowing money to buy an asset. It is usually a long-term lease, where the lessee is expected to pay over enough cash to have been sufficient to purchase the asset in the first place.

Operating Leases

Operating leases are any leases that are not finance leases, ie they are leases that are not equivalent to borrowing money but are just short-term rental agreements.

4 THE BENEFITS OF LEASING

Tax Efficiency

It may be the case that a lease can be structured to benefit the lessor and lessee at the expense of the Inland Revenue. This was the main reason why the leasing industry initially became successful in the United Kingdom.

If a company buys a fixed asset, it is entitled to charge capital allowances (ie depreciation for tax purposes) against its taxable profit, based on the cost of the asset. If the company is not making large profits, it may be unable to take advantage of the whole of its capital allowances entitlement in any one year.

It may be possible for a company making larger profits to buy the asset and receive the capital allowances instead. It can then lease the asset on to the smaller company, which will be allowed to charge the lease rentals paid as a taxable expense instead of the capital allowances.

The lease rentals can be structured to ensure that the smaller company is able to reduce its tax liability efficiently in each year of the lease. The net result is that both the larger and smaller company receive tax relief in a way that is most efficient to them. Both companies can share out the benefits of this arrangement (received at the expense of the Inland Revenue) between them.

It is also possible to construct a 'double dip' lease across national borders. The idea is that both the lessor and the lessee gain tax advantages from the tax treatment of leases in their own tax regime.

Convenience

Convenience is typically an advantage for a short-term lease. It is much more convenient to rent rather than buy an asset that is only going to be used for the short term.

Ability to Cancel

The ability to cancel a lease on obsolete equipment is valuable to a company. Again, this will typically be the advantage of an operating lease, since finance leases are usually not cancellable until the bulk of the asset has been paid for by the lessee. Otherwise, the lessor would be too much at risk. In the case of the operating lease, the rental payments will be sufficiently large to compensate the lessor for this risk.

Provision of Maintenance

Lessors of specialist equipment are able to include maintenance of the equipment as part of the lease package. They will be able to provide this service relatively cheaply since they are specialists in their own area.

Low Administration and Transaction Costs

Typically, lenders will have to conduct detailed credit analysis before lending money to a business. The lessor has the advantage that a lease is often based around a saleable object, such as a car. Risk assessment need not focus solely on the lessee but can also focus on the nature of the asset being leased and its likely resale value at various points of time in the lease. If the lessee defaults, the lessor has the automatic right to reclaim the asset, since they are still the legal owner. In addition, the lessor can construct a standard lease agreement to apply to all leases, rather than having separate detailed loan agreements for each borrower.

Accounting Impact

Where a lease is an operating lease, it is not shown on the balance sheet of the lessee and the rental payments are charged as an expense against the profit and loss account. This makes the company's asset base look lower and hence its use of assets to generate turnover and profits (ie return on capital employed) appears superior. In addition, it makes reported gearing levels lower and reduces the interest charge in the profit and loss account compared to when a company borrows money to purchase assets.

When a lease falls into the definition of a finance lease, it is required to be treated as if the company had borrowed money to buy the asset. Consequently, assets and debt levels will increase, meaning that 'off balance sheet finance' is not a possibility.

5 Lease Evaluation

Introduction

Leases can be evaluated using discounted cash flow techniques. The basic idea is to identify the impact of the lease on the cash flows of the company and calculate the net present value of the impact. In order to do this, we first need to identify how a lease will affect the cash flows of a company, and secondly what discount rate should be used to appraise the lease. All we then have to do is to calculate its net present value.

Relevant Cash Flows

The relevant cash flows to use when appraising a lease are the changes in cash flows that will arise when compared to the alternative, which is borrowing money to buy an asset. The cash flows relating to buying an asset are as follows.

Cash Flows When Buying an Asset

Time	Narrative	Cash Inflow/(Outflow)
0	Purchase asset	(x)
1–n	Tax relief due to capital allowances	x

Cash Flows When Leasing an Asset

The cash flows when an asset is leased are as follows.

Time	Narrative	Cash Inflow/(Outflow)
1–n	Lease rentals	(x)
1–n	Tax relief on lease rentals	x

Relevant Cash Flows for Lease Evaluation

The relevant cash flows to use when evaluating a lease are the **difference** between these two sets of flows, as follows.

Time	Narrative	Cash Inflow/(Outflow)
0	Saved purchase cost	x
1–n	Lost tax relief on capital allowances	(x)
1–n	Lease rentals paid	(x)
1–n	Tax relief on lease rentals	x

Identifying the Discount Rate

The relevant discount rate to use for investment appraisal is based upon the risk of the cash flows in question. The cash flows of a lease are generally assumed to be in the same risk category as cash flows on debt instruments. This may not be exactly correct, since it assumes that the company in question has sufficient taxable profits to mean that any relevant tax-based flows are effectively guaranteed to occur. However, it is a useful simplification for most companies.

This means that the relevant discount rate to use when evaluating the post-tax flows of the lease as noted above is the company's **post-tax cost of debt**.

Sale and leaseback

A company may have a significant amount of its net worth represented by non-current assets used in its commercial activities, such as factories or a head office. It may choose to sell one or more of its properties to a property company or bank, and then lease it from the new owners. This will have the effect of raising an immediate cash sum, although the cost of leasing the property back will dilute earnings in future years.

A company might choose to enter into a sale and leaseback agreement when:

- It is seeking to raise cash to repay debt. It will seek to ensure that the leasing costs are lower than the interest on the debt repaid
- It wishes to raise cash for an expansion of the business, or to improve a long-term liquidity position

Types of debt

The following types of debt instrument are considered, including their terms, rights, conditions of use and factors impacting valuation:

- Floating rate notes (FRNs)
- Zero-coupon bonds
- Convertible bonds
- Mandatory convertible bonds
- Exchangeable bonds
- MTNs
- Eurobonds
- Securitisation
- Money Market instruments

Floating Rate Notes (FRNs)

A FRN is a particular types of bond where the coupon is not fixed at the outset, but floats in line with market rates and is re-fixed on a regular basis. Every few months, the market rate of interest is assessed, often using a measure such as LIBOR, and adding to it a margin. LIBOR represents the rate the largest banks are prepared to lend to each other (the interbank deposit rate is called LIBID) and, therefore, provides a benchmark for market interest rates. The margin added reflects the additional risk the investor is taking in lending to a company.

With a fixed rate bond, a change in interest rates will cause the price of the bond to change (so that the yield reflects the market rate of interest). With a FRN, however, the coupon will change in line with market interest rates. This will result in the value of the bond remaining constant at around the par value.

Zero-coupon bonds

These are bonds that carry no coupon rate but are issued at a discount to their face value. The discount reflects the interest that is liable over the life of the bond. The tax treatment of zero-coupon bonds is that the company receives corporation tax relief on a notional interest charge each year, while the investor suffers income tax (not capital gains tax) on the gain made, but only in the year the bond is redeemed.

The same effect is achieved if the bond is redeemed at a premium to its nominal value. For example, if a bond of £100 nominal value has a redemption premium of 15%, at redemption the issuer will pay back £115.

Convertible bonds

One way in which a company that is paying a high coupon on its debt may be able to reduce the coupon rate is by attaching conversion rights or warrants to the bond. A conversion right will give the holder of the bond the right, at a date in the future, to convert the bond into shares at a specified rate. In effect, the purchaser of this bond receives two instruments.

Firstly, the holder is the owner of a reasonably low coupon bond and secondly, he has an option into the equity of the company enabling him to convert at a specified price in the future. The attraction of having this option along with the straight bond is that the issuer of convertible stock can obtain a lower yield cost on the bond than would otherwise be the case.

This 'equity kicker' may also come in the form of a warrant. A warrant is a long-term call option, giving the holder the right to buy shares at a specified price up to a certain date in the future. The principal difference between a warrant and a conversion right is that a warrant may be split away from the bond and traded separately. Conversion rights by their very nature must always trade with the underlying bond.

The basic intention of this structure was to make the investor believe that he had a two-way option. If the share prices rose significantly then the conversion right would be a valuable one. However, if the share price were to fall, the investor would always be able to put the bond back to the issuer, at the premium rate. Conversion rights tend to be issued in the belief that they will be exercised. From the point of view of the company issuing the debt, this makes sense because if the conversion right is exercised, there will be no need to refinance the loan when it matures, as at that point, it will be converted into shares.

Mandatory convertible bonds

However, sometimes the bondholder will be required to convert the nominal value into ordinary shares of the company at a set redemption date. These are known as mandatory convertibles.

For example, equity contract notes will be redeemed for the equivalent of the bond's nominal value in current market value of shares of the company.

The appeal for the investor of 'mandatories' is that the company takes the risk of the share price volatility in the period between issuance and conversion. Mandatories are often issued in conjunction with equity in an IPO to attract investors who would not otherwise be interested in the IPO.

Exchangeable bonds

Exchangeable bonds are ones that are convertible into the ordinary shares of a subsidiary or associate company of the issuer. This is therefore a **different company to the issuer** of the bond.

The use of exchangeable bonds can be to provide a way for a group to divest an unwanted investment. There is no dilution of control for the shareholders of the issuer.

Medium Term Notes/Shelf Programmes

Medium Term Notes (MTNs) are not strictly a type of security. Instead, the term describes a facility enabling the issuer to issue a range of stock from one global facility. In the US, the facility can cover short-term, commercial paper out to 30-year debt.

The issuer sets up a **shelf programme**. When the programme is initially set up, relevant documentation is prepared to enable the issuer to issue a wide variety of different instruments in terms of:

- Maturity (eg from one week to ten years)
- Currency (sterling, US dollars, euro)
- Coupon (coupon-paying or zero coupon)
- Instrument (commercial paper, long-term bonds)

The implication of this is that the costs of setting up the programme are relatively high compared to the cost of a large Eurobond issue (see below).

However, the benefit is that the programme offers **greater flexibility** and **lower cost** to the issuer **in the long run**. As a result, it is more suitable for issuers who need funding flexibility over a period of time. In contrast, a large issuer might find a one-off large Eurobond issue more suitable.

Eurobonds

In essence, a Eurobond is a debt instrument issued by a borrower (typically a government or a large company) normally, or predominantly, outside the country in whose currency it is denominated. For example, a US dollar Eurobond could be issued anywhere in the world except for the US. As such, a better name for it might be an 'international bond'. Eurobonds frequently carry no security, other than the name and credit rating of the issuer.

Another important feature of bonds issued in this market is that, for the most part, they are issued in **bearer form**, with no formal register of ownership held by the company. These bearer documents are immobilised at central depositories, such as Euroclear and Clearstream, which provide clearing and stocklending facilities.

It should be noted that for a number of pragmatic reasons, the clearing houses in the Euromarkets do maintain a form of register of ownership. However, this register is not normally open either to government or tax authorities. Combined with the feature of being bearer documents, a vital aspect of the Eurobond is that, unlike most government bonds, it does not attract withholding tax. **Eurobonds pay coupons gross** and usually **annually**.

Most Eurobonds are issued in **bullet form**, redeemed at one specified date in the future. However, a number of issues have alternative redemption patterns. Some bonds are redeemed over a number of years, with a proportion of the issue being redeemed each year. Whilst Eurobonds are not issued in registered form, each will have an identifying number. A **drawing** of numbers is made every year from the pool of bonds in issue. The numbers drawn are published and the bonds are called in and redeemed. This redemption process is known as a drawing on a Eurobond.

Advantages of Eurobonds

(a) Eurobonds are 'bearer instruments', so the owner does not have to declare his identity.

(b) Interest is paid gross.

(c) Eurobonds create a liability in a foreign currency to match against a foreign currency asset.

(d) They are often cheaper than a foreign currency bank loan because they can be sold on by the investor, who will therefore accept a lower yield in return for this greater liquidity.

(e) They are also extremely flexible. Most eurobonds are fixed rate but they can be floating rate or linked to the financial success of the company.

(f) They are typically issued by companies with excellent credit ratings and are normally unsecured, which makes it easier for companies to raise debt finance in the future.

(g) Eurobond issues are not normally advertised because they are placed with institutional investors and this reduces issue costs.

Disadvantages of Eurobonds

Like any form of debt finance there will be issue costs to consider (approximately 2% of funds raised in the case of Eurobonds) and there may also be problems if gearing levels are too high. A borrower contemplating a eurobond issue must consider the foreign exchange risk of a long-term foreign currency loan. If the money is to be used to purchase assets which will earn revenue in a currency different to that of the bond issue, the borrower will run the risk of exchange losses if the currency of the loan strengthens against the currency of the revenues out of which the bond (and interest) must be repaid.

Securitisation

Securitisation is the process of converting illiquid assets into marketable securities. These securities are backed by specific assets and are normally called asset-backed securities (ABS). Securitisation started with banks converting their long-term loans such as mortgages into securities and selling them to institutional investors. One of the problems of banks as financial intermediaries, is the fundamental mismatch between the maturities of assets and liabilities. Securitisation of loans and sale to investors with more long-term liabilities reduces the mismatch problem and a bank's overall risk profile.

The oldest and most common type of asset securitization is the mortgage-backed bond or security (MBS), although today one can expect virtually anything that has a cash flow to be a candidate for securitisation.

The development of securitisation has led to disintermediation and a reduction in the role of financial intermediaries as borrowers can reach lenders directly. Disintermediation describes a decline in the traditional deposit and lending relationship between banks and their customers and an increase in direct relationships between the ultimate suppliers and users of financing.

Cash flows before securitisation

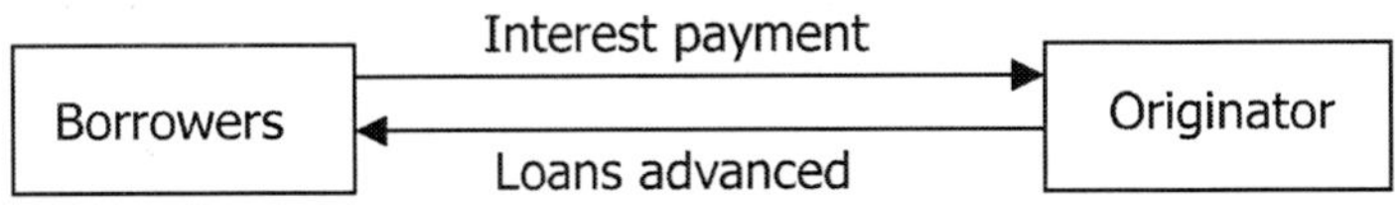

Cash flows after securitisation

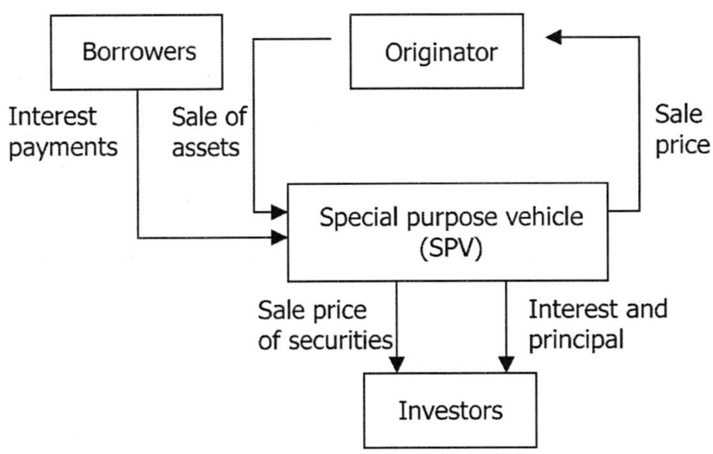

6 Money Market Instruments

Money markets are the markets where short-term instruments are traded. Money markets are over the counter markets and the transactions take place between institutions rather than individual investors. The main characteristic of money market instruments apart from their short maturities (up to 12 months) is that they normally have only one cash flow. Money market instruments can be either negotiable or nonnegotiable. They can also be coupon bearing or discount instruments.

Discount instruments do not pay interest. They are issued and traded at a discount to the face value. The discount is equivalent to the interest paid to the investor and is the difference between the purchase price of the instrument and the price at maturity. The table below shows some of the money market instruments in the UK.

Coupon Bearing	Discount	Derivatives
Money Market Deposits	Treasury Bill (T-bill)	Forwards and Futures
Certificate of Deposit (CD)	Banker's Acceptance (BA)	Swaps
Repurchase Agreement (Repo)	Commercial Paper (CP)	Options

Money market deposits

Money market deposits are very short-term loans between banks or other institutions including governments. These deposits can either be fixed, where the rate of interest and maturity dates are agreed at the time of the transaction or call deposits where the interest is variable and the deposit can be terminated if notice is given.

Certificates of deposit

A Certificate of Deposit (CD) is a certificate of receipt for funds deposited at a bank or other financial institution for a specified term and paying interest at a specified rate.

Certificates of deposit can be either negotiable or non-negotiable. The holder of a negotiable CD has two options: to hold it until maturity, receiving the interest and the principal or to sell it before maturity at the market price. The coupon is expressed as an annual percentage rate and needs to be adjusted to reflect the fact that its maturity is less than a year.

Repos

A repurchase agreement (repo) is a loan secured by a marketable instrument, usually a treasury bill or a bond. The typical term is 1-180 days and is an attractive instrument because it can accommodate a wide spectrum of maturities. A repurchase agreement is an agreement between two counterparties under which one counterparty agrees to sell an instrument to the other on an agreed date for an agreed price, and simultaneously agrees to buy back the instrument from the counterparty at a later date for an agreed price.

The flows in a repo are shown in the following diagram.

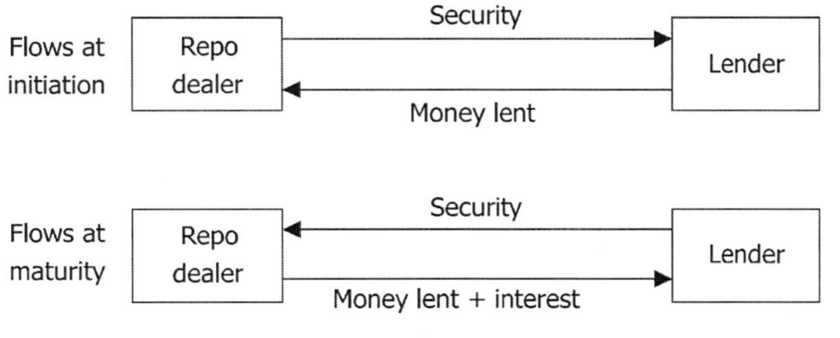

In a reverse repo, the dealer purchases the security initially and then sells it on maturity. Because the two parties in a repo agreement act as a buyer and a seller of the security, a repo to one party is a reverse repo to the other.

Treasury bills

Treasury bills are debt instruments issued by the government with maturities ranging from one month to one year.

Commercial paper

Commercial paper is short-term unsecured corporate debt with maturity up to 270 days. The typical term of this debt is about 30 days. Commercial paper can only be issued by large organisations with good credit ratings, normally to fund short-term expenditure. The debt is issued at a discount that reflects the prevailing interest rates.

Banker's acceptance

Banker's acceptances are negotiable bills issued by companies and guaranteed by a bank.

They are issued by firms to finance commercial transactions such as imports or the purchase of goods. The name derives from the fact that the bank has guaranteed the payment to the holder of the banker's acceptance; that is the bank has accepted responsibility for the payment. Banks guarantee the payment by the company for a fee.

Banker's acceptances are sold on a discounted basis like T-bills and commercial paper. Because banker's acceptances are negotiable instruments, they can be bought and sold until they mature. The rates on banker's acceptances are low because, as they are guaranteed by a bank, the credit risk is low. The typical term is 30 to 180 days and they are issued by firms that do not have a sufficiently high credit rating to issue commercial paper.

PRIVATE EQUITY

chapter 6

Contents

1 INTRODUCTION

Venture capital investment is very risky. The possibility of business failure is high and even if the business is successful, the investment is illiquid. Shares in a private company are not easily re-sold, and their value will consequently be proportionately less than the market price of shares in a comparable quoted company. In addition, the investments are often not viewed as attractive lending options by traditional bankers for a number of reasons:

- Little asset backing
- Personal guarantees of varying worth, since the directors will already have invested much of their own finance in the business
- Little trading history
- Inexperienced management

As a result, equity finance from investors who are used to dealing with risk and assessing the viability of investments from such a viewpoint is necessary.

Hands-on Management

The venture capitalist will often have financial and organisational skills that will be of value to the company. In addition, the entrepreneur will have given up a sizeable stake of his company to the investor and may expect something more in return than just the initial cash finance. Active management participation and a seat on the board for the venture capitalist will often be attractive to both sides.

Capital Gains

A young company is unlikely to have significant cash surpluses for distribution to investors. Any cash generated is likely to be reinvested in the business to achieve growth or to pay off debt. This means that a venture capital investor will need to achieve most of his return through selling his investment in the future and achieving a high capital gain. Only a small part of the overall return will be in the form of a running yield, through a preference dividend for example.

Exit Routes

Given the investor's need for a capital gain, a feasible exit route is vital from the very start. The exit is likely to be either a flotation, a trade sale to another company or a restructuring whereby the investor's shares are repurchased by the company. The most likely of these is a trade sale since many companies will not be sufficiently large to be floated or may be unsuitable for flotation for some other reason. A share repurchase scheme may not realise a realistic sum unless the company gears up to an unacceptable extent.

Required Rates of Return and the Principle of Leverage

In order to compensate for the high-risk levels, the return on the investment will need to be substantial. The actual return required will vary from investment to investment but an internal rate of return of around 30% to 35% would not be unusual. The venture capitalist will aim to maximise this return by introducing debt funding to help partly fund the purchase price. Since debt finance is repaid at par value on exit, any upside can be for the benefit of the Ordinary shareholders, namely the venture capitalist and the management. This is known as the 'Principle of Leverage'.

2 Types of Venture Capital Investment

Venture capital funding can be provided at all stages of a company's development, but typically, is necessary to take the business to a new stage. The existing owners may be unable to fund all the finance the business needs and the banks may be reluctant to lend due to high credit risk.

Venture capital investments can be categorised according to the stage of development the business has reached when risk capital funding is required.

Seedcorn

Seedcorn funding is invested to help develop a business idea, for example making a prototype or conducting initial market research.

For a venture capitalist investing in seed capital is very high risk. Commencement of trading (and therefore cash generation) is some way off and the feasibility of the business idea is unlikely to be explored fully. Most seedcorn funding will come from the entrepreneurs themselves.

Start-Ups

Financing could be provided to a company in the process of setting up, or at a stage where its product or service has not yet been sold commercially. The product or service exists and, in contrast to a seedcorn business, no research and development (R&D) expenditure is needed before the company becomes operational.

Other Early Stage Projects

Companies that have completed product development and begun marketing might want more funds to manufacture and sell the product on a commercial scale. These companies will not yet be making a profit, and cannot finance their development out of operational cash flows. They must, therefore, rely on external funding.

Expansion Financing

Finance could be required for the growth and expansion of an established business. A company might wish, for example, to increase its manufacturing capacity, develop its marketing channels or invest more in working capital. Expansion financing is usually low-risk venture capital, compared with early stage investments and turnarounds. Most venture capital investments are for expansion purposes.

Turnarounds

A company that has been in decline might develop plans for halting the decline and staging a recovery. In the early stage of a recovery programme, the original backers will have to provide the extra finance required. If the recovery appears successful, other venture capitalists could be willing to inject extra funds. Turnaround financing is comparatively rare.

Refinancing Bank Debt

An established company burdened by bank debts, possibly reaching maturity, might seek venture capital funding to repay the banks.

Secondary Purchase

In a secondary purchase, existing shares in a company are purchased by one venture capital firm from another, or from another shareholder (or shareholders) in the company. Although venture capital finance is being invested, it replaces existing capital and does not provide any additional capital to the company concerned.

Acquisitions ('Buyouts')

Venture capital funding can be invested to finance a change of control of the company in an acquisition or buyout situation. Two examples of acquisition funding are as follows:

- A management buyout (MBO) is the purchase of an existing company or a business unit by a group of its managers, with the support of external investors.
- A management buy-in (MBI), in contrast, is the purchase of an existing company or a business unit by an external management team, with financing from venture capitalists and banks. The buy-in team must have the necessary experience and/or expertise to run the business they are purchasing.

An alternative is the buy-in management buyout (BIMBO), where the existing management team is supplemented with outside expertise.

Public to Private Transactions

A public to private transaction involves the buyout of a quoted company. The following is a list of scenarios when a public to private transaction might be appropriate:

- The company is a small cap share that has been underperforming the market as a result of general underperformance in the small cap sector.
- There is poor liquidity in the shares such that it is difficult for shareholders to realise value other than through some form of offer for the shares.
- There is at least one major shareholder who can influence the outcome of the bid.
- The proportion of shares in public hands falls below a minimum percentage.
- The institutional investors can add something to the company that it does not have in a public context as a separate entity, such as management skills or links to other companies.

Institutional Buyouts (IBOs)

Here, an institution identifies a possible company, arranges the finance and then approaches a potential management team. IBOs tend to be the larger venture capital deals, with management often receiving a very small share of the overall equity.

3 Buyouts – Regulatory Issues

Relevant regulatory issues affecting venture capital-funded acquisitions are as follows:

- There is a conflict of interest arising, since the directors of the company are wishing to buy the company at the lowest price the shareholders will accept. However, they have a duty to the shareholders to act in their best interests.
- The Takeover Code will be relevant for management buyouts of public limited companies.
- There are potential issues to consider in respect of financial assistance under the Companies Act.

City Code Issues

The City Code provisions are only relevant when there is a change of control in a public limited company.

- *Rule 25.2* (*note 5*) highlights that the directors of the company subject to the bid face a conflict of interest in their duty to act in the best interest of shareholders, as they are also the offeror.
- *Rule 3* specifies that an independent adviser should be appointed as soon as possible to ensure the shareholders' interests are looked after.
- *Rule 20.3* of the City Code states that, in an MBO, the offeror or potential offeror must, on request, promptly furnish the independent directors of the offeree company or its advisers with all information that has been furnished by the offeror or potential offeror to external providers of finance, whether equity or debt.
- Where there is a competing offer, *Rule 20.2* states that information passed by the offeree company to external providers of finance, whether equity or debt, should be given equally and promptly to the competing offeror, even if that offeror is less welcome. The competing offeror will, however, have to specify exactly what information it requires, rather than asking in general terms for all the information supplied to the external providers of finance for the MBO.
- As with any MBO, the venture capital provider will usually want to incentivise the MBO team by having them take an equity stake in the buy-out vehicle. Rule 16 however prohibits a bidder from making arrangements with shareholders if there are favourable conditions attached which are not available to all shareholders. However, in certain situations, the offeror may wish to retain the services of director shareholders of the offeree and to motivate them by means of an 'earn out' deal where they receive a higher price for their shares if the company's profits hit specified targets.
- Such special deals may be permitted as long as relevant details of the arrangements are disclosed and an independent adviser states that, in his opinion, the terms are fair and reasonable. Where the value of the arrangements entered into is significant and/or unusual in the context of industry practice, then the Panel must be consulted and consent to the arrangements be obtained. The Panel may require, as part of this process, that the arrangements be approved at a general meeting of the company's shareholders (*Rule 16.2*).
- Full details of management shareholdings must be disclosed in the offer document (*Rule 24.2*).

Financial Assistance

The Companies Act 2006 states that it is illegal for a public limited company to give financial assistance for the acquisition of shares in itself or its holding company.

Financial assistance includes gifts, loans, guarantees, indemnities and any other assistance that reduces a company's net assets to a material extent.

Private companies are permitted to give financial assistance for the purchase of their own shares. This exception usually becomes important in the case of management buyouts when the assets of the company are used as security for loans received to buy the company's shares. It is likely that the company subject to the buyout will have to be converted to a private company, prior to the buyout taking place, in order for the financial assistance to be lawful.

In order to convert the company to private status, it will be necessary to have an acceptance condition that the offer is conditional on acceptances being received in respect of 90% of the shares to which the offer relates. This will enable the company to be taken private without any problems from minority shareholders.

4 Venture Capital Organisations

Although venture capital can be provided by individuals and investment institutions, the main providers are specialist venture capital organisations. The major sources of venture capital can be categorised as follows.

There are five broad types:

- Independents
- Captives
- Semi-captives
- Government departments or agencies
- Venture Capital Trusts

They differ in how they raise funds and who controls their investment decisions.

Independents

Independent venture capital organisations raise their funds from more than one source, mainly institutional investors. No single shareholder or investor has a dominant position in the ownership of the fund. The funds are managed independently, and management is free to choose how the money should be invested. Wholly independent funds can be set up in either of two ways:

- A group of experienced venture capitalists seek backing from several investment institutions. The institutions put money into a fund, which the venture capitalists manage on their behalf.
- A group of financial institutions agree to set up a fund, and recruit a management team to make the investments. The fund managers then decide how to invest the money in business ventures.

Investors in the funds are paid returns out of the proceeds from investing in business ventures, ie dividends on shares, interest on loans and the cash proceeds from the eventual sale or redemption of the investments.

Independent funds have several other features. They are usually 'close-ended', with a specified initial capital base. For example, a £200m fund might be established. After the initial fundraising, no further money will be sought for the fund, and management will invest in business ventures until the money in the fund is used up.

- They are primarily equity oriented, and seek long-term capital gain rather than a regular flow of annual dividend income.
- They are often established with a maximum life, typically ten years. At the end of this time, the fund is liquidated, and the proceeds distributed (in cash or as unsold securities owned by the fund) to the fund investors and managers in a pre-arranged proportion. Management can, if it wishes, set up a new fund to attract fresh venture capital.
- During the life of the fund, management also charges a fee, typically 2%–2½% of the funds invested in a smaller fund, and perhaps 1%–1½% for a larger fund.

Some independents are companies investing their own funds in business ventures. For example, 3i Group plc is a public company with share capital. Funds are obtained by issuing shares, borrowing or reinvesting the proceeds of realised investments in earlier business ventures. Their aim is to make profits on investing in ventures in order to provide a return to their own shareholders.

Captives

A captive venture capital organisation obtains its funds from a parent organisation, usually a financial institution, and manages them on behalf of the parent. The management is appointed by and accountable to the parent, which expects the fund to provide a suitable return.

Captive funds may be more concerned than independents about an annual 'running yield', ie dividend income, from their investments, although capital gain is an important part of the overall return.

Semi-Captives

A semi-captive venture capital organisation invests funds on behalf of a parent, but also manages independently, funds obtained from other sources. An investment bank or other investment institution could set up a fund and appoint a management team, and then invite a number of other investment institutions to join the fund.

Government

Some venture capital organisations receive their funds from national or local governments and use the money to invest in businesses in their region.

Venture Capital Trusts

Venture Capital Trusts (VCTs) are quoted funds which hold investments in unquoted businesses, and are controlled and managed by venture capital firms. The regulations covering VCTs are considered below.

Advisory Services

Instead of investing funds under its management, a venture capitalist could also act as adviser to other fund managers or venture capital investors. One example is a 'gatekeeper' that specifically advises investors on funds or provides opportunities to invest in a 'fund of funds'.

5 Approaching Investors – The Business Plan

When trying to raise funds for his business, the entrepreneur's first point of contact with potential investors will be his business plan. The business plan is a marketing document that aims to make the business seem attractive and a worthy investment opportunity. It will be competing with many other proposals and will need to immediately stand out to the venture capitalist. Key areas to include in the plan are as follows:

- **Executive Summary.** A one-page summary of the document, including the main reasons for the business' likely success, the investment required, the timespan to exit and key financial details, as well as what the unique opportunity is that this investment provides.
- **Company Background.** History and main events in the company's history.
- **The Product or Service.** What it is and why there is demand for it. What advantages it has over rival products/services. Development information.
- **The Market and Demand.** Whether the market is stable, growing or declining. What is the market segment and size? Who constitutes the customer base? What factors affect demand and cause the customers to buy the product? Commercially sensitive information about customers will not be included.
- **Marketing Plan.** How the business is going to be developed and how the customers will be approached and persuaded to do business with the company. The venture capitalist will consider the sales strategy carefully to see how the business could be grown to give a good return on the initial investment.

- **Competition.** Who the competitors are, what size they are, how important the market place is to them, and how likely they are to fight to defend their position against any new entrant. If there is no competition, why this is the case? How can this business meet the competitive threat? What barriers to entry exist?
- **Suppliers.** Who are the principal suppliers for the business, how numerous are they, and are they in a strong position when negotiating prices?
- **Company Structure.** Legal structure and ownership details.
- **Management.** Even if the market is right, it is vital to have a management team capable of developing the business. Many venture capitalists say that the three most important success ingredients for a company are the three M's – management, management and management. Profiles of all key staff and their experience and qualifications for running such a business should be included. A management weakness in one area, such as finance or organisational expertise, can often be filled by the venture capital provider.
- **Operations.** This includes such areas as: production process and capacity; facilities details; and other organisational details that are key to the business, for example, administration facilities.
- **Financial Projections.** The purpose of the financial projections is to estimate:
  - How much finance will be needed
  - Annual revenues, costs and profits of the business
  - The cash flows, including all capital expenditure and working capital requirements

  The projections should include a summary profit and loss statement, a cash flow and usually a balance sheet. A forecast period of between three and five years would be typical.
- **Risks and Opportunities.** A summary of the key strengths of the business and the opportunities available to it. Importantly, how they will be capitalised on. Also, the key risks and weaknesses and how they will be mitigated.
- **Investment Required and Exit Routes.** The level of investment required, the time to realisation of investment and how realisation is going to be achieved.

6 The Ideal MBO Candidate

The ideal MBO candidate is one where the risks of the investment can be successfully mitigated whilst still allowing the venture capital and debt investors to realise a satisfactory return. Desirable characteristics for a company to have are as follows:

- A stable or growing market place
- Potential for cost saving or synergistic restructuring
- Cash generation
- Large asset backing as security for loans
- The ability to restrict fixed asset expenditure over the years subsequent to the buyout to minimise cash outflows in the critical early years
- The ability to squeeze working capital in the early years to generate additional cash to pay back loan finance
- The existence of surplus assets that can be sold to pay down debt
- A strong, well-balanced management team
- A feasible exit route, ie the company should be of sufficient size to be floated or should be an attractive purchase for other acquisitive companies

Progressing the Deal

Financiers and Advisers

Before making an offer and negotiating with the vendor, the management team should aim to meet with the potential financiers. They can then inspect the business plan and establish whether or not finance is likely to be available.

It may be useful at this stage to use professional advisers, such as accountants or lawyers. The advantage of this is that they will be expert at representing the management's interests. The risk is that heavy fees will be incurred which will have to be met by the management personally if the bid does not succeed.

Offer to the Vendors

After meeting with the potential financiers, an offer can be made to the vendors. This will cover the following points:

- Details of the assets or shares to be purchased
- Details of trademarks or other brand names to be included in the deal
- Which employees and attached obligations (such as redundancy payments) are to be included in the deal
- Pre-conditions for the sale, such as an investigation or tax clearances
- The purchase price and payment terms

When setting the price, the management will have to value the company using various valuation techniques. This, however, will only give a base guide and the final price will be determined by a range of factors. The negotiating strength of each party will be paramount.

7 Illustration of a Venture Capital Deal

Initial Appraisal

Having established that the venture is a reasonably sound proposition by analysing the business plan, the venture capitalist will identify the total investment requirement in cash terms, how the deal is to be structured (what other sources of finance are likely to be available), and what sort of return he can expect to achieve over the life of the investment. He will then compare the return calculated from the investment to his required return to ascertain whether the deal represents a viable business proposition.

Profit Forecasts

Consider a company that is seeking finance for an MBO and predicts the following income statement figures.

Income Statement Forecasts	Year 1 £'000	Year 2 £'000	Year 3 £'000	Year 4 £'000	Year 5 £'000
Revenue	500	800	1,200	1,900	2,500
EBIT	85	160	300	510	725
Net income	30	70	110	150	190

Net income for the latest year was £26,500.

Investment Required

The capital outlay required is £560,000, which includes the purchase cost of £400,000, paid to the vendors, and expansion capital for the business of £100,000. The remaining £60,000 is estimated to cover fees.

Funding Requirements	£'000
Purchase consideration	400
New non current assets (machinery)	70
Working capital	30
Costs (professional fees, etc.)	60
Total financing requirements	560

Sources of Finance

As a venture capitalist, you assess that the minimum interest cover ratio (defined as EBIT divided by interest expense) acceptable to the banks, is likely to be 4×. Market rates indicate that loan finance could be raised at a cost of 9.0% per annum. The maximum amount the entrepreneur can afford to invest is £30,000, which he will raise by taking out a second mortgage on his home.

Financing Scheme

A possible financing scheme would be as follows.

Funding Requirements	£'000
Equity (note 1)	
Entrepreneur	30
Venture capitalist – Ordinary shares	45
Venture capitalist – preference shares	255
	330
Debt	
Bank debt – term loan (note 2)	180
Leasing of machinery (note 3)	50
	230
Total finance	560

Note 1 – Equity

The entrepreneur is only investing £30,000 out of the total financing of £560,000. Although his investment is relatively small compared to the other sources of finance, it is very high in proportion to his overall wealth. His own personal assets are at stake and he will therefore be entitled to a relatively high shareholding in the business to reflect the risk. The entrepreneur will receive Ordinary (voting) shares in return for his investment, based on an ownership split negotiated with the venture capitalist. If we assume management have agreed a 40% stake, then the Ordinary shareholding of the venture capitalist is 60%, ie £45,000 $\left(30 \times \frac{60}{40}\right)$. The balance of venture capitalist funding will be invested as preference shares or loan notes (if gearing covenants permit).

Note 2 – Debt

The bank debt is structured as a term loan. This term loan would account for most of the fixed requirements of the business such as leasehold and fixed asset purchases and financing the permanent core of working capital in the business. Repayments would link into the expected cash flows of the business.

The bank would need to justify its lending. Using the assumptions of a minimum interest cover ratio of 4×, and loan finance being available at 9% per annum, we can calculate the maximum debt available to the company.

$$\text{Interest cover} = \frac{\text{Forecast EBIT}}{\text{Maximum interest cost}}$$

$$\text{Maximum interest cost} = \frac{£85,000}{4}$$

$$= £21,250$$

$$\text{Maximum debt} = \frac{\text{Interest charge}}{\text{Borrowing rate}}$$

$$= \frac{£21,250}{0.09}$$

$$= £236,111$$

The proposed loan of £180,000 is more than covered by this.

Note 3 – Leasing

Leasing is often an excellent way of reducing the initial funding requirements. However, care should be taken that the cost of leasing is not excessive. Leasing companies will often attempt to charge interest rates of 30% or more. Leases will therefore increase the gearing and reduce the interest cover of the business.

Forecasting Free Cash Flows and Debt Repayment

We now forecast the cash flow generated by the investment, deducting from this the repayment of interest and debt capital in accordance with the terms of the debt instruments.

Continuing the example above, assume the term loan (£180m at 9% interest) is repayable in equal instalments to include both capital and interest. Assume a tax rate of 30% is applicable.

The annual repayment on the term loan is calculated by dividing the capital sum by the five-year annuity factor at 9%.

$$\text{Annual repayment} = \frac{£180\text{m}}{3.89} \text{ (see working)}$$

$$= £46\text{m}$$

Working

Annuity factor $= \frac{1}{r}\left(1 - \frac{1}{(1+r)^n}\right)$

$= \frac{1}{0.09}\left(1 - \frac{1}{1.09^5}\right)$

$= 3.89$

The repayment of capital and interest, together with the associated tax shield on the interest, can be scheduled as follows.

Scheduling Repayment of Capital and Interest

Year	Term Loan Balance b/f	Interest (tax relief)	Cash Payment	Term Loan Balance c/f
1	180	16.2 (4.86)	46	150.2
2	150.2	13.5 (4.06)	46	117.7
3	117.7	10.6 (3.2)	46	82.3
4	82.3	7.4 (2.2)	46	43.7
5	43.7	3.9 (1.2)	46	–

We can now forecast the free cash flow from the investment to ascertain if there is sufficient cash flow to repay this debt.

Forecasting Free Cash Flow

	Time				
	1	2	3	4	5
EBIT	85	160	300	510	725
Less tax (30%)	(26)	(48)	(90)	(153)	(218)
Free cash flow	59	112	210	357	507
Less: Repayment of capital and interest	(46)	(46)	(46)	(46)	(46)
Add: Tax relief on interest	4.9	4.0	3.2	2.2	1.2
Retained cash	17.9	70.0	167.2	313.2	462.2

The forecasts make the following assumptions.

- Depreciation is equal to capital expenditure.
- The business has no additional working capital requirements.
- Tax relief is available on the interest as soon as it arises.

The forecasts indicate that the business will have sufficient cash flow to repay the term loan prior to exit at the end of Year 5.

Calculating the Venture Capitalist's Return

In order to assess whether or not the above deal is acceptable, the venture capitalist needs to assess what his overall rate of return is going to be by calculating the internal rate of return of the cash flows of his investment.

The venture capitalist's internal rate of return (IRR) will largely depend on the value of the business in five years' time, assuming that a sale or flotation occurs at that date.

Assuming the business is exited on a P/E ratio similar to the purchase price.

$$\text{P/E ratio at entry} = \frac{\text{Purchase consideration}}{\text{PAT (latest year)}}$$

$$= \frac{400{,}000}{26{,}500}$$

$$= 15.1\times$$

$$\text{P/E ratio at exit} = \frac{\text{Exit value}}{\text{PAT (Year 5)}}$$

$$\text{Exit value} = 15.1 \times £190{,}000$$

$$= £2{,}869{,}000$$

We can now calculate the share of the exit value attributable to the venture capitalist. This calculation assumes all borrowings have been paid off over the life of the investment.

	£
Total exit value	2,869,000
Less: Preference shares	(255,000)
Balance to equity holders	2,614,000
Less: Entrepreneur share (40%)	(1,045,600)
Venture capitalist (equity)	1,568,400
Total venture capitalist cash on exit (Preference and equity shares)	1,823,400

Calculating the IRR of the venture capitalist's cash flows, is as follows.

Time		Cash Flow (£)
0	Cash outflow for purchase	(300,000)
5	Cash inflow on sale	1,823,400

IRR = 43%

As this return is in excess of normal minimum requirements, say, of 30%, the deal is likely to be acceptable to the venture capitalist at this stage.

This calculation assumes that the venture capitalist does not receive a dividend from their shares during the five-year investment period. A dividend would give rise to additional cash flows and therefore increase the overall return of the investment.

Use of Ratchets

The venture capitalist could be prepared to offer incentives to management to motivate them towards making the venture successful. These can take the form of a ratchet.

A ratchet is an arrangement whereby managers get a larger share of the company's equity if the business performs well and achieves certain specified targets in the business plan. The ratchet allows the exact division of the Ordinary share capital between the entrepreneurs and the venture capitalists to be decided after the success (or failure) of the venture is known.

EXAMPLE

A company is the subject of an MBO. It is currently making annual after-tax profits of £2m, which are forecast to rise to £5m after three years. The venture capital organisation financing the buyout has estimated that to achieve its target return on investment, it would have to own 40% of the company's Ordinary share capital if annual profits are £5m at the end of three years. However, if annual profits are £6m, it will only need to own about 30% of the Ordinary share capital to earn its target return.

SOLUTION

A ratchet arrangement could be agreed whereby for every £100,000 of profits over £5m p.a. after three years, up to a ceiling of £6m, management should be entitled to an extra 0.5% of the equity. If profits reach £6m, management will therefore raise their stake in the Ordinary share capital from 60% to 65%.

Ratchets are often structured using convertible shares.

Advantages of a Ratchet

- A ratchet motivates the entrepreneur, who will probably be optimistic about the business and believe that it will do very well.
- A ratchet also protects the return of the venture capitalist.

Disadvantages

- A ratchet can encourage short-termism.
- The entrepreneur only concentrates on achieving the ratchet profits to the exclusion of all other considerations.
- The definition of profits can be manipulated.
- If the business does less well, then the entrepreneur may become less motivated since more gains are going to the venture capitalist.

8 Sources of Finance and Deal Structuring

The major sources of finance used in venture capital deals are as follows:

- Equity (Ordinary and preference shares)
- Senior debt
- Mezzanine debt

- High yield bonds
- Venture capitalist loan notes
- Vendor loan notes
- Others

Equity Finance

The equity finance will typically be split between the management team and the venture capitalists, although it may be the case that the vendor wishes to retain an interest in the company. The bulk of the finance will be supplied by the venture capitalists. They will largely be concerned to ensure that they earn a satisfactory rate of return on an IRR basis taking into account the risk being incurred. On top of this, they will need to ensure that the management is well motivated to succeed by owning an appropriate proportion of the equity.

Additional elements in the equity package may be as follows:

- **Share Options or Convertible Loan Sock**

  These will enable the financiers to increase their percentage of the company at low cost. The conversion or exercise rights can be altered depending on whether the company achieves agreed performance targets.

- **Redeemable Preference Shares**

  These enable the venture capitalists to obtain repayment of their investment if equity returns are inadequate. They will give a running yield that will increase overall returns. They may include a conversion option.

- **Ratchets**

  These may enable the deal to satisfy both the management team and the venture capitalists.

Senior Debt

Senior debt will be supplied by banks on a secured basis. In order to assess the debt capacity of the company, banks will look at ratios such as the following:

- Interest cover, both on a profits and cash flow basis
- The ratio of free cash flow to total debt repayments (interest + scheduled capital repayments)
- The ratio of total debt to EBITDA

The senior debt lender is likely to specify these ratios for the senior debt facility and also for the total debt of the venture, thereby controlling the total amount of debt raised. For example, the senior debt agreement may stipulate a minimum interest cover of 5× for the senior debt and 2.5× for all debt.

Since the company being acquired is giving a charge over its assets to the banks, there are S151 issues with respect to financial assistance for the purchase of a company's shares. This is considered in more detail in the chapter, Other Takeover Regulations.

Mezzanine Finance

Mezzanine finance is financing that ranks below senior debt for repayment and interest payment, but ahead of equity. It usually takes the form of a loan from a bank or specialist finance house or venture capital firm, at a higher interest rate than the senior debt and with lower or subordinated security. Frequently it will include an 'equity kicker'. This is an entitlement for the lender to take an equity stake in the venture capital investment, usually through the issue of warrants exercisable on the venture capitalist's exit or on repayment of the mezzanine debt.

Mezzanine finance is often part of the funding mix for a buyout. It is popular because debt is inherently cheaper than equity as the interest charge is tax-deductible, and equity providers always seek the maximum leverage compatible with the risk profile of the company, to maximise the returns on equity.

Generally, the team will first establish the maximum amount of senior debt available, based on interest cover and in some cases asset backing. The next step is to establish whether any mezzanine debt can be raised. This will be determined by the attitude of the senior lender, who will have imposed restrictions on the company's overall borrowings in the form of gearing covenants and (most importantly) overall interest cover covenants.

Mezzanine debt is often accompanied by a **PIK** ('payment-in-kind') interest structure. Here, the interest payment is not paid in cash as it arises, but rather accrues as part of the capital of the loan, thereby increasing the capital redemption value of the loan at the maturity date of the loan. A lender will want to ensure the investment has excellent cash flow potential and growth prospects to be able to repay both the initial loan investment, plus the accrued PIK interest, at the date of the investment horizon. The interest rate attaching to the PIK loan would be substantially higher than for secured debt, to reflect the increased risk to the lender.

EXAMPLE

Newco Limited is forecasting EBIT of £1.5m for the current financial year. The senior lender has imposed a senior interest cover of 3x and overall interest cover of 2.0x. Interest rates on secured debt are currently 10%.

The maximum amount of senior debt can be calculated, as interest cannot exceed one third of EBIT of £1.5m. Thus, the maximum interest that can be paid on the senior debt is £500,000. With interest rates at 10%, the maximum senior debt available is £5m.

The maximum mezzanine debt can now be calculated. Total interest cannot exceed half of EBIT of £1.5m, ie £750,000. Of this, £500,000 is being paid to the senior lender, so we have surplus interest capacity of £250,000. Mezzanine debt is typically 3%–4% more expensive than senior debt – say, 14%. The maximum mezzanine debt available is therefore £250,000 @ 14% = £1.785m. To encourage the mezzanine provider to fund the debt more cheaply, an equity kicker might be offered and the terms would be agreed in negotiation.

High Yield Bonds in the Funding Mix

'High yield' bonds are issued by companies with a credit rating below what is called 'investment grade'. High yield bonds are widely used in the funding mix in the US and to a more limited extent in continental Europe, but only used infrequently in the UK. Because bonds are issued to the public through the capital markets, they will only be available to the largest private equity deals, where a company is of potential interest to the public. Typically, however, they will not form a part of the initial purchase consideration, but will be a means of refinancing the buyout shortly after the deal has completed.

This is as a result of the following:

- The time and expense involved in arranging a public offer of securities, which equity investors will not wish to incur until they have actually obtained ownership of the MBO vehicle
- The timing problem – investors will not wish to lend to a 'Newco' until it has actually acquired the assets
- The risk of the market for bonds changing adversely prior to the issue, which could wreck the transaction

Where high yield bonds are available, they are popular as a part of the funding mix because:

- Interest is tax deductible and there may be possibilities for structuring the bond tax effectively in other respects
- Covenants will be limited and therefore less restrictive for the company
- The overall cost of debt for a large issue is typically lower than mezzanine finance would be (although the initial issue costs are higher)

The maximum amount of high yield bonds that can be issued will be determined in exactly the same way as mezzanine finance, ie by reference to interest cover imposed by the senior lender.

Venture Capitalist Loan Notes

The venture capitalist may also, if loan covenants on existing debt permit, invest cash as loan notes. This has the following advantages for the company:

- Flexibility. The debt instrument can be structured to the expected cash flow of the business.
- Interest holidays can be used in early years.
- Tax efficiency. Loan interest may be offset against profits to reduce the business' tax liability.

In considering whether the venture capitalist can invest funds as loan notes, it is important to have regard to the loan covenants on debt facilities. The senior lender is likely to specify a minimum interest cover ratio for all borrowing that the venture has outstanding.

Vendor Loan Notes

This is where the vendor supplies finance at a reduced rate of interest for several years by accepting deferred consideration. It is more common in a recession, reflecting the inability of vendors to negotiate a better deal with management when no alternative purchasers are available.

Other Sources of Finance

Other sources of finance include the following:

- Leasing
- Grants from government and regional bodies
- Sale and leaseback
- Debt factoring

Deal Structuring – Conclusion

When constructing a financing package for a venture capital transaction, the following principles are usually adhered to:

- Maximise 'cheap' capital for the company
- Reduce the outlay from the venture capitalist, thereby maximising the venture capitalist's IRR

Most venture capital deals will usually, therefore, aim to raise the maximum debt compatible with the company's risk profile. Reducing the venture capitalist investment generally gives an increased IRR to the venture capitalist. This is because debt is redeemed at par value and can be paid down over the life of the investment, if cash flows permit. Any upside in the exit valuation is therefore for the benefit of the equity providers alone.

These principles give the following pecking order in raising finance for most venture capital transactions:

1. Maximise cheapest capital first: senior debt.
2. Next cheapest finance: maximum other debt (eg mezzanine) permitted within loan covenants (minimum interest cover ratios and maximum gearing levels will be specified).
3. Management equity stake, based on a negotiated ownership split with venture capitalist.
4. The balance from the venture capitalist as Ordinary shares, preference shares or loan notes.

9 Exit Routes

The two main exit routes whereby investors can realise their capital gain in a successful MBO are the flotation or the trade sale to another company. The attractiveness of each depends to an extent on market conditions.

The factors to take into account when considering which exit route is the more suitable include the following.

	Flotation	Trade Sale
Size of Company	Large	Any size
Timing of Exit	Market determined	Flexible
Business weaknesses	Unacceptable	Can be accommodated
Management Quality	Essential	Not essential, but will be reflected in the price
Independence	Arguable	Ends
Realisation	Partial	Full
Price	Arguable, but possibly small discount to market	Arguable, but possibly at a premium

Given the small size of most venture capital transactions, flotation is unlikely to be feasible most of the time. Therefore, most exits are via trade sales. For this reason, venture capitalists are particularly attracted to investments in sectors that are consolidating and therefore offer identifiable potential purchases for the business at exit date.

Alternative exit routes are as follows:

- **Refinancing:** The company is raising new debt to buy out the venture capitalist.
- **Repurchase:** The management buys out the venture capital interest.
- **Secondary purchase:** A second venture capital company buys out the venture capital interest.
- **Insolvency**

Public Equity

chapter 7

Contents

1 Introduction

In this chapter on public equity, we initially consider the listing process, together with the rationale for applying for a listing and the advantages and disadvantages of being a listed company. We look at the main stages in an Initial Public Offering (IPO), together with the common methods of issuing shares and methods to price an IPO. We also look at secondary methods of issuing equity, including rights issues, placings, open offers and vendor consideration issues. Share repurchases are examined and the chapter concludes with a section on secondary and dual listings.

2 Applying for a Listing

Reasons for Wanting a Listing

When a new company is formed, particularly with the assistance of venture capitalists, one of the aspirations of the director shareholders may be for the company to seek a stock market listing in the future. In reality, very few companies ever actually come to the market and it is important to consider the reasons why a listing may or may not be appropriate.

The Advantages of a Listing

(a) Exit route

Flotation of the company could enable investors to realise a large part of their investment and become rich beyond their wildest dreams. Realisation is absolutely vital when the company has some venture capital investors who need to realise their funds in a set time scale. One of the first questions a venture capitalist will ask when assessing a business is the feasibility of various exit routes, including flotation.

(b) Immediate source of long-term capital for the business

In addition to existing shareholders realising part of their investment, the company will be able to issue new shares and obtain long-term capital for the business. This will enable the business to expand its markets, make acquisitions and reduce gearing levels.

(c) Ongoing source of capital

The ability to issue new shares in the future, subject to investor sentiment, or to issue listed debt will give the company more flexibility in its financing options. This will translate into lower costs and will assist the company in its expansion plans.

(d) Share-for-share acquisitions

The ability to issue shares as consideration when making an acquisition will give the company more options when implementing a strategy of growth.

(e) High profile

The listing will give the company more credibility with its customers and suppliers and will also be a source of publicity, leading to lower costs and higher revenues.

(f) Share incentive schemes

It is easier to introduce share option schemes for employees and directors with a listed company, since there is a readily ascertainable market price and a liquid market in which to dispose of a holding.

(g) Personal factors

The directors of the company may feel attracted to the prestige and kudos of being the directors of a listed company.

The Disadvantages of a Listing

(a) Time and cost spent preparing a flotation

The planning of a flotation is a lengthy procedure and will probably last for at least six months. Throughout this time, a significant amount of management effort will need to be diverted into the flotation process. This will take the management's eye off the underlying business. In addition, advisers will be spending time and charging bills. These may be rolled up and only be payable if the flotation goes ahead, but at some time the cost will come through.

(b) The cost of the flotation itself

The flotation process itself is very expensive, involving fees to advisers, the stock market regulator and the underwriters and marketing expenses.

(c) The ongoing cost of maintaining a listing

The company must pay annual fees to the stock market regulator. In addition, the directors of the company will need to spend a significant amount of management time communicating with investors and ensuring that the company is being marketed properly.

(d) Satisfying the needs of external shareholders

The needs of external shareholders depend on the nature of those investors – whether they want income or capital growth, whether they are pension funds, insurance companies, unit trusts or private investors. The company must identify their needs and tailor the strategy of the company to meet those requirements. This may be at odds with the desires of the directors who previously made decisions by reference to their own personal situations. In particular, the need to achieve short-term results at the expense of the long-term development of the business may be a problem.

(e) Accountability

The requirement to have non-executive directors on the board and to justify performance, executive pay and other decisions to outside shareholders may be an interference to directors used to running the company their own way.

(f) Lack of secrecy

The disclosure requirements set by the FCA and under the Financial Services and Markets Act 2000 (FSMA 2000) and the fact that the company is subject to the scrutiny of analysts and the public, means that the company will not have the benefits of secrecy and discretion accorded to a private company.

(g) The risk of takeover

If the directors do not perform satisfactorily, the company may be subject to a hostile bid. Once listed, the directors are answerable to a public shareholder base who may be persuaded by a predator's arguments that a change of control of the company could be in the shareholders' interest.

(h) Different culture

The culture of the business is likely to change, since the directors will be answerable to outside shareholders. Previously, the business may have been run as a 'lifestyle' company, with lavish benefits to the directors and their families. Such advantages disappear on listing.

(i) Tax planning

The scope for tax planning is much wider in an unquoted company with a small group of shareholders and an uncertain market value. Tax implications are likely to be an important consideration with respect to any possible flotation, and early advice should be sought.

Alternatives to a Listing

Depending on the situation of the company, a number of alternative routes may be available. Each will have advantages and disadvantages.

- **Trade sale to another company**

  The trade sale is the alternative means of realising any investment and is, in fact, the more common occurrence in practice for a successful company. The decision whether to float or sell the company depends on a number of factors. The following table highlights the key differences between the two routes.

	Flotation	Trade Sale
Size of Company	Large	Any size
Timing of Exit	Market driven	Flexible
Business Weaknesses	Unacceptable	Can be accommodated
Management Quality	Essential	Not essential, but will be reflected in the price
Independence	Arguable	Ends
Realisation	Partial	Full
Price	Depends on market sentiment	Possibly at a control premium

- **Debt finance**

  Where the purpose of the listing is to raise additional finance, use of debt may be an alternative. The advantages of debt in this context are that it:

  - Is cheap to raise
  - Keeps control of the company with existing shareholders
  - Ensures that all the benefits of success stay with the existing shareholders

  The disadvantages of debt are that it:

  - Is only available in limited quantities up to acceptable gearing levels
  - Exposes the company to the risk of insolvency should operating profits and cash flows fall
  - Is only issued with strict loan agreements defining ratio covenants to which the business must adhere

- **Unquoted equity finance**

  If the company is unwilling or unable to raise sufficient debt, an alternative is to use a provider of equity expansion finance. The key advantage of this approach is that it expands the equity capital base of the company, meaning that additional debt can also be raised and increasing the possibilities for expansion. Furthermore, an equity investor can be selected whose vision for the business matches that of the existing shareholders. For example, a long-term investor may be ideal for a company with expansion plans that involve significant cash outflows but where benefits will only accrue in the distant future. A business with highly volatile earnings, such as in the airline industry, may find it better to have an investor who understands this and is not going to sell out just because one year's figures do not meet short term expectations.

The disadvantages of such equity finance are that it will dilute the interests of existing shareholders, introduce new investors who will probably want a seat on the board and commit the company to focusing on its new investors' needs. In addition, the level of funds that can be raised in this way is probably less than the level that would be possible by releasing the majority of the company's shares on the market place.

Key Stages for an Initial Public Offering

- **Appoint advisers.** Key advisers to appoint are:
  - **Sponsor.** The sponsor will frequently be an investment bank and will co-ordinate the flotation as well as advising on complex issues. The role of the sponsor is discussed in more detail below.
  - **Broker.** The broker will advise on pricing, timing and market conditions, assist in representing the issuer with potential investors, give guidance on the most appropriate method of marketing the issue, advise on FCA, Stock Exchange and any other relevant requirements and ensure that the market for the shares is liquid.
  - **Reporting Accountant.** The reporting accountant will carry out due diligence, as discussed earlier.
  - **Lawyer.** The lawyer carries out the legal due diligence on the company, reviews the issuer's legal status, reviews service contracts, re-registers the issuer as a public company if necessary, completes the document verification process and prepares all other relevant legal agreements. Separate lawyers would normally represent the directors of the company, the issuer and the advisers to the issuer.
  - **Public relations.** Public relations will advise on the selling of the issue to investors, liaise with the press and analysts and ensure that the marketing tone of any documents is appropriate.

  The importance of each of the advisers and the specific role that they adopt will depend on the nature and size of the company to be floated. For example, in a relatively small flotation, the broker can act as the sponsor, lead underwriter and overall co-ordinator of the listing. Alternatively, a firm of accountants or lawyers may take on a more central role.
- **Planning.** This involves preparing a detailed timetable, lists of key documents required, potential problem areas, and clear allocation of responsibilities.
- **Consultation with regulators.** This must be at an early stage, to fix the timing and level of disclosure required, and to confirm suitability for listing.
- **The long form report.** The responsibility of the accountants, this is a very detailed document covering every aspect of the company, its finances and its operations. It will be used by the sponsor to assist in his assessment of the company's suitability for listing and will also be used as a base for much of the information in the prospectus or listing particulars.
- **Draft documents.** The exact scope of the documents required is detailed below. The main documents to be prepared are the long form report, draft prospectus, working capital letter, responsibility letters and derogation letters. The purpose of the derogation letters is to obtain permission from the regulators to omit certain specified information from the prospectus and other documents.
- **Verification.** This is the process of checking on a line-by-line basis that all statements made in the prospectus are fair, accurate and complete, ensuring that the directors have fully discharged their legal responsibilities in respect of the prospectus.
- **Completion meeting.** This is the final meeting when all documents are signed and the final decision to float is taken.

The following table provides an indicative timetable for a listing for a company.

Application for Listing – Summary Timetable	
Time Before Listing	**Action**
24 weeks	Appoint advisers Planning Consult regulators (FCA) Commence long form report
	↓
8 to 12 weeks	Draft documents prepared Drafts submitted to FCA Public relations campaign starts
	↓
1 to 6 weeks	Draft prospectus Verification Formal submission of documents to FCA
	↓
Final week	Approval of documents by FCA Completion meeting Underwriting agreement signed Investment presentations Allocation lists open and basis of allocation is announced Formal application for listing Listing granted Dealing commences

3 Methods of Bringing Securities to Listing

The methods used to bring securities to listing depend on whether the issuer is a new applicant (ie coming to the market for the first time) or making a secondary offering.

New Applicants for Listing

The regulator wishes to ensure that on a new application for listing, the shares will be marketable. The main methods which will ensure this are:

- Offer for subscription or offer for sale
- Placing
- Intermediaries offer
- Introduction
- Reverse takeover

Any other method which is acceptable to the FCA may also be proposed; these methods are not prescriptive and are no longer detailed in the Listing Rules.

Offer for Sale

In an offer for sale the company issues shares to an issuing house (typically an investment bank) which then offers the shares for sale to the retail investing public. These may be shares newly issued by the company, to raise finance for the company, or they may be shares originally held by the existing shareholders, being sold to allow them to realise some of their investment.

The offer for sale can be represented diagrammatically as follows:

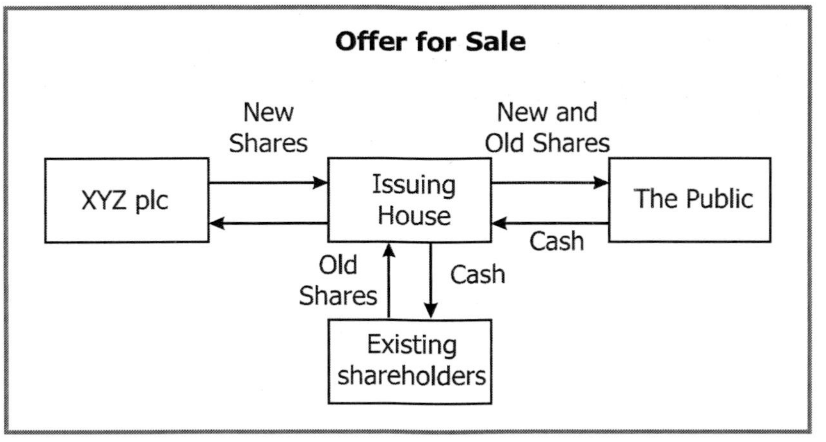

Offer for Subscription

An offer for subscription is similar to an offer for sale, but in this case the company issues new shares to new shareholders directly, in response to the applications for these shares.

This method is most typically used by investment companies. The requirements concerning offers for sale and subscription are the same. It can be represented diagrammatically as follows.

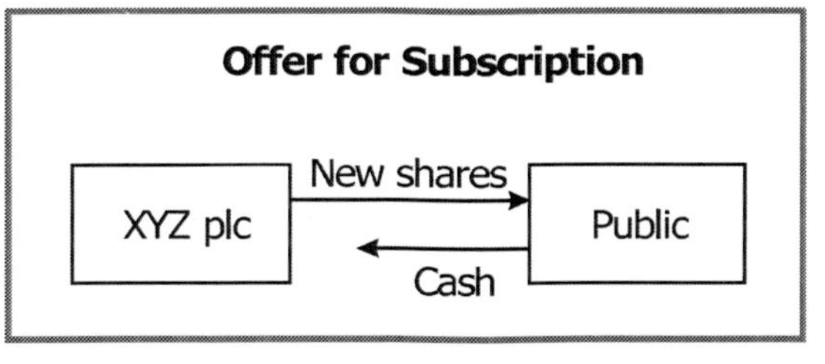

Placing

It is very common for an offer for sale to be accompanied by a placing. A placing involves the selective identification of interested investors from amongst the issuing house's institutional clients and contacts. Securities are then marketed to this smaller number of larger investors. A placing may be represented as follows.

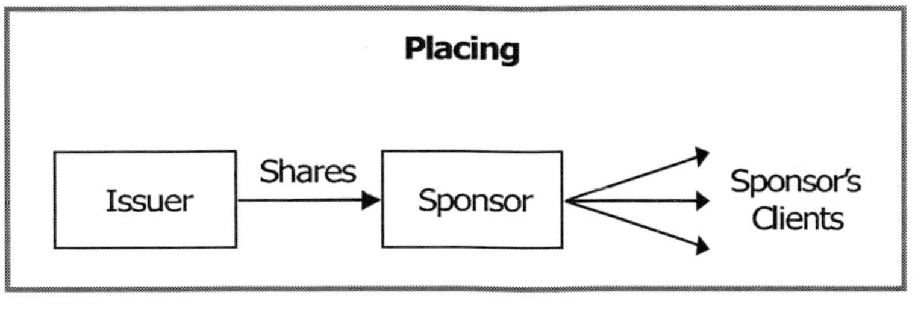

The Advantages of a Placing

The main advantages of a placing for the company are:

- **Cost.** The placing method is far cheaper than the offer for sale since it involves selling the shares to a limited number of investors rather than having to undertake a widespread general marketing and advertising campaign. In addition, the ongoing costs of maintaining and servicing a share register with a large number of small shareholders will be substantially more.
- **Targeting of investors.** The placing gives the company the opportunity to target an appropriate investor base and to select its shareholders more carefully.
- **Speed.** The placing may be carried out much more quickly than a public offering.

Intermediaries Offer

An intermediaries offer is where the shares are offered only to intermediaries such as stockbrokers, who apply to subscribe for shares on behalf of their own clients for onward sale to them. It is somewhat quicker and cheaper for the issuer than an offer for sale but gives more opportunity for the public to participate than with a placing. It can be represented diagrammatically as follows.

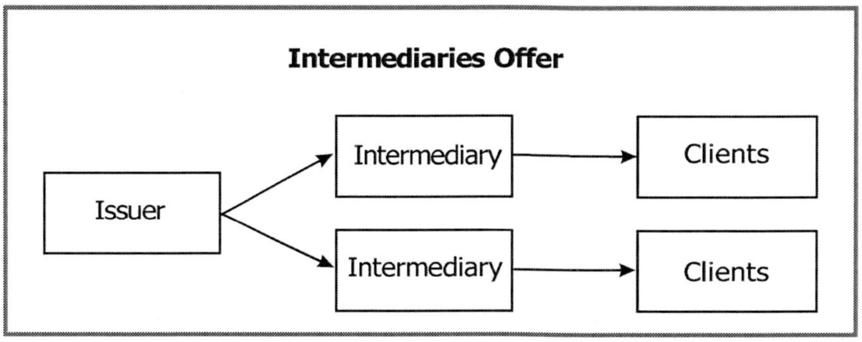

Introduction

Offers for sale/subscription, placings and intermediaries offers are all marketings of shares in that the company receives cash and issues shares in exchange. Where an issuer is not seeking to raise cash, it may elect to come to the market through an introduction. This does not involve marketing, since no new shares are issued. All that happens is that existing shares continue to be owned by the existing shareholders but are 'introduced' to trading on a Recognised Investment Exchange such as the Stock Exchange.

To ensure sufficient liquidity in the shares, the FCA will therefore only allow an introduction to be used as a means of achieving a listing if the securities are of such an amount and are so widely held that they will be marketable when listed. A shareholder statement confirming this must be submitted to the FCA.

Examples of situations where this may be appropriate include:

- A large, perhaps employee-owned, private company that has a substantial shareholder base
- A demerger, where one listed company distributes shares in a major subsidiary to its own existing shareholders and seeks a listing for that subsidiary
- An overseas company which already has a listing overseas and wishes to access the UK markets
- An AIM-traded company seeking to move to the main market

Reverse Takeovers

Introduction

A reverse takeover is typically a situation where a listed company makes a share-for-share offer for the shares of an unlisted company. The unlisted company, however, is substantially larger than the listed company making the offer. This means that the unlisted company's management and its shareholders effectively control the new listed company. The major purpose of carrying out the transaction in such a way that the smaller listed company makes the acquisition rather than the other way round is to achieve a listing for the unlisted company.

An example of this was when Star Computer Group plc, a listed company, acquired PizzaExpress Limited, an unlisted company, plus some other smaller companies associated with PizzaExpress, and then renamed itself PizzaExpress plc. In this case, of the 53 million shares in issue in PizzaExpress plc (née Star) after the acquisition, 36 million were issued as a result of the acquisition of PizzaExpress Limited and the other companies. It can be seen that the original shareholders of the listed company had therefore lost control through the acquisition.

Before

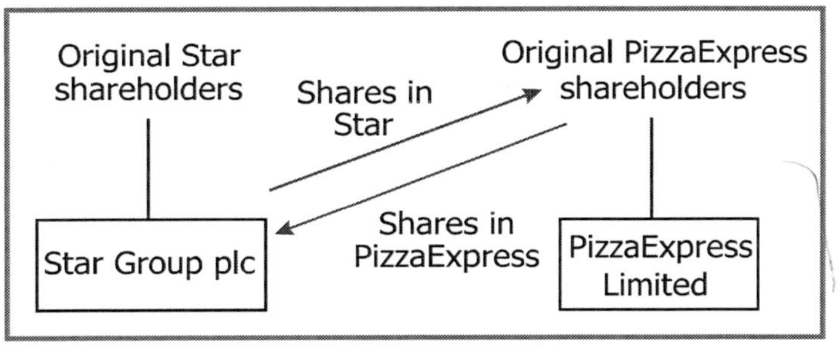

After

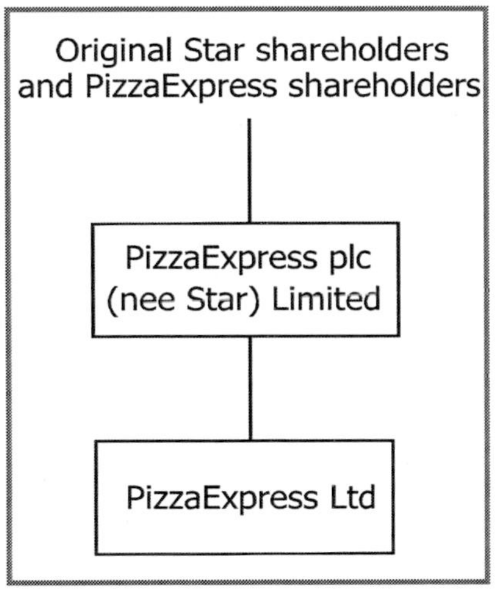

Rationale for a Reverse Takeover

A reverse takeover does not in itself necessarily make obtaining a listing any easier, since the enlarged group must apply for listing for the new shares issued as if it were a new applicant for listing. Unless there are specific benefits related to the reverse takeover, then it may be better for a private company to apply for a listing itself and complete a share issue.

Circumstances that may favour a reverse takeover are as follows:

- An existing listed company has lost its direction and lacks investor confidence with its existing business offering no scope at all.
- The listed company has a large cash balance, which can be released into the private company's business, providing funds for expansion, rather than being paid out to shareholders of the listed company.
- The listed company has a good shareholder base for the private company to access.
- The listed company has tax losses which may become available to the private company to shelter profits.

In these circumstances, the reverse takeover can be useful for both the private company's and the listed company's shareholders. However, there are potential risks, as follows:

- There may be unknown liabilities in the accounts of the listed company.
- There may be a risk that a mandatory offer will arise under Rule 9 of the City Code.
- There may be two sets of advisers' fees to be paid, for both sets of shareholders, leading to increased costs.
- The private company itself must be suitable for listing as an independent entity and, for example, must have three years' results and trading history.

Definition of a Reverse Takeover

A 'reverse' is defined in the Listing Rules (*LR5.6.4*) as where any of the following ratios give a figure of 100% or more.

- The value of the gross assets acquired by the listed company compared with the gross assets of the acquiring listed company itself.
- Net profit before tax attributable to the assets acquired compared with net profit before tax of the acquiring company.
- The consideration given compared with the market value of the Ordinary share capital of the acquiring company.
- The gross capital (see below) of the acquired assets compared with the gross capital of the acquiring company. Gross capital for the acquired company is given by the aggregate of the consideration, the value of any shares or debt not being acquired, all other liabilities (excluding current liabilities but including minority interests and deferred tax) and, if applicable, net current liabilities. Gross capital for the acquiring company is calculated in a similar way, being the aggregate of its shares and debt, all other liabilities and, if applicable, net current liabilities.

In addition, a reverse takeover will occur where there is a fundamental change in the business or a change in board or voting control for the listed company. The FCA considers that the following factors are indicators of a fundamental change (LR 5.6.5):

- The extent to which the transaction will change the strategic direction or nature of its business; or
- Whether the business will be part of a different industry sector following the completion of the transaction; or
- Whether its business will deal with fundamentally different suppliers and end users.

Requirements for Reverse Takeovers

Once the decision has been taken to complete the reverse takeover, it must be announced publicly. Listing of the acquiring company's shares will then be suspended until, it has prepared and published a class 1 circular, after which it will be restored. The transaction must then be approved by shareholders, at an EGM, following which the new shares will be issued (with listing particulars being prepared).

Pricing the Flotation

The offer price may be set in either of the following ways.

Fixed Price or Tender Offer

A fixed price offer is where the price per share is fixed by the company in advance of the offer and the public is invited to subscribe at that price. A tender offer is where the public are invited to tender for shares, offering whatever price they think is appropriate subject to a minimum tender price set by the company. The company will set a strike price for the offer based on tenders received and all successful tenderers will pay the same strike price. Investors who tendered at higher prices will receive preference.

Illustration of a Tender

XYZ plc wishes to issue 1,000 shares by way of tender and sets a minimum tender price of £2.00 per share. The following tenders are received.

Tendering Investor	No. of Shares Tendered for	Price per Share
A	500	£4.00
B	700	£3.00
C	700	£3.00
D	600	£2.00

XYZ plc could theoretically set the strike price at £3.00 per share, issue 500 shares to A and 250 shares each to B and C at this price, with no shares being issued to D. In practice, the price may be set at below £3.00, say at £2.90, in order to stimulate trading in the after market.

The Advantages of Each Method

The advantages and disadvantages of each method can be compared as follows:

Fixed Price	Tender
Certainty of price	Uncertain price
Easier for private investors to understand	Harder for the private investor, but no problem for professionals
More difficult to price	Price is set by the market
Stagging is possible	Less scope for stagging

Overall, if the company and its existing investors wish to achieve wide share ownership and to appeal to the public in general, the fixed price offer is likely to be the better alternative. If the company wishes to target its investor base more carefully and to ensure that it issues shares so as to obtain best value for existing shareholders, the tender approach is likely to be superior.

Bookbuilding

The bookbuilding approach is, to some extent, a merging of the two above methods, the fixed price offer and the tender. It is especially relevant for very large issues of securities that would be difficult to underwrite because of their size. The idea of bookbuilding is that the issuing house gauges demand for the issue prior to setting a fixed price for the offer. Investors are asked to indicate, either on a firm or uncommitted basis, the best price that they will offer and the maximum number of shares that they will buy at particular prices. This information enables the issuing house to build up a demand curve and establish the most appropriate offer price for the issue.

The advantages of using bookbuilding are that it can build up creative tension and increase demand for the shares and the final issue price. It is highly suitable for large issues where underwriting would not be possible due to the size of the risk to which the underwriters would be exposed. It is already well established as a technique in the US and, now that it has been used successfully in a large number of issues, has become accepted in the UK.

The technique does have potential problems. While creative tension may drive the issue price up for a popular share, there is the possibility that investors will all wait to see what others do, particularly with a doubtful issue and uncertain markets. If no-one is prepared to take a lead then the issue may never get off the ground. In addition, it is possible for investors to sell the stock short prior to the issue in an attempt to drive the price down for the new issue. After the issue, the shares can be repurchased at a lower price.

In order to combat these problems, the issuing house must:

- Establish an anchoring market place to get the issue off the ground
- Have a sophisticated computer system to enable global demand to be accurately tracked on an instantaneous basis
- Have in place detection techniques to identify sellers of the stock prior to the issue. This will require good relations with market participants so that all sellers can be identified.
- Have the muscle to punish institutions that sell short in the above fashion
- Have the ability to stabilise the after market, possibly by use of call options on a tranche of shares. This is often referred to as a **greenshoe option**.

Greenshoe Option

A greenshoe option arises where there is an overallocation of shares into the market by the issuing house, typically representing around 15% of the whole issue. The issuing house is short the shares as a result, but is covered through holding a call option on the same number of shares, exercisable on the company. If the share price in the market falls, the issuing house will close its short position by buying shares in the market, hence increasing demand and stabilising the price. If the share price rises, the issuing house will exercise its call option, buying additional shares from the company. In this case, no stabilisation takes place and the company has actually issued more shares into the market.

Secondary Offerings

If a company already has a listing, the FCA is concerned to protect the interests of existing shareholders. It therefore confirms the pre-emption rights requirement of the Companies Act 2006, which provide that whenever a company issues new shares for cash, these shares are offered in the first instance to the existing shareholders in proportion to their existing shareholders. Thus the main methods for a secondary offering are pre-emptive issues – ie offers to existing shareholders in line with their pre-emption rights. Any non pre-emptive issue must be approved by shareholders.

Rights Issues

A rights issue is an offer to existing shareholders to subscribe for new shares in the company in proportion to their existing shareholdings. Shareholders have the right, but not the obligation, to acquire new shares or to sell their entitlement to the shares. Rules for rights issues are found both in the Companies Act 2006, and in the Listing Rules.

Procedures for a Rights Issue

Initially shareholders are sent a circular which provides full details of the rights issue and proposals by the issuer. The contents of the circular are specified by the Listing Rules (*LR 13*) and its issue must be approved by the FCA before posting. The circular is accompanied by a provisional allotment letter (PAL), setting out each shareholder's entitlement to a specified number of new shares, proportionate to their existing holding.

A PAL is a temporary document of title. This means that until definitive share certificates are produced, this letter is proof of the shareholder's entitlement to the new shares. It is renounceable, which means that the shareholder may renounce his entitlement by selling it to someone else. In practice, the holder of the renounceable letter has a number of options:

- Take up the rights to subscribe himself. In this case, he pays the company for the new shares and receives a receipted PAL in exchange. He may then either continue to hold this PAL until definitive share certificates are issued, or sell the receipted PAL to another shareholder, who will then notify the issuer of his right to claim the definitive share certificate instead.
- Without paying for the new shares, simply sell the PAL to a third party. This results in the sale of the rights to subscribe at the set price to that third party; it is then up to the third party to take up the rights issue, pay for the new shares and notify the issuer of his right to receive the definitive share certificates. This is referred to as selling the rights 'nil paid'; the FCA may grant a listing for the securities in nil paid form *(LR 9.5.3 G)*.
- Do nothing. In this case, the company must sell the rights shares attached to the letter in the market place for the best price possible, or place then with underwriters. Any premium achieved over the subscription price is then remitted to the person to whom the rights related and who received the PAL. However, if the surplus is very small (£5.00 or less), the company need not send it to the shareholder but can retain it for the benefit of the company *(LR 9.5.4.R)*.

Indicative Timetable for a Rights Issue

Rights Issue – Summary Timetable	
Time	**Action**
Impact –1	Board meeting to approve issue Underwriting agreement signed
	↓
Impact day	Announcement Circular posted
	↓
+17 days	EGM for section 551 authority *(if required)* Post provisional allotment letters
	↓
+21 days	Dealings commence nil paid
	↓
+38 days	Last acceptance day Sell rump of issue Place unsold shares with underwriters
	↓
+59 days	Last registration of renunciation
	↓
+80 days	Issue new share certificates

Additional Rules for Rights Issues

Directors' authority to allot shares. Section 551 of the Companies Act 2006 gives authority for directors to issue and allot shares in the company, provided it is granted by an ordinary resolution of shareholders in general meeting. Such authority may be general or specific. A general authority is granted by shareholders at the company's AGM and is applicable at least for the following year up to a permissible maximum of five years. If general authority has not been granted, an EGM must be called to grant specific authority for the issue of new shares. The notice period for an EGM where only ordinary resolutions are proposed is 14 days.

Disapplication of pre-emption rights. Under s571 of the Companies Act, shareholders in listed companies may pass a special resolution dis-applying pre-emption rights for a maximum period of **five years**. This maximum period is also confirmed in the Listing Rules.

However, listed companies will normally be allowed to dis-apply pre-emption rights only for issues of new shares amounting to a maximum of 5% of the issued share capital in any one year, or 7½% on a rolling three-year basis, so long as they obtain shareholder approval. In addition, the Listing Rules do not normally permit non-pre-emptive issues at a discount of more than 10% to the middle market price of the shares. Any discount greater than 10% requires shareholder approval.

The Pre-Emption Group was set up in 2005 to produce a statement of principles to be taken into account when considering the case for dis-applying shareholders' pre-emption rights. The main points are as follows.

A request to issue up to 5% (10% for AIM listed companies) is considered to be routine. Shareholders will have to vote in favour at a special company meeting to dis-apply routine pre-emption rights. The Pre-emption Group permits a discount of 5% from the market price.

For any secondary offerings outside of these sizes or pricings, the Group requires a strong business case to be presented before approval can be obtained in a general meeting.

Exemption for Overseas Companies. Where an overseas company has a UK listing but does not have pre-emption rights in its own country, the FCA provides an exemption from the requirement for pre-emption rights.

Disclosure. The market must be notified without delay of any proposed or completed rights issue, though a Regulatory Information Service (RIS).

Last acceptance day. Shareholders must be given a reasonable time to decide on their options, and this is set as at least 21 days after posting of the PAL. No other deadlines are prescribed by law, but must be set by the company and stated in the PAL.

Last registration of renunciation. A shareholder who decides to sell his rights to another individual, whether nil paid or paid, must register the renunciation of his rights by a deadline specified by the company in the PAL. Otherwise the new share certificates will be issued in the name of the original holder of the rights.

Open Offers

An open offer is a pre-emptive offer, which is not allotted on renounceable documents. This means that although shareholders are offered shares on a pre-emptive basis, they cannot sell on the right to subscribe for the open offer shares, unlike in a rights issue.

Requirements for Open Offers

The Listing Rules state that the timetable for an open offer must be approved by the Recognised Investment Exchange (RIE) concerned (*LR 9.5.7 R*). An open offer will not be permitted where the offer price is at a discount of more than 10% to the middle market price of the shares when the offer is announced *(LR 9.5.10 (1) R*).

Placings

Providing shareholders approval the disapplication of their pre-emption rights, a company may issue shares to new investors through an institutional placing. The process here is the same as for a primary placing.

For a company which already has a listing, the FCA will not usually grant permission for a placing which is at a discount of more than 10% unless the issuer obtains specific shareholder approval for that transaction (*LR 9.5.10 R*). A general authority to dis-apply the 10% discount rule would not be acceptable. This prevents existing shareholders from losing part of their company at a price significantly lower than its market value.

Vendor Placings

A vendor placing (also called a vendor consideration placing) occurs in the context of an acquisition. The purchaser wishes to pay for the target using its own shares, however, the vendor shareholders wish to receive cash. In order to satisfy both parties to the deal, the acquirer pays for the target in newly issued shares, but arranges through its bankers for the vendor to on-sell those shares to third party investors in a pre-arranged, underwritten deal. Hence they receive the desired cash.

The transaction can be shown diagrammatically.

A Vendor Placing

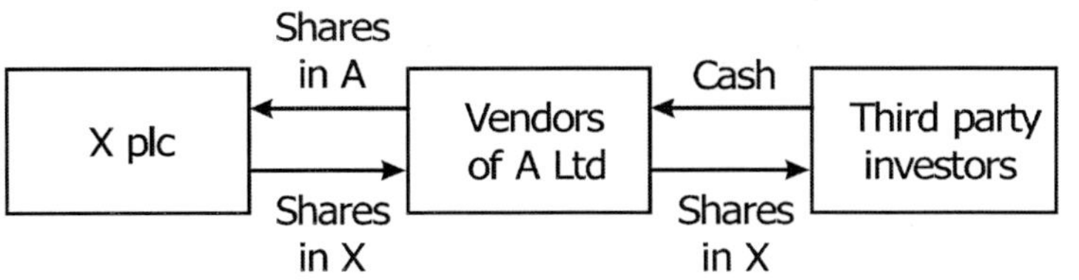

Requirements for a Vendor Placing

The Listing Rules required that all vendor shareholders must have equal opportunity to participate in the placing (*LR 9.5.9 R*). The placing must not usually be at a discount of more than 10% to the middle market price at the time of the placing, unless permitted by the FCA.

Vendor Consideration Issue

Where the vendors of A Ltd keep the shares in X plc then it is referred to as a vendor consideration issue. Alternative names for this are an acquisition or merger issue, a share-for-share exchange or a paper offer.

Clawback

When a company issues convertible loan stock which could increase the equity of the company by more than 10%, then existing shareholders have the right to subscribe for the convertible loan stock in order to protect their investment in the company.

Likewise, when a company completes a vendor placing which increases its share capital by more than 10% or is at a discount to the market price of more than 5%, then the existing shareholders may exercise clawback rights and subscribe for the shares. This will usually be achieved by means of an open offer to shareholders on a pro rata basis to their existing holdings in the company.

4 PRE-EMPTION RIGHTS

A Legal Requirement

The Basic Law

Section 561 of the Companies Act 2006 states that where a company issues shares **for cash**, then it is obliged to offer them first to existing shareholders on a pro rata basis to their existing holding in the company. The shareholders must be given at least 21 days to decide whether to purchase the shares. If they do not, then the shares can be sold to outsiders, but the price must not be better than that offered to existing shareholders.

The objective of this law is to protect the interests of existing shareholders and prevent shares in the company being issued by the directors to new shareholders, possibly at cheap prices, thus diluting the existing shareholders' interests.

Exemption for Private Companies

A private company is able to exclude the requirement for these pre-emption rights in its Memorandum and Articles if it so desires. However, it is often the case that private company Memorandum and Articles contain even more stringent rules about share issues and transferability of shares than a listed company. This is in order to protect the individual shareholders from being oppressed by a majority of other shareholders.

Exemption for Public Companies

The shareholders may pass a special resolution dis-applying pre-emption rights for a maximum period of five years, under the Companies Act 2006 and the Listing Rules.

Exemption for Overseas Companies

Where an overseas company has a UK listing but does not have to follow pre-emption rights in its own country, the FCA relaxes the requirement to give pre-emption rights to shareholders.

The Advantages and Disadvantages of Pre-Emption Rights

Arguments for Pre-Emption Rights

- Existing shareholders have the right to decide what happens to their ownership of a company, not the directors.
- Issue of shares to new investors will be at a discount to market price, to encourage them to subscribe. This means that shares are being sold on the cheap, resulting in a transfer of value from old to new shareholders.
- Pre-emption rights are a right enshrined in UK statute.

Arguments Against Pre-Emption Rights

- Very few countries actually have pre-emption rights for existing shareholders.
- Pre-emption rights merely perpetuate the stranglehold of UK institutions on UK listed companies.
- Pre-emption rights prevent companies from increasing their shareholder base. An increased shareholder base should result in greater marketability and liquidity for the shares, increasing their price.
- Companies are unable to issue shares into strategically important market places such as the US or China, where they have a commercial presence.
- Companies lack the flexibility to issue shares in the most attractive market place where the shares are in most demand.
- High overseas demand for the shares will mean that they do not need to be issued at a significant discount to market value. Any transfer of value is more than offset by increases in share price due to accessing a greater pool of demand and improving the shares.

5 Share Repurchases

General Rules

Legal requirements covering repurchase of its own shares by a company are contained in the Companies Act 2006. The purpose of the legal rules is to protect creditors of the company by ensuring that the company does not reduce its share capital and non-distributable reserves (known collectively as the **'creditors' buffer'**) as a result of the repurchase.

A repurchase may be completed **off-market** or **on-market**. An off-market purchase is where the shares are either not purchased on a recognised investment exchange (RIE) or purchased on an RIE, but are not subject to a marketing arrangement on that RIE. A marketing arrangement is where the shares are listed on the exchange or the company has been afforded dealing facilities on the exchange.

For an off-market purchase, the terms of the contract of purchase must be approved by special resolution prior to the purchase taking place. For a public company, the authority to make the repurchase must expire within 18 months of the resolution being passed.

For an on-market purchase, an ordinary resolution is required, specifying the maximum number of shares to be purchased, the maximum and minimum prices to be paid and the date on which the authority expires. For a public company, this cannot be greater than 18 months after the resolution is passed.

Public Companies

Public listed companies can repurchase shares and rather than cancel them, hold up to 10% of their issued share capital as treasury shares. The company is then permitted to sell the treasury shares at a later date.

Private Companies

Private companies may repurchase their own shares even if the creditors' buffer is reduced as a result. The extent by which the creditors' buffer is to be reduced is known as the permissible capital payment. However, if a private company wishes to reduce its creditors' buffer, it must comply with certain requirements:

- As much of the repurchase as possible must be financed from distributable reserves, ie the distributable reserves must be zero before the creditors' buffer can be reduced.
- Any capital payment must be approved by special resolution.
- The directors must make a statutory declaration that there are no grounds on which the company could be found unable to pay its debts and can continue as a going concern for the next year. A director who makes such a declaration without having reasonable grounds for doing so is liable to imprisonment and/or a fine.
- An auditors' report must be annexed to the statutory declaration stating that the auditors have inquired into the company's affairs, the capital payment has been properly calculated and they are not aware of anything to indicate that the directors' declaration is unreasonable.

Accounting Requirements

The examples below show the accounting treatment, firstly for a public listed company that repurchases shares and cancels them, and secondly, if the same company repurchases shares, holds them as treasury shares and then subsequently sells them.

EXAMPLE

Share Repurchase and Cancelling of Shares

We will illustrate a share repurchase by considering a company which has 1 million £1 Ordinary shares in issue at a current market price of £3, and which has the following summarised balance sheet.

Summarised Balance Sheet	£'000
Net Assets	2,500
Share Capital	1,000
Share Premium	500
Profit and Loss	1,000
	2,500

Our company wishes to repurchase 100,000 shares from a particular shareholder at the current share price of £3. The repurchase will be financed out of cash reserves.

SOLUTION

Repurchase Old Shares

We are repurchasing 100,000 old shares, at a price of £3 per share. Hence, the impact will be reducing the creditors' buffer by £100,000.

	£
Cash down	300,000
Share capital down	100,000
Profit and loss reserve down	200,000

Maintain Creditors' Buffer

The net effect is that our creditors' buffer has been reduced by £100,000 and this now needs to be reinstated by transferring £100,000 from the profit and loss reserve into a capital redemption reserve. The impact of this will be:

	£
Capital redemption reserve up	100,000
Profit and loss reserve down	100,000

Summary

The overall position is illustrated below.

	Before £'000	Repurchase £'000	Maintain Buffer £'000	After £'000
Net assets	2,500	(300)	–	2,200
Share capital	1,000	(100)		900
Share premium	500			500
Capital redemption reserve	–	–	100	100
Creditors' buffer	1,500	(100)	100	1,500
Profit and loss	1,000	(200)	(100)	700
	2,500	(300)	–	2,200

This illustration shows that the creditors' buffer is being maintained at £1.5m following the repurchase. Also the repurchase itself (costing £300,000) has been financed from the distributable reserves – the profit and loss account (reduced by £300,000) satisfying the general rule above.

EXAMPLE

Share Repurchase and Holding Shares as Treasury Shares

Using the same company, the following illustrates the accounting if the company were to hold the shares as treasury shares rather than cancel them. We also illustrate what the accounts would look like if the company subsequently sold the treasury shares for £4 each, a higher price than they were acquired for.

Repurchase Shares

We are repurchasing 100,000 shares at a price of £3 per share. Hence, the impact will be:

	£
Cash down	300,000
Profit and loss reserve down	300,000

There is no reduction to the creditor's buffer because the shares have not been cancelled and therefore, there has been no impact on the share capital account.

Subsequent Sale of Shares

We are selling all 100,000 shares for a higher price of £4. Hence, the impact will be:

	£
Cash down	400,000
Share premium up	100,000
Profit and loss reserve up	300,000

The distributable reserves are replenished up to the amount that they were previously written down on acquiring the shares (£300,000). Any sales proceeds in excess of this amount are included in the share premium account.

Summary

The overall position is illustrated below.

	Before	Repurchase	After Repurchase	Sale	After Sale
	£'000	£'000	£'000	£'000	£'000
Net assets	2,500	(300)	2,200	400	2,600
Share capital	1,000	–	1,000	–	1,000
Share premium	500	–	500	100	600
Creditors' buffer	**1,500**	**–**	**1,500**	**100**	**1,600**
Profit and loss	1,000	(300)	700	300	1,000
	2,500	(300)	2,200	400	2,600

This illustration shows that the creditor's buffer is being maintained at £1.5m following the repurchase, just as in the previous example. Also, the repurchase itself has been financed from the distributable reserves. The advantage of holding shares as treasury shares is that when they are subsequently sold, the distributable reserves are replenished up to the amount that they were previously reduced by, as a result of the repurchase (£300,000). However, if in the first Example the company were to subsequently issue shares, these would have to be brand new shares and the accounts would simply be:

Cash up
Share capital up
Share premium up

Hence, the profit and loss reserve would not be replenished and would still be reduced by £300,000.

Listing Rules Requirements

General Requirements for Buy-Backs

The rules relating to share buy-backs apply to companies with equity or preference shares listed.

A decision by a company to seek shareholder permission to purchase its own shares must be disclosed through its RIS without delay, and shareholder approval is required before shares may be repurchased.

Shareholders must be sent a notice of the EGM, together with a circular stating the following (*LR 13.7.1 R*).

- The directors' intentions, where the authority sought is general (ie where the intention is to buy shares in the market)
- The names of the vendors of the shares and the details of the contract, where the authority is specific (ie where specific vendors are identified)
- Details concerning the maximum and minimum prices to be paid

In general, no share repurchases may be made in any period prohibited by the Model Code for directors' dealings (*LR 12.2.1 R*). This is covered in more detail below.

Where less than 15% of the company's share capital is to be repurchased in a year and the purchases are made on market, the price paid must not be more than 5% above the average market price for the five business days prior to the purchases (*LR 12.4.1 R*). Where 15% or more is to be published, the repurchase must be by means of a tender offer to all shareholders (*LR 12.4.2 R*). Where the repurchase is made by way of tender offer to all shareholders, this pricing limit does not apply.

Where shareholder approval is granted, but prior to any actual purchases, the issuer must disclose the grant of the approval by no later than 07:30 on the day following the approval by shareholders, stating the reason for the purchase, the maximum and minimum price to be paid for shares, the maximum number of shares to be acquired, and the date of expiry of the authority.

Purchases actually made must be disclosed publicly (through an RIS) by no later than 07:30. on the business day following the day of the purchase (*LR 12.4.6 R*). This must state the date of purchase, the number of shares purchased, the average price paid, the number of shares purchased for cancellation and the number to be held as treasury shares.

Legal Requirements for Share Buy-Backs

Public limited companies may generally only fund a repurchase of shares out of distributable profits. A limited company may fund a repurchase out of share capital and undistributable reserves but the directors must make a solvency statement for the company, reported on by the auditors.

Where a company intends to make repurchases on-market, it must seek shareholder approval, through the passing of an ordinary resolution specifying the maximum and minimum price which will be paid and the maximum number of shares to be repurchased.

Where a company intends to make repurchases off-market, the specific purchase contract must be approved by a special resolution of shareholders, requiring a 75% majority voting in favour.

Once shares have been repurchased, the company must give details of the purchases in its next annual report, and must notify the Registrar of Companies of any repurchases made.

Treasury Shares

Companies carrying out a buy-back may hold such shares as treasury shares, as long as the following criteria are met:

- Treasury shares must comprise no more than 10% of the company's issued share capital.
- Shares must be UK listed, AIM shares or EEA listed; private or unlisted companies may not have treasury shares.

If the criteria are not (or cease to be) met, the shares must be cancelled. The company's officers will be liable to a fine if the company is in default.

The company will appear as a member of itself on its share register in respect of the shares; they cannot be held by a nominee on the company's behalf, so may only be held through CREST if the company is a CREST member or sponsored member. Treasury shares do not carry the normal voting, dividend or pre-emption rights associated with their class; however, if the shares are redeemable the company is entitled to redemption proceeds if they are redeemed while in treasury. Any bonus shares allotted in respect of treasury shares are be treated as if they too were treasury shares purchased at the time of allotment.

The treasury shares may not be pledged as security.

The shares will be shown as a deduction to shareholders' equity in the accounts and will reduce the distributable reserves of the business. The company's accounts must show the number and nominal value of any shares held in treasury.

Selling Treasury Shares

Resale of the shares for cash is covered by the Companies Act 2006, whereby existing shareholders' pre-emption rights must be adhered to, unless a disapplication is in place. This excludes shares used to fulfil obligations under an employee share scheme.

ABI guidelines governing the size of non pre-emptive issues (no more than 5% in any one year) also apply to the sale of treasury shares. However, the rolling limit of 7.5% in any three years may be exceeded at the ABI's discretion, to cater for sales or cancellations of treasury shares.

Any sale of treasury shares must be for cash. The corresponding entry in the balance sheet is a restatement of distributable profits. Any excess of the selling price over the buyback price will be credited to the share premium account; otherwise the proceeds are a realised profit.

General Reasons for Repurchasing Own Shares

Reasons for purchasing own shares include the following:

- To pay surplus cash to shareholders as an alternative to dividends
- To increase the level of financial gearing, borrowing cash to finance the repurchase
- To signal to investors that the share price is too low and the company is undervalued
- To increase the share price and earnings per share. (This will be achieved if the interest received on cash surpluses used to finance the repurchase is lower than the returns generated on the main operations of the company.)
- To buy back unwanted share holdings in a private company that cannot be sold on the Stock Exchange
- To provide an exit route for venture capitalists
- Part of a capital reorganisation where a company repurchases preference shares and issues new equity shares
- An employee share scheme where a company buys back the shares from employees when they leave the company

Reasons for Holding Shares as Treasury Shares rather than Cancelling Them

Reasons for holding shares as treasury shares are:

- These shares are available for subsequent sale for cash or transfer into an employee share scheme.
- Provides the company with greater flexibility in managing their share capital, leading to a reduction in the cost of funding for the company.
- The accounting treatment is such that a company has the potential to restore the distributable profits used when the shares were bought back. When the shares are sold out of treasury, the sales price replenishes the distributable reserves up to the amount lost on their acquisition.

Taxation Implications

The exact tax implications depend on the precise nature of the transaction. Where the repurchase is considered as off market for tax purposes, investors will receive a tax credit. Where the repurchase is considered as on market, investors will be treated as making a capital gain on disposal of the shares.

6 Secondary Listing

An issuer generally seeks a primary listing of securities in its country of incorporation. It then may choose to obtain additional, secondary listings on other markets overseas. The issuer must still meet the regulatory requirements for listing on this additional market, thus a secondary listing entails additional costs and regulatory burdens. This is particularly true of foreign companies seeking a listing in the US, where issuers must prepare detailed US GAAP reconciliations for their financial statements. Secondary listings may be direct listings of the securities concerned, or they may be listings of GDRs or ADRs.

There are various motivations for seeking a secondary listing:

- **Access to a new investor base**

  A company with global operations can potentially appeal to a global investor base and thus a global investment fund. However, foreign investors are dissuaded from investing in an overseas companies' shares because of their unwillingness to hold foreign paper (and thus receive foreign dividends) and the consequent illiquidity that would result. A secondary listing thus makes it easier for the firm to meet its capital requirements by issuing shares to local investors traded on local markets and denominated in local currency.

- **Cheaper finance and enhance company value**

  A secondary listing can reduce a company's cost of capital by increasing the liquidity of the shares. Generally speaking, however, liquidity remains strongest in the market where the company has its primary listing. Empirical studies show that a secondary listing on the US market generally leads to an increase in share price in the domestic market of the issuer. This is likely to be more pronounced for foreign issuers domiciled in countries perceived to have weaker regulatory regimes and disclosure rules.

- **Improved investor confidence**

  Firms can use a secondary listing on markets with stringent disclosure requirements to improve their information flow to the market and thus signal their quality to outside investors. It also enables firms to demonstrate compliance with more stringent corporate governance regimes.

- **Greater publicity**

  Secondary listings tend to be associated with increased media attention, greater analyst coverage, improved accuracy of analysts' forecasts and higher quality of accounting information.

- **Facilitate foreign expansion**

  A secondary listing can make it easier to expand abroad. An acquirer can offer its own paper as consideration for a takeover. Generally, otherwise, a foreign purchaser would need to fund an overseas acquisition via cash. A foreign listing also demonstrates to local suppliers and customers that a company has a long term commitment and interest in the foreign market.

- **Improve employee retention**

  A secondary listing can improve employee relations in foreign countries by introducing share and option plans as part of the remuneration package for foreign employees.

7 Dual Listing

A dual listing company has two equal listings in different markets, ie neither is primary nor secondary. The legal structure supporting a dual listing can be complex and usually involves having two separate holding companies, each of which is listed in a different market. There are complex legal agreements supporting the structure to ensure that profits and dividends are shared appropriately. There needs to be a unified board and voting rights must be allocated appropriately between the two holding companies. Legal agreements covering the commercial activities of both entities must also be in place.

Dual listed companies often result from mergers of two existing companies, for example Unilever and Reed Elsevier (UK/ Dutch) and Rio Tinto (UK/ Australian), as opposed to being set-up as a good in their own right. A dual listing enables local investor tax advantages to be preserved and separate national heritages to be respected. Dual listed companies do offer access to additional liquidity from two separate foreign markets, but as markets become more global and secondary listings become easier additional liquidity can be achieved in this way instead. The benefit of additional liquidity is counteracted by the additional bureaucracy that results from the way the organisation is structured. In additional there can be problems with the valuation of the shares, with the possibility that the shares on one market trading at a discount to the shares in another market.

In general, investors prefer the additional transparency that comes from secondary listings and are fearful of the complexity surrounding dual-listed entities. Shell abandoned its dual listing structure in favour of unification, on the grounds that it would become more responsive and it would have clearer reporting lines. The change was welcomed by its investors.

The Listing Rules

chapter 8

Contents

1 Introduction

This chapter compares and contrasts the different listing regulations that exist, governing the main market, AIM and Plus. We look at requirements for a listing and the processes governing the issue of a prospectus. A listing timetable is considered, along with the main stages necessary to achieve a listing, including the role of the sponsor. A listed company's continuing obligations are examined, which includes rules on announcements, dealing with inside information, material transactions, related party transactions and directors' obligations.

2 The Structure of the Listing Rules

The Financial Conduct Authority (FCA) is the UK Listing Authority (UKLA) and, as such, has overall responsibility for regulating the UK stock market. The London Stock Exchange operates two markets: the Main Market and the Alternative Investment Market (AIM). FCA regulation relating to Main Market listings is set out in the Listing Rules, contained within the FCA Handbook.

To be able to list on the Main Market, a company must satisfy the admission for listing requirements from the Listing Rules. In addition, the company will also need to apply to the London Stock Exchange for admission to trading of its shares. The Stock Exchange has its own trading rules, which act in conjunction with the FCA's Listing Rules.

The Listing Rules are organised into three sections:

- **Listing Rules.** This includes twenty chapters of provisions for listing and continuing obligations, with rules and guidance shown in a single text.
- **Disclosure Rules.** This provides rules and guidance for the dissemination of price-sensitive and other information, compliant with the EU Market Abuse Directive.
- **Prospectus Rules.** This contains the rules on the format, content and approval of prospectuses, in line with the EU Prospectus Directive.

3 Standard and Premium Listings

Companies listing on the main market can choose between two types of listing: a 'premium' or a 'standard' listing. **Premium listings** are only available for listing equity shares and require adherence to a set of 'super-equivalent' rules which provide a higher regulatory hurdle than the EU minimum requirement for listing.

Standard listings cover the issuance of shares, Global Depositary Receipts (GDRs), debt and securitised derivatives that are required to comply with EU minimum requirements. A Standard listing allows issuers to access the Main Market by meeting EU harmonised standards only rather than the higher hurdle for premium listings.

Both Premium and Standard listings are available to UK and overseas domiciled companies. Both Premium and Standard listings require that a prospectus is prepared in line with the Prospectus Rules.

The Listing Rules apply to Premium and Standard listings but not all of the provisions apply to Standard listings. The following table summarises the main regulatory between the two types of listing.

Rule	Premium Listing	Standard Listing
Country of domicile	Any	Any
Inclusion in UK indices	Yes	No
Minimum market capitalisation	£700,000	£700,000
Free transferability of shares required	Yes	Yes
Historical audited financial information	Required for the last 3 years	Not required

Rule	Premium Listing	Standard Listing
Three year revenue earning record	Required for 75% of business	Not required
Three year control over majority of assets	Required	Not required
Working capital statement	Required	Not required
Proportion of shares in public hands	25%	25%
Sponsor required?	Yes	No
Publish a prospectus for admission	Yes – Prospectus Rules apply	Yes – Prospectus Rules apply
Publish preliminary and interim financial results	Yes	Yes
Announce price sensitive information	Yes	Yes
Corporate governance	Compliance with Combined Code required	A corporate governance statement should be made
Rules on directors' share dealings	The Model Code applies	No
Significant transaction rules apply	The Class Tests apply	No
Stock Exchange trading rules apply	Yes	Yes

A premium listing thus encompasses much more comprehensive regulatory requirements and compliance with the Listing Rules provisions therefore is more expensive and time-consuming. The additional cost of a premium listing may be offset by a reduction in the cost of capital due to greater investor confidence from compliance with the ;gold standard; rules.

Listing Principles

The purpose of the Listing Principles (*LR 7.2*) is to set out the overall responsibilities of listed companies in maintaining market confidence and ensuring fair and orderly markets. The Listing Principles apply to companies with a premium listing for equity shares (*LR 7.1.1 R*).

The Listing Principles state that an issuer must:

1 A listed company must take reasonable steps to establish and maintain adequate procedures, systems and controls to enable it to comply with its obligations

2 A listed company must deal with the FCA in an open and co-operative manner

There are additional listing principles for Premium Listed Companies as follows

1 A listed company must take reasonable steps to enable its directors to understand their responsibilities and obligations as directors

2 A listed company must act with integrity towards the holders and potential holders of its premium listed shares premium listed shares

3 All equity shares in a class that has been admitted to premium listing must carry an equal number of votes on any shareholder vote

4 Where a listed company has more than one class of equity shares admitted to premium listing, the aggregate voting rights of the shares in each class should be broadly proportionate to the relative interests of those classes in the equity of the listed company

5 A listed company must ensure that it treats all holders of the same class of its listed equity shares that are in the same position equally in respect of the rights attaching to those listed equity shares

6 A listed company must communicate information to holders and potential holders of its listed equity shares in such a way as to avoid the creation of a false market in those listed equity shares

The Listing Principles are designed to ensure adherence to the spirit – as well as the letter – of the rules in the interests of promoting a transparent and fair market.

4 Minimum Requirements for Listing

The basic conditions for a listing are given in chapters 2 and 6 of the Listing Rules. They are divided into generic requirements for all issuers of securities (Chapter 2) and additional requirements for commercial companies seeking a premium listing (Chapter 6). Key requirements are as follows.

The Issuer

The applicant must be incorporated (*LR 2.2.1 R*) as a public limited company (for UK issuers only). Private limited companies (those designated Limited or Ltd) are not permitted to issue shares to the public. Therefore, a private company must re-register as a public limited company (plc) before it can apply for a listing.

There are some additional requirements for premium listings:

- **The business must have a trading history.** Apart from in exceptional circumstances, the applicant must have published audited accounts which cover at least three years (*LR 6.1.3 R*) and the latest accounts must be in respect of a period ended not more than six months before the date of the listing particulars. This requirement exists to ensure that there is evidence of a company's stability and likely future success.
- **The business must be independent.** Apart from in exceptional circumstances, the applicant must be an independent revenue generating business supported by a historic revenue earning record covering at least 75% of its business and with control over the majority of its assets throughout at least the last three years (*LR 6.1.4 R*).
- **The business must be liquid.** The applicant must supply a working capital statement that indicates that the company will have sufficient working capital for at least the next twelve months (*LR 6.1.16*).

Companies that cannot meet the additional Premium listing criteria will still be eligible to apply for a standard listing.

The Shares/Securities

These regulations apply to both premium and standard listings:

- Securities must **conform to the law** in the company's place of incorporation (*LR 2.2.2 R*).
- The whole class of securities **must be admitted to trading** on the London Stock Exchange (*LR 2.2.3 R*).
- The securities must be **freely transferable** (*LR 2.2.4 R*). Many private companies' Articles stipulate that shares may only be transferred with the approval of the board of directors, or that shares to be sold must first be offered to existing shareholders prior to being made available to outsiders. Both of these conditions prevent free transferability and are not permitted for listed companies.
- The securities must have a **market capitalisation of at least £700,000 in the case of shares and £200,000 in the case of debt** securities (*LR 2.2.7 R*). These limits may be

disapplied if the FCA is satisfied that securities of a lower market value would be adequately marketable, although this would be unusual.

- **All of** the **securities** of any **class** must be **listed** (*LR 2.2.9 R*).
- **Convertible securities** are only to be admitted to listing if the securities into which they are convertible (or the securities to which they relate) are already or will be listed. (*LR 2.2.12 R*).

There are additional regulations for premium listings only:

- A **sufficient number of the shares must be in the hands of the public**, to ensure that the secondary market for the shares is sufficiently liquid and the shares are marketable (*LR 6.1.19 (3) R*). This requirement is known as the 'free float' requirement and will be satisfied where at least 25% of the shares are in public hands. A lower percentage than 25% may be permitted if the shares will nevertheless be sufficiently marketable.
- **Warrants or options to subscribe for shares must not exceed 20% of the issued equity.** Rights under employee share schemes are not included in this (*LR 6.1.22*)
- In the case of UK applicants, shares must be **eligible for electronic settlement** (*LR 6.1.23*).

5 Prospectuses

When is a Prospectus Required?

The Prospectus Rules section of the Listing Rules details when a prospectus is required, the contents and format of a prospectus, the processes for approval, publication and advertising, and other relevant provisions.

A prospectus is a detailed document required by the Prospectus Directive, in the following circumstances:

- **When an offer of securities is made <u>to the public</u> in any EU member state.** An 'offer' includes any 'communication to persons in any form and by any means, presenting sufficient information on the terms of the offer and the securities to be offered, so as to enable an investor to decide to purchase or subscribe to these securities'. 'Securities' means transferable securities – eg equities and debt securities, or tradable warrants or options – not stock options.
- **When securities are admitted to trading <u>on a regulated market</u> in the EU.** This includes admission to trading on domestic 'second markets' and trading facilities, provided that they are a 'regulated market' as defined in the Investment Services Directive. This does therefore include Premium and Standard listings on the Main Market of the London Stock Exchange; but not the Alternative Investment Market, which is an 'Exchange-Regulated Market'.

There are a number of exceptions to this requirement. In particular, issues of securities with a maturity of less than 12 months such as short-dated debt instruments are excluded; so are corporate issuers offering debt and equities where the total size of the offer is less than €2.5m over a 12-month period.

Additionally, the Prospectus Directive provides a number of exemptions which apply as long as the securities are **not** admitted to trading on an EU regulated market. In particular, these include:

- Offers to 'qualified investors' only. Qualified investors are defined as legal entities which are authorised or regulated to operate in the financial markets, as well as other entities whose corporate purposes are solely to invest in securities, national and regional governments and central banks.
- Offers to fewer than 100 people per EU member state, excluding qualified investors

- Offers where the minimum subscription per investor, or minimum denomination per unit of stock, is at least €50,000 ('wholesale' issues)
- Offers where the total consideration is under €100,000 over a 12-month period

Further exemptions from the requirement for a prospectus apply where the securities **are to be** admitted to trading on an EU regulated market. These apply to secondary issues in certain circumstances, such as:

- Conversion of existing securities
- Merger and takeover issues
- Employee share issues
- Admission to trading of shares involving less than 10% of a class already issued, over a 12-month period

Generally speaking, then, primary issues of equity, most significant secondary issues of equity, and substantial issues of debt, **will** require the production and approval of a prospectus whose format and content is in line with the Prospectus Directive.

Format of the Prospectus

The prospectus can be a single document or comprise three separate documents (*PR 2.2.1 R*). The prospectus must contain: a **summary** of approximately 2,500 words using non-technical language which gives information on the directors, advisors, financial performance, reasons for the offer, risks and prospects; a **registration document** containing the detailed information on the issuer and valid for up to twelve months; and a **securities note** containing a description of the securities for which listing is sought (*PR 2.2.2 R*).

Where a three-part prospectus is used, the issuer may file a registration document in advance, with or without approval by FCA. At the time of issue of securities, the issuer must then seek approval for its securities note and summary (and registration document, if not already approved). Each must be approved separately, but jointly they comprise a valid prospectus.

All necessary information must be provided in the documents to enable investors to make an informed assessment of various factors (*PR 2.1.1 R*). It is also acceptable to incorporate information by reference, meaning that the prospectus could refer potential investors to recently published documents, for example financial statements (*PR 2.4.1 R*).

Contents of the Prospectus

The Prospectus Rules set out the minimum information to be included in a prospectus, but this varies according to the type of issuer, the nature of the securities and the size of the issue.

Appendix 3 to the Prospectus Rules provides a building block approach, whereby issuers consult a number of different Annexes, according to the type of securities to be issued and the circumstances involved, to extract the information requirements for the relevant section of their particular prospectus.

(1) Persons responsible

There will be a declaration by those accepting responsibility for the document, stating that it is in accordance with fact and that there are no material omissions. Primary responsibility for the document rests with the directors of the issuer. This will be accompanied by details of the auditors and any other advisers (for example the sponsor, bankers or legal advisers) whose statement or report forms part of the prospectus.

(2) Information relating to the issuer

The detailed requirements include:

- Incorporation details
- Domicile and legal form
- Summary of important events in history
- Investments
- Business overview (including principal activities and markets)
- Organisational structure
- Operating and financial review
- Significant assets
- Capital resources
- Details of directors, including experience and remuneration policies
- Board structure and practices
- Corporate governance information, including internal controls and statement of compliance with regulation
- Major shareholders
- Related party transactions

(3) Trend Information

Details of significant historical trends and information about the issuer's prospects in the current financial period. Forecast information does not have to be included but, if it is, assumptions must be detailed and the forecast must be accompanied by an accountants' report.

(4) Risk Factors

There must be prominent disclosure of risk factors that are specific to the issuer or its industry.

(5) Financial Information

- The latest audited three year historic accounts, accompanied by the audit reports
- Most recent interim results if applicable
- Pro-forma financial information, to show how the transaction is expected to impact the balance sheet and income statement of the issuer
- Details of dividend policy
- Details of any significant change to the trading or financial position from the latest reporting period end

(6) The Issuer's Share Capital

- Details of issued share capital, and authorised but unissued share capital
- Changes to share capital in the last three years
- Details of outstanding convertibles, warrants etc

(7) Material Contracts and Display Documents

There needs to be included a summary of all material contracts entered into in the last two years and details of all documents available to be inspected (including the memorandum and articles of association, directors' service contracts and previous years' audited accounts.)

Omission of Information

The FCA permits information to be omitted from a prospectus, where the inclusion of it would be against the public interest, or it is of minor importance, or would be seriously detrimental to the interests of the issuer. Additionally, the Prospectus Directive allows omissions of information which is inappropriate to the issuer's legal form, its activity, or the securities concerned (*PR 2.5.1-2 R/D*). FCA permission to omit must be sought in advance of publication of the prospectus.

Approval of a Prospectus: 10/20 Day Documents

Where a prospectus is required for an offering of shares, it must be approved by FCA in advance. In this respect, a wide range of documents needs to be submitted to the FCA in draft form. In a primary (initial) offering, or where there are complex issues involved, the deadline is 20 business days prior to the intended publication of the prospectus (*PR 3.1.3 R*). Where a company is not a new applicant, but is seeking admission to listing of additional new securities, the drafts need to be submitted 10 business days in advance. The documents required must be submitted in draft but substantially in final form, and in duplicate in hard copy or electronic format. They are as follows (*PR 3.1.1 R*):

- A completed 'Form A' seeking approval
- The prospectus
- A cross-reference sheet, linking items in the prospectus to those in the schedules and building blocks in the PD Regulation
- Any letter seeking the authorisation of omission of information from the prospectus
- A non-applicable letter confirming that items excluded from the prospectus are not applicable to the issuer
- Contact details for individuals within the issuer's firm who are knowledgeable and available to answer queries (between the hours of 07:00 and 18:00)
- Any other information required by FCA
- The fee required for approval of the prospectus

This information must also then be submitted to the FCA in final form before midday on the day when approval is required to be granted.

Passporting

Under the Prospectus Directive, prospectuses approved in one EU member state may be 'passported' into another 'host' member state. If an issuer wishes to take advantage of this, he may request a 'certificate of approval', either on filing the application for approval of the prospectus, or after the approval. In the former case, the certificate will be granted within one day of the approval of the prospectus; in the latter case, it will be issued within three days of the request. In either case, the certificate is provided to the competent authority in the host member state.

Where it is in the best interests of investors to do so, the FCA has the power to transfer the responsibility for approving a prospectus to a competent authority in another EU member state, at the request of the issuer or the competent authority.

6 Pathfinder Prospectus

The FCA may formally approve the issue of pathfinder prospectuses in certain circumstances. A pathfinder is a 'preliminary offering circular' or draft prospectus which is, broadly speaking, the entire text of the prospectus omitting only the final pricing details. Pathfinder documents must be approved by the FCA if they are to distributed beyond a 'tightly limited' number of investors. These must therefore include information as required in the Prospectus Rules.

The Prospectus Directive permits the approval of prospectuses where the final offer price and amount of securities to be offered remain to be determined; but these must contain information set out in the prospectus rules.

7 Publication of the Prospectus

Once the prospectus is approved, it must be filed with the FCA and made available to the public as soon as practicable, and before the offer of securities to the public or the admission to trading of the securities (*PR 3.2.2-3 R).*

8 Continuing Obligations

We examine here the obligations of a company once it is listed. We will look at the following areas:

- **Announcements to shareholders** – inside information and when other announcements are required
- **Significant transactions** – the existence and application of the class tests
- **Related party transactions –** definition and additional regulatory requirement
- **Directors' obligations –** directors' statutory obligations and the operation of the Model Code, including prohibited dealings

9 Announcements to Shareholders

The Disclosure Rules provide rules and guidance for the dissemination of price-sensitive and other information, compliant with the EU Market Abuse regulation. The rules apply to a premium and a standard listing on the Main Market, but not to AIM.

The overall purpose of the Disclosure Rules is stated as being to 'promote prompt and fair disclosure of relevant information to the market; and set out specific circumstances when issuers can delay public disclosure of inside information and requirements to ensure that such information is kept confidential in order to protect investors and prevent insider dealing' (*DR 2.1.3 G*).

This reinforces S397 of the Financial Services and Markets Act (FSMA), which makes it a criminal offence to conceal information dishonestly in order to create a false market, or to take a course of action which has the effect of distorting the market. In addition, Section 118 of FSMA states that action or inaction which abuses the markets is a civil offence.

Announcements of Inside Information

The primary rule within the Disclosure Rules is that **an issuer must notify a Regulatory Information Service (RIS) as soon as possible of any inside information which directly concerns the issuer** (*DR 2.2.1 R*).

Information is deemed to be 'inside' if it meets each of the tests set out in the S118 of FSMA. Specifically, these are as follows. Information which is:

- **Of a precise nature and not generally available.** The Code of Market Conduct states that generally information is available if it has been disclosed to the market, in public records, available via the internet or by payment of a fee or observable without infringing any rights of privacy.

And either:

- **For investments other than commodity derivatives** – relates directly or indirectly to one or more issuers of the investment or to one or more qualifying investment and would if generally available be likely to have a significant effect on the price of the investments (or related investments); or
- **For investments which are commodity derivatives** – relates directly or indirectly to such derivatives and users of the relevant markets would expect to receive that information in accordance with accepted market practices on **those** markets.

The definition of accepted market practice would require consideration of the level of transparency in the relevant market, the need to ensure a proper operation of supply and demand and what the regulators in that country have indicated accepted market practice is.

In addition the rules make clear that inside information could include information which that client has conveyed in connection with an order, eg to a broker. This would be the case where the information indicates circumstances that may exist and is specific enough to enable a conclusion to be drawn as to the possible effect of those circumstances on the price of qualifying or related investments.

The rules provide guidance on how issuers should interpret this definition, in deciding whether disclosure is required in each circumstances. Disclosure will generally be required, however, **where the information would be likely to be used by a reasonable investor**, and would therefore be likely to have a significant impact on the price of the qualifying investments (known as the 'reasonable investor test') (*DR 2.2.4 G*). To apply the reasonable investor test, issuers must exercise their own judgement, but should take into account the size, status and position of the company concerned in deciding what information would be significant to an investor, whilst assuming the investor is acting to maximise his own economic interests. Further, the issuer's directors and advisers should continuously monitor changes in the issuer's position, to check whether and when announcements should be made.

Specific factors to take into account include:

- The assets and liabilities of the issuer
- Expectations of future performance
- The issuer's financial position
- The course of business of the issuer
- Any major new developments in its business
- Information already disclosed to the market

Dissemination of Inside Information

The prescribed method of dissemination of inside information is that all disclosures should be made as soon as possible, through a Regulatory Information Service (RIS) (*DR 2.2.1 R*). An issuer's disclosure obligation is fulfilled as soon as the relevant announcement has been forwarded by them to the RIS.

In addition, issuers must publish all inside information disclosed through an RIS, on its own internet site no later than the close of the business day following the RIS announcement, and this information should be available on the issuer's website for at least one year following the posting. This is not an alternative to the RIS disclosure, nor should it be posted here in advance of the RIS disclosure (*DR 2.3 R*).

Where possible, all inside information disclosed should be announced at the same time in all jurisdictions where its investments are traded or listed.

Exceptions

There may be cases where public disclosure of inside information would be **detrimental to the legitimate interests of the issuer**. This might include impending developments or negotiations in progress, in particular in relation to refinancing. In these circumstances, the issuer may delay the disclosure, provided that the delay would not be likely to mislead the public, and that the issuer is able to ensure the confidentiality of the information. Moreover, if any person (such as an adviser) receives this information, it is regarded as having a duty of confidentiality towards the issuer. However, any decision to delay disclosure of information remains the responsibility of the issuer.

Delay will not be permissible when there is rumour or speculation in the market about the inside information, where the price of investments is already reacting, or where the issuer cannot ensure the confidentiality of the information (*DR 2.6.2R*). It is also not permissible to delay public disclosure of worsening financial condition, or financial difficulty.

Where disclosure is reasonably delayed, the issuer may selectively disclose this inside information to persons owing it a duty of confidentiality, provided that this is in the normal course of his duties; this would include advisers to that transaction, interested regulators, etc.

Control of Inside Information

Issuers have an obligation to have in place effective systems and controls, to ensure (*DR 2.6 R*):

- Preservation of the confidentiality of the information, by preventing unauthorised third parties gaining access to it
- Disclosure via a RIS of all inside information revealed to any third party, subject to the exemptions available above
- Immediate disclosure via a RIS, where it becomes impossible to maintain the confidentiality of the inside information
- All persons with access to inside information understand and acknowledge the duties, and the sanctions available

Insider Lists

Under the Market Abuse Directive the issuer is required to maintain an insider list. This is a list of those persons working for the issuer, whether employees, advisers or otherwise, who have access to inside information relating directly or indirectly to the issuer, whether regularly or occasionally (*DR 2.8.1 R*).

The list should show the identities of the insiders, the reason for their being on the list, and the date the list was last updated. It must be provided to the FCA on request.

Where the company includes an adviser on its insider list, it must record the name of the principal contact at that firm on its own list, and make contractual arrangements for the adviser to also maintain a list of those of its staff and associates who are also insiders in relation to that issuer, to be provided to the issuer on request. Persons on the list must be both acting for the issuer and have access to inside information. Moreover, all employees on the insider list must be trained as to the rules in relation to insider dealing.

The list should be updated whenever there is a change to the list and it should be kept for at least five years from when it was last updated.

Other Announcements

The Listing Rules and Disclosure Rules detail a number of specific announcements that must be made by issuers, which include the following:

- **Changes in share capital and capital structure**, such as new issues or redemptions of equity or debt securities (*LR 9.6.4 R*).
- **Corporate actions**, including details of dividends to be paid (*LR 9.7A.2 R*).
- **Changes** to the company's name, board of directors, details of directors, reporting dates, key advisers or directors' responsibilities (*LR 9.6.11 – 19 R*).
- **Financial Results**, including a requirement for interim results to be announced no later than two months from the period end (DTR 4.2.2). The company must publish its annual report and accounts as soon as possible after they have been approved, and in any event no later than four months from the financial year end (*DTR 4.1.3 R*). The consolidated accounts must be prepared in accordance with IFRS (DTR 4.1.6 R).

10 SIGNIFICANT TRANSACTIONS

Shareholders in listed companies delegate responsibility for the company's day-to-day decisions to directors. However, when the directors wish to enter into a material acquisition or disposal, outside the normal day-to-day activities of the company, it may require separate shareholder approval. The FCA is concerned to capture all transactions by **premium listed** companies outside the normal course of business that change a shareholders' economic interest in the assets and liabilities of the company.

Whether the transaction requires shareholder approval is dependent on its materiality, which is established by comparing the size of the business/assets being bought/sold to the size of the listed company, using a number of different means of measuring size. These measures are known as the **Class Tests**, as they allow us to divide transactions into a number of classes, each with different requirements.

Transactions covered by the Class Tests include acquisitions and disposals outside the ordinary course of business, of assets or businesses by the issuer or by its subsidiaries. It also includes entering into joint ventures, where the entire joint venture is compared to the size of the issuer.

The Tests

The tests used to determine the materiality of a transaction are:

(a) Gross Assets

The gross assets which are the subject of the transaction, divided by the gross assets of the listed company. This refers to the total fixed assets plus the total current assets of each of the listed company and of the subject of the transaction, irrespective of the percentage interest being bought or sold.

(b) Profits

The profit before taxation and extraordinary items attributable to the assets acquired or disposed of, divided by those of the listed company. Note that if the transaction involves an interest in a subsidiary company which would be or is consolidated, the whole of the profit of the business acquired or disposed of should be included in the test, regardless of the actual interest bought or sold.

(c) Consideration to market capitalisation

The consideration (including the maximum amount of any deferred consideration) divided by the aggregate market value of all the ordinary shares (excluding treasury shares) for the listed company at the close of business on the day before the announcement of the transaction. If no maximum consideration is shown, then the transaction is treated automatically as a Class 1 transaction.

(d) Gross capital

The gross capital of the company or business being acquired compared with the gross capital of the listed company. Note that this test only applies to **acquisitions** of a company or business. Gross capital for the acquired company is given by the aggregate of the consideration, the value of any shares or debt not being acquired, all other liabilities (excluding current liabilities but including minority interests and deferred tax) and, if applicable, net current liabilities. Gross capital for the listed company is calculated in a similar way, being the aggregate of its shares and debt, all other liabilities and, if applicable, net current liabilities.

Results – Classifying Transactions

Class 1

If any test amounts to 25% or more, the transaction is usually a Class 1 transaction.

Class 2

If any test amounts to at least 5% but all are less than 25%, it ranks as a Class 2 transaction.

Class 3

Any transaction where none of the tests comes to 5% ranks as a Class 3 transaction.

Related Party Transactions

Chapter 11 of the Listing Rules provides additional requirements for related party transactions. Any transaction with a director or other closely connected person is a related party transaction, and requires shareholder approval if any one of the tests shown above comes to 5% or more. These are discussed further below.

Reverse Takeovers

In the case of acquisitions of unlisted companies, where any of the tests come to 100% or more, the transaction is classed as a reverse takeover.

Other points

Where an **anomalous result** would arise due to the application of these tests (eg where the test would involve comparing profits with losses), the FCA has the discretion to substitute other relevant indicators of size.

When considering the class of transaction, the FCA will **aggregate all transactions** with the same person or with connected persons, or involving a particular business or new business line, entered into **in any 12 month period**. If the aggregated transactions require shareholder approval, this is required only for the latest transaction.

Class 3 Transactions

Class 3 transactions do not require any announcement unless the transaction involves an acquisition, where the consideration to be paid includes securities for which admission to listing will be sought or a press release is to be made to the public. If an announcement is made, it must include details of any securities being issued and brief details of the transaction.

Class 2 Transactions

Announcement

A Class 2 transaction requires disclosure through the company's RIS without delay once terms have been agreed. The announcement should give details of the following:

- The business being acquired and its trade
- The consideration being paid and how it is to be satisfied
- The net profits and net assets attributable to the business
- The expected benefits from the transaction
- For a disposal, the application of the sale proceeds
- If the consideration for a disposal includes shares or securities, a statement as to whether these will be sold or retained

Shareholder approval, of the premium listed company undertaking the transaction, is not required.

Class 1 Transactions and Reverse Takeovers

Announcement, Circular to Shareholders and Shareholders' Approval

Reverse takeovers and Class 1 transactions are sufficiently material to require all of the following:

- An announcement in the same form as for a Class 2 transaction
- A circular to be sent to shareholders, after approval by the FCA
- The **transaction to be made conditional on approval by shareholders in general meeting** (ordinary resolution)
- On the completion of a reverse takeover where the target is an unlisted company, UKLA will generally cancel the listing of the securities (*LR 10.6.3 G*) and require the company to re-apply for listing as if it were a new applicant.

Contents of the Circular to Shareholders

The circular to shareholders must be approved by the FCA before it may be sent to shareholders (*LR 13.2.1 R*). It comprises a letter from the chairman of the listed company explaining the transaction to its shareholders, and seeking approval by shareholders in a general meeting. It is further backed up by detailed additional information on the issuer and the target of the transaction.

The main contents of the circular are as follows:

- The information contained in the announcement
- A summary of the acquired company's income statement record for the last three years, in the case of an acquisition of a new subsidiary
- A summary of the acquired company's most recent balance sheet, in the case of an acquisition of a subsidiary
- For disposals and other smaller acquisitions, a summary of any relevant financial information and confirmation that the value of the relevant business justifies the consideration received or paid
- A working capital letter covering the adequacy of working capital for the new group, after taking into account the acquisition or disposal
- Statement of indebtedness
- The combined group's prospects
- A statement of the effect of the acquisition or disposal on the earnings and assets and liabilities of the group (typically a pro forma statement)
- A statement by the directors acknowledging responsibility for the information contained in the circular
- Where any profit forecast has previously been published, this profit forecast must be either included or disclaimed.
- Where any synergy statement or profit forecast is included in the circular, this must be reported on by the company's advisers, and the figures included in the next published annual accounts; if the results for the period differ by 10% from the forecast, issuers should also include an explanation of the difference.

If the company to be acquired is unlisted and there has been a significant change in its business or its accounts have been qualified or unaudited in the last three years, an accountant's report must be prepared, and included in the circular.

11 Related Party Transactions

A related party transaction refers to a transaction, or an arrangement, between the company and a related party, other than one of a revenue nature in the ordinary course of business.

A related party is a director (of any company in the group); 50:50 joint venture partner and its subsidiaries; a substantial shareholder (10% or more); or an associate of each of these.

An associate is a spouse, a child, a trustee of a trust in which the related party is interested or a company where he or she (plus spouse and children) owns 30% or more of the voting rights or has control of the Board.

Where the related party is a joint venture partner, transactions requiring approval include any amendments to the joint venture agreement, exercise of any put or call options in relation to the agreement, and further investment in the joint venture.

Announcement, Circular to Shareholders and Shareholders' Approval

When a company with equity shares listed agrees to enter into a related party transaction, the FCA will normally require that an announcement is made, a circular is sent to shareholders and shareholder approval is obtained for the transaction. The circular should explain the nature of the transaction and contain a statement that the directors have been advised by an independent adviser that the transaction is fair and reasonable. An ordinary resolution must be passed at an extraordinary general meeting of the company.

The related party, and its associates, should abstain from any vote in relation to the transaction.

Exceptions to the Rule

The rules relating to related party transactions do not apply to a company if:

(a) It does not have equity shares listed

(b) It is a standard listed company

(c) The transaction relates to the issue of securities for cash that is available to other holders of securities of the same class on the same terms or relates to the conversion of or subscription rights attached to a class of security

(d) The transaction involves the receipt of shares by the director or is the grant of an option to the director under an employee share scheme that does not confer benefits only or mainly on directors

(e) The transaction is giving of credit on commercial terms or on terms no more favourable than to other employees of the company

(f) The transaction is the granting of indemnity for the director to protect him when conducting business for the company

(g) The transaction is a normal commercial underwriting transaction

(h) The transaction is small, where the tests for class purposes above all come to 5%. However, if any of the tests reaches 0.25% the transaction must be notified to UKLA, together with written confirmation from an independent adviser acceptable to the FCA that the terms of the transaction are fair and reasonable so far as the shareholders are concerned. In this case details of the transaction must also be included in the next published financial accounts.

12 Summary

Transaction	Approval of Shareholders	Circular to Shareholders	RIS Announcement
Related party transaction	Yes	Yes	Yes
Reverse takeover	Yes	Yes	Yes
Class 1	Yes	Yes	Yes
Class 2	No	No	Yes
Class 3	No	No	If new equity issued or if announced to the press

13 DIRECTORS' OBLIGATIONS

The implied duty of a director is as an agent of the company and therefore one of skill and care. In exercising their powers, directors must demonstrate fiduciary duties. If directors fail to use their powers appropriately, they can end up finding themselves personally liable for their actions. This liability may fall due to the members of the company (the shareholders, for the negligent use of the company's assets) or indeed maybe to third parties where the third party, in dealing with the company, has incurred a loss.

With regard to the liability to third parties, the extent of a director's authority is set out in several key documents:

- Articles of Association,
- Service Contracts; or
- Special Resolutions of a Company.

All of these are publicly available documents.

Directors' Duties

The duties of directors arise from both the common law and statute. Additional obligations apply to directors of listed companies, and these are found within the Listing Rules.

Common Law

Under a common law there is a general duty of skill and care attached to any agent. The level of skill and care required from a director is difficult to define and does depend very much on the director and the firm involved.

The Fiduciary Duties of Directors

Directors have a duty of utmost good faith to the Company (not to the shareholders). There are three broad areas where this applies:

- Directors are to exercise their powers for the benefit of the company as a whole,
- Directors are not to make secret profits; and
- Directors are to avoid conflicts of interest.

This final point is covered by statute in the form of the Companies Act, which requires directors to state their interests in any contract into which the company enters. The Companies Act has wide powers to excuse Directors for negligence, default, breach of duty or breach of trust, provided that the Director acted reasonably and honestly.

General Obligations Imposed by the Listing Rules

Additional obligations for directors of listed companies are dealt with in Chapter 9 – *Continuing Obligations* of the Listing Rules. Key areas are as follows:

Board Changes

Changes in the composition of the Board or the significant roles or responsibilities of its members must be notified without delay through the company's RIS *(LR 9.6.11 R)* and by no later than the end of the following business day following the decision or receipt of notice by the company.

In respect of any new director appointed, or existing director, the company must announce details of (*LR 9.6.13 R*):

- Any directorships held by him in any other quoted company during the last five years, including his current status;
- Any unspent convictions in relation to indictable offences;
- Details of any receiverships, administrations, compulsory liquidations etc in relation to companies where the director was an executive director at the time or in the previous 12 months, or for partnerships where he was a partner in the same timescale; and
- Details of any public statutory or regulatory criticisms of the director, including designated professional bodies and whether he has ever been disqualified as a director.

The disclosure must be made within five business days of the decision to appoint the new director, or as soon as possible in the case of an existing director.

Disclosure of Directors' Interests

Under the Disclosure Rules, all transactions in the shares of the company by the issuer's senior executives and their close associates, must be disclosed by them to the issuer within four business days of the day of the transaction. The disclosure must show the name of the person and issuer concerned and full details of the transaction in the shares.

Senior executives includes directors and also those who are not directors but who have regular access to the company's inside information, and the authority to make managerial decisions.

Close associates include any relative who has shared the same household as a director or senior executive in the preceding 12 months, and any company connected with a director or a senior executive.

Once an issuer receives such a notification, it is required to disclose it as soon as possible via a RIS, and not later than the end of the business day following the receipt of the disclosure.

Directors Dealing in Their Own Company's Securities – The Model Code

It is desirable that directors should own shares in their company, to align their interests with those of the company that they run. However, due to the privileged level of knowledge possessed by directors, restrictions must be placed on their dealings in shares. It is not sufficient for directors to have integrity in their share dealings; they must also be seen to have integrity.

Listed companies are therefore required to have internal rules which restrict the ability of directors to trade freely in the shares of that company. The Listing Rules provide that a listed company must *'require every person discharging managerial responsibilities, including directors, to comply with the Model Code and to take all proper and reasonable steps to secure their compliance.'* (*LR 9.2.8 R*)

A listed company may impose more rigorous obligations than those required by the Model Code. (*LR 9.2.9 G*)

Prohibitions on Dealing

The Model Code requires that directors of the listed company should not deal in its shares on considerations of a short-term nature (eg an investment with a maturity of one year or less).

Additionally, employees of the listed company or its subsidiaries who, by virtue of their position in the company, are likely to receive price sensitive information will be treated in the same way as directors for the purpose of the Model Code, and are referred to as relevant employees. Jointly, they are referred to as restricted persons.

Specifically, a restricted person will not be allowed to deal in the shares of his own company:

- In the 60 days immediately preceding the preliminary announcement of the company's annual results or half year results or, if shorter, the period between the financial period end and the results announcement. This is known as the **close period**.
- For companies reporting on a quarterly basis, in the 30 day period prior to the announcement of results or, if shorter, the period from the financial period end to the announcement (except for the last quarter of the year, which is covered by the point above). Where relevant this would also be included in the close period.
- Prior to the announcement of matters of an exceptional nature involving unpublished price sensitive information
- At any time when in possession of price sensitive information about the shares and hence prohibited from dealing by insider dealing legislation (this, together with the close period, is known as the **prohibited period**)
- Without notifying the Board of his intention to deal and receiving clearance

Procedures to be Followed on Dealing

If a restricted person wishes to deal in the company's shares, then he must first notify the chairman of the company or a designated director of his intention to do so and receive clearance in advance of the trade. Clearance or refusal to trade must be given within five business days of the request. Once clearance is given, the restricted person must deal within two business days of it being received.

For persons below Board level, the company secretary may grant or withhold approval to deal.

Clearance should not be given in any situation where the above prohibitions apply, even if the restricted person is not aware of the reason for the prohibition.

The company must keep written records to show that notification was received and clearance was given to the restricted person concerned, and a copy given to the restricted person concerned.

Exceptions to the Rules

The following dealings may be permitted:

- Exercise of share options or convertible securities where the expiry date falls within a prohibited period
- Dealings in an approved employee share scheme
- Taking up entitlements to rights
- Acceptance of a takeover offer
- Selling (but not buying) shares to meet a director's pressing financial commitment that can only be satisfied through the sale of the securities, provided that disclosure of the dealing and the circumstances is made through an RIS. The disclosure of this dealing is only required in the close period, but not in the prohibited period when the disclosure would create speculation in the market. The FCA should be consulted at an early stage in this case.

14 AIM AND ISDX

Alternative Investment Market

The Alternative Investment Market is regulated by the London Stock Exchange and provides an alternative market place for companies to trade their shares publicly. AIM offers similar benefits to a full listing but without imposing the full regulatory burden of listing on the main market. **AIM Rules are more flexible and less complex** than the Listing Rules which apply to premium and standard listings on the main market.

An admission to trading on AIM used to be regarded as a stepping stone towards obtaining a full listing. Companies now choose to remain on AIM rather than progress to the Main Market; indeed recent years have seen an increase in traffic of companies transferring the other way - from the main market to AIM, attracted by the lighter touch regulation and also the **tax advantages offered to investors.** Shareholders in an AIM-listed company only need to pay Capital Gains Tax on gains of 10 per cent, rather than the usual 40 per cent. Certain AIM holdings are also free from inheritance tax.

Market Data

Since its launch in 1995, AIM has played host to more than 3,500 companies with more than £88 billion having been raised. Of those currently on the market, about a quarter are from overseas. Many of these companies do not fit the traditional 'niche' profile of AIM companies. As at November 2015, 22 AIM companies had a market capitalisation exceeding £500m. The largest of these was Asos plc with a market capitalisation of £2.8bn. Most AIM companies have a market capitalisation in the range £5-50m.

Regulation

All AIM companies must appoint a **nominated adviser** (termed a 'nomad') to advise on the company's admission to AIM and then the on-going responsibilities of meeting the AIM requirements. The nomad must advise the London Stock Exchange on the company's initial suitability for listing to gain admission to AIM. Otherwise, there are limited initial listing requirements, for example there is no free float threshold, nor minimum market capitalisation required.

A comparative summary of listing regulation is shown below, to help you understand how the AIM requirements to compare to those of the main market.

Rule	Main market: Premium listing	Main market: Standard listing	AIM
Minimum market capitalisation	£700,000	£700,000	None
Track record required?	Yes	No	No
Free transferability of shares required	Yes	Yes	No
Requirement for 25% of shares in public hands	Yes	Yes	No
Working capital statement required	Yes	Yes	Yes
Sponsor/ nomad required	Yes	No	Yes (at all times)
Corporate governance requirements	Yes	Yes	Yes
Class tests apply	Yes	No	Yes (light – 10% threshold)
Related party rules apply	Yes	No	Yes (light – 5% threshold)
Disclosure rules apply	Yes	Yes	No
Requirement to announce price sensitive information without delay?	Yes	Yes	Yes

Rule	Main market: Premium listing	Main market: Standard listing	AIM
Prospectus rules apply	Yes	Yes	Only for public listings, otherwise an admission document is required
Half yearly financial reporting required?	Yes	Yes	Yes

ISDX

ISDX (ICAP Securities and Derivatives Exchange) was created in late 2012 after the inter-dealer broker ICAP acquired and re-branded PLUS Stock Exchange (PLUS-SX), which has been described as London's third stock market after the LSE main market and AIM. The market is lightly regulated and was established (as PLUS-SX) to help smaller companies raise capital. However, PLUS-SX struggled to attract listings thanks, in part, to the success of AIM. ISDX has said it is targeting entrepreneurial companies typically seeking access to equity capital of between £150,000 and £5 million. This would place its target market at the lower end of the companies on Aim.

ISDX describes itself as a London-based stock exchange providing UK and international companies with access to European capital through a range of fully listed and growth markets.

ISDX Growth Market

The **ISDX Growth Market** aims to provide growing **small- and medium-sized enterprises (SMEs)** from all industry sectors with a source of equity finance for companies coming to a public market for the first time, as well as being a venue for existing issuers to raise further funds.

ISDX admits companies to its ISDX Growth Market in accordance with the ISDX Growth Market Rules for Issuers, which include its application requirements and continuing obligations requirements. A fast-track admission procedure is available to applicants from the Alternative Investment Market of the London Stock Exchange (AIM), and the Access Market of the Munich Stock Exchange (Bayerische Boerse).

ICAP now have three market makers (including Peel Hunt and Shore Capital) making continuous two-way prices to maintain liquidity provision on the venue and to ensure that it operates as a primary and secondary market.

ISDX faces the prospect of competition as a **listing venue for SMEs** from NYSE Euronext's Entrepreneurial Exchange (launched in May 2013), and from the LSE, which is believed to be considering possibilities of improving opportunities for SMEs to raise equity.

Benefits of ISDX (for issuers and investors)

- Reduced regulatory requirements – there is no requirement for companies to issue a full prospectus to join ISDX
- Lower cost – ISDX is, for some companies, a cost effective flotation venue which compares favourably with other Stock Markets including AIM
- No minimum market capitalisation – the ISDX rules currently do not stipulate the minimum size of company that may be admitted to the market
- No minimum trading record - there is no minimum trading history required for companies prior to joining the market

- Tax incentives – investors in ISDX companies benefit from a range of tax advantages as ISDX is an unquoted market for tax purposes
- A potential exit route for existing Shareholders – ISDX provides existing shareholders in the company with a potential exit or part exit route if required, either at the time of the flotation or at a later time of their choosing

The main negative associated with listing on ISDX is the lack of liquidity in the market, with more delistings than listings since the market was launched at the end of 2012.

Entry requirements

Companies are required to publish an 'ISDX Growth Market Admission Document'. This is the key admission document that will contain information about the company, its operations and its strategy. Although the ISDX admission document is comprehensive, it is considerably less onerous than undertaking the preparation of a full prospectus.

In addition, the following rules apply:

- Companies are required to publish audited financial reports no more than nine months prior to the date of their admission to ISDX.
- Companies must demonstrate appropriate levels of corporate governance including having at least one independent Non-Executive Director on their board, (currently AIM companies require two Non-Executive Directors).
- Companies are required to demonstrate that they have at least 12 months adequate working capital.
- No restrictions are permitted on the transferability of shares.
- Company shares must be traded via electronic settlement.

ISDX Main Board

The **ISDX Main Board** is an **EU Regulated Market** aims to provide companies and other issuers with lower-cost admission to trading through the UKLA's Official List, or other European Competent Authority.

Issuers will be subject to the Listing Rules and the regulator's Disclosure and Transparency Rules. To join the ISDX Main Board, issuers will be required to produce a prospectus approved by the UK Listing Authority (UKLA), or other EU body that is a competent authority under the Prospectus Directive.

The application for admission to the ISDX Main Board will be made in conjunction with the issuer's application to the UKLA (or other EU competent authority for listing) for admission to the Official List under a Premium or Standard Listing.

The Advisory Team

chapter 9

Contents

1 Introduction

This chapter distinguishes between the activities of the corporate finance advisory team, namely:

- Financial advisers, including the role of sponsors and nomads
- Stockbrokers
- Lawyers
- Reporting accountant
- PR advisers
- Other specialist advisers

2 Financial Adviser

The financial adviser's responsibilities will entail the following:

- Determining the **appropriate capital structure**, taking into account the operating risks of the business. The financial adviser will suggest how best to implement any proposed changes and how to communicate these plans effectively to investors.
- **Capital and fund raising**. The financial adviser will often act as a 'sponsor' for new issues of capital (equity and debt). The role of the sponsor is set out in listing regulation and includes establishing the suitability of the applicant for listing; planning the flotation; co-ordinating other advisers; liaising with the regulatory authorities including the relevant exchange. The sponsor has other duties relating to the listing of the securities and supervision of the after-market: these will usually be fulfilled by the stockbroker (see below). The financial adviser will also supervise any secondary issues of capital (for example by a rights issue).
- **Originating and transacting mergers and acquisitions**. Deal origination refers to when the investment bank searches for potential acquisition targets for its clients. Transacting relates to the advice that the financial adviser gives its client in the process of an offer. Particular areas where the adviser can be of use include the following: planning of a bid; general 'housekeeping' to deter unwanted bids; timing of a bid; preparation of a bid and defence documents; market announcements; pricing and nature of consideration to be offered; general conduct during the bid; adherence to takeover regulation; representations to the Takeover Panel.
- **Restructuring and corporate reorganisations**. Restructuring advice includes identifying non-core activities for disposal, paying special cash dividends to shareholders, repurchasing of shares or demerging a quoted group into two separate entities. In particular, the financial adviser can devise the original restructuring idea; advise on timing; advise on implementation; prepare documents; seek appropriate taxation and legal advice; market the idea and communicate it to investors. The financial adviser will also assist in advice to companies in financial difficulties, including insolvency situations.
- **Valuations**. Many financial advisers have specialist sector valuation teams.
- **Compliance and regulatory matters**. For many corporate finance departments, the bread and butter work is general advice on compliance matters and the impact of financial transactions. Whenever a listed company is intending to complete any major transaction outside of its normal trading activities, it needs to be aware of its obligations under the regulatory framework. It also needs to consider what investor reaction is likely to be to certain announcements and how such information can be communicated effectively to investors.

The financial adviser may also fulfil a listed company's requirement to have a 'sponsor'.

Obligations of a sponsor

The sponsor is the primary adviser to an issuer of equity securities in the UK. A sponsor has responsibility for guiding the issuer as to the regulatory requirements in the Listing Rules, Prospectus Rules and Disclosure Rules. The sponsor is required to report to the FCA that the issuer has met its responsibilities under the Listing Rules (*LR 8.3.1 R*). The FCA expects the Sponsor to be its main point of contact in relation to the proposed listing (*LR 8.3.2 G*).

A sponsor is required for an issuer seeking a premium listing of shares where (*LR 8.2.1 R*):

- An issuer makes an application for listing of equity securities that requires production of a prospectus, or equivalent document
- An issuer produces a circular in connection with a Class One transaction, a reconstruction or a major share buyback, or is proposing to undertake a substantial or related party transaction
- A transfer of listing from a Standard listing to a Premium listing
- The issuer has breached listing rules and the FCA decides that a sponsor is needed to advise the company

A sponsor is needed to report to the FCA in relation to a particular transaction. For example, if a prospectus contains a profit forecast, then a sponsor must confirm to the FCA that the forecast has been prepared after due and careful enquiry.

Issuers are encouraged to retain, on an ongoing basis, a sponsor fully experienced in market practice but this is not mandatory. For transactions other than those listed above, a sponsor is not required.

Qualifications of a sponsor

A sponsor must be authorised by the FCA, or a member of a designated professional body. To qualify, a firm must satisfy the FCA that it is competent to act as such and has appropriate systems and controls to carry out its duties (*LR 8.6.5 R*).

The FCA will consider a sponsor to be competent if it has a broad range of relevant expertise in providing advice to listed companies and on the listing rules (*LR 8.6.7 R*).

Principles for sponsors

The Listing Rules set out principles for sponsors, as follows (*LR 8.3.3-6 R*):

- The sponsor is required to provide all of its services, including guidance or advice to an issuer in relation to the rules, with **due skill and care**.
- Where the sponsor gives advice or guidance to an issuer on the application of the rules, it must take all reasonable steps to satisfy itself that the directors **understand** the nature and extent of their responsibilities in this regard; and it should provide **updates** to the issuer where there are major changes to the listing or disclosure rules, or when a new director is appointed to the board.
- It should deal with the FCA in an **open and co-operative way**; deal with all enquiries raised by the FCA promptly; and disclose promptly to the FCA any material information of which it has knowledge which addresses non-compliance with the Listing Rules or Disclosure Rules.
- It should identify and manage **conflicts of interest** that could adversely affect its ability to perform its role, by putting in place adequate organisational and administrative arrangements eg Chinese walls. Disclose of the existence of a conflict is not enough.

Specific responsibilities of the sponsor

On an application for listing, the sponsor should ensure that:

- The company has satisfied all conditions and requirements for listing (*LR 8.4.2 R*)
- The directors of the company have established procedures which enable them to comply with the Listing Rules and Disclosure Rules on an ongoing basis (*LR 8.4.2 R*)
- In the case of a new applicant, the directors have established procedures to enable them to make proper judgements on an ongoing basis as to the financial position and prospects of the company (*LR 8.4.2 R*)
- The directors have concluded that the company has adequate working capital for its present requirements and the confirmation has been made after due and careful enquiry by the directors (*LR 8.4.2 R*)
- All matters relevant to the application for listing have been disclosed with sufficient prominence in the prospectus (*LR 8.4.3 (3) R*)

The Alternative Investment Market

There are also requirements for companies listed on AIM to have a financial adviser:

All AIM companies must appoint a **nominated adviser** (termed a 'Nomad') to advise on the company's admission to AIM and then the on-going responsibilities of meeting the AIM requirements. The Nomad must be retained by the AIM company at all times (the shares will be delisted by the London Stock Exchange if the company does not comply with this requirement).

To act as a Nomad, the financial adviser must be approved as a Nomad by the London Stock Exchange. To gain approval the financial adviser must:

- Be a firm or company, not an individual,
- Have practised corporate finance for at least the last two years,
- Have acted on at least three relevant transactions during that two year period, and
- Employ at least four 'qualified executives'.

Under the AIM Rules, the Nomad has a number of specific responsibilities both during a company's application for listing and then, once listed, relating to its continuing obligations:

1. The Nomad must advise the London Stock Exchange on the company's initial suitability for listing to gain admission to AIM. This will include that the company's admission document meets all regulatory requirements.
2. The Nomad should review announcements made by the company to the market via a Regulatory Information Service prior to the release of the statement. The Nomad is not required review every routine announcement if it is satisfied that the directors have 'appropriate knowledge and experience'.
3. The Nomad must monitor the trading in the company's shares particularly when there is price sensitive information that is not yet in the public domain.
4. The Nomad must ensure directors are aware of all of their responsibilities under the AIM rules and when they are required to consult the Nomad for advice.
5. The Nomad should advise the company on any changes to its board of directors. This would include ensuring that proposed new directors are suitable for the company and are fit to be a director of a public company.
6. Where an AIM company is in breach of any of the AIM Rules, the Nomad is required to inform the London Stock Exchange immediately.

3 Stockbrokers

Stockbrokers undertake a range of activities, some of which overlap with those of the financial adviser. Indeed, a stockbroker and the financial adviser may both be part of the same investment bank. Typically, a stockbroker's activities are based around the distribution of equity shares and other capital instruments in the secondary market.

Application for a Listing

When a company applies for a listing for its shares, it is required to have a sponsor. As discussed above, this may be the financial adviser. In addition, the broker will be an obvious candidate for the role. Typically the broker will be engaged in the following activities: the pricing and timing of the issue; give marketing advice; suggest the method of issue to be used; arranging and participating in underwriting; ensuring the after-market is satisfactory. Once the company has a listing, it will find it useful to keep a broker to assisting with announcements and the presentation of information to investors and to act as a source of authoritative research on the company.

Buy-Side and Sell-Side Analysts

Research on listed companies is compiled from two viewpoints. On one side there are 'buy-side' analysts who work for fund managers, recommending which courses of action to take. On the other side there are the 'sell-side' analysts who work for brokers and whose primary aim is to stimulate dealing in shares, thus generating commission income.

Authoritative Research?

All major companies will be covered by analysts from all major brokers. However, certain research departments have a reputation for being very strong in a particular sector and certain brokers have strong links with particular companies (for example, a company's nominated brokers). Reports from these sources tend to be treated as being particularly authoritative and can heavily influence a company's share price.

Communication with Analysts

It is important for a company to have a close relationship with brokers' research departments to ensure that it can communicate its message about the company's results and prospects effectively. Accordingly, analyst meetings are common and finance directors will often be very keen to assist analysts in understanding the implications of changes in economic variables and other factors for their company.

In 2012, Google released its financial results to the stock market earlier than scheduled, a mistake it blamed on its printers. The trading results showed that the company's third quarter results were well short of expectations. The report was planned to be released after the market closed (at 4pm), to allow time for analyst briefings to explain the results and give some market background to the trading performance. Instead the results were released during normal trading hours at 12.30pm. The shares dropped by 9% before trading was suspended for around two hours.

Equity Sales

The major role of the sales department is to be in regular contact with clients. As such, they will have strong links with the research department, using analyst reports as a means of drumming up interest in a particular company's shares. The objective of the sales department is to encourage trading of shares to generate commission income.

Corporate Finance

The corporate finance department of a broker is essentially the same as that of an investment bank. One key difference between the two is that traditionally they each have a different customer base. Typically, brokers have always had close links with the fund managers and investors, on whose behalf they have acted in the past. By contrast, investment banks have always had close links with the companies, their natural clients in the past.

4 ACCOUNTANTS

The traditional role of the accountant has been that of auditing and giving advice on accounting aspects of transactions. Accountancy firms often now take on a wider corporate finance role by becoming sponsors for new applicants for a listing. Accountants have successfully developed their corporate finance business, building on the large client base from their auditing activities and the fact that the audit partner often has close links with a company's board.

Accountancy firms do not have access to capital and are therefore unable to execute and underwrite deals.

Accountants' Reports

The Short Form Report

Accountants may be required to complete a report for inclusion in the prospectus/ listing particulars. The contents of the report comprise a review of a company's results, financial position and cash flows over the last three years. The short form report examines the working capital cycle and will give a conclusion on the overall solvency and liquidity position of the business. If a profit forecast has been made, the accountants will be required to examine the forecast and confirm in a letter that the forecast has been prepared correctly on the basis of the stated assumptions (but not that the forecast will be achieved).

The Long Form Report

In addition to the above, the accountant is also usually required to prepare a 'long form report' for a listing. This is a very detailed document containing the financial due diligence. It will contain a detailed financial analysis of the historical results and forecasts, together with an appraisal of financial systems and historic variances in forecasting. The assumptions upon which the forecasts are based will be examined. The scope of the report will also include other matters pertaining to the company, including details of a company's organisation, commercial activities, directors, employees, non-current assets, off balance sheet liabilities, future prospects and any other relevant areas. The report will be used by the sponsor to assist in establishing whether the company is suitable for listing and will be a useful basis for much of the content of the prospectus.

Investigations

Accountants may be required to complete a due diligence investigation into a company, typically in the context of an acquisition. Acquisitions of private companies will often be subject to satisfactory completion of an accountant's investigation. The objective of the investigation is to ensure that the company being bought is as it is described by the vendor and in its financial accounts. The investigation and subsequent report will cover all aspects of the company, including details of its assets and liabilities, results, future prospects, personnel, etc, much in the same way as the long form report referred to above.

5 Lawyers

Lawyers are likely to become involved in any transaction at a very early stage. With a flotation, the lawyers will be concerned that any documents are phrased in an exact and acceptable form from a legal viewpoint. Many hours will be spent at drafting meetings ensuring that the final version is satisfactory in this respect. In an acquisition, the lawyers will produce an acquisition agreement, which will be negotiated between the acquirer and vendor, the former trying to ensure that adequate warranties and conditions have been included and the latter trying to minimise his or her liability.

The lawyers will conduct a 'verification' exercise on all transaction documents to ensure that statements contained therein can be substantiated by underlying evidence. There will be a detailed legal due diligence exercise where all company documentation will be scrutinised including customer and supplier agreements, employee contracts, directors' service agreements and documents of title. Lawyers will advise on the employment law ramifications of a transaction, including TUPE (transfer of undertakings – protection of employment) rules.

In addition to specific legal advice on transactions, lawyers will often give tax advice and in this respect are competing with accountants.

As with accountants, lawyers who are authorised persons and on the regulator's list of approved sponsors may act as sponsors for new applicants for listing.

6 Public Relations Advisers

Public relations can be divided into two main categories, investor relations and public relations. The former is concerned with marketing of the company's shares to its investor base. The latter is concerned with presentation of a company's message to the financial world at large.

Investor Relations

The objective of investor relations is to market the shares effectively and achieve increases in the share price of the company. The role of the adviser is to identify an appropriate investor base for a company and bring the company to the attention of these investors in the most effective way.

Public Relations

The public relations (PR) adviser has a more general role and is concerned with making sure that the company presents itself effectively to the outside world. The adviser will:

- Ensure announcements are phrased effectively
- Ensure announcements are presented effectively
- Follow up announcements with analyst meetings and press briefings
- Arrange interviews with reputable newspapers for the company
- Ensure consistent and favourable coverage in newspapers and periodicals

In addition to this ongoing role, the PR adviser will aim to get involved in special projects such as rights issues and acquisitions at an early stage, to ensure that the marketing angle is developed at the very start.

7 Other Advisers/Support Services

Corporate finance transactions often draw in the services of other specialists eg sector valuation specialists, technical experts, IT consultants, strategy consultants, environmental advisers, actuaries, to name but a few. Each will prepare a report addressed to the financial adviser/company to ensure all relevant information has been sourced and is available prior to completion of the transaction.

In addition to the advisers above, a company will need a range of support services to ensure that corporate finance transactions run smoothly. Such support services include: security printers who specialise in overnight runs of confidential material; receiving bankers to accept applications for shares on a public offer; registrars to register share issues and paying agents to arrange payment of interest to debt investors

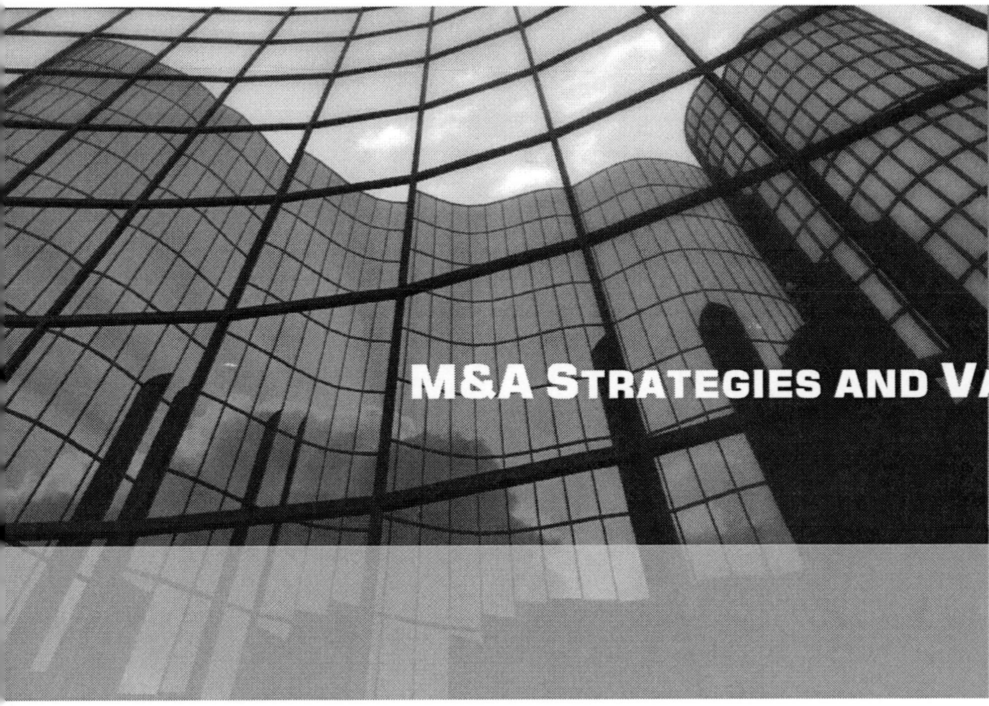

M&A Strategies and Valuation Issues

chapter 10

Contents

1 Mergers and Acquisitions as a Method of Corporate Expansion

Although growth strategy through acquisition requires high premiums, it is widely used by corporations as an alternative to internal organic growth. Companies may decide to increase the scale of their operations through a strategy of internal organic growth by investing money to purchase or create assets and product lines internally. Alternatively, companies may decide to grow by buying other companies in the market thus acquiring ready-made tangible and intangible assets and product lines.

Which is the right strategy? The right answer is not easy to arrive at. Organic growth in areas where the company has been successful and has expertise may present few risks but it can be slow, expensive or sometimes impossible. On the other hand acquisitions require high premiums that make the creation of value difficult. Irrespective of the merits of a growth strategy by acquisition or not, the fact remains that this is used by corporations extensively.

Advantages of Mergers as an Expansion Strategy

As an expansion strategy, mergers are thought to provide a quicker way of acquiring productive capacity and intangible assets and accessing overseas markets. There are four main advantages that have been put forward in the literature and these are summarised below:

Speed

The acquisition of another company is a quicker way of implementing a business plan, as the company acquires another organization that is already in operation. An acquisition also allows a company to reach a certain optimal level of production much quicker than through organic growth. Acquisition as a strategy for expansion is particularly suitable for management with rather short time horizons.

Lower cost

An acquisition may be a cheaper way of acquiring productive capacity than through organic growth. An acquisition can take place for instance through an exchange of shares which does not have an impact on the financial resources of the firm.

Acquisition of intangible assets

A firm, through an acquisition, will acquire not only tangible assets but also intangible assets, such as brand recognition, reputation, customer loyalty and intellectual property which are more difficult to achieve with organic growth.

Access to overseas markets

When a company wants to expand its operations in an overseas market, acquiring a local firm may be the only option of breaking into the overseas market.

Disadvantages of Mergers as an Expansion Strategy

An expansion strategy through acquisition is associated with exposure to a higher level of business and financial risk. The risks associated with expansion through acquisitions are:

Exposure to business risk

Acquisitions normally represent large investments by the bidding company and account for a large proportion of their financial resources. If the acquired company does not perform as well as it was envisaged, then the effect on the acquiring firm may be catastrophic.

Exposure to financial risk

During the acquisition process, the acquiring firm may have less than complete information on the target company, and there may exist aspects that have been kept hidden from outsiders.

Acquisition premium

When a company acquires another company, it normally pays a premium over its present market value. This premium is normally justified by the management of the bidding company as necessary for the benefits that will accrue from the acquisition. However, too large a premium may render the acquisition unprofitable.

Managerial competence

When a firm is acquired, which is large relative to the acquiring firm, the management of the acquiring firm may not have the experience or ability to deal with operations on the new larger scale, even if the acquired company retains its own management.

Integration problems

Acquisitions can be beset with problems of integration as each company has its own culture, history and ways of operation.

Types of Mergers

Mergers and acquisitions can be classified in terms of the company that is acquired or merged with, as horizontal, vertical or conglomerate. Each type of merger represents a different way of expansion with different benefits and risks.

Horizontal mergers

An example of a horizontal merger was the $160 billion 2015 merger between Pfizer Inc and Botox-maker Allergan plc. Another horizontal merger example was the $108 billion 2015 merger in the beverages sector between Anheuser-Busch and SABMiller plc.

Vertical mergers

Vertical mergers are mergers between firms that operate at different stages of the same production chain, or between firms that produce complementary goods such as a newspaper acquiring a paper manufacturer. Vertical mergers are either backward when the firm merges with a supplier or forward when the firm merges with a customer.

An example of a vertical merger is the merger between Time Warner Incorporated and the Turner Corporation, which produced CNN, TBS, and other programmes. In this merger, the Federal Trade Commission (FTC) was alarmed by the fact that such a merger would allow Time Warner

to monopolize much of the programming on television. Ultimately, the FTC voted to allow the merger but stipulated that the merger could not act in the interests of anti-competitiveness to the point that public good was harmed.

Conglomerate mergers

Conglomerate mergers are mergers which are neither vertical nor horizontal. In a conglomerate merger a company acquires another company in an unrelated line of business.

2 Evaluating the Acquisition Proposal

Expansion either by organic growth or by acquisitions should only be undertaken if it leads to an increase in the wealth of the shareholders. This happens when the merger or acquisition creates synergies which either increase revenues or reduce costs, or when the management of the acquiring company can manage the assets of the target company better than the incumbent management, thus creating additional value for the new owners over and above the current market value of the company. We look at some of the aspects that will have an impact on the competitive position of the firm and its profitability in a given acquisition proposal.

Market power

The impact on market power is one of the most important aspects of an acquisition. By acquiring another firm, in a horizontal merger, the competition in the industry is reduced and the company may be able to charge higher prices for its products. Competition regulation however may prevent this type of acquisition. To the extent that both companies purchase for the same suppliers, the merged company will have greater bargaining power when it deals with its suppliers.

Barriers to entry

A second aspect of an acquisition proposal and related to the previous one is the possibility of creating barriers to entry through vertical acquisitions of production inputs. Aspects of a merger that will have an impact on the firm's competitive position include increased market power, the creation of barriers to entry, supply chain security and economies of scope and scale.

Supply chain security

A third aspect that has an impact on the competitive position of a firm is the acquisition of a firm which has an important role in the supply chain. Companies acquire suppliers to ensure that there is no disruption in the supply of the inputs that will threaten the ability of the company to produce, sell and retain its competitive position. Although the risk of disruption can be eliminated by long-term contracts, acquisition is still considered an important option.

Economies of scale

The merged company will be bigger in size than the individual companies and it will have a larger scale of operations. The larger scale of operations may give rise to what is called economies of scale from a reduction in the cost per unit resulting from increased production, realized through operational efficiencies. Economies of scale can be accomplished because as production increases, the cost of producing each additional unit falls.

Economies of scope

Scope economies or changes in product mix are another potential way in which mergers might help improve the performance of the acquiring company. Economies of scope occur when it is more economical to produce two or more products jointly in a single production unit than to produce the products in separate specializing firms. Scope economies can arise from two sources:

(a) The spreading of fixed costs over an expanded product mix; and
(b) Cost complementarities in producing the different products.

Economies of scope have been invoked as the main reason driving mergers in the financial sector. The fixed capital of a bank branch for example, or its computer systems are more fully utilized when they issue not just banking products such as deposits and loans but also insurance products and investment services. These additional services allow the spreading of fixed costs over a larger number of activities reducing the unit cost of each activity.

Financial synergy: tax and debt benefits

The final aspect in an acquisition proposal has to do with the existence of financial synergies which take the form of diversification, tax and debt benefit synergies.

3 Developing an Acquisition Strategy

A coherent acquisition strategy could be based on one of these motives.

Acquire Undervalued Firms

This is one of the main reasons for firms becoming targets for acquisition. If a predator recognises that a firm has been undervalued by the market it can take advantage of this discrepancy by purchasing the firm at a 'bargain' price. The difference between the real value of the target firm and the price paid can then be seen as a 'surplus'.

For this strategy to work, the predator firm must be able to fulfil three things:

- **Find firms that are undervalued.** This might seem to be an obvious point but in practice it is not easy to have such superior knowledge ahead of other predators. The predator would either have to have access to better information than that available to other market players, or have superior analytical tools to those used by competitors.
- **Access to necessary funds.** It is one thing being able to identify firms that are undervalued – it is quite another obtaining the funds to acquire them. Traditionally, larger firms tend to have better access to capital markets and internal funds than smaller firms. A history of success in identifying and acquiring undervalued firms will also make funds more accessible and future acquisitions easier.
- **Skills in executing the acquisition.** There are no gains to be made from driving the share price up in the process of acquiring an undervalued firm.

Diversify to Reduce Risk

Firm-specific risk (unsystematic risk) can be reduced by holding a diversified portfolio. Predator firms' managers believe that they may reduce earnings volatility and risk – and increase potential value – by acquiring firms in other industries.

Can diversification be achieved more efficiently at company level or at individual investor level? Obviously individual investors can diversify much more cheaply than companies can. All they have to do is buy shares in companies in different industries, whereas companies have to go through long, complicated and expensive processes in order to acquire other companies. There are two exceptions to this:

(a) Owners of private firms with all or most of their wealth invested in the firm. The owner is exposed to all the risk therefore there is a greater case for diversification.

(b) Incumbent managers who have large amounts of their wealth invested in the firm. If these managers diversify through acquisition, they will reduce their exposure to total risk.

This opens up other arguments as to whether these managers are acting in the best interests of the other shareholders, if the other shareholders do hold well diversified portfolios of other shares.

Criteria for Choosing an Appropriate Target for Acquisition

There are a number of different aspects to successful target identification. The criteria that should be used to assess whether a target is appropriate will depend on the motive for the acquisition. The main criteria that are consistent with the underlying motive are:

- **Benefit for acquiring undervalued company.** The target firm should trade at a price below the estimated value of the company when acquired. This is true of companies which have assets that are not exploited.
- **Diversification.** The target firm should be in a business which is different from the acquiring firm's business and the correlation in earnings should be low.
- **Operating synergy.** The target firm should have the characteristics that create the operating synergy. Thus the target firm should be in the same business in order to create cost savings through economies of scale. Or it should be able to create a higher growth rate through increased monopoly power.
- **Tax savings.** The target company should have large claims to be set off against taxes and not sufficient profits. The acquisition of the target firm should provide a tax benefit to acquirer.
- **Increase the debt capacity.** This happens when the target firm is unable to borrow money or is forced to pay high rates. The target firm should have capital structure such that its acquisition will reduce bankruptcy risk and will result in increasing its debt capacity.
- **Disposal of cash slack.** This is where a cash rich company seeks a development target. The target company should have great projects but no funds. This happens when for example the target company has some exclusive right to product or use of asset but no funds to start activities.
- **Access to cash resources.** A company with a number of cash intensive projects or products in their pipeline, or heavy investment in R&D might seek a company that has significant cash resources or highly cash generative product lines to support their own needs.
- **Control of the company.** In this case the objective is to find a target firm which is badly managed and whose stock has underperformed the market. The management of an existing company is not able to fully utilize the potential of the assets of the company and the bidding company feels that it has greater expertise or better management methods. The bidding company therefore believes that the assets of the target company will generate for them a greater return than for their current owners. The criterion in this case is a market valuation of the company which is lower than for example the value of its assets.
- **Access to key technology.** Some companies do not invest significantly in R&D but acquire their enabling technologies by acquisition. Pharmaceutical companies who take over smaller biotechs in order to get hold of the technology are a good example of this type of strategy.

Creating Synergies

The three main types of synergy to be gained from acquisitions or mergers are revenue, cost and financial synergies. The existence of synergies has been presented as one of the two main explanations that may increase shareholder value in an acquisition. Indeed the identification, quantification and announcement of these synergies are an essential part of the process as shareholders of the companies need to be persuaded to back the merger.

Revenue Synergy

Revenue synergy exists when the acquisition of the target company will result in higher revenues for the acquiring company, higher return on equity or a longer period of growth. Revenue synergies arise from:

(a) Increased market power
(b) Marketing synergies
(c) Strategic synergies

Revenue synergies are more difficult to quantify relative to financial and cost synergies. When companies merge, cost synergies are relatively easy to assess pre-deal and to implement post-deal. But revenue synergies are more difficult. Will customers actually buy the new, expanded 'total systems capabilities,' and how much of the company's declared cost savings will be demanded in price concessions (this is common in automotive supplier M&A where the customers have huge purchasing power over the suppliers). Nevertheless, revenue synergies must be identified and delivered. The stock markets will be content with cost synergies for the first year after the deal, but thereafter they will want to see growth.

Cost Synergy

A cost synergy results primarily from the existence of economies of scale. As the level of operation increases, the marginal cost falls and this will be manifested in greater operating margins for the combined entity. The resulting costs from economies of scale are normally estimated to be substantial.

Financial Synergy

Diversification

Acquiring another firm as a way of reducing risk cannot create wealth for two publicly traded firms, with diversified stockholders, but it could create wealth for private firms or closely held publicly traded firms. A takeover, motivated only by diversification considerations, has no effect on the combined value of the two firms involved in the takeover. The value of the combined firms will always be the sum of the values of the independent firms. In the case of private firms or closely held firms, where the owners may not be diversified personally, there might be a potential value gain from diversification.

Cash Slack

When a firm with significant excess cash acquires a firm, with great projects but insufficient capital, the combination can create value. Managers may reject profitable investment opportunities if they have to raise new capital to finance them. It may therefore make sense for a company with excess cash and no investment opportunities to take over a cash-poor firm with good investment opportunities, or vice versa.

The additional value of combining these two firms lies in the present value of the projects that would not have been taken if they had stayed apart, but can now be taken because of the availability of cash.

Assume that Softscape Inc, a hypothetical company, has a severe capital rationing problem, that results in approximately $500 million of investments, with a cumulative net present value of $100 million, being rejected. IBM has far more cash than promising projects, and has accumulated $4 billion in cash that it is trying to invest. It is under pressure to return the cash to the owners. If IBM takes over Softscape Inc, it can be argued that the value of the combined firm will increase by the synergy benefit of $100 million, which is the net present value of the projects possessed by the latter that can now be taken with the excess cash from the former.

Tax Benefits

The tax paid by two firms combined together may be lower than the taxes paid by them as individual firms. If one of the firms has tax deductions that it cannot use because it is losing money, while the other firm has income on which it pays significant taxes, the combining of the two firms can lead to tax benefits that can be shared by the two firms. The value of this synergy is the present value of the tax savings that accrue because of this merger. The assets of the firm being taken over can be written up to reflect new market value, in some forms of mergers, leading to higher tax savings from depreciation in future years.

Debt Capacity

By combining two firms, each of which has little or no capacity to carry debt, it is possible to create a firm that may have the capacity to borrow money and create value. Diversification will lead to an increase in debt capacity and an increase in the value of the firm. This has to be weighed against the immediate transfer of wealth that occurs to existing bondholders in both firms from the stockholders. When two firms in different businesses merge, the combined firm will have less variable earnings, and may be able to borrow more (have a higher debt ratio) than the individual firms.

4 Explaining High Failure Rate of Acquisitions

A number of theories have been put forward to explain the high failure rate of acquisitions in enhancing shareholder value. These include agency theory, errors in valuing a target firm, the pre-emptive theory and market irrationality.

One of the most common empirical findings is that in an acquisition the shareholders of the acquiring company seldom enjoy any benefits, whereas the shareholders of the target company do. What is the reason for the failure to enhance shareholder value? We said earlier that there must be some evidence of synergies or concrete proof of managerial superiority in the acquiring firm to produce an acquisition that would enhance shareholder value. A number of alternative theories explain the phenomenon of failure by postulating that the main motive of the management of a company when they bid for another company is not maximisation of the shareholder value but other motives which have been found to be consistent with empirical evidence.

Agency Theory

Agency theory suggests that takeovers are primarily motivated by the self-interest of the acquirer's management. Reasons that have been advanced to explain the divergence in the interests of the management and the shareholder of a company include:

- Diversification of management's own portfolio
- Use of free cash flow to increase the size of the firm
- Acquiring assets that increase the firm's dependence on management

The common idea of these explanations is that acquisitions is a process that results in value being transferred from the shareholder of the acquiring firm to the managers of the acquiring firm.

The implication of agency theory is that, because the target firm knows that a bid is in the interest of the management rather than the shareholders of the acquiring firm, it sees this bid opportunity to extract some of the value that would have gone to acquiring firm management. How much value the target firm can extract depends on the bargaining power they have.

Errors in Valuing a Target Firm

Managers of the bidding firm may advise their company to bid too much as they do not know how to value an essentially recursive problem. A risk-changing acquisition cannot be valued without revaluing your own company on the presupposition that the acquisition has gone ahead. The value of an acquisition cannot be measured independently. As a result the merger fails as the subsequent performance cannot compensate for the high price paid.

Market Irrationality

If a rational manager observes that his firm's stocks are overvalued in the short run, he has an incentive to exchange the overvalued stocks to real assets before the market corrects the overvaluation. A merger therefore occurs in order to take advantage of market irrationality and it is not related to either synergies or better management. The lack of the latter may in the end lead to a failing merger even though the acquired firm was bought cheaply through the exchange of over-valued shares.

Pre-emptive Theory

This theory explains why acquiring firms pursue value-decreasing horizontal mergers even if managers are rational and are trying to maximize shareholders' value. If large cost savings can be achieved through the merger by several potential acquiring firms, these firms will compete for the opportunity to merge with the target. The winning firm who acquires the target could become a lower cost producer, improve its product market position and gain market share from the rivals. Intuitively, if a firm fears that one of its rivals will gain large cost savings or synergies from taking over some other firm, then it can be rational for the first firm to pre-empt this merger with a takeover attempt of its own.

Window Dressing

Another reason for the high failure rate is that companies are not acquired because of the synergies that they may create, but in order to present a better financial picture in the short term.

Poor Integration Management

In order to integrate two or more organisations effectively there must be effective integration management and a recognition that successful integration takes time. Where management is poor or there is an attempt to do too much too soon, potentially successful mergers can actually fail.

Inflexibility in the application of integration plans drawn up prior to the event can be damaging. Once the merger has taken place, management must be prepared to adapt plans in the light of changed circumstances or inaccurate prior information. Poor man-management can be detrimental to successful integration. Keeping staff informed in what may be a very unsettling period is important. Lack of communication of goals and future prospects of employees, and failure to recognise and deal with their uncertainties and anxieties can lead to employees being unclear of what is expected of them. Hostilities may develop between the two groups of staff, with a unwillingness to adapt to new procedures and practices.

5 The Impact of an Acquisition or Merger upon the Risk Profile of the Acquirer

An acquisition may have an impact on both the financial and the business risk. There are three possibilities which also characterise the type of acquisitions:

(1) **Type I acquisition**

These are acquisitions that do not disturb the acquirer's exposure to financial or business risk.

(2) **Type II acquisition**

These are acquisitions that affect the acquirer's exposure to financial risk but it does not affect the exposure of the firm to business risk.

(3) **Type III acquisition**

These are acquisitions that affect the acquirer's exposure to both financial and business risk.

The business risk of the combined entity will be affected by the betas of the target and predator first and the beta of the synergy that results from the acquisition. The asset beta of the combined firm is the weighted average of the betas of the target firm, the predator firm and the synergy generated from the acquisition.

Valuation of a Type I Acquisition of both Quoted and Unquoted Entities

A type I acquisition does not affect the acquiring company's exposure to business or financial risk.

Type I acquisitions may be valued using one of the following valuation methods:

- Book value-plus models
- Market relative models
- Cash flow models, including EVA$_{TM}$, MVA

EXAMPLE

Macleanstein Inc is considering making a bid for 100% of Thomasina Inc's equity capital. Thomasina has a P/E ratio of 14 and earnings of $500m. It is expected that $150m in synergy savings will be made as a result of the takeover and the P/E ratio of the combined company is estimated to be 16.

Macleanstein currently has a P/E ratio of 17 and earnings of $750m.

Required

(a) What is the maximum amount that Macleanstein should pay for Thomasina?
(b) What is the minimum bid that Thomasina's shareholders should be prepared to accept?

SOLUTION

(a) **Maximum amount to be paid**

Macleanstein must consider the synergies to be made from the combination when determining the maximum amount to pay.

Value of Thomasina to Macleanstein = value of combined company – current value of Macleanstein

Value of combined company = new P/E ratio x combined earnings

= 16 × (500m + 750m + 150m) = $22,400m

Current value of Macleanstein = 17 × $750m = $12,750m

Value of Thomasina to Macleanstein = $22,400 - $12,750m = $9,650m

Therefore the maximum amount that Macleanstein should pay for Thomasina is $9,650m.

(b) **Minimum amount that Thomasina's shareholders should accept**

= current value of Thomasina's equity

= 14 × $500m = $7,000m

The final amount paid will probably fall between these two extremes.

Market to Book Ratio – based on Tobin's Q Ratio

Market value of a target company = market to book ratio x the book value of assets of target company

Market to book ratio = market capitalisation/book value of assets for a similar company

An industry average could also be used in the absence of a similar company.

The **Q ratio** is defined as the market value of a firm/total asset value of the firm

As a guideline for valuing a potential target, a firm with a Q <1 is vulnerable since the assets of a company can be acquired at a cheaper price than they were bought on their own as assets. So, high-Q firms usually buy low Q-firms. In fact empirical studies have shown that in more than two thirds of all mergers the acquirer's Q exceeded the target's Q.

Free Cash Flow Approaches to Valuation

In order to produce a cash flow-based valuation of a company, it is first necessary to estimate the cash flows the business can generate from its operations. This calculation is often referred to as 'free cash flow' and it can be estimated in the following three ways:

(1) Free cash flow to the enterprise (including capital allowances)
(2) Free cash flow to the enterprise (assuming depreciation is tax deductible)
(3) Free cash flow to equity

We will provide definitions of all three measures, then look at when each might be appropriate to use.

Definition 1 – Free Cash Flow to the Enterprise, including Capital Allowances

Free cash flow to the enterprise or free cash flow to the firm (FCFF) is the total amount of cash the company generates after funding purchases of non-current assets and any required increases in working capital, but before any financing flows such as interest, dividends or debt capital repayments. It is termed 'free cash flow to the enterprise' as it gives the flows available to all providers of capital (ie both debt and equity).

A proforma calculation for FCFF including capital allowances is as follows:

FCFF	**£**
Earnings before interest and tax	x
+/– Non-cash items	x
Cash EBIT	x
Less: Cash taxes (Cash EBIT x tax rate)	(x)
Add: Tax relief for capital allowances	x
Less: Capital expenditure	x
Less/add: (Increase)/decrease in working capital	x
Free cash flow to the enterprise	x

Cash EBIT

The starting point for the calculation is the firm's operating profit (EBIT). This is then adjusted for non-cash items, such as depreciation, impairment costs and increases/ decreases in provisions. For instance, depreciation and impairment expenses should be added back and the release of an unused provision should be deducted. This gives us a 'Cash EBIT' figure.

Tax

We can then estimate the cash taxes figure by multiplying the Cash EBIT figure by the prevailing tax rate. The calculated tax figure will differ from the tax charge in the income statement as it is based on a measure of profit pre-financing costs and it excludes accounting adjustments, which are largely disallowable for tax purposes. The calculated tax figure will also differ from the actual tax paid because no credit has been allowed for tax depreciation and this must be adjusted for in the next line in the proforma via capital allowances.

Capital Allowances

The company will save tax through capital allowances. Relief is generally available for a company's non-current assets at a rate of 25% on a reducing balance. The impact on the free cash flow calculation will be the tax saving that this represents at the company's marginal cost of taxation.

TASK

A company purchases a machine for £10,000 which it expects to use for a three-year project at the end of which it will be sold for an estimated £2,000. If the company pays tax at a rate of 30%, what is the impact of the capital allowances on its free cash flow?

Year	Asset Pool		Capital Allowances Available	Tax Saving in Free Cash Flow	
	£		£	£	
1	10,000				
	(2,500)		2,500	750	(Time 1)
2	7,500				
	(1,875)		1,875	563	(Time 2)
3	5,625				
	(2,000)	Note 1			
	3,625	Note 2	3,625	1,088	(Time 3)

Note 1 – the disposal proceeds

Note 2 – the remaining asset value, available for tax relief as a balancing allowance. If the disposal proceeds exceeded the tax written down value of £5,625, the allowances would be clawed back from the company via a balancing charge, giving rise to a cash outflow in the final period.

Capital Expenditure

This is the total amount of cash spent on purchasing new non-current assets less the proceeds from assets disposed of. When analysing past cash flow for a company, total capital expenditure should be included. However, when forecasting, it may be appropriate to limit capital expenditure to a replacement level, on the basis that any additional investment represents an application of free cash flow. This will be the case if a business has reached a state where there is no opportunity for rapid growth in its markets through expansion of the asset base.

Working Capital

Any increase in working capital levels represents increased investment in the asset base of the business and means that a certain amount of profits has not yet been realised in cash. Working capital should only reflect those items that are included in the profit before interest and tax referred to above. This means that it will include inventories, receivables and payables. It will not, however, include short-term investments or cash balances, unless they are an essential part of working capital, eg for a cash retailer. These represent surplus assets in the business and are not linked to operating flows. In addition, it does not include short-term interest bearing liabilities such as bank overdrafts. All of these are dealt with separately in the valuation.

The market value of any deposits or investments is added into the firm's total value. Overdrafts are treated as being part of debt, which is considered in more detail below.

Non-Operating Cash Flows

Any items excluded from the operating profit figure above need to be taken into account separately for the purpose of the cash flow valuation of the business. Where this is a series of one-off cash flows, they will need to be highlighted and valued as such. Where the cash flows relate to investments and deposits, the market value of the underlying investment is added into the investment, as noted above.

TASK

Calculate the free cash flow to the enterprise of ABC Ltd, where the following data is given.

EBIT	£100m
Depreciation	£40m
Accounting tax charge	£10m
Tax rate	30%
Capital expenditure	£30m
Capital allowances available in year	£50m
Increase in working capital pa	£2m

SOLUTION

	£m
EBIT	100
+ Depreciation	40
Cash EBIT	140
– Tax (*30% × cash EBIT*)	(42)
+ Capital allowances relief (30% × 50m)	15
– Capital expenditure	(30)
– Increase in working capital	(2)
Free cash flow to the enterprise	81

Note: The accounting tax charge is irrelevant since it is not a cash flow.

Definition 2 – Free Cash Flow to the Enterprise, excluding Capital Allowances

The second way to calculate free cash flow is commonly used where information on the company's capital allowances is not available.

It is calculated as follows:

FCFF	£
Earnings before interest and tax	x
+/– Non-cash items	x
Cash EBIT	x
Less: Taxes (*EBIT x tax rate*)	(x)
Less: Capital expenditure	x
Less/add: (Increase)/decrease in working capital	x
Free cash flow to the enterprise	x

The figures used are the same as method (1) above, with the important distinction in the tax calculation. Method (1) based the tax calculation on the **cash EBIT** number and adjusted separately for tax relief on non-current assets ie capital allowances. However, we will not always have access to capital allowance information (for example if carrying out a valuation from publicly available financial information). In this case, method (2) is more appropriate. Here, we base the tax calculation on the **EBIT** number and in doing so assume that depreciation is tax deductible (ie accounting depreciation = tax depreciation). There is thus no need for an additional capital allowances adjustment. We also assume that there are no other tax disallowable items impacting EBIT. In practice, this is not likely to be true – especially for UK companies – but it is generally assumed that the differences are not so significant as to invalidate the overall calculation.

Definition 3 – Free Cash Flow to Equity

The third calculation is of Free Cash Flow to Equity (FCFE). This calculates the total amount of cash the company generates after funding purchases of non-current assets and any required increases in working capital, and **including** any financing flows such as interest, preference dividends and debt capital repayments. It is termed 'free cash flow to equity' as it gives the flows available to all providers of equity capital (ie after payments to other providers of capital).

It is calculated as follows:

FCFE	£
Net income	x
+/– Non-cash items	x
	x
Less: Capital expenditure	x
Less/add: Changes in working capital	x
Less: debt principal repayments	x
Add: new debt raised	x
Free cash flow to equity	x

The calculation starts from net income, in other words it is already after tax and interest. The non-cash items adjusted for in the next line, will therefore include non-cash operating expenses, finance costs and tax expenses. Capital expenditure and working capital are adjusted for as previously. Finally, as we are calculating free cash flow to equity, changes in debt capital in the year are included, with repayments shown as a cash outflow and any new debt raised as a cash inflow.

Which Method to Choose

For valuation purposes, free cash flow to the enterprise is a much more useful calculation. It gives us a valuation independent of the financing structure, which may alter as a result of the proposed acquisition etc. Considering free cash flow to the enterprise enables us to consider the value of the operations as a whole and then consider the financing structure separately.

Importantly, different types of cash flow should be discounted at different discount rates:

- **Free cash flow to the enterprise**, should be discounted at the **weighted average cost of capital** to give an **enterprise value.**
- **Free cash flow to equity** should be discounted at the **cost of equity** to give an **equity value.**

6 Valuation of Type II Acquisitions

A type II acquisition affect the acquiring company's exposure to financial risk only – it does not affect exposure to business risk.

Type II acquisitions can be valued used the Adjusted Present Value (APV) model.

Valued by discounting the Free Cash Flows to the firm by the ungeared cost of equity and then adding the present value of the tax shield. The net present value is given by APV = Value of acquired company if all–equity financed + Present Value of Debt Tax Shields – Initial investment

If the APV is positive then the acquisition should be undertaken.

The APV method involves two stages:

STEP 1 Evaluate the project first of all as if it was all equity financed, and so as if the company were an all equity company to find the 'base case NPV'

STEP 2 Make adjustments to allow for the effects of the method of financing that has been used

We will look at an example of APV in relation to a project to demonstrate how the method works.

Example

APV method

A company is considering a project that would cost $100,000 to be financed 50% by equity (cost 21.6%) and 50% by debt (pre-tax cost 12%). The financing method would maintain the company's WACC unchanged. The cash flows from the project would be $36,000 a year in perpetuity, before interest charges. Tax is at 30%.

Appraise the project using firstly the NPV method and secondly the APV method.

Solution

We can use the **NPV method** because the company's WACC will be unchanged.

	Cost %	Weighting	Product %
Equity	21.6	0.5	10.8
Debt (70% of 12%)	8.4	0.5	4.2
WACC			15.0

Annual cash flows in perpetuity from the projects are as follows

		$
Before tax		36,000
Less tax (30%)		10,800
After tax		25,200
NPV of project	= –$100,000 + (25,200 ÷ 0.15)	
	= –$100,000 + £168,000	
	= $68,000	

Note that the tax relief that will be obtained on debt interest is taken account of in the WACC *not* in the project cash flows.

Since $100,000 of new investment is being created, the value of the company will increase by $100,000 +$68,000 = $168,000, of which 50% must be debt capital.

The company must raise 50% x $168,000 = $84,000 of 12% debt capital, and (the balance) $16,000 of equity. The NPV of the project will raise the value of this equity from $16,000 to $84,000 thus leaving the gearing ratio at 50:50.

The APV approach to this example is as follows:

(a) First, we need to know the cost of equity in an equivalent ungeared company. We can use the Modigliani and Miller formula for degearing and regearing betas to establish this is as follows:

Cost of ordinary (equity) share capital in a geared firm (with tax):

$$k_e = k_e^i + (1+T)(k_e^i - k_d)\frac{V_d}{V_e}$$

Remember

k_d = the **pre-tax** cost of debt. Using the information from the question:

$$21.6\% = k_e^i + (k_e^i - 12\%) \times \left[\frac{50 \times 0.7}{50}\right]$$

$$21.6\% = k_e + 0.70k_e - 8.4\%$$

$$1.70\,k_e = 30\%$$

$$k_e = 17.647\%$$

(b) Next, we calculate the NPV of the project as if it were all equity financed. The cost of equity would be 17.647%

$$NPV = \frac{\$25{,}200}{0.17647} - \$100{,}000 = \$42{,}800$$

(c) Next, we can use the theories of Modigliani and Miller on the relationship between the value of geared and ungeared companies, to establish the effect of gearing on the value of the project. £84,000 will be financed by debt.

V_g (APV) = V_u + (value of debt × corporate tax rate)
= $42,800 + ($84,000 × 0.30)
= $42,800 + $25,200
= $68,000

The value of debt x corporate tax rate represents the present value of the tax shield on debt interest, that is the present value of the savings arising from tax relief on debt interest.

This can be proved as follows:

Annual interest charge = 12% of $84,000 = $10,080

Tax saving (30% × $10,080) = $3,024.00

Cost of debt (pre-tax) = 12%

PV of tax savings in perpetuity = $3,024/0.12 = $25,200

Make sure you use the cost of debt to discount the tax relief on interest costs and not the cost of equity.

Suppose in the above example the cash flows only lasted for five years, and tax was payable one year in arrears. Calculate the present value of the tax shield.

The tax saving will now only last for years 2 to 6. (Remember interest will be paid in years 1 to 5, but the tax benefits will be felt a year in arrears).

PV of tax savings = 3,024 × Annuity factor years 2 to 6
= 3,024 × (Annuity factors years 1 to 6 – Annuity factor year 1)
= 3,024 × (4.111 – 0.893)
= $9,731

The APV and NPV approaches produce the same conclusion.

APV and Changes in Gearing

However, the APV method can also be adapted to allow for financing which changes the gearing structure and the WACC. In this respect, it is superior to the NPV method. Suppose, for example, that in the previous example, the entire project were to be financed by debt. The APV of the project would be calculated as follows:

(a) The NPV of project if all equity financed is:

$$\frac{\$25,200}{0.17647} - \$100,000 = +\$42,800 \text{ (as before)}$$

(b) The adjustment to allow for the method of financing is the present value of the tax relief on debt interest in perpetuity.

DT_c = $100,000 × 0.30 = $30,000

(c) APV = $42,800 + $30,000 = + $72,800

The project would increase the value of equity by $72,800.

Example

A project costing $100,000 is to be financed by $60,000 of irredeemable 12% loan stock and $40,000 of new equity. The project will yield an after-tax annual cash flow of $21,000 in perpetuity. If it were all equity financed, an appropriate cost of capital would be 15%. The tax rate is 30%. What is the project's APV?

	$
NPV if all equity financed: $21,000/0.15 – $100,000	40,000
PV of the tax shield: $60,000 × 12% × 30%/0.12	18,000
APV	58,000

The advantages and disadvantages of the APV method

The main advantages of the APV are as follows:

(a) APV can be used to evaluate all the effects of financing a product including:

(i) Tax shield
(ii) Changing capital structure
(iii) Any other relevant cost

(b) When using APV you do not have to adjust the WACC using assumptions of perpetual risk-free debt.

The main difficulties with the APV technique are:

(a) Establishing a suitable cost of equity, for the initial DCF computation as if the project were all equity financed, and also establishing the all-equity β

(b) Identifying all the costs associated with the method of financing

(c) Choosing the correct discount rates used to discount the costs

Using APV to value companies

EXAMPLE

The management of XERON Inc is considering the acquisition of NERON Inc. an unquoted company. The owners of NERON want $500 million for the business. The analysis of the prospects of NERON by XERON is reflected in the following financial statements.

INCOME STATEMENT

	Current Year			Years			
	20X7	**20X8**	**20X9**	**20Y0**	**20Y1**	**20Y2**	**20Y3**
Sales	620.00	682.00	750.20	825.22	907.74	998.52	998.52
Less: cost of goods sold	(410.00)	(441.00)	(475.10)	(512.61)	(553.87)	(599.26)	(599.26)
Gross profit	210.00	241.00	275.10	312.61	353.87	399.26	399.26
Operating expenses	133.00	(144.30)	(156.53)	(169.78)	(184.16)	(199.78)	(199.78)
EBIT	77.00	96.70	118.57	142.83	169.71	199.48	199.48
Less interest expense	–	(32.00)	(26.88)	(20.19)	(11.73)	(1.27)	–
Earning before tax	77.00	64.70	91.69	122.64	157.98	198.21	199.48
Less taxes	(21.56)	(18.12)	(25.67)	(34.34)	(44.23)	(55.50)	(55.85)
Net income	55.44	46.58	66.02	88.30	113.75	142.71	143.63

STATEMENT OF FINANCIAL POSITION

	Current Year			Years			
	20X7	**20X8**	**20X9**	**20Y0**	**20Y1**	**20Y2**	**20Y3**
Current assets	100.00	100.00	100.00	100.00	100.00	242.90	404.55
Non-current assets	400.00	378.00	354.00	328.00	300.00	270.00	238.00
Total Assets	500.00	478.00	454.00	428.00	400.00	512.90	642.55
Debt	400.00	335.95	252.35	146.63	15.94	–	–
Equity	100.00	142.05	201.65	281.37	384.06	512.90	642.55
Total assets	500.00	478.00	454.00	428.00	400.00	512.90	642.55

Other information

Growth rate for sales	10%
Depreciation expense (20X7)	$40m
Interest rate on debt (all debt is interest-bearing)	8%
Tax rate	28%
Capital expenditures/year (depreciation charged at 10% per annum)	$20m
All available cash flow is applied to repaying debt until repaid in full	
Ungeared beta	1.1
Terminal value reflects level perpetuity equal to year 6 cash flow	
Risk free rate	6.0%
Market risk premium	7.5%
There are no disposals of non-current assets for the duration of the project	
XERON proposes to take over NERON in 20X8	

STEP 1 Calculation of NPV as if ungeared

Don't forget to include the terminal value before calculating the final NPV in this step.

	20X8	20X9	20Y0	20Y1	20Y2	20Y3
EBIT(1 – Tax rate)						
Plus: Depreciation Expense	42.00	44.00	46.00	48.00	50.00	52.00
Less: CAPEX	(20.00)	(20.00)	(20.00)	(20.00)	(20.00)	(20.00)
Firm free cash flow	91.62	109.37	128.84	150.19	173.63	175.63
Discount factor (14%)(W1)						
Net present value	80.35	84.11	86.97	88.91	90.11	80.09
Total NPV before terminal value	510.54					

$$\text{Terminal value} = \frac{\$175.63}{0.14} = \$1{,}254.5\text{m}$$

The present value of the terminal value is:

$$\frac{\$1{,}254.5\text{m}}{(1.14)^6} = \$571.53\text{m}$$

Total NPV = $510.54 + $571.53 = $1.082.07m

W1 The discount factor can be calculated using CAPM

$$E(r_i) = R_f + \beta\ (E(R_m - R_f))$$

$$E(r_i) = 6 + 1.1 \times 7.5$$

$$E(r_i) = 14.25\%\ (\text{say } 14\%)$$

STEP 2 PV of tax saved on debt interest

The tax shield is discounted at the gross cost of debt (8%)

	20X7 $m	20X8 $m	20X9 $m	20Y0 $m	20Y1 $m	20Y2 $m	20Y3 $m
Interest tax savings	–	8.960	7.530	5.650	3.280	0.360	–
Discount factor at 8%	–	0.923	0.857	0.794	0.735	0.681	–
Present value	–	8.300	6.450	4.490	2.410	0.250	–
Total PV of tax shield	21.9						
Add PV from Step 1	1,082.07						
Total PV	1,103.97						

STEP 3 Deduct current debt and cost of acquisition to obtain equity value

Equity value = $1,103.97m – $500m – $400m = $203.97m

Conclusion – as NERON's equity value exceeds the price paid and the debt, XERON should proceed with the acquisition.

Valuation of Type III Acquisitions using Iterative Revaluation Procedures

A type III acquisition affects both the financial and business risk exposure of the acquiring company.

Steps for valuing a type III acquisition

In a type III valuation both the **business** and the **financial risk** of the acquiring company change. The following steps are followed in order to value an acquisition.

STEP 1 Calculate the asset beta of both companies

STEP 2 Calculate the average asset beta for the group post-acquisition

STEP 3 Regear the beta to reflect the group's post-acquisition gearing

STEP 4 Calculate the group's new WACC

STEP 5 Discount the group's post-acquisition free cash flows using the new WACC

STEP 6 Calculate the group's revised NPV and subtract debt to calculate the value of the equity

EXAMPLE

Omnivore Inc is considering the acquisition of Sweet Meals Co. The management of Omnivore have estimated that the cash flows of Sweet Meals will grow much faster than theirs over the next 10 years, and that considerable savings will be realised by integrating their distribution networks and marketing operations. The estimated cash flows for Omnivore, Sweet Meals and the synergies in the case of a merger are shown below. It is estimated that on acquisition Omnivore will be able to sell one of its storage sites realising an instant income of $5 million.

Year	Sweet Meal $m	Synergies $m	Omnivore $m	Cash flows of combined entity $m
20X5		5		5.00
20X6	12.00	6	42	60.00
20X7	14.400	6	45	65.40
20X8	17.28	6	48.01	71.29
20X9	20.74	6	50.97	77.71
20Y0	24.88	6	53.81	84.69
20Y1	29.86	6	56.46	92.32
20Y2	35.83	6	58.79	100.62
20Y3	29.41	6	64.27	109.68
20Y4	43.36	6	70.20	119.56
20Y5	45.52	6	78.79	130.31
Terminal value	682.86	50	1,663.97	2,396.84

The following information is available.

	Omnivore $m	Sweet Meals $m
Debt	100	20
Equity	900	280
Asset beta	0.9	2.4

Omnivore has decided to make a cash offer of $380 million to the shareholders of Sweet Meals for the purchase of 100 percent of their shares. The cash offer will be funded by additional borrowing.

The tax rate is 30%. Risk-free rate is 5% and the required rate of return for the combined company is 9%.

Cost of debt for the combined company is expected to be 7%.

Calculate the change in equity for Omnivore's shareholders that would result from the acquisition.

SOLUTION

The **asset beta of the combined company** is:

$$\frac{\text{Total value of Omnivore}}{\text{Total combined value}} \times \text{Beta(Omnivore)} + \frac{\text{Total value of Sweet Meals}}{\text{Total combined value}} \times \text{Beta (Sweet Meals)}$$

$$= \frac{1{,}000}{1{,}300} \times 0.9 + \frac{300}{1{,}300} \times 2.4 = 1.25$$

Geared beta of combined company

$$\text{Asset beta} \times \left(1 + (1 - T) \times \frac{\text{Total debt}}{\text{Total equity}}\right) = 1.25 \times \left(1 + 0.7 \times \frac{500}{1{,}180}\right)$$ (Total debt includes $380m for 100% of Sweet Meals shares)

$$= 1.62$$

Cost of equity (using CAPM)

$K_e = 5 + 1.62 \times 4 = 11.48\%$

$$\text{WACC} = \frac{1{,}180}{1{,}680} \times 11.48 + \frac{500}{1{,}680} \times 7 \times 0.7 = 9.52\%$$

Discount cash flows at WACC to find the value of the combined firm = $1,422.76 million

Value of equity = Value of firm – value of debt

= $1,422.76 – 500

= $922.76 million

Omnivore's shareholders' value has increased by ($922.76 – 900) million = $22.76 million

Nessie Inc

Nessie Inc is considering making a bid for 100% of Patsy Inc, a company in a completely different industry. The bid of $200 million, which is expected to be accepted, will be financed entirely by new debt with a rate of 7%.

Pre-acquisition information

Nessie

Nessie has debt finance totalling $60 million at a pre-tax rate of 7.5%. There are 50 million equity shares with a current market value of $22 each and an equity beta of 1.37.

Post-tax operating cash flows are as follows.

Year 1 $m	Year 2 $m	Year 3 $m	Year 4 $m	Year 5 $m
60.3	63.9	67.8	71.8	76.1

Patsy

Patsy has an equity beta of 2.5 and 65 million shares with a total current market value of $156 million.

Current debt – which will also be taken over by Nessie – is $12.5 million.

Post-acquisition information

Land with a value of $14 million will be sold.

Post-tax operating cash flows of Patsy's current business will be

Year 1	Year 2	Year 3	Year 4	Year 5
$m	**$m**	**$m**	**$m**	**$m**
15.2	15.8	16.4	17.1	17.8

If the acquisition goes ahead, Nessie will experience an improvement in its credit rating and all **existing** debt will be charged at a rate of 7%.

Cash flows after Year 5 will grow at a rate of 1.5% per annum.

General information

The risk-free rate is 5.2% and the market risk premium is 3%. Corporation tax rate is 28%. Debt beta is 0.

Required

Should Nessie go ahead with the acquisition of Patsy? Give reasons for your answer.

(1) **Calculate asset betas of both companies**

Assuming a debt beta of 0, asset beta can be calculated using the following formula.

$$\beta_a = \left(\frac{Ve}{(Ve + Vd)1 - T))}\right) be$$

Nessie = (1,100m/[1,100m +(60m × 0.72)]) × 1.37 = 1.32

Patsy = (156m/[156m + (12.5m × 0.72)]) × 2.5 = 2.36

(2) **Combined asset beta**

Combined beta = 1.32 × (1,100/[1,100 + 156]) + 2.36 × (156/[1,100 + 156]) = 1.45

(3) Regear beta to reflect group post-acquisition gearing

Using pre-acquisition debt and equity weightings

Equity beta = 1.45 / (1,256/[1,256 + [(60 + 12.5 + 200) × 0.72]) = 1.68

(4) **Calculate the group's new WACC**

Ke = 5.2 + (1.68 × 3) = 10.24%

WACC = (10.24 × 1,256/[1,256 + 272.5]) + (7 × 272.5/[1,256 +272.5])

= 8.4144 + 1.2480

= 9.66%

(5) Discount group's post-acquisition cash flows using this WACC

Post-acquisition NPV

Year	1 $m	2 $m	3 $m	4 $m	5 $m	Year 6 onwards $m
Combined cash flow	75.5	79.7	84.2	88.9	93.9	95.3
Annuity (1/r-g))						12.3
Value as at time 5						1,172.2
At 9.66%	0.912	0.832	0.758	0.692	0.631	0.631
PV	68.9	66.3	63.8	61.5	59.3	739.7
Total PV	1,059.5					
Sale of land	14.0					
Nessie's debt	(60.0)					
Patsy's debt	(12.5)					
New debt to fund acquisition	(200.0)					
Net value	801.0					

The net value of the combined companies is less than Nessie's individual value (50 million shares x $11 = $1,100m) therefore the acquisition of Patsy should not go ahead.

In the first example above, however, we have introduced an inconsistency in the calculation of the WACC because we have assumed that equity represents 70 percent of the value of the firm (1180/1680) and debt represents 30 percent of the value of the firm (500/1680).

In the values we have derived the value of the equity represents 65 percent of the value of the firm (922.76/1422.76) and debt represents 35 percent of the value of the firm. That is, the WACC weights are not consistent with the values derived.

If the two sets of weights differ significantly, the valuation is **internally inconsistent.** In such circumstances, we need to adopt **an iterative procedure** that takes into account the interrelation between the market value of the firm and the WACC. In the iterative procedure we must go back and re-compute the beta using a revised set of weights that are closer to the weights derived from the valuation. This process is then repeated until the assumed weights and the weights calculated from the derived values are approximately equal. A change in the WACC affects the market value of the equity, which alters the equity weight, and thereby affects the WACC.

The iteration proceeds as follows:

(a) The market value of FCF is initially set equal to its book value and the capital structure weights are computed.

(b) Then, given the capital structure weights, the WACC is calculated and used to discount the forecast cash flows to present value.

(c) Finally, the market value of the firm calculated from the discounting process is used to compute a revised value of the equity by subtracting the value of the debt. Based on this revised value, the initial assumption for the value of the equity is set equal to the original equity value plus one-half of the difference between the original value and the revised value and the program is rerun. This procedure is repeated until the change in the market value of the equity is less than a specified small value.

Fortunately this iterative procedure need not be done manually. It can be calculated in excel using the Tools/Options/Calculation commands. The iteration box needs to be ticked and the maximum number of iterations to be set to a large number, 10,000 to ensure convergence. In practice since the iteration requires recalculation of the equity values, if the book values do not differ too much from the market values a few iterations will suffice for convergence.

The internally consistent results of the iterative procedure are presented below.

Value of the firm	$1,395.45 million
Value of equity	$1,395.45 – 500 = $895.45 million
Geared beta	1.73
Cost of equity	11.93%
Weighted average cost of capital	9.41%

The value of equity is reduced now to $895.45 million below pre-acquisition value of Omnivore. The increased debt has increased the leveraged beta and the cost of equity, but it has slightly reduced the WACC as a result of the larger proportion of debt.

The iterative procedure has shown that at this price, the acquisition of Sweet Meals is not in the interest of the Omnivore shareholders.

7 Valuation of High Growth Start-ups

Due to their unique characteristics high growth start-ups presents a number of challenges. The valuation of start-ups presents a number of challenges for the methods that we have considered so far due to their unique characteristics which are summarised below:

(1) Most start-ups typically have no track record
(2) Ongoing losses
(3) Few revenues; untested products
(4) Unknown market acceptance, unknown product demand
(5) Unknown competition
(6) Unknown cost structures, unknown implementation timing
(7) High development or infrastructure costs
(8) Inexperienced management

Projecting Economic Performance

All valuation methods require reasonable projections to be made with regard to the key drivers of the business. The following steps should be undertaken with respect to the valuation of a high-growth start-up company:

Identifying the drivers

Any market-based approach or discounted cash flow analysis depends on the reasonableness of financial projections. Projections must be analysed in light of the market potential, resources of the business, management team, financial characteristics of the guideline public companies, and other factors.

Period of projection

One characteristic of high growth start-ups is that in order to survive they need to grow very quickly.

Start-ups that do grow quickly usually have operating expenses and investment needs in excess of their revenues in the first years and experience losses until the growth starts to slow down (and the resource needs begin to stabilise). This means that long-term projections, all the way out to the time when the business has sustainable positive operating margins and cash flows, need to be prepared. These projections will depend on the assumptions made about growth. However, rarely is the forecast period less than seven years.

Forecasting growth

Forecasting growth in earnings can be accommodated in the framework we have already explained for the prediction of earnings. The growth in earnings will be:

g = retention rate x ROIC

For most high growth start-ups, the retention rate = 1, as the company, in order to achieve a high growth rate, needs to invest in research and development, expansion of distribution and manufacturing capacity, human resource development to attract new talent, and development of new markets, products, or techniques.

If the retention rate is equal to 1, the sole determinant of growth is the return on invested capital (ROIC). The ROIC can be estimated from industry projections from securities analysts or from an evaluation of the company's management, marketing strengths, and level of investment.

Estimation of the ROIC is possible by decomposing it further to get an insight:

ROIC = EBIT/ Invested capital

= EBIT/ sales x sales/ invested capital

That is the ROIC is determined by the profit margin and by revenue growth.

Valuation Methods

Once growth rates have been estimated, the next step is to consider which is the most appropriate of the valuation approaches we have considered so far: net-assets, market or discounted cash flows.

Asset-based method

The asset based method is not appropriate because the value of capital in terms of tangible assets may not be high. Most of the investment of a start-up is in people, marketing and /or intellectual rights that are treated as expenses rather than as capital.

Market-based methods

The market approach to valuation also presents special problems for start-ups. This valuation process involves finding other companies, usually sold through private transactions, that are at a similar stage of development and that focus on existing or proposed products similar to those of the company being valued. Complicating factors include comparability problems, differences in fair market value from value paid by strategic acquirers, lack of disclosed information, and the fact that there usually are no earnings with which to calculate price-to-earnings ratios (in this case price-to-revenue ratios may be helpful).

Discounted cash flows

Using the DCF methodology, free cash flows are first projected and are then discounted to the present using a risk-adjusted cost of capital.

Our discussion of the high growth start-up indicates that the growth rates of revenues and costs may vary.

Since FCF = Revenue – Costs = R – C, the value of company will be given by:

$$V = \frac{R - C}{r - g}$$

Now assuming that the growth rate of revenues g_R is different than the growth rate of costs g_C:

$$V = \frac{R}{r - g_R} - \frac{C}{r - g_C}$$

Valuation of start-ups

QuickLeg is an internet legal services provider which next year expects revenue of $100 m and costs of $500 m. The revenues of the firm are expected to rise by 21 percent every year but costs will remain at the same level. The required rate of return is assumed to 22 percent. What is the value of QuickLeg?

$$V = \frac{\$100m}{0.22-0.21} - \frac{\$500m}{0.22-0} = \$7{,}727.27\text{million}$$

The above model seems to capture the phenomenon observed in many start-ups of high losses in the first year of operations with high values of the company. A very important problem with the discounted flow approach is the sensitivity of the valuation model to the underlying assumptions. Changes in the growth rate induced by changes in demand, technology, and management of other causes can have a dramatic effect on the value of the start-up. For example suppose that the growth rate of revenues falls from 21 percent to 20 percent. The value of the company now is:

$$V = \frac{\$100m}{0.22-0.20} - \frac{\$500m}{0.22-0} = \$2{,}727.27\text{million}$$

That is the company has lost $5 billion. Another problem with the discounted cash flow is that it cannot reflect managerial flexibilities and the strategic options to expand, delay, abandon, or switch investments at various decision points. The best way of incorporating uncertainty into the discounted cash flow analysis for a new company, technology, or product is to assign probabilities of success to each of the various possibilities.

Probabilistic Valuation Methods (expected values)

In a probabilistic cash flow model, we assume a number of scenarios for the drivers of value and derive a value under each scenario. The next step is to assign probabilities to each scenario and arrive at a weighted average value. The procedure to be followed is similar to the Monte Carlo methodology.

EXAMPLE

Suppose you have calculated three valuations of QuickLeg over a 10 year forecast period. Based on your analysis of value drivers, strategies, competition, and other variables, you have assigned the following values to each scenario:

Scenario	Probability	Value Derived from Scenario	Expected value
Conservative	0.2	1,000	200
Normal	0.7	1,600	1,120
High Growth	0.1	2,200	220
	Overall value		1,540

Assigning the above values and respective probabilities to each scenario, the expected overall value of Quickleg is $1,540 million.

8 INTANGIBLE ASSETS

The valuation of intangible assets and intellectual capital presents special problems. Various methods can be used to value them including the relief from royalties, premium profits and capitalisation of earnings methods.

Valuation of Intangibles

The book value method discussed earlier specifically excluded most intangible assets from the computation. This rendered this method unsuitable for the valuation of most established businesses, particularly those in the service industry. Here we consider the various types of intangible assets that a business may benefit from and how they might be valued.

Intangible Assets and Goodwill

Intangible assets are identifiable non-monetary assets without physical substance which must be controlled by the entity as the result of past events and from which the entity expects a flow of future economic benefits. (*IAS 38*)

Goodwill (acquired) is future economic benefits arising from assets that are not capable of being individually identified and separately recognised. (*IFRS 3*)

The above definition of intangible assets distinguishes:

(a) Intangible assets from tangible assets, by the phrase 'do not have physical substance'.

(b) Intangible assets from goodwill, by the word 'identifiable', an identifiable asset is legally defined as one that can be disposed of separately without disposing of a business of the entity.

The strict accounting distinctions do not need to concern us here. We are interested in any element of business that may have some value. Certain intangible assets can be recorded at their **historical cost.** Examples include patents and trademarks being recorded at **registration value** and franchises being recorded at **contract cost.** However over time these historical values may become poor reflections of the assets' value in use or of their market value.

Intellectual Capital

Intellectual capital is knowledge which can be used to create value. Intellectual capital includes:

(a) **Human resources**: the collective skills, experience and knowledge of employees

(b) **Intellectual assets**: knowledge which is defined and codified such as a drawing, computer program or collection of data

(c) **Intellectual property**: intellectual assets which can be legally protected, such as patents and copyrights (*OT 2005*)

As the demand for knowledge-based products grows with the changing structure of the global economy, knowledge plays an expanding role in achieving competitive advantage. Employees may thus be extremely valuable to a business, and they should be included in a full assets based valuation.

The principles of valuation discussed below should be taken as applying to all assets, resources or property that are defined as intangible assets or intellectual capital, which will include:

- Patents, trademarks and copyrights
- Franchises and licensing agreements
- Research and development
- Brands
- Technology, management and consulting processes
- Know-how, education, vocational qualification
- Customer loyalty
- Distribution channels
- Management philosophy

Measurement of Intangible Assets of an Enterprise

The expanding intellectual capital of firms accentuates the need for methods of valuation for comparative purposes, for example when an acquisition or buy-out is being considered.

Ramona Dzinkowski (*The measurement and management of intellectual capital*, Management Accounting) identifies the following three indicators, which are derived from audited financial statements and are independent of the definitions of intellectual capital adopted by the firm.

- **Market-to-book values**
- **Tobin's 'Q'**
- **Calculated intangible value**

Market-to-Book Values

The value of a firm's intellectual capital is defined as **the difference between the book value of tangible assets and the market value of the firm**. Thus, if a company's market value is $8 million and its book value is $5 million, the $3 million difference is taken to represent the value of the firm's **intangible** (or intellectual) assets.

Although obviously **simple**, this method's simplicity merely serves to indicate that it fails to take account of **real world complexities.** There may be imperfections in the market valuation, and book values are subject to accounting standards which reflect historic cost and amortisation policies rather than true market values of tangible non-current assets.

In addition, the accounting valuation does not attempt to value a company as a whole, but rather as a sum of separate asset values computed under particular accounting conventions. The market, on the other hand, values the entire company as a going concern, following its defined strategy.

Tobin's 'Q'

The Nobel prize-winning economist James Tobin developed the 'Q' method initially as a way of predicting investment behaviour. 'Q' is the ratio of the **market capitalisation of the firm** (share price x number of shares) to the **replacement cost** of its assets.

If the replacement cost of assets is **lower** than the market capitalisation, **'Q' is greater than 1** and the company is enjoying higher than average returns on its investment ('monopoly rents'). Technology and so-called 'human-capital' assets are likely to lead to high 'Q' values.

Tobin's 'Q' is affected by the **same variables** influencing market capitalisation as the **market-to-book** method. In common with that method, it is used most appropriately to make comparisons of the value of intangible assets of companies within an industry which serve the same markets and have similar tangible non-current assets. As such, these methods could serve as performance benchmarks by which to appraise management or corporate strategy.

Calculated Intangible Values (CIV)

CIV calculates an 'excess return' on tangible assets. This figure is then used in determining the proportion of return attributable to intangible assets.

A step-by-step approach would be as follows:

STEP 1 Calculate average pre-tax earnings over a time period

STEP 2 Calculate average year end tangible assets over the time period using statement of financial position figures

STEP 3 Divide earnings by average assets to get the return on assets

STEP 4 Find the industry's return on assets

STEP 5 Multiply the industry's return on asset percentage by the entity's average tangible asset

Subtract this from the entity's pre-tax earnings to calculate the excess return

STEP 6 Calculate the average tax rate over the time period and multiply this by the excess return

Subtract this from the excess return to give the after-tax premium attributable to intangible assets

STEP 7 Calculate the NPV of the premium by dividing it by the entity's cost of capital

EXAMPLE

CIV method

Jools Inc is trying to value its intangible assets and has decided to use the CIV method. Details for Jools over the last three years are as follows:

	20X6 $m	20X7 $m	20X8 $m
Pre-tax earnings	350.0	359.8	370.6
Tangible assets	1,507.5	1,528.9	1,555.9

The current return on assets ratio for the industry as a whole is 21%. Jools' WACC is 8%.

Calculate the fair value of Jools Inc's intangible assets, assuming an average tax rate of 30%.

SOLUTION

Average pre-tax earnings =

(350.0 + 359.8 + 370.6)/3 = $360.13 million

Average tangible assets =

(1,507.5 + 1,528.9 + 1,555.9)/3 = $1,530.77 million

Return on assets =

360.13/1,530.77 = 23.5%

Excess return = 360.13 – (0.21 × 1,530.77) = $38.67 million

After-tax premium = 38.67 – (0.3 × 38.67) = $27.07 million

NPV of premium = 27.07/0.08 = $338.38 million

Problems with the CIV approach

Whilst this seemingly straightforward approach, using readily available information, seems attractive, it does have two problems:

(a) It uses average industry ROA as a basis for computing excess returns, which may be distorted by extreme values.

(b) The choice of discount rate to apply to the excess returns to value the intangible asset needs to be made with care. To ensure comparability between companies and industries, some sort of average cost of capital should perhaps be applied. This again has the potential problems of distortion.

Lev's Knowledge Earnings Method

Lev's knowledge earnings method involves separating the earnings that are deemed to come from intangible assets and capitalise these earnings. This method involves separating the earnings that are deemed to come from intangible assets and capitalise them. This model does produce results that are very close to the quoted share price, suggesting that it is a good method of valuation.

The main problem with this technique is that it can be very complicated and in the end unrealistic. In practice most valuations come from intense negotiations between the interested parties rather than complex calculations.

Valuation of Individual Intangible Assets

Relief from royalties method

This method involves trying to determine:

(a) The value obtainable from licensing out the right to exploit the intangible asset to a third party; or

(b) The royalties that the owner of the intangible asset is relieved from paying through being the owner rather than the licensee.

A **notional royalty rate** is estimated as a percentage of revenue expected to be generated by the intangible asset. The estimated royalty stream can then be **capitalised**, for example by discounting at a risk-free market rate, to find an estimated market value.

This relatively simple valuation method is easiest to apply if the intangible asset is already subject to licensing agreements. If they are not, the valuer might reach an appropriate figure from other comparable licensing arrangements.

Premium profits method

The premium profits method is often used for **brands**. It bases the valuation on capitalisation of the **extra profits generated** by the brand or other intangible asset in excess of profits made by businesses lacking the intangible asset or brand.

The premium profits specifically attributable to the brand or other intangible asset may be estimated (for example) by comparing the price of branded products and unbranded products. The estimated premium profits can then be capitalised by discounting at a risk-adjusted market rate.

Capitalisation of earnings method

With the capitalised earnings method, the **maintainable earnings accruing to the intangible asset** are estimated. An **earnings multiple** is then applied to the earnings, taking account of expected risks and rewards, including the prospects for future earnings growth and the risks involved. This method of valuation is often used to value **publishing titles.**

Comparison with market transactions method

This method looks at **actual market transactions** in similar intangible assets. A multiple of revenue or earnings from the intangible asset might then be derived from a similar market transaction. A problem with this method is that many **intangible assets are unique** and it may therefore be difficult to identify 'similar' market transactions, although this might be done by examining acquisitions and disposals of businesses that include similar intangible assets.

The method might be used alongside other valuation methods, to provide a comparison.

9 Firms with Product Options

A product option is where a firm has the option to sell a product in the future but does not have the obligation to do so. Traditional valuation techniques may not be suitable for valuing firms with product options – the option-based approach may be more suitable. Examples of product options are patents and copyrights, and firms owning natural resources. Firms that have product options are often research and technology-based. When a firm has a product option that is not currently generating cash flow, there is a risk that a discounted cash flow approach to valuation will not fully reflect that full value of the option. This is because a DCF approach may not incorporate all the possible future cash flows of the company.

Problems with traditional DCF techniques

The value of a firm usually comes from two different sources, as follows:

- The current assets of the business. Typically, the value of the current assets can be captured in the current cash flows of the firm.
- The present value of any future growth opportunities. Typically, the value of future growth opportunities is captured by the growth in cash flows in the future.

In the context of a product option, this approach is not fully appropriate, for the following reasons:

- The options represent a current asset of the business, but are not generating any cash flows.
- Any cash flows expected to be generated by the product could be outside of the detailed forecasting period.

Possible Solutions to the Valuation Problem

There are three possible methods of valuing product options:

- **Value the option on the open market.** This is only possible if there is a traded market in such options. If there is no active market or if the option is difficult to separate from the other operations of the firm, this approach is probably not feasible.
- Use a traditional **DCF framework** and factor in a higher growth rate than would be justified given the existing assets of the firm. The problem with this is that any growth rate used will be subjective. In addition, it expresses contingent cash flows as expected cash flows.
- Use an **option-based approach** to valuation. This is considered below.

Use of Option Pricing Models

Benefits and problems of option pricing models

The benefit of using option pricing models is that the approach is based on **contingent claim valuation**, which reflects the situation more precisely than a DCF approach.

The problems of using option pricing models, such as Black-Scholes, are as follows:

(a) **They need the underlying asset to be traded.** This is because the model is based on the principle of arbitrage, which means that the underlying asset must be easy to buy and sell. This is not a problem when valuing options on quoted shares. However, the underlying asset in the context of product options will not be traded, meaning that arbitrage is not possible.

(b) **They assume that the price of the underlying asset follows a continuous pattern.** While this maybe a reasonable approximation most of the time for quoted shares, it is clearly inappropriate in the context of product options. The impact of this is that the model will undervalue deeply out-of the- money options, since it will underestimate the probability of a sudden large increase in the value of the underlying asset.

(c) **They assume that the standard deviation of price of the underlying asset is known** and does not vary over the life of the option. While this may be a reasonable assumption in the context of short-dated equity options, it is not appropriate for long-term product options.

(d) **They assume that exercise occurs at a precise point in time.** In the case of product options, exercise may occur over a long period of time. For example, if a firm has the right to mine natural resources, it will take time to extract the resources. This will reduce the present value of the asset.

Using option pricing models to value product patents

When valuing product patents as options, the key inputs for an option pricing will need to be identified, being the underlying asset price, the strike price, the expected volatility of the underlying asset price and the time to expiry. The following approach could be adopted.

STEP 1 **Identify the value of the underlying asset.** This will be based on the expected cash flows that the asset can generate. Given the uncertain nature of the cash flows and the distant time periods in which they may arise, it clearly will be difficult to value the underlying asset precisely.

STEP 2 **Identify the standard deviation of the cash flows above**. Again this will be difficult to identify, owing to changes in the potential market for the product, changes in technology and so on. It would, however, be possible to use techniques such as scenario analysis. The higher the standard deviation, the more valuable the asset.

STEP 3 Identify the **exercise price of the option.** This is the cost of investing in the resources needed to produce the asset. It is typically assumed that this remains constant in present value terms, with any uncertainty being reflected in the cash flows of the asset.

STEP 4 **Identify the expiry date of the option.** This is when the patent expires. Any cash flows after this date are expected to have an NPV of zero, since there will be generic competition after patent protection ends.

STEP 5 **Identify the cost of delay.** If the product is not implemented immediately, this will reduce the value of the cash flows from the project as competing products will enter the market in future years. A similar approach could be adopted to valuing other product options, such as natural resources. Where a company is investing in research and development, but has no patents developed, the same approach will apply, but the value of the option is clearly even more uncertain due to the greater uncertainty of the inputs.

A similar approach could be adopted to value other product options, such as natural resources. Where a company is investing in research and development, but has no patents developed, the same approach will apply, but the value of the option is clearly even more uncertain due to the greater uncertainty of the inputs.

Deal Structuring

chapter 11

Contents

1 Introduction

This section considers the relative merits of a share purchase versus structuring a deal as the purchase of assets. We also examine different forms of transaction consideration and why each might be appropriate to use. We look at deal effects and how the rationale for a transaction can be substantiated by financial analysis. We finish off by considering the ways that public deals can be put into effect – contrasting takeover offers and schemes of arrangement and a consideration of bid tactics.

2 Structuring the Deal

Shares versus Assets Purchases

When buying a business in a private deal, it is possible to acquire either the shares of the company that is conducting the business or to buy the business and the related assets from the company. The factors to consider in deciding which route to follow include the following.

Share Deal

- The transaction will put the cash directly in the hands of the vendor, whereas selling assets would keep the cash in the company selling the assets. Taking the cash out of the company will involve additional tax charges. Receiving cash directly will only incur capital gains tax liabilities. If the consideration being paid is not cash, but shares or loan stock, then any capital gains tax liability may be deferred.
- The share deal will preserve tax losses in the business being sold, if applicable. Selling the business would mean that the acquirer would probably be unable to use these losses.
- Transferring shares may make it easier to keep the business of the target company intact, eg preserving long-term contracts with key customers.
- Given the business is transferring intact, the sale and purchase agreement will include detailed warranties and indemnities regarding the nature of the business to be sold.
- Transferring shares will avoid potential problems with loss and clawback of capital allowances that may occur with an asset sale.

Assets Purchase

- The acquirer can pick and choose which business assets he wishes to buy. The exception to this is the target company's staff, who will transfer automatically in the UK under 'TUPE' employment regulation – Transfer of Undertakings (Protection of Employment) Regulations 2006.
- The target company's liabilities are not transferred without explicit agreement.
- The business can be put into a 'clean' company and, hence, there is no risk of unpleasant surprises or liabilities in the future. This avoids the need for many of the detailed warranties and indemnities in the sale agreement.
- If the acquirer has previously disposed of certain business assets, such as land and buildings or plant and machinery, then it may be able to claim roll-over relief when it replaces these by purchasing the assets of the target company.
- Purchase of assets will result in different capital allowances being received when compared to the purchase of shares in the company, which may be disadvantageous.
- Purchase of assets will create goodwill in the acquirer's accounts, whereas this may be avoided in the case of a shares purchase.
- The target company will remain in existence, unless liquidated.

- The vendor effectively is subject to two tax charges: there will be an immediate gain on the asset sale arising in the target company, amounting to the difference between the sales price and the book value of the assets. A subsequent gain will arise if the proceeds are distributed to shareholders in the form of a dividend or a liquidation distribution.

3 Offer Consideration

We are concerned here with how the offer is to be financed. This will usually be a choice between cash or equity.

Cash Bid

- The vendor's connection with the company is severed. He will, therefore, feel no concern as to whether or not the company does well in the future. Cash consideration provides the vendor with an exit route from the business and a way to realise his investment.
- The vendor will have to pay capital gains tax immediately on any gain.
- The acquirer's gearing will increase, if borrowings have been raised to finance the purchase. For a group with little debt, this may have the desirable effect of lowering the overall WACC of the company. For a highly geared company, the increase in financial risk of the entity may have a negative impact on credit rating and therefore overall cost of capital. In the latter scenario, it may be appropriate to raise the cash via a rights issue, termed a 'cash underpinning'.
- The earnings of the acquiring group will be boosted by the profits of the target but reduced by the additional interest expense on increased borrowings or the lower interest income due to reduced cash balances. The net effect is likely to be an increase in earnings per share, but the quality of the earnings will have fallen as a result of the increased gearing.
- All the gains of the acquisition after allowing for the cost of the deal will go to existing shareholders of the acquirer. Their interest in the group has not been diluted through the introduction of additional shareholders.

Shares Bid

- The fortunes of the vendor are tied in with the acquirer. It is, therefore, in his interests to ensure that the company does well in the future. It provides a way for the acquirer to incentivise the existing owners to maximise value in the post-acquisition period. Typically, the vendor of a private company will not be allowed to sell the shares for several years via a 'lock-in' arrangement.
- The vendor will be able to roll over any capital gains tax liability until the shares are disposed of. This will assist in tax planning.
- The gearing of the acquirer will reduce as a result of issuing shares, although this does depend on the level of gearing in the acquired company.
- The earnings of the acquirer will be boosted by the profits of the acquired company, but these will be spread over more shares, with the effect on earnings per share being uncertain. Generally, if a company acquires another company on a P/E ratio lower than its own, then the earnings per share subsequent to the acquisition should improve.
- It may be possible to use merger accounting in the group accounts as an alternative to acquisition accounting. This will give the acquirer more flexibility in how it prepares its accounts. Merger accounting is only available for share-for-share deals.
- The gains arising from the acquisition will have to be shared with the new shareholders. The interests of the existing shareholders will have been diluted by the issue of new shares to outsiders.
- The total dividend will need to be increased in order to maintain dividend per share after the acquisition.

Loan Stock

Instead of borrowing from outside providers of finance to fund a cash bid, the acquirer may issue loan stock to the vendor. Loan stock is an 'IOU' from the acquirer to the target company shareholders. Loan stock enables the vendor to defer any capital gains tax liability until the loan stock is disposed of. It may also reduce the effective price of the acquisition if the coupon on the loan stock is below a market rate of interest.

4 Earn Outs and Deferred Consideration

Advantages of Earn Outs

It is possible for a transaction to be structures so that the final consideration for a deal is paid several years after completion and is linked to the profit performance of the acquired company. This is termed as 'contingent' consideration or using an 'earn out'. The obvious advantage for the acquirer is that it ensures that a full price will only be paid if certain financial targets are met in the post-acquisition period. It will also often mean that the vendor will stay on to manage the acquired company for several years. This will ensure continuity of management, enable a smooth transition to be made in terms of management over the period of the earn out and keep in the company an individual who may well be instrumental in the company's past success.

Deals can also be structured using deferred consideration where there is certainty at the outset as to the total consideration to be paid; however this is paid in instalments, thus helping the cash flow of the bidding company.

Problems of Earn Outs

- Calculation of profits for the purpose of working out the deferred consideration will need to be exactly defined. The temptation is for both sides to adjust the profits to suit themselves. The vendor, who is still the key director of the acquired company, may argue for reduced provisions for doubtful debtors, etc, whereas the acquirer may seek to impose excessive management charges against the company.
- The level of integration of the subsidiary with the group will need to be established. The group will want to integrate it as fully as possible in order to realise the anticipated benefits of the acquisition. However, it will need to be kept separate for the purposes of profit calculations. If central services are provided by the group, then this will reduce the costs in the subsidiary but a management charge will be made. Such charges can be difficult to negotiate and be seen as fair.
- The acquiring company's directors will seek to control the direction in which the subsidiary is heading, for the benefit of the overall group. This may conflict with the desire of the vendor to maximise profits over the period of the earn-out. It will be difficult to ensure goal congruence between the vendor and the acquirer.
- The vendor will find it difficult to operate within the constraints of a large organisation and with budgets imposed from outside. His or her ability to run a successful business may have stemmed from the ability to make decisions quickly without reference to any outsiders. Furthermore, the vendor's status in the company will have changed and this may be hard for him or her to take.
- Earn outs can work against the long-term good of the business. The managers may be incentivised to focus too much on short-term profit targets and avoid making difficult decisions that have a detrimental impact on profit today but benefit the business as a whole in the long term. For example, if targets are based on a measure of free cash flow, capital expenditure could be put off until after the earn-out period is completed.

5 Analysing Deal Effects

When commentators are appraising public company acquisitions, they will look to financial analysis to substantiate the commercial justification for the transaction. Pro-forma numbers are helpful here. Pro-forma numbers calculate key ratios to provide a comparison between a company on a stand-alone basis and as part of a pro-forma merged entity. This makes a direct comparison possible – is there a direct financial justification for the deal? We often use the latest historical financial results for the calculation, to develop some 'what if?' scenarios for consideration. The most common deal effects that are computed are:

- Pro-forma earnings per share
- Pro-forma gearing
- Pro-forma statement of net assets

Other factors that commentators consider are the size of any bid premium, the P/E ratio post-acquisition and dividend policy.

Calculating Pro-forma Earnings Per Share

Commentators will want to know if a transaction is earnings 'enhancing' or 'accretive' (EPS is improved) or if it is earnings 'dilutive' (EPS worsens). For an acquisition, we can make this conclusion by comparing the earnings per share of the acquirer on a standalone basis, versus the pro-forma earnings per share of the enlarged entity.

- Where the earnings per share of the acquirer $<$ the earnings per share of the acquirer and target on a pro-forma basis, the transaction is said to be **earnings enhancing**
- Where the earnings per share of the acquirer $>$ the earnings per share of the acquirer and target on a pro-forma basis, the transaction is said to be **earnings dilutive**

When calculating the pro-forma earnings per share of the combined entity, bear in mind the following considerations:

- The post-tax impact of any **synergies** should be included. For the EPS calculation, we are looking at the impact on earnings and thus synergies need to be incorporated on an accruals basis. Remember that synergies can be negative, as well as positive.
- The post-tax impact of the **financing structure on earnings** needs consideration. For example, the interest on new borrowings should be factored in, as well as the interest receivable lost on cash consideration paid out as part of the transaction terms.
- The pro-forma number of **ordinary shares** must take account of the financing structure ie any new shares to be issued as offer consideration must be included.

In the current low interest rate climate, potential acquirers have found that many acquisitions are earnings enhancing, given the poor return that businesses earn on their retained cash.

For a transaction where the consideration is new acquirer shares, if the target company has a higher P/E ratio than the acquirer, then the transaction will be earnings dilutive. This is because the acquirer has to pay more for each pound of target company earnings than the market currently rates its own earnings. In terms of the calculation, the pro-forma number of shares (denominator) will go up by more than the pro-forma earnings (numerator), causing EPS to decline.

EXAMPLE

Giant Inc takes over Tiddler Co by offering two shares in Giant for one share in Tiddler. Details about each company are as follows.

	Giant Inc	Tiddler Co
Number of shares	2,800,000	100,000
Market value per share	$4	–
Annual earnings	$560,000	$50,000
EPS	20p	50p
P/E ratio	20	

By offering two shares in Giant worth $4 each for one share in Tiddler, the valuation placed on each Tiddler share is $8, and with Tiddler's EPS of 50c, this implies that Tiddler would be acquired on a P/E ratio of 16. This is lower than the P/E ratio of Giant, which is 20.

If the acquisition produces no synergy, and there is no growth in the earnings of either Giant or its new subsidiary Tiddler, then the EPS of Giant would still be higher than before, because Tiddler was bought on a lower P/E ratio. The combined group's results would be as follows.

	Giant group
Number of shares (2,800,000 + 200,000)	3,000,000
Annual earnings (560,000 + 50,000)	610,000
EPS	20.33c

If the P/E ratio is still 20, the market value per share would be $4.07 (20.33 × 0.20), which is 7c more than the pre-takeover price.

The process of buying a company with a higher P/E ratio in order to boost your own EPS is known as bootstrapping. Whether the stock market is fooled by this process is debatable. The P/E ratio is likely to fall after the takeover in the absence of synergistic or other gains.

You might think that dilution of earnings must be avoided at all costs. However, there are three cases where a dilution of earnings might be accepted on an acquisition if there were other advantages to be gained.

(a) Earnings growth may hide the dilution in EPS

(b) A company might be willing to accept earnings dilution if the quality of the acquired company'searnings is superior to that of the acquiring company

(c) A trading company with high earnings, but with few assets, may want to increase its assets base by acquiring a company which is strong in assets but weak in earnings so that assets and earnings get more into line with each other. In this case, dilution in earnings is compensated for by an increase in net asset backing.

Calculating Pro-forma Gearing

Pro-forma gearing ratios assess the change in financial risk as a result of the transaction. A comparison is made between the acquirer's existing gearing ratio, calculated as interest-bearing borrowings divided by shareholders' funds and the pro-forma gearing ratio, which considers the borrowings and shareholders' funds of the enlarged group. If the gearing ratio has increased, the acquirer's shareholders will need to be convinced that forecast cash flows for the combined entity are sufficient to service the levels of borrowings. They will be mindful of the existing operating leverage of the business (how volatile are earnings?) and the current asset-backing. Combining different earnings streams can reduce volatility and therefore the risk appetite of shareholders for debt may increase.

The following considerations impact the calculation:

- The pro-forma debt number should be based on the borrowings of the enlarged entity, namely the acquirer borrowings and any borrowings necessary to fund the transaction.
- The pro-forma equity number should include any new equity to be issued. In addition, shareholders' funds should be adjusted to include accrued profits in retained earnings, between the balance sheet date and the date of the transaction.
- Gearing ratios can be distorted by accounting policy choices and therefore the ratios should be computed eliminating accounting policy differences between the two companies.

Calculating Pro-forma Net Assets Per Share

Pro-forma net assets per share gives an idea of the relative size of the enlarged entity, versus the acquirer. It also provides the basis for other calculations, for example, pro-forma gearing and pro-forma return on equity.

The following considerations are relevant:

- The net assets of the two companies need to be added together, taking account of fair value adjustments and aligning accounting policies.
- The net assets need to be adjusted for profit accruals between the last balance sheet date and the proposed transaction date.
- Any goodwill arising on the acquisition should be capitalised as an intangible asset, calculated as the difference between the fair value of the acquisition consideration and the fair value to the acquirer of the net assets of the business that is to be acquired.

Other Factors

Other factors that commentators consider are the size of any bid premium, the P/E ratio post-acquisition and dividend policy.

Bid premium

Where the target company is listed, the acquirer will consider the size of the bid premium. The bid premium is calculated as the increase in bid price over the pre-announcement share price of the target company. The share price chosen is the last closing share price prior to a market announcement relating to the transaction. Sometimes, the bid premium is calculated by comparing the bid price to the average of the target's share price over a period time, often six months', in the pre-announcement period. This is to ensure the impact of any market rumours is excluded. Once computed, the bid premium can be compared to comparable market transactions to see if it is reasonable.

P/E Ratio Post Acquisition

A combine P/E ratio for the combined entity can be calculated by weighting the existing P/E ratios of both companies by their market values. This gives a basic means to assess the market rating of the new entity.

EXAMPLE

Acquirer market value	= \$2.1bn, with a P/E ratio of 9x
Target market value	= \$250m, with a P/E ratio of 6x
Combined P/E	= {(2,100 × 9) + (250 × 6)}/(2,100 + 250)
	= 8.7x

Dividend Policy

Commentators will assess the relative dividend policy by looking at the payout ratios of the two businesses. The payout ratio is calculated as the dividend per share divided by the earnings per share. A view can then be taken on what the likely payout ratio of the combined group will be.

6 Sharing of Merger Gains

The financial gains expected to arise from the acquisition will not necessarily all accrue to the acquirer company shareholders. The nature of the acquisition consideration will determine the basis of sharing of merger gains between acquirer and target company shareholders.

This concept is best illustrated by an example.

EXAMPLE

Africa plc pays €1.2m cash consideration to purchase Botswana plc. The existing market value of Africa is €10m and existing market value of Botswana is €875,000. Africa has 1 million shares in issue and anticipate that €500,000 merger gains will arise from the transaction.

(i) What is the bid premium?

(ii) What proportion of total acquisition gains go to Africa shareholders?

(iii) What would be the bid premium if the transaction was instead funded by 120,000 new Africa shares?

SOLUTION

(i) Bid premium = acquisition consideration – market value of target (pre-bid)
= 1,200,000 – 875,000
= €325,000

(ii) Gains to Africa = 500,000 – 325,000
= €175,000

(iii) With equity consideration, Botswana shareholders will now participate in the future gains and losses of the combined entity.

New bid premium = original bid premium + B's share of A's merger gains
= 325,000 + {(120/1,120) × 175,000}
= €343,750

7 Calculating Control Premia

The per share value for a controlling stake is greater than the per share value for a minority stake. A controlling stake gives the power to decide business strategy; acquisitions and disposals; the level of dividends; who to appoint as a director; how much to pay directors; which business options to pursue. A minority stake gives only the right to receive dividends and capital gains.

When an acquirer agrees the deal consideration, the acquisition price should include a control premium. A control premium is often quantified by looking at comparable transactions. However establishing true comparability is very difficult due to differences in individual circumstances caused by different synergies; strategies etc. In addition, unless the comparable transaction is very recent, comparability is likely to have been eroded by changing market conditions.

The control premium must be justified to acquirer shareholders by a quantification of deal synergies. The bid premium should never exceed the present value of the estimated synergistic benefits that are expected to arise.

In practice, the need to apply a control premium to the valuation that is computed, will depend on the valuation method chosen. The following table provides guidance for you on this matter:

Valuation Method	Control premium?
Discounted cash flow	A DCF calculation values a business on a controlling basis already. There is therefore no need to add on a separate control premium
Comparable company multiples	Comparable company multiples assume a minority holding. A separate control premium must be added on to the valuation.
Comparable transaction multiples	Already includes a control premium

Marketability Discounts

For valuations of unlisted companies, a marketability discount is sometimes applied to the final valuation to reflect the fact that there is not an active market in which to trade the company's shares. It is therefore harder to value the company and the investment is illiquid.

In practice, the marketability of all investments has improved, as markets become more homogenous and liquid. The appropriate size of a marketability discount is thus getting smaller. The size of discount in any scenario (if any) is therefore up for individual negotiation. If appropriate, marketability discounts should be applied to valuations computed by both discounted cash flow and multiples methods.

8 Takeovers of Public Limited Companies

There are two main methods to takeover public limited companies in the UK: **a takeover offer** to the shareholders of the target company or a **scheme of arrangement**. A takeover offer is structured as an invitation to the offeree shareholders by the offeror and a scheme of arrangement is a proposal by the target company to its own shareholders and/or creditors.

For a takeover offer to be successful, offeree company shareholders amounting to the specified acceptances level must vote to accept the offer. For a scheme to be successful, offeree shareholders must vote in a general meeting to accept the scheme and the scheme needs court approval.

If successful, both methods will result in the takeover of the offeree by the offeror and both methods are subject to the provisions of the City Code on Takeovers and Mergers.

The following section of the material, Regulation, Governance and Ethics, considers the provisions of the City Code in detail. In this chapter, we concentrate on the overall process of a public company takeover and consider how this differs from the private company acquisition process covered earlier.

9 Takeover Offer

We have looked already at the acquisition process for private companies. By necessity, this process is collaborative, and the terms of the transaction are worked out in negotiation between the offeror company and the offeree directors. With public companies, it is likely that there is a separation between the offeree company directors and offeree shareholders (who have ownership). Offers for public companies thus follow a different process, with the offeror appealing directly to the offeree shareholders who will determine the bid outcome. Offeror shareholder approval is also necessary if the transaction is particularly material for the offeror (required by the Listing Rules).

All takeover offers for UK public limited companies (both listed and unlisted) are covered by the City Code on Takeovers and Mergers. The City Code contains detailed provisions relating to the way an offer is conducted to ensure fair treatment of offeree shareholders and to avoid the creation of a false market in offeree company shares during the course of the bid. Offeree directors are required to communicate their views on the offer to the shareholders, but are prevented from undertaking action designed to frustrate the bid. Shareholders must be allowed to decide for themselves on the merits of the bid. In addition, the offeror must treat all offeree shareholders of the same class, as far as possible, equally – so no special deals with significant shareholders are allowed.

The takeover offer is an invitation by an offeror company to the shareholders of the offeree public limited company. The offer will include the price and terms of the offer, including the nature of the consideration to be paid. The offer will also incorporate an acceptances condition. The acceptances condition will specify the percentage of share capital which the offeror requires for the offer to be declared 'unconditional as to acceptances'. This acceptances level can be chosen by the offeror; it must be a minimum of 50%, but is usually set at 90%. A 90% level of acceptances, allows an offeror to evoke the compulsory purchase provisions available under the Companies Act 2006, thus gaining 100% of the offeree company.

The main due diligence exercise carried out by the offeror is undertaken from publicly available information prior to the launch of the offer. Due diligence is limited once the offer process commences. In particular, offeree companies will be mindful of the provisions of the City Code, which state that information given to one offeror or potential offeror must also be given on request to another offeror or bona fide potential offeror, regardless of whether or not their offer is welcome (*City Code, Rule 20.2*). The offeror must request the information specifically and cannot frame a request in general terms.

Public company takeovers do not have a sale and purchase agreement, as is used in private company acquisitions. The legal document is the 'offer document' which contains the offer conditions, such as regulatory clearances and information that is to be furnished to the offeror. In a voluntary offer, the offeror can include whatever conditions they wish to, provided that the conditions do not depend solely on subjective judgements by the directors of the offeror or if the fulfilment of the condition lies in their hands (*City Code, Rule 13*). If this proviso were not in existence, it would be easy for offerors to withdraw their offers at will and at any time by setting subjective conditions. If the conditions are met, the transaction completes and a change in ownership is affected.

10 Schemes of Arrangement

A Scheme of Arrangement is a statutory procedure, under Part 26 (*Sections 895–901*) of the Companies Act 2006, which allows a company to make an arrangement or compromise with its shareholders or creditors. Once the Scheme is approved by the requisite majority of shareholders or creditors and sanctioned by the court, the Scheme is binding on all, whether or not they have voted in favour of it. The requisite majority is 75% in value of members or creditors present and voting at the relevant court meeting, either in person or by proxy. Schemes can be used to effect a number of processes, including a takeover, an alteration of the rights of creditors, share buybacks, a debt restructuring and a compulsory purchase of minority shareholdings.

In a takeover context, the offeree company's shares are cancelled and then reissued to the bidder, in return for which the bidder pays the consideration to the target's shareholders. A scheme of arrangement can really only be used for an agreed bid, because the application to the court must be made by the company whose shares are being re-organised (ie the offeree). A Scheme does, however, have some advantages for the offeror: for example, there is a greater finality of outcome – either the scheme will be agreed or not. The offeror does not risk being left with a large stake but not 100% ownership. Once a scheme is sanctioned, the offeror is guaranteed 100% control of the target. Minority shareholders are bought out under the terms of the Scheme, whether they like it or not.

The need to seek court approval adds extra complication to a takeover via a Scheme, as opposed to a takeover offer. Scheme documentation is lengthy and complex, containing the same information as a takeover offer document, and also the relevant notices for shareholder meetings and the court hearing. As such, a Scheme is most expensive to effect in terms of advisers' fees and regulatory costs. However, on almost all Schemes stamp duty (at 0.5 per cent of the target's value at the offer price) can be saved. A takeover offer would generally be expected to provide the offeror with control of the offeree company quicker than a scheme. However acquiring, dissenting, outstanding minority shareholdings could substantially extend the timetable of the takeover offer beyond that of the scheme.

Schemes are less suitable to use where changes in terms of the offer are expected mid-way through the process. Changing offer terms, for example because a rival bidder has emerged, requires changing the terms of a scheme mid-way through the process and is likely to require the parties to go back to court.

Takeovers of UK public limited companies via Schemes of Arrangement are still subject to the provisions of the Takeover Code. Specific rules for Scheme of Arrangement takeovers are in Appendix 7 of the Code.

Recent years have seen a significant increase in the number of takeover deals effected by Schemes of Arrangements.

11 Agreed or Hostile Bid

Private Companies

In the case of a bid for an unlisted company, it is highly likely that the bid will need to be approved by the board of the company. This is because the board will probably own a significant number of shares and other shareholders will tend to follow the board's lead. If the board does not approve the bid, then the chances of success are usually so low that it will be best to find a different target.

Listed Companies

A bid for a listed company does not need to be approved, since the directors will probably not own a significant number of shares and the shareholder base is unlikely to have emotional or other attachments to the company. Instead, it is the fiduciary duty of directors to advise whether the bid is in the best interests of shareholders. If the bid is recommended by directors, it is termed an 'agreed' offer. If directors do not support the bid, then it is 'unrecommended' and, if to proceed, will do so on a 'hostile' basis.

Advantages of an Agreed Offer

Notwithstanding this, there can be advantages in obtaining board approval for a bid, as follows:

- There is a greater chance that shareholders will accept the bid.
- It may act as a disincentive for a hostile bidder to join the fray or persuade them to pull out.
- It will avoid the risk of the bidding company coming out worse in a public relations battle and damaging its reputation.
- More information will be forthcoming on the target company and make for an easier due diligence process.
- Integration of the target into the acquiring company's group may be easier.

Problems with Trying to Achieve an Agreed Offer

Against this, certain disadvantages must be considered:

- If talks fall through, then the bidder will have probably released information about itself to the target.
- It will give the target advance warning of the impending bid and, should the approach fail, enable the board to prepare their defence.

Surprisingly perhaps, obtaining board approval for a bid does not make it any cheaper for the bidder to acquire the company. It is true that, in a hostile situation, the bidder will be obliged to make the price sufficiently attractive to overcome opposition to the bid. However, in an agreed bid, the price will need to be set sufficiently high to deter other bidders from coming in. It will also need to ensure that the bid can be sold successfully to the target's shareholders without accusations of their board negotiating a bad deal.

12 Hostile Bid Tactics

A number of tactics can be adopted to enhance the chances of a bid's success as follows.

Stakebuilding

This can either be undertaken gradually or rapidly, via a dawn raid. In the case of the gradual build-up of interests, the danger is that the demand for the shares will be picked up by the company which will use its powers under S793 of the Companies Act 2006 to identify the acquirer. In any case, if 3% or more of the company is acquired, then the acquirer will be legally obliged to notify the company of its interests. This regulation sacrifices any element of market surprise.

In the case of a dawn raid, the company will quickly be identified and may be unable to acquire a significant number of shares if the market becomes aware of what is happening. It can be very time-consuming to accumulate shares from daily trading of the free float in the market.

Tender Offer

A bidder can consider making a tender offer directly to target shareholders. This is an invitation to shareholders to sell their shares to the bidder at a certain price within a specified time frame. In the UK, the Takeover Panel's consent is required for any tender offer. This consent is unlikely to be forthcoming for a tender offer for over 30% of the share capital of the target company. Tender offers have been used extensively in other jurisdictions, for example the United States, as a way to circumvent management and gain control even when managers oppose the takeover.

Advertising

The City Code prohibits advertising of a controversial nature about the bid *(Rule 19.4)*, but the company's image can be improved by selected and tasteful advertising of a more general nature.

Lobbying

In order to persuade politicians that the bid will be in the target's and the country's interests and prevent a referral to the Competition Commission or a subsequent blocking of the bid.

Public Relations Campaign

This may obtain press support and favourable press comment.

Investor Relations

This may persuade the bidding company's own shareholders of the validity of the bid and assure the target's investors of the bid's advantages.

Offer Document

In the case of superior performance of the bidder and its management, which will be relevant if the offer is shares and not just cash. It will also criticise the past performance of the target and illustrate the benefits of the bid for the target's shareholders.

Offer Price

It is important to ensure that the price is sufficiently competitive to:

- Make it unattractive for competing bidders to enter the fray or to stay in the frame, if already bidding
- Encourage target shareholders to accept

However, the price should not be so expensive as to result in the company overpaying.

White Knight

A bidder can portray itself as the saviour of the company subsequent to another hostile bidder announcing an offer.

13 DEFENCE STRATEGY AND TACTICS

General Housekeeping Before a Bid

The most effective method of defence is to ensure that the company is not perceived as being a bid target in the first place. The way to achieve this is to ensure that the company is fully and fairly valued by investors. If this is the case, then it is unlikely that any company will be motivated to bid, since there will be no prospect of satisfactory gains to be made from the acquisition. There are various ways of achieving this.

Investor Relations

Effective communication with the company's investor base will ensure that they understand its business and strategy, appreciate the reasons for short-term falls in profitability and will not sell out on the cheap just before results start to improve.

Investor Management

This will ensure that the shareholder base is appropriate for the company, so that they will be happy to stay committed for the longer term and not sell out at the first opportunity. It may be appropriate to develop friendly shareholdings with other companies. The danger of this is that a cross-holding ties up capital and a large shareholder who was originally perceived as friendly may either sell out on a bid or use its stake to launch a bid itself.

Group Strategy

Developing a clear and consistent group strategy will add value to the company and increase the share price. This strategy will, of course, need to be explained and communicated to investors.

Public Relations

The company should ensure that announcements, interim statements and final published accounts are produced in an attractive way that fully emphasises the strengths of the company. In addition, it should ensure that announcements are followed up appropriately with interviews and analysts' meetings.

Dividend Policy

The company should ensure that its dividend policy is suitable for its earnings stream and reflects investors' needs and expectations.

Specific Bid Preparation

In addition to the above points, techniques which can be used specifically to assist in defending against a bid include:

- Checking the share register for undesirable investors and identifying trends in share transactions. Powers to investigate shareholdings under S793 of the Companies Act 2006 can be used to identify undesirable shareholders
- Keeping a draft defence document ready to be tailored to meet a specific bid situation
- Keeping files of information on possible bidders ready for use
- Having a contingency plan ready for a bid, to be put into action at a moment's notice. This will include allocation of responsibilities for defence, setting up a defence committee and allocating everyday tasks in managing the business to others who will be less concerned with the bid defence. The details are often maintained in what is commonly referred to as a company's Defence Manual or 'Black Book'.

14 Bid Defence

After the bid has been launched, the company will only have a limited amount of time (around 60 days) to conduct its defence against the specific bidder. By contrast, the bidder may have spent a substantial amount of time identifying the target and putting together an attractive and feasible bid. This underlies the importance of good housekeeping before a bid to ensure that the company is as prepared as possible. Once the bidder has been identified, possible tactics include the following. There are rules relating to the contents and other matters related to Defence Document and Profit Forecasts released by a company in a potential transaction to which the Takeover Code applies.

Defence Document

It is, of course, vital to have a well-argued and cohesive defence document subsequent to receiving the offer document from the bidder.

Profit Forecast

The company may decide to issue a profit forecast. The danger with this is that it will need to be sufficiently optimistic in order to prevent the bidder's offer from seeming attractive, but must not be too ambitious. Otherwise it will either lose credibility in the short-term or act as a hostage to fortune in the longer term, when the company has to achieve those results.

Attack as a Form of Defence

In a share bid, attacking the bidder's management, strategy and accounting policies (used to show improving profits) can be particularly effective.

Public Relations

Lobbying, effective public relations and advertising may assist in turning the tide of investor opinion or may cause the bid to be referred to the Competition Commission.

Restructuring

The company may announce an intention to restructure itself, by selling off a major division or demerging the company into separate divisions, each with a listing.

White Knight

The company could encourage a counter bid from a friendly bidder or white knight, although this will mean that the company will lose its independence. An alternative would be the purchase of a large block of target shares by a 'white squire', who does not take control but agrees to vote in alignment with target management. The white squire can disrupt the hostile takeover process and help the company retain its independence.

Dividend Increases

Increases in dividends may pacify investors. However, this may be seen as too little, too late. Also, if the increase is too large, it may beg questions as to why it has only been done now and raise doubts as to whether the larger dividend is sustainable in the future.

Frustrating Action

The City Code prohibits the board of the target company from taking actions which would frustrate a bona fide offer or prevent its shareholders from deciding on the bid's own merits. Therefore, actions such as disposals of significant business assets in the course of a bid will need shareholder approval. In addition, preferential treatment of certain shareholders will go against the basic principle of equal treatment for all offeree shareholders. This means that many frustrating action techniques used in other jurisdictions (eg the US), would not be possible in the UK.

Examples of frustrating action:

- Changes to a company's constitutional documents that limit the ability of a predator to gain control. For example, changes in the voting rights of shares in the event of a hostile bid to effectively block a predator gaining control or the use of dual class voting shares.
- Golden parachutes, granting management generous severance payments if they lose their jobs in the event of a hostile bid.
- Crown jewels defence; where key assets are sold from the business prior to a hostile bidder gaining control.
- Leveraged recapitalisation; the target company draws down a significant amount of debt and uses it to pay a special dividend to shareholders. This means the bidder acquires a much larger debt burden than expected. Leveraged recapitalisations can be structured to include 'poison puts' whereby the debt becomes immediately repayable on a change of control of the company.
- Greenmail. Here the target company buys back shares from the bidder at an inflated premium not available to other shareholders. Greenmail will temporarily repel an intruder but will not stop other potential purchasers. Again, under the Takeover Code this is not permitted, as it is against the interests of the other shareholders of the offeree.

Takeover and Disclosure Rules

chapter 12

Contents

1 INTRODUCTION

This chapter examines the regulatory issues that govern the conduct of much corporate finance activity in the UK, namely the Disclosure and Transparency Rules, the Companies Act 2006 and the Takeover Code.

2 DISCLOSURE RULES AND TRANSPARENCY RULES (DTR)

The Transparency Directive was introduced in 2007 and led to the enforcement by the FCA of The Disclosure Rules and Transparency Rules (DTR). The relevant requirements of the DTR are covered below. Issuers are generally required to disseminate regulatory announcements through an approved Regulated Information Service (RIS), of which the following are examples:

- Regulatory News Service (RNS) of the LSE
- ONE – part of Thomson Reuters
- PR Newswire Disclose
- Business Wire Regulatory Disclosure

Shareholdings Notification Requirements

Notification requirements for major shareholdings are included in DTR 5. Where a person's holding of financial instruments on the relevant market:

- **Reaches or falls below 3%** of the voting rights; or
- **Increases or reduces across one full percentage point** above 3% (eg: 4.9% to 5.2%).

then they must **notify the company within two business days**. They need to use a prescribed form available on the FCA website, and also **file a copy electronically with the FCA**.

The rules apply to a **wider range of issuers** than the Transparency Directive requires, as it applies to issuers on all regulated and prescribed markets, thus including the Alternative Investment Market (AIM) and PLUS-SX. The Transparency Directive requires the disclosure of holdings of shares to which voting rights are attached. Notification is required in respect of indirect holdings, which **includes holdings by 'concert parties'**. Under DTR, a person is an indirect holder of shares held by a third party if they agree that they should adopt, by concerted exercise of the voting rights they hold, a 'lasting common policy towards the management' of the company in question.

There are some exclusions to these provisions. For instance voting rights are normally disregarded for shares that are held by market makers, but only up to a threshold of 10% of voting right and held by a custodian (or nominee) in its custodian (or nominee) capacity.

Company's Power to Request Information on Shareholders

Section 793 CA 2006 states that where a public company knows or has reasonable cause to believe that someone has **at any time in the previous three years** had an interest in the company's share capital, then they can send a notice to the person requiring them to confirm whether or not this is the case. If the person has had an interest in the shares, then the notice can also require him to **disclose details of his holding, whether it is part of a concert party holding and to whom he sold the interest**, if relevant.

The person should reply **within the time limit set** by the notice, which should be reasonable. If he fails to do so then the **company can suspend the shares' voting and other rights** (s794 CA 2006). Once the company has obtained information in this manner, it should enter the details on its share register.

Shareholders of the company **holding at least 10% of the voting rights** can require a company to use its powers under s793 Companies Act 2006 to identify another shareholder.

Compulsory Purchase Provisions

Sections 974-991 CA 2006 provide that, where a person making a takeover bid has acquired at least 90% of the shares in each class to which an offer relates and 90% of the voting rights, then the offeror is entitled to acquire the remaining shares compulsorily. In addition (s983 CA 2006), when a offeror acquires at least 90% in value of the shares or of a class of shares of the company, then the relevant minority shareholders can force him to purchase their shares.

Given these legal rights it is likely that, when an offeror manages to acquire 90% of the shares bid for, they will automatically move to a 100% holding.

Further requirements

The offeror must notify the remaining shareholders within three months of reaching the 90% figure that they intend to use the compulsory purchase provisions. They must pay the same consideration as that given to the other shareholders.

Statutory Protection of the Minority

Majority rule is the basis of democracy. However, there must be provisions to ensure that minorities are protected from exploitation. Company law seeks to protect minority shareholdings in a number of ways. First, it imposes restrictions on certain company actions. Where these are particularly significant, the approval by 75% of shareholders of a special resolution is required. In addition, a dissenting minority has the option of complaining to the Courts.

In addition to the general requirements set out above, there are also statutory remedies contained in the company law legislation. In particular, ss994–998 CA 2006 allow shareholders to bring court proceedings for unfairly prejudicial conduct.

3 European Takeover Directive

The European Takeover Directive came into force in 2004. Each Member State was required to implement the Directive in their domestic legislation. The Directive was a framework measure setting minimum requirements for Member States, but allowing them latitude to adopt additional and more stringent requirements. It included a set of General Principles (derived from the UK Takeover Code) and a limited number of specific requirements.

There were few material changes of substance to the Takeover Code in the UK. Key points of interest were as follows:

- The Panel was given statutory powers to make and amend takeover rules.
- The Directive's six General Principles replaced the Panel's ten General Principles but there was no material difference in substance between the two.
- The Panel was given power to be able to require bidding companies to pay compensation to target shareholders where there is a breach of rules and may apply to the courts to enforce its rulings.
- The Panel was given formal statutory power to require parties to provide information to it, where this information would otherwise not be forthcoming. All parties subject to the Code were also under an obligation to disclose to the Panel any information of which the Panel might reasonably expect notice of.

- The Directive allowed opt-outs from some important areas such as frustration and the use of golden share structures. This means it arguably failed to harmonise EU takeover regulation. Taking frustration as an example, the initial draft of the Directive effectively prevented a company from taking defensive action during a hostile bid without the prior approval of the shareholders. The final wording of the Directive prohibits frustration without shareholder approval but allows Member States to opt out of this provision.
- It became a criminal offence to publish an offer document which is not compliant with certain content requirements of the Directive.
- Offeror and offeree companies required to provide information to employees about the bid and offeree companies must give their employees a chance to comment.

Acquisitions Directive

The EU adopted the Acquisitions Directive in 2007, and its provisions were implemented in the UK in 2009.

The Directive precludes Member States from unreasonably preventing acquisitions of financial services firms. It aimed to encourage more cross-border mergers and acquisitions activity by improving transparency, consistency and the process of approvals. It also ensures that potential acquirers who are declined permission are given the information they need to challenge that decision if they wish to.

4 The Panel on Takeovers and Mergers

The Panel on Takeovers and Mergers ('the Panel') is responsible for regulating takeovers in the UK. Backing the Panel is the Bank of England, which appoints the Chairman and Deputy Chairmen. In addition, its membership draws from representatives of key City institutions. The purpose of the Panel is to monitor adherence to the general principles and detailed rules laid down in the City Code on Takeovers and Mergers ('the City Code" or 'the Code'). The Code is designed to provide an orderly framework within which takeovers are conducted. In addition, it is designed to promote, in conjunction with other regulatory regimes, the integrity of the financial markets.

The Panel has statutory authority from the Companies Act 2006. In addition, it has the support of regulatory authorities such as the Financial Services Authority (FCA), meaning that adherence to the City Code is indicative of best market practice. The FCA requires that all investment businesses follow best market practice and it may be that anyone who breaches the Code could have the facilities of the market withdrawn from them ('cold shouldering').

The Panel operates via a system of consultation and the City Code requires advisers and parties to a bid to discuss in advance any course of action related to a bid if there is uncertainty as to how the Code might apply. There are a number of advantages of the system of Takeover Regulation administered by the Panel, as follows:

- **Flexibility** – the Code can quickly be adapted to take account of changing circumstances. The law can only be changed very slowly.
- **Consultation in advance** – the Panel can be consulted in advance to ensure that the rules in the City Code are not going to be broken, albeit unintentionally
- **Quick decisions** – due to the system of consultation, the Panel can come up with speedy judgements
- **Focus on principles** – the Panel applies general principles of fairness in making its decisions. Companies must comply with the General Principles which represent the "spirit" of the code. An action can be deemed inappropriate if it does not uphold these principles.
- **Practitioner involvement** – this makes the City Code and its application more realistic, acceptable and effective
- **Links with other regulatory bodies** – the FCA requires compliance with the City Code and may cold-shoulder people who are severely censured by the Panel

5 When Does the Code Apply?

All UK, Channel Island and Isle of Man incorporated public companies which have securities admitted to trading on a multilateral trading facility (which includes AIM and the ISDX Growth Market) in the UK are subject to the Takeover Code, **irrespective of the company's place of central management and control**. The Code applies to all public and private companies if:

- They are registered in the UK, the Channel Islands or the Isle of Man; and
- Their securities are admitted to trading on a UK multilateral trading facility,

regardless of the location of that company's central management or control.

The Code also applies to offers for any private limited company (Ltd) resident in these areas if:

- The company's equity share capital has been listed on the London Stock Exchange at any time during the ten years prior to the offer being announced
- Dealings and/or prices in the company's shares have been published on a regular basis for a continuous period of at least six months in the last ten years
- The company's shares have been afforded dealing facilities on a recognised investment exchange in the last ten years.
- The company has filed a prospectus to issue equity shares in the last ten years

The objective of these rules is to cover any company where the public may have had an opportunity to purchase shares in the recent past.

It should be noted that if the Code applies to a transaction, then it will apply to **all parties** involved with that transaction (including the directors of the offeror and offeree and all of the professional advisers) regardless of where the offeror is incorporated or based.

The Code applies to all takeover and merger transactions, including partial offers for less than 100% of a company's shares and situations where **control** of a company is to be obtained or consolidated. However, it does not usually relate to offers for non-voting or non-equity shares.

Control is defined in the definitions as where **at least 30%** of the company's voting rights are held. Although, strictly speaking, control only becomes legally possible when more than 50% of the voting rights are held, the Panel believes that effective control can be achieved at this much lower percentage.

Waiver of the Code

The Panel has indicated that it is prepared to consider a waiver of the Code for a public company in the following circumstances:

- There are ten or less shareholders in the company; and
- All shareholders have confirmed in writing that they are happy to waive their rights under the Code.

Waivers are only available for specific transactions and not as a 'general' waiver. Panel permission to seek a waiver from shareholders must be sought in advance.

6 The Spirit of the Code

The main overriding principle of the Code is that all shareholders of the target company ("offeree shareholders") are treated fairly during the offer process and are not denied an opportunity to decide on the merits of a takeover.

There are six General Principles of the Code. The existence of the Principles recognises that it is impossible to devise rules that cover every situation. The General Principles assist companies and the Panel in interpreting and applying the spirit of the Code. Three key propositions of the Code sum up the spirit of the Code:

- Equal treatment for all offeree company shareholders
- Adequate and timely advice and information
- No false markets

Equal treatment for all shareholders

General Principle 1 states that all holders of securities of an offeree company of the same class must be afforded equivalent treatment; moreover, if a person acquires control of a company, the other holders of securities must be protected.

Adequate and timely advice and information

General Principle 2 states that shareholders must have sufficient time and information to enable them to reach a properly informed decision. General Principle 3 states that the board of an offeree company must act in the interests of the company (as opposed to, for instance, the directors' personal interests). They must allow shareholders the opportunity to consider the merits of the bid. Unapproved frustrating action is not permitted.

General Principle 6 states that the offeree company must not be hindered in the conduct of its affairs for longer than is reasonable by a bid for its securities. Takeover offers must be conducted in reference to the bid timetable set out in the Code.

No false markets

General Principle 4 provides that false markets must not be created in the securities of the offeree company, of the offeror company or of any companies concerned by the offer, in such a way that the rise or fall of the prices of the securities becomes artificial and the normal functioning of the markets is distorted. As a further point, General Principle 5 states that an offer should be announced by an offeror only once it can fulfil in full any cash consideration, if offered, and after taking all reasonable measures to secure the implementation of any other type of consideration.

7 The Offer Process

The method in which a company should make an offer is included in section D of the City Code. This covers how approaches should be made, what announcements are required and what advice should be sought by the offeree board.

The Approach (Rule 1)

Any approach must first be made to the board of the offeree company or to its advisers. The identity of the offeror must be disclosed.

Announcements (Rule 2)

In order to prevent leakage of price-sensitive information, it is vital that absolute secrecy is maintained prior to an offer being announced (*Rule 2.1*). The advisers to the offeror or offeree should always warn their clients of the importance of this. They are required to draw their clients' attention to the Code and to highlight the rules restricting share dealings (these rules are dealt with below). This is to ensure a false market does not develop in offeree company shares.

When an Announcement is Required

An announcement is required in the following circumstances (*Rule 2.2*). Consultation with the Panel to clarify whether an announcement is required is encouraged.

(a) A firm intention to make an offer has been notified to the offeree board from a serious source. The offeree board is obliged to make an announcement that it has received the offer regardless of its attitude to the offer.

(b) The offeror should make an announcement where an obligation to make an offer has arisen as a result of *Rule 9*, manadatory offers. The announcement should be made immediately after the obligation has been incurred.

(c) Where there is rumour and speculation or the offeree's share price moves untowardly (for example, by more than 5% in any one day or by more than 10% above the lowest price since an approach was made to the potential offeree), an announcement may be required in the following circumstances:

- If there has been an approach to the offeree company, in which case the offeree board should make an announcement.
- If no approach has yet been made but the potential offeror has reason to believe that its actions are causing the rumours or price changes, in which case the offeror should make an announcement. Where there is any doubt in this respect, the Panel should be consulted.

(d) Where negotiations or discussions are being extended to include more than a very restricted number of people outside of those in the company who need to know and their immediate advisers, then the offeree should make an announcement.

(e) Where a purchaser is being sought for a holding or aggregate of holdings which have 30% or more of the voting rights in the company or where a company is seeking potential offerors, then the offeree company will be required to make an announcement in any of the following circumstances:

- The company is subject to rumour and speculation or there is untoward movement in its share price.
- The number of offerors being approached is increasing beyond a very restricted number.

Contents of the Announcement of a Firm Offer

Where there is a firm intention to make an offer, a detailed 'firm intention' announcement is required. The announcement should contain details of the terms and conditions of the offer, the identity of the offeror and any existing holdings in the offeree which the offeror (or people acting in concert with him) owns, controls or has options to buy (*Rule 2.7*).

Contents of an Announcement of a Possible Offer

All 'possible offer' announcements made under *Rule 2.4* of the Code, which commence an offer period, will be required to identify a potential bidder. The possible offer announcement, whether released by the prospective offeror or offeree, will trigger an automatic 28 day 'put up or shut up' deadline by which time the named bidder must either commit to a 'firm intention to make an offer' announcement, or publicly withdraw from the offer process (*Rule 2.6*).

Offeror's Obligations

An offeror should only announce an offer if he knows that he has the ability to see the offer through, for example financing arrangements are in place. After an announcement has been made, an offeror must proceed with the offer unless permitted to withdraw by the Panel (*Rule 2.7*). Once an offeror has stated that he does not intend to make an offer, he will normally be bound by that statement for at least six months or until there is a material change in circumstances (*Rule 2.8*).

The purpose of this rule is to avoid uncertainty and the possibility of vexatious offers, which may create a false market in the offeree's shares.

Independent Advice (Rule 3)

After an offer has been received, the offeree board must obtain **competent and independent advice** on the offer (*Rule 3.1*). The substance of this advice must be made known to their shareholders. This is particularly important in the case of a management buyout (MBO), where the MBO directors will have a conflict of interest and will be unable to give advice to their shareholders.

If an adviser receives a fee dependent on the failure of a hostile bid, this will give an impression of a conflict of interest. Such an adviser will normally be disqualified from acting as a *Rule 3* adviser. In addition, the Panel will require such arrangements to be disclosed in a defence document.

Reverse Takeovers

A reverse takeover is typically a situation where a listed company makes a share offer for an unlisted counterpart. As a result of the offer, the original shareholders of the unlisted company end up owning more than 50% of the shares of the listed company. Effectively, the unlisted company becomes the acquirer and obtains a listing through being taken over in this way.

Where the offer is effectively a reverse takeover or the offeror directors have a conflict of interest, then the **offeror** must also obtain competent independent advice (*Rule 3.2*). The basis of this is that the offeror is effectively the offeree.

8 THE OFFER AND DEFENCE DOCUMENTS

General Obligation as to Information

Documents from the offeror and offeree boards are covered in section J of the Code. *Rule 23* states that shareholders must be given sufficient information and advice to enable them to reach a properly informed decision as to the merits of an offer. This information must be made available early enough for them to make a decision in good time.

The offer and defence documents are both essentially sales documents. As such, much of the required information below, which is not necessarily exciting to shareholders, will be relegated to the small print at the back of the document.

The Responsibility of the Directors

Any document or advertisement issued in connection with an offer must state that the directors of the offeror or offeree company, as appropriate, accept responsibility for the information contained in the document. It must also state that, to the best of the directors' knowledge, the information is in accordance with the facts and does not omit anything likely to affect the importance of the information (*Rule 19.2*).

If the information relates to another company and has been taken from published sources, then this responsibility is limited to ensuring that the information is correctly and fairly reproduced (*Note 3* to *Rule 19.2*).

9 The Offer Document

The offer document must be sent to offeree shareholders within 28 days of the announcement of a firm's intention to make an offer (*Rule 24.1*). On the day of publication, the offeror must publish the offer document on a website (usually its own) in accordance with *Rule 30.4*; and announce via a RIS that the offer document has been so published.

The principal contents are as follows:

(a) **The intentions of the offeror for the offeree company and its employees (*Rule 24.2*)**

This will include any major changes to be introduced and plans for continued employment of employees. The document should give the long-term commercial justification for the bid.

Typically, offer documents will make rather bland statements concerning the offeror's plans for existing employees. For example, they may just state that the existing rights of employees will be safeguarded. The commercial justification for the offer will be more fully developed, particularly in a share for share offer.

(b) **Financial and other information on the offeror and offeree company (*Rule 24.3*)**

- Names of directors
- Nature of the business and the financial and trading prospects
- The website address where the audited consolidated accounts for the last two years have been published
- The website address where an interim statement and/or preliminary announcement made since the date of the last published audited accounts have been published
- For a securities exchange offer, a description of any known significant change in the financial or trading position that has occurred since the end of the last financial period
- A pro-forma statement of earnings and net assets for the offeror
- Details of material contracts for the offeror for the two year period prior to the offer
- Rating agencies' outlooks and any changes made during the offer period

(c) **Offer conditions** (*Rule 24.3d*)

(d) **The terms of the offer** (*Rule 24.3d*), including the consideration offered and how this is to be paid

(e) **Share price comparisons.** The offeree historic share price for the first business day in the each of the six months immediately before the date of the offer document and for the last business day before the commencement of the offer period and for the last date before the publication of the offer document (*Rule 24.3d*)

It is often the case that the value of the offer is compared to the share price of the offeree. If this is done, there must be a comparison with the offeree share price on the last business day before the offer was announced along with any other comparison that may be made. This is meant to prevent solely unfair comparisons being made. (*Rule 24.3g*) The problem is that the share price of the offeree will often have moved before the announcement in anticipation of the offer. As a result, this share price will already contain an element of bid premium, reducing the validity of the comparison.

(f) **How the offer is to be financed (*Rule 24.3f*)**

There must be details of how the offer is to be financed and the source of any finance. This includes details of any debt instruments entered into in order to finance the offer.

Where the offer is for cash or includes an element of cash then the offeror's bankers or another appropriate adviser should confirm that resources are available to satisfy full acceptance of the offer *(Rule 24.8)*.

(g) **Details of any relevant shareholdings and dealings (*Rule 24.4*)**

These include shareholdings in the offeree by the offeror company and shareholdings in the offeror or the offeree company by the offeror's directors or people acting in concert with the offeror. It also includes dealings in derivatives referenced to the shares.

(h) Whether and in what manner the **emoluments of the offeror directors** will be affected by the acquisition of the offeree company or other associated transaction (*Rule 24.5*).

(i) **Responsibility statement (*Rule 19.2*)**

A statement that the directors of the offeror accept responsibility for the information contained within the document must be included in each document the offeror sends to shareholders.

(j) Fees and expenses (*Rule 24.16*). The offer document should contain an estimate of the fees and expenses expected to be incurred by the offeror, analysed by different fee categories.

10 THE DEFENCE DOCUMENT

The defence document should be sent to shareholders within 14 days of the publication of the offer document (*Rule 25.1*). On the day of publication, the offeree company must publish the document on a website (usually its own) in accordance with *Rule 30.4*; and announce via a RIS that the defence document has been so published.

The main contents of the defence document are as follows:

- **The views of the offeree board** on the offer and their reason for this view. An opinion on the effects of the implementation of the offer on the company's interests, including employment and an opinion on the offeror's strategic plans for the offeree company. (*Rule 25.2a*)
- Substance of the advice received by the board from the *Rule 3* **independent adviser** (*Rule 25.2b*).
- A description of any known **significant change in the financial or trading position** of the offeree company which has occurred since the end of the last financial period for which either audited financial information or interim financial information has been published, or the directors need to give an appropriate negative statement (*Rule 25.3*).
- **Relevant shareholdings and dealings** should be disclosed (*Rule 25.4*). These include shareholdings in the offeror held by the offeree or its subsidiaries and any shareholdings in the offeror or offeree company held by the offeree's directors or people acting in concert with the offeree. It also includes derivatives referenced to the shares.

- **Directors' service contracts**, including the name of the relevant director and the remuneration payable under the contract (*Rule 25.5*).
- **Responsibility statement** (*Rule 19.2*) is also required.

11 PROFIT FORECASTS AND EARNINGS ENHANCEMENT STATEMENTS

There are specific regulations in the City Code regarding the inclusion of financial forecast information in published documents. The subjectivity associated with making forecasts necessitates clear reporting requirements regarding the forecast and how it has been prepared to ensure shareholders understand the information that has been provided.

The Code distinguishes between 'profit forecasts' and 'earnings enhancement statements'.

Definition of a Profit Forecast

The definition of a profit forecast is fairly wide-ranging and is covered in *Rule 28.6*. A statement that includes no figures, but indicates how the profits have performed may constitute a forecast. Key factors to consider include whether the statement:

- Puts a ceiling or floor on the possible profit
- Gives information enabling an approximate profit figure to be calculated

For example, a statement that profits will be higher than last year is likely to be considered a forecast.

Even if the period for which the estimate of profit is being made has already expired, the estimate will still be a forecast. However, preliminary or interim announcements made by companies that comply with the Listing Rules' requirements for such announcements will not be treated as forecasts. Likewise, dividend forecasts will not normally be included unless they are accompanied by an estimate of dividend cover.

Requirements relating to Profit Forecasts

A profit forecast must be compiled with due care and consideration by the directors *(Rule 28.3)*. It must be fairly presented to the highest standards of accuracy. The responsibility for this lies with the directors making the forecast, but the advisers must satisfy themselves that it is the case.

The assumptions upon which the forecast has been based must be stated in the document giving the forecast *(Rule 28.4)*.

Where an offer is solely for cash, then any forecast made by the offeror need not be reported on *(Rule 28.1)*. In all other cases, the accounting policies and calculations for the forecast must usually be examined and reported on by the auditors for the company. If another financial adviser has been mentioned in the document, then that person must also report on the forecast.

A report by a financial adviser will not confirm that the profit forecast is correct. It will typically state that the adviser has discussed the bases and assumptions relating to the forecast with the directors of the company and that he considers the forecast to have been prepared after due and careful enquiry.

The accountant's report is likewise fairly limited in its scope. It merely states that the accountant has confirmed that the figures in the forecast have been properly compiled on the basis of the assumptions made by the directors and that the report has been prepared on a basis consistent with the usual accounting policies of the company.

The reports must be published in the document giving the forecast *(Rule 28.1)*. The reports must be accompanied by a statement that those making them have given and not withdrawn their consent to publication. If a company's forecast is published first in an announcement, it must be repeated in full, together with the reports, in the next document published in connection with the offer by that company.

Exception

The Takeover Code has been changed so that third party advisers' confirmation reports are not required on profit forecasts made outside an offer period.

Instead, a directors' confirmation regime applies (*Rule 28.1c*). Directors must confirm that:

- The forecast has been properly compiled on the basis of the assumptions; and
- The basis of accounting used is consistent.

The rationale behind the change is to encourage listed companies to provide greater guidance to the market about their future expectations, thus improving market transparency and valuations, without the company worrying about the Takeover Code implications on profit forecasts if an unforeseen offer materialises in the future.

If an offer does subsequently arise, any document or announcement published during the offer period which refers to the profit forecast must:

- Repeat the forecast and include certain confirmations from the directors; or
- Include a statement by the directors that the forecast is no longer valid and an explanation as to why that is the case; or
- Include a new forecast for the relevant period, which will then need to be accompanied by the relevant third party advisers' reports.

However, where a company **regularly publishes 'earnings guidance' statements** as part of their normal shareholder communications the need for third party reports may not arise. The new rules allow that if all parties agree (or the Takeover Panel considers reporting would be disproportionate), the profit forecast need not be reported on and only the directors' confirmations set out above for pre-approach forecasts are required.

The Panel will normally grant a waiver from Rule 28 reporting regimes for a forecast relating to a future financial period, which ends more than 15 months from the date of publication. Instead directors' confirmations must be provided. However, if a subsequent offer document or announcement repeats the forecast, the document must include a profit forecast for the current year and any intervening year and these forecasts are potentially subject to the Rule 28 reporting regime.

Rule 28 reporting requirements will always apply in an MBO scenario: in other words third party reports are required and directors' confirmation statements alone are insufficient.

Quantified Financial Benefits Statements

Quantified Financial Benefits Statements

Where a party makes a statement concerning the expected financial benefits of a takeover or merger (for example by quantifying the synergies expecting to arise), the following disclosures are required *(Rule28.6)*.

- The bases of the belief supporting the statement (including sources of information)
- Reports by financial advisers and accountants
- An analysis and explanation to enable shareholders to understand the statement
- A base figure for any comparison drawn

These requirements also apply to target companies quantifying financial benefits from cost savings and all quantification of financial implications should a bid fail. Those wishing to make quantified financial benefits statements should consult the Panel in advance.

12 Restrictions on Share Dealings

Restrictions on the Offeror and Concert Parties During the Offer Period (Rule 4.2)

During the offer period, the offeror or persons **acting in concert** (see below) may not sell securities in the offeree without prior permission from the Panel, and only then after 24 hours' public notice has been given that the sales may take place. If the bid is a mandatory bid under *Rule 9* (see below), then no sales will be allowed at all.

If there is an announcement that sales may be made, then no further purchases of securities will be permitted and it is highly unlikely that the Panel will permit the offer to be revised. This means that the only way the offeror can acquire shares in the offeree after the announcement will be if shareholders accept the existing offer.

The rationale behind these rules is to prevent an offeror from driving up the price of a target's shares via announcing an offer and then selling subsequently at a profit.

Acting in Concert

The definition of acting in concert for the purpose of the City Code (section C) includes persons who, pursuant to an agreement or understanding, cooperate to acquire shares in a company to obtain or consolidate control. Note that this is not the same as the legal concept of acting in concert, which merely refers to an agreement between two or more people to acquire interests in shares (Companies Act).

Specific Examples

In certain cases, people will be deemed to be acting in concert unless it is shown to be otherwise. Specific examples include the following:

(a) A company, together with its parent, subsidiaries and fellow subsidiaries plus any company that is an associated company of any of the above, or a company which itself owns 20% of any of the above. An associated company is defined as a company in which the investing company owns at least 20% of the voting rights.

The relationships described above can be demonstrated on a diagram.

Companies Acting in Concert with Each Other

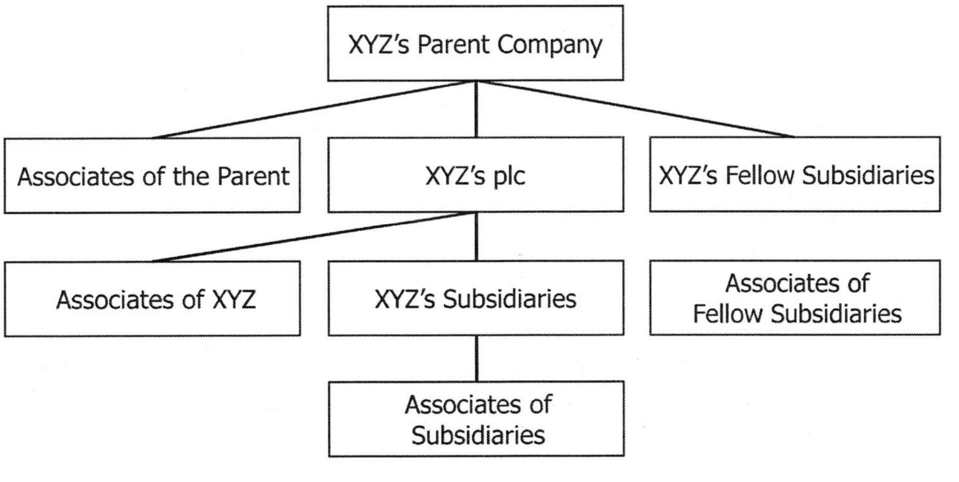

Each of the above companies will be presumed to be acting in concert with any other member of the total grouping.

(b) A company will be presumed to be acting in concert with its directors and their close relatives.

(c) The directors of a company subject to, or likely to be subject to, an offer, are presumed to be acting in concert.

(d) A company with any of its pension funds, or any pension funds of the companies mentioned in (a) above.

(e) A 'connected' adviser with its client. This normally relates to a financial adviser and corporate broker advising an offeror or offeree or concert party on a specific transaction. It excludes exempt fund managers and exempt principal traders acting in such capacity.

(f) A fund manager (including an exempt fund manager) is presumed to be acting in concert with any person whose investments it manages on a discretionary basis.

Standstill Agreements

A standstill agreement is an agreement between a company and a shareholder which maintains the status quo ie restricts a shareholder's ability to acquire further shares in the company or to sell any shares in the company.

If a Standstill agreement is in place, the Panel will not normally consider a concert party to exist between the parties to the agreement, provided that the agreement does not restrict any of those parties from either accepting an offer for the company's shares at any stage or agreeing to accept any offer for the company's shares either before or after announcement (Practice Statement 16). The Panel should be consulted.

Dealings by Connected Exempt Principal Traders and Connected Exempt Fund Managers

A principal trader is a person who:

1. Is registered as a market-maker with a recognised investment exchange, or is accepted by the Panel as a market-maker; or
2. Is a member firm of a recognised investment exchange dealing as principal in order book securities. An exempt principal trader is recognised by the Panel as exempt for the purposes of the Code.

An exempt fund manager is a fund manager who deals on a discretionary basis for clients and is recognised as such by the Panel.

Fund managers, who manage investment accounts on a discretionary basis, and principal traders must apply to the Panel to obtain 'exempt' status. Exempt status is only relevant if the sole connection between a fund manager or principal trader is that they are in the same group as a financial adviser or corporate broker to an offeror, offeree or concert party thereof.

The main effect of having exempt status is that the definition of acting in concert will not apply.

Connected, exempt principal traders must comply with *Rule 38* of the Code. A principal trader, who is connected with the offeror or offeree, must not carry out dealings with the purpose of assisting the offeror or offeree company (*Rule 38.1*). An offeror and persons acting in concert must not deal as principal with a connected exempt principal trader (*Rule 38.2*).

If a principal trader or fund manager is connected but not exempt, rule 7.2 of the Code applies. On commencement of the offer period both connected principal traders and connected fund managers will be presumed to be concert parties and Code restrictions on dealings will be relevant (*Rules 5, 6, 9, 11, 36*).

Dealings in Offeree Securities by Financial Advisers of the Offeree (Rule 4.4)

Financial advisers to the offeree, apart from exempt principal traders and exempt fund managers, may not do the following during the offer period:

- Purchase any securities of the offeree or deal in derivatives and options referenced to the securities during the offer period on their own account
- Lend money to others to enable them to deal in the shares other than on normal commercial term
- Enter into any agreement to induce someone else to deal or refrain from dealing in the shares

This rule prevents advisers from purchasing shares or adopting other related methods designed to prevent the offeror from obtaining sufficient acceptances to declare the bid unconditional.

Prohibited Dealings by People Other than the Offeror (Rule 4.1)

Dealing in the Shares of the Offeree

Any person who possesses confidential price-sensitive information concerning an offer or possible offer is prohibited from dealing in any way in the securities of the offeree, including dealing in options. In addition, they are also prohibited from making recommendations to other people to deal.

Dealing in the Shares of the Offeror

Dealings in the securities of the offeror company will be permitted so long as the offer is not price sensitive to the relevant securities, for example, in a wholly cash bid.

Insider Dealing

This rule reinforces the Criminal Justice Act 1993, which broadly states that nobody in possession of inside information may deal in the relevant company's securities.

Summary: Dealings in Offeror and Offeree Securities

The table below summarises the main provisions relating to dealings in offeror and offeree securities in the offer period.

Dealings by	Offeror Securities	Offeree Securities
Offeror	N/A	• Sales – prohibited • Purchases – allowed subject to *Rules 5, 9, 6* and *11*
Financial Advisers to Offeree	N/A	Dealings – prohibited
Any holder of Price-Sensitive Information	Dealings – prohibited*	Dealings – prohibited

* Unless the offer is not price-sensitive to the offeror

Restrictions on Acquisitions

Restrictions on Obtaining Control

The Code contains restrictions on companies amassing substantial shareholdings in target companies without making an offer for all of the shares. Two Code rules work together here – *Rules 5* and *9*.

The objective of *Rule 5* is to prevent a person obtaining control or consolidating control over a company except in a number of acceptable circumstances. The basic rule states that when a person (including people acting in concert with him) holds shares or rights over shares that carry less than 30% of the voting rights in a company, he may not acquire any shares or rights over shares, which would mean that he would hold 30% or more of the voting rights in the company.

It should be noted that the definition of 'effective control' as being control of 30% of the voting rights is essentially arbitrary. The Panel has considered changing this percentage in the past but has concluded that the 30% test has 'stood the test of time'.

If a person already holds shares or rights over shares with between 30% and 50% inclusive of the voting rights then he may not increase his percentage holding in the company.

Exceptions to the Restrictions

There are a number of exceptions where the above basic rule does not apply, allowing a stake of over 30% to be acquired. These are as follows (*Rules 5.1 and 5.2*):

(a) Where a person already holds shares with more than 50% of the voting rights, since they already have legal control (*Note 1* to *Rule 5.1*).

(b) Where there is a vote of independent shareholders, ie excluding the acquirer, which approves the acquisition (*Note 4* to *Rule 5.1*) – a 'whitewash' – see dispensations from *Rule 9* later in this chapter.

(c) Where the purchase of shares or rights over shares is from a single shareholder and it is the only purchase in a seven-day period (*Rule 5.2a*). Where such a purchase is made, then no subsequent purchases will be permitted unless the situations given below apply (*Rule 5.3*).

(d) Where the purchase is immediately before or at any time after a firm announcement to make an offer or during an offer and either the offer itself or a competing offer will be/has been recommended by the offeree board (*Rule 5.2b/c*). Where the purchase is immediately before the announcement, it must be conditional on the offer being made.

(e) Where an offer has been announced, and the first closing date of the offer or a competing offer has passed (*Rule 5.2c*).

(f) During an offer that is unconditional in all respects (*Rule 5.2c*).

(g) Where the acquisition is by way of a shareholder accepting an offer, as opposed to selling in the market (*Rule 5.2d*).

(h) Where the acquisition replenishes a previously held shareholding, as long as it is a very small purchase (less than 1% of issued voting share capital) (*Rule 9.1, note 11*).

Rights Over Shares

It should be noted that *Rule 5* refers to shares or rights over shares. This will include options over existing shares but will not include warrants to subscribe for new shares in the company or convertible debt (since the shares are not yet in existence in these cases). Exercise of such warrants or conversion rights would, however, be relevant for the purpose of *Rule 5*, when they would be treated as an acquisition from a single shareholder. The exercise of options over existing shares would not be relevant, since the options themselves have already been included as rights over shares.

EXAMPLE

	Before %	Exercise Options %	Exercise Warrants %
Shares owned	25	29	32
Options over existing shares	4	–	–
Total for *Rule 5* purposes	29	29	32
Warrants over shares	3	3	–

Since the options are already included in the *Rule 5* total, the exercise of the options has no effect on the holder's position. By contrast, exercise of the warrants increases the shares and rights over shares held and brings the total to 30% or over. This in itself would be permitted by *Rule 5*, since the exercise of the warrants is treated as a purchase from a single shareholder. However, the restrictions on future purchases outlined above would subsequently apply.

13 THE MANDATORY OFFER

The mandatory offer is required by *Rule 9* of the Code. Where a person obtains control of a company, then he must make an offer for the shares of all other shareholders. This means that other shareholders will not:

- Be forced to keep a shareholding in a company where somebody else effectively controls the company's operations and financial policy; or
- Have to sell shares subsequently at a lower price that reflects the fact that there is a dominant investor who does not intend to make an offer for the other shares.

When the Mandatory Offer is Required

Acquiring or Consolidating Control

Rule 9 covers two situations:

- When a person originally acquires effective control of a company (defined as holding 30% or more of the voting rights)
- When a person consolidates control (defined as increasing a holding of between 30% and 50% inclusive of the voting rights by any percentage)

The rule specifically states that:

- Where a person acquires shares which, when taken in aggregate with his existing holdings and those of people acting in concert, carry 30% or more of the voting rights of a company; or
- Where a person or people acting in concert already hold shares with between 30% and 50% (inclusive) of the voting rights and the person or people acting in concert acquire shares which result in an increase in their percentage holding,

then that person must make an offer to all the holders of any class of equity share, or voting non-equity share in which he or people acting in concert have a holding.

Contrast to Rule 5

This rule links in strongly with *Rule 5*. There are, however, some important distinctions between the two. *Rule 5* basically prohibits purchases that take a holding to 30% or over except in certain circumstances. If a person takes advantage of one of the exceptions, they can purchase the shares. However, they will still be subject to *Rule 9* and will be required to make a mandatory offer for the company in question.

A second difference is that *Rule 5* refers to shares or rights over shares (such as options) but *Rule 9* refers to shares. Thus, a purchase of options taking a person over 30% would be relevant for *Rule 5* purposes, but would not usually be covered by *Rule 9*, unless the buyer of the option had effectively acquired control of the shares (*Note 10* to *Rule 9.1*). If the options were exercised, however, then the resultant acquisition of shares could trigger a *Rule 9* bid.

EXAMPLE

	Before %	Exercise Options %	Exercise Warrants %
Shares owned (= Rule 9 total)	25	25	31
Options over existing shares	–	6	–
Total for *Rule 5* purposes	25	31	31
Warrants over shares	3	3	–

The purchase of the options has no effect on the total for *Rule 9* purposes and hence no mandatory offer is required. It will, nevertheless, be relevant for *Rule 5* purposes. If the options are purchased from more than one shareholder, then the purchase would probably not be permitted. If the purchase was from only one person, then it would be permitted but subsequent acquisitions would not usually be possible, in accordance with *Rule 5*.

The later exercise of the options is irrelevant for *Rule 5* purposes, but increases the total of shares to 30% or over. Hence, a mandatory offer will probably be required under *Rule 9*.

Moving from a Voluntary Offer to a Mandatory Offer

Note that a person may make an offer on a voluntary basis and then purchase shares in the market bringing his holding in the company to 30% or more. This will trigger *Rule 9* and mean that the offer will become mandatory. Mandatory offers can only have a limited number of conditions attached and must have a cash alternative (see below).

Should an offeror plan to incur such an obligation, it should consult the Panel in advance (*Note 9* to *Rule 9.1*).

Acquisitions of Shares by People Acting in Concert

The prime responsibility for making a mandatory offer rests with the person who made the purchase that took the total concert party holding to 30% or over and triggered the offer (*Rule 9.2*). The obligation may, however, be extended to include any other member of the concert party, especially where the person with prime responsibility is a relatively minor member of the group.

Reduction or Dilution of a Controlling Shareholding

It may happen that a controlling stake of between 30% and 50% is diluted as a result of a new issue of shares by the company or by a sale of part of the shareholding. In these circumstances, the controlling shareholder (or concert party) is permitted to make limited purchases without incurring a *Rule 9* obligation (*Note 11* to *Rule 9.1*).

Such shareholders may purchase up to 1% of the shares in any one year, subject to the proviso that the total percentage owned does exceed the highest percentage owned in the previous 12 months. As a result, such controlling shareholders will not be able to increase their percentage holdings from one year to the next. They can only reinstate the holding to its previous percentage level. For example, if a holding was reduced from 37% to 36.5%, it could be reinstated to a maximum level of 37% within the next year.

Advisers with Recognised Intermediary Status

Shares held by a recognised intermediary acting in a client-serving capacity will not be treated as interests in shares for the purpose of deciding if a *Rule 9* bid is required (*Note 1* to *Rule 7.2*). Note that the shares must be held by the intermediary in a client-serving capacity and as such this exclusion would not apply to shares held by an intermediary for proprietary trading purposes. If any part of the trading operations of a bank or securities house wishes to be accepted by the Panel as a recognised intermediary, it must apply to the Panel to be granted such status and it will have to comply with any requirements imposed by the Panel as a condition of its granting such status.

Dispensations from Making a Mandatory Offer

The dispensations from *Rule 9* give a number of situations when acquiring 30% or more of the voting rights in a company, or increasing a holding with 30% or more of voting rights by any percentage, will not necessarily trigger a mandatory offer. In all cases, the dispensation is not an automatic right but is granted by the Panel.

Whitewash

Where there is an issue of new securities by the company as consideration for an acquisition and a shareholder is set to acquire 30% or more of a company. No mandatory offer will be required if there is a vote of independent shareholders, ie not including the person making the acquisition or people acting in concert with him, which approves the shareholding. This type of proposal is known as a 'whitewash'. A 'whitewash will also be given provided there has been a vote of independent shareholders, in cases involving the underwriting of an issue of shares.

Foreclosure on Security for a Loan

Where a lender forecloses on security for a loan and takes control of 30% or more of the company. This exception will not apply if the lender had reason to believe that foreclosure was likely when the loan was made.

Rescue Operations

Where a person acquires 30% or more of a company as a result of a rescue operation when the company is in financial difficulty.

Inadvertent Mistake

Where the person made a genuine mistake in incurring an obligation to make an offer. However, the shares must be sold in a limited period of time to people unconnected to the original purchaser.

Where 50% of Shareholders Will Not Accept

Where holders of shares carrying 50% or more of the voting rights in the company have confirmed in writing that they will not accept any offer. This would mean that a mandatory offer would be bound to fail, since it must be a condition of the offer that the offeror and people acting in concert end up with more than 50% of the voting rights (see below).

Enfranchisement of Non-Voting Shares

Where shares that were previously non-voting are enfranchised, giving a person 30% or more of the voting rights. However, the person should not have acquired the shares with reason to believe that they would be enfranchised.

Repurchase of Shares

Where a company repurchases its own shares and a person not acting in concert with the directors ends up owning 30% or more of the company as a result. Such a person will not be required to make an offer for the company, unless he acquired the shares with the expectation of the share repurchase taking place (*Notes 1 and 2* to *Rule 37.1*). Note that a director obtaining 30% or more of the company may be required to make a mandatory offer in such a situation, unless there is a whitewash vote.

Required Conditions for a Mandatory Offer

There are only two conditions permitted with a mandatory offer:

Referral to Competition and Markets Authority Competition and Markets Authority or the European Commission

The mandatory offer must be made subject to a referral to the Competition and Markets Authority Competition and Markets Authority or the European Commission, before the later of the first closing date of the offer and the date that it becomes unconditional. If the bid is referred before this date, it will lapse (*Rule 9.4*).

Acceptances Condition

It must also be conditional on the offeror and people acting in concert holding shares with more than 50% of the voting rights after the offer (*Rule 9.3*).

Required Consideration to be Offered

The offer must be for cash or with a cash alternative (*Rule 9.5*). The cash offer must be at a price not less than the highest price paid for shares in the offeree in the last 12 months by the offeror or persons acting in concert with him.

14 The Voluntary Offer

A voluntary offer is any offer not subject to *Rule 9*, Mandatory Offers. There are required conditions for a voluntary offer, and then the offeror may choose to add in additional conditions.

Referral to the Competition and Markets Authority

Where an offer comes within the statutory provisions for a referral to the Competition and Markets Authority or to the European Commission, then it must be a term of the offer that it will lapse should such a referral take place before the later of the first closing date of the offer and the date that the offer becomes or is declared unconditional (*Rule 12*).

Acceptance Condition

The offer must contain an 'acceptances condition'. A usual condition of the offer is that it will not become unconditional as to acceptances unless the offeror has acquired or agreed to acquire shares such that he will hold more than 50% of the voting rights in the company (*Rule 10*).

Although the acceptance condition must specify that the offeror holds more than 50% of the company, it may specify a higher percentage. A typical acceptance condition would state the following.

> The offer is conditional upon the offeror acquiring 90% or more of the shares to which the offer relates (or such lesser percentage as the offeror sees fit), so long as the offeror holds more than 50% of the voting rights in the offeree.

Contrast between Voluntary Offer and Mandatory Offer Acceptance Provision

In a mandatory offer, there is no option to have an acceptance level in excess of 50%.

Note that the offeror in a voluntary offer will be required to control more than 50% of the shares himself, excluding any people acting in concert. This is a contrast to *Rule 9* where the requirement is that the offeror together with persons acting in concert control more than 50% of the shares. If there are reasons why a person acting in concert cannot or will not transfer the shares to the offeror, this will make it easier for the mandatory offer to succeed than the voluntary offer.

Example

An illustration of this would be a situation where B plc, an associated company of A plc, owns 29.4% of X plc. A plc wishes to bid for X plc, but to leave at least 25% of the shares in public hands, in order to maintain X plc's listing. The problem is that, if A plc makes a voluntary offer, it will have to acquire more than 50% of X plc's shares. This means that a maximum of <20.6% of the shares will remain in public hands, after taking into account A plc's holding of >50% and B plc's holding of 29.4%.

A solution may be for A plc to purchase an additional 0.6% of X plc's shares in the market. Together with the associate's holding of 29.4%, this comes to a total of 30% and incurs a mandatory offer requirement. In this case, it would be possible to acquire only an additional 21% of the shares, since B plc's holding can be taken into account for the purpose of the acceptance condition, leaving well over 25% of the shares in public hands. The deal would of course need to be structured to make it attractive for existing shareholders not to fully accept the offer and leave A plc owning all of the shares in X plc.

In the actual case from which this illustration was drawn, the offeror gave investors two choices as part of the mandatory offer. They could either sell all their shares or they could sell 3/5ths of their holding and retain the other 2/5ths. The second alternative, which was the preferred option for the offeror, would mean that only 3/5ths of the remaining shares would need to be purchased, ie (3/5 × 70%) 42%, leaving a total of 28% of the shares in public hands.

Note that such an offer may be considered to be a partial offer by the Panel and, hence, be covered by the rules on partial offers, covered below.

Other Possible Conditions

In addition to the above, the offeror can set any conditions he wants, provided that the condition does not depend solely on subjective judgements by the directors of the offeror or if the fulfilment of the condition lies in their hands (*Rule 13*). If this proviso were not in existence, it would be easy for offerors to withdraw their offers at will and at any time by setting subjective conditions.

Minimum Price to Be Offered

Where an offeror or people acting in concert have purchased shares in the offeree within the three months prior to the announcement, then the offer price should be on terms no less favourable than for those purchases (*Rule 6*). Note that, even if the purchases are for cash, there is no requirement in these circumstances for a cash alternative.

The Panel may extend the three-month period if it feels that this is necessary to ensure similar treatment to all shareholders, as required in the first general principle (*Note 1 to Rule 6*). An example of this may be where purchases were made from directors of the offeree company in the fourth month prior to the offer.

Purchase of Shares in the Offer Period

If the offeror or people acting in concert purchase shares after the announcement of the offer at higher than the offer price, then the offer must be revised to at least the highest price paid for the purchases (*Rule 6.2*). The revised offer will apply to all offeree shareholders, including those who have already accepted the offer (*Rule 32.3*). This prevents the offeror arranging a better deal with a particular shareholder by waiting until other shareholders have accepted an inferior offer and then purchasing his shares in the market place.

Requirement for a Cash Alternative

This requirement usually arises where the offeror or people acting in concert have either purchased any shares for cash during the offer period or have purchased for cash shares with 10% or more of the voting rights in the company in the 12 months prior to the announcement of the offer (*Rule 11*).

Where shares have been purchased for cash during the offer period but the 10% threshold has not been breached, the offer must be for cash or there must be a cash alternative to the offer at a price not less than the highest price paid by the offeror or persons acting in concert during the offer period. Where the 10% threshold is breached, the offer must be for cash or have a cash alternative set at not less than the highest price paid by the offeror or persons acting in concert in the last 12 months.

The Panel may, in addition, require a cash offer or cash alternative in any circumstances where it feels this is necessary to ensure similar treatment for all shareholders. This will be in similar circumstances to those noted above for the minimum price to be offered, eg where directors have sold their shares for cash.

Requirement for a Securities Alternative

When an offeror has acquired 10% of shares in the last three months in exchange for securities, securities must be offered to all other shareholders.

Similar Treatment for All Shareholders

General principle 1 of the Code requires that all holders of the securities of an offeree company of the same class must be afforded equivalent treatment. This principle must be adhered to for all offers, mandatory and voluntary.

Different Classes of Share Capital and Convertibles

All classes of share capital must be given comparable (but not necessarily identical) treatment (*Rule 14.1*). In addition, the interests of convertible debt and warrants investors should be safeguarded (*Rule 15*).

Special Deals with Favourable Conditions

Favourable conditions should not generally be extended to any particular group of shareholders (*Rule 16*). However, in certain situations, the offeror may wish to retain the services of director shareholders of the offeree and to motivate them by means of an 'earn out' deal where they receive a higher price for their shares if the company's profits hit specified targets.

Such special deals may be permitted as long as relevant details of the arrangements are disclosed and an independent adviser states that, in his opinion, the terms are fair and reasonable. Where the value of the arrangements entered into is significant and/or unusual in the context of industry practice, then the Panel must be consulted and consent to the arrangements be obtained. The Panel may require, as part of this process, that the arrangements be approved at a general meeting of the company's shareholders (*Rule 16.2*).

Summary of Differences Between Mandatory and Voluntary Offers

	Mandatory Offer	Voluntary Offer
Nature of Consideration	Cash or cash alternative required	No cash offer required except under *Rule 11*
Price to be Offered	Highest price paid by the offeror in the last 12 months	Highest price paid by the offeror in the last three months, unless *Rule 11* applies
Competition and Markets Authority Referral Condition	Yes	Yes
Acceptances Condition	Offeror and concert parties own more than 50% of the voting rights in the offeree	Offeror sets acceptance condition, subject to it being at least owning more than 50% of the voting rights in the offeree
Other Conditions	No	Yes, so long as not subjective and fulfilment does not lie in hands of offeror's directors

15 Conduct During the Offer

Disclosure of Shareholdings

Opening Position Disclosure

An offeror (*Rule 8.1a*), an offeree (*Rule 8.2a*) and a 1% security-holder in any party to the offer (*Rule 8.3a*) must make an Opening Position Disclosure relating to its interests in or rights to subscribe for any relevant securities of any party to the offer. Shares or other securities of a cash offeror will not be treated as 'relevant securities' for the purposes of *Rule 8* (*Rule 8, note 1*). The Opening Position Disclosure must be made by no later than 12 noon on the day falling 10 business days after the commencement of the offer period or the announcement that first identifies the offeror (*Rule 8, note 2*).

Dealings during the Offer Period

As well as the Opening Position Disclosure, announcements are required relating to relevant dealings during the offer period. Public dealing disclosures must be made by certain parties, including:

- The offeror (*Rule 8.1b*)
- The offeree (*Rule 8.2b*)
- Any person who holds an interest in 1% or more of any class of relevant securities of any party to the offer (*Rule 8.3b*)
- Any person acting in concert with a party to the offer dealing for his own account or for the account of discretionary investment clients (*Rule 8.4*)

Shares or other securities of a cash offeror will not be treated as 'relevant securities' for the purposes of *Rule 8* (*Rule 8, note 1*).

The disclosure is required to be made no later than 12 noon on the business day following the day of dealing.

Both the offeror and offeree are obliged to assist the Panel in identifying those persons interested in 1% or more of any class of relevant securities of the offeror or offeree (*Rule 22*). The offeror and offeree have a responsibility to send those persons an explanation of their disclosure responsibilities under *Rule 8*.

16 Irrevocable Commitments

Irrevocable commitments and letters of intent are commitments to accept or not to an offer, and often include a commitment to vote in a certain way relating to the shares. An irrevocable undertaking may be either hard (binding in all circumstances), soft (ceases to be binding if a higher offer emerges) or semi-hard (ceases to be binding if a higher offer emerges which exceeds the existing offer by an agreed amount).

An irrevocable commitment which relates only to acceptance of an offer will not, in itself, normally result in a shareholder being considered to be acting in concert with an offeror under the definition of 'acting in concert' in the Code.

However, the Panel considers that a shareholder who enters into an irrevocable commitment to accept an offer, which includes a voting undertaking, to be acting in concert with the offeror, if the voting undertaking is restricted to the period of the offer or it is limited to matters which relate to ensuring that the offer succeeds.

During an offer period, if any party to the offer or any person acting in concert with it procures an irrevocable commitment or a letter of intent, the relevant party to the offer must publicly disclose the details in accordance with the Notes on *Rule 2.11*. The announcement must be made no later than 12 noon on the business day following the date of the transaction.

Any irrevocable commitments or letters of intent received before the commencement of the offer period, must be disclosed in the Opening Position Disclosure (*Rule 2.11* and *Rule 8, note 5a(viii)*).

Standards of Care and Responsibility

Highest Standards of Accuracy and Fair Presentation

Whenever any document or advertisement is issued or any statement is made during the course of an offer, the highest standards of accuracy must be satisfied and any information must be presented adequately and fairly (*Rule 19.1*). Parties to an offer or potential offer must take care not to issue statements which, although not inaccurate, may mislead shareholders and the market or create uncertainty (*Rule 19.3*).

It may be the case that a document is true and correct but nevertheless misleading. Consider the following graph of a company's earnings per share performance.

X plc – Earnings per Share

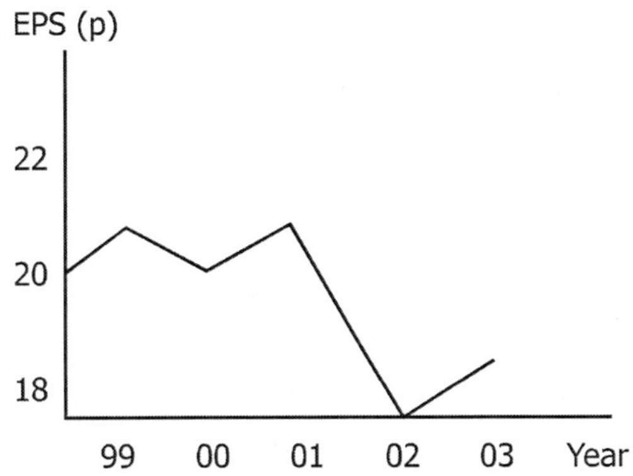

While the graph may truthfully portray the earnings per share performance of the company, the decision to make 18p the base line of the y-axis means that the presentation may be misleading, giving the impression that the earnings have almost fallen to nil.

Similarly, the selection of the base year when calculating dividend growth rates, for example, must be made with care to ensure that misleading growth rates are not quoted.

The Responsibility of the Directors

Any document or advertisement issued in connection with an offer must state that the directors of the offeror or offeree company as appropriate accept responsibility for the information contained in the document and that to the best of their knowledge the information is in accordance with the facts and does not omit anything likely to affect the import of the information (*Rule 19.2*).

If the information relates to another company and has been taken from published sources, then this responsibility is limited to ensuring that the information is reproduced correctly and fairly (*Note 3* to *Rule 19.2*).

Advertisements

In the past, a number of controversial advertisements have threatened to reduce the credibility of the City in the eyes of the public and to trivialise takeover bids. As a result, advertisements connected with the offer may not be published unless they fall within a number of specific categories (*Rule 19.4*). These include the following:

- Product advertisements not bearing on the offer. The advert will need to be cleared with the Panel in advance of publication if in doubt.
- Corporate image advertisements not bearing on the offer
- Advertisements confined to non-controversial information about an offer, eg a reminder of closing dates
- Advertisements comprising preliminary or interim results and their accompanying statements, so long as the statement does not contain argument or invective about the offer
- Advertisements giving information that is required or specifically permitted to be published by the FCA

Telephone Campaigns

There is an obvious danger that telephone calls by overzealous salesman may result in misleading information being released to offeree shareholders or additional information being made available to some shareholders, but not to others. The purpose of the City Code is to ensure that all callers are properly briefed about their responsibilities under the Code.

Telephone campaigns should only be conducted by staff of the financial adviser who are fully conversant with the requirements of and their responsibilities under the Code (*Rule 19.5*). The Panel may consent to other callers being used, but only if they have a prepared script and information from which they are not allowed to depart.

Only previously published information that is still accurate may be used during the telephone call. Shareholders must not be put under pressure and must be encouraged to consult their own advisers.

Interviews and Debates

The unscrupulous nature of some editors in pursuing the art of sensational television leads to risks that fairly ordinary interviews may be rearranged so that they are no longer a fair representation and will appear controversial as a result.

When interviewed, parties involved in the offer should seek to ensure that the sequence of the interview is not broken by the insertion of comments by others not made during the interview (*Rule 19.6*). Joint interviews and confrontations between the offeror and offeree or competing offerors should be avoided.

Equality of Information to All Shareholders and to Competing Offerors

Information about companies involved in the offer must be made available, as far as possible, to all shareholders at the same time and in the same manner *(Rule 20.1)*. Notwithstanding this, an offeree company can make available information on a confidential basis to a potential offeror or vice versa.

Interviews and Meetings

There is a clear danger that, when meeting with important shareholders, new information may be released that is not yet available to all shareholders. *Rule 20* aims to ensure that new information is not released or, if it has been, that it is then immediately made available to all shareholders.

Rule 20 states that great care must be taken during interviews and meetings to ensure that no significant new information is released (*Note 3* to *Rule 20*). If significant new information does emerge, then a circular must be sent to shareholders as soon as possible.

A representative of the company's financial adviser should **always** attend meetings and confirm in writing to the Panel by 12 noon of the next business day whether in their opinion significant new information was forthcoming at the meeting.

Information to Different Offerors

Information given to one offeror or potential offeror must also be given on request to another offeror or bona fide potential offeror, regardless of whether or not their offer is welcome (*Rule 20.2*). The offeror must request the information specifically and cannot frame a request in general terms.

For example, it would not be possible for one offeror to request 'all the information given to company Y'. Rather than such a general request, the offeror would have to list a specific series of questions. It is of course possible for the offeror to compile an exceedingly long list of questions!

The objective of making sure that information is disseminated equally is to ensure that all offerors are in a position to make a fair offer. This will ensure that the offeree shareholders are not disadvantaged and forced to accept a lower offer than might otherwise have surfaced.

Frustrating Action

If an offer is in process, or the board of the offeree company has reason to believe that an offer is imminent, then the board must not attempt to frustrate the bid without the permission of the shareholders by any of the following actions (*Rule 21.1*):

- Issue any authorised but unissued shares or grant options on these shares
- Issue securities with the right to convert into shares
- Sell, dispose of or acquire/agree to sell, dispose of or acquire assets of a material amount. The Panel will normally consider relative values of 10% or more as being of a material amount.
- Enter into contracts other than in the ordinary course of business

Inducements

An inducement fee is where the offeree company agrees to pay an offeror a sum of money should certain events cause the offeror's bid to fail. For example, a fee might be payable if the offeree company's directors recommend a competing bid that is higher.

Under *Rule 21.2*, any commitment by a prospective target to pay the bidder a break fee, or inducement, should a transaction abort is prohibited under the Code. There are some very limited exceptions: payments to a 'white knight' coming in to rescue a target from a hostile bidder, or where a potential target puts itself up for auction, and in both cases subject to a 1% de minimis limit.

17 Timetable of an Offer

Summary Bid Timetable

The following summary highlights the main dates in an offer. These and other important dates are dealt with in more detail as follows.

Summary Bid Timetable

28 days	Announcement of offer
	↓
'D' day	Publication of offer document
	↓
D + 14	Posting of defence document
	↓
D + 21	First closing date
	↓
D + 39 offeree	Last date for announcements by
	↓
D + 46	Last date for revision of the offer
	↓
D + 60	Last day an offer can be declared unconditional as to acceptances

Posting the Offer Document ('D' Day)

The offer document should normally be sent to shareholders within 28 days of the announcement of a firm intention to make an offer (*Rule 24.1*).

Offeree Board Circular (D + 14)

The defence document should be sent to shareholders within 14 days of the publication of the offer document (*Rule 25.1*).

First Closing Date (D + 21)

The offer must initially be open for at least 21 days following the date on which the offer document is posted (*Rule 31.1*). If there is any announcement of an extension to the offer, then the next closing date must be stated (*Rule 31.2*). If the offer has been declared unconditional as to acceptances, then a statement may be made that the offer will remain open until further notice. In this case, at least 14 days' notice must be given in writing to shareholders who have not yet accepted before the offer is closed.

Purchase of Shares in the Market

After the first closing date has passed and provided that the bid has not been referred to the Competition and Markets Authority, the restrictions on purchasing shares carrying more than 30% of the votes in *Rule 5* is lifted (*Rule 5.2*). However, such purchases could trigger a mandatory offer.

Unconditional Acceptance Period

After an offer has become or is declared unconditional as to acceptances, the offer must remain open for acceptance for at least 14 days after the date it would otherwise have expired, unless it has been unconditional from the outset (*Rule 31.4*).

Fulfilment of Conditions

Except with the consent of the Panel, all conditions must be fulfilled or the offer must lapse within 21 days of the later of the first closing date and the date the offer becomes or is declared unconditional as to acceptances (*Rule 31.7*).

Withdrawal of Acceptances

If an offer has not become unconditional by 21 days after the first closing date, then an acceptor must be entitled to withdraw his acceptance from this date (*Rule 34*).

Offeree Board Announcements (D + 39)

The offeree board should not, without the Panel's consent, announce any material new information (including trading results, profit or dividend forecasts and any material acquisition or disposal) after the 39th day following the posting of the initial offer document (*Rule 31.9*). Where such an announcement is made, the Panel will normally be prepared to grant an extension to 'Day 46' and/or 'Day 60'.

Revision of Offers and Final Revision Date (D + 46)

There is no requirement for an offer to be revised or extended (*Rule 31.3*). However, if an offer is revised, then it must remain open for at least 14 days following the date the revised offer document is posted (*Rule 32.1*). This means that the latest possible date that an offer can be revised is 46 days after the initial offer, since the time limit for the bid is 60 days after that date (see below).

On revision of an offer, all shareholders who accepted the original offer must be entitled to the revised consideration (*Rule 32.3*).

Where it has been stated that an offer will not be extended or increased, then only in exceptional circumstances will the Panel permit the offer to be extended or increased (*Rules 31.5* and *32.2*). It is usual for a 'no extension' or 'no revision' statement to be accompanied by a rider stating that the offeror specifically reserves the right to extend or revise the offer, should a competing offer emerge. The Panel will normally accept this (*Notes 2* and *4* to *Rule 31.5*).

When an offer includes shares, the offeror will have to ensure that it does not release information after D + 46, which will affect the value of the share consideration. For example, the issue of interim results that are better than expected might increase the share price and effectively revise the offer. Release of such sensitive information will only be possible if it: fits in with the offeror's normal results timetable; every effort was made to ensure that the release date was not after Day 46; and it is not likely to affect, materially, the outcome of the offer.

Final Time Limit (D + 60)

An offer may not become or be declared unconditional as to acceptances after midnight on the 60th day after the day the initial offer document was posted, without the Panel's consent (*Rule 31.6*). The Panel will normally consent to an extension beyond this if:

- There is a competing offer, in which case both offerors will normally have to follow the timetable of the competing offer
- The board of the offeree company consents to the extension
- The board of the offeree company has made an announcement of material new information more than 39 days after the initial offer document was posted

In establishing whether acceptance conditions have been satisfied, the offeror can only take into account acceptances or share purchases where the relevant documents are received by its receiving agent by 13:00 on the 60th day.

Settlement of Consideration

The consideration must be posted within 14 days of the later of:

- The first closing date
- The date the offer becomes or is declared unconditional
- The date an acceptance is received (*Rule 31.8*)

Impact of CMA Investigation on Timings

It is often the case that there is a significant delay before a decision is made subsequent to an investigation by the competition authorities. In such a case, the Panel will typically rule that, should the offer be cleared, Day 39 will be two days after the clearance and subsequent dates will be adjusted accordingly to maintain the usual relationship thereafter (*Note 3* to *Rule 31.6*).

18 RESTRICTIONS FOLLOWING OFFERS

Delay of 12 Months Before Making New Offer

Where an offer is unsuccessful or an announcement is made that raises the possibility of an offer but no offer is forthcoming within a reasonable period, then the offeror or any person acting in concert with it should not within 12 months (*Rule 35.1*):

- Make an offer for the company
- Acquire shares in the company if this would result in an obligation to make an offer under *Rule 9*

Partial Offers

The above restrictions also apply where a partial offer has been made that could have resulted in a holding of between 30% and 50% inclusive of the voting rights of the offeree, regardless of whether the offer has been successful or not (*Rule 35.2*).

Dispensations

The 12-month waiting period may be dispensed with if the Panel consents. Circumstances when consent is likely to be forthcoming include where (*Notes a* and *b* to *Rules 35.1* and *35.2*):

- A new offer is to be recommended
- A competing offer has been announced
- A 'whitewash' proposal, whereby another shareholder will acquire 30% or more of the company without the requirement to make a mandatory offer, is announced
- There has been a material change in circumstances

Delay of Six Months Before Buying Shares Above the Offer Value

If a person or people acting in concert hold shares carrying more than 50% of the voting rights of a company, then they may not acquire shares in the company or make an offer for it on better terms than those available under a previous offer within six months of the closure of the previous offer which became unconditional (*Rule 35.3*). Should they do so, then the Panel may require that the better terms are offered to the shareholders who accepted the previous offer.

As with the rules concerning purchases above the offer price during the offer period, the purpose of this is to ensure equality of treatment for all offeree shareholders.

19 Conflicts of Interest and Management Buyouts

Independent Advice and Conflicts of Interest

Rule 3.1 states that the board of the offeree company must obtain competent independent advice on any offer. The Panel will not regard as being independent either of the following (*Rule 3.3*):

- Someone from the same group as the financial adviser to the offeror company
- Someone who has a significant interest or financial connection with either an offeror or the offeree company so as to create a conflict of interest

This means that any directors who will continue as part of the management team are unlikely to be able to offer advice to their existing shareholders. In addition, any adviser working for a management buyout team will be unable to give independent advice to the shareholders.

Where the transaction is a reverse takeover or the directors of the offeror company have a potential conflict of interest, then the board of the offeror must also seek independent advice (*Rule 3.2*).

Management Buyouts

Clearly, a management buyout (MBO) presents special problems in ensuring that shareholders are given a fair deal. The MBO directors will possess a level of knowledge about the company and its value to which shareholders can only aspire. In addition, the directors are unlikely to be keen to pay the full market value of the company.

Rule 20.3 states that, in an MBO, the offeror or potential offeror must, on request, promptly furnish the independent directors of the offeree company or its advisers with all information that has been furnished by the offeror or potential offeror to external providers of finance, whether equity or debt.

Where there is a competing offer, *Rule 20.2* states that information passed by the offeree company to external providers of finance, whether equity or debt, should be given equally and promptly to the competing offeror, even if that offeror is less welcome. The competing offeror will, however, have to specify what information it requires, rather than asking in general terms for all the information supplied to the external providers of finance for the MBO.

20 Partial Offers

Panel's Consent

Offers for Less than 30% of a Company

The Panel's consent is required for any partial offer (*Rule 36.1*). This will normally be granted if the offer will not result in the offeror holding shares with 30% or more of the voting rights in the offeree.

Offers for 30% or More

Consent will not normally be granted for offers for 30% or more when the offeror or persons acting in concert have acquired significant numbers of shares in the offeree in the 12 months preceding the application for consent (*Rule 36.2*).

Share Dealings Around the Offer Period

The offeror and persons acting in concert may not purchase shares in the offeree company during the offer period (*Rule 36.3*). They are also not permitted without Panel consent to make purchases in the 12-month period after the offer if the offer is successful. Panel consent will normally be granted where the original offer resulted in a holding of less than 30%.

The objective of this is to ensure fair treatment for all shareholders, preventing the offeror from buying all the shares from one shareholder and only making a partial offer to other shareholders.

Offers for Between 30% and 50%

Acceptance Condition

Where the offer could result in a holding of between 30% and 50% inclusive, then the precise number of shares offered for must be stated and the offer can only be declared unconditional when acceptances are received for at least the stated number of shares (*Rule 36.4*).

Shareholder Approval

An offer for 30% or more of the company should be made conditional on shareholders carrying at least 50% of the voting rights not held by the offeror or persons acting in concert indicating that they approve of the offer (*Rule 36.5*).

Tender Offers (Appendix 5)

Fixed and Maximum Price Tenders

A fixed price tender is where the offeror agrees to buy shares for cash at a fixed price of, say, £2.50 per share. People can submit tenders if they believe this price to be attractive. A maximum price tender is where the offeror invites people to submit the price at which they are prepared to sell their shares, subject to a defined maximum price that the offeror is prepared to pay. The final strike price of the tender will depend on the prices submitted by the existing shareholders.

Oversubscription for a Tender

If the tenders received exceed the number offered for, then with a fixed price offer all the tenders must be scaled down pro rata. If a maximum price tender is oversubscribed, then the striking price will be the lowest price at which the number of shares offered for is met. All who tender at or below that price will receive that price. Tenders made at the striking price will be scaled down pro rata if necessary.

Consider the following example where the offeror wants to purchase 1,000 shares in XYZ plc and has specified a maximum tender price of £5.00 per share. The following tenders to sell shares to the offeror are received.

Tendering Shareholder	Number of Shares Tendered	Price at which Tendered
A	400	£2.00
B	500	£4.00
C	500	£4.00
D	200	£5.00

The minimum price at which 1,000 shares can be purchased is £4.00 per share. This becomes the common strike price for all successful tenders. The offeror, therefore, buys 400 shares from A at a price of £4.00, and 300 shares each from B and C at a price of £4.00. D's offer to sell 200 shares at a price of £5.00 each is not taken up.

Undersubscription for a Tender

If the tender is undersubscribed, then all tenders will receive the maximum or fixed price, subject to the minimum acceptance condition in (d) above.

Code Regulation on Tender Offers

The Panel's consent is required for any tender offer. The Panel's consent will normally be granted where:

(a) The tender offer could not result in the offeror and concert parties being interested in shares carrying 30% or more of the voting rights of the company on the closing date of the tender; or

(b) The tender offer is by a person holding shares carrying more than 50% of the voting rights of a company, is for less than all the shares carrying voting rights held by the minority and the Panel believes the circumstances justify the use of a tender offer.

Advertising Requirements

Any tender offer must be published by a paid advertisement in two national newspapers and the advertisement must include the following details:

- The name of the offeror and its broker
- The name of the offeree
- The maximum number of shares being offered
- A statement that if tenders totalling less than 1% (or higher if the offeror wishes, but not usually over 5%) of the offeree's voting rights are received, then the tender will be void (no other conditions will be allowed)
- The fixed or maximum price offered
- Details of the offeror's existing holding in the offeree
- The closing day and time for the tender

Minimum Duration of a Tender Offer

The minimum period for which a tender offer can remain open is eight calendar days, from the date it is advertised to the date it closes (inclusive).

Schemes of Arrangement (Appendix 7)

A scheme of arrangement is a transaction effected by means of statutory provisions in the Companies Act 2006. The provisions of the Code apply to offers effected by schemes of arrangement in the same way as they apply to contractual offers, except as set out in Appendix 7.

The offer document should normally be sent to shareholders within 28 days of the announcement of a firm intention to make an offer (*Rule 24.1*). This rule also applies to the scheme document. A scheme must include a term that it will lapse if there is a competition reference before the shareholder meetings.

There is no maximum time limit for the holding of shareholder meetings and/or the fulfilment of other scheme conditions in the absence of a competitive situation. So there is no equivalent to the 60 day limit (*Rule 31.6*) as there is for contractual offers.

Section 5 of *Appendix 7* requires the offeree to make announcements following three key events in a scheme, namely (a) the shareholder meetings (b) the court sanction hearing and (c) the date of effectiveness of the scheme. In relation to the announcement following the shareholder meeting, the announcement should specify whether the resolutions had been passed by the requisite majorities, the voting results and, in relation to the court-convened meeting and the number of shareholders who voted for and against the resolution.

Section 10 of *Appendix 7* requires consideration to be posted to offeree shareholders within 14 days of the effective date of the scheme. It also requires the terms of the scheme to reflect this, so it may be enforced by offeree shareholders.

An obligation to make a mandatory offer under *Rule 9* may not be satisfied by a scheme of arrangement unless the Panel consents. The factors that the Panel would take into account when considering giving their consent would include the likely timetable and the views of the offeree board and its *Rule 3* adviser.

There is a specific obligation on an offeror to consult the Panel when it is considering announcing an offer (or possible offer) to be implemented by a scheme, but without first obtaining the support of the offeree board. This requirement is set out in section 13 of *Appendix 7*.

Practice Statements

Practice Statements are issued by the Panel Executive to provide informal guidance to companies involved in takeovers and practitioners as to how the Executive normally interprets and applies relevant provisions of the Takeover Code in certain circumstances.

Practice Statements do not form part of the Code. Accordingly, they are not binding on the Executive or the Panel and are not a substitute for consulting the Executive to establish how the Code applies in a particular case.

Tutors' note

You are expected to be familiar with the content of the Practice Statements for your exam. It is recommended that you read the Practice Statements in full. The current up to date version of the statements can be found on the Panel's website at www.thetakeoverpanel.org.uk.

Directors' Duties and Corporate Governance Issues

chapter 13

Contents

1 Separation of Ownership from Control

In most public limited companies, the owners do not actually manage the company. Whilst the equity shareholders own the company, the day to day operations are managed on their behalf by the board of directors. The directors and managers within the organisation have their own personal goals that may conflict with those of the shareholders. Whilst managers are privy to privileged information about the company, shareholders have to rely on publicly available details such as annual reports and press articles, a situation known as **information asymmetry.**

Commentators point to the following evidence of managers running businesses for their own interests, as opposed to those of the shareholders:

(1) **Decisions driven by short-termism**

There is evidence that in many companies the primary driver of decision-making has been to increase share prices and hence managerial rewards in the short-term. The longer-term benefits of investment in research and development may be ignored in the short-term drive to cut costs and increase profits thus jeopardising the long term prospects of the company.

(2) **Sales maximisation goal**

This strategy is often employed by managers to increase market share and therefore the importance of the company within its sector. An increase in importance for the company will mean greater status for management but will not necessarily be in the best interests of the shareholders.

(3) **Overpriced acquisitions**

Takeovers are another manifestation of the non-alignment of the interests of shareholders and managers. Empirical evidence shows that many takeovers or mergers fail to increase shareholder value. The rationale for transactions can be driven by other motivations, including 'empire-building'.

(4) **Resistance to takeover approaches**

The management of a company may tend to resist takeovers if they feel that their position is threatened even if in doing so shareholder value is also reduced.

(5) **Poor relationships with other stakeholders**

Many companies' pursuit of short-term profit maximisation may lead to difficult relationships with their wider stakeholders. Relationships with suppliers may be disrupted by demands for major improvements in terms and in reduction of prices. Employees may be made redundant in a drive to reduce costs and customers may be able to buy fewer product lines and have to face less favourable terms. These policies may aid short-term profits, but in the long-term suppliers and employees are able to take full advantage of market conditions and move to other companies, and customers can go elsewhere.

2 Agency Theory

The relationship between management and shareholders is sometimes referred to as an agency relationship, in which managers act as 'agents' for the 'principals', the shareholders. In the **agency theory** set up, shareholders as the main providers of capital, enter into contractual agreements with managers so as the managers manage the assets of the company in a way that maximises the utility of shareholders. The agency problem arises when agents do not act in the best interests of their principals, but instead are driven by self-interest. The goal of agency theory is to find **governance structures** and **control mechanisms** that minimise the problem caused by the separation of ownership and control. In that sense agency theory is the cornerstone of the theory of corporate governance. More specifically agency theory tries to find means for the owners to control the managers in such a way that the managers will operate in the interest of the owners.

The agency theory implies heavy **monitoring costs** of the agents by the principals as well as high costs of enforcing the **negotiated contracts.** The resulting corporate structure is designed to monitor and control.

Stewardship theory

This view of the corporate world by the agency theory is, however, not universally accepted. The **stewardship theory** for example maintains that the interests of managers and shareholders are not always at variance, and management may have incentives such as **responsibility**, **altruism** or **recognition** that do not conflict with the interests of the shareholders. According to this theory, the managers of a company are the **stewards** of the company.

Transaction cost economics

The transaction cost economics theory postulates that the governance structure of a corporation is determined by **transaction costs.** The theory of transaction cost economics explains the organisational structure of a firm and its behaviour as a result of the costs that are incurred when the owners of the firm are making transactions. These transaction costs include search and information costs, bargaining costs and policing and enforcement costs. Bargaining costs arise from the process of agreeing (bargaining) on a contract, and the enforcement costs, are the costs of ensuring that every party complies with the contract. Transaction costs imply limited liability for shareholders and limited liability enables investors to diversify. Diversification allows investors to ignore the idiosyncratic risks of individual companies. This implies that investors require relatively little direct monitoring of the operations of individual business firms.

3 Strategies for the Resolution of Stakeholder Conflict

The **resolution** of the **agency problem** arising when agents do not act in the best interests of their principals is to bring about **goal congruence** between the objectives of the shareholders and those of management by devising **appropriate mechanisms.** In addition, the relevant authorities should enforce good **corporate governance** practice.

Firm induced strategies

Goal congruence is accordance between the objectives of agents acting within an organisation and the objectives of the organisation as a whole.

Remuneration

Goal congruence can be achieved by using remuneration incentives:

(a) **Profit-related/economic value-added pay**

Pay or bonuses related to the size of profits or, to prevent short-termism, economic value-added.

(b) **Rewarding managers with shares**

This might be done when a private company 'goes public' and managers are invited to subscribe for shares in the company at an attractive offer price. In a **management buy-out** or buy-in managers become owner-managers. The takeover code allows special equity deals to be agreed with directors, even if equity is not available to all shareholders.

(c) **Approved Company Share Option Plans (CSOP)**

Directors receive options to buy shares in the company, with favourable tax treatment. Again this will help to align directors and shareholders interests in improving company share price.

4 Corporate Governance

Adoption of a corporate framework of decision making that restricts the power of managers and increases the role of independent external parties in the monitoring of their duties. This can be achieved for example by establishing 'management audit' procedures, by introducing additional reporting requirements, or by seeking assurances from managers that shareholders' interests will be foremost in their priorities.

Corporate governance can be defined broadly as the system by which an organisation is directed and controlled. It is concerned with systems, processes, controls, accountability and decision making at the heart of and at the highest level of an organisation. It is therefore concerned with the way in which top managers execute their responsibilities and authority and how they account for that authority to those who have entrusted them with assets and resources. In particular, it is concerned with the potential abuse of power and the need for openness, integrity and accountability in corporate decision making.

The King Report

In 2009, the King Report was published in South Africa. This was the culmination of a series of reports on corporate governance, spanning nearly two decades. The King reports are widely recognised as being an effective summary of the best international practices in corporate governance.

King identified seven characteristics of good corporate governance:

(a) **Discipline**, adherence to correct and proper behaviour including the underlying principles of good corporate governance.

(b) **Transparency**, ease with which analysis can be made of actions, economic fundamentals, and non-financial matters. This reflects how good management is at making necessary information available.

(c) **Independence**, reflecting mechanisms to minimise or avoid conflicts of interest such as composition of board, appointments to board committees and relations with auditors.

(d) **Accountability**, mechanisms allowing investors to query and assess actions of board.

(e) **Responsibility**, including responsibility to stakeholders. Governance should permit corrective action and penalising of mismanagement.

(f) **Fairness**, balanced systems that take into account everyone having an interest in the company.

(g) **Social responsibility**, in particular ethical standards, but also laying stress on being non-discriminatory and non-exploitative.

King had the following additional recommendations:

The board

A unitary board ensures positive interaction and diversity of views. The board must give strategic direction, retain full and effective control over the company, monitor management, ensure that the company complies with all relevant laws, regulations and codes of practice and communicate with shareholders and relevant stakeholders openly and promptly. The board should consider whether its size, diversity and demographics make it effective. The board should consider developing a code of conduct, covering conflicts of interest of management. The board should identify key risk areas and key performance indicators, and identify and monitor non-financial aspects of these.

Board composition

The board should comprise a mix of executive and non-executive directors, particularly independent non-executives, to protect shareholder interests. Formal appointment procedures, including a nomination committee, should be in place. Board continuity should be ensured by a director rotation programme.

Chairperson and chief executive

There should be a clear division of responsibilities, with preferably separation of the roles of chairperson and chief executive and the chairperson being an independent non-executive director. The chairperson's performance should be appraised regularly, the chief executive's at least annually.

Directors

No one individual or block of individuals should dominate the board's decision-taking.

Non-executive directors should have calibre and credibility and have the necessary skill and experience to assess all strategic, operational and conduct issues.

Remuneration

Remuneration should be sufficient to attract, retain and motivate executives of the required quality. A remuneration policy should be established and a remuneration committee should make recommendations; the chief executive can be consulted but should not fix his own remuneration. Full disclosure should be made in the accounts. Performance-related elements should constitute a substantial part of executives' total remuneration packages. Executive directors' fixed term service contracts should not exceed three years.

Board meetings

Boards should meet at least once a quarter. Non-executive directors should have access to management. Boards should regularly review processes and procedures to ensure the effectiveness of the company's system of internal controls. The board should receive relevant non-financial information, going beyond assessing the financial and quantitative performance of the company, looking at qualitative measures that involve broader stakeholder interests.

Board committees

Boards should not shelter behind board committees, but there should be a formal procedure for certain functions of the board to be delegated. At a minimum boards should have audit and remuneration committees. All board committees should preferably be chaired by an independent non-executive director.

Company secretary

The company secretary has a pivotal role in corporate governance, in providing detailed guidance on responsibilities, inducting new directors and assisting the chairperson.

Risk management

The board is responsible for the total process of risk management and for forming its opinion on the effectiveness of the process. Management is responsible for integrating the risk management process into the activities of the company. Risk strategy policies should be communicated to all employees.

The board should make use of generally accepted models to assess whether organisational objectives are being achieved. The board should at a minimum assess the following risks:

- Physical and operational
- Business continuity
- Human resource
- Credit and markets
- Technology
- Compliance

A board committee should aid the board in risk assessment. Boards should consider the need for a whistle-blowing process. A comprehensive system of control should be established to ensure risks are mitigated and objectives obtained. Risks should be assessed on an on-going basis and control activities respond to risks, with relevant information about risks being identified, captured and communicated. Management should report on significant risks, system effectiveness and weaknesses found.

Boards should acknowledge their accountability for risk management and state that there is an on-going process for identifying, evaluating and managing risks and there is an adequate system of internal control in place to mitigate risks.

Internal audit

Companies should have an effective internal audit function, with access to the chief executive, chairman and audit committee. There should be adequate segregation of duties if internal and external audit are carried out by the same firm. Internal audit should seek assurance that management processes are adequate to identify and monitor significant risks, confirm the effective operation of control systems, review processes for feedback on risk management and assurance, and confirm that the board receives the right quality of information. The audit plan should be risk-based and linked to the board's risk assessment.

Sustainability reporting

Companies should report at least annually on the nature and extent of its social, transformation, ethical, safety, health and environmental management policies and practices. These include concerns such as workplace accidents, impact of HIV/AIDS, environmental concerns, black economic empowerment, human capital development and equal opportunities policies. Each company should introduce a code of ethics and disclose adherence to it.

Accounting and auditing

The audit committee should recommend the appointment of external auditors and should encourage consultation between external and internal auditors. The audit committee should set out principles for whether non-audit services should also be supplied by auditors. The majority of members of the audit committee should be independent non-executive directors and should be financially literate. It should be chaired by an independent non-executive director who is not the chairperson of the board. The committee should have formal terms of reference.

Relations with shareowners

Companies should maintain a dialogue with institutional shareholders. They should explain each item of special business and consider using polls to approve special business.

Accounts

Boards should present a balanced and understandable assessment of the company's position and a comprehensive and objective assessment of the activities of the company. Reports must be made in the context of society demanding greater transparency and accountability from companies regarding their non-financial matters.

Development of Corporate Governance in the UK

Three reports published in the 1990s – Cadbury, Greenbury and Hampel – recommend best practice in UK corporate governance, financial reporting and accountability. Many of the principles contained therein reflect the conclusions of King. The Cadbury Report defines corporate governance as 'the system by which companies are directed and controlled'. The **Cadbury and Hampel reports** covered general corporate governance issues, whilst the **Greenbury report** concentrated on remuneration of directors. The recommendations of these three reports were merged into a **Combined Code** in 1998, with which companies listed on the London Stock Exchange are required to disclose compliance with.

Since the publication of the Combined Code a number of reports in the UK have been published about specific aspects of corporate governance:

- The **Turnbull report** focused on risk management and internal control
- The **Smith report** discussed the role of audit committees
- The **Higgs report** focused on the role of the non-executive director

The Combined Code was renamed **the UK Corporate Governance Code** when a new version was published in 2014.

The UK Corporate Governance Code

The provisions of the UK Corporate Governance Code are divided into five sections, as follows:

A Leadership

A1 Role of the board

All listed companies should be led by an effective board, responsible for providing entrepreneurial leadership, within a framework of prudent and effective controls, enabling risk to be assessed and managed. The board is responsible for setting strategic aims, ensuring sufficient resources are available, setting values and standards and ensuring obligations to shareholders. The board should meet regularly, with a formal schedule of matters reserved for it. The annual report should explain how the board operates, and give details of members and attendance.

A2 Division of responsibilities

A clear division of responsibilities should exist so that there is a balance of power, and no one person has unfettered powers of decision. The roles of chairman and chief executive should not be exercised by one person.

A3 The chairman

The chairman is responsible for leading the board and ensuring its effectiveness. The chairman should establish the board's agenda, and ensure there is adequate time for discussion, particularly of strategic matters. The chairman should promote openness and debate, help non-executive directors contribute effectively and promote constructive relations between executives and non-executives. The chairman should ensure that the board receives accurate, timely and clear information and should ensure communication with shareholders is effective. The chairman should meet the independence criteria for non-executive directors. A chief executive should not go on to become chairman.

A4 Non-executive directors

Non-executive directors should scrutinise management's performance and constructively challenge strategy. They should obtain assurance about the integrity of financial information and that financial controls and risk management systems are robust and defensible. Other important tasks include determining executive remuneration and playing a significant role in decisions about board changes.

One of the independent non-executives should be appointed as senior independent director, to act as an intermediary with other directors and shareholders. The chairman should hold meetings with the non-executives without the executives being there, and the non-executives should meet without the chairman to appraise the chairman's performance. Directors should ensure that concerns they have that cannot be resolved are formally recorded.

B Effectiveness

B1 Composition of the board

The board and its committees should have a balance of skills, experience, independence and knowledge of the company. The board should be of sufficient size to operate effectively, but not so large as to be unwieldy. The board should have a balance of executive and non-executive directors so that no individual or small group is dominant. Decisions on committee membership should take into account the need to avoid undue reliance on particular individuals. At least half the board of FTSE 350 companies should be independent non-executive directors. Smaller listed companies should have at least two independent non-executive directors.

B2 Appointments to the board

There should be a clear, formal procedure for appointing new directors. A nomination committee should make recommendations about all new board appointments. The majority of members of this committee should be independent non-executives. Directors should be appointed on merit, against objective criteria, and considering the value of diversity, including gender diversity. There should be an orderly succession process in place.

B3 Commitment

Directors should allocate sufficient time to the company to discharge their duties effectively. In particular the nomination committee should assess the time commitment expected of the chairman, and the chairman's other commitments should be disclosed to the board and shareholders. Non-executives' letters of appointment should set out the expected time commitment and non-executives should undertake to have sufficient time to fulfil their responsibilities. Their other significant commitments should be disclosed to the board. A full time executive director should not take on more than one non-executive directorship of a FTSE 100 company, nor the chairmanship of a FTSE 100 company.

B4 Development

All directors should be properly inducted when they join the board and regularly update their skills and knowledge. The chairman should agree training and development needs with each director.

B5 Information and support

The board should be promptly supplied with enough information to enable it to carry out its duties.

Information volunteered by management will sometimes need to be supplemented by information from other sources. The chairman and secretary should ensure good information flows. Directors should be able to obtain independent professional advice and have access to the services of the company secretary. The company secretary is responsible for advising the chairman on all governance matters. The whole board should be responsible for appointing and removing the company secretary.

B6 Evaluation

There should be a vigorous annual performance evaluation of the board as a whole, individual directors (effective contribution and commitment) and board committees. Evaluation of the board of FTSE 350 companies should be externally facilitated at least once every three years. The chairman should take action as a result of the review, if necessary proposing new board members or seeking the resignation of directors.

B7 Re-election

All directors should submit themselves for re-election regularly, and at least once every three years.

Directors of FTSE 350 companies should be subject to annual election by shareholders.

C Accountability

C1 Financial and business reporting

The board should present a balanced and understandable assessment of the company's position and prospects in the annual accounts and other reports such as interim reports and reports to regulators. The directors should explain their responsibility for the accounts, and the auditors should state their reporting responsibilities. The directors should explain the basis on which the company generates or preserves value and the strategy for delivering the company's longer-term objectives. The directors should also report on the going concern status of the business.

C2 Risk management and internal control

The board is responsible for determining the nature and extent of the significant risks it is willing to take to achieve objectives. Good systems of risk management and control should be maintained. The directors should review effectiveness annually and report to shareholders that they have done so. The review should cover all controls including financial, operational and compliance controls and risk management.

C3 Audit committee and auditors

There should be formal and clear arrangements with the company's auditors, and for applying the financial reporting and internal control principles. Companies should have an audit committee consisting of independent non-executive directors. One member should have recent and relevant financial experience. The committee should monitor the accounts, review internal financial controls and also other internal controls and risk management systems if there is no risk committee. The audit committee should make recommendations for the appointment and remuneration of the external auditor, and consider the auditor's independence and objectivity, the effectiveness of the audit process and whether the external auditor should provide non-audit services. The audit committee should also review internal audit's work. If there is no internal audit function, the audit committee should consider annually whether it is needed. The audit committee should also review 'whistleblowing' arrangements for staff who have concerns about improprieties.

D Directors' remuneration

D1 Level and components of remuneration

Remuneration levels should be sufficient to attract directors of sufficient calibre to run the company effectively, but companies should not pay more than is necessary. A proportion of remuneration should be based on corporate and individual performance. Comparisons with other companies should be used with caution. When designing performance-related elements of remuneration, the remuneration committee should consider annual bonuses and different kinds of long-term incentive schemes. Targets should be stretching. Levels of remuneration for non-executive directors should reflect time commitment and responsibilities, and should not include share options or performance-related options. Boards' ultimate objectives should be to set notice periods at one year or less. The remuneration committee should consider the appropriateness of compensation commitments included in the contracts of service.

D2 Procedure

Companies should establish a formal and clear procedure for developing policy on executive remuneration and for fixing the remuneration package of individual directors. Directors should not be involved in setting their own remuneration. A remuneration committee, staffed by independent non-executive directors, should make recommendations about the framework of executive remuneration, and should determine remuneration packages of executive directors and the chairman. The board or shareholders should determine the remuneration of non-executive directors.

E Relations with shareholders

E1 Dialogue with shareholders

The board should keep up a dialogue with shareholders, particularly major (institutional) shareholders.

The board should try to understand issues and concerns, and discuss governance and strategy with major shareholders.

E2 Constructive use of the AGM

The AGM should be a means of communication with investors. Companies should count all proxies and announce proxy votes for and against on all votes on a show of hands, except when a poll is taken. Companies should propose a separate resolution on each substantially separate issue, and there should be a resolution covering the report and accounts. The chairmen of the audit, nomination and remuneration committees should be available to answer questions at the AGM. Papers should be sent to members at least 20 working days before the AGM.

Compliance with the Code

UK Listing Regulation does not require companies to comply with the Code. However, there are disclosure requirements in respect of the Code. The following statements must be included in a listed company's report and accounts:

(a) A narrative statement of how the company **applied** the **principles** set out in the UK Corporate Governance Code. This should provide explanations which enable the company's shareholders to assess how the principles have been applied.

(b) A statement as to whether or not the company **complied throughout** the **accounting period** with the provisions set out in the UK Corporate Governance Code. Listed companies that did not comply throughout the accounting period with all the provisions must specify the provisions with which they did not comply, and give **reasons** for **non-compliance**.

Remuneration Committees

The role of remuneration committees was originally emphasised by the Greenbury Report, which required a remuneration committee consisting exclusively of non-executive directors to determine on behalf of shareholders the company's policy on executive remuneration and the remuneration of specific executive directors.

The chairman of the committee should account directly to shareholders for the committee's decision. He should attend the company's AGM to answer shareholders' questions about directors' remuneration.

The non-executive directors should have no personal financial interest other than as shareholders in the matters to be decided and no conflicts of interest through cross-directorships.

The remuneration committee should make a report to shareholders each year that should form part of or be annexed to the company's Annual Report and Accounts. The report should set out key details of the company's policy on executive remuneration, including levels, comparator groups of companies, performance criteria and contracts of service. The report should also contain full details of all elements of the remuneration package of each director by name, including share options and pension entitlements.

Remuneration Policy

Packages must be provided to attract, retain and motivate directors of the quality required but should avoid paying more than is necessary for this purpose. The remuneration committee should be sensitive to the wider scene, including pay and employment conditions elsewhere in the company. Performance related elements of the package should be designed to align the interests of shareholders and directors and give directors keen incentives to perform at the highest levels. Executive share options should never be issued at a discount. The impact of salary increases on pension commitments for the company should be considered, especially for directors nearing retirement.

Service Contracts and Compensation

The remuneration committee should consider what compensation payments, if any, should be available on the early termination of directors' contracts of service, particularly in the case of unsatisfactory performance. There is a strong case for setting notice or contract periods of one year, although in some cases up to two years may be appropriate.

5 US Corporate Governance: Sarbanes-Oxley Act

The Sarbanes–Oxley Act of 2002 is a United States federal law that set new or enhanced standards for all U.S. public company boards, management and public accounting firms. It is narrower in scope that the UK Corporate Governance Code, focussing exclusively on financial reporting and firm's internal control over the financial reporting process. Corporate scandals in the United States, particularly the Enron and Worldcom scandals, led to enactment of Sarbanes-Oxley and also to consequent changes to the listing rules that companies quoted on Wall Street have to fulfil.

A summary of the Act's key provisions are as follows:

Public oversight board

A Public Oversight Board has been established to register and regulate accounting firms.

Auditing standards

Audit firms should retain working papers for several years, have quality control standards in place, and as part of the audit review internal control systems to ensure that they reflect the transactions of the client and provide reasonable assurance that the transactions are recorded in a manner that will permit preparation of the financial statements.

Non-audit services

Auditors are expressly prohibited from carrying out a number of services including internal audit, bookkeeping, systems design and implementation, appraisal or valuation services, actuarial services, management functions and human resources, investment management, legal and expert services.

Provision of other non-audit services is only allowed with the prior approval of the audit committee.

Partner rotation

There should be rotation of lead or reviewing audit partners every five years.

Auditors and audit committee

Auditors should discuss critical accounting policies and alternative treatments with the audit committee.

Audit committees

All members of audit committees should be independent. At least one member should be a financial expert. Audit committees should be responsible for the appointment, compensation and oversight of auditors. Audit committees should establish mechanisms for dealing with complaints about accounting, internal controls and audit.

Corporate responsibility

The chief executive officer and chief finance officer should certify the appropriateness of the financial statements and that those financial statements fairly present the operations and financial condition of the issuer. If the company has to prepare a restatement of accounts due to material non-compliance with standards, the chief finance officer and chief executive officer should forfeit their bonuses.

Transactions not included in accounts

There should be appropriate disclosure of material transactions and other relationships.

Internal control reporting

Annual reports should contain internal control reports that state the responsibility of management for establishing and maintaining an adequate internal control structure and procedures for financial reporting. Annual reports should also contain an assessment of the effectiveness of the internal control structure and procedures for financial reporting. Auditors should report on this assessment.

Companies should also report whether they have adopted a code of conduct for senior financial officers and the content of that code.

Whistleblowing provisions

Employees of listed companies and auditors will be granted whistleblower protection against their employers if they disclose private employer information to parties involved in a fraud claim.

6 Comparison between UK and USA Models

The voluntary code-based UK approach can be contrasted with the American approach, very much founded in regulation and legislation. The following is a comparison of the main points of UK and US guidance.

	UK guidance:	US guidance:
	UK Corporate Governance Code and Turnbull report (unless indicated otherwise)	Sarbanes-Oxley
Scope	All types of internal control including financial, operational and compliance	Internal control over financial reporting
Audit committee	Smith report states should consist of independent non-executive directors, at least one having relevant and recent financial experience	Should consist of independent directors, one of whom should be a financial expert
Audit rotation	Ethical guidance states lead audit partner should be rotated at least every five years, other key audit partners at least every seven years	Rotation of lead partner required every five years
Non-audit services	Audit committee should review non-audit services provided by auditor to ensure auditor objectivity and independence is safeguarded. Accountancy bodies state that executing transactions or acting in a management role not compatible with being an objective auditor; other services (custody, preparing accounting records) cast doubts on objectivity	Auditors forbidden by law from carrying out a number of non-audit services including internal audit, bookkeeping, systems design/implementation, valuation, actuarial, management, expert services
Reports on internal control	Accounts include statement of responsibility of management for internal controls; also disclosure that there is a process for identifying, evaluating and managing risks and the process board has applied to review this	Accounts include statement of responsibility of management for internal controls and financial reporting; accounts should also include audited assessment of effectiveness of financial reporting controls
Code of ethics	No equivalent guidance	Companies should adopt a code of ethics for senior financial officers
Certification by directors	Under UK legislation directors required to state in directors' report that there is no relevant audit information that they know and that auditors are unaware of	Certification of appropriateness and fair presentation of accounts by chief executive and chief finance officer
Sanctions	No equivalent UK provision	If accounts have to be restated, chief executive and chief finance officer forfeit their bonuses

7 Corporate Governance Internationally: Comparisons with Other Countries

The establishment of a voluntary code of practice on corporate governance in the UK characterises a different approach to that adopted in many other countries.

(a) In **continental Europe**, reporting requirements tend to be more statutorily based in tax law, although all EU members are subject to EU company law directives.

(b) **Japanese** companies are characterised by what is sometimes called a flexible approach to corporate governance, with a low level of regulation. All stakeholders are supposed to collaborate in the company's best interests.

(c) The **South African** regime relies heavily on disclosure as a regulatory measure.

(d) The **Organisation for Economic Co-operation and Development** (OECD) has issued a set of nonbinding principles that are intended to provide guidance to governments, stock exchanges, investors and companies in various countries.

Germany: institutional differences

A significant difference between companies in the UK and many German companies is the distribution of power between workers and managers, and shareholders and managers. In the UK, ownership is something which can be easily traded on the Stock Exchange in the form of shares. Buyers of shares seek the best combination of risk and return. While managers have most power for practical purposes, in theory they are acting in the shareholders' interests. From the company's point of view, the stock market is the principal source of investment capital, especially for large companies. Banks generally provide credit, not capital.

In Germany the role of stock markets in company finance and management is not so important. German banks specialising in lending to industry and commercial enterprises have a relatively long-term interest in a company, and might even have an equity investment in it, as the sign of a long-term business relationship. It is argued that this makes them more sympathetic to a company's problems.

Institutional arrangements in German companies, typified by the two-tiered board, allow employees to have a formal say in the running of the company. A supervisory board has workers' representatives, and perhaps shareholders' representatives including banks' representatives, in equal numbers. The board has no executive function, although it does review the company's direction and strategy and is responsible for safeguarding stakeholders' interests. An executive board, composed entirely of managers, will be responsible for the running of the business.

Japan: cross shareholdings

The main emphasis of Japanese corporate governance is on management by consensus rather than directors following voluntary codes or statutory regulations. In Japan, the stock market does have an important role to play, particularly in savings. However, the separation between investment and management is in practice drawn differently to the UK. The stock market is less 'open'. The corporate sector has close links with the banks, who are often represented on boards of directors.

There are three different types of board of director:

- Policy boards – concerned with long-term strategic issues
- Functional boards – made up of the main senior executives with a functional role
- Monocratic boards – with few responsibilities and having a more symbolic role

Japanese companies generally set up long-term business relationships with banks, suppliers and customers, even to the extent of buying each other's shares as a symbol of the relationship. When share prices fall, friendly companies do not sell shares in each other. If the web of interrelated companies is large enough, it may possibly include a bank which provides credit to participants in the group. In Japan the long-term interests of the company are stressed rather than the short-term preferences of shareholders. These arrangements have enabled some companies to be protected from the rigours of profit-performance, so that long-term objectives such as market share have been traditionally favoured instead. There is evidence, however, that this system is gradually coming to an end.

South Africa

South Africa's major contribution to the corporate governance debate has been the King report, first published in 1994 and updated in 2010 to take account of developments in South Africa and elsewhere in the world. The King report differs in emphasis from other guidance by advocating an integrated approach to corporate governance in the interest of a wide range of stakeholders – embracing the social, environmental and economic activities of a company's activities. The report encourages activism by shareholders, business and the financial press and relies heavily on disclosure as a regulatory measure.

OECD Guidance

The Organisation for Economic Co-operation and Development (OECD) has developed a set of principles of corporate governance that countries and companies should work towards achieving. The OECD has stated that its interest in corporate governance arises from its concern for global investment. Corporate governance arrangements should be credible and should be understood across national borders. Having a common set of accepted principles is a step towards achieving this aim. The OECD developed its Principles of Corporate Governance in 1998 and issued a revised version in 2004. They are non-binding principles, intended to assist governments in their efforts to evaluate and improve the legal, institutional and regulatory framework for corporate governance in their countries. They are also intended to provide guidance to stock exchanges, investors and companies. The OECD principles deal mainly with governance problems that result from the separation of ownership and management of a company. Issues of ethical concern and environmental issues are also relevant, although not central, to the problems of governance.

The OECD principles are grouped into five broad areas:

(a) **The rights of shareholders**

Shareholders should have the right to participate and vote in general meetings of the company, elect and remove members of the board and obtain relevant and material information on a timely basis. Capital markets for corporate control should function in an efficient and timely manner.

(b) **The equitable treatment of shareholders**

All shareholders of the same class of shares should be treated equally, including minority shareholders and overseas shareholders. Impediments to cross-border shareholdings should be eliminated.

(c) **The role of stakeholders**

Rights of stakeholders should be protected. All stakeholders should have access to relevant information on a regular and timely basis. Performance-enhancing mechanisms for employee participation should be permitted to develop. Stakeholders, including employees, should be able to freely communicate their concerns about illegal or unethical relationships to the board.

(d) **Disclosure and transparency**

Timely and accurate disclosure must be made of all material matters regarding the company, including the financial situation, foreseeable risk factors, issues regarding employees and other stakeholders and governance structures and policies. The company's approach to disclosure should promote the provision of analysis or advice that is relevant to decisions by investors.

(e) **The responsibilities of the board**

The board is responsible for the strategic guidance of the company and for the effective monitoring of management. Board members should act on a fully informed basis, in good faith, with due diligence and care and in the best interests of the company and its shareholders. They should treat all shareholders fairly. The board should be able to exercise independent judgement; this includes assigning independent non-executive directors to appropriate tasks.

8 Remuneration Code 2011

The 2011 Remuneration Code requires financial firms to put in place a remuneration policy that:

- Is consistent with and promotes sound and effective risk management, and
- Does not encourage risk-taking that exceeds the level of tolerated risk of the firm.

Other Principles in the Code include:

- Avoidance of conflicts of interest
- Ensuring that a firm's remuneration practices do not endanger its capital base
- Basing assessments of financial performance on profit; and
- Ensuring that employees undertake not to use personal hedging strategies to offset the risk-based approach to their compensation.

Controversially, Principle 12 sets out the following new requirements for remuneration structures, which must be adhered to subject to the principle of proportionality:

- Remuneration must be structured so as to promote effective risk management
- Performance-related remuneration must take into account individual, business unit and firm-wide performance and must encompass non-financial performance metrics
- Guarantees should be exceptional, for new hires only and limited to a year
- Firms must set appropriate ratios between fixed and variable elements of total compensation
- Early termination payments should not reward failure
- At least 50% of both the deferred and non-deferred elements of variable remuneration should consist of shares, ownership interests, share-linked instruments and/or equivalent non-cash instruments that are subject to a retention policy to align incentives with the firm's long-term interests
- At least 40% of variable remuneration should be deferred over a minimum period of 3 to 5 years and deferred remuneration must vest no faster than on a pro-rata basis
- For staff whose remuneration has a variable component of over £500,000, 60% should be deferred
- Variable remuneration should be paid or vest only if justified by the performance of the firm, business unit and employee; the firm should adjust unvested elements of remuneration if warranted by subsequent circumstances

The Remuneration Code covers staff whose professional activities have a material impact on the firm's risk profile and who fall into one of four categories:

- Senior management,
- Risk takers,
- Staff engaged in control functions; and
- Any employee whose remuneration is in the same bracket as senior management and risk-takers.

INVESTOR PROTECTION

chapter 14

Contents

1 Introduction

We consider the importance of an ethical code of conduct in relation to the work of corporate financiers. We also look at the Bribery Act and rules on insider trading, misleading statements and market abuse provisions. In each case we consider how each of the regulations applies in practice, together with the relevant defences and remedies that are available. The chapter concludes with a consideration of the changes to the regulatory regime that are in the process of being enacted.

2 Ethics

Ethics are the moral principles that govern a person's conduct. Ethical behavior in the financial services industry has come under scrutiny in recent years, particularly in light of a series of financial scandals and business collapses which has turned the spotlight on the way the financial services industry operates.

Poor ethical standards clearly have detrimental effects. They pose risks to market confidence and consumer protection. They can increase the scope for financial crime and have a negative impact on public awareness and confidence.

Behaving ethically in a business scenario can run counter to personal interest. A finance professional is in a position of trust with the client, employer and general public. Consequently, the highest standards of professional behavior are expected. Written codes have been formulated in an attempt to systematize standards of ethical behavior and provide practical examples of the ethical dilemmas that could arise.

CISI Ethics

Members of the Chartered Institute for Securities & Investment (CISI) are required to meet the standards set out within the CISI's 'Lord George' Principles.

The Principles		Stakeholder
1	To act **honestly** and **fairly** at all times when dealing with clients, customers and counterparties and to be a good steward of their interests, taking into account the nature of the business relationship with each of them, the nature of the service to be provided to them and the individual mandates given by them.	**Client**
2	To act with **integrity** in fulfilling the responsibilities of your appointment and to seek to avoid any acts, omissions or business practices which damage the reputation of your organisation or the financial services industry.	**Firm** – Industry
3	To **observe applicable law, regulations and professional conduct standards** when carrying out financial service activities, and to interpret and apply them to the best of your ability according to principles rooted in trust, honesty and integrity.	**Firm** – Industry, Regulator
4	To observe the standards of **market integrity**, good practice and conduct required or expected of participants in markets when engaging in any form of market dealings.	**Market** – Participant
5	To be alert to and **manage fairly** and effectively and to the best of your ability **any relevant conflict of interest**.	**Client**
6	To attain and actively manage a level of **professional competence** appropriate to your responsibilities, to commit to continuing learning to ensure the currency of your knowledge, skills and expertise and to promote the development of others.	**Client** – Colleagues, Self
7	**To decline to act in any matter about which you are not competent** unless you have access to such advice and assistance as will enable you to carry out the work in a professional manner.	**Client** – Firm, Industry
8	To strive to uphold the **highest personal and professional standards**.	**Self**

The CISI state that material breach of the Code of Conduct would be incompatible with continuing membership of the CISI and may result in disciplinary action.

Members who find themselves in a position which might require them to act in a manner contrary to the Principles are encouraged by the CISI to:

1 Discuss their concerns with their line manager

2 Seek advice from their internal compliance department

3 Approach their firm's non-executive directors or audit committee

4 If unable to resolve their concerns and, having exhausted all internal avenues, contact the Chartered Institute for Securities & Investment for advice at principles@cisi.org

ICAEW Ethical Code

The Institute of Chartered Accountants in England and Wales has developed a Code of Ethics, effective from 2011. The Code is based around five fundamental principles as follows. A professional accountant shall comply with the following fundamental principles:

- **Integrity** – to be straightforward and honest in all professional and business relationships
- **Objectivity** – to not allow bias, conflict of interest or undue influence of others to override professional or business judgments
- **Professional competence and due care** – to maintain professional knowledge and skill at the level required to ensure that a client or employer receives competent professional services based on current developments in practice, legislation and techniques and act diligently and in accordance with applicable technical and professional standards
- **Confidentiality** – to respect the confidentiality of information acquired as a result of professional and business relationships and, therefore, not disclose any such information to third parties without proper and specific authority, unless there is a legal or professional right or duty to disclose, nor use the information for the personal advantage of the professional accountant or third parties
- **Professional behaviour** – to comply with relevant laws and regulations and avoid any action that discredits the profession

FCA's Ethical Framework

The Financial Services and Markets Act 2000 and the FCA's principles and commitments embody a framework of core values. In summary they can be seen as:

- Being open, honest, responsive and accountable;
- Being committed to acting competently, responsibly and reliably; and
- Relating to colleagues and customers fairly and with respect.

The following questions are set out in the FCA paper 'An Ethical Framework for Financial Services', published in 2002. The questions are designed to help practitioners recognise, apply and balance values in everyday decisions and actions:

Open, honest, responsive and accountable

- Who is left out or kept in the dark? Why?
- How happy are we to be associated with our decisions/actions?
- Are we listening or just hearing?
- What can we learn? How do we help others to understand us?
- How do we recognise and deal with conflicts of interest?

Relating to colleagues and customers fairly and with respect

- Do we treat everyone as we would like to be treated?
- Do we deal with people with respect and without prejudice?
- How do we keep rights and obligations in balance and proportionate?
- When do we hold to our commitments and resist 'fudging'?
- Who benefits and who loses out? Should they?

Committed to acting competently, responsibly and reliably

- Do we do what we say we will do?
- Under pressure do we swap co-operation for coercion?
- Do we dither or delay? How is error treated?
- Do people trust us? If not, why not?
- Can we meet our commitments and plans?

3 Ethical Behaviour in Corporate Finance

Some key themes can be developed out of the above codes of conduct that impact particularly on corporate finance work.

Conflicts of Interest

Conflicts of interest prevent an adviser **acting objectively**, or, as importantly, **being perceived to be acting objectively**. Conflicts of interest can arise between the adviser and the client or between two different clients of an adviser.

Conflicts between the adviser and the client

A conflict can exist due to some arrangement which an adviser has entered into which might prevent them giving a client unbiased and objective advice. An example might be an arrangement whereby the adviser receives commission from introducing the client to a third party, or from performing some other service. Any such arrangements must always be disclosed to the client.

Conflicts between two different clients of an adviser

If the interests of two clients are in dispute with each other (for example different sides of a takeover bid) the objectivity of the adviser may be perceived to be impaired. Conflicts can sometimes be managed via internal arrangements, for example by using separate advisory teams and proper record keeping, but if a material conflict exists an appointment should be declined. The Takeover Code requires that offeree shareholders be represented by an independent (rule 3) adviser and a material conflict of interest would prevent the adviser being perceived as independent.

A disclosure to the client that a conflict of interest exists is not always sufficient to ensure that the perception of objectivity is upheld.

Confidentiality

A corporate financier is privy to much confidential information about a client. This information should not be disclosed without express consent from the client, unless there is a legal duty to disclose the information, for example if breaches of the law come to light. Confidential information acquired in the course of professional work should neither be used nor appear to use that information for personal advantage or for the advantage of a third party. In some situations disclosing confidential information can be a crime; legislation exists in respect of insider dealing and market abuse.

Corporate financiers are often dealing with price sensitive information. The takeover code sets out the importance of secrecy relating to all matters concerning a bid prior to initial announcement to prevent false markets in the company's shares.

Fee Arrangements

Fee arrangements with clients must not be designed in a way that might be perceived to detract from the impartiality and objectivity of the advice that is given. Fee estimates should be set out in advance of work being undertaken and should specify the scope of work that is expected. It is acceptable to charge differential fees with different rates for different services that are to be undertaken. It is acceptable to charge fees on a percentage or contingent basis. However, contingent fees may give rise to a self-interest threat to objectivity. The significance of this threat should be evaluated and safeguards considered. Success fees payable to advisers are likely to prevent an adviser being seen as 'independent' under rule 3.2 of the takeover code.

4 The Bribery Act 2010

The Bribery Act was enacted in 2010 to modernize the regulations on bribery and became effective in July 2011.

Bribery is defined as **giving someone a financial or other advantage to encourage that person to perform their functions or activities improperly or to reward that person for having already done so**. A bribe therefore does not have to be monetary in nature but could include an offer of employment, other contractual entitlement or gift. **Function or activity** includes any function of a public nature and any activity connected with a business. **Improper** performance of functions occurs where the expectation of good faith or impartiality has been breached, or when the function has been performed in a way not expected of a person in a position of trust.

The Act is very wide in jurisdiction and will apply if any part of an organisation's business takes place in the UK, regardless of where the organisation is incorporated and regardless of where the bribe took place. The offence applies to both making and receiving bribes.

The penalties for committing bribery are a maximum of ten years' imprisonment, along with an unlimited fine, and the potential for the confiscation of property under the Proceeds of Crime Act 2002, as well as the disqualification of directors under the Company Directors Disqualification Act 1986.

The Act also introduces a **corporate offence** of failure to prevent bribery. A company may be guilty even if no one within the company knew of the bribery. There is a defence, if the company can show that it has in place 'adequate procedures designed to prevent persons associated with [the organisation] from undertaking such conduct'. The government has provided guidance as to what constitutes 'adequate procedures' and each organisation needs to have a code of conduct in place that appropriately reflects this guidance and to ensure its personnel are fully conversant with the risks and adequately trained. Failure by an organization to prevent bribery is punishable by an unlimited fine.

5 Insider Dealing

Insider dealing is the offence of acting with information that is not freely and openly available to all other participants in the market place. This is an offence under the Criminal Justice Act 1993. The Act makes it a criminal offence for connected persons who receive inside information to act on that information. The penalties are imprisonment for a maximum of seven years and/or an unlimited fine. The purpose of requiring inside information to be announced to the market as soon as possible is to allow investors the opportunity to make informed investment decisions.

The legislation covers the following instruments:

- Shares
- Debt securities issued by the private or public sector
- Warrants
- Depository receipts
- Options, futures or contracts for a difference on any of the above

An insider is defined as an **individual** (not a company) who has **information** in his possession that he **knows** is **inside information** and **knows** is from an **inside source.** Inside information in this context refers to unpublished price-sensitive information that is specific or precise and relates to a security or its issuer.

For the purposes of determining what is **published** information the following information is deemed to be published:

- Information published via a regulated market, eg an RIE
- Information contained in public records
- Information that can otherwise be readily acquired by market users, eg in the financial press.
- Information derived from public information
- Information that can only be acquired by expertise or by the payment of a fee
- Information that is published only to a section of the public, rather than the public in general, or published outside the UK
- Information that can be acquired by observation, eg a factory burning down

An **inside source** is an individual and would include a director, employee or shareholder of an issuer of securities or a person who has access to the information by virtue of their employment, office or profession. A person will also be an inside source if he receives the information directly or indirectly from one of the above and in addition satisfies the general definition above.

If a person satisfies the definition of an insider it is an offence to:

- **Deal** in the affected securities either on a regulated market or through a professional intermediary
- **Encourage another** person to deal with reasonable cause to believe that dealing would take place on a regulated market or through a professional intermediary
- **Disclose the information** to another person other than in the proper performance of their duties

An individual is not guilty of insider **dealing** if he can show:

- That he did not, at the time, expect the dealing to result in a profit attributable to the fact that the information was price sensitive
- That, at the time, he believed on reasonable grounds that the information had been disclosed widely enough to ensure that none of those taking part in the dealing would be prejudiced by not having the information
- That he would have done what he did even if he had not had the information

A similar series of defences are available to the charge of **encouraging** another to deal in price-affected securities.

An individual is not guilty of insider dealing by virtue of a **disclosure** of information if he shows:

- That he did not, at the time, expect any person, because of the disclosure, to deal in securities either through a regulated market or via a professional intermediary
- That although he had such an expectation at the time, he did not expect the dealing to result in a profit attributable to the fact that the information was price sensitive in relation to the securities

An individual is not guilty of insider dealing if he can show:

- He acted in good faith as a market maker
- The information, gained as an insider, was market information and it was reasonable to act in that way despite having information as an insider
- That he acted in connection with an acquisition or disposal and the information was market information arising directly from the involvement with the acquisition or disposal
- He acted in conformity with the price stabilisation rules

There are obligations on companies to manage access to and disclosure of inside information.

Examples of Insider Dealing Prosecutions

Rifat

In 2014, The Financial Conduct Authority (FCA) prosecuted former Moore Capital trader, Julian Rifat for passing on inside information during the course of his employment. The FCA said he had passed on information on eight companies, including Barclays, Volkswagen, Metro and Iberdrola, to an associate, Graeme Shelley, who worked as a broker at Novum Securities. Shelley, then traded on the information for their joint benefit using contracts for difference. Rifat received a custodial sentence, whilst Shelley received a suspended sentence. The case involved other prosecutions and fines to recover illegal profits made, as part of 'Operation Tabernula'.

Pignatelli

In 2006, the FCA fined equity salesman Sean Pignatelli £20,000 for failing to comply with internal compliance procedures and passing on information from an e-mail to clients with the suggestion that it constituted inside information. In fact, the FCA found, the e-mail did not contain inside information, but Mr Pignatelli had not turned his mind to whether or not it did.

Depending on the evidence, a broker in such a situation might be considered guilty of 'encouraging' another to engage in insider trading.

Motorola

Following the 2007 introduction of Sabre (replaced by ZEN in August 2011), its new computer system for detecting abnormal share trading, the FCA doubled the number of its criminal prosecutors for pursuing insider dealing cases. The Authority launched its first ever criminal prosecution for insider dealing in January 2008, in a case involving accusations of trading ahead of an offer by Motorola for TTP Communications in 2006. Another criminal prosecution, of an ex-Cazenove trader, followed in July 2008.

Ex-hedge fund trader sentenced for insider dealing: June 2010

On 22 June 2010, in a case brought by the FCA, Anjam Saeed Ahmad, an ex-hedge fund trader and risk manager with AKO Capital LLP (AKO), was sentenced to 10 months imprisonment, suspended for two years, 300 hours of unpaid work in the community and fined £50,000 for insider dealing. Between 15 May 2009 and 22 August 2009 he conspired with another individual to deal in at least 19 different securities, based on inside information obtained by Ahmad in his role as a trader at AKO about forthcoming transactions by AKO in those securities.

Insider Lists

Issuers of financial instruments are required by the Disclosure Rules and Transparency Rules (DTR 2.8) to set up insider lists of persons, whether they are employees or not, with access to inside information about the issuer. This would cover where information is received on either a regular or occasional basis.

The definition of issuer here relates to any entity which has its financial instruments trading on a regulated market (or has applied to have them trading on a such a regulated market). Regulated markets include the LSE, Liffe, NYSE Euronext London and PLUS-listed market (operated by PLUS Markets plc), but not AIM.

The list must be provided to the FCA on request, and must show:

- Each person's identity
- Reason for the person being on the list
- Date of creation and updating of the list

For insiders working for another firm, it is sufficient to record a principal contact, provided the other firm maintains its own list of the insiders (eg its principal contact at an advising investment bank or law firm). The issuer should also make (usually contractual) arrangements for such businesses to maintain their own lists of insiders with inside information regarding the issuer and provide copies of that list to the issuer on request.

The list must be updated promptly for changes, and must be kept for at least five years.

The issuer firm must ensure that employees with inside information acknowledge the legal and regulatory duties entailed. The firm must establish effective arrangements to deny access to inside information to anyone who does not require it to do their job. There must also be procedures to make a public disclosure if the firm cannot ensure confidentiality of information – for example, if they become aware of a breach of confidence.

There have been concerns regarding the cost to businesses of implementing this requirement, as it results in significant additional administration and may result in amendments to contacts of employment and advisers' engagement letters, amongst other documents.

Delayed Disclosure of Inside Information

Under DTR 2.5, an issuer may delay the public disclosure of inside information, such as not to prejudice its legitimate interests, provided that the public would not be likely to be misled and the issuer is able to ensure the confidentiality of the information.

For example, if the firm's financial viability is in 'grave and imminent danger', although not within the scope of the applicable insolvency law, public disclosure of information may be delayed for a limited period where such a public disclosure would seriously jeopardise the interest of shareholders by undermining the conclusion of specific negotiations designed to ensure the firm's long-term financial recovery.

Delayed Disclosure Example: Photo-Me

In June 2010, the FCA fined Photo-Me International plc (Photo-Me) £500,000 – the largest fine yet of this type – for failing to disclose inside information to the market as soon as possible, resulting in a false market in Photo-Me's shares for 44 days.

In late 2006, Photo-Me made announcements that created an expectation in the market that it would benefit from the winning of large minilab (photo-processing) sales contracts and strong minilab sales generally. These announcements underpinned Photo-Me's share price in the relevant period and were based on Photo-Me's expectation that it would conclude a contract with a large US-based retailer (the Albertsons contract) for the sale of 200 minilabs.

In January 2007, Photo-Me was informed that it was no longer engaged in exclusive negotiations for the Albertsons contract: Photo-Me was one of at least five competitors for the business. This, as well as downward revisions of minilab sales which were known by 12 February 2007, comprised inside information and should have been disclosed as soon as possible. The company finally issued a profit warning on 2 March 2007 and the share price closed 24% lower that day.

UK Enforcement Compared with USA

An FCA study found that, in 2008, 29% of UK corporate takeover announcements were preceded by suspicious share trading activity – indicating that there is much enforcement work to be done.

It is arguable that more rigorous past enforcement in the USA compared with the UK is a matter of differing attitudes of the regulators in each jurisdiction, at least in the past. The FCA has had broader powers than US regulators, in significant respects. Trading while in possession of any market-moving non-public information is market abuse under the UK regime, while in the US enforcement authorities must show that a duty to keep information confidential was violated. Additionally, the SEC in the USA can only bring civil cases, and must bring in the Department of Justice to effect custodial sentences.

6 Misleading Statements and Impressions

Misleading Statements

Section 89 of the Financial Services Act 2012 covers misleading statements. Under s89, it is an offence to:

- Make a statement which the person making the statement 'P' knows to be false or misleading in a material respect.
- Make a statement which is false or misleading in a material respect, being reckless as to whether it is; or
- Dishonestly conceal any material facts whether in connection with a statement made by P or otherwise.

P commits an offence if P makes the statement or conceals that facts with the intention of inducing, or is reckless as to whether making it or concealing them may induce, another person:

- To enter into or offer to enter into, or to refrain from entering or offering to enter into, a relevant agreement; or
- To exercise, or refrain from exercising, any rights conferred by a relevant investment.

Misleading Impressions

Section 90 of the Financial Services Act 2012 covers misleading impressions.

A person (P) who does any act or engages in any course of conduct which creates a false or misleading impression as to the market in or the price or value of any relevant investments commits an offence if P intends to create the impression.

Manipulation of Benchmark Ratios

Finally, in response to the LIBOR scandal, s91 creates a new offence which deals with the manipulation of benchmark rates. In summary, offences are committed if misrepresentations are made in the course of setting the benchmark, or if false impressions as to the value of an investment may in due course have an impact upon the benchmark rate.

Penalties

This is a criminal offence and the maximum penalty is **seven years'** imprisonment and/or an unlimited fine. The fine is often referred to as the 'statutory fine'.

7 Market Abuse

Certain types of behaviour, such as insider dealing and market manipulation, can amount to market abuse. Types of conduct constituting market abuse are set out in section 118 of the Financial Services and Markets Act 2000 and in the Market Abuse Directive.

In June 2014 new European legislation seeking to strengthen the fight against market abuse was agreed. The Market Abuse Regulation (MAR) will apply in the UK and across the EU from 3 July 2016

Market abuse is a civil offence under s118 of FSMA which provides an alternative civil regime for enforcing the criminal prohibitions on insider dealing and market manipulation. The UK market abuse rules implement the EU Market Abuse Directive.

The **territorial scope** of market abuse is very wide. It covers everyone, not just authorised firms and approved persons. Furthermore, firms or persons outside the UK are also covered by the offence.

As market abuse is a **civil offence**, the FCA must prove, on the balance of probabilities, that a person:

- Engaged in market abuse; or
- By taking or refraining from action required or encouraged another person to engage in market abuse.

The Definition of Market Abuse

Market abuse is behaviour, whether by one person alone or by two or more persons jointly or in concert, which occurs in relation to:

- Qualifying investments admitted to trading on a prescribed market; or
- Qualifying investments in respect of which a request for admission to trading on a prescribed market has been made; or
- Related investments of a qualifying investment (strictly, this is only relevant to the offences of 'Insider Dealing' and 'Improper Disclosure', see below).

And falls within one or more of the offences below.

The Seven 'Offences' of Market Abuse

The seven types of behaviour which can constitute market abuse are:

1 **'Insider Dealing'**. This is where an insider deals, or attempts to deal, in a qualifying investment or related investment on the basis of inside information.

2 **'Improper Disclosure'**. This is where an insider discloses inside information to another person otherwise than in the proper course of the exercise of his employment, profession or duties.

3 **'Misuse of Information'**. This fills gaps in '1' or '2' above and is where the behaviour:

   (a) Is based on information which is not generally available to those using the market but which, if available to a regular user of the market, would be regarded by him as relevant when deciding the terms on which transactions in qualifying investments should be effected; and

   (b) Is likely to be regarded by a regular user of the market as a failure on the part of the person concerned to observe the standard of behaviour reasonably expected of a person in his position.

4 **'Manipulating Transactions'**. This consists of effecting transactions or orders to trade (otherwise than for legitimate reasons and in conformity with accepted market practices) which:

   (a) Give, or are likely to give a false or misleading impression as to the supply, demand or price of one or more qualifying investment; or

   (b) Secure the price of one or more such investment at an abnormal or artificial level.

5 **'Manipulating Devices'**. This consists of effecting transactions or orders to trade which employ fictitious devices or any other form of deception.

6 **'Dissemination'**. This consists of the dissemination of information by any means which gives, or is likely to give, a false or misleading impression as to a qualifying investment by a person who knew or could reasonably be expected to have known that the information was false or misleading.

7 **'Misleading Behaviour'** and **'Distortion'**. This fills any gaps in '4', '5' and '6' above is where the behaviour:

   (a) Is likely to give, a regular user of the market a false or misleading impression as to the supply of, demand for or price or value of, qualifying investments; or

   (b) Would be regarded by a regular user of the market as behaviour that would distort the market in such an investment and is likely to be regarded by a regular user of the market as a failure on the part of the person concerned to observe the standard of behaviour reasonably expected of a person in his position.

Qualifying Investments and Prescribed Markets

Behaviour will only constitute market abuse if it occurs in the UK or in relation to qualifying investments traded on a prescribed market. The term 'behaviour' is specifically mentioned as the offence of market abuse can cover both action and inaction.

Qualifying investment means any investment traded on a UK RIE or a regulated market. Regulated markets cover the main European exchanges.

The definition of prescribed market and qualifying investment are amended slightly with reference to the offences of 'Misuse of Information' and 'Misleading Behaviour' and 'Distortion'. Here, a prescribed market means any UK RIE. Thus these offences are only relevant to the UK markets.

As behaviour must be in relation to qualifying investments, the regime is not limited to on-market dealings. For instance, abusive trades on foreign exchanges could constitute market abuse if the underlying instrument also trades on a prescribed market. This makes the regime much wider than the criminal law offences.

Defences

Under S123 of FSMA, the FCA may not impose a financial penalty in relation to market abuse where it is satisfied that the person believed, on reasonable grounds, that his behaviour did not amount to market abuse or he took all reasonable precautions and exercised all due diligence to avoid engaging in market abuse.

The FCA also has a Code of Market Conduct which sets out:

- Descriptions of behaviour that, in the opinion of the FCA, do or do not amount to market abuse. Descriptions of behaviour which do not amount to market abuse are called 'safe harbours'
- Descriptions of behaviour that are or are not accepted market practices in relation to one or more identified markets
- Factors that, in the opinion of the FCA, are to be taken into account in determining whether or not behaviour amounts to market abuse

The Code does not exhaustively describe all types of behaviour that may or may not amount to market abuse.

Enforcement and Penalties

The FCA may impose one or more of the following penalties on those found to have committed market abuse:

- An unlimited fine
- Issue a public statement
- Apply to the court to seek an injunction or restitution order
- Where an authorised/approved person is guilty of market abuse, they will also be guilty of a breach of the FCA's Principles and they could, in addition to the above penalties, have disciplinary proceedings brought against them, which may result in withdrawal of authorisation/approval

Note that as market abuse is a civil offence, offenders cannot be sent to prison unlike the criminal laws of insider dealing and the rules on misleading statements and impressions. Civil offences are also easier to prosecute.

In addition to being able to impose penalties for market abuse, the FCA is given criminal prosecution powers to enforce insider dealing and the rules on misleading statements and impressions. The FCA has indicated that it will not pursue both the civil and criminal regime. In terms of the enforcement process for market abuse, this is the same as the FCA's disciplinary process.

Reporting Suspicious Transactions (market abuse)

A firm which has reasonable grounds to suspect that a transaction might constitute market abuse must notify the FCA without delay. The notification must include a description of the transaction and reasons for the suspicion. The firm must not inform any other persons of this notification, in particular the person on behalf of whom the transaction has been carried out.

Statutory Exceptions

If a person is within one of the statutory exceptions set out in the Code of Market Conduct (also known as safe harbours) they are not committing market abuse. Generally, there are no rules in the Takeover Code which permit or require a person to behave in a way which amounts to market abuse.

However, the following rules provide safe harbour meaning that behaviour conforming with that rule does not amount to market abuse.

FCA Rules

Behaviour caused by the proper operation of a Chinese wall or behaviour which relates to the timing, dissemination or content to a disclosure under the Listing Rules will not amount to market abuse.

Takeover Code

Behaviour conforming with any of the rules of the Takeover Code about the timing, dissemination or content of a disclosure does not, of itself, amount to market abuse. This is subject to the behaviour being expressly required or permitted by a rule and provided it conforms to the General Principles of the Takeover Code.

Price Stabilisation

Behaviour which conforms with the Buyback and Stabilisation Regulation (in the Market Conduct Sourcebook of the FCA's Handbook) will not amount to market abuse.

However, buyback programmes which do not follow the Buyback and Stabilisation Regulation are not automatically seen as market abuse, but do not have an automatic safe harbour.

The Market Conduct section of the FCA Handbook sets out how and when a lead manager in an initial public offering may purchase securities to stabilise a price without abusing the market.

- Where the offer is for cash.
- Where the offer is public on a qualifying exchange.
- When it is for a limited period.
- When adequate prior disclosure is given to the market in the prospectus.
- When information on stabilising activity is given to the issuer, although this would not include identifying individual clients.

Price stabilisation is often achieved through a process of over-allotment, backed up by a greenshoe option over further shares for the stabilising manager.

By allotting to new investors more than 100% of the shares actually created by the issuing company, the stabilising manager has left itself 'short' of these extra shares it has sold but does not yet have. This means the manager will go into the market and buy these extra securities from any new shareholders willing to sell their allocation. This creates an artificial demand to support the price.

Of course, this leaves the stabilisation manager exposed to having to buy the extra shares needed at above the issue price, incurring a loss. To protect against this risk, the manager will hold 'greenshoe' options to buy more shares from the issuing company at the issue price.

Greenshoe options may be used for other purposes besides stabilisation, but the reason must be disclosed to the issuer.

Market Abuse Regulation (MAR)

Market Abuse Regulation seeks to increase market integrity and investor protection, while ensuring a single rulebook and level playing field across the EU. MAR contains the following main provisions.

Inside Information and Disclosure

The definition of inside information is broadly unchanged, but has been widened to capture inside information for spot commodity contracts. Issuers must notify the regulator after delaying disclosure of inside information, and financial institutions must seek consent from the regulator prior to delaying disclosure due to financial stability concerns.

Inside Dealing and Unlawful Disclosure

It is clarified that the use of inside information to amend or cancel an order shall be considered to be insider dealing. It is also clarified that recommending or inducing another person to transact on the basis of inside information amounts to unlawful disclosure of inside information

Market Manipulation

The manipulation offence has been extended to capture attempted manipulation. Benchmarks, and in some situations spot commodities, are now in scope of the manipulation offence. Examples of behaviours and activities that shall be considered as market manipulation are set out, eg acting in collaboration to secure a dominant position over the supply or demand of a financial instrument, and certain algorithmic trading strategies which disrupt the functioning of a trading venue.

Market Soundings

Introduces a framework for persons to make legitimate disclosures of inside information in the course of market soundings.

Buy-Back Programmes and Stabilisation Measures

Makes revisions to the existing framework for conducting buy-back programmes and stabilisation measures.

Accepted Market Practices (AMPs)

Continues to permit regulators to establish an accepted market practice which is subject to certain criteria and conditions.

Insider Lists

Places an obligation on issuers to draw-up and maintain a list of all those persons working for them that have access to inside information. Issuers on SME growth markets will only be required to draw up a list when it is requested by the regulator.

Suspicious Transaction and Order Reports (STORS)

Extends the existing obligation to report suspicious transaction reports, to include suspicious orders too. Trading venues are also caught by the obligation to submit STORs.

Managers' Transactions

Persons discharging managerial responsibilities within issuers (PDMRs), and persons closely associated with them, must notify the issuer and the regulator of relevant personal transactions they undertake in the issuer's financial instruments. The issuer in turn must make that information public within three business days.

Investment Recommendations

Continues to require persons producing or disseminating investment recommendations to ensure information is objectively presented, and to disclose any conflicts of interest.

Whistleblowing

Places requirements on regulators and firms to be able to receive whistleblowing notifications.

8 The UK Regulatory Regime

The Financial Conduct Authority (FCA)

The late 2000s was a period of turmoil for the international financial services sector, stemming in large part from excessive lending by banks, particularly to sub-prime borrowers, and from the 'securitisation' or packaging of mortgages by lenders for selling on to investors who were insufficiently aware of the risks attached to the securities.

In mid-2010 it was announced by the Conservative-Liberal Democrat coalition that there was to be a complete overhaul of the regulation of the UK financial services industry and that the Financial Services Authority (FSA) in its existing form would be abolished. The changes came into force with the enactment of the 2012 Financial Services Act, which came into effect in 2013.

The main provisions of the Act were as follows:

- **Bank of England**. Significant new powers were granted to the Bank of England. The Bank is now responsible for identifying potential crises and developing and implementing contingency plans. The Bank has been made **responsible for ensuring the stability of the financial system**, and is empowered to lead the response in a financial crisis. Responsibility for regulating settlement systems and recognised clearing houses has been transferred to the Bank of England.
- The **Financial Policy Committee (FPC)** was established within the Bank of England, with responsibility for macro-prudential oversight of the regulatory system. The FPC has more flexibility regarding appointments of committee members to allow for swift changes in membership. The Government renews the FPC's remit annually. In an effort to make its workings transparent and accountable, records of FPC meetings are published. The FPC publishes two **Financial Stability Reports (FSRs)** a year, including a summary of its activities and an assessment of the effectiveness of its actions in the period since the last report. (The FPC can exclude confidential or market-sensitive information from what it publishes.) The Role of the FPC is considered further below.
- The **Prudential Regulation Authority (PRA)** was set up as a **subsidiary of the Bank of England** to conduct prudential regulation of firms which manage significant balance sheet risk as a core part of their business. This includes banks, insurers and the more complex investment firms. The PRA has the power to designate firms that should fall within its scope, subject to certain procedural safeguards. The role of the PRA is considered further below.
- The Financial Services Authority (FSA) legal entity became the **Financial Conduct Authority (FCA)**, which is now responsible for consumer protection in financial services, the regulation of conduct of business (including in firms regulated by the new PRA) and market conduct. The **FCA** specialises in protecting customers and promoting confidence in financial services and markets, and promoting competition. The listing function (hitherto performed by the FSA in its UKLA role) is conferred on the FCA. The role of the FCA is considered further below.
- The reforms emphasised the need for **coordination between the regulatory bodies**, as well as extensive **coordination with other bodies**, such as the Financial Ombudsman Service (FOS) and the Bank of England.

- The **Financial Ombudsman Service (FOS)** is one of a **range of organisations** that has the power to raise with the FCA **matters causing significant detriment** and the FCA is required to consider appropriate action, which may include consumer redress.
- **Financial promotions power**. The FCA has the power to take regulatory action to prevent consumers from being misled and to publicise the action taken. Safeguards have been introduced to reflect concerns raised by respondents over potential reputation damage to them in the use of this power.
- **Competition scrutiny**. The Government made the competition scrutiny regime, which will applies to the PRA and FCA, more up-to-date and effective. The regime allows the competition authorities to monitor the impact of regulatory practices and provisions upon competition in financial services. While the promotion of competition is a key duty of the FCA, the Authority's primary objective remains as the protection and enhancement of the UK financial system.

The Financial Policy Committee (FPC)

The creation of the **Financial Policy Committee** was motivated by the perception that the absence of any effective macro-prudential agency was a major failing in the UK, EU and US before the 2008 financial crisis. This lack was highlighted with the inability of the authorities to deal with asset price bubbles, especially in the property market, and the accumulation of debt and leverage across the financial system.

The FPC includes the FCA Chief Executive and representatives from HM Treasury. The FPC also has some external representation and meets four times annually and at times of crisis.

S9C Bank of England (BoE) Act 1998 (as amended by FSA 2012) provides that the FPC is to exercise its functions with a view to:

- Contributing to the achievement by the Bank of England of the **Financial Stability Objective**; and
- Subject to that, supporting the economic policy of the Government, including its objectives for growth and employment.

The BoE's **Financial Stability Objective** is stated in s2A Bank of England Act 1998 (as amended by FSA 2012), which states that an objective of the Bank shall be: **To protect and enhance the stability of the financial system of the UK.**

The responsibility of the Committee in relation to the achievement by the Bank of the Financial Stability Objective relates primarily to the identification of, monitoring of, and taking of action to remove or reduce, **systemic risks** with a view to protecting and enhancing the resilience of the UK financial system (s9C(2) BoE Act 1998).

Those systemic risks include, in particular:

- Systemic risks attributable to structural features of financial markets, such as connections between financial institutions
- Systemic risks attributable to the distribution of risk within the financial sector; and
- Unsustainable levels of leverage, debt or credit growth (s9C(3) BoE Act 1998).

Systemic risk here means a risk to the stability of the UK financial system as a whole or of a significant part of that system, whether the risk arises in the UK or elsewhere.

The **FPC** has the following **tools** at its disposal:

- Setting system-wide cyclical capital requirements, reducing capital buffers required in a crisis while toughening them in more favourable economic times
- Altering risk weights, enabling the Bank to force banks to hold more capital against specific classes of assets in apparently frothy markets

- Setting limits on leverage as a backstop against excessive lending where changing risk weights might not be effective
- Requiring forward-looking loss provisioning to prepare for future losses when lending growth is strong
- Setting limits on borrowing, eg with maximum loan-to-value ratios for mortgages
- Setting limits on lending through regulation

The **Chancellor of the Exchequer** retains the right to **overrule the Bank of England Governor** in a crisis.

Prudential Regulation Authority (PRA)

The PRA – established in 2013 as a subsidiary of the Bank of England – is responsible for the prudential regulation of banks, insurance companies and large investment firms.

The PRA has a statutory **general objective** that is fundamentally different from that of earlier regulatory regimes:

Promoting the safety and soundness of PRA-authorised firms

The PRA meets this objective primarily by seeking to minimise any adverse effects of firm failure on the UK financial system and by ensuring that firms carry on their business in a way that avoids adverse effects on the system.

The PRA focuses on the stability of the system overall, albeit through the mechanism of the supervision of individual firms. This requires close coordination with the **Financial Policy Committee** whose role is to manage the risks in the system as a whole. The PRA is a key contributor to the information and analysis on which the Financial Policy Committee bases its judgements.

The PRA's supervisory efforts relating to financial stability focuses particularly on **large international banks.** In the case of UK subsidiaries of overseas banks, links of the UK entity with the group as a whole as well as the group's viability are an integral part of the PRA's supervisory assessment.

In order to deliver its objective of stability of the financial system, the PRA uses a new framework to assess risks to financial stability.

Key elements of PRA risk assessment framework

- Potential impact on the financial system of a firm coming under stress or failing
- Impact on the viability of a firm's business model of the macroeconomic and business risk context
- A firm's overall safety and soundness, which may act to mitigate the potential risk a firm poses to financial stability

Key mitigants assessed by the PRA

- Degree of resolvability of a firm (working closely with the Bank's Special Resolution Unit)
- The firm's financial strength (including its ability to generate capital through earnings, its capital held against future risks, the quality of its liquid assets and its liquidity management)
- The quality of a firm's risk management and governance (including the competence of its senior management)

Risks to a firm are identified using:

- Baseline monitoring
- Investigation and assurance
- The macroeconomic and business context

The PRA takes a forward-looking and **judgment-based approach to supervision.** Baseline monitoring is undertaken for all firms, including those that can be resolved with minimal disruption to the financial system (eg credit unions and small deposit-takers). This monitoring includes a review of a firm's resolvability (at least) once a year, analysis of a firm's financial position, discussions with senior management and ensuring compliance with minimum prudential standards for capital, liquidity and large exposures, as well as early interventions where necessary.

Financial Conduct Authority (FCA)

The **Financial Conduct Authority (FCA)** is the **conduct regulator** for the UK financial services industry. The FCA also has responsibility for the **prudential regulation** of investment exchanges, many investment firms and other financial services providers.

Although set up by statute, the FCA is not regarded as acting on behalf of the Crown. Its members, officers and staff are, therefore, not Crown or civil servants. Like its predecessor – the FSA – the FCA is structured as a **company limited by guarantee**, and is given its powers by FSMA 2000.

The FCA is **accountable to the Treasury** and, through the Treasury, to **Parliament.**

The FCA is governed by a **Board** that is appointed by the Treasury. The majority of the Board members are non-executive. One of the non-executive members is a senior non-executive.

The FCA's Board sets the policy of the Authority. Day-to-day decisions and staff management are the responsibility of the FCA's **Executive Committee.**

The Authority is operationally independent of Government and is funded entirely by the firms it regulates.

The FSA 2012 gives the **Financial Conduct Authority (FCA)** a single **strategic objective**:

'Ensuring that the relevant markets function well' (s1B(2) FSMA 2000, as amended by FSA 2012)

'Relevant markets' include the financial markets and the markets for regulated financial services.

The strategic objective of the FCA is supported by three **operational objectives** (s1C-E FSMA 2000):

- **The consumer protection objective**: securing an appropriate degree of protection for consumers
- **The integrity objective:** protecting and enhancing the integrity of the UK financial system
- **The competition objective**: promoting effective competition in the interests of consumers in the market for regulated financial services and for services provided by a recognised investment exchange

The Authority also has duties to **promote competition** (which may involve analysing pricing) and to **address financial crime.**

A spokesperson for the regulator explained that the FCA was set up to work with firms with the aim of ensuring that they put consumers at the heart of their business.

Underlining this are three outcomes:

- Consumers get financial services and products that meet their needs from firms they can trust.
- Firms compete effectively with the interests of their customers and the integrity of the market at the heart of how they run their business.
- Markets and financial systems are sound, stable and resilient with transparent pricing information.

Dividend Policy

chapter 15

Contents

1 WHAT IS DIVIDEND POLICY?

Target Dividend

Dividend policy is a strategy developed by a company's directors for the level of dividends they will pay each year. Dividend policy may be expressed in terms of a desired growth rate, eg 5% annual growth in real terms. It may be expressed as a cover ratio, eg dividends will be covered by a ratio of at least 2× when compared to earnings for the year. Whatever way they do it, the directors will have some target dividend rate.

Reasons for Setting a Dividend Policy

The reason that directors set a dividend policy for their company is that they believe that shareholders like to have a stable or steadily growing dividend each year. Typically, they will look at past dividend growth, this year's earnings and expected future earnings levels and from these three factors aim to set an acceptable level of dividend this year which will grow at a roughly constant rate in the future.

The dividend decision is really an interaction between the investment decision and the financing decision, as the amount of money paid out as dividends will affect the level of retained earnings available for investment.

This chapter considers dividend policy from a theoretical viewpoint first of all before moving on to look at the practical factors that affect a company's dividend.

2 THE DIVIDEND VALUATION MODEL (DVM)

Introduction

The impact of dividends on share price is summarized in the dividend valuation model.

The dividend valuation model states the following:

$$MV_{xd} = \frac{D_1}{k_e - g}$$

Where

MV_{xd} = the ex-div market value of the shares that may need to be calculated using

$$MV_{xd} = Mv_{cum\ div} - D_0$$

Where

$MV_{cum\ div}$	= the cum div market value of the shares
D_0	= the dividend about to be paid now if we are cum div
D_1	= the expected dividend in one year's time which may need to be calculated as $D_1 = D_0 \times (1 + g)$
K_e	= the investors' required rate of return
g	= the expected annual growth rate of the dividends

The growth in dividends is usually estimated by using the following formula

$$g = r \times b$$

Where

r = rate of return on reinvested capital

b = proportion of profits retained and reinvested (= 1 – Payout ratio)

It can be seen that there is a trade-off between current dividends and growth. Paying a higher dividend at Time 1 will increase the d_1, increasing the share price. However, it will reduce the value of b, by increasing the payout ratio. This will reduce growth, reducing the share price.

Optimal Dividend Policy

The optimal dividend policy is one that strikes a balance between paying dividends and retaining earnings to achieve future growth, such that the share price is maximised. This balance will depend on the rate of return on investment and the amount of investment that is possible at that rate of return.

TASK

Marlon Ltd, an all equity company, has free cash flow available at Time 0, ie now, of £1,000. It is currently paying out all of its annual free cash flow as a dividend to shareholders. The free cash flow is expected to remain constant at £1,000 p.a. to infinity. The shareholders' required rate of return is 10%. Calculate the value of the company today on the basis that Marlon Ltd.

(a) Maintains its current policy of paying out all of its free cash flow as a dividend.

(b) Decides to retain 40% of its cash flow each year, starting now, and reinvesting this to earn a return of 20%, ie in excess of shareholders' required returns.

(c) Decides to retain 40% of its cash flow each year, but only earns a return on this of 5%, ie below shareholders' required returns.

(d) Decides to retain 40% of its cash flow each year and earns a return on this of 10%, ie equal to shareholders' required returns.

SOLUTION

(a) Market value = $\frac{1{,}000}{0.1}$ + 1,000 = £11,000

Note that the additional £1,000 needs to be added on to reflect the dividend flow at Time 0.

(b) Growth rate in dividends = rb = 0.2 × 0.4 = 0.08 or 8%

Market value = $\frac{600 \times 1.08}{0.1 - 0.08}$ + 600 = £33,000

The value of the dividend at Time 1 is given by the revised dividend of £600 today increased by the growth rate of 8%.

(c) Growth rate in dividends = rb = 0.05 × 0.4 = 0.02 or 2%

$$\text{Market value} = \frac{600 \times 1.02}{0.1 - 0.02} + 600 = £8,250$$

(d) Growth rate in dividends = rb = 0.1 × 0.4 = 0.04 or 4%

$$\text{Market value} = \frac{600 \times 1.04}{0.1 - 0.04} + 600 = £11,000$$

Conclusion

The above calculations indicate an unsurprising conclusion. When a company's new investments earn a rate of return greater than that required by shareholders, the investments have a positive net present value and undertaking the investments increases shareholder wealth. When the new investments earn a substandard rate of return, they have a negative net present value and reduce shareholders' wealth. When the required rate of return equals the expected return, the new investments have a net present value of nil and shareholders are indifferent as to whether or not the investment is made.

The illustration also demonstrates how increasing dividends can reduce the share price. This is when a company sacrifices investment in projects with positive net present values and future growth in order to pay a dividend this year.

3 THEORETICAL VIEWS ON DIVIDEND POLICY

Dividend Irrelevancy Theory

Introduction

The dividend irrelevancy theory argues that a firm's value and Weighted Average Cost of Capital (WACC) is independent of any dividend policy the firm may adopt. Hence, dividend policy is irrelevant.

The Importance of Investment and Gearing Policy

The theory argues that directors maximize the wealth of their employers, the shareholders, by ensuring that they invest in profitable projects – those with a positive net present value. On top of this, they should ensure that the company has an appropriate capital structure. Having established these two policies, they will have minimized their WACC and maximized the present value of future cash flows.

If a company has established its desired level of investment and how much of this is going to be funded by debt, then the balance will need to be funded by shareholders. If this means that a dividend cannot be paid because there are insufficient cash resources in the company, this does not matter. Shareholders will not be concerned about not receiving a dividend since they know that their money is being invested wisely.

Broadly speaking, a company's value is determined by its earnings power and its business risk, not by how it splits its earnings between dividends and retained profits.

The Level of Dividends in Any One Year is Irrelevant

The theory does not imply that a company does not need to pay dividends or that dividends are irrelevant. It merely says that the level of dividend in any one year should be determined by reference to the resources in the company after taking into account planned investment and debt raising activities.

If a company has surplus resources, then the surplus should be paid out as a dividend. The only alternative is to keep the money in the firm, earning a return equal to the required return. Such an investment will give a nil NPV and hence neither creates nor destroys shareholder value.

If a company has insufficient resources to invest in all of the projects it wants to, then it should actually raise money from its shareholders rather than pay a dividend. In such circumstances, paying a dividend would either mean that the company has to forsake profitable projects or it will have to undertake an even larger share issue – in other words, taking back with the left hand what the right hand gave as a dividend. In this case, the shareholder has not received any cash after allowing for the share issue.

In both cases, the dividend decision was irrelevant, so long as the company followed an appropriate investment and gearing policy.

The approach to dividend payments based on any surplus resources after investment levels have been decided is known as the **residual theory.**

Manufacture of Dividends/Homemade Dividend Policy

One potential argument against the theory is that some investors may need cash and, hence, require a dividend payment. However, if for some reason investors have a pressing need for cash, then they can manufacture a homemade dividend by selling part of their shareholding.

The need to pay cash is not therefore a constraint on the company. Indeed, if the company has concentrated on its investment and gearing policy, then it will have done this investor a service, since presumably the share price will be higher and he will receive more cash than would otherwise be the case.

Likewise, if an investor does not wish to receive a cash dividend, he can reinvest the cash in the company by buying more shares.

Assumptions Underlying Dividend Irrelevancy

The above theory is fairly simplistic and relies on a number of assumptions about the world which clearly do not apply in practice:

- In theory, buying and selling shares is assumed to be a costless transaction. In the real world, investors have to pay commission to their brokers, meaning that selling shares is not a perfect substitute for receiving a dividend.
- There are no tax distortions. In reality, the tax treatment of dividend income and capital gains or losses on sale of shares is likely to be different, meaning that the post-tax receipt to the investor is different.
- Investors are rational and have perfect information. This is why investors are happy if they do not receive a dividend. They know that the company is investing their money wisely elsewhere. In practice, investors may not know exactly what the directors are doing with their money and may assume the worst.

4 Investor Preference for Immediate Cash

Introduction

This theory is sometimes known as the bird in the hand theory. It argues that investors prefer immediate cash to uncertain future capital gains. It argues that the cost of equity will be lower for companies with higher dividend payouts as a result of the reduced risk this entails for investors.

Using the dividend valuation model, the value of a share is the present value of all the future dividends. Hence, a company with higher dividends in the near future and a lower cost of equity for these dividends will be worth more.

Arguments Against the Bird in the Hand Theory

- Very few people need income from dividends. It is possible for such people to manufacture dividends. There are many mutual funds that do this with fairly low transaction costs. Notwithstanding this, the transaction costs of manufacturing dividends may make it a less preferable route. In addition, the tax impacts of each route would need to be considered.
- Other investors (institutions, for example) tend to reinvest dividends in the shares of the same or other firms.
- The risk of returns to investors is determined by the underlying risk of the operating cash flows of the company. Paying higher dividends now cannot alter the underlying risk of the investments. Hence, the cost of equity is unaffected by dividend policy.

Tax Preference Theory

Arguments in Favour of Lower or Higher Payouts

Different tax treatments due to dividend payments may affect the desirability of paying dividends. For example, an investor may be taxed more highly on dividend income than capital gains made from selling shares or vice versa. A company may incur higher or lower tax bills if it pays a dividend.

Personal Taxation

In the UK, the treatment of dividend income and capital gains is different.

Tax-free investors who receive dividends will not pay any further tax on the dividends, but will not be able to reclaim any tax credit. Starting rate or basic rate taxpayers will not be liable to pay any additional tax on dividends received, since their full tax liability is covered by the tax credit. Higher rate payers will have to pay additional tax, which will be equal to 25% of the net dividend gains (or 32.5% of the gross dividend).

When tax-free investors make capital gains, they will not be liable to tax, making them indifferent between dividends and capital.

When starting rate and basic rate payers make capital gains in excess of any tax-free amount, they will be liable to pay capital gains taxes. This will make them prefer dividends, since they suffer no further tax on dividends.

When higher rate payers make capital gains in excess of any tax-free amount, they will be liable to pay tax at 40% of the gain, compared to the 25% gain for dividends. Therefore, they will prefer dividends.

Summary of Theories

- **Irrelevancy theory** – argues that share prices and cost of equity are unaffected by dividend policy
- **Bird in the hand theory** – argues that share prices are increased by high payouts and the cost of equity reduced by high payouts
- **Tax preference theory** – argues that dividend policy is affected by tax factors

Empirical research on whether investors are indifferent to dividend policy, or have a preference for high or low payouts, is difficult to conduct. This is because when evaluating share prices and required returns and how they are affected by dividend policy, all other factors such as business risk need to be allowed for. This is difficult to do. In addition, it is difficult to measure different firms' costs of equity to establish whether or not they are different due to dividend policy.

Generally, research has not indicated a marked preference for a particular level of dividend payouts, offering support to the dividend irrelevancy hypothesis. However, it is clear that individual investors do have their own preferences.

5 Practical Factors Affecting Dividend Payouts

The Availability of Cash and Gearing Levels

In order to pay a cash dividend to its shareholders, a company must have the cash resources to do so. These resources may be in the form of cash deposits or the availability of overdraft facilities, but the company must be able to write the cheques. A dividend will either reduce cash balances or increase debt. Excessive dividend payments could increase gearing levels to an intolerable level.

Maintaining Control

If existing shareholders want to retain control, they will not want to issue new equity. Hence, they will prefer to raise debt or retain profits, giving a lower payout ratio.

Legal Factors

Some investors have a legal requirement to invest in shares that pay dividends. This would favour higher payouts.

Companies must have legally distributable profits to finance a dividend. This will restrict payouts to a lower level.

Availability of Investment Opportunities

A firm that has many investment opportunities with high rates of return should have lower payout ratios.

Where investments can be accelerated or delayed, this will assist in achieving a stable dividend policy.

Clientele Effect

Investors tend to buy shares in companies that suit their investment requirements and one of these requirements may be a particular form of dividend policy, be this for tax reasons or whatever.

If an investor buys shares in a company to receive high dividends, then he will not be very happy if the company suddenly changes its dividend policy and decides to retain all its profits for reinvestment. As far as the investor is concerned, dividend irrelevancy theory does not matter. He will probably sell the share and invest elsewhere. This could be inefficient due to transaction costs and capital gains tax. In addition, new shareholders may not be attracted by the new dividend policy.

What this suggests is that the actual dividend policy followed by a company is less important than communicating that policy to investors and adhering to it. The clientele effect then predicts that investors who are attracted by that dividend policy will gravitate to the company.

Note that this does not imply that a company could increase its share price by increasing its dividends to attract high payout investors. These investors' needs are already being satisfied by companies offering high payouts and from a company's viewpoint, one clientele is as good as another.

Information Content

Directors usually have superior information to that held by shareholders about a company's prospects. If they believe that the company is going to do well in the future, then one way they can tell investors about this good news is by increasing the dividend. Shareholders will see the higher dividend and reason that the directors have only increased it on the basis that it can be maintained in future years. As a consequence, the share price will rise. This is sometimes referred to as signalling.

Note that in these circumstances, it is not the increase in dividend that has in itself caused the share price to rise. Rather, it is the expectation that future earnings will rise. All the dividend increase has been is a vehicle for communicating this information to investors. If the information content in the dividends is false, then investors will realize this in future years and the market price of the share will fall back to its previous level.

If the dividend is cut, this will be seen as imparting negative news about the company's future prospects and cause the share price to fall. Once again, however, the fall is due to lower expected cash flows in the future, not due to the dividend cut itself.

Capital Raising

If a company pays out excessive dividends now, it may need to raise external equity finance later. The issuance of shares will incur flotation costs, which means that it would have been better not to pay the higher dividends initially. In addition, issuing new shares will mean that existing shareholders lose control.

Loan Agreements

Clauses in loan agreements may restrict payments of dividends via covenants.

Tax Rules

Tax rules prevent small private companies from not distributing earnings, merely to avoid tax payable on dividends received by the owners.

6 Deciding on Dividend Levels

Residual Approach

The residual approach to paying dividends states that a company first establishes its investment policy and then how this is going to be financed. Dividends are the residual figure after making investments.

The residual approach bases dividends on the following three factors:

- Investment opportunities
- Target capital structure
- Availability and cost of external capital

A fourth possible factor, being investor preferences for dividends or capital gains, is ignored.

EXAMPLE

Assume that a company has earnings available for dividends of £10,000. It maintains an ongoing debt-to-equity ratio of 50%. If it retains all of the £10,000, it would also raise £5,000 of debt to maintain the debt-to-equity ratio. This would give a maximum of £15,000 available for new investment, assuming no external equity was raised.

Assume that the company wished to invest only £9,000 in new investments. This would be financed by £6,000 of equity and £3,000 of debt, ie the ongoing debt-to-equity ratio. The company would therefore retain £6,000 of equity, pay out a dividend of £4,000 and raise new debt of £3,000.

If the company wished to invest £18,000 in new investments, it would finance this with £12,000 of equity and £6,000 of debt. Since the profit for the year is only £10,000, it would need to raise £2,000 of external equity and not pay a dividend.

The problem with applying the residual theory each year is that it will give rise to unstable dividends each year, as the level of investment opportunities varies. As a result, it should be used to determine a long-run target payout ratio, rather than the payout in any one year. Investment opportunities are forecast out through time, the target capital structure is established and an achievable target payout ratio is identified from this.

Large stable firms, eg utilities, have few investment opportunities. Therefore, they should make higher payouts. New firms in high growth industries will have more investment opportunities. Therefore, they should retain more of their earnings and have lower payout ratios.

Dividend Stability

Directors tend to believe that a stable dividend policy is in the interest of shareholders and, hence, will not follow the residual policy noted above, which could give highly unstable dividends.

As a result, they will aim to maintain a constant or gradually growing dividend through time, regardless of earnings fluctuations. They will forecast their expected earnings growth through time and link their dividend payments to this.

In order to achieve dividend stability, companies may pay low regular dividends which can easily be maintained. On top of this, they will then make extra dividend payments in good years. This would be designated as a special dividend, with no assurance that it will be repeated.

The two key components of dividend stability are as follows

- Is the growth rate in dividends dependable?
- How likely is it that the dividend will be cut so that dividends fall in the future?

Compromise Approach

Many firms adopt an approach that represents a compromise between the above two approaches. They have several objectives, ranked in approximate order of importance.

- Invest in projects with positive net present values.
- Do not cut dividends.
- Do not sell new equity.
- Maintain a target debt-to-equity ratio.
- Maintain a target dividend payout ratio.

It can be seen that the objectives will conflict. For example, if earnings fluctuate, a constant dividend payout ratio will result in a changing debt-to-equity ratio, since the level of dividends will change each year and will not be linked to total reinvestment levels including debt.

As a result, the dividend payout ratio will not be constant, with dividend growth lagging behind earnings growth.

7 METHODS OF PAYING DIVIDENDS

Cash Dividends

The Benefit of Cash Dividends

The benefit to the investor of a cash dividend is that he receives cash in hand. However, this will mean that any tax effects will crystallize. Furthermore, if the investor wishes to reinvest the cash in the same company, he will incur transaction costs on buying new shares.

Types of Cash Dividend

Companies usually pay a regular cash dividend. This implies that it is an ongoing dividend paid in the regular course of business, often on a semi-annual basis.

Special dividends are even more unusual and almost certainly will not be repeated.

Dividend Reinvestment Plans

This is where shareholders can automatically reinvest their dividends in the shares of the company, rather than receiving the cash. Most companies offer this facility, although the level of take-up by investors varies from company to company.

A high take-up rate for a reinvestment plan would suggest that the company should be adopting a lower payout policy.

Dividend reinvestment plans have even been extended to allow shareholders to buy further shares in the company with new cash investment, rather than just using cash from dividends.

Scrip Dividends

A scrip dividend is where the company gives investors the choice of receiving a cash dividend or new shares to the value of the cash dividend.

The impact on the company is that where the scrip dividend is taken, the company retains more cash and equity finance in the business than where the cash dividend is taken.

Where companies wish to encourage investors to take a scrip alternative, it may be made as an enhanced alternative. This is where the value of the shares exceeds the value of the cash dividend.

Where there is an enhanced scrip alternative, investors will almost certainly take the scrip alternative, or they will suffer a transfer of value to other shareholders.

The tax treatment for a scrip dividend is the same as for a cash dividend.

Share Repurchase

A share repurchase can be thought to be very similar to a cash dividend, in that cash passes from the company to its shareholders. In fact, ignoring transaction costs and taxes, the two approaches are identical.

One difference is that a dividend is paid to all investors whereas a share repurchase will only apply to investors who wish to sell their shares. This gives the share repurchase scheme more flexibility.

Earnings per Share Impact

Share repurchases will usually increase earnings per share. However, this in itself should not mean that they are worthwhile, since it is purely an accounting effect.

TASK

A company has cash balances of £1,000 earning interest at 5% (ignore tax). The total earnings are £500, being £50 of interest and £450 of earnings from business operations. The current share price is £10 and there are 250 shares in issue. What will be the impact of buying back 100 shares at a total cost of £1,000 on earnings per share and share price?

SOLUTION

Current earnings per share are $\frac{500}{250}$ = £2 per share.

After the buyback, earnings will fall to £450 and the number of shares in issue will fall to 150 shares.

Earnings per share after the buyback are $\frac{450}{150}$ = £3 per share.

However, the total market capitalisation of the company should fall by £1,000, reflecting the cash outflow to buy the shares. The previous market capitalisation was £2,500, meaning that the new market capitalization will fall to £1,500. With 150 shares in issue, the share price will remain at £10.

The risk to total earnings has increased, since the risk-free source of return (cash balances on deposit) has been removed. The increase in earnings is counterbalanced by an increase in risk, meaning that there is no net gain to shareholders. The P/E ratio has fallen from 5× to 3.3×.

Advantages of Repurchases

- Signal to the market that the management believes that the company is undervalued.
- Investors can choose whether or not to receive the cash by selling their shares, unlike a dividend.
- Can be used to remove an 'overhang', where there is a large block of shares available for sale in the market.
- Achieves the same end as a special dividend, since there is no implication that a repurchase will be repeated.

- Gives the company more flexibility in determining its total distribution policy rather than just relying on dividends.
- Can result in major changes in capital structure, either eliminating large amounts of surplus cash or increasing debt levels by borrowing money to finance a repurchase.

Disadvantages of Repurchases

- Dividends are seen as a more dependable form of distribution than repurchases, meaning that the share price might rise more if dividends are increased.
- Selling shareholders may not be fully aware of the implications of the repurchase.
- The shares are repurchased at an excessively high price.

EMPLOYEE SHARE OPTION SCHEME

chapter 16

Contents

1 Introduction

The purpose of this chapter is to look at the main forms of option and profit sharing schemes that are in existence and the restrictions imposed on the schemes (mainly by the tax authorities).

The benefits of having a scheme approved by HMRC is that certain tax advantages will accrue to the beneficiaries of the scheme. However, to obtain approval, certain constraining conditions must be adopted. The benefit of unapproved schemes is that they offer greater flexibility in terms of the number of share options granted to individual employees, the strike price of the options and the performance targets set for such options to be exercised.

2 Approved Company Share Option Plans (CSOP)

Participation in company share option schemes can be restricted to a limited number of employees ie the scheme is operated on a discretionary basis. The other schemes covered below, by contrast, have to be open to all types of employee within the company, providing they have served a minimum service period.

To qualify to grant an option under a CSOP scheme, a company must either be a listed company or, if unlisted, must be independent and not controlled by another company. The shares issued under that option must also fulfil certain conditions, including that they must:

- Form part of the ordinary share capital of the company and be fully paid up
- Not be subject to restrictions other than those attaching to all shares of the same class, or certain restrictions limited to the disposal of the shares following the end of the participant's employment with the company

The big advantage to the recipient of the options is that any growth in value is income-tax and national insurance contribution free up to a £30,000 threshold. Any options granted above this limit will be subject to income tax in the usual way.

Normal capital gains tax (CGT) rules will apply at the date of disposal of the shares if there has been an increase in the market value of the shares between the time the share option was exercised and when the shares were disposed of.

The advantage to the company is that the employees will theoretically be motivated to achieve improvements in the company's share price, since this will increase their own personal wealth.

Approved Schemes

The requirements for a scheme to be approved are broadly as follows:

- The scheme can only be open to full-time employees and directors. It does not, however, need to be open to all full-time employees. (Full-time broadly means working more than 25 hours a week for employees and 20 hours a week for directors.)
- Options cannot have an exercise price at a discount to the market price of the shares at the date that the option is granted.
- The options must be exercisable in the period from three to ten years after being granted to be exempt from income tax.
- An employee can only be granted options once every three years.
- The market value of the shares, which would be obtained under the options, must not exceed £30,000 at any one time.

Institutional Guidelines

The institutions have sought to encourage the use of share option schemes to motivate employees while placing a cap on the dilution that can occur to their own holdings. The following guidelines are in place:

- Such options should not be more than 5% of the share capital when issued.
- There should be real growth in earnings per share in the three-year period following the issue of the options for the options to be exercised.
- Options should not be issued with an exercise price at a discount to the market price of the shares at the date of issue.

3 Savings Related Share Option Schemes

When employees of a company save money in a Save As You Earn (SAYE) scheme, they are issued with options to subscribe for shares in the company at a future date. The savings will then be used to exercise the options which will be at a discount to the market price of the shares.

Tax Restrictions

If a scheme is approved, then any profits made by the employees from the options will not be liable to income tax.

The requirements for a scheme to be approved are as follows:

- It must be available to all employees and directors who have been with the company for at least five years and it must not be structured so as to discourage some individuals from joining.
- The amount invested on a monthly basis must be less than £500 per employee.
- The exercise price must not be less than 80% of the market price of the shares at the date of issue.
- The exercise date of the options must be at least three years after the start of the SAYE scheme for the employee.

Institutional Guidelines

- Shares issued under SAYE schemes must not represent more than 10% of the share capital at the date when the shares are issued on a ten-year rolling basis.
- The maximum monthly investment is £500.

4 Share Incentive Plans (SIPs)

Share Incentive Plans enable employers to give 'free shares' to their employees up to a maximum value of £3,600 per year. The value of share received is free from income tax and national insurance contributions. Eligibility for the scheme must be for all employees on similar terms.

Employees who keep their shares in the plan for five years pay no income tax, NICs or capital gains tax when their shares are taken out of the plan. If shares are taken out of the plan between three and five years, an employee pays income tax and NICs only on the market value of the shares when they were awarded or the then market value of the shares, whichever is lower. If the shares are withdrawn from the plan before three years has passed, income tax and NICs are charged on the market value of the shares at that time.

In addition employees may buy up to £1,800 of 'partnership shares' each year from their pre-tax salary. Employers may give up to two additional matching shares for each partnership share an employee buys. Therefore the maximum possible combined entitlement in any tax year under a SIP amounts to £9,000.

Dividends paid on SIP shares can be re-invested in further shares known as Dividend Shares. These shares are free of Income Tax and National Insurance at the date of purchase. No tax is payable on dividends that are then reinvested into further shares, subject to limits.

5 Enterprise Management Incentives (EMI)

This initiative allows small, higher risk companies to offer up to £3m worth of share options to help them recruit and retain the high calibre people that they need to make their company successful and grow.

Nature of the Scheme

Key features of the EMI option scheme are as follows:

- Share options can be issued to all employees.
- The shares over which options are granted can have a value of up to £250,000 per employee. This refers to the value at the time the options are granted. The total value of shares (for the whole company) over which options can be granted is £3m.
- The price at which options may be exercised may be more or less than market value at the time the options are granted.
- The only income tax charge is on exercise of the options and is equal to the difference between the shares' market value at the time of grant, less the exercise price. If the options are granted at the market value, no tax is payable.
- There are also significant CGT benefits for the employees. The shares acquired by the employees qualify for the business asset rate of taper relief. The period of ownership is deemed to start from when the share options are granted (the rules for other share option schemes are that the period starts when the shares are acquired).

Tax Restrictions

Only certain companies can operate the scheme:

- The company must be independent and not under the control of another company.
- It must be carrying on a qualifying trade and this trade must be carried on mainly in the UK.
- Its gross assets cannot exceed £30m at the time the options are granted.
- The company must have fewer than 250 employees.

Investor Relations

chapter 17

Contents

1 INTRODUCTION

'Investor relations' is the process of marketing the company's shares to its investor base. This can be distinguished from public relations – the process of ensuring that the company puts its marketing and other messages across in an effective way.

2 IDENTIFYING THE INVESTOR BASE

There are five main sources of investors:

- Pension funds
- Insurance companies and life funds
- Unit trusts
- Investment trusts
- Private investors

The equity markets in the UK are dominated by institutional investors falling into the first four categories above. Between them they own more than 75% of shares in issue.

Pension Funds

Pension funds are by far the largest of all investors in UK shares. The pensions industry in the UK has developed over a number of years and is far more significant than in any other country in Europe.

Pension funds are usually managed by external fund managers. These professional managers are retained by companies to manage their own pension schemes. The alternative is for a company to manage its own pension scheme, although this is relatively rare.

In-house fund managers only have responsibility for meeting the long-term pension liabilities of their own company's employees. This means that they have the luxury of being able to adopt a long-term approach to investment.

Although professional fund managers have a similar structure of liabilities to the in-house managers, they are constrained by the fact that they are largely rated on the basis of quarterly performance. If they do not achieve good returns each quarter it is likely that new investors will not be attracted to their fund and existing investors will switch to the competition.

This means that professional fund managers tend to adopt a fairly short-term approach to investment.

Life Funds and Insurance Companies

Life funds and insurance companies are essentially long-term savings schemes. They receive premiums from their customers and pay out on claims when policies mature.

The investment timescale of life funds is therefore relatively long term. There is no absolute requirement to make short-term gains and the fund managers can afford to take a long-term view.

This makes such companies ideal investors for companies which are experiencing short-term pressure on profits due to adverse market conditions or due to high capital investment. The insurance companies can afford to sit out the short term on the basis that there are good long-term prospects.

Unit Trusts

Unit trusts are collective investment schemes that raise money from investors by selling units. The investor buys the units, the trust invests the funds received and hopefully the units will rise in value as the trust's investments give capital gains and dividend income. The investor realises his or her investment by selling the units back to the trust, which will redeem them at the quoted price.

The benefit to the investor of investing in a unit trust is that it enables a small investment in a diversified portfolio, reducing risk. As such, unit trusts are very popular as a form of monthly savings.

Unit trusts are referred to as 'open-ended' because the value of funds that can be received from investors is theoretically unlimited, since the trust can always create new units for sale. Conversely, when investors wish to redeem their units, the assets of the trust are reduced in order to buy the units back. This can be a problem, especially in times of uncertain or pessimistic markets, when the unit trust will be forced to sell investments at low prices to meet its commitments to redeem units.

The unit trust consequently has a high exposure to short-term investor sentiment. In times when stock market investment is booming, it will attract many new investors. In times of recession, many investors will disinvest. Again, a poorly performing fund will lose investors to its more successful rivals. This means that unit trusts tend to adopt relatively short-term investment strategies in order to attract and keep investors.

Investment Trusts

Investment trusts are similar to unit trusts in that they invest in the shares of listed companies and increase the size of their net assets through making capital gains and receiving dividend income. As with unit trusts, the benefit of the investment trust to the small investor is that it provides a ready means of obtaining a diversified portfolio.

However, a key difference is that investment trusts are actually public limited companies. When they are originally set up, investors will subscribe for shares, much in the same way as they will buy units in a unit trust. However, investors do not realise their investment by selling it back to the company. Rather, they will have to sell the shares in the secondary market or hold onto the shares and receive dividend income.

It is this feature of investment trusts that means that they are called 'closed-ended'. Once the money has been invested, the company has no concern that investors may wish to disinvest. Whereas the unit trust will have to sell assets to fund redemptions of units, sales of the investment trust's shares in the secondary market will not impact on the company. This means that investment trusts can afford to take a longer term view of a company's prospects than a unit trust.

Whereas unit trusts are priced by reference to the value of the fund's net assets (as required by the FCA), the price of shares in investment trusts is determined by supply and demand factors. Historically, investment trusts tend to have traded at a discount to net asset value, but in recent years their rising popularity as an investment vehicle has meant that some have, at times, traded at a premium.

Open-Ended Investment Companies (OEICs)

In the UK, the usual forms of collective investment scheme or mutual fund are unit trusts and investment trusts. However, continental European investors are unused to either unit trusts or investment trusts. They are much more familiar with Open-Ended Investment Companies (OEICs), which are now also referred to as Investment Companies with Variable Capital (ICVCs). In effect, these are a cross between the two forms. Unlike unit trusts there is a full secondary market and not solely a link to the fund manager. Equally, unlike investment trusts, which are constrained by the Companies Act rules for companies, the manager is capable of issuing more shares and redeeming shares at any stage.

In order to accommodate the OEICs into the system, a special company structure has been introduced in order to allow a company continually to issue, and redeem, its own shares. The end result is an investment product that is more flexible and more appealing to the continental market.

Unlike both unit and investment trusts, OEICs are able to adopt an 'umbrella' structure, offering unprecedented switching speed and convenience between markets. Under an umbrella fund there may be sub-funds investing in, say, UK equities, Asian equities, US equities, corporate bonds, cash, etc. which the investor will easily be able to switch between. This will be much quicker and cheaper than, say, selling a UK equities unit trust and buying another trust investing in US equities. Fund managers no longer need to offer a range of different trusts, they are able to offer them all under one simple structure.

Private Investors

Private investors are a relatively small part of the investor base in the UK and for most companies represent a very small proportion of the share register in terms of shares held, if not in terms of number of investors. Privatised industries and other companies where a large offer for sale was marketed to the general public will possibly have up to 25% of shares in private hands, but for most companies the percentage will be substantially lower.

Most private investors are not active investors. It is often the case that they own a very small number of shares in very few companies, and do not trade at all.

A large contingent of passive private investors can be very useful to a company that is going through a period of low profits.

3 Selling to the Investors

Having identified its investor base, a company will need to market itself effectively to those investors. Methods of marketing and communication can be classified into two main categories:

- Formal methods, being those prescribed by the FCA, statute and other regulatory bodies
- Informal methods, being ad hoc or planned communications with specific investors, subject to rules on announcements and disclosure of price-sensitive information

It is often the case that formal methods, such as the requirement to announce interim results, will be complemented by an informal method of communication, such as an analysts' meeting.

Formal Methods of Communication

Announcements of Results

A listed company must announce its results twice yearly in the UK – interim results for the first six months of the year and the annual results for the year.

The preliminary statement of annual results:

(1) Must be published as soon as possible after it has been approved by the board;

(2) Must be agreed with the company's auditors prior to publication;

(3) The statement must show the figures in the form of a table, consistent with the presentation to be adopted in the annual accounts for that financial year; and

(4) The statement must include any significant additional information necessary for the purpose of assessing the results being announced.

(LR 9.7A)

Analysts consider these announcements to be amongst the most important forms of communication they receive from a company. The announcements will typically be combined with analysts' presentations and press briefings to ensure maximum favourable publicity for the company.

Annual Report

All companies are required by law to prepare an annual report to be sent to shareholders and the registrar of companies. A company must make public its annual financial report at the latest four months after the end of each financial year (*Disclosure Rules 4.1.3*). The annual report must remain publically available for at least five years (*Disclosure Rules 4.1.4*).

The annual report must contain

- The audited financial statements;
- A management report; and
- Responsibility statements.

In addition, the annual report will usually contain a detailed review of operations, photographs of the directors and other marketing information. Most of this is not required by statute or the FCA, but reflects the company's desire to present an attractive face to the public. Listed companies will also have a section on corporate governance, reflecting the requirements of the Combined Code on corporate governance.

Notwithstanding the lack of interest from analysts, the annual report is a useful tool for communicating with smaller private investors. Along with the six-monthly results sent to shareholders, it will typically be the listed company's main means of communication with this investor group. The use of the annual report as a marketing tool in this area has been enhanced by the ability to send out summarised annual reports to shareholders.

Interim Report

A company must make public a half-yearly financial report covering the first six months of the financial year. The half-yearly financial report must be made public as soon as possible, but no later than two months, after the end of the period to which the report relates. An issuer must ensure that the half-yearly financial report remains available to the public for at least five years (*DTR 4.2.2*).

Interim Management Statements

A company must make public a statement by its management during the first six-month period of the financial year and another statement by its management during the second six month period of the financial year (*DTR 4.3.2*). The interim management statement must provide:

(1) An explanation of material events and transactions that have taken place during the relevant period and their impact on the financial position of the group, and

(2) A general description of the financial position and performance of the group during the relevant period.

Regulatory Information Service Announcements

The continuing obligations for listed companies in the Listing Rules require that announcements are made to investors via a Primary Information Provider (PIP) in certain circumstances. Announcements are required to ensure that a false market does not develop in a company's shares and to appraise investors of any unusual events that may impact on the price of the company's shares.

The means by which such information is disseminated is strictly controlled to ensure that all investors have an equal opportunity to receive the information and act upon it.

Informal Methods of Communication

A company is free to meet its investors at any time to discuss the company and its prospects. Good communication should always be a two-way affair, with the company and analysts regularly discussing the company's prospects.

Constraints on Informal Communication

The major constraints on companies and analysts in such situations are the UKLA's rules on announcements and the law regarding insider dealing. If price-sensitive information is inadvertently disclosed on a selective basis, for example to an analyst or journalist, the company should take immediate steps to ensure that a full announcement is made so that all users of the market have access to the same information.

Methods of Informal Communication

The major methods of communicating with investors include the following:

- Analysts' presentations
- Press briefings
- Press interviews

Responsibility within the company for communication with analysts and the press should be clearly defined. Special care should be taken during meetings with analysts to minimise the risk of providing price-sensitive information not available to a wider audience. Companies should decline to answer analysts' questions where the answers would provide price-sensitive information. Precautionary procedures should be implemented, such as keeping records of all discussions that take place.

The UKLA encourages companies to open up analyst meetings to include a wider audience, eg the press and the public via the internet. This will help refute allegations that there is selective release of price-sensitive information during analyst briefings.

Correction of Analysts' Forecasts

In most circumstances, the company is not obliged to make an announcement correcting public forecasts by analysts. It can draw their attention to any public sources of information that may challenge the basis on which the forecasts have been prepared. However, if the error is of sufficient magnitude to cause serious misapprehension in the market, the company should consider making an announcement.

4 International Investor Relations

The Benefits of an International Shareholder Base

The advantages of having a wide investor base include the following:

- Access to different capital markets, enabling funds to be raised cheaply and efficiently
- Increased liquidity and marketability of shares, increasing the company's share price
- Evidence of a commitment to the local market place may improve relations with suppliers and customers
- A local stock market quote may improve local investors' perceptions generally, improving the rates at which a company can borrow locally, for example

- Increased publicity and awareness may result in improved business prospects
- Improved prospects for making overseas acquisitions in countries where the company has an investor presence

The Problems of an International Shareholder Base

- Increased costs of running an effective investor relations exercise.
- Cultural differences between different investor bases may make marketing of the company on a worldwide basis difficult.
- The existence of local regulations and the cost of complying with these. Since the UK has a fairly stringent regulatory background, the cost of this can be limited through reciprocal arrangements between regulators. Nevertheless, particularly in the US, it can be a major factor to consider.
- The risk of 'flowback' where overseas investors lose interest in a company and sell their shares back into the home market. This reduces prices and liquidity and goes against all the advantages of having overseas investors in the first place.
- The need to alter the company's accounting policies to fit in with the requirements of the relevant country eg by providing profit reconciliations and restate of results.

Managing International Investors

- The initial issue of shares in an overseas market will need to be prepared carefully in order to educate the overseas investors on the company, its products and its market places.
- Having successfully completed the initial distribution of shares, regular contact will need to be kept with important overseas investors. This will need to be done by important figures within the company to demonstrate its absolute commitment to the overseas market.
- It is important to understand the cultural bias of each overseas investor base. One obvious example of this is language. Each country's investor base will have different concerns. Whereas UK and US investors may be heavily focused on earnings performance, German and Japanese investors may prefer a more detailed story about the company's overall strategy and intentions for the future.
- Use of local advisers will be of great assistance in enabling the company to understand the needs of the investing community and the best ways in which to approach them. Local advisers will often be able to provide a fast track to the key investors and to working around local regulations and requirements.

5 The Stewardship Code

The Stewardship Code is a set of guidelines for institutional investors. The Code aims to enhance the quality of engagement between institutional investors and companies to help improve long-term returns to shareholders and the efficient exercise of governance responsibilities. The Code was issued by the Financial Reporting Council in 2010 and subsequently revised in 2012.

Principles of the Stewardship Code

- Principle 1: Institutional investors should **publicly disclose** their policy on how they will discharge their stewardship responsibilities.
- Principle 2: Institutional investors should have a robust policy on **managing conflicts of interest** in relation to stewardship and this policy should be publicly disclosed.
- Principle 3: Institutional investors should **monitor** their investee companies.
- Principle 4: Institutional investors should establish clear guidelines on when and how they will **escalate their activities** as a method of protecting and enhancing shareholder value.
- Principle 5: Institutional investors should be willing to **act collectively** with other investors where appropriate.
- Principle 6: Institutional investors should have a clear policy on **voting** and disclosure of voting activity.
- Principle 7: Institutional investors should **report periodically** on their stewardship and voting activities.

The FRC sees the UK Stewardship Code as complementary to the UK Corporate Governance Code for listed companies and, like that Code, it should be applied on a 'comply or explain' basis. Since 2010 all UK-authorised Asset Managers are required under the FCA's Conduct of Business Rules to produce a statement of commitment to the Stewardship Code or explain why it is not appropriate to their business model.

Advanced Corporate Performance Techniques

chapter 18

Contents

1 INTRODUCTION

In this chapter we look at a number of advanced corporate performance techniques:

- Economic value added
- Cash Flow Return on Equity
- Real Options Approach

The chapter provides a rigorous analysis of these theories, which entails, at times, some fairly complex numerical examples. You will not have to replicate this level of calculation in your exam but numerical examples have been included to deepen your understanding of these important techniques and to help you formulate an opinion on how useful, as corporate performance and evaluation techniques, they are likely to be in practice. You should be prepared to discuss relative merits and demerits and provide substantiated analysis on all techniques included in this chapter.

2 ECONOMIC VALUE ADDED

Introduction

Economic Value Added (EVA - *note that the abbreviation is a registered trademark*) is a measure of performance which is designed to identify the economic profit a company is earning. It was primarily designed to be a measure of management performance, genuinely assessing the value which management have brought to a company's shareholders by their actions. The benefit of using economic profit for this purpose is that, if carefully calculated, it will be less affected by accounting choices in the way that accounting profits are.

However, in recent times, EVA is commonly used as part of an assessment of a company's expected future returns. The methodology of EVA focuses on some basic ideas, as follows:

- Capital invested
- Cost of capital
- Economic profitability, after allowing for the cost of capital

The idea is that management have to generate a positive return to investors after charging an interest charge against profits, based on the cost of capital multiplied by the capital invested in the business.

EVA = Net Operating Profit After Tax – (Capital Invested × Cost of Capital)

With an EVA calculation, management are charged for the capital they are using in the business when their performance is assessed. This should encourage management to use capital efficiently, raising capital where they believe they can earn high returns compared to the cost of capital and repaying capital if the rate of return on investment is too low.

3 CAPITAL INVESTED

The Objective of Calculating Capital Invested

Capital invested is designed to measure the economic book value of all cash invested in the company's business activities. It is based on the accounting balance sheet adjusted for certain items which do not reflect economic reality.

Definition of Capital Invested

Capital invested can be calculated in two ways, from an operating or from a financing perspective. From an operating perspective it may be defined as follows:

CAPITAL	
Current assets	x
less: Non-interest bearing current liabilities (NIBCLS)	(x)
Net Working Capital	x
add: Net property, plant and equipment*	x
add: Other assets, including net goodwill	x
Total assets less non-interest bearing current liabilities	x
Adjustments for Equity Equivalents	
add: Deferred tax reserves/provision	x
add: LIFO reserve	x
add: Previously amortised goodwill	x
add: Unrecorded goodwill	x
add: Cumulative R&D or other expenditure	x
add: Successful effort to full cost accounting adjustments	x
add: Other equity equivalents	x
	x
less: Marketable securities	(x)
Capital	x

** Including the present value of non-capitalised lease payments*

Note that the above adjustments are simply the main ones advocated by Stern, Stewart & Co. They have identified well in excess of 200 adjustments that should be made to arrive at a true invested capital figure.

The first section of the calculation up to total assets less non-interest bearing current liabilities represents a broadly conventional accounting view of capital employed. Non current assets are taken net of depreciation since depreciation represents a valid economic charge for use of a deteriorating asset. Non-interest bearing current liabilities (or NIBCLS as Stern, Stewart & Co. refer to them) provide a natural source of financing within capital (hence mitigating the need to raise permanent finance) and are thus deducted from capital. It should be noted, however, that non-capitalised leases of a long term nature should be capitalised since from an economic viewpoint these are a long-term asset (and debt) equivalent.

In order to achieve an economic capital invested figure on a cash basis certain adjustments need to be made to the accounting information - referred to as 'Equity Equivalents'. These adjustments to the balance sheet information also impact on the appropriate measure of returns on capital and will be discussed later.

The alternative way of calculating capital invested is to add together all the sources of finance on the balance sheet and make the same adjustments for equity equivalents.

In this case, the calculation of capital invested is as follows.

CAPITAL	
Book value of common equity	x
add: Non-equity/Preferred stock	x
add: Minority interest	x
add: Interest bearing liabilities*	x
	x
Adjustments for Equity Equivalents and marketable securities (as above)	x
Capital invested	x

** Including capital/finance leases and the present value of non-capitalised lease payments*

4 Net Operating Profit After Tax (NOPAT)

NOPAT is a measure of economic, not accounting return. The main distinctions between economic and accounting returns are as follows.

- Economic return allows for implicit as well as explicit costs, whereas accounting return only allows for explicit costs. Indeed, when moving from economic return to economic profit a charge will be made for implicit cost of using the capital.
- Economic profit recognises reserves and costs on a cash basis, as opposed to an accruals basis.

Definition of NOPAT

NOPAT is defined as follows:

NOPAT	
Earnings available to equity shareholders	x
add: Interest on debt (including all leases)	x
less: Tax adjustment in respect of interest	(x)
add: Non-equity/Preference dividends	x
add: Minority interest in profit	x
	x
add: Increase in equity equivalents	x
less: Income from marketable securities	(x)
NOPAT	x

It can be seen that we commence with accounting earnings available to equity or ordinary shareholders on an accruals basis. Two groups of adjustments need to be made as follows:

- Adjust the earnings to those available to all providers of finance
- Adjust the accruals basis earnings to a cash based economic return

It should be noted that NOPAT is after charging depreciation. As noted above, depreciation (or amortisation) is considered an economic cost, charging for usage of a deteriorating asset over the period.

Interest on Debt

Interest on debt must be added back to generate a return measure available to equity and debt-holders consistent with the definition of capital. Moreover, only by looking at an overall return can the worst gearing distortions be removed to create a measure which is comparable from company to company.

It should be noted that the interest figure includes interest on operating leases. Any operating lease rental expense is treated as being partly depreciation and partly interest cost. The implied interest cost is added back to earnings to avoid making any finance charges against NOPAT. The implicit interest cost is estimated by calculating the present value of future operating lease payments using the cost of debt. (Stern, Stewart & Co. recommend using the cost of secured indebtedness). The interest charge is then the cost of debt multiplied by the present value of future lease payments.

Tax Adjustment in Respect of Interest

Payment of interest reduces taxable profits and hence reduces the company tax bill. Unless this reduction in the company's tax bill is reversed a distortion will occur in looking at the earnings of geared and ungeared companies. The benefits of gearing in reducing tax liabilities are more properly reflected in the cost of capital as discussed later.

It should be noted that the tax adjustment should be computed in respect of all interest including imputed interest on the non-capitalised leases. The tax adjustment is therefore

Interest on Debt (as above) × Marginal Total Tax Rate of Company

Non-Equity Dividends/Minority Interests

Earnings must be grossed up for deductions of non-equity/preference dividends and minority interest in profits for consistency with a total capital invested figure including minority and non-equity capital.

Income from Marketable Securities

Since capital is defined as being net of marketable securities then any income generated from marketable securities must also be deducted from the earnings figure for consistency.

Equity Equivalent Adjustments

These adjustments are required both to generate an economic capital figure and an appropriate cash based NOPAT figure. The logic of each of these shall be examined in turn.

Deferred Tax Provision

Deferred tax provision arise from accounting for tax on an accruals basis. However, it does not represent actual capital expended and should therefore be added back to capital invested and the movement on the provision should be removed from the tax charge. This should leave the tax charge within NOPAT as net only of cash taxes paid, not accounting provisions.

LIFO Reserve

In an inflationary environment a company holding inventory will achieve economic holding gains as the price of inventory in hand increases. This gain should be booked to the return for the year and the capital should reflect the economic value of inventory at year end prices.

Where a company uses a FIFO method to generate inventory values no adjustment would normally be needed to the accounting earnings or capital invested (as inventory would be shown at what is broadly their economic value). However, where a company uses a LIFO method to generate inventory values, capital invested needs to be adjusted to uplift inventory to their economic value, and earnings need to be uplifted to reflect the economic holding gain.

In US accounts this adjustment is easily ascertained as companies using a LIFO method to generate inventory values must disclose a 'LIFO reserve' - being the difference between inventory values using LIFO and FIFO methods.

Amortised Goodwill

Whilst Stern, Stewart & Co. believe depreciation and amortisation charges are an appropriate economic cost for deteriorating assets, goodwill is not viewed as a deteriorating asset. Nor, indeed, is amortisation of goodwill a cash cost to be charged against economic return.

In order to restate capital to the cash invested by the providers of finance, any goodwill previously amortised needs to be added back to capital invested. In order to restate the return onto a cash basis, any goodwill amortisation for the period also needs to be added back.

In circumstances where goodwill might be deteriorating over time it would be appropriate to estimate an **economic** amortisation charge which relates to the rate of deterioration. This would only rarely equate the actual charge in the accounts which is governed by accounting conventions.

Unrecorded Goodwill

Where what is essentially an acquisition is accounted for under pooling of interest or merger accounting methods, substantial goodwill will be unrecorded. For consistency with acquisition accounting methodologies one can imagine that the shares issued as consideration are issued for cash at market value and the acquisition consideration is cash rather than shares. This approach will generate a goodwill figure to be added into capital invested.

Research and Development and Other Intangibles

From an economic viewpoint all R&D spending represents investment in a capital asset, not an expense to be charged against economic return (we do not need to be concerned with issues of prudence). It is appropriate, however, to amortise the R&D asset over the useful life of successful projects developed (Stern, Stewart & Co. believe five years represents a reasonable proxy).

The unamortised value of R&D should, therefore, be added into capital invested and the economic return should have the R&D expense added back and an R&D amortisation charge shown in its place (these should be substantially the same once a company reaches a steady state).

Stern, Stewart & Co. go on to say that this treatment should also be applied to any new product development or up front marketing costs (such as the millions of dollars spent by Gillette on marketing its sensor razor). Moreover, they even advocate adding in a time value adjustment just as one might include the cost of interest on loans used to fund the building of plant in the cost of plant.

Successful Effort to Full Cost Accounting

Where companies write off unsuccessful effort costs (such as the costs of unsuccessful explorative oil drilling or product development) they fail to properly reflect in capital the true cash investment made. Such write-offs should, therefore, be reversed out of returns and added back into capital – full cost accounting.

Furthermore, where firms recognise unusual losses or gains in their accounts then the return measure is distorted - investors capitalise expected future returns from ongoing business. It is, therefore, also necessary to reverse out unusual gains and losses from NOPAT but also to reverse out cumulative unusual gain/loss adjustments from capital (after tax).

Other Equity Equivalents

Precautionary reserves (such as bad debt, warranties, inventory obsolescence, deferred income etc.) obscure the actual timing of cash movements. Any changes in such reserves should, therefore, be reversed out of returns to arrive at a cash based NOPAT figure. It will also be necessary to add back such reserves to properly measure economic capital invested

Illustration

	£
Warranty reserve at the start of the year	100,000
Increase in reserve for year (charged against profits)	22,000
Cash expended in meeting warranty claims	(12,000)
Warranty reserve at the end of the year	110,000

Capital must be increased by £110,000 to arrive at economic capital invested.

Returns for the year must be increased by £10,000 (the overall increase in the warranty reserve from start to end of the year). It should be noted that NOPAT is still net of a £12,000 warranty expense charge (having reserved out only £10,000 of the overall charge against profits of £22,000) properly reflecting actual cash expended to meet warranty claims.

SUMMARY OF EQUITY EQUIVALENT ADJUSTMENTS

Increase in CAPITAL for Equity Equivalents:	Increase/(Decrease) in NOPAT for Increase/(Decrease) in Equity Equivalents:
Deferred Tax Provision	Increase/(Decrease) in deferred tax provision
LIFO Reserve	Increase/(Decrease) in LIFO Reserve
Cumulative Goodwill Amortisation	Goodwill amortisation charge for year
Unrecorded goodwill	N/A
Capitalised intangibles net of amortisation	Increase/decrease in net capitalised intangibles
Full cost reserve	Increase in full cost reserve
Cumulative unusual (gains)/losses after tax	Unusual (gain)/loss for year after tax
Other precautionary reserves	Increase/(decrease) in precautionary reserves

5 Cost of Capital

Weighted Average Cost of Capital

The cost of capital is the weighted average cost of capital of the firm. It is defined as follows:

$$\textbf{WACC} = \textbf{ke} \times \frac{\textbf{E}}{\textbf{V}} + \textbf{kd} \times \frac{\textbf{D}}{\textbf{V}}$$

Where

k_e is the cost of equity, ie the equity shareholders' required return.

k_d is the post-tax cost of debt, ie the debtholders' required return after the effects of tax relief.

E is the market value of the firm's equity.

D is the book value or market value of the firm's debt.

V is the total market value of the firm (V= E + D).

It should be noted that all the tax benefits of gearing are accounted for in a lower cost of capital (via a lower cost of debt). This is consistent with **not** reflecting tax advantages in the NOPAT.

Obtaining Appropriate Estimates

Stern, Stewart & Co. suggest the debt to equity ratio could be taken from the average ratio (in market value terms) over the three preceding years.

The cost of debt is based on the pre tax cost of debt less the marginal tax rate. The pre tax cost of debt is based on the yield of long term bonds issued by companies of similar credit quality to the company in question. It is essentially the rate at which the company can raise new debt finance.

Stern, Stewart & Co. recommend using the Capital Asset Pricing Model to derive the cost of equity. It is thus based on the long term yield on government bonds plus a risk premium. The risk premium is based on the stock's beta multiplied by the market risk premium.

Problems in Identifying the WACC

Identification of a company's WACC is always going to be difficult. This means that EVA and economic profit approaches are sensitive to the WACC used. Problems in identifying the WACC are as follows.

- Identifying a risk free rate for use in CAPM – this should theoretically be the return on a zero beta portfolio with a duration the same as that of the investor. This is difficult to identify so a more usual approach is the government bond yield, as noted above. A ten year bond yield is probably most appropriate since it matches the duration of the market portfolio. A Treasury bill yield would not satisfy this criteria.
- Identifying the market risk premium – historical estimates of market risk premia can be calculated but we need to use the expected risk premium.
- Identifying the appropriate debt to equity ratio – should it be based on book values or market values. The usual answer is to base it on market values, since this reflects the true marginal cost of funds today.

6 Calculating Economic Value Added

Economic Value Added (EVA) can be defined as follows.

ECONOMIC VALUE ADDED	
NOPAT	x
Less: cost of capital in monetary terms (capital invested × WACC)	(x)
Economic Value Added	x

Economic value added may therefore be thought of as the economic returns generated in excess of the economic return required to satisfy the providers of economic capital.

Stern, Stewart & Co. also provide a rearranged method of calculating of EVA as follows:

EVA = (Return on Capital* - WACC) × Capital Invested

** Return on capital is calculated as NOPAT ÷ Capital Invested*

7 Improving EVA

There are a number of means by which a company may seek to improve its EVA:

- Raise capital to invest in new areas where the economic return exceeds the cost of additional finance raised

- Terminating investment in areas where the economic return is below the cost of the finance provided. In such circumstances the capital should be released and possibly returned to the providers of finance.
- Reducing the cost of capital

The first strategy may be appropriate where a firm is a growth industry or enjoys some form of competitive advantage. The latter strategies are likely to be appropriate for mature companies whose competitive advantage has been eroded. In particular, Stern, Stewart & Co. firmly believe in the theories of Modigliani and Miller. As such, they recommend the use of aggressive debt finance to not only lower the cost of capital (due to the tax savings interest payments will yield – although it should be noted that this is reflected in a lower WACC in the EVA model) but also to focus the company on generating cash and economic returns in order to service that debt.

8 Application of EVA

Stern, Stewart & Co. developed the EVA model as a management tool. Its aim is to harmonise the focus of company management with the focus of the company's shareholders.

If management can use EVA as a tool for decision-making, and in particular as a tool for assessing managerial performance, then they will also be focusing on maximising wealth for their shareholders and maximising the company's share price.

Stern, Stewart & Co. have done extensive consultancy work worldwide in helping such companies as Coca Cola develop EVA management systems. In particular, where management remuneration can be tied to their ability to create EVA, then management can be turned into 'owners' of the business, and their rewards will be coincident with their creation of wealth for shareholders.

One potential problem with the use of EVA in this context, however, is that if management rewards systems are too short term, managers may be tempted to enhance short term EVA at the expense of longer term benefit. For example, managers may avoid highly beneficial investments where returns are not generated for some time following the investment of capital since this would temporarily reduce EVA. Conversely, they may be tempted to invest in areas which, whilst not beneficial in the long term, provide high returns quickly. Care must, therefore, be taken to ensure management are assessed in their ability to enhance long term EVA.

9 EVA Return on Capital

EVA return on capital is defined as follows:

$$\textbf{EVA return on capital} = \frac{\textbf{EVA}}{\textbf{Capital}}$$

It represents the amount by which the actual return on capital for the year in question exceeds the required return on capital, being the WACC.

The benefits of looking at EVA return on capital instead of purely focusing on EVA as an absolute figure are as follows:

- The EVA return on capital can be tracked through time, identifying how the company is doing compared to the past.
- The EVA return on capital allows for comparisons across companies with different amounts of capital invested, identifying which company is earning greater excess returns, ie which company has the largest economic profit per unit of capital invested.

An important point to note in relation to the second benefit is that the best company is not necessarily the one which maximises the EVA return on capital. A company may maximise EVA return on capital by only investing in highly restricted projects with very high rates of return. However, it could be ignoring investments which have a rate of return in excess of the cost of capital but by less than the current EVA return on capital of the firm. These investments are good because they have positive net present values, but the firm rejects them because they will reduce the EVA return on capital.

10 MARKET VALUE ADDED

Definition of Market Value Added

Market Value Added (MVA) is defined as the difference between the market capitalisation of the firm's equity plus debt less the capital invested.

MARKET VALUE ADDED	
Total market capitalisation of equity plus debt	x
less: Capital	(x)
Market Value Added	x

This measures the amount by which the management have increased the value of the capital invested in the firm. It is done by investing in projects with positive net present values, ie where the required return exceeds the WACC.

The Market Value Added is the present value of all the expected future EVA from the firm's operations, as the example in the next section demonstrates.

The performance of the management can be measured by looking at the change in the MVA year on year. If new capital of £1 million is added to the firm in the year but the total market value of debt plus equity increases by £1.5 million, the management have increased MVA by £0.5 million and hence have increased the wealth of shareholders.

MVA can be linked to the price to book ratio, the Tobin Q ratio and the CFROI Value/Cost ratio in the way it compares the market value of the firm with the value of its assets. As with these ratios, the reason why the MVA is positive is because the management has invested capital received from investors in projects which have positive net present values, where the expected rate of return exceeds the required rate of return.

One feature of MVA is that it can only be calculated on a firmwide basis, since it is based on the market value of the firm. It cannot be performed on a divisional basis, unlike the other measures highlighted.

11 RECONCILING EVA WITH MVA AND LINKING THEM TO NPV ANALYSIS

EVA and MVA are simply net present value analysis expressed with a slightly different methodology. This can be seen from a simplified example.

EXAMPLE

A company has capital invested of £1,000. It is capable of generating net operating profits after tax (NOPAT) of £110 per year to infinity, without changing the level of capital in the business. Its weighted average cost of capital is 10%.

- Value the firm using NPV analysis
- Identify the Market Value Added of the firm
- Link the Market Value Added with the expected future EVAs

SOLUTION

Value of the firm

The value of the firm using NPV analysis is the present value of the future free cash flows. Since the company is not changing its level of capital invested, the free cash flow will be equal to the NOPAT.

$$\textbf{Value} = \frac{\textbf{Free cash flow}}{\textbf{WACC}} = \frac{\textbf{110}}{\textbf{0.1}} = \textbf{£1,100}$$

Market Value Added

Market Value Added is the difference between the value of the firm and its capital invested, as follows:

Market Value Added = 1,100 – 1,000 = £100

Linking MVA to future EVAs

The MVA is the present value of all the future EVAs, discounted at the WACC.

Each year's EVA is calculated as follows:

	£
NOPAT	110
less: Capital charge (10% × 1,000)	(100)
EVA	10

The present value of these is as follows:

$$\textbf{Present value} = \frac{\textbf{EVA}}{\textbf{WACC}} = \frac{\textbf{10}}{\textbf{0.1}} = \textbf{£100}$$

Note that, since MVA is determined in part by interest rates, it will change year on year partly as a result of changing interest rates, not just due to changes in the ability of the firm to deliver profits relative to its capital invested.

12 PROBLEMS WITH LINKING MVA AND EVA

The basic link between MVA and EVA noted above is that MVA is the present value of all the future EVAs discounted at the WACC. This was demonstrated by a simple example assuming a perpetuity.

$$\textbf{MVA} = \frac{\textbf{EVA}}{\textbf{WACC}}$$

This link is certainly correct in theoretical terms. However, the problem is that it is difficult to identify future EVAs in the real world.

The assumption of a perpetuity based on this year's EVA would not be reasonable in reality, since a firm will be unable to generate a positive economic profit indefinitely as its competitive advantage declines.

In addition, in practice EVA is a single period measure, looking at economic profit generated in one year, using accounting data and an estimated WACC. (Note that Stern, Stewart & Co. do not advocate its use as a single period measure as will be discussed below). In contrast, MVA is a forward looking measure based on actual market values and the current capital invested. MVA is therefore in reality a more forward looking measure than EVA.

13 Using EVA and MVA as Analysis Tools

Dangers in Interpreting EVA

Great care must be taken when using EVA as a method of identifying companies that are creating value. In particular:

- A company which generates a positive EVA may be destroying value
- A company whose return on capital exceeds its WACC may be destroying value

The above points are most easily demonstrated by way of an illustration. Let us consider an all equity company with the following features.

- Economic capital invested = £100m
- Market value of shares = £200m
- Required return of shareholders (WACC) = 10%
- Economic return generated = £15m

The following figures can be derived for the above company.

Return on capital = $\frac{£15m}{£100m}$	=	15%
WACC	=	10%
Spread		+ 5%
EVA = Spread × capital invested = 5% × £100m	=	£5m

What should be noted, however, is that the WACC is calculated based on the market value of the company. If a shareholder were to buy all the shares they would pay £200 million. **In order to achieve the required return of 10% the company would have to generate a return of 10% × £200m = £20m.**

What may be seen for the above company is that the actual economic return generated is actually **£5m short** of the amount required to satisfy its providers of capital. Despite a positive EVA and a return on capital which exceeds the WACC the company is actually **destroying value.**

The seemingly counter-intuitive results of the above illustration are easily explained. The market value of shares may reflect the expectation of investors that the company could generate returns of £20m in perpetuity. This would lead to a valuation as follows.

$$\textbf{Market Value} = £20m \times \frac{1}{0.1} = £200m$$

The market value can be sub-analysed into capital invested of £100m and MVA of £100m. As noted earlier, MVA is the present value of all future EVAs discounted at the WACC of 10%. Since the company only has £100m of capital invested, £10m (10% × £100m) constitutes a break-even return on invested capital and the remaining £10m of the anticipated return constitutes anticipated future EVAs in perpetuity. Therefore,

$$\textbf{MVA} = \frac{EVA}{WACC} = \frac{£10}{0.1} = £100m$$

When the company only achieves a return of £15m, whilst this will yield a positive EVA, the EVA is short of market expectation. Assuming that expectations of future EVAs are revised down to £5m per annum, the market value of the shares will fall from £200m to £150m and the MVA will fall from £100m to £50m.

Revised Market Value $= £15m \times \frac{1}{0.1} = £150m$

Revised MVA $= \frac{£5m}{0.1} = £50m$

Whilst the above illustration shows simplistic analysis of positive EVAs and spreads can be very misleading, it should be noted that it does **not generate any problems** in using EVA for its **intended purpose** – to facilitate management decisions consistent with creating value for shareholders. At the point of initial investment in a particular project the prospective capital to be invested and its market value are entirely equivalent. If a project can provide returns which exceed the cost of capital then any prospective investment will indeed create value for shareholders.

14 Using EVA and MVA to Identify Winners

Whilst some investment houses have applied some of the basic ideas of EVA in their analysis work, there is a propensity to use it in an excessively simplistic manner which is susceptible to the misinterpretation noted above.

In order to identify a company which will perform well in the future, analysis work must focus on identifying companies whose MVA fails to reflect the true level of future EVAs. The following steps must therefore be taken:

- Forecast the length of the competitive advantage period over which the company can feasibly generate positive EVAs (or will continue to generate negative EVAs)
- Prepare detailed forecasts of economic returns, capital invested and WACCs for the competitive advantage period
- Calculate all prospective EVAs and discount at the WACCs to generate an MVA for comparison with the actual MVA observed

Where the above analysis process generates MVAs which exceed the MVA observed in the current market values, then the company should increase in value as (or rather if) the market recognises that the MVA is understated.

Whilst the above approach clearly shares much in common with discounting free cash flow to generate enterprise values, Stern, Stewart & Co. believe it has one **key advantage** – you do not have to forecast beyond the competitive advantage period. By removing the need to calculate a terminal value (which will normally form a crucial element of the enterprise value) the extreme sensitivity of conclusions to terminal value assumptions is also removed.

15 Cash Flow Return on Investment (CFROI)

CFROI stands for Cash Flow Return on Investment and is a measure developed initially by Holt Value Associates (now Credit Suisse Holt). CFROI is essentially an internal rate of return (IRR) of projected cash flows from existing investment in assets. One key difference, however, between CFROI and a conventional IRR measure is that CFROI is expressed in constant dollars or money. This means that CFROI avoids distortions in the return measure caused by inflation through time.

Having calculated CFROI, it is then necessary to compare the return to a benchmark cost of capital. This cost of capital must also be expressed in constant dollar or money terms and must reflect the risk inherent in the forecast cash flow. Holt believe conventional cost of capital methodologies based on the Capital Asset Pricing Model (CAPM) are counter-intuitive and flawed, and have, therefore, developed their own methodology.

Calculating CFROI

There are six stages in using CFROI, as follows:

- Estimate the life of the assets in the company
- Estimate the gross cash flow
- Calculate the total of non-depreciating assets
- Calculate gross cash investment
- Calculate the IRR of the flows, which is the CFROI
- Compare the CFROI with the cost of capital/WACC

The CFROI measure attempts to quantify the return the company is able to generate on the gross investment it has made in its assets. It is, therefore, a performance measure based on historic investment decisions. In order to do this, however, an analysis horizon needs to be established. This is taken to be the life of the company's existing assets.

Estimating the Life of the Assets

Estimating the life of a company's depreciable non-current assets is obviously difficult from the accounting information. However, few companies disagree with an approximation based on the cost of depreciable plant non-current assets in the balance sheet and the associated depreciation charge in the profit and loss account.

Which particular non-current assets are examined in establishing an analysis horizon would obviously depend on the type of company being examined. For manufacturing companies, for example, gross plant, property and equipment would be examined.

Illustration

Details of a company's gross plant non-current assets and associated depreciation charges over the last three years are as follows:

	2010	**2011**	**2012**
	£	**£**	**£**
Gross plant, property equipment	20,000	21,000	22,000
less: Land and other non-depreciables	(1,000)	(1,000)	(1,400)
	19,000	20,000	20,600
Depreciation charge	4,000	4,200	4,300
Estimated life (= depreciable assets ÷ expense)	4.75 years	4.76 years	4.79 years

Holt generally uses the median of the estimated asset life over the last three years (as this is less likely to be distorted by unusual observations than a simple average). This results in an estimated asset life of 4.76 years. This has been rounded up to five years for simplicity in the following calculations.

A slightly more complex method is also used by Holt, whereby lives are ascertained from disclosed depreciation policies for various asset types. These lives are then weighted by the gross value of the component assets to arrive at a weighted average life. It may be difficult, however, to split disclosed asset depreciation categories into similar gross values.

Holt maintains a database of industry averages for asset lives. Where the results of the above calculations are outside the normal industry range, the life will be taken as the upper or lower end of the industry range as appropriate. For example, a chemicals company has a calculated average asset life of 12 years. Since this falls outside of the bulk chemicals industry range of 14–18 years, the company's asset life is taken to be 14 years for the analysis.

Note that an actual asset life calculation is likely to be much longer than five years in practice. For the sake of keeping the illustration simple, a short asset life has been established.

Estimate of Gross Cash Flow

Having established an analysis horizon, it is then necessary to forecast expected cash flow returns. The estimate of gross cash flow would be estimated from the most recent year's accounting information as follows. (Note that the numbers are once again arbitrary).

Gross Cash Flow for 2012	£
Net income	1,300
Add: Depreciation and amortisation	5,300
Add: Interest expense	800
Add: Operating lease rental expense	200
Add: Minority interest	300
Add/less: After tax impact of special/exceptional items	175
Add/less: Monetary holding gains/(losses)	(30)
less: Inventory adjustment	(25)
Gross cash flow (current £ terms)	8,020

Depreciation and Amortisation

Depreciation and amortisation are added back to net income since they do not represent cash outflows. Note that this will be all depreciation and amortisation in the accounts, not simply that associated with plant, property and equipment. It will normally, therefore, exceed the depreciation charge used in establishing the life of assets.

Interest Expense

Interest expense is added back as this is a financing, not operating, flow. Whether the company generates sufficient cash to cover its financing costs is considered in the final stage of the analysis when comparing CFROI to a cost of capital.

Note that no adjustment is made to the tax charge in respect of tax savings generated from interest payments. This represents a different approach to that used by Stern, Stewart & Co. in arriving at economic return for EVA analysis. The reason why the Holt approach leaves the tax benefit of interest payments in gross cash flow whilst the benefit of tax savings on interest is reversed for EVA analysis is found in the different approaches to calculating a cost of capital; namely

- Holt calculates a cost of capital which is based upon required returns of investors which is **not** reduced for tax savings enjoyed by the company on interest payments. They, therefore, match higher returns with a higher cost of capital.
- Stern Stewart & Co. use a benchmark cost of capital based on the cost to the company of servicing its investors which **is** reduced for the tax benefit of interest payments. They, therefore match lower returns with a lower cost of capital.

It should, therefore, be noted that if a conventional cost of capital (derived by applying the theories of Modigliani and Miller) is to be used as the benchmark for comparison to the CFROI, then it will be necessary to also reduce gross cash flow by removing the tax benefit that interest payments will yield.

Operating Lease Rentals

The decision to lease an asset rather than purchase it with debt funding essentially represents a financing decision. By contrast to the approach used in EVA analysis, the whole of the lease rentals are added back to arrive at gross cash flow in CFROI analysis. This is because in EVA analysis the rentals are viewed as part interest and part depreciation, and economic profit is net of depreciation but gross of interest payments. CFROI gross cash flow is gross of both interest **and** depreciation, and hence both elements of the operating rental expense must be added back to arrive at a cash-based operating return.

Minority Interest

If the starting point for gross cash flow is profit after minority interest then it will be necessary to add back any minority interest deduction. This must be done since the investment in assets derived from the balance sheet will include assets belonging to the minority (as shown later). For consistency, therefore, both returns and investment will be calculated gross of minority interests.

Note that following the logic of the above adjustment, it will be necessary to include within the capital invested figure any investment in associated undertakings, since the return figure will include income from associated undertakings.

Exceptional/Special Items

To avoid distortions in gross cash flow any unusual items which are unlikely to recur over the analysis period should be reversed. Note that this will also require an adjustment for the tax associated with any such distorting items.

Monetary Holding Gains/Losses

Since CFROI analysis is designed to avoid distortions due to inflation through time, the gross cash flow figure needs to be adjusted to reflect monetary holding gains on liabilities and losses on assets being held. It will only be possible to make an accurate comparison of companies if the disadvantages of holding monetary assets in an inflationary environment are reflected in the return measure.

Holt recommends multiplying the net monetary assets excluding debt finance by the GDP deflator change for the year for US companies. This adjustment should, however, be capped to a maximum of 10% of gross cash flow as a reasonable maximum. Where the monetary holding gain or loss exceeds the 10% cap, the company will need to be investigated carefully. Large adjustments may indicate the presence of a financial subsidiary which must be dealt with under a separate framework.

Inventory Adjustment

Where a company uses a LIFO method to ascertain the cost of inventory, then the cost of closing inventory may be based on out of date prices but the cost of goods sold (which impacts on the profit figure used as the basis for gross cash flow) will be at broadly current prices. No adjustment is therefore needed to arrive at gross cash flow based on current dollars or pounds (Note, however, an adjustment will need to be made to closing inventory to ascertain a current dollar value).

Where a company uses a FIFO method to ascertain the cost of inventory, then the cost of closing inventory will be at broadly current prices but the cost of goods sold will be based on out of date prices. An adjustment will, therefore, need to be made to the gross cash flow measure to reflect an uplift of this cost to 2012 constant pound terms.

Holt recommends multiplying the estimated FIFO value of inventory by the change in the PPI (UK; RPI) for the relevant year. Once again, they also recommend a cap of 10% of gross cash flow.

Calculation of Non-Depreciating Assets

In order to generate returns companies must invest cash in non-depreciating assets, such as working capital and land as well as depreciating assets such as plant, property and equipment. One key distinction, however, is that whilst depreciating assets will have been exhausted by the end of the analysis horizon, non-depreciating assets will be available to liquidate back into cash.

Once again, to avoid distortions due to inflation, adjustments will need to be made to ensure the value of non-depreciating assets is expressed in constant 2012 pounds or monetary units. The calculation of non-depreciating assets is as follows.

Non-Depreciating Assets	£
Monetary short-term assets	1,800
less: Non-debt short-term liabilities	(1,100)
Net monetary assets excluding debt	700
Inventory	600
Current £ mark up on inventory	–
Land	600
Current £ mark up on land	300
Investments	20
Non-depreciating assets, current £	2,220

Adjustments to 2012 Pounds

As noted earlier, where a company uses a LIFO method to ascertain the cost of inventory, no adjustment needs to be made to gross cash flow. However, since inventory costs will be out of date they will require adjusting to constant 2012 pound terms.

The cost of land, too, is likely to be based on out of date costs. It will also be necessary to adjust land costs to 2012 pound terms in a similar manner.

Calculation of Gross Cash Investment

Gross cash investment represents the immediate cost or outflow at the outset of the IRR calculation. It is composed of the entire investment in both depreciating and non-depreciating assets made by the company from which it can generate gross cash flow throughout the analysis horizon. Gross cash investment is calculated as shown below.

Gross Cash Investment	£
Non-depreciating assets, current £	2,220
Gross plant, property, equipment etc.	22,000
Current £ adjustment to gross plant	7,280
Gross intangibles	1,000
Current £ adjustment to intangibles	400
Present value of operating leases	916
Gross cash investment, current £	33,816

Current £ Adjustments

The intention of the adjustments applied to tangible and intangible assets is to bring the out of date cost information for each layer of assets to a 2012 constant £ cost. Holt estimates the appropriate adjustments using a combination of the project life established, smoothed past real growth rates, and the GDP deflator. The first two factors would be used to estimate how the cost of assets was built up over time (the total cost presumably having been built up on a straight line basis over the project life as adjusted for real growth such that each year's investment exceeds the previous year's investment by real growth) and the latter factor applied to the investment profile to bring costs up to current £ figures.

Operating Leases

Following the logic of the adjustment to gross cash flow (namely to reverse operating lease payments out) operating lease rentals are capitalised and treated as part of the cash investment. For consistency with all other elements of the CFROI calculation, operating leases are capitalised at the present value of the operating lease payments discounted at the real cost of debt (or more precisely, the real return required by debtholders) for the company. From the gross cash flow calculation it can be seen that operating lease rentals amount for £200. These are the discounted over the analysis horizon (that is to day the estimated life of the assets) which is 5 years in this case.

Assuming a 3% real debt rate, the calculation would proceed as follows:

Present Value of Operating Leases

Time	Cash Flow £	Discount factor @ 3%	Present Value £
1	200	0.971	194
2	200	0.943	189
3	200	0.915	183
4	200	0.888	178
5	200	0.863	172
			916

Calculating the IRR of the Cash Flows

There are four inputs into the IRR calculation:

- Current £ gross assets
- Gross cash flow (in current £ terms)
- Current £ non-depreciating assets (as an inflow in the final year)
- The estimated life of the assets

The layout of the cash flows based on the above four inputs can be represented as follows:

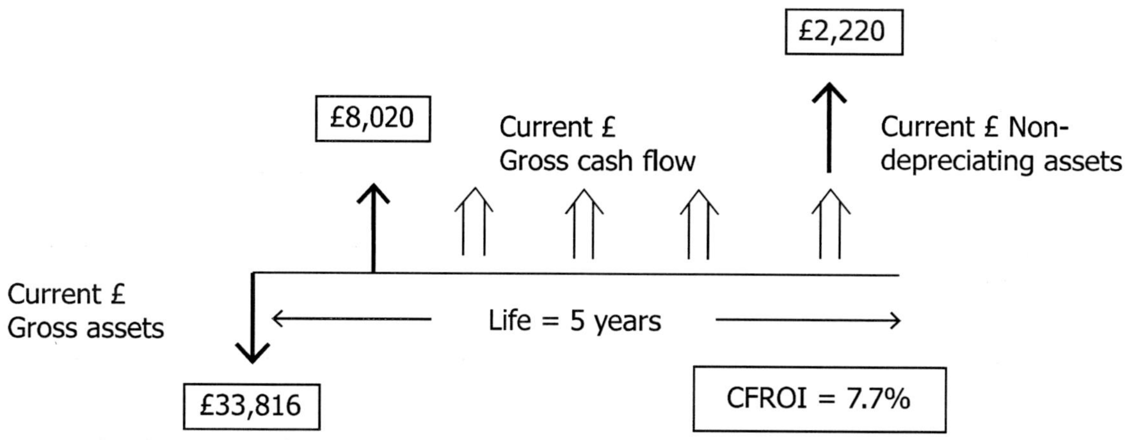

Based on the above cash flows the resultant CFROI ca be calculated as approximately **7.7%**. Whilst this may appear low in terms of conventional returns, it must be remembered that this is a **real return** based on the investment in assets.

Growth in Cash Flows

It should be noted that it would be entirely inappropriate to apply any form of growth to the gross cash flow over the analysis horizon period. The gross cash flow (and, indeed, all cash flows) are expressed in constant £s or monetary units, and hence no inflationary increase is appropriate. Secondly, the analysis seeks to estimate the return on the existing investment in assets. It would, therefore, be entirely inappropriate to include any form of growth which would result from future investment in assets.

Establishing a Benchmark Cost of Capital

Holt have developed their own method of calculating a cost of capital since they believe a conventional cost of capital based upon the Capital Asset Pricing Model and the theories of Modigliani and Miller have a number of weaknesses:

- Betas used in CAPM are historic, whereas the cost of capital needed is one which applies in the future.

- Betas often prove counter-intuitive in assessing the risk faced with regard to an investment in practice.

- A cost of debt net of the tax benefits enjoyed by the company is a less useful figure than using the required return of debtholders.
- Nominal costs of capital are susceptible to distortions caused by inflation over time and across international boundaries.
- The cost of capital to be used in a valuation methodology should be consistent with the rest of the valuation methodology, not founded on some entirely separate theory.

Holt have, therefore developed a benchmark cost of capital measure which attempts to overcome the above perceived weaknesses. The exact nature of the calculation remains largely proprietary, but the broad approach can be shown.

Finding a Benchmark Cost of Capital

Firm's Equity Discount Rate	=	Market Average Discount Rate	+/-	Risk Differential ↙ ↘ • Gearing • Size
Firm's Debt Discount Rate	=	Market Average Discount Rate	+/-	Risk Differential ↓ • Company Characteristics

Market Average Discount Rate

Since the Holt methodology looks at the cash flows available to all providers of finance, the market average discount rate is calculated for a firm as a whole (it is not actually necessary to split this into individual debt and equity rates).

The market average discount rates are derived by equating the market values of firms (debt and equity) to the present value of projected cash flows for firms (cash flows available to debt and equity). The resultant discount rate is hence the 'market derived' average cost of capital.

Holt actually calculate twenty market average rates for twenty different 'fade classes' of firms. Fade classes are discussed in detail below, but the categorisation of firms into twenty classes splits firms according to the rate at which the firms' returns tend towards break-even (ie the manner in which a firm's competitive advantage or disadvantage is competed away, such that the firm provides returns which equal the cost of capital).

For each fade class Holt will then project cash flows based on projected CFROIs as determined by the fade class. Using sustainable growth estimates (based on assumptions of stable capital structure and stable dividend payout ratios) and CFROI estimates aggregate cash flows can be calculated for all the companies in a fade class. These aggregate cash flows are then equated to the aggregate firm values for a fade class and a market derived discount rate is then calculated.

Risk Differentials

The company-specific discount rate is the market derived rate for a particular company's fade class adjusted for a risk differential (which can be positive, negative or nil). The resultant rate is a weighted average cost of capital (debt and equity rates) which can then be used for comparison with the CFROI.

As noted above, Holt use two key factors to determine the risk differential to be applied to a company's cost of capital – namely size and gearing/leverage. These two factors suggest themselves as risk differentials since they are factors that cannot be eliminated by portfolio diversification.

Whilst higher gearing levels will lead to higher gross cash flows (since the tax burden of the company will fall due to the tax deductibility of interest payments), financial leverage will cause the discount rate to rise once financial distress is experienced.

Larger companies are more able to withstand economic shocks or management errors than smaller companies, and hence have lower risk of insolvency. In addition, Holt suggest that since transaction costs associated with investment in smaller companies is greater, investors require a higher return to compensate.

Holt believe they have found strong empirical evidence to support their belief that size and gearing are important determinants of the risk differential. Indeed, the risk differentials to be applied are empirically derived and suggest that large size and low gearing imply lower than average risk, and hence a negative risk differential.

Two points are worth noting concerning the Holt discount rate. Firstly, despite the fact that it is a real discount rate using a gross of tax debt rate, if Modigliani and Miller's theories apply in the real world, one would anticipate the cost of capital to fall due to increased gearing or leverage. This does not appear to happen in any consistent manner even at the most modest gearing levels (there is some support for this notion if a comparison of the lowest gearing decile is made to the second lowest decile for the size deciles highlighted in boxes).

Secondly, the concept of financial distress would suggest that the cost of capital will rise at higher gearing levels. This is certainly borne out by the empirically derived costs of capital.

Splitting the Cost of Capital

Whilst it is not necessary to split the overall cost of capital into its components, this can be achieved by deriving the cost of debt independently. By looking at the company characteristics which would be pertinent to deriving a credit rating, it should be possible to ascertain an approximate rating even if not published. By using this credit rating it should then be possible to ascertain an appropriate pre-tax debt yield for similar debt.

Once a debt rate and gearing level are known, the equity rate can be derived from the overall weighted average cost of capital as a balancing figure.

Real Cost of Capital

It should be remembered that however a benchmark cost of capital or discount rate is calculated, it must be a **real** figure for comparability to the real CFROI.

Interpreting the CFROI Spread

On a simple basis, those companies that generate CFROIs in excess of the real cost of capital benchmark represent companies that are adding value for shareholders. The investments they have made are expected to generate returns in excess of the risk adjusted required returns of the investors.

It should be noted, however, that a positive spread between CFROI and the real cost of capital alone is not very meaningful, and can be misleading.

In common with EVA analysis, the return measure (based on actual invested capital) and the cost of capital measure (based on market values) are not calculated in a consistent manner. As illustrated for EVA analysis, this lack of consistency can cause problems where a simplistic interpretation is applied. A company which generates a **positive** CFROI over cost of capital spread could find its share price **fall** if the spread is less than the market had anticipated.

In order to interpret CFROI meaningfully, it will always be necessary to view the CFROI spread (be it positive or negative) in the light of the positive or negative spread the market value exhibits over the company's assets. This approach is discussed in more detail in the following sections.

The CFROI Life Cycle

Introduction

Whilst the calculation of the CFROI above enables calculation of a current spread between a firm's return on assets and its cost of capital, the marked value of a firm actually depends on how this spread will change throughout time – the CFROI life cycle.

The CFROI life cycle is based on the economic life cycle of firms. In the long-term competition will diminish any spread between the cost of capital and the return on assets (positive or negative). Hence, a positive spread between returns and costs of capital is only sustainable whilst any competitive advantage persists.

The Value/Cost Ratio

Holt's have developed the value/cost ratio as a measure to determine where a company lies in its CFROI life cycle. The value/cost ratio is defined as the firm's total market value (debt plus equity) divided by its net assets marked up to current dollar/monetary terms using a general price level deflator (this is done to ensure that both numerator and denominator are expressed in current units of purchasing power, hence removing any inflation distortions).

Holt's liken the value/cost ratio to a bond trading above or below par according to the relation of coupon to market yields. The value/cost ratio should be in excess of unity if a company has a positive spread of CFROI over cost of capital, and the ratio should be less than unity if the firm has a negative CFROI spread.

The value/cost ratio can be calculated as follows (note that any numbers not previously used are arbitrary).

The Value/Cost Ratio	**£**
Equity market value using average of high and low stock prices for the year	14,938
Short term debt at book/market value	729
Long term debt at book/market value	6,027
Debt value of leases (916 ÷ 2)	458
Other liabilities	314
Total debt	7,528
Total market value = Equity + Total Debt	22,466
Current £ Non-depreciating assets	2,220
Current £ Gross plant	29,280
less: Current £ Depreciation reserve	(14,590)
Net leased property (916 ÷ 2)	458
Current £ intangibles	1,400
less: Current £ Depreciation reserve	(650)
Total current £ net assets	18,118
$\frac{\text{Value}}{\text{Cost}} = \frac{\text{Total Market Value}}{\text{Current £ Net Assets}} = \frac{22,466}{18,118} =$	1.24

Many of the inputs to the value cost ratio are self-evident (equity value, debt at market value or book value if not traded) or have been explained earlier (gross plant, non-depreciating assets, intangibles). Other elements, however, merit further discussion.

Debt Value of Leases/Net Leased Property

These inputs both relate to the capitalised operating leases. For consistency with CFROI calculation, the operating leases must be treated as assets and associated debt in the value/cost ratio.

Note that for the gross cash investment calculation for CFROI we generated a **cost** of assets as £916. In the value cost ratio we are not interested in cost, but rather the **outstanding debt** and the **net book value** of the assets. For simplicity, it has been assumed that at any given point the average net book value and debt outstanding is half of the original amount (which was the 'cost' of £916 calculated earlier).

Other Liabilities

Firms may well have other liabilities which should be regarded as debt finance. Perhaps the most significant of these is **pension liabilities**, particularly where a firm's scheme is unfunded. Even with a funded scheme, any shortfall between scheme assets at market value and the present value of projected benefits would also need to be accounted for if information is available.

Current £ Depreciation Reserves

Just as assets must be stated in current £ terms, so must depreciation reserves. Holt's method (as described for establishing the current £ cost of non current assets) uses estimates of project life, past real growth rates and the GDP deflator.

Locating a Company in the CFROI Life Cycle

Once the value/cost ratio (and CFROI) have been calculated, it should be possible to locate the firm in the CFROI life cycle.

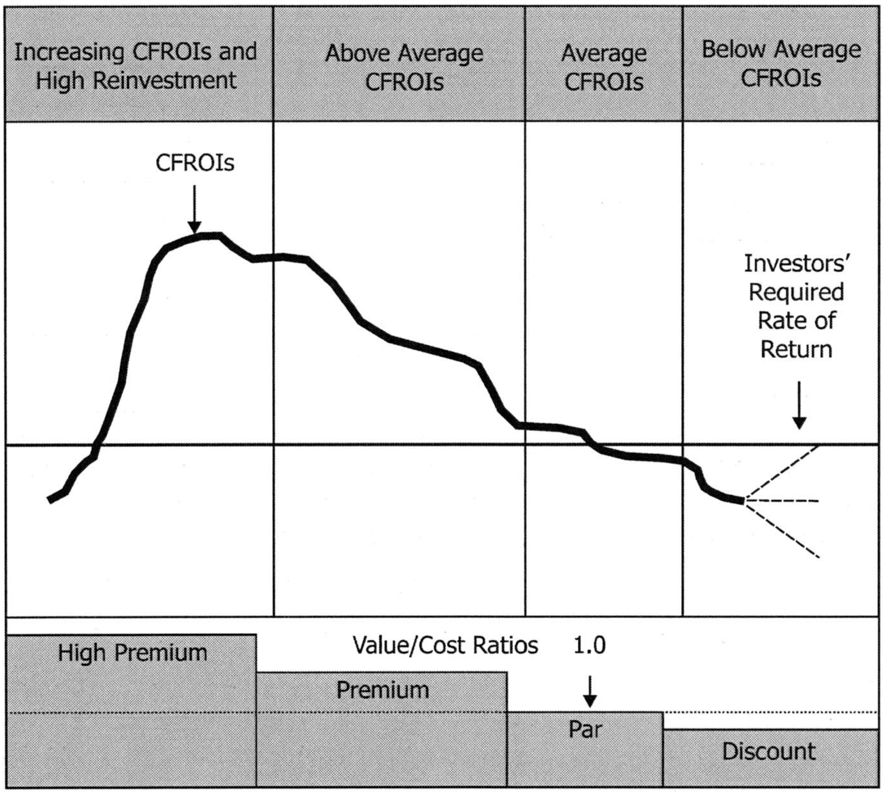

An important point to note is that if Holts are correct in their linkage between CFROI and the value/cost ratio, then positive CFROI spreads cannot be linked to increasing value cost ratios. As can be seen from the above diagram, as the firm moves from the increasing CFROI to the above-average CFROI stage, the value/cost premium is declining. This could, therefore, indicate a stock where all benefits of positive CFROI spreads are accounted for in the market value at the outset, and as CFROI spreads decline, the market value may also decline since CFROIs are below market expectation.

Fade Rates

Holt have undertaken research to establish how CFROI can be used to distinguish winners from losers in terms of stock market performance. Their work indicates that the determinant of a winner is how CFROI over time behaves when compared to expectation. For example, those companies that manage to sustain positive CFROIs beyond the expected competitive advantage period should provide above average overall returns to shareholders (by way of dividends and capital growth).

Holt term the change in CFROI over time the 'fade rate'. There are three factors which can be used to determine what fade rate class a security belongs to, namely:

- Historic CFROIs
- Variability of CFROIs
- Growth rate for the company

Holt generate twenty different fade classes based on the above by splitting historic CFROIs into quintiles as shown below.

Fade Classification

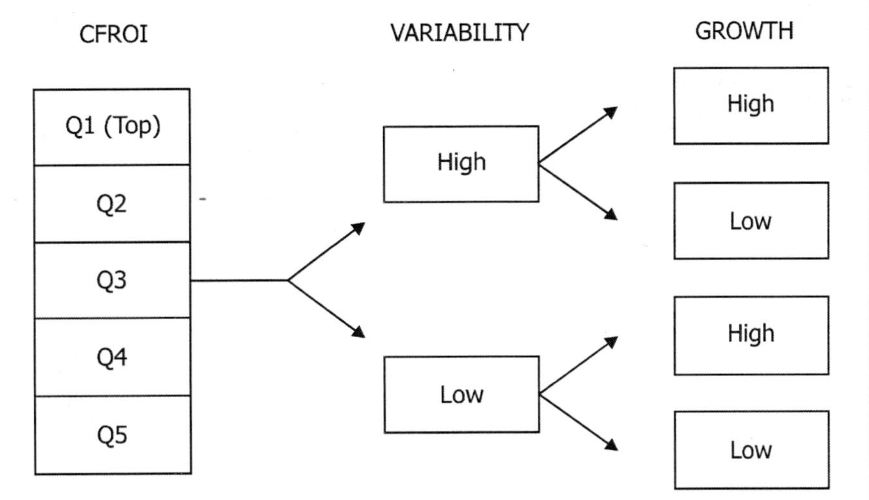

Holt's work on how CFROIs change over time provides some useful (and intuitive) insights. The first, and most basic conclusion that can be drawn from their empirical work is that competition over time compresses all CFROIs towards the average. This, therefore, suggests:

- Companies with top quintile CFROIs are likely to experience a relative decline in future CFROIs
- Companies with bottom quintile CFROIs are likely to experience a relative rise in future CFROIs

However, it is essential to predict how quickly the CFROIs will fade towards the average in the future – the fade rate. Holt's research strongly indicates that the more extreme (high or low) the existing or historic CFROI is, the more quickly it will tend towards the average. In other words, extreme CFROIs are generally not sustainable.

The other determinants of fade rate are relative variability and growth. Whilst their impact appears relatively unimportant when looking at companies with low historic CFROIs, Holt's work indicates they are important determinants of fade rate for companies with historically high CFROIs, namely:

- High growth and variability cause quick fade rates
- Low growth and variability dampen fade rates

The above seems intuitively sensible. In high growth markets, one would anticipate greater competition than low growth markets, and the greater the level of competition the greater the decline of competitive advantage.

Winners and Losers

The work undertaken by Holt clearly shows that those companies which can improve or sustain their CFROI compared to peers in their fade class are the companies that provide the best stock market performance. How, then, are winners identified?

The following extract from *The CFROI Life Cycle* by Bartley J Madden of Holt provides some insights.

Past CFROI	Variability	Growth	Winner/Loser Ratio
Q1	High	High	0.55
Q1	Low	Low	1.32
Q2	High	High	0.57
Q2	Low	Low	1.71
Q3	High	High	0.89
Q3	Low	Low	1.63
Q4	High	High	0.69
Q4	Low	Low	1.97
Q5	High	High	0.67
Q5	Low	Low	1.39

Source: The Journal of Investing

For the above table a winner (loser) is defined as a stock that is in the top (bottom) quartile of shareholder return for all stocks in the universe over the four year period following CFROI classification.

What appears to be the case is that, based on the research undertaken, regardless of current or past CFROI levels, low variability and growth produce more winners than high variability and growth. It appears that the market tends to undervalue stocks with low variability and growth compared to those with relatively high levels.

The CFROI Valuation Model

Introduction

The ultimate aim of examining a company's current CFROI and understanding the CFROI life cycle is to generate a valuation. In order to generate a valuation the current and anticipated CFROIs must be converted into cash flows. The key steps in determining the cash flows are:

- Determine future cash flows from the current CFROI
- Determine future sustainable real growth in assets
- Determine future CFROIs given anticipated fade rates and convert into incremental wealth cash flows

Once the cash flows have been determined, then these may be discounted to arrive at a valuation.

Determination of Cash Flows from Current CFROI

In order to break the current CFROI down into component cash flows, it is necessary to understand how the gross cash investment has been built up over previous years. The overall dynamic of the current CFROI can then be applied in miniature to the gross cash investment made in previous years. The methodology is most easily understood by way of a simple example.

Illustration

Let us begin with the current CFROI of a simplified company, A Plc for later reference. All the numbers are arbitrary and are unrelated to earlier examples.

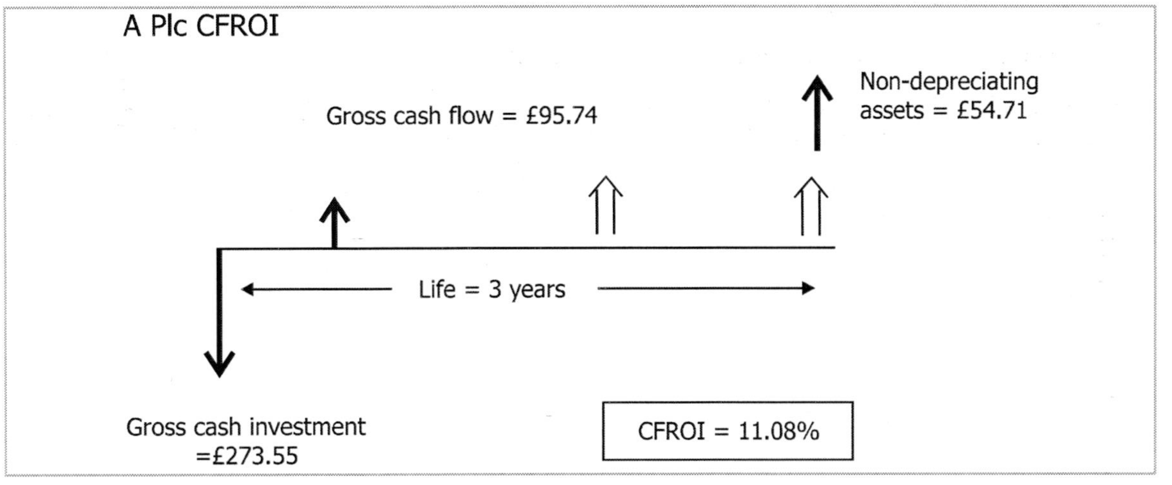

The overall dynamic of the CFROI can easily be established by extracting the relationships of the relevant cash flows. If we take gross cash investment to be 100%, then gross cash flow and non-depreciating assets can be expressed as relative proportions of the investment.

- Gross cash flow = $\frac{£95.74}{£273.55}$ = 35%

- Non-depreciating assets = $\frac{£54.71}{£273.55}$ = 20%

The next step is to establish how the gross cash investment has been built up over time. This will already have been done when calculating the CFROI itself in order to generate the current £ adjustments to gross plant, etc within gross cash investment. As noted earlier, the build up of the gross cash investment is a function of the project life and smoothed real growth in assets. For the illustration above, we have a three-year life, and let us assume that real asset growth has been 10%. The current £ amounts of gross cash investment can then be broken out of the overall figure as follows.

t_{-2} gross cash investment	$= £273.55 \times \frac{1}{(1+1.1+1.1^2)}$	=	£82.64
t_{-1} gross cash investment	$= £273.55 \times \frac{1.1}{(1+1.1+1.1^2)}$	=	£90.91
t_{-0} gross cash investment	$= £273.55 \times \frac{1.1^2}{(1+1.1+1.1^2)}$	=	£100.00
Overall gross cash investment			£273.55

Given a three-year life any investment prior to t_{-2} will have already been retired and will have ceased to generate further cash flows. It is, therefore, not part of the overall gross cash investment which has been sub-analysed above.

It is now possible to turn the original CFROI into cash flows for valuation purposes by applying the dynamics of the overall CFROI to the sub-analysed gross cash investments.

	t_{-2} £	t_{-1} £	t_0 £	t_1 £	t_2 £	t_3 £
Gross cash investment	(82.64)	(90.91)	(100.00)	–	–	–
Gross cash flow (35%)						
For £82.64 invested	–	28.92	28.92	28.92	–	–
For £90.91 invested	–	–	31.82	31.82	31.82	–
For £100.00 invested	–	–	–	35.00	35.00	35.00
Non-depreciating assets (20%)	–	–	–	16.53	18.18	20.00
	(82.64)	(61.99)	(39.26)	112.27	85.00	55.00

Only those cash flows from t_1 onwards form part of the valuation. A discounted cash flow valuation values the firm as the present value of **future cash flows** which are only those highlighted within the working.

Determination of Future Sustainable Real Growth in Assets

It is necessary to establish future growth in assets in order to translate future CFROIs into cash flows for discounting. Factors such as acquisitions, divestitures and capital structure changes make observed actual growth in assets volatile. However, by assuming that the debt/equity ratio within a firm stays constant and by assuming relative dividend payouts are constant, Holt are able to calculate a 'sustainable' real growth rate which is more stable.

The calculation of sustainable real growth is a function of several key inputs explained below.

P (Ploughback) = Net income + depreciation + minority interest – dividend.

This represents cash retained from operations which is available for investment in assets.

R (Retirement) = The current £ value of assets being retired this year and hence requiring replacement in order to keep the asset base stable.

D (Debt change) = Debt/Equity ratio × (P-R)

If P exceeds R then the excess represents the additional gross assets funded by equity. Taken alone this would increase the value of equity relative to debt. In order to maintain the debt equity ratio, a proportionate amount of gross assets must also be funded by debt (hence giving the change in debt).

A (Gross assets) = The year end current £ value of gross assets.

By introducing some numbers we can establish sustainable growth for A Plc, our simplified company (note that numbers not previously introduced are arbitrary).

Net income = 50.42

Depreciation = 72.95 ($\frac{1}{3}$ of depreciating gross investment given 3 yr life).

Minority interest = 0

Dividend = 50.00

Debt/Equity = 0.5

R(Retirements) = 60.11

A (Gross assets) = 218.84 (depreciating element of gross cash investment).

P (Ploughback) = 50.42 + 72.95 + 0 – 50.00 = **73.37**

P – R = 73.37 – 60.11 = 13.26 (increase in assets funded by equity)

D = 0.5 × 13.26 = 6.63 (increase in assets funded by debt)

The growth in assets is 13.26 + 6.63 (ie P-R+D) = 19.89. However, these assets are included in A (year end gross assets). In order to calculate growth we need the start of year assets.

A (end of year assets)	218.84
Less P-R+D (increase in assets for the year)	(19.89)
Start of year assets	198.95

Finally, growth can be calculated

Sustainable real growth $= \frac{P-R+D}{A-(P-R+D)} = \frac{19.89}{198.95} =$ **10%**

Determination of Cash Flows from Future CFROIs

The third stage of a CFROI valuation necessitates prediction of future CFROIs. The changes in CFROI are predicted using the life cycle model discussed earlier. By inputting the current CFROI, the CFROI variability (assigned a value between high and low) and the growth (assigned a value between high and low also), the Holt software will produce a 'fade factor' based on their empirical research.

This fade factor is then used to profile CFROIs over the next five year period (Holt term this the 'fade window'). Beyond five years Holt will then fade the CFROI to a long-term market average for a thirty-five year period using a 10% exponential fade rate. Growth rates are also faded to a long-term average over the forty year period.

CFROI and Growth Fade

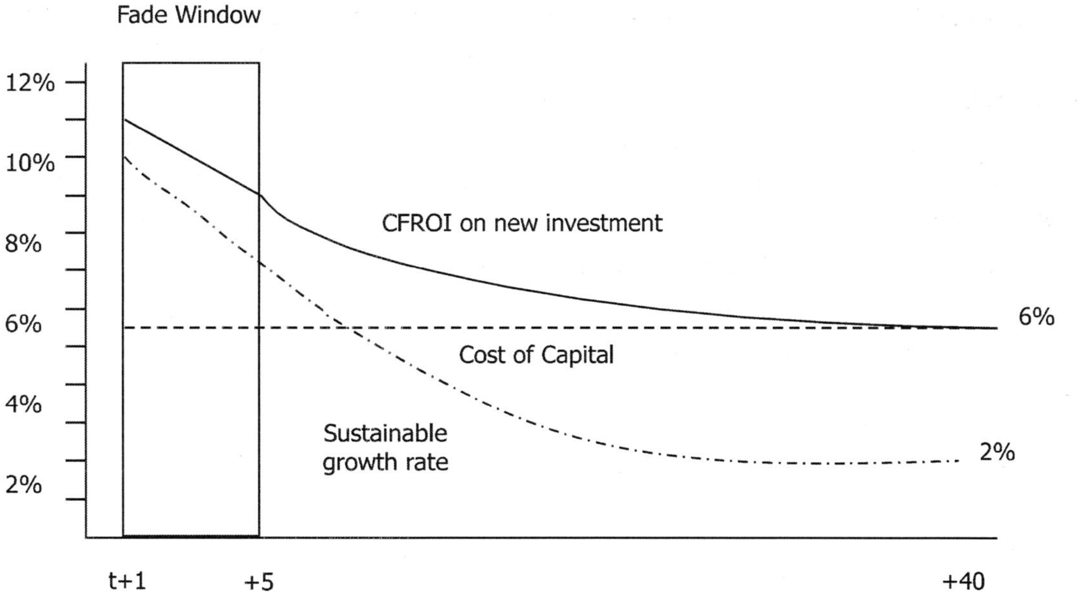

As can be seen from the diagram above, the long-term CFROI and cost of capital will be equal. In line with all other methodologies, Holt believe competitive advantage will be eroded until ultimately no excess return can be generated. In addition, growth is also assumed to fade to a long-term market estimate of real growth – taken as 2% in the illustration.

Fade Factors

Holt believe share price movements are mostly influenced by near term CFROI movements and therefore devote particular attention to the five year fade window. The fade factor produced from current CFORI, CFROI variability and growth predicts how CFROIs will change over the next five years. If we assume long-term market average costs of capital (and therefore CFROIs) are 6%, but current

CFROIs are 11%, then the fade factor expresses how much of the existing excess will be lost in the next five years.

Application of Fade Factors		Example 1	Example 2
1.	Current CFROI	11%	3%
2.	Long-term CFROI	6%	6%
3.	Current excess ((1) – (2))	5%	-3%
4.	Fade factor	0.5	0.8
5.	CFROI after 5 years ((1) – (3) × (4))	8.5%	5.4%

Converting Future CFROI and Growth Predictions into Cash Flows

As noted above, the CFROI valuation model will predict CFROIs and growth over the forthcoming forty years. In order to keep all numbers manageable, the method for turning CFROI and growth predictions into cash flows is illustrated for our initial example – A plc – over just three years.

Application of Fade Factors	Existing	1 Year	2 Years	3 Years
	Existing	***1 Year***	***2 Years***	***3 Years***
CFROI	11.08%	11.08%	8.60%	6.09%
Growth	10%	10%	7%	2%

Beyond year 3 it is assumed growth and CFROIs remain stable. The growth and CFROI at time 3 (the terminal point – in practice it is time 40 for Holt model) therefore represent long-term estimates of real growth and return. The CFROI at the terminal point also represents the assumed long-term real cost of capital.

Having established future CFROIs, the dynamic of the CFROIs can be built if we assume the proportion of gross cash investment in non-depreciating assets remains stable at 20% and the life of the assets remains stable at three years. If we know the CFROI (internal rate of return) of the cash flows, the gross cash investment (100%), and the non-depreciating asset proportion (20%), the gross cash flow proportion can be found as a balancing figure assuming a continued three year life.

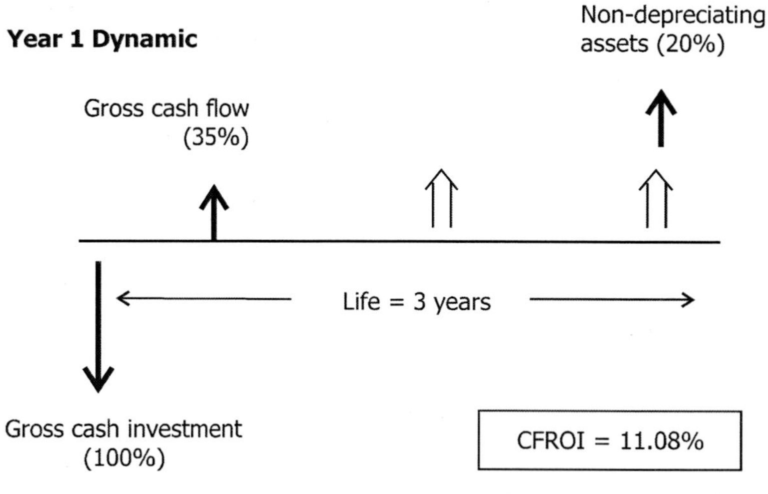

Year 2 Dynamic

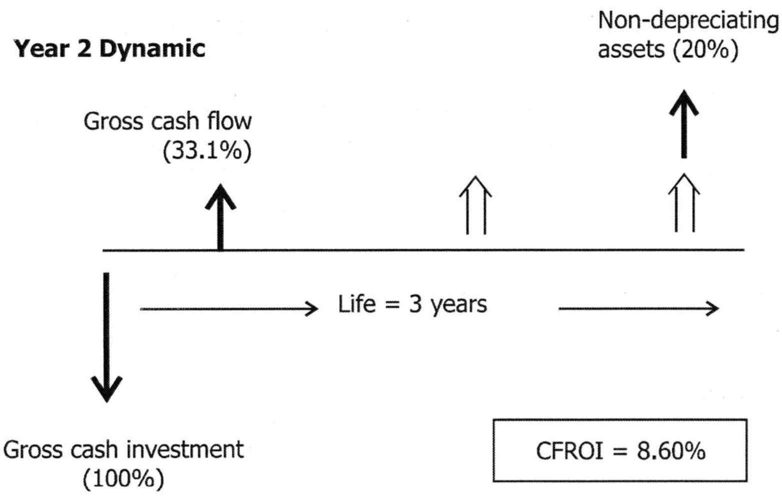

Year 3 Dynamic

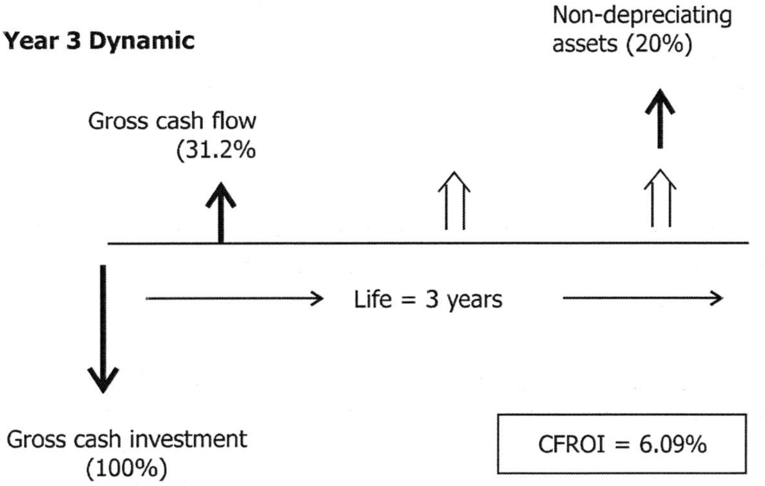

The final stage in converting the CFROI predictions into cash flows is to overlay the growth predictions (which represent the growth in gross cash investment) onto the CFROI dynamics already derived. This allows prediction of the cash flows in respect of gross cash investment as shown below.

Gross Cash Investment

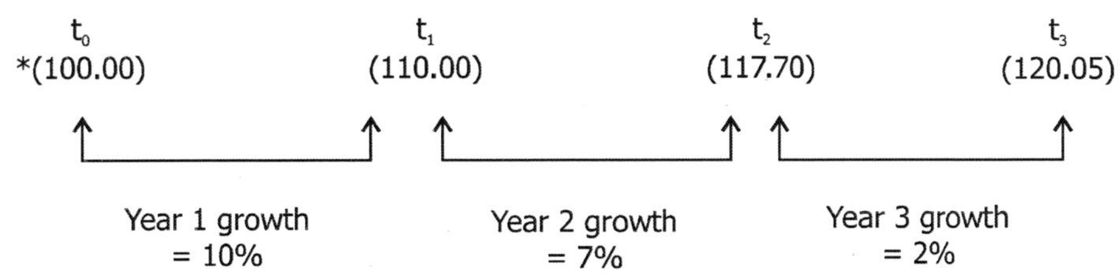

* From the decomposition of the current CFROI as derived earlier.

Once gross cash investment has been derived, it is also possible to derive the gross cash flow and non-depreciating assets by applying the CFROI dynamics to the gross cash investment.

The resultant cash flows represent the return achieved on investment made over the next three years. The CFROI valuation model assumes no further investment beyond the terminal point, since such investment would only achieve a return equal to the cost of capital. As such, it would add no value for the shareholders. It is therefore assumed that at the terminal point the company terminates investment and simply winds down, returning any surplus cash to shareholders.

	t_1 £	t_2 £	T_3 £	T_4 £	T_5 £	T_6 £
Gross cash investment	(110.00)	(117.70)	(120.05)			
Gross cash flow						
For t_1 invested	–	38.50	38.50	38.50		
For t_2 invested	–	–	38.96	38.96	38.96	
For t_3 invested	–	–	–	37.46	37.46	37.46
Non-depreciating assets	–	–	–	22.00	23.54	24.01
	(110.00)	(79.20)	(42.59)	136.92	99.96	61.47

Discounting the Cash Flows to Derive a Valuation

Using standard discounting theory, the value of the company (debt and equity) can be determined as the present value of the cash flows discounted at the weighted average cost of capital. Since the long-term CFROI at the terminal point must be equal to the long-term real cost of capital, the cost of capital is taken to be 6.09% for A Plc.

This real cost of capital can now be used to discount the future cash flows from existing investment in assets and the future cash flows from future investment as shown below.

The CFROI Model Valuation	t_1 £	t_2 £	T_3 £	T_4 £	T_5 £	T_6 £
Cash flow from existing investment	112.27	85.00	55.00	–	–	–
Cash flows from future investment	(110.00)	(79.20)	(42.59)	136.92	99.96	61.47
	2.27	5.80	12.41	136.92	99.96	61.47
Discount factor at 6.09%	0.9426	0.8885	0.8375	0.7894	0.7441	0.7014
Present Value	2.14	5.15	10.39	108.09	74.38	43.11
Company Value (Debt and Equity)						243.26

The value of the equity can then be derived by deducting the value of the debt from the overall value.

	£
Total Company Value	243.26
less: Value of debt (say)	(81.09)
Value of equity	162.17

Finally, a share price can be calculated by dividing by the number of shares in issue (say 100). Holt term this the warranted price.

Warranted price for A plc = 162.17 ÷ 100 = 162p

Terminal Point Assumption

As already noted above, the CFROI model assumes that once a company can only return the cost of capital it will terminate any further investment and wind down. Whilst this is highly unlikely in practice, it can be shown that this is exactly equivalent to assuming the company continues in operation and generates cash flows consistent with a stable CFROI and equal real cost of capital.

If it is assumed that A Plc continued to make investments which were growing at 2% beyond the third year, and assumed that the third year CFROI dynamic continued to apply to the cash flows, then the cash flows resulting from investment beyond time 4 would all grow at 2%.

Below the cash flows for A Plc have been projected out to time 8 by applying the assumptions of 2% growth and a stable CFROI of 6.09% beyond the third year.

	t_1 £	t_2 £	t_3 £	t_4 £	t_5 £	t_6 £	t_7 £	t_8 £
Gross cash investment	(110.00)	(117.70)	(120.05)	(122.46)	(124.90)	(127.40)	(129.95)	(132.55)
Gross cash flow								
t_1 investment	–	38.50	38.50	38.50	–	–	–	–
t_2 investment	–	–	38.96	38.96	38.96	–	–	–
t_3 investment	–	–	–	37.46	37.46	37.46	–	–
t_4 investment	–	–	–	–	38.21	38.21	38.21	–
t_5 investment	–	–	–	–	–	38.97	38.97	38.97
t_6 investment	–	–	–	–	–	–	39.75	39.75
t_7 investment	–	–	–	–	–	–	–	40.54
Non-depreciating assets	–	–	–	22.00	23.54	24.01	24.49	24.98
Cash from existing investment in assets	112.27	85.00	5.00	–	–	–	–	–
	2.27	5.80	12.41	14.46	13.27	11.25	11.47	11.69
						2% cash flow growth →		

As can be seen from the above projections, the cash flows from time 6 onwards grow at a constant 2%. This is what would be anticipated, since by time 7 all the cash flows are the result of investments at time 4 and beyond, which are themselves growing at 2%.

Once the pattern of the cash flows from time 6 onwards has been established as growing at a compound annual rate of 2%, the cash flows based on continued investment can also be discounted to produce a valuation. The discounting techniques to be applied here are entirely consistent with producing a valuation from free cash flow projections.

Valuation Based on Continued Investment

	t_1	t_2	t_3	t_4	t_5	$t_{6-\infty}$
Cash flow	2.27	5.80	12.41	14.46	13.27	11.25
Discounted at 6.09%	$\frac{1}{1.0606}$	$\frac{1}{1.0609^2}$	$\frac{1}{1.0609^3}$	$\frac{1}{1.0609^4}$	$\frac{1}{1.0609^5}$	$\frac{1}{1.0409} \times \frac{1}{1.0609^5}$
Present value	2.14	5.15	10.39	11.41	9.87	204.67
Company value						243.67

It should be noted that the valuation based on continued investment (£243.67) is only different to the valuation based on wind-down (£243.26) due to rounding of the input numbers. It can be seen, therefore, that the CFROI valuation model assumption of wind down is entirely consistent with a free cash flow terminal value assumption.

Using Holt's CFROI Valuation Model in Analysis

Advantages of the Model

The CFROI Valuation Model has a number of advantages. Some of these derive from the fact that the valuation model is computerised and all of Holt's latest estimates are fed into the model for clients of Holt.

Rigour

The CFROI valuation model requires a rigorous examination of companies' past results in order to derive many key inputs (asset life, CFROI levels, CFROI fade rates, growth in investment, etc). Whilst the model may be complex, at least the source of inputs can be determined.

Flexibility

The computerised model allows pre-established inputs to be varied. For example, the level of CFROI variability and growth can be altered to determine a different CFROI fade rate. This enables sensitivity analysis to be undertaken with great ease for any of the inputs which can be varied.

The model is also capable of being used in reverse to decompose from the actual share price what, for example, market expectations of future CFROIs are.

Empirically Based

Many of the inputs to the CFROI valuation model have some empirical base in market information (costs of capital, CFROI fade rates, etc). As such, the values derived are at least linked to valuation behaviour that has been observed in the market.

No Terminal Value

By assuming that a company winds down at time 40, once CFROIs and the cost of capital are equal, Holt eliminate the need for continued projection of cash flows. Whilst, as already shown, this is theoretically consistent with assuming continued investment, it does remove a potential source of estimation error in forecasting future CFROIs and growth.

Real Measure

Since the CFROI valuation model uses real cash flows and costs of capital, it is independent of estimates of future inflation. Like the avoidance of a terminal value, this approach removes another potential source of estimation error in forecasting future inflation. It should be noted, however, that inflation estimates only represent a problem if inflation implicit in the cash flows is not consistent with inflation in the cost of capital.

Research

Research undertaken by independent parties has shown that the CFROI model yields a high coefficient of determination for the S&P 500 Index. Research by Rawley, Thomas and Marvin Lipston found the following abilities of analytical tools to explain movements in US share prices.

Variable	R^2
EPS	0.09
ROE	0.19
ROI	0.34
CFROI	0.65

Problems in Using the CFROI Model for Analysis

Complexity

The first, and most obvious, drawback of using the CFROI model is its complexity. The model is extremely information hungry and it would be very time-consuming to either generate or audit the information being used. Whilst the Holt software provides the necessary inputs, the inputs may not be transparent within the system or otherwise difficult to audit.

Circularity

It may not be entirely surprising that the CFROI model produces valuations that explain actual prices relatively well. The model would be expected to do so since the cost of capital is derived by using CFROI derived cash flows and actual market prices. The cost of capital is then used to discount CFROI derived cash flows for a particular company to arrive at a warranted value. It is only due to the fact that discount rates are derived for a universe of companies rather than individual companies that prevents the model being entirely circular.

Rigidity

Unless the user of the CFROI valuation model is willing to adjust default inputs, the model is excessively rigid. Points which may require additional consideration from the user include:

- Using time 40 as the terminal point
- Using derived sustainable growth (which assumes no changes in debt to equity ratios)
- Using the derived fade rate (given knowledge of the industry, competition against the company and management skill)

Built In Assumptions

The model has a large number of built in assumptions. Many of these appear arbitrary or not entirely supportable in practice. Some of the key assumptions are considered below:

- **No changes in the project lives** – In order to turn projected CFROIs into cash flows, the project life is kept stable. With changing technologies in industries, this assumption may be unreasonable.
- **No change in the proportion of investment that is non-depreciating** – This assumption is also required to turn projected CFROIs into cash flows. As companies move through their life cycle, it is likely that the proportion of investment in depreciating and non-deprecating assets might change (with initially heavy investment in depreciating assets then declining as would be the case for a telecommunications company building a network).
- **No change in the debt/equity ratio of companies** – This assumption is used in generating sustainable growth. Not only is it unrealistic, but even the assumption itself is questionable within the CFROI theoretical framework. The sustainable growth formulation equates amounts of equity and debt invested in assets to changes in the value of debt and equity. This equality can only exist if the investment were to yield a zero NPV, otherwise the ratio of debt to equity value changes would be given by taking debt invested against equity invested + or – the NPV.
- **10% exponential fade of CFROIs beyond the fade window** – Whilst this assumption may not have any very significant impact on the valuation, it does appear somewhat arbitrary.

Growth Fade Rate

Nothing as yet published by Holt explains how the growth estimate fades down to the economy average of around 2%.

Applicability of the Model

Whilst the whole CFROI framework can be easily applied to many industries and sectors, its appropriateness to certain sectors appears limited. In particular, the approach of determining investment horizons by examination of the average life of non-current assets does not have obvious applicability to service sectors.

Holt have adapted their model to encompass financials by focusing on the equity rather than equity and debt (since debt is not properly a source of finance, but rather more like working capital for financials). However, the whole CFROI framework seems ill-fitted to such companies.

16 Real Options Evaluation

Real option approaches are intended to supplement discounted cash flow valuation. Natural resource companies (oil, gas, gold etc.) have been applying option pricing models since their development in the 1970's. In more recent times, many technology companies have harnessed the same techniques to evaluate strategic options available to them.

Discounted cash flow methodologies do not attempt to reflect the value of flexibility that is a crucial driver of value within such companies and consequently practitioners are seeking to harness alternative frameworks such as option valuation models to capture this feature of many natural resource and new economy enterprises.

A second application of option pricing methodologies to value the equity of a company as a whole is also considered in this chapter. Whilst the advocates of this later model (Aswath Damodaran) suggest it has general application, the model is almost certainly at its most useful in evaluating companies which are the subject of significant financial distress.

Discounted Cash Flow Shortcomings

Nobody questions the validity of a discounted cash flow valuation framework, indeed, option valuation models utilise discounted cash flow to generate the value of options. The problem, however, with conventional discounted cash flow approaches is that they rely on a number of assumptions with regard to known inputs which become less and less acceptable when applied to scenarios where a company has strategic choices or real options.

Known Cash Flows

A discounted free cash flow valuation framework requires input of a single set of future cash flows expected from an enterprise in the future. Firstly, there are likely to be areas within a company's future operations that the company is as yet uncommitted to. In addition, these prospective areas of operation may be very difficult to predict with extremely wide feasible parameters. Secondly, the company may or may not engage in such prospective areas of operation. The discounted cash flow framework can either include or exclude any relevant cash flows associated with such operations, but it is incapable of valuing the real world flexibility that managers have in waiting to see whether such operations become worthwhile. The managers of these companies will be making strategic choices as the development of markets and the economy as a whole unfolds. In other words, the managers will be exercising options.

The problem of the DCF framework is that it relies on an assumed certainty with regard to strategic decisions which have not yet been made. We can either include or exclude the cashflows associated with such decisions but we cannot allow for the uncertainty associated with the decision itself.

Cost of Capital

A discounted cash flow valuation framework utilises the required return of the finance providers as a discount rate at which to generate the present value of future returns. Unfortunately, the most widely used methodology for generating a cost of equity capital, the CAPM, requires a substantial history of trading to generate an ex-post risk measure – the beta. Where the prospective operations being reviewed are entirely new we may have no useful indication of the risks involved as expressed within a beta.

Valuing Flexibility

The essential difference between standard discounted cash flow valuation models and option valuation models is that option valuation models attempt to capture the value associated with uncertainty. Option valuation methodologies are based on the fundamental ability to wait and see before exercising a choice with regard to a company's strategic direction. Whilst they were developed to value instruments which give the holder the right to buy or sell an underlying asset, they can be used to value management's options to start up, expand, contract, sell off or close down activities. Option valuation models have been created to value flexibility. They are designed to capture the value associated with a contingent decision – in other words they value the ability to wait and see how a present uncertainty unfolds before deciding upon a course of action. This is often the just the flexibility which form a fundamental feature of many technology companies and which a standard discounted cash flow approach fails to address.

A possible expansion of operations may appear to have no value if the company is assumed to make a decision today. A DCF approach will therefore attach no value to the possibility of expansion. However, strategic decisions can be deferred. The management of the company can wait and see if the music distribution business is worth expanding into by waiting to see how the demographic reach of the

Internet changes over time. Effectively, the management of the company has a valuable option with good prospective payoffs. Real options valuation attempts to model and value these options which a discounted cash flow approach will attribute no value to.

The essential difference between a discounted cash flow approach and a real options approach is that by allowing for contingent decision-making, a real options approach turns what could have been either a substantial loss or a substantial gain under the DCF framework into a situation with capped losses.

Real options analysis creates an asymmetrical payoff profile exactly like the profile of a standard call option. A crucial distinction results from the analysis of, for example, a technology company under the real options approach to analysis under a DCF framework. Whereas increased uncertainty reduces value in a DCF framework, increased uncertainty increases value within an options valuation framework.

Types of Real Options

Real options analysis has attempted to classify the types of options available to management into various types. Whilst being able to analyse a particular option available to management into one of these particular types does not generally influence the value of the option, the classifications provide a checklist which can be used to try to identify the real options available to the management of a company.

Real Options Classification:
Grow, Defer or Quit

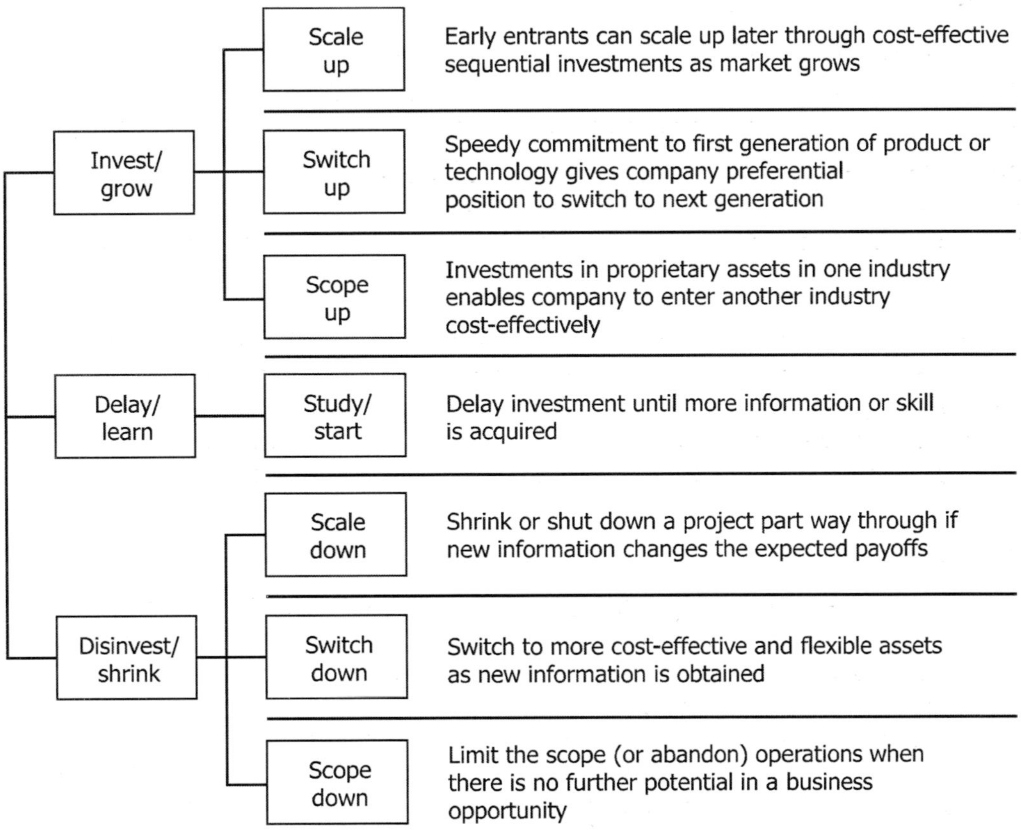

Once the options available to a company have been identified, the next stage is to ascertain their value. It should be noted that the options can only have value if the decision to scale or scope up or down is based on uncertain future events and where the uncertainty reduces through time. If the uncertainty remained at the later date, the future decision would be as uninformed as a decision today and would not produce enhanced expected payoffs.

It should be noted, however, that for an option of any kind to have value, it must be owned. One potential problem with the analysis of real options is that many strategic options are simply not proprietary.

Types of Financial Options

The essential similarity between financial options and real options is that in both cases there is no obligation to exercise the option. With a financial option if the value of the underlying share falls below the agreed price at which the option holder can buy the share, then the holder of the option would not exercise their right to buy.

Financial options which give the right to buy an asset are referred to as call options. The valuation models used to value call options are therefore appropriate for real options which enable a company to scale, switch or to scope up their activities, or to study/start with respect to potential future investment opportunities. Financial options conferring the right to sell an asset are referred to as put options. Valuation models for valuing put options are therefore appropriate for real options enabling an enterprise to scale, switch or scope down its operations.

Financial Options Valuation Models

There are two key types of financial option valuation models which are available to derive the value of real options:

- The Cox-Ross-Rubenstein or binomial model
- The Black Scholes Pricing Model

Each of these is now considered in detail both as a financial options valuation model and as a model for valuing real options.

Binomial Model

The binomial model starts from the assumption that the share price can only be one of two values at the end of a period based on its value at the start. This may seem a little unrealistic since share prices may move over a considerable range in a period. However, by shortening the length of each period from years to weeks to days to seconds etc. and correspondingly increasing the number of periods we may be able to get a useful model.

Single Period Illustration

Imagine that a stock has a current price of 100p and it is known that at the end of one month it will be either 120p or 90p. The risk free rate is 8% p.a. with continuous compounding. What is the value of a one month European* 95p call?

**Note that European options can only be exercised at the end of the option life. We will consider American options, which can be exercised at any time later*

Diagrammatically

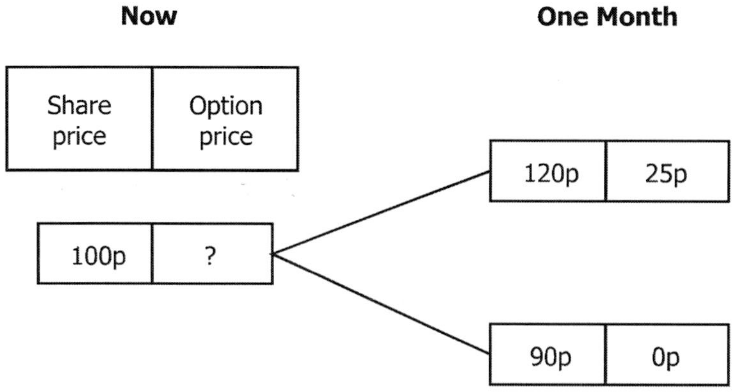

We can see that the value of the call at its expiry in one month's time will be either 25p (the intrinsic value of the 95 call if the stock is 120) or 0p. What we need to do is attribute a weighting to the particular outcomes by determining the probability of an upmove and a downmove.

To do this we use the following formula:

$$p = \frac{R - d}{u - d}$$

where

p = the probability of an upmove

R = the continuously compounded risk free rate of interest for the period

u = the expected percentage upmove, eg 1.1 for a 10% upmove, or for our example $(\frac{120}{100}) = 1.20$

d = the expected percentage downmove, eg 0.91 for a 9% downmove, or for our example $(\frac{90}{100}) =$ 0.90

Using the figures from above

$R = e^{rt}$

where r = annual interest rate

t = period as a fraction of a year

$$R = e^{0.08 \times 1/12}$$

$$= 1.0067$$

Inserting into formula

$$p = \frac{1.0067 - 0.90}{1.20 - 0.90}$$

$$p = \frac{0.1067}{0.30}$$

$$P = 0.3557$$

Consequently the chance of a downmove is 1 – p, ie 0.6443.

Now we have the probabilities to weight the potential outcomes

$0.3557 \times 25 + 0.6443 \times 0$

Signifying that there is 0.3557 chance of an upmove and consequently an expiry value of 25p, and a 0.6443 chance of a downmove to give zero intrinsic value.

These values are brought back to present value, by discounting at the continuously compounded rate for the period, R.

$$\text{Call} = \frac{(0.3557 \times 25) + (0.6443 \times 0)}{1.0067}$$

Call = 8.83p

The above example used continuous compounding. It would have been possible to use discrete compounding.

This would give

$$p = \frac{(1.08)^{1/12} - 0.90}{1.20 - 0.90}$$

p = 0.3547

$$\text{Call} = \frac{(0.3547 \times 25) + (0.6453 \times 0)}{(1.08)^{1/12}}$$

Call = 8.81p

A similar process may be used for a put.

The current price of a stock is 50p, and at the end of a six month period it will be either 45p or 55p. The risk free rate is 10% p.a. continuously compounded. What is the value of a European style six month put?

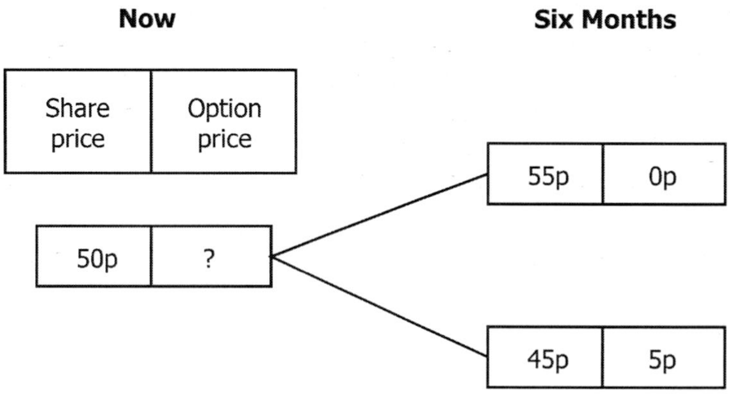

Calculate p

$$p = \frac{R - d}{u - d}$$

$$p = \frac{1.0513 - 0.9}{1.1 - 0.9}$$

$$p = \frac{0.1513}{0.20}$$

$$p = 0.7565$$

$$1 - p = 0.2435$$

$$\text{Put} = \frac{(0.7565 \times 0) + (0.2435 \times 5)}{1.0513}$$

$$\text{Put} = 1.16$$

Using the Single Period Binomial to Value Real Options

Required Inputs

The simple binomial model used above to generate the value of financial options required several inputs, namely known future share prices, an exercise price of the option, the duration of the option and a risk-free discount rate. The table below summarises how the first two of these inputs can be generated for a real option.

Input		Estimation Process
1.	Known future share price possibilities	Present value of the cash **inflows** from exercising the option to undertake the project under the various scenarios that may unfold (Note 1).
2.	Exercise price of the option	Cost of making the necessary investment to undertake the project (Note 2).

Note 1

The present value of the possible outcomes must be calculated as at the real option expiry, namely at the point in time by which the decision must have been made or the point at which the relevant uncertainty will have been removed. It is worth noting that in order to calculate these inputs a risk adjusted discount rate needs to be ascertained.

Note 2

The cost of undertaking the project is assumed to be constant, just as the price at which a share can be bought or sold under a financial option is constant.

Note 3

It should be noted that with respect to real options it will not be possible to derive the probabilities of upmoves and downmoves utilising the formula utilised for the share options. The derivation of the formula relies on the assumption that the share price today is a reflection of the possible share prices at a future date. Clearly, since under a conventional valuation framework the share price today and at a future date are both driven by the expected future returns from the share, it is reasonable to assume that today's share price is a function of the future share price. There is no necessary linkage or relationship between the cost and expected returns of non-traded projects which a company may chose to undertake.

In applying the binomial in a real options scenario it will therefore be necessary to calculate or estimate the probabilities associated with different outcomes independently from the outcomes themselves at this stage.

Applying the Binomial

Multi-period illustration

The continuously compounded rate of interest is 8% p.a. A stock is priced at 100 and pays no dividends and has an annual volatility of 25%. What is the current value of a European style 95 call two months before expiry, taking a period as being one month?

In this example the expected value of the stock is provided obliquely through the volatility figure. Consequently we need to derive the monthly percentage movement from the annual volatility figure and thus derive u and d.

Using the formula $u = e^{\sigma \sqrt{t}}$

where

σ = annualised standard deviation of returns expressed in decimal

t = time in each period expressed as a fraction of a year

Thus $u = e^{0.25 \times 0.2887}$

$u = 1.0748$ (ie it is expected to move up by 7.48% each period)

To find d is more straightforward if a lognormal distribution is presumed, d is simply

$$d = \frac{1}{u}$$

$$d = \frac{1}{1.0748}$$

$$d = 0.9304$$

(**Note.** This is the same as saying $d = e^{\sigma^{\sqrt{t}}}$)

Now we can solve for p.

$$p = \frac{R - d}{u - d}$$

$$p = \frac{1.0067 - 0.9304}{1.0748 - 0.9304}$$

$$p = \frac{0.0763}{0.1444}$$

$$p = 0.528$$

and $1 - p = 0.472$

Having now found p and 1 – p, let us consider the two period lattice.

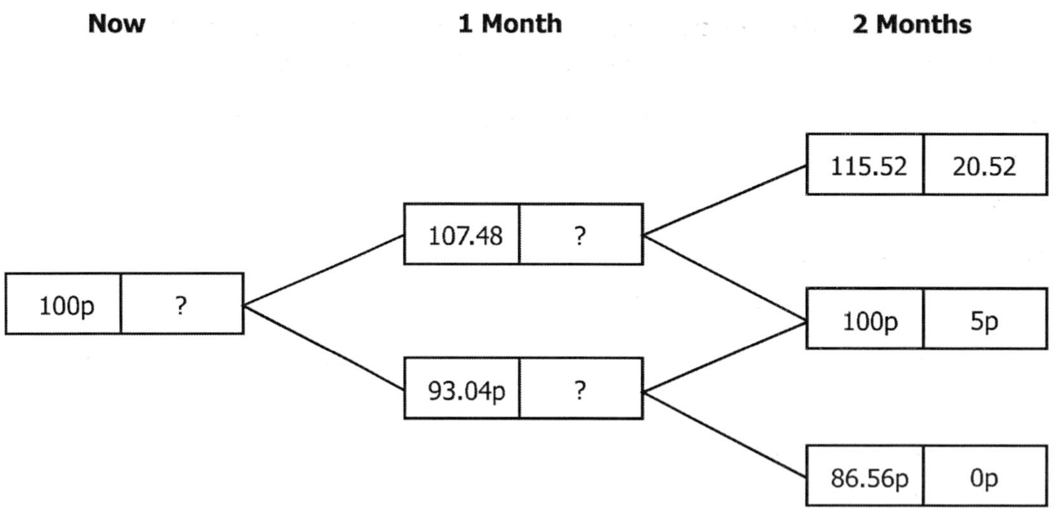

The three possible stock prices after two periods are found as follows:

(i) Upmove followed by upmove

$100 \times 1.0748 \times 1.0748 = 115.52p$

(ii) Upmove followed by downmove

$100 \times 1.0748 \times 0.9304 = 100p$

(this value could be reached by a downmove followed by an upmove).

(iii) Downmove followed by downmove

$100 \times 0.9304 \times 0.9304 = 86.56p$

The intrinsic value of the 95 call at expiry would be 20.52 if the stock is 115.52, 5 if the stock is at 100, and 0 if the stock is at 86.56.

Value of the 95 call after an upmove in the first period is

$$\frac{(0.528 \times 20.52) + (0.472 \times 5)}{1.0067}$$

= 13.11p

Value of the 95 call after a downmove in the first period is

$$\frac{(0.528 \times 5) + (0.472 \times 0)}{1.0067}$$

= 2.62p

Value of the 95 call now is

$$\frac{(0.528 \times 13.11) + (0.472 \times 2.62)}{1.0067}$$

= 8.10

It is worth noting that when calculating a *non-annual interest rate* from an annual rate it is simply time apportioned.

Eg annual rate = r = 12%

rate for six months = $r \times \frac{1}{2}$

rate for three months = $r \times \frac{1}{4}$

rate for one month = $r \times \frac{1}{12}$

This has been seen above where the continuous compounded rate for one month based on an annual rate of 8% = $e^{rt} = e^{0.08 \times 1/12}$ = 1.006688 (rounded to 1.0067 in above example).

However, when calculating *non-annual volatility* from annual volatility it is ***not*** simply time apportioned. The correct relationship is given by

σ 6 months = σ annual $\sqrt{1/2}$

σ 3 months = σ annual $\sqrt{1/4}$

σ month = σ annual $\sqrt{1/12}$

The reason for the square root is that risks combine by adding variances (σ^2) rather than adding standard deviations (σ).

To understand the above we can state that

σ^2 annual = $12 \times \sigma^2$ monthly (ie the variances are added)

σ^2 monthly = σ^2 annual $\times$ $1/12$

σ monthly = σ annual $\sqrt{1/12}$

The above idea can be extended as follows:

Eg σ Sept = 0.8%

σ Oct = 0.9%

What is the volatility for September and October, ie for a two-month period.

σ^2 Sept + σ^2 Oct = $\sigma^2$2 months

Therefore, σ 2 months = $\sqrt{\sigma^2}$ Sept and σ^2 Oct

Using the Multi-Period Binomial to Value Real Options

The multi-period binomial allows for much more realistic modelling of possible future share prices and by extension it also allows for much more realistic modelling of outcomes from deciding to invest in a project.

It should be noted that with the above illustration the future share prices were generated from a share volatility measure – the standard deviation or variance of the share. This was then applied to the current share price to derive the share price one period forward.

In attempting to apply this idea to our real options illustration we could estimate a 'most likely' scenario to generate the payoff today (which would be equivalent to today's share price) and then estimate a variance of payoffs around this figure. The multi-period binomial therefore requires different inputs as described below

Input		Estimation Process
1.	Current value of the underlying asset	Present value of **inflows** from exercising the option to undertake a project now.
2.	Exercise price of the option	Cost of making the necessary investment to undertake the project.
3.	Variance in the value of the underlying asset	Variance of the possible values of cash inflows under various scenarios (Note 1).
4.	Risk free rate	Estimated from government bond yields.
5.	Life of option	The period of time over which the company has the option to invest in the project or not.

Note 1

This variance could be estimated from the variance in the cash flows of companies with similar activities to the project under consideration (though it is unlikely there is any good comparator) or by some kind of simulation of possible outcomes such as Monte Carlo simulation. In either case it is a very difficult input to estimate with a reasonable degree of confidence.

Binomial Model - Variations

All the examples outlined so far have focused on valuing an option where the underlying asset has been a share. What has not been included in these calculations is any dividend paid on the underlying shares. This idea of including the yield from the underlying asset can be extended to cover equity index options, currency options and options on futures.

Options on Income Yielding Assets

When calculating the probability of an upmove we need to reflect the fact that we are receiving the yield from the underlying asset. To do this the following formula is used.

$p = \frac{e^{(rt - yt)} - d}{u - d}$ where y = dividend yield

Example $r = 8\%$ pa

$y = 5\%$ pa

$t = 1$ month

$s = 100$

$u = 1.05$

$d = 0.90$

What is the value of a 95 call?

$$p = \frac{e^{(0.08 \times 1/12 - 0.05 \times 1/12)} - 0.90}{1.05 - 0.90}$$

$p = 0.6834$

$1 - p = 0.3166$

$$\text{Call} = \frac{(0.6834 \times 10) + (0.3166 \times 0)}{e^{0.08 \times 1/12}}$$

Call = 6.788

The above example looked at a stock option index where the yield was the dividend yield. The logic would be exactly the same if the underlying was currency. The yield then would be the interest rate of the currency.

Application to Real Options

The first consideration in applying the binomial adjustment for underlying assets which are yield-bearing is to consider what, by analogy, can be considered to be the yield on the asset.

One approach, advocated by Professor Alexander Ljungqvist of Stern School of Business, New York University, is to draw an analogy between the real option and the equity option. With regard to an equity, the dividend yield is the cash based return from early exercise of the option. The dividend yield can, therefore, be considered to be the effective cost of delaying exercise. The analogy would then suggest that the cost of delaying the real option is the loss of one year's cash flows from the project. Hence

$$\text{Dividend yield} = \frac{\text{dividend}}{\text{price}} = \frac{\text{PV lost dividend}}{\text{PV of all future dividends}}$$

$$\text{Cost of delaying} = \frac{\text{PV lost project cash flow}}{\text{PV of all future project cash flows}}$$

If we assume that the option is allowed to expire, then the total cost of delays

$$= \frac{\text{PV all future cash flows lost}}{\text{PV of all future cash flows}} = 1$$

The final step is to assume smoothed cash flows such that PV of lost cash flows in each year is the same, then the cost of delay in every year is

$$\frac{\text{PV of lost cash flow over 1 year}}{\text{PV of lost cash flow p.a.} \times \text{No. years to expiry}} = \frac{1}{\text{No. years to expiry}} = \frac{1}{n}$$

This line of reasoning makes for very straightforward calculation of the cost of delay with respect to real options.

The above analogy, however, does not work well if there is no finite life to cash flows. For example, returning the original financial option over an equity, the above approach would calculate the dividend yield as $1/n$ where n is the option life in years. This would clearly give absurd dividend yields of over 100%.

The problem arises because the cash flows from the equity extend far beyond the option expiry. With real options it is likely that the cash returns will extend far beyond the point by which the business is effectively forced to make a decision.

Applying the same analogy based upon equity options and dividend yields, the cost of delay can still be treated as the lost cash flow of a year's delay. However, rather than proceeding on the basis that even after the option has expired there would still be cash flows from the project (though not worth exercising the option to capture them), then

$$\frac{\text{PV lost cash flows over option life}}{\text{PV of all cash flows}} \neq 1$$

Instead, however, the idea of the cost of delay as a dividend yield can be pursued in another direction.

$$\text{Dividend yield} = \frac{\text{dividend}}{\text{price}} = \frac{\text{PV lost cash flow}}{\text{PV of all future cash flows}}$$

Now we can flexibly describe the PV of all future cash flows (which are equivalent to share price and can be expressed just as share price can be expressed). For example, assuming cash flows from the project continue in perpetuity at the same level, then

$$\text{Cost of delay} = \frac{\text{CF}}{\text{CF}/\text{r}} = r$$

r is the required return of shareholders for financial options, and an appropriate risk adjusted discount rate reflecting the risk of cash flows from the project for real options.

Alternatively, if it is assumed that cash flows from real option would grow in perpetuity, then

$$\text{Cost of delay} = \frac{\text{CF}}{\text{CF}/\text{r} - \text{g}} = r - g$$

Where r is the risk adjusted discount rate appropriate for the project and g is the perpetual growth rate of the cash flows.

Given that some kind of cash flow projection has to be made to derive the value of the project today, the cost of delay can generally be stated as

$$\frac{\text{PV lost project cash flow}}{\text{PV of cash flows today}}$$

It is worth noting that with the binomial, another possibility exists – to reflect the cost of delay within a higher exercise or strike price. Within the binomial it is possible to have different strike prices at different points in time. If the cost of delay would include additional costs in exercising the option, this can be built into the model.

Summary

The binomial model has a number of advantages over the Black Scholes model discussed below. It can allow for early exercise, and also allows for different interest rates and volatility levels in each period. A major disadvantage is the formula's reliance on repetitive numerical calculations, rather than just a single formula.

As the number of periods increases, the answers derived from the binomial model get close to the Black Scholes model which uses the properties of a normal distribution to calculate the fair values of options.

17 Black Scholes

The Model

As we increase the number of stages in the binomial expansion it tends towards the normal distribution. Similarly as we increase n by taking smaller and smaller time intervals, the Cox-Ross-Rubenstein model tends to converge to the Black Scholes model.

The Black Scholes model and its variants is highly popular as in one formula we are able to replicate the results of the binomial model but at a fraction of the effort.

To the non-mathematician however, the Black Scholes formula appears exceedingly complex; certainly a proof of it would be! For our purposes, however, all we need to be able to do is apply it. Such an application need not be unthinking and indeed within the model we will see many of the things we have already considered albeit at a more intuitive level.

The most basic Black Scholes model relates to European options on non-dividend paying stocks and can be expressed as follows

$$C = SN(d_1) - Xe^{-rt}N(d_2)$$

Where

- $d_1 = \dfrac{\ln(\frac{S}{X}) + (r + 0.5\sigma^2)t}{\sigma\sqrt{t}}$
- $d_2 = \dfrac{\ln(\frac{S}{X}) + (r - 0.5\sigma^2)t}{\sigma\sqrt{t}}$ or $d_2 = d_1 - \sigma\sqrt{t}$
- S = underlying share price
- X = exercise price
- r = continuously compounded risk-free rate expressed on an annual basis
- t = time to expiry in years
- σ = risk of the underlying stock, measured as the annual volatility
- N(d) = cumulative probabilities that deviations less than d will occur in a normal distribution with a mean of 0 and a standard deviation of 1

Alternatively, d_1 and d_2 can be written as follows:

- $$d_1 = \frac{1n(\frac{S}{X}) + rt}{\sigma\sqrt{t}} + 0.5\sigma\sqrt{t}$$

- $$d_2 = \frac{1n(\frac{S}{X}) + rt}{\sigma\sqrt{t}} - 0.5\sigma\sqrt{t} \text{ or } d_2 = d_1 - \sigma\sqrt{t}$$

Into this formula we enter details on underlying price, strike price, interest rate, time to expiry and volatility, and out comes a fair or theoretical value.

Whilst many of these symbols are ones we have already come across, some require a little explanation.

In (s/x): This is the natural logarithm of the ratio of the stock price to the strike price. The logarithm is used to create a lognormal distribution of prices; a distribution deemed more reasonable than a normal distribution as it prevents negative values and biases the prices to the upside. The 'ln' function is found on most calculators.

N (d): This is the cumulative normal distribution function. From this function we calculate the probability that the call will be in the money at expiry. The application of this function is very similar to our use of normal distribution tables in our earlier discussion of probabilities.

We can see that one of the inputs we require is a figure for the annualised volatility (σ). How do we obtain this figure? The first thing to notice is that what we will need to know is future volatility. We should be pricing options based on the volatility that is expected over the future life of the option. How do we determine this? A good starting point for predicting future volatility is to consider past, or historic, volatility. If we are pricing a two monthly option we need to consider what volatility will be over the next two months.

What period revival should be used? There is no single correct answer to this question. The volatility of the most recent two months might well be different from a two-month period three or six months ago. What the investor must do is to allot a period from the past that they believe best reflects the future conditions they are expecting. Having selected an appropriate period in the past, it is then necessary to decide whether to calculate volatility based on daily, weekly or even monthly price change observations. In practice, investing usually uses daily prime data to calculate volatility. This is then converted into annual volatility and that figure input into the pricing model.

Example

A call option with an exercise price of 40p expires in three months. The current price and risk of the underlying share are 36p and 50% respectively. The annual continuously compounded risk-free rate is 5%. What is the fair price of the call option?

Solution

$$d_1 = \frac{\ln(\frac{S}{X}) + (r + 0.5\sigma^2)t}{\sigma\sqrt{t}}$$

$$d_1 = \frac{\ln(\frac{36}{40}) + (0.05 + 0.5(0.50)^2)\,0.25}{0.50\sqrt{0.25}}$$

$$d_1 = \frac{-0.10536 + (0.175)\,0.25}{0.25}$$

$$d_1 = \frac{-0.10536 + 0.04375}{0.25}$$

$$d_1 = \frac{-0.06161}{0.25}$$

$d_1 = -0.246$ (round to -0.25)

Hence

$d_2 = -0.246 - 0.5\sqrt{0.25}$

$d_2 = -0.496$ (round to -0.50)

We now need to look up these values for d_1 and d_2 in a **cumulative** normal distribution table. The mean in this distribution is zero, therefore, a negative value (eg –0.25) simply implies the value is to the left of the mean; a positive value implies it is to the right of the mean.

An extract from a cumulative normal distribution table is shown below.

X	N(x)	X	N(x)
0.0	0.5000	0.5	0.6915
0.1	0.5398	0.6	0.7257
0.2	0.5793	0.7	0.7580
0.3	0.6179	0.8	0.7881
0.4	0.6554	0.9	0.8159

The values given in the N(x) column represent the area to the left of the x value and hence the probability of it occurring.

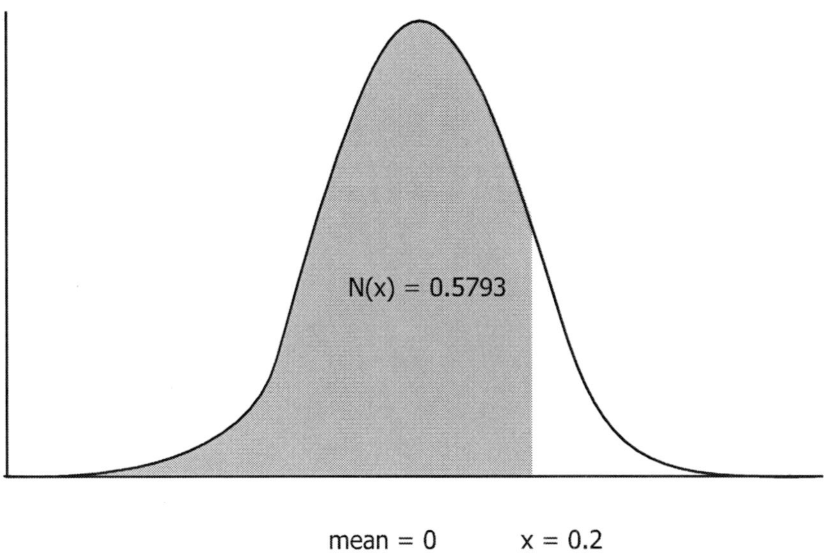

Note that negative values for x are not given in the table. This poses no problem. As the distribution is symmetrical about the mean a negative value can be interpreted as 1 – N (x). If we had an x value of –0.2, the probability of that event occurring is 1 – 0.5793 re 0.4207

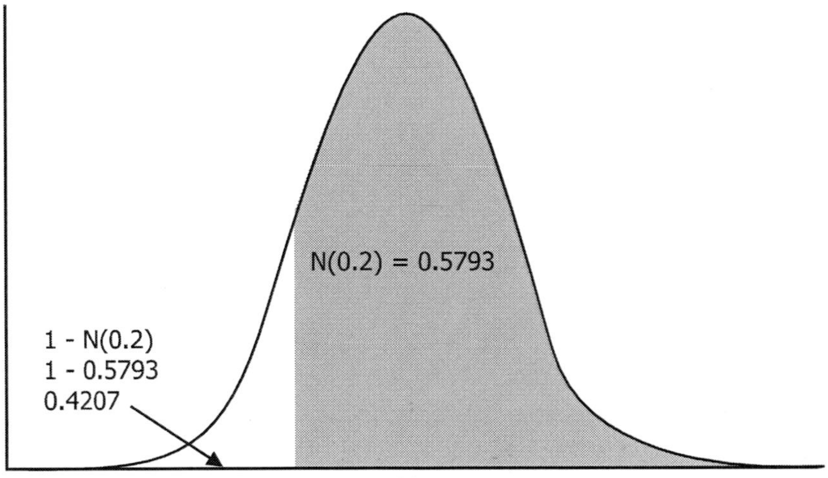

Using the limited data that the table provides it will be necessary to interpolate between two values. It is easiest to do this in a linear fashion.

$d_1 = -0.25$

$N(d_1) = N(-0.25)$

$= 1 - N(0.25)$

$= 1 - 0.5986$

$= 0.4014$

$d_2 = -0.50$

$N(d_2) = N(-0.50)$

$= 1 - N(0.50)$

$= 1 - 0.6915$

$= 0.3085$

Hence

$$C = SN(d_1) - \frac{X}{e^{rt}} N(d_2)$$

gives

$$C = 36 \times 0.4014 - \frac{40}{e^{0.05 \times 0.25}} \times 0.3085$$

C = 2.26p

The above example calculated $N(d_1)$ and $N(d_2)$ from a **cumulative** probability table. As stated before, a cumulative probability table gives the area to the left of the x value which is what $N(d_1)$ and $N(d_2)$ represent.

It is possible that the values for $N(d_1)$ and $N(d_2)$ will have to be calculated from a standard (ie non-cumulative) normal distribution table.

Using probability tables to calculate $N(d_1)$ and $N(d_2)$ for the above example we get the following:

$d_1 = -0.25$

$d_2 = -0.50$

Looking these up in the table and remembering that negative numbers are to the left of the area we get

$N(d_1) = 0.40129$

$N(d_2) = 0.30854$

These are the same as before.

It is further possible that the distribution table might give the area under the curve **between** the mean and the x value – an extract of this type of table is shown below.

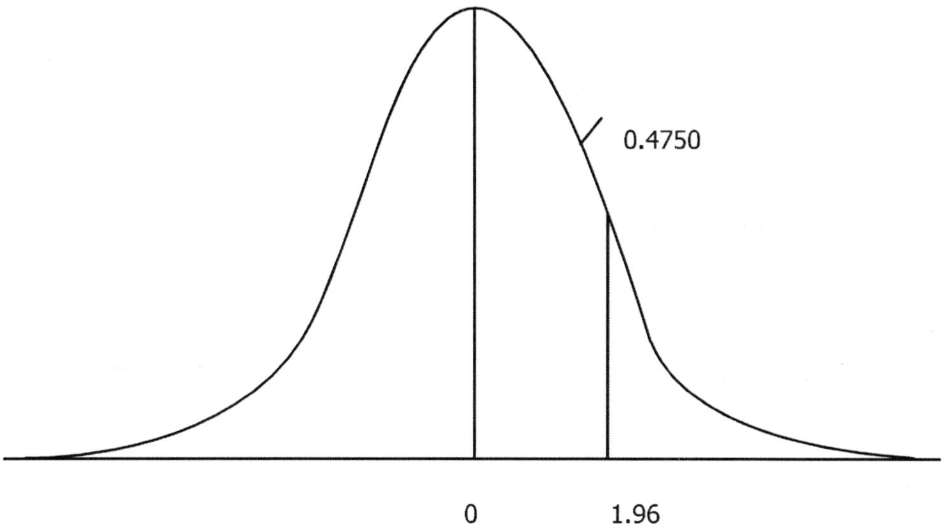

EXAMPLE

Pr $(0 \leq x \leq 1.96) = 0.4750$
Pr $(x \geq 1.96) = 0.5 - 0.4750 = 0.025$

x	.00	.01	.02	.03	.04	.05	.06	.07	.08	.09
0.0	.0000	.0040	.0080	.0120	.0160	.0199	.0239	.0279	.0319	.0359
0.1	.0398	.0438	.0478	.0517	.0557	.0596	.0636	.0675	.0714	.0753
0.2	.0793	.0832	.0871	.0910	.0948	.0987	.1026	.1064	.1103	.1141
0.3	.1179	.1217	.1255	.1293	.1331	.1368	.1406	.1443	.1480	.1517
0.4	.1554	.1591	.1628	.1664	.1700	.1736	.1772	.1808	.1844	.1879
0.5	.1915	.1950	.1985	.2019	.2054	.2088	.2123	.2157	.2190	.2224

Using this table

$d_1 = -0.25$, value from table = 0.0987
$d_2 = -0.50$, value from table = 0.1915

As the above values for d_1 and d_2 are negative and we want the area under the curve to the left of these values

$N(d_1) = 0.5 - 0.0987 = 0.4013$
$N(d_2) = 0.5 - 0.1915 = 0.3085$

Again, these are the same values as before.

If we plot the call values derived from this model against the value of the underlying share we get the following, which we can see is very similar to the binomial situation above.

Diagrammatically

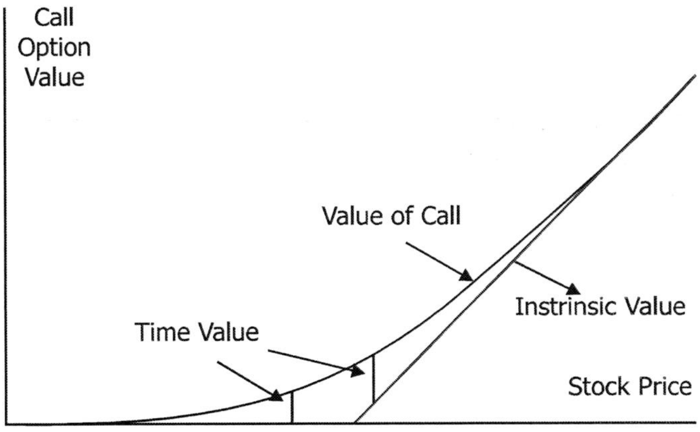

To consolidate our understanding of the model, let us try another example.

Calculate the value of a European style call with a strike of 95 given the following information.

- S = 92
- X = 95
- t = 50 days (0.137 of a year)
- r = 7.12%
- σ = 35%

SOLUTION

$$d_1 = \frac{\ln\left(\frac{S}{X}\right) + (r + 0.5\sigma^2)}{\sigma\sqrt{t}}$$

$$d_1 = \frac{\ln\left(\frac{92}{95}\right) + \left(0.0712 + 0.5(0.35)^2\right) \times 0.137}{0.35\sqrt{0.137}}$$

$$d_1 = \frac{-0.0321 + 0.0181456}{0.129}$$

$$d_1 = \frac{-0.0139544}{0.129}$$

$d_1 = -0.1082$

$d_2 = d_1 - \sigma\sqrt{t}$

$d_2 = -0.1082 - 0.129$

$d_2 = -0.2372$

By interpolation from the tables

$N(d_1) = 0.4570$

$N(d_2) = 0.4063$

$$C = 92 \times 0.4570 - \frac{95}{1.0098} \times 0.4063$$

$C = 42.04 - 38.22$

$C = 3.82$

The Valuation of a Put Option

The examples so far have been to calculate the value of a call. It is possible to rearrange the basic Black Scholes formula to allow for the valuation of a put.

$P = Xe^{-rt} N(-d_2) - SN(-d_1)$

EXAMPLE

A put option with an exercise price of 50p expires in three months. The current price of the underlying share is 48p and annual volatility is 20%. The risk-free rate is 5%. What is the fair price of the put option?

$$d_1 = \frac{\ln\left(\frac{S}{X}\right) + (r + 0.5\sigma^2)}{\sigma\sqrt{t}}$$

$$d_1 = \frac{\ln\left(\frac{48}{50}\right) + (0.05 + 0.5 \times 0.2^2) \times 0.2}{0.2\sqrt{0.25}}$$

$$d_1 = \frac{-0.040822 + 0.0175}{0.1}$$

$d_1 = -0.23322$

$d_2 = -0.23322 - 0.1$

$d_2 = -0.33322$

$N(-d_1) \quad = N(0.23322)$

$\quad = 0.5921$

$N(-d_2) \quad = N(0.33322)$

$\quad = 0.6304$

$P = -48 \times 0.5921 + 50 \times e^{-0.05 \times 0.25} \times 0.6304$

$P = 2.71\text{p}$

Applying the Black Scholes Pricing Model to Real Options

Firstly, let us specify the inputs required to value an option using the Black Scholes pricing model and their equivalents in the context of a real option

Input		Estimation Process
1.	Current value of the underlying asset	Present value of **inflows** from exercising the option to undertake the project now.
2.	Exercise price of the option	Cost of making the necessary investment to undertake the project.
3.	Variance in the value of the underlying asset	Variance in the value of cash inflows from the project under various scenarios.
4.	Risk free rate	Estimated from government bond yields.
5.	Life of option	The period of time over which the company has the option to invest or not.

Note that these are the same input requirements as we had for the multi period binomial model. More detail on how to ascertain the input values has therefore already been discussed.

Problems with Black Scholes

The Black Scholes option pricing model is based on a number of restrictive assumptions:

1. The underlying asset does not pay dividends or accrue interest payments.
2. The option being valued is European style.
3. The risk free interest rate is constant over the life of the option.
4. Volatility is constant over the life of the option.
5. The underlying asset price is log normally distributed.
6. Perfect markets with continuous trading and no costs/taxes.
7. Short selling of securities with no restrictions is permitted.

Assumption 1

This can be overcome by reducing the stock price by the present value of the dividends. More broadly, the original model designed for stock options has been modified to deal with options on futures (Black model) and other variants.

In a real options context the current present value of inflows from the project can be reduced by the present value of the cash flows lost by deferring the decision over the option life

Assumption 2

Whilst generally this assumption is not restrictive as early exercise is not normally optimal, where early exercise may be rational other models may be more appropriate.

Early exercise of real options therefore presents a problem with respect to use of the Black Scholes pricing model. Where the possibility of early exercise is significant, the multi period binomial will allow for more reasonable modelling.

Assumption 3

To assume interest rates are constant it is an obvious weakness which has two consequences, first on the premiums and secondly on certain underlying assets such as currencies and bonds.

With respect to premiums, a rise in interest rates will have various effects dependent on the option being examined.

Aside from the influence that changes in interest rates has on premiums it will also have an effect on most underlying assets. This however, is a risk associated with trying to evaluate the underlying asset, rather than an option on that contract.

These same problems also impact upon use of the Black Scholes pricing model for real options. The value of the future cash flows from the project (ie the underlying with respect to the real option) will vary as the discount rate applied to the cash flows varies. The most common methodology to derive a discount rate is the CAPM which uses a risk free interest rate as an input.

Assumption 4

Perhaps a necessary simplification, but not one borne out in reality. Most assets will have periods of movement, followed by periods of inactivity during an option's life. As an option's sensitivity to volatility changes varies over time (long dated options are most sensitive) a period of high volatility in the first part of its life would have an effect on its value, whilst a change in volatility late in its life may not. By assuming constant volatility options may, for a given period, be either over or undervalued.

Once again, this problem carries over into real options application. It should be noted that the multi period binomial can deal with different volatility estimates over the life of the option.

Assumption 5

There may be assets such as bonds which do not 'fit' the log normal distribution. This is for two reasons, firstly, in the real world interest rates tend to a long term average. For example, if bond yields in the UK were 25% the most logical next move in yields would normally be for them to go lower. Conversely if bond yields were 1% one might reasonably suggest that the next move would be upwards. This attribute of interest rate products is known as mean reversion. The other bond specific problem that arises from using a log normal distribution is that it takes no account of the pull to par as redemption gets nearer.

The assumption of log normality does not truly fit the behaviour of the potential returns from investment in a project. Whilst the set-up costs of a venture are considered to be the exercise price of the option, the operational cash flows from investment in a project can become negative.

Assumption 6

Perfect or efficient markets are a device used in many elegant theories, but do not fully exist in practice. Implicit in this idea is a belief that markets move randomly, that trading is continuous and that there are no 'jumps' in an asset's price. Events in the UK and global stock markets since 2008 prove such things do happen. The problem that jumps cause to the model is that the Black Scholes model assumes that one is able to constantly readjust a position to maintain delta neutrality (broadly, this equates to having a hedged position. The Black Scholes pricing model is based on the possibility of being able to dynamically hedge a position using derivatives) this may be impossible in practice.

In the context of real options assumptions of continuous pricing and perfect capital markets are clearly even less acceptable. However, there is little that can be done to adapt the model in these respects since the ability to dynamically hedge a position is the very basis of the Black Scholes pricing model.

Assumption 7

Short selling is not available to all participants. In the UK, the ability to go short is limited in stock markets to registered market makers.

Clearly, it will not be possible to short sell a real options project. Once again, however, this assumption cannot be relaxed without dispensing of the entire model.

Overcoming the Restrictions

European Style Calls on Income Yielding Assets

The Black Scholes model can be adjusted to take account of dividends by reducing the stock price throughout the formula by the present value of the dividends paid before expiry. The discounting should be from the anticipated payment date and not the ex dividend date. This variation is sometimes described as the Known Dividend Model. It does not allow for early exercise.

The rationale behind this is that the share's expected value at expiry (after the ex-date) will be lower to the extent of dividends whose ex-date is already past.

As already noted, an equivalent adaptation is possible with respect to real options where there is an effective cost of delay. The present value of cash flows foregone or lost over the option life can be deducted from the present value of the cash flows from going ahead with the project today (which is the equivalent of the current stock price).

American Style Calls on Dividend Paying Stocks

These can be evaluated using Black's approximation. This is indeed an approximation and should be seen as a relatively crude method. American style calls on dividend paying stocks should rationally be exercised just prior to the ex-dividend date if the present value of the dividends is greater than the time value which would be lost.

In this method two calculations are done; the price of a European style call that expires on the expiry date is calculated as well as the price of a European style call that expires just before the stock goes ex dividend (in this case no adjustment for dividends is made). The higher of these two values is the price of the American call. This is sometimes known as the Pseudo-American Model.

This style of adjustment will be difficult in a real options application. It is unlikely that cash flows from a project would be as lumpy as dividends and therefore this crude adjustment is unlikely to be reasonable.

European Style Call on a Stock Index

The normal method for dealing with the dividend flows on an index is to subtract the dividend yield from the continuously compounded risk free rate. This is analogous to the procedure involved in pricing a stock index future.

The formula therefore becomes

$$C = Se^{-dt}N(d_1) - x\,e^{-rt}N(d_2)$$

$$d_1 = \frac{\ln\left(\frac{S}{X}\right) + (r - d + 0.5(\sigma)^2)t}{\sigma\sqrt{t}}$$

$$d_2 = d_1 - \sigma\sqrt{t}$$

Where d = expected annual dividend yield expressed as a decimal

This approach is much more likely to be appropriate for dealing with real options where there is likely to be an implicit cost with regard to deferring a decision. The calculation of the relevant cost associated with delaying the decision is discussed in detail within the adjusted multi period binomial for income yielding assets

Other Models

So far in this text mention has been made of the following models.

(i) Binomial model or Cox-Ross-Rubenstein model.

(ii) Black Scholes model - basic model for non-dividend paying stock.

(iii) Known dividend model - extension of basic Black Scholes to allow for a known dividend paid on a discrete date before expiry. The possibility of early exercise is ignored.

(iv) European style income yielding asset adaptations of the Black Scholes model.

In addition, there exist other models which attempt to overcome some of the assumptions previously mentioned or evaluate more exotic options

Implied Volatility

Implied volatilities are calculated by using a pricing model, but instead of using it normally to compute a theoretical premium based on the inputs discussed above, the formula is used to find volatility. When used in this form, users input time to expiry, exercise price, underlying price, interest rates and the actual market price of the option. The formula then determines the unknown; namely volatility. In this way users can find out what the market's perception is of future volatility; this may at times be better than relying on historic volatilities which may not fully incorporate the impact of information recently released to the market.

One would assume that in an efficient market, the implied volatilities of all options on the same asset would be the same. However, empirically this is not the case. In some cases the implied volatilities of either deeply in or deeply out-of-the-money options show much higher implied volatilities than at-the-money options.

This phenomenon, known as skew, springs from a suggested defect in the Black Scholes model; namely its assumption of log normally distributed price changes. Whilst this model of distributions is reasonably accurate, the market place, from their own experience, seem to recognise that the chance of either a big up or big down move is more likely than the normal distribution would suggest.

The phenomenon gives rise to something often referred to as the volatility smile. It has been stated that the market puts a higher value on deep in and deep out-of-the-money options than the Black Scholes model would suggest.

When calculating the implied volatility from the market prices Black Scholes will, therefore, produce lower figures for the at-the-money options and higher implied volatilities for in and out-of-the-money options. Graphically this can be shown as

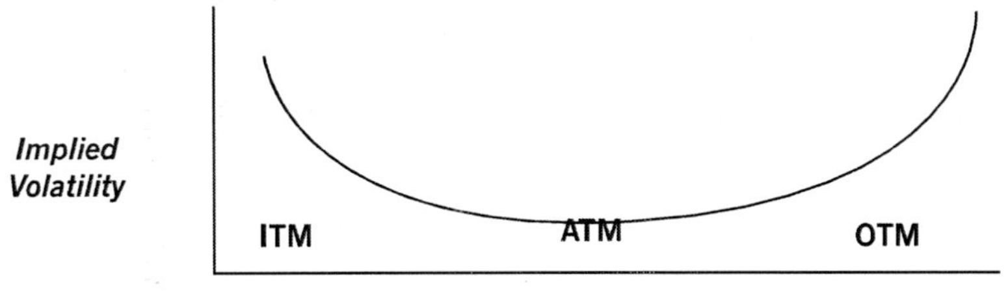

The propensity of implied volatility distributions to show higher volatilities for deeply in or out-of-the-money options is known as 'Kurtosis' or more colloquially as 'fat tails'. The distribution would look like

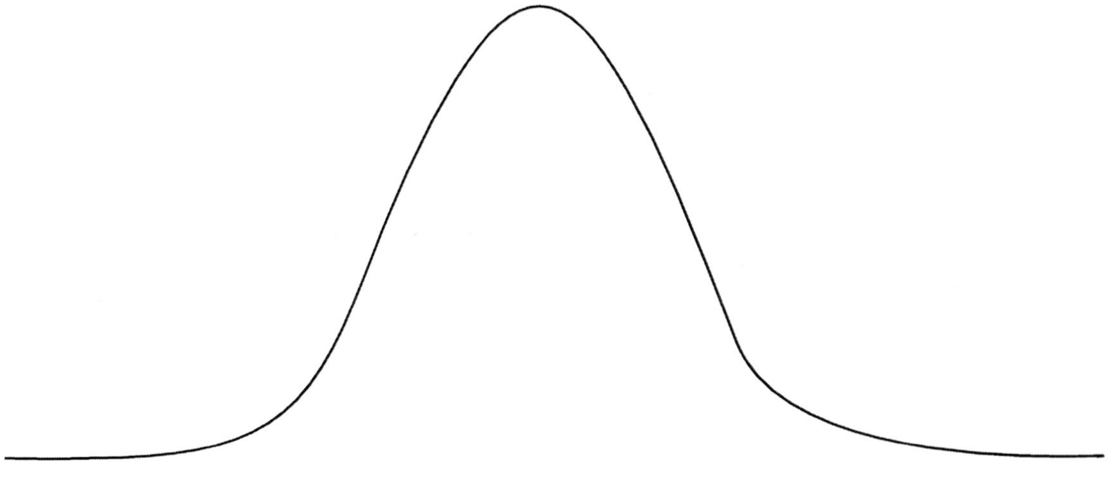

Two further evaluative tools shall be examined in this chapter:

- Evaluating equity as an option
- Tobin's Q ratio

The first of these requires complex inputs and makes several assumptions. Its use is, therefore, limited and only the basic principles of this approach will be examined.

Evaluating Equity as a Call Option

Introduction – Call Options

As already discussed, a call option is an instrument which confers the right to acquire an asset at an agreed fixed price (the 'strike price' or X) up to a specified expiry date. For example, consider the right to buy a share at 100 pence which costs 15 pence to buy. At the expiry date, the value of the option is determined by the value of the underlying share as follows:

- If the underlying share price is below 100 pence then an option conferring the right to buy the share at 100 pence (ie paying more than the market price) confers no benefit at all. The option holder will have lost their initial investment.
- If the underlying share price is above 100 pence then the option confers a benefit - namely the right to buy the share for less than its market price. The level of benefit to be derived depends upon the difference between the underlying share price (S) and the strike price (X). The table below summarises the potential benefits the option may confer and the overall profit or loss that results once the cost of the option (15 pence) has been deducted.

Share Price (S)	Strike Price (X)	Benefit (S-X)	Profit/(loss)
100	100	0	(15)
105	100	5	(10)
110	100	10	(5)
115	100	15	0
120	100	20	5
125	100	25	10

The profile of potential profits and losses from purchasing the option can be represented graphically as shown below.

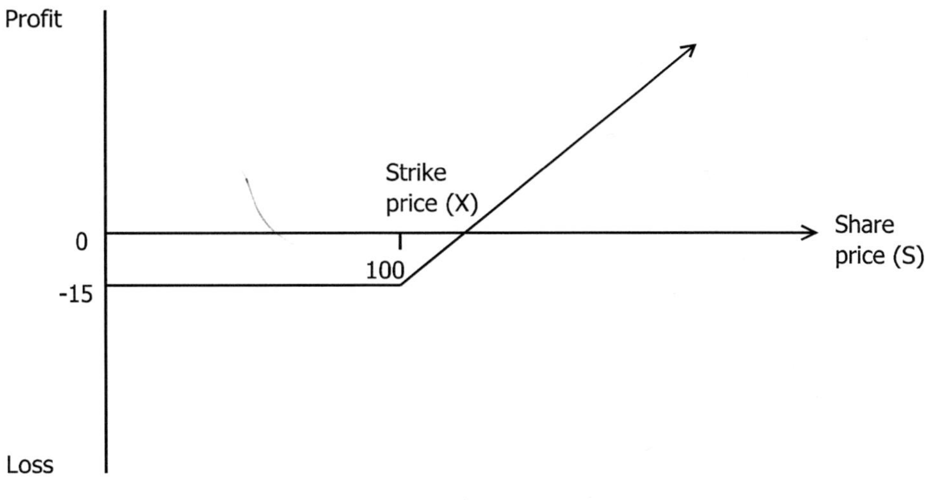

Viewing Equity as a Call Option

If we now consider buying all the shares in a company at a cost £15 million, where the company has £100m nominal 10 year zero coupon debt in issue, similar pay-offs can be observed at expiry of the debt in 10 years' time (which is analogous to the option expiry).

- If the total value of the firm (debt and equity) is less than £100m, then the firm will be unable to meet the debt repayment. However, due to the concept of limited liability the shareholders will simply lose their initial investment of £15 million, but would not be required to meet the shortfall on debt.

- If the total value of the firm exceeds £100m then the equity will have some value, since once the debt is repaid any balance belongs to equity holders. Once again, the value of equity on 'expiry' depends on the difference between the total value of the firm and the debt outstanding of £100m. The pay-offs can again be tabulated, after deduction of the £15 million cost of the shares.

Total value of firm (S)	Face value of debt (X)	Benefit (S-X)	Profit/(loss)
100	100	0	(15)
105	100	5	(10)
110	100	10	(5)
115	100	15	0
120	100	20	5
125	100	25	10

Once again, a graphical representation would look as shown below.

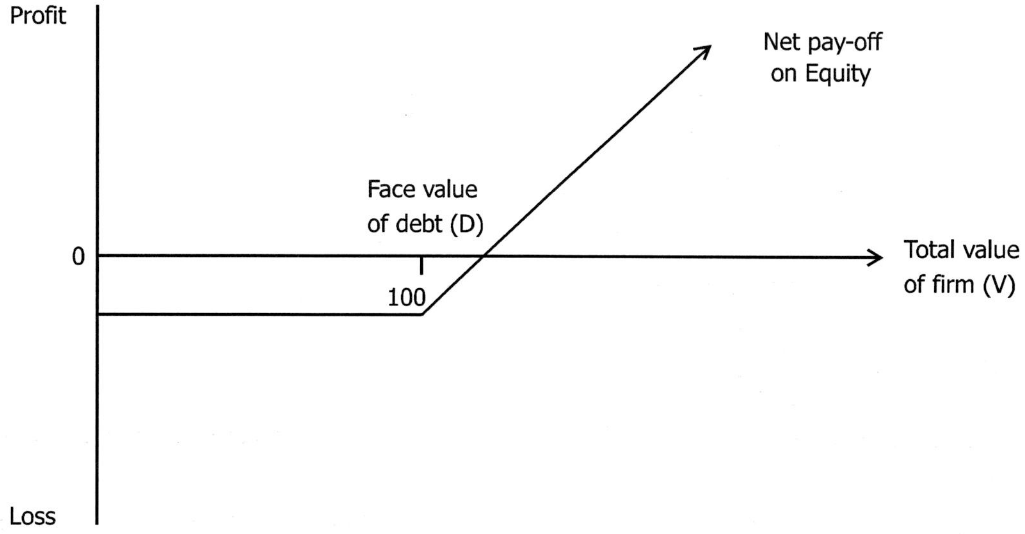

Applying Options Valuation Model

Having established the equivalence between a call option and the equity in a firm, it should then be possible to apply options pricing techniques to value the equity in a firm.

In applying the analogy of option pricing to equity pricing, the equivalent required inputs of the Black Scholes Pricing Model are:

Share price	=	Enterprise value
Strike Price	=	Redemption value of debt
Share price volatility	=	Enterprise value volatility
Time to expiry	=	Time to debt redemption
Risk free rate	=	Risk free rate

Black Scholes Pricing Model

$$= S\,N(d_1) - Xe^{-rt}\,N(d_2)$$

Put simply, the model values the call option as the expected difference between the share price at expiry and the strike price. The model, then, can be applied to value the equity of a company as the difference between the total expected market value of the firm at the debt redemption point and the value of the debt.

For a simple company scenario the Black Scholes model can then be applied to inputs relating to a company to arrive at a value of equity.

Illustration

- A firm is currently valued at £100 million (debt plus equity).
- The firm has £80m nominal of 10 year zero coupon debt (maturing in 10 years' time).
- The model also requires inputs for the risk free rate (10% has been assumed) and variability of the total market value (50% has been assumed).

Inputting this information into the Black Scholes model produces the following values:

$N(d_1) = 0.9411$

$N(d_2) = 0.4932$

Hence

$SN(d_1) - Xe^{-rt}(N(d_2)$

$= (100 \times 0.9411) - (80\ e^{-0.1 \times 10} \times 0.4932)$

$= 94.11 - 14.51$

= £79.6 million equity value

Advocates of the model suggest other information can also be derived, namely

Value of debt = £100m total value – £79.6m equity value = **£20.4m**

Interest rate on debt = $\sqrt[10]{\frac{80}{£20.4}} - 1 =$ **14.64%**

Whilst the model may be limited in its application, there are number of important points brought out by the model.

- Higher levels of risk/variability will actually result in higher apportionments of value to equity rather than debt as shown in the table below.

	25% variability	**50% variability**
Equity Value	£71.64m	£79.6m
Debt Value	£28.36m	£20.4m
Total Value	£100.00m	£100.00m

- Equity has value even if the total market value of the firm falls well below the face value of debt. The values in the table below are derived assuming total market values well below the £80m level, and indeed even below the values of debt indicated above (note that 50% variability is assumed).

	V = £50m	**V = £20m**
Equity Value	£32.55m	£4.31m
Debt Value	£17.45m	£15.69m
Total Value	£50.00m	£20.00m

- Conglomerate mergers which reduce the variability of the asset values by diversification may actually cause a transfer of wealth from shareholders to bond holders. The table below shows how the split of value between debt and equity holders would alter if two companies with profiles outlined in the earlier illustration were to merge (it is assumed no synergies arise. It has been assumed that the correlation coefficient of the cash flows of the two firms is 0.3.)

	Value A	Value B	Derived A + B	Value transfer
Equity Value	£79.6m	£79.6m	£151.9m	–£7.3m
Debt Value	£20.4m	£20.4m	£48.1m	+£7.3m
Total Value	£100.0m	£100.0m	£200.0m	£0.0m

Problems with an Options Based Approach

The options based valuation approach applied some simplifying assumptions, namely:

- There are only two claim holders – debt and equity.
- Debt had a known maturity and could be retired at face value.
- Debt had a zero coupon and no special features.
- The total value of the firm and the standard deviation in the value can be estimated.

The chief problem lies in the final assumption. The options based approach only-sub-analyses an enterprise value into its components. It does not provide an objective valuation alone. The model, therefore, relies on some other means to ascertain a valuation in the first place (be it a market value, a value derived from discounting free cash flow or some other method).

The simplifying assumptions with regard to debt maturity are also problematic. Where companies have coupon bearing debt with a variety of maturities, advocates of the model suggest it is possible to use the weighted average duration of the debt as the proxy for option expiry. This does not, however, accord in any meaningful way to the manner in which an option strike price is actually paid.

Conclusions

The proposed model for evaluating the equity of a company as a whole using option pricing suffers from a number of serious problems. The analogy itself becomes extremely strained in any realistic scenario and too many of the assumptions of the Black Scholes Pricing Model are breached. In such circumstances it becomes very questionable that the numerical results achieved can be of any reliability.

Furthermore, some of the conclusions of the model (namely that if the enterprise value becomes more volatile, the equity value will increase) are either in direct opposition to standard valuation paradigms, (namely that higher risk will lead to investors ascribing a lower value to the entity) or appear to make no intuitive sense (such as the idea that a company with longer dated debt will be more valuable than an equivalent company with shorter dated debt).

Financial distress scenarios

Why does an option pricing model appear to be inappropriate tool for valuing equities and why does it yields such unreasonable conclusions? One likely reason is that the analogy between the majority of equities and options may be fundamentally misguided. Whilst the significant risk of losing all money invested is a standard feature of option investment, it is not a usual feature of equity investment. Option pricing models naturally place substantial importance on the capped losses associated with option investment, but limited shareholder liability is not normally a key consideration when valuing equities.

In circumstances of significant financial distress, however, the concept of limited shareholder liability becomes relevant. When evaluating a company which is suffering distress, the implications of using option pricing models cease to be in opposition to standard thinking with respect to valuation.

The application of the model to equities results in the implication that longer dated debt renders a company more valuable. This implication appears entirely intuitive. If a company were to find itself unable to repay its outstanding debt facility at a proximate due date, but later was able to announced that it had negociated to defer repayment until a later date, one would expect the share price to rally in response.

Equally, where a company is the victim of significant financial distress and where the share price has collapsed, shareholders would be likely to view a risky rescue package favourably. A package which would produce dramatic financial improvement but which carried a risk of substantial losses which left the company unable to repay its debtholders would offer high potential returns for shareholders whilst transferring much of the risk of failure to the debtholders. The conclusion that higher volatility would benefit the equity value can thus also be seen to have some resonance with conventional thinking with respect to equity evaluation.

Tobin's Q Ratio

Introduction

One of the earliest value added measures is based on the Nobel Prize winning work of the economist James Tobin. Tobin's Q is often used as a measure of the real value created by a firm's management. The ratio expresses the relationship between the market value of a firm's assets and the replacement cost of those assets.

$$\text{Q Ratio} = \frac{\text{Market Value of Assets}}{\text{Replacement Cost of Assets}}$$

Calculation of the Q Ratio

Calculation of the market value and replacement cost of assets may be difficult in practice.

$$\text{Q ratio proxy} = \frac{\text{Book Value of Debt} + \text{Book Value of Non - Equity} + \text{Market Value of Equity}}{\text{Total Assets}}$$

The problem of the above ratio is that it deviates significantly from the conceptual framework of Tobin's Q and somewhat resembles a price to book or EV to capital employed ratio.

Using the Q Ratio

The Q ratio shows how particular firms have been able to add value based on the investment in assets expressed in current price units.

Q ratios above unity show that the market values the firm at a premium due to factors such as goodwill, quality of management and future investment opportunities. The reverse is obviously the case where the firm is at a discount to replacement cost of assets.

Tobin suggested that where a Q ratio is above one further investment of the same sort (ie where the **marginal** Q ratio is also above one) should be undertaken. However, due to competition, the Q ratio would tend towards unity. A Q ratio greater than one suggest an opportunity for others to replicate the observed value added - investment in similar assets (at replacement costs) could result in market values exceeding the original investment.

Ranking firms according to their Q ratios should provide a ranking based upon their future cash flow generation relative to the value of assets being used to generate those cash flows. Moreover, looking at changes in the Q ratio over time will indicate how the firm's investment opportunities are changing. As always, however, the problem lies in establishing whether the market is under or over-estimating the investment opportunities and future returns a firm is able to generate. Empirical research on book value/market value ratios shows that as Tobin proposed, there is a tendency towards unity. Moreover, the relationship of book value/market value is related to security returns. High book value/market value (therefore, low Tobin's Q) are associated with high returns and vice versa (Rosenberg, Reid and Lanstein; Fama and French).

Haugen proposed that the market consistently overestimates the persistence of above average returns, hence explaining why low book value/market value (high Tobin's Q) can be observed to underperform high book value/market value (low Tobin's Q) firms.

Conclusions

Tobin's Q ratio provides information on how the market values the future opportunities of a firm as compared to the investment in assets made to date. It measures value added by a firm to date but does not alone indicate if the company can continue to add value in the future.

Empirical research would indicate that the market tends to overestimate the ability of companies to sustain high returns, and hence high Tobin's Q ratios may indicate overvaluation, and low Tobin's Q ratios may indicate undervaluation.

Reconstructions

chapter 19

Contents

1 INTRODUCTION

Reconstruction schemes are undertaken when companies have got into difficulties or as part of a strategy to enhance the value of the firm for its owners.

Not all businesses are profitable. Some incur losses in one or more years, but eventually achieve profitability. Others remain unprofitable, or earn only very small and unsatisfactory profits. Other companies are profitable, but run out of cash. A company which runs out of cash, even if it is profitable, might be forced into liquidation by unpaid creditors, who want payment and think that applying to the court to wind up the company is the best way of getting some or all of their money. In such a situation, the company might be able to attract fresh capital and to persuade its creditors to accept some securities in the company as 'payment', and achieve a capital reconstruction which allows the company to carry on in business.

Reconstruction schemes may also be undertaken by companies which are not in difficulties but as part of a strategy to create value for the owners of the company.

2 TYPES OF RECONSTRUCTION

Depending on the actions that a company needs to take as part of its reconstruction plans, these schemes are usually classified in three categories:

(a) Financial reconstruction which involves changing the capital structure of the firm

(b) Portfolio reconstruction, which involves making additions to or disposals from companies' businesses, for example through acquisitions or spin-offs

(c) Organisational restructuring

Financial Reconstructions

A financial reconstruction scheme is a scheme whereby a company reorganises its capital structure, including leveraged buyouts, leveraged recapitalisations and debt for equity swaps.

Leveraged Recapitalisations

In a leveraged recapitalisation a firm replaces the majority of its equity with a package of debt securities, consisting of both senior and subordinated debt. Leveraged capitalisations are employed by firms as defence mechanisms to protect them from takeovers. In the UK companies subject to the takeover code would not be able to undertake a leveraged recapitalisation in an offer period without shareholder permission. Such action would be deemed to be frustrating action and thus against the spirit of the Code. Internationally, leveraged recapitalisations are common. The high level of debt in the company discourages corporate raiders who will not be able to borrow against the assets of the target firm in order to finance the acquisition. In order to avoid the possible financial distress arising from the high level of debt, companies that engage in leveraged recapitalisation should be relatively debt free, they should have stable cash flows and they should not require substantial ongoing capital expenditure in order to retain their competitive position.

Debt-Equity Swaps

A second way of changing its capital is to issue a debt/equity or an equity/debt swap. In the case of an equity/debt swap, all specified shareholders are given the right to exchange their stock for a pre-determined amount of debt (ie bonds) in the same company. A debt/equity swap works the opposite way: debt is exchanged for a predetermined amount of equity (or stock). The value of the swap is determined usually at current market rates, but management may offer higher exchange values to entice share and debt holders to participate in the swap. After the swap takes place, the preceding asset class is cancelled for the newly acquired asset class.

One possible reason that the company may engage in debt-equity swaps is because the company must meet certain contractual obligations, such as a maintaining a debt/equity ratio below a certain number. Also a company may issue equity to avoid making coupon and face value payments because they feel they will be unable to do so in the future. The contractual obligations mentioned can be a result of financing requirements imposed by a bank, or may be self-imposed by the company, as detailed in the company's prospectus. A company may self-impose certain valuation requirements to entice investors to purchase its stock. Debt/equity swaps may also be carried out to rebalance a firm's WACC.

Leveraged Buy-outs

A leveraged buy-out is a transaction in which a group of private investors uses debt financing to purchase a company or part of a company. In a leveraged buy-out, like a leveraged capitalisation, the company increases its level of leverage, but unlike the case of leveraged capitalisations, the company does not have access to equity markets any more.

Financial Reconstruction and Firm Value

The impact of a financial reconstruction scheme on the value of the firm can be assessed in terms of its impact on the growth rate of the company, its risk, and its required rate of return.

The growth rate following a financial restructuring can be calculated from the formula

$$g = b\left(ROA + \frac{V_D}{V_E}\left(ROA - r(1-T)\right)\right)$$

Where ROA is the return on the net assets of the company

b = the retention rate

V_D = the book value of debt

V_E = the book value of equity

r = the cost of debt

T = the corporate tax rate

Changes in the level of debt will be reflected in the growth rate through its impact on the debt ratio D/E. Similarly, changes in dividend policy can be reflected in the earnings growth rate. Changes in the dividend policy will change the value of b. Decreasing dividends (a higher b) will increase the growth rate, and increasing dividends will decrease the growth rate.

EXAMPLE

A firm currently has a debt-equity ratio of 0.12 and a return on assets (ROA) equal to 15 percent. The optimal debt ratio is however much lower than the optimal level, since it can raise the debt-equity ratio up to 0.30 without increasing the risk of bankruptcy. The firm plans to borrow and repurchase stock to get to this optimal ratio. The interest rate is expected to increase from 7 percent to 8 percent. The tax rate is 25 percent and the retention rate is 50 percent. Find the impact of the increase in debt on the growth rate.

Before the increase in the debt ratio we have:

ROA = 0.15

b = 0.50

D/E = 0.12

r = 0.07

T = 0.25

$$g = b\left(ROA + \frac{V_D}{V_E}(ROA - r(1-T))\right) = 0.5\ (0.15 + 0.12\ (0.15 - 0.07\ (1 - 0.25)) = 0.08085$$

After the increase in the debt ratio we have:

ROA = 0.15

b = 0.50

D/E = 0.30

r = 0.08

T = 0.25

$$g = b\left(ROA + \frac{V_D}{V_E}(ROA - r(1-T))\right) = 0.5\ (0.15 + 0.30\ (0.15 - 0.08\ (1 - 0.25)) = 0.0885$$

The increase in the debt-equity ratio will raise the growth rate from 8.085 percent to 8.85 percent, that is by nearly one percentage point.

Continuing the previous example, suppose that the firm plans to reduce its dividend payout to 30 percent instead of increasing the debt ratio. What is the impact on the growth rate?

SOLUTION

The growth rate before the reduction in the dividend payout ratio is 0.08085. The growth rate after the decrease in the payout rate (ie increase in b) is:

$$g = b\left(ROA + \frac{V_D}{V_E}(ROA - r(1-T))\right) = 0.7\ (0.15 + 0.12\ (0.15 - 0.07\ (1 - 0.25)) = 0.1132$$

The increase in the retention rate will raise the growth rate from 8.085 percent to 11.32 percent, that is over three percentage points.

Effect on Systematic Risk

The impact of changes in financial policy on the value of the firm can be assessed through one of the valuation models that we have considered in previous chapters. For example the growth rate following a financial restructuring can be calculated from the formula

$$\beta_e = \beta_a\left(1 + \frac{V_D}{V_E}(1-T)\right)$$

Where β_a = is the asset beta and

β_e = is the geared beta

A higher level of debt relative will increase the geared beta of the company, and a lower level of debt will reduce it.

A firm currently has a debt equity ratio of 0.12 and an asset beta of 0.9. The optimal debt ratio is however much lower than the optimal level, since it can raise the debt/equity ratio up to 0.30 without increasing the risk of bankruptcy. The firm plans to borrow and repurchase stock to get to this optimal ratio. The tax rate is 25%. Find the impact of the increase in debt on the geared beta.

Before the increase in the debt ratio we have:

D/E = 0.12

T = 0.25

β_a = 0.9

$$\beta_e = \beta_a\left(1+\frac{V_D}{V_E}(1-T)\right) = 0.9\ (1 + 0.12\ (1 - 0.25)) = 0.981$$

After the increase in the debt ratio we have:

D/E = 0.30

T = 0.25

β_a = 0.9

The new beta following the change in the level of debt will be:

$$\beta_e = \beta_a\left(1+\frac{V_D}{V_E}(1-T)\right) = 0.9\ (1 + 0.30\ (1 - 0.25)) = 1.1025$$

Leveraged Buy-outs (LBOs)

In an LBO a publicly quoted company is acquired by a specially established private company. The private company funds the acquisition by substantial borrowing. A public company 'goes private' when a small group of individuals, possibly including existing shareholders and/or managers and with or without support from a financial institution, buys all of the company's shares. This form of restructuring is relatively common and may involve the shares in the company ceasing to be listed on a stock exchange.

Advantages of leveraged buy-outs

(a) The costs of meeting listing requirements can be saved.

(b) The company is protected from volatility in share prices which financial problems may create.

(c) The company will be less vulnerable to hostile takeover bids.

(d) Management can concentrate on the long-term needs of the business rather than the short-term expectations of shareholders.

(e) Shareholders are likely to be closer to management in a private company, reducing costs arising from the separation of ownership and control (the 'agency problem').

Disadvantages of leveraged buy-outs

The main disadvantage with leveraged buy outs is that the company loses its ability to have its shares publicly traded. If a share cannot be traded it may lose some of its value. However, one reason for seeking private company status is that the company has had difficulties as a quoted company, and the price of its shares may be low anyway.

Market Response to Financial Reconstruction

The market response to financial reconstruction has been estimated from empirical studies of the behaviour of share prices. The available empirical evidence shows that the market reacts positively to firms raising their level of debt up to a certain level, since the constraint that debt imposes on future cash flows makes companies choosier when selecting investment opportunities.

A number of studies have dealt with the performance of **leveraged buyouts.** Since the company becomes private as a result of the leveraged buyout we cannot assess the impact of the market. However, most studies show that a company does significantly better after the leveraged buyout. More specifically leveraged buy-outs result in increases in free cash flow, improved operational efficiency and a greater focus on the company's core business. The causes of the improvement following financial restructuring are reportedly benign and cannot be attributed to lay-offs of employees – rather the increased efficiency of operations coupled with improved control of capital expenditure seem to account for much of the difference.

The empirical evidence also shows that leveraged buy-outs which involve divisions of companies seem to display larger improvement gains than corporate leveraged buy-outs. On the other hand, the authors do enter a caveat, as the risk of bankruptcy and financial disaster with leveraged buy-outs seems to be greater. Moreover, leveraged buy-outs would appear to under-invest in long-term assets where the risk is greater.

The market reaction to dividend changes has been studied extensively. Most studies show abnormally high returns for dividend increases and abnormally low returns for dividend decreases around the announcement days.

EXAMPLE

Financial reconstruction schemes

Crosby and Dawson Co is a private company that has for many years been making mechanical timing mechanisms for washing machines. The management was slow to appreciate the impact that new technology would have and the company is now faced with rapidly falling sales.

In July 20X1, the directors decided that the best way to exploit their company's expertise in the future was to diversify into the high precision field of control linkages for aircraft, rockets, satellites and space probes. By January 20X2, some sales had been made to European companies and sufficient progress had been made to arouse considerable interest from the major aircraft manufacturers and from NASA in the USA. The cost, however, had been heavy. The company had borrowed $2,500,000 from the Vencap Merchant Bank plc and a further $500,000 from other sources. Its bank overdraft was at its limit of $750,000 and the dividend on its cumulative preference shares, which was due in December, had been unpaid for the fourth year in succession. On 1 February 20X2, the company has just lost another two major customers for its washing machine timers. The financial director presents the following information. If the company remains in operation, the expected cash flows for the next five periods are as follows.

	9 months to	Years ending 31 December			
	31.12.X2 $'000	20X3 $'000	20X4 $'000	20X5 $'000	20X6 $'000
Receipts from sales	8,000	12,000	15,000	20,000	30,000
Payments to suppliers	6,000	6,700	7,500	10,800	18,000
Purchase of equipment	1,000	800	1,600	2,700	2,500
Other expenses	1,800	4,100	4,200	4,600	6,400
Interest charges	800	900	700	400	100
	9,600	12,500	14,000	18,500	27,000
Net cash flow	(1,600)	(500)	1,000	1,500	3,000

The above figures are based on the assumption that the present capital structure is maintained by further borrowings as necessary.

STATEMENTS OF FINANCIAL POSITION

	31.12.X0 $'000	31.12.X1 $'000	31.3.X2 Projected $'000
Assets employed			
Non-current assets			
Freehold property	2,780	2,770	2,760
Plant and machinery	3,070	1,810	1,920
Motor vehicles	250	205	200
Deferred development expenditure	–	700	790
Current assets			
Inventory	890	970	1,015
Receivables	780	795	725
	1,670	1,765	1,740
Current liabilities			
Trade payables	1,220	1,100	1,960
Bank overdraft (unsecured)	650	750	750
	1,870	1,850	2,710
	(200)	(85)	(970)
	5,900	5,400	4,700
Long-term liabilities			
10% debentures 20X8 (secured on Freehold property)	(1,000)	(1,000)	(1,000)
Other loans (floating chargers)	–	(3,000)	(3,000)
	4,900	1,400	700

	$'000	$'000	$'000
Ordinary shares of $1	3,500	3,500	3,500
8% Cumulative preference shares	1,000	1,000	1,000
Accumulated reserves/(accumulated deficit)	400	(3,100)	(3,800)
	4,900	1,400	700

Other information:

1 The freehold property was revalued on 31 December 20X0. It is believed that its net disposal value at 31 March 20X2 will be about $3,000,000.

2 A substantial quantity of old plant was sold during the second six months of 20X1 to help pay for the new machinery needed. It is estimated that the break-up value of the plant at 31 March 20X2 will be about $1,400,000.

3 The motor vehicles owned at 31 March 20X2 could be sold for $120,000.

4 Much of the work done on the new control linkages has been patented. It is believed that these patents could be sold for about $800,000, which can be considered as the break-up value of development expenditure incurred to 31 March 20X2.

5 On liquidation, it is expected that the current assets at 31 March 20X2 would realise $1,050,000. Liquidation costs would be approximately $300,000.

Required

Suggest a scheme of reconstruction that is likely to be acceptable to all the parties involved. The ordinary shareholders would be prepared to invest a further $1,200,000 if the scheme were considered by them to be reasonable.

SOLUTION

The first step is to ascertain the likely result of Crosby & Dawson Co going into liquidation as at 31 March 20X2.

Break-up values of assets at 31 March 20X2	$'000
Freehold	3,000
Plant and machinery	1,400
Motor vehicles	120
Patents	800
Current assets	1,050
	6,370

Total liabilities at 31 March 20X2	$'000
Debentures	1,000
Other loans	3,000
Bank overdraft	750
Trade payables	1,960
	6,710

If the company was forced into liquidation, the debentures and other loans would be met in full but that after allowing for the expenses of liquidation ($300,000) the bank and trade creditors would receive a total of $2,070,000 or 76c per dollar. The ordinary and preference shareholders would receive nothing.

If the company remains in operation, the cash position will at first deteriorate but will improve from 20X4 onwards. If the figures can be relied on and the trend of results continues after 20X6 the company will become reasonably profitable.

In the immediate future, after taking into account the additional amounts raised from the existing ordinary shareholders, the company will require finance of $400,000 in 20X2 and $500,000 in 20X3.

Vencap might be persuaded to subscribe cash for ordinary shares. It is unlikely that the company's clearing bank would be prepared to accept any shares, but as they would only receive 76c per dollar on a liquidation they may be prepared to transfer part of the overdraft into a (say) five year loan whilst maintaining the current overdraft limit. It is unlikely that a suitable arrangement can be reached with the trade payables as many would be prepared to accept 76c per dollar, rather than agree to a moratorium on the debts or take an equity interest in the company.

A possible scheme might be as follows:

1 The existing ordinary shares to be cancelled and ordinary shareholders to be issued with $1,200,000 new $1 ordinary shares for cash.

2 The existing preference shares to be cancelled and the holders to be issued with $320,000 new $1 ordinary shares at par.

3 The existing debentures to be cancelled and replaced by $800,000 15% secured debentures with a 15-year term and the holders to be issued with $400,000 of new $1 ordinary shares at par.

4 The loan 'from other sources' to be repaid.

5 The Vencap Bank to receive $2,000,000 15% secured debentures with a 15-year term in part settlement of the existing loan, to be issued $680,000 new ordinary shares in settlement of the balance and to subscribe cash for $800,000 of new ordinary shares.

6 The clearing bank to transfer the existing overdraft to a loan account repayable over five years and to keep the overdraft limit at $750,000. Both the loan and overdraft to be secured by a floating charge.

Comments

1 **Debenture holders**

The debentures currently have more than adequate asset backing, and their current nominal yield is 10%. If the reconstruction is to be acceptable to them, they must have either the same asset backing or some compensation in terms of increased nominal value and higher nominal yield. Under the scheme they will receive securities with a total nominal value of $1,200,000 (an increase of $200,000) and an increase in total yield before any ordinary dividends of $20,000. The new debentures issued to Vencap can be secured on the freehold property (see below).

2 **Loans from other sources**

It has been suggested that the 'loans from other sources' should be repaid as, in general, it is easier to arrange a successful reconstruction that involves fewer parties.

3 **Vencap**

Vencap's existing loan of $2,500,000 will, under the proposed scheme, be changed into $2,000,000 of 15% debentures secured on the property and $680,000 of ordinary shares. This gives total loans of $2,800,000 secured on property with a net disposal value of $3,000,000. This is low asset cover which might increase if property values were to rise. The scheme will increase the nominal value of Vencap's interest by $180,000 with an improvement in security on the first $2,000,000 to compensate for the risk involved in holding ordinary shares. It has also been suggested that Vencap should be asked to subscribe $800,000 for new ordinary shares. The money is required to repay the 'loans from other sources' and to provide additional working capital. The issue of share capital would give the bank a total of 1,480,000 ordinary shares or 43.5% of the equity. From the company's point of view issuing new equity is to be preferred to loan stock as it will improve the gearing position.

4 **The clearing bank**

In a liquidation now, the clearing bank would receive approximately $573,000. In return for the possibility of receiving the full amount owed to them they are being asked under the scheme to advance a further $750,000. By way of compensation, they are receiving the security of a floating charge.

5 **Preference shares**

In a liquidation at the present time, the preference shareholders would receive nothing. The issue of 320,000 $1 ordinary shares should be acceptable as it is equivalent to their current arrears of dividend. If the preference shares were left unaffected by the scheme, the full arrears of dividend would become payable on the company's return to profitability, giving preference shareholders an undue advantage.

6 **Ordinary shareholders**

In a liquidation, the ordinary shareholders would also receive nothing. Under the scheme, they will lose control of the company but, in exchange for their additional investment, will still hold about 35.3% of the equity in a company which will have sufficient funds to finance the expected future capital requirements.

7 **Cash flow forecast, on reconstruction**

	$'000
Cash for new shares from equity shareholders	1,200
Cash for new shares from Vencap	800
	2,000
Repayment of loan from other sources	(500)
Cash available	1,500

The overdraft of $750,000 is converted into a long-term loan, leaving the company with a further $750,000 of overdraft facility to use.

8 **Adequacy of funds**

The statement of financial position below shows the company's position after the implementation of the scheme but before any repayments of short-term debt.

	$'000	**$'000**
Non-current assets		
Free hold		2,760
Plant and machinery		1,920
Motor vehicles		200
Deferred development expenditure		790
		5,670
Current assets		
Inventory	1,015	
Receivable	725	
Cash	1,500	
	3,240	
Less current liabilities: Trade payables	(1,960)	
		1,280
		6,950
Less long-term liabilities		
15% debentures		(2,800)
Loan from clearing bank		(750)
		3,400
Ordinary shares of $1		3,400

It would seem likely that the company will have to make a bigger investment in working capital (ignoring cash) for the following reasons:

- Presumably a substantial proportion of the sales will be exports which generally have a longer collection period than domestic sales.
- It is unlikely that the trade creditors will accept the current payment position (average credit takes over two months) in the long term.

9 **Will the reconstructed company be financially viable?**

Assuming that net current assets excluding cash and any overdraft will, by the end of 20X2, rise from the projected figure of –$220,000 (1,015,000 + 725,000 – 1,960,000) to $500,000 and increase in proportion to sales receipts thereafter, that the equipment required in 20X2 and 20X3 will be leased on five year terms and that the interest charges (including the finance elements in the lease rentals) will be approximately the same as those given in the question, then the expected cash flows on implementation could be as shown below.

	9 months to 31.12.X2 $'000	20X3 $'000	20X4 $'000	20X5 $'000	20X6 $'000
Receipts from sales	8,000	12,000	15,000	20,000	30,000
Purchase of equipment			1,600	2,700	2,500
Payments to suppliers	6,000	6,700	7,500	10,800	18,000
Other expenses	1,800	4,100	4,200	4,600	6,400
Interest charges	800	900	700	400	100
Lease rentals (excluding finance element) (say)	200	360	360	360	360
Bank loan repayment (say)	150	150	150	150	150
Invt. In working capital	720	250	190	310	630
	9,670	12,460	14,700	19,320	28,140
Net movement	(1,670)	(460)	300	680	1,860
Cash balance b/f	1,500	(170)	(630)	(330)	350
Cash balance c/f	(170)	(630)	(330)	350	2,210

These figures suggest that with an agreed overdraft limit of $750,000 the company will have sufficient funds to carry it through the next five years, assuming that the figures are reliable and that no dividends are paid until perhaps 20X4 at the earliest.

This scheme of reconstruction might not be acceptable to all parties, if the future profits of the company seem unattractive. In particular, Vencap and the clearing bank might be reluctant to agree to the scheme. In such an event, an alternative scheme of reconstruction must be designed, perhaps involving another provider of funds (such as another venture capitalist). Otherwise, the company will be forced into liquidation.

Business Reorganisation

Business reorganisations consist of portfolio restructuring and organisational restructuring. Reorganisations of the operations and the structures of business is a constant feature of business life. Companies are restructuring in the pursuit of long term strategy in order to achieve a higher level of performance or in order to survive when existing structures and activities are problematic. Corporate restructuring is usually the result of extreme changes in corporate governance such as takeovers and bankruptcy, but it can also be initiated as a response to product market pressures and internal corporate controls. Companies which experience negative earnings due to competition, overexpansion, high costs and excessive debt respond in many ways such as cutting research and development expenditure, reducing debt levels, reducing employment levels and introducing changes in the internal organisation.

Organisational Restructuring

Organisational restructuring consists of changes in the organisational structure of the firm, such as divisional changes and hierarchical structures. As part of such a restructuring a company may redraw divisional boundaries, it may flatten the hierarchical structure, it may streamline processes, it may adopt a different system of corporate governance and it may reduce employment. Organisational restructuring on its own does not always have a significant effect on the performance of the company. However when used in conjunction with other forms of restructuring, it is a more potent means of increasing performance.

Portfolio Restructuring

Portfolio restructuring consists of changes in the mix of assets owned by the firm or the lines of business in which the firm operates in order to increase the performance of the firm. This can entail the acquisition or disposal of assets or business units by a company in the form of divestments, demergers, spin-offs or management buy-outs. The different ways that portfolio restructuring can be achieved are considered below.

Divestments

Divestment is the partial or complete sale or disposal of physical and organisational assets, the shutdown of facilities and reduction in workforce in order to free funds for investment in other areas of strategic interest. In a divestment the company ceases the operation of a particular activity in order to concentrate on other activities. The rationale for divestment is normally to reduce costs or to increase return on assets. Divestments differ from the other forms of restructuring because they do not require the formation of a new company.

Divestments are undertaken for a variety of reasons. They may take place as a corrective action in order to reverse unsuccessful previous acquisitions, especially when the acquisition has taken place for diversification purposes. Divestments may also be take place as a response to a cyclical downturn in the activities of a particular unit or line of business. However, divestments may be proactive in the sense that a company may want to exit lines of business which have become obsolete and redeploy resources to activities with a higher return on invested capital.

Where divestments are part of a strategic response for business realignment, the issue of which assets to divest is as important as the decision of which assets to acquire. A company has to decide what constitutes core activities and where the next growth opportunities exist. The growth opportunities may be realized by concentrating on the core business, organic growth and development of the right product lines, or by acquisitions and investment in the right markets.

Demergers

A demerger is the splitting up of corporate bodies into two or more separate bodies, to ensure share prices reflect the true value of underlying operations. For example, the ABC Group plc might demerge by splitting into two independently operating companies AB plc and C plc. Existing shareholders are given a stake in each of the new separate companies.

Demerging, in its strictest sense, stops short of selling out, but is an attempt to ensure that share prices reflect the true value of the underlying operations.

Cadbury agreed financing with five banks for a £5.4 billion demerger of its US drinks business. The new US drinks company Dr Pepper Snapple Group was listed on the New York Stock Exchange with net debt of £1.9 billion. Cadbury was listed on the London Stock Exchange with debt of £1.65 billion. The demerger cost Cadbury over £1 billion (almost 10% of its market value), with approximately £370 million of this arising from unwinding tax synergies. Refinancing resulted in an increased annual cost of debt of around £17.5 million.

Aurora Fashions, the group that includes the Oasis and warehouse chains announced a demerger including the sale of the fashion brand Karen Millen and the creation of Coast as a separate fashion business (2014).

Advantages of demergers

The main advantage of a demerger is its greater operational efficiency and the greater opportunity to realise value. A two-division company with one loss making division and one profit making, fast growing division may be better off by splitting the two divisions. The profitable division may acquire a valuation well in excess of its contribution to the merged company.

Disadvantages of demergers

(a) Economies of scale may be lost, where the demerged parts of the business had operations in common to which economies of scale applied.

(b) The smaller companies which result from the demerger will have lower revenue, profits and status than the group before the demerger.

(c) There may be higher overhead costs as a percentage of revenue, resulting from (b).

(d) The ability to raise extra finance, especially debt finance, to support new investments and expansion may be reduced.

(e) Vulnerability to takeover may be increased. The impact on a firm's risk maybe significant, when a substantial part of the company is spun off. The result maybe a loss in shareholder value, if a relatively low beta element is unbundled.

Sell-offs

A sell-off is a form of divestment involving the sale of part of a company to a third party, usually another company. Generally, cash will be received in exchange.

Sell-offs arise for a number of reasons:

- Not seen to be core to business strategy
- Consolidates control over the remaining businesses
- Disposal of a loss-maker
- Protection from takeover
- Raise cash
- Reduce operating cash flow volatility of the business
- Realise a profit following a takeover

In 2010, BP announced a £20 billion asset sale to help pay for the cost of the oil spill in the Gulf of Mexico. The plan, which is to take place over an 18 month period, includes the sale of businesses that are 'worth more to other companies than they are to BP'. Part of the proceeds of the sales were used to reduce BP's £15 billion debt to between £6.4 billion and £9.6 billion.

Liquidations

The extreme form of a sell-off is where the entire business is sold off in a liquidation. In a voluntarydissolution, the shareholders might decide to close the whole business, sell off all the assets and distribute net funds raised to shareholders.

Spin-offs

A spin-off is the creation of a new company, where the shareholders of the original company own the shares. In a spin-off, a new company is created whose shares are owned by the shareholders of the original company which is making the distribution of assets.

In a spin-off:

- There is no change in the ownership of assets, as the shareholders own the same proportion of shares in the new company as they did in the old company
- Assets of the part of the business to be separated off are transferred into the new company, which will usually have different management from the old company
- In more complex cases, a spin-off may involve the original company being split into a number of separate companies

For a number of possible reasons, listed below, a spin-off appears generally to meet with favour from stock market investors:

(a) The change may make a merger or takeover of some part of the business easier in the future, or may protect parts of the business from predators.

(b) There may be improved efficiency and more streamlined management within the new structure.

(c) It may be easier to see the value of the separated parts of the business now that they are no longer hidden within a conglomerate.

(d) The requirements of regulatory agencies might be met more easily within the new structure, for example if the agency is able to exercise price control over a particular part of the business which was previously hidden within the conglomerate structure.

(e) After the spin-off, shareholders have the opportunity to adjust the proportions of their holdings between the different companies created.

Time Warner announced that it would spin off AOL as a separate independent company. Jeff Bewkes, Time Warner Chairman and CEO stated that, with the spin-off, Time Warner had 'returned to [its] roots as one of the leading content companies in the world ... [and believed] that AOL will have greater operational and strategic flexibility as a standalone company'.

Carve-outs

A carve-out is the creation of a new company, by detaching parts of the company and selling the shares of the new company to the public. In a carve-out, a new company is created whose shares are owned by the public with the parent company retaining a substantial fraction of the shares. Parent companies undertake carve-outs in order to raise funds in the capital markets. These funds can be used for the repayment of debt or creditors or it can be retained within the firm to fund expansion. Carved out units tend to be highly valued.

3 Unbundling and Firm Value

The main effect of unbundling on the value of the firm comes through changes in the return on assets and the asset beta. The impact of unbundling on the value of the firm can be assessed through one of the valuation models that we considered earlier. For example the growth rate following a restructuring can be calculated from the formula:

$$g = b\left(ROA + \frac{V_D}{V_E}\left(ROA - r\left(1 - T\right)\right)\right)$$

Where ROA is the return on the net assets of the company

b = is the retention rate

V_D = is the market value of debt

V_E = is the market value of equity

r = is the cost of debt

T = is the corporate tax rate

When firms divest themselves of existing investments, they affect their expected return on assets, as good projects increase the return on assets, (ROA) and bad projects reduce the return –and any investment decision taken by firms affects their riskiness and therefore the asset beta.

EXAMPLE

A firm is expected to divest itself of unrelated divisions, which have historically had lower returns on assets. As a result of the divestment the return on equity is expected to increase from 10 percent to 15 percent. Calculate the effect on the earnings growth rate if the debt to equity ratio is 0.30, the tax rate is 0.25, the retention rate is 0.50 and the interest rate on debt is 8 percent.

SOLUTION

Before the restructuring the growth rate is equal to:

$$g = b\left(ROA + \frac{V_D}{V_E}\left(ROA - r\left(1 - T\right)\right)\right) = 0.5\ (0.10 + 0.3\ (0.10 - 0.08\ (1 - 0.25))) = 0.056$$

After the restructuring the growth rate is equal to:

$$g = b\left(ROA + \frac{V_D}{V_E}\left(ROA - r\left(1 - T\right)\right)\right) = 0.5\ (0.15 + 0.3\ (0.15 - 0.08\ (1 - 0.25))) = 0.0885$$

The restructuring has increased the growth rate from 5.6 percent to 8.85 percent.

EXAMPLE

The business risk of an oil company which has diversified into a number of other activities such as leisure and tourism is 1.3. If the oil company divested itself of all other activities and concentrated on its core business, its beta, based on the observed beta of oil companies with similar financial structure is expected to be 1.4. If the tax rate is 0.25 and the debt to equity ratio is 0.30, calculate the business risk following the divestment of business.

SOLUTION

The beta of the company is related to its business beta through the relationship:

$$\beta_e = \beta_a\left(1 + \frac{V_D}{V_E}(1 - T)\right)$$

The business risk is calculated from:

$$\beta_a \frac{\beta_e}{\left(1 + \frac{V_D}{V_E}(1 - T)\right)} = \frac{1.4}{\left(1 + 0.3\left(1 - 0.25\right)\right)} = 1.143$$

After the restructuring the business risk of the company is reduced from 1.3 to 1.143, implying a lower cost of equity and consequently a higher value of equity.

INDEX